Aircraft of the Luftwaffe,
1935–1945

ALSO BY JEAN-DENIS G.G. LEPAGE
AND FROM McFARLAND

Hitler Youth, 1922–1945: An Illustrated History (2009)

The French Foreign Legion: An Illustrated History (2008)

*German Military Vehicles of World War II:
An Illustrated Guide to Cars, Trucks, Half-Tracks,
Motorcycles, Amphibious Vehicles and Others* (2007)

The Fortifications of Paris: An Illustrated History (2006)

*Medieval Armies and Weapons in Western Europe:
An Illustrated History* (2005)

*Castles and Fortified Cities of Medieval Europe:
An Illustrated History* (2002)

Aircraft of the Luftwaffe, 1935–1945

An Illustrated Guide

Jean-Denis G.G. Lepage

McFarland & Company, Inc., Publishers
Jefferson, North Carolina, and London

LIBRARY OF CONGRESS CATALOGUING-IN-PUBLICATION DATA

Lepage, Jean-Denis.
Aircraft of the Luftwaffe, 1935–1945 :
an illustrated guide / Jean-Denis G.G. Lepage.
p.   cm.

Includes bibliographical references and index.

ISBN 978-0-7864-3937-9
softcover : 50# alkaline paper ∞

1. Airplanes, Military—Germany—History—20th century.
2. Germany. Lutfwaffe—History—20th century.
3. World War, 1939–1945—Aerial operations, German.   I. Title.
UG1245.G4L47 2009   623.74' 6094309043—dc22   2008052744

British Library cataloguing data are available

©2009 Jean-Denis G.G. Lepage. All rights reserved

*No part of this book may be reproduced or transmitted in any form
or by any means, electronic or mechanical, including photocopying
or recording, or by any information storage and retrieval system,
without permission in writing from the publisher.*

On the cover: Digital illustration by Jerry Boucher of
two Messerschmitt Bf 109E-7Bs during the 1941
Balkans Campaign (www.the-vaw.com)

Manufactured in the United States of America

*McFarland & Company, Inc., Publishers
Box 611, Jefferson, North Carolina 28640
www.mcfarlandpub.com*

Table of Contents

Acknowledgments vi
Introduction 1

1. Historical Background 5
2. Basic Technical Data 33
3. Regalia and Uniforms 70
4. Bombers 106
5. Fighters 205
6. Jet Fighters 244
7. Seaplanes 314
8. Transport Aircraft 335
9. Miscellaneous Aircraft 358

Bibliography 395
Index 397

Acknowledgments

My gratitude to Jeannette and Jan à Stuling, Eltjo de Lang and Ben Marcato, Wim Wiese, and Peter De Laet. A special thanks to Dan Johnson's internet site (www.Luftwaffe46.com), and his team of computer artists, who were of great help providing data and inspiration for the illustrations for the sections about German experimental and jet aircrafts.

Introduction

One of the most significant innovations in warfare has certainly been the appearance of air power during the First World War (1914–1918). Demanding resources and technical and financial investment on a whole new scale, the expansion of military activity in the sky also fundamentally changed the nature of war itself. On the battlefield, the aircraft became critical to intelligence, reconnaissance and artillery direction, and soon for ground-support operations and bombing raids. The introduction of strategic long-range bombers also helped to initiate "total war" involving civilians as industrial weapons producers and therefore as targets.

The period 1939–1945, an era of rapid change and experiments, is still of great fascination for the student of weapons in general and military aircraft more particularly. The Second World War provided an arena for the airplane to prove its deadly worth, and such a period may never recur. Weapons are now too expensive, large and complicated to ever be treated with the same degree of experiment as they were then. The German Luftwaffe saw unparalleled changes in the design and use of aircraft. Hitler's reign from 1933 to 1945 was a period of unusual, prolific advances in aircraft design. In 1935 German airmen used planes much the same as had been used by their fathers in 1918 by the end of World War I. By 1945, the changes had been profound, culminating in the world's first jet fighter, the Messerschmitt Me 262.

The subject of World War II German aircraft is vast and sometimes hopelessly complicated, and my intention is to approach it in as simple a way as possible. In this book the most familiar and best-known Luftwaffe aircraft are all included, and sorted by type: bombers, fighters, jet fighters, seaplanes, transport aircraft, and miscellaneous. Together with the most important aircraft, such as the Bf 109, Ju 87, Fw 190 and Me 262, great attention is also paid to large numbers of lesser-known planes, never-developed replacements, rarities, and experimental designs—some totally extravagant and lunatic, others potentially viable but much too ahead of their time. In short, the reader will encounter in these pages almost all Luftwaffe aircraft.

The objective of the work is to provide a reliable and stimulating source of information and reference for serious students and the interested lay reader alike. It is my hope that this comprehensive survey of almost every facet of the German World War II Luftwaffe might be of interest for military historians, specialists, collectors of militaria, aircraft "buffs," and war-gamers, as well as to provide the wide circle of interested and curious readers—those with little specific knowledge in this subject—with a general overview on German World War II aircrafts. Each entry is illustrated with my black-and-white drawing made from existing photographs, and explained in compact text describing type, origin, dimensions and weight (both in metric and imperial), as well as engine used, performance, armament, and history, when known. The first three parts of this book provide some basic historical background and general information.

The experts can skip this, but those less conversant with Hitler's Third Reich aircrafts in general and Luftwaffe in particular may find this helpful. The sheer number of Luftwaffe aircraft built and used, and those only designed or envisioned, has demanded a measure of information selectivity and brevity. The most difficult problem in preparing this book was one of selection. A work of this kind can never be complete in every detail. It has been necessary in certain cases to limit technical data, to approximate information and to omit certain details and particularities. I hope readers will remember that oversimplification is an almost inescapable result of compression. To facilitate this work's readability, I have adopted a narrative approach and avoided the temptation of footnotes. However, a bibliography at the back of the book will provide the interested reader with some of the background material used in the preparation of this study, as well as with suggestions for further reading.

The Luftwaffe, as all other aspects of Hitler's regime, is one historical subject where claims to absolute objectivity and technical detachment sound somewhat artificial and forced, not to say dishonest. It is true that the Luftwaffe is astonishing by the excellency of its designs, produced under pressure of rapid and unpredictable events. By the end of its single decade of existence, Hitler's air force advanced from wood and fabric biplanes to operating futuristic jet-powered aircraft. Its legacy is not precisely measurable, but German aircraft—particularly the jet designs—opened up a new dimension of air warfare. Knowledge and techniques acquired during World War II were doubtless the inspiration for the first generation of subsonic rocket and jet-powered aircraft in the late 1940s and early 1950s. During 1935–1945, the achievements were amazing and demonstrated a technical prowess. There is now no denying the fact that from the aviation history point of view, Germany from 1935 to 1945 is an extremely interesting place and time which on purely technical and historical grounds has been given a lot of attention. One should, however, neither overestimate nor be blinded by technical exploits and remarkable achievements. As in all aspects of Hitler's regime, there is a dark side to the German air force. Owing its existence and independent development to the Nazi regime, the Luftwaffe was necessarily in unconditional allegiance to Hitler.

From the start, the highly-regarded Luftwaffe was directed by Hermann Göring, a fanatical Nazi from the first hour and officially second in the Nazi hierarchy. The air force thus enjoyed better access to the seat of power than the German army and the navy. Certainly when it came to the allocation of funds, the Luftwaffe was at the head of the line. It was also one of Hitler's most disciplined weapons, intended to destroy, kill and devastate, an instrument created to secure the Nazi's *Lebensraum* (living space), a predatory expansionism dictated by the Nazi claim of a superior German race. The Luftwaffe's leadership did not shun mass killing by bombarding civilian cities. Technological designs and manufacture were ordered by a monstrous political system which concentrated all its strength on the military, and which was spurred by hatred, totalitarianism, racism and anti–Semitism, megalomania and nihilism. Unquestionably the Luftwaffe had many brave aircrew spurred more by patriotism than adherence to the criminal Nazi ideology, but it should be remembered that during World War II an important part of the German industrial production was carried out by slave labor, ruthlessly treated and working in atrocious conditions. Millions of forced workers were rounded up all over occupied Europe by Friedrich Sauckel (1894–1946), the Third Reich's Plenipotentiary for the Mobilization of Labor, who was given full responsibility by Hitler in March 1942 for finding workers to support Albert Speer's armaments and ammunition program at any cost. Concentration camp slave labor was provided by the SS on a contract basis to assist most major firms, including Messerschmitt, Heinkel, Junkers, and others.

Various medical research departments of the German air force, headed by SS doctors and physicians Hans Wolfgang Romberg, Gerhard Rose, Hermann Becker-Freyseng, Wilhelm Beiglböck, Siegfried Ruff, Sigmund Rascher and many others, conducted human medical experimentation and deadly tests in SS concentration camps. Himmler personally assumed the responsibility for supplying "asocial individuals and criminals" to die for these experiments. At KZ Dachau, prisoners were used to find out the capacity of the human body to endure and survive high altitude, and a low-pressure chamber was used to simulate conditions of up to 20 km (68,000 feet). Prisoners were submitted to enormous G-forces in barbaric test machines to research the limits of human resistance. In 1942, in order to find out how long a ditched airman could hold on, innocent humans were plunged into ice-cold water tanks or placed naked in the open with temperatures below freezing while doctor recorded temperatures, heart action, respiration, etc. Experiments were conducted to study various methods of making sea water drinkable, using healthy inmates. At KZ Buchenwald in 1943 and 1944, experiments were conducted on prisoners to test the effect of phosphorus burns from incendiary bombs. Healthy inmates were deliberately infected with dangerous diseases to test vaccines. Inevitably many test persons died. In this regard, it is obvious that the Luftwaffe was not only a military arm but also a part of the Nazi system of terror and annihilation. At the Doctors' Trials held in Nuremberg from December 1946 to August 1947, several Luftwaffe and SS doctors who had violated the Hippocratic Oath were condemned to long prison sentences.

Until the end of the war, the Luftwaffe remained a huge arm, including not only the air force proper, with an enormous number of ground and administrative personnel, but also the Flak artillery, airborne troops, and Luftwaffe infantry field divisions, forming Reichsmarschall Hermann Göring's own empire within the Nazi state. The private empire was never relinquished or merged with the other arms of the Wehrmacht, for reasons of political pride, and Göring's belief that the army was not fully committed to Nazi Party ideals.

The German Luftwaffe started off on very professional lines, with high ambitions and great expectations during the 1930s, and reached the peak of its power in the years 1939–1941. From 1943 onward it was forced into an increasingly defensive role, and—hampered by lack of firm direction and long-term planning—it ended in a complete shambles. Fortunately, technical superiority was often bedeviled by administrative muddle, and achievements came often to nothing through inter-service rivalries and an utter lack of vision at the top. World War II was lost by Germany in part because the German High Command never fully understood how to master problems generated by overextended conquests. The history of the Luftwaffe is the story of a total failure, as the air force proved itself incapable of meeting the demands placed upon it.

Jean-Denis G.G. Lepage
Groningen
The Netherlands

1

Historical Background

A Short History of the Luftwaffe

The Luftwaffe, unlike the Heer (army) and the Kriegsmarine (navy), was purely a Nazi creation. According to the stipulations of the Treaty of Versailles in 1919, Germany had no right to possess an air force. By forbidding the design and construction of airplanes, the peace treaty had invested this arm with considerable glamour. From then on, the airplane was read about, written about and discussed behind locked doors. During World War I, though its development was rapid, airpower was only in its infancy. Twenty years later it had become adult, and the interwar period saw airpower theorists and enthusiasts promote the effectiveness of military aviation in an atmosphere which made airplanes seem both glamorous and omnipotent. A remarkable achievement illustrating Germany's focus on aviation could be seen in the activities of the civilian airline company Lufthansa (see below).

What later would become the Luftwaffe started in the early 1920s, at first covertly, within the framework of Lufthansa, and—in the mid–1920s—the Deutscher Luftsportverband (DLV, German Air Association). German manufacturers, who were not allowed to produce war airplanes under the terms of the Treaty of Versailles, could however do a fruitful business and acquire useful experience by designing and producing war airplanes for foreign powers. For example, the Heinkel He 8 floatplane, designed in 1928, was intended to be a mail plane, but it was no problem to modify the aircraft for military purposes in the role of reconnaissance floatplane when purchased by the Danish air force.

Another organization, the Nationalsozialistische *Fliegerkorps* (NSFK, Nazi Flyers Corps), was founded in the early 1930s and grew after Hitler's seizure of power in 1933 as the Nazis incorporated all existing civilian aviation, ballooning and gliding clubs. The NSFK, closely associated with the Hitler Youth, was placed under tutelage of the future leader of the air force, Hermann Göring (1893–1946), a glamorous and distinguished ex–World War I pilot, a prominent Nazi leader and member of Hitler's inner circle. Heroes such as Bruno Lörzer and Ernst Udet joined the Corps and played a significant role in the creation of the Luftwaffe in 1935.

Before the official promulgation of the Luftwaffe, both NSFK and DLV promoted interest in—and development of—air sports, involving model building, educational classes related to aeronautics, and building and flying gliders and balloons. Under cover of the NSFK and DLV, anti-aircraft machine-gun companies were formed in the early 1930s, thereby helping to start the clandestine training of Flak gunners. These organizations also rallied World War I veteran mechanics and pilots for propaganda aims, and were used as a means to channel energy, to exploit youth enthusiasm in aeronautics, and—in the long term—in the formation of future combat pilots and technical ground personnel. When the Second World War started, the NSFK provided a constant flow of skilled personnel for the Luftwaffe, functioning as a reserve pool for them.

In 1933, the Deutsche Forschungsanstalt für Segelflug (DFS, German Institute for Glider Flight) was formed, which centralized and coordinated all technical research on gliders in the new Reich. DFS was created by nationalizing the Rhön-Rossitten Gesellschaft (RRG). During the war, DFS produced military gliders and conducted research and experimentation on jet and rocket propulsion.

Before 1933, in order to train its pilots on modern experimental combat aircraft, Germany ironically solicited the help of its future enemy, the USSR. A secret training airfield was established at Lipetsk in 1924 and operated for approximately nine years, using mostly Dutch and Russian—but also some German—aircrafts before being closed in 1933. Conditions thus existed for the rapid development of a German military air force, and upon the abrogation of the Versailles Treaty in 1935, the existence of the Luftwaffe was revealed. The new corps was organized and commanded by the charismatic but militarily limited Reichsmarschall Göring. Closely related to the Nazi Party, the air force was consequently looked on much more favorably than the other two armed services, the Heer and Kriegsmarine. Thanks to Göring's dynamism and Field Marshal Erhard Milch's realistic approach, the Luftwaffe's rise in the 1930s was meteoric. However, the new arm was also a confused one, as Göring never gave firm leadership. The Reichsmarschall was more flamboyant showman than a consistent and competent planner. Göring—who was both chief of the Luftwaffe and RLM (Minister of Aviation)—often failed to make a clear distinction between the functions of the two posts. He deliberately left the

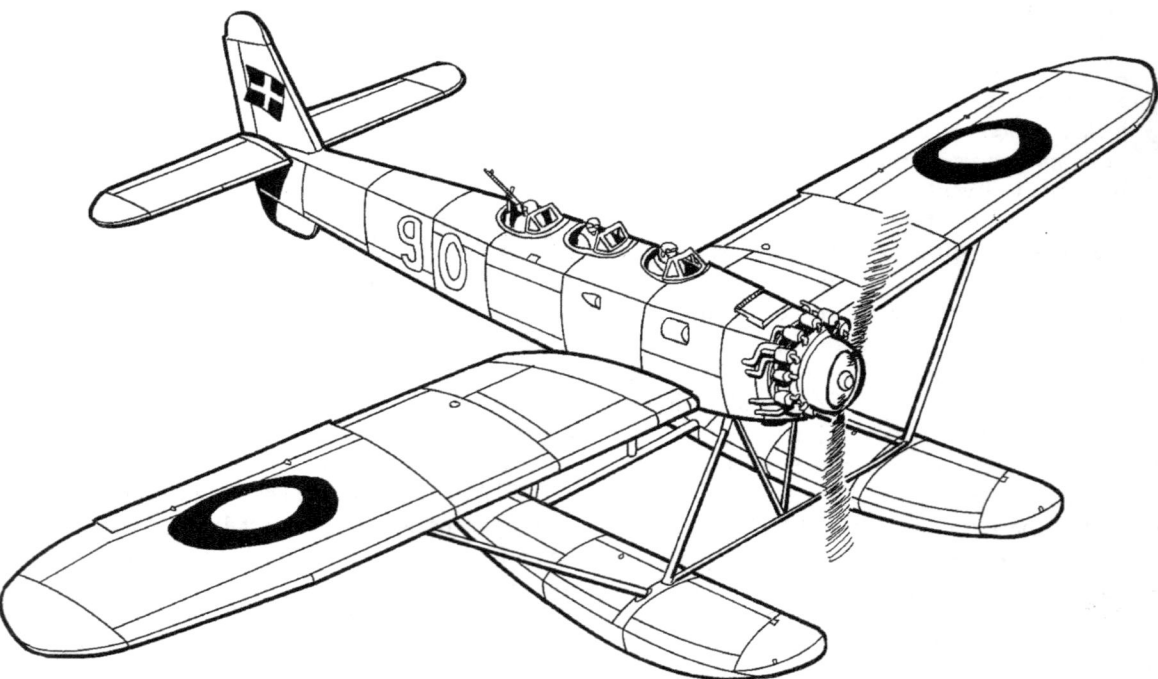

Heinkel He 8 (Danish H.M. II). The Heinkel He 8, used by the 1st Flotilla of the Danish Naval Air Service based at Copenhagen, was designated H.M. II, and was used until 1940. The low-wing monoplane had a span of 9.15 m, a length of 11.65 m and a height of 4.40 m. Powered by one Armstrong-Siddeley Jaguar IVC, it had a maximum speed of 210 km/h. The H.M. II was operated by a crew of three, placed in open cockpits, including pilot, radio-operator, and rear gunner. Armament included two 8 mm light machine guns. The sturdy H.M. II, although designed as a maritime reconnaissance aircraft, could carry eight 12.5 kg bombs in underwing racks. Six units were built by the Heinkel Werke in Germany and sixteen were built at the Danish Naval Dock Yard under license.

structure of authority under him unclear, and as a result the arbitrary crossing of administrative, technical and military boundaries created uncertainty and acute personal rivalry within air force departments.

In 1936, Hitler sent military support, a force called Legion Condor, with a strong Luftwaffe element, to support the rebellious Spanish nationalist, General Franco. The Spanish Civil War became a valuable proving ground for new German aircraft designs and tactics, and to accustom personnel to real combat conditions. A grim foretaste of the systematic bombing of cities during World War II came in April 1937 when a combined force of German and Italian bombers under nationalist Spanish command destroyed most of the Basque city of Guernica in northeast Spain. This bombing received worldwide condemnation, and the collective memory of the horror of the bombing of civilians has ever since been aided via the famous painting named after the town, by the artist Pablo Picasso.

In the late 1930s, the full potentialities of the airplane were finally realized and air power had become capable of taking over a share of the functions of artillery, namely the function of supporting tanks and motorized infantry. As a flying artillery, planes could do what guns used to do in Napoleon's hands: blast open a breach in the enemy's position for a decisive maneuver. At the outbreak of the war, the German air force was an efficient instrument and one of the keys to the successful *Blitzkrieg*, a deadly, efficient combination of fast-moving ground attack with a furious and frightening air assault. The Germans regarded their Luftwaffe as an extension of the land arm; its function was to give close support to the Heer in the field, as another form of long-range artillery. They put considerable faith in the airplane as a tactical instrument, particularly for short campaigns with two-engined medium bombers and dive bombers which destroyed communications, prevented counter-attacks, aided tank and infantry assaults, and paralyzed morale everywhere. The Luftwaffe, virtually unopposed by modern aircraft, performed its intended tactical role, and contributed a lot to German victories from September 1939 to June 1940. The first campaigns of World War II resulted in the conquest and occupation of large parts of Europe and the creation of a not entirely deserved reputation of invincibility for the Luftwaffe that was to have repercussions in the ensuing conflict. After the fall of France, Hitler turned his eyes to the British Isles, and an invasion was prepared, but the Luftwaffe suffered its first defeat during the Battle of Britain. British cities, ports and industrial sites were bombed, causing great damage and civilian casualties but to no military advantage. At the end of September 1940 Hitler conceded defeat by canceling the invasion, to allow him to prepare for Operation Barbarossa, the planned invasion of the Soviet Union. In 1941, the violent Blitzkrieg was replicated on a smaller scale in the Balkans, North Africa and with enormous success during the opening stage of the Russian campaign. Although initial successes were achieved, the Luftwaffe was unable to repeat. For one thing, the attacks in Russia were made on a very broad front, instead of the short, sharp thrusts of the previous Blitzkrieg campaigns. And as the war continued, the German air force was called upon to operate on too many widely dispersed fronts, sapping its ability to achieve further decisive victories. The German air superiority was especially felt during the first two years on the Eastern front, as long as the Luftwaffe enjoyed an advanced technical standard compared to the Russian air force, and could employ highly trained and experienced pilots. Even during the initial period, however, Luftwaffe resources were never sufficient to guarantee complete control of the air space over the front line, unlike what it had achieved in 1939–40. The air force authorities continued to think that strategic bombing could be separated from tactical operations and as a result the Luftwaffe failed to hit the Russians hard enough and at the proper time. It became obvious that the longer the war lasted, the more stretched resources would be, particularly when the United States entered the war by the end of 1941.

From 1943 onward, Luftwaffe superiority slipped away, as the Russian air force recovered from its devastating initial losses, and Soviet factories provided planes to the front that could compete with their German counterparts. From then on to the end of the war, Hitler's air force enjoyed several local successes, but the Luftwaffe became increasingly unable to carry the fight to the enemy or even to defend the homeland against Allied air attacks. Like so much in the Third Reich, the Luftwaffe was not ready for the type of war that developed after 1941, and serious preparations were only put onto efficient footing when the war had effectively been lost. After 1943, the Luftwaffe lost its original numerical and qualitative superiority, and tactics shifted increasingly to the defensive. It was unable to go on the offensive, except occasionally and on a limited scale. Thus, the Luftwaffe tactics were modified from one of bold attack to one of conservation of strength, assuming risks only when decisive results appeared obtainable. Between 1940 and 1945 the Luftwaffe saw action on many fronts, including in North Africa in support of ground operations conducted by General Erwin Rommel's Afrika Korps, where its fortune rose and sank with those of the "Desert Fox," and in the offensives against Yugoslavia and Greece prior to the invasion of the USSR in June 1941. Many Luftwaffe units were stationed in Italy, including after the Italians switched sides in September 1943, and remained there until the end of the European war in May 1945. Following some early experience in support of the war at sea during the Norwegian Campaign, the Luftwaffe contributed small forces to the Battle of the Atlantic, claiming minor successes by long-range maritime attacks and patrols, and fighter and seaplane cover for U-boats venturing out into and returning from the Atlantic. But the Germans had not fully developed the concept of air cover for their navy. Nor did they have the adequate long-range aircraft to provide it; consequently, the Allies won the crucial Battle of the Atlantic largely by superior airpower that defeated the German submarines.

From 1940 to 1944, the Luftwaffe also had to continually increase the resources made available to counter the Allied strategic bombing campaign, first carried out alone by RAF Bomber Command under Sir Arthur Harris, but eventually joined by the U.S. 8th Air Force. The air offensive—which was intended to win the war quickly and without the need for an invasion of mainland Europe—was far below expectation. For years, however, it was the only way in which the war could be carried home to the German people, and this undoubtedly was of the highest importance to Allied morale. Until the development of Allied long-range fighters, the Luftwaffe remained relatively efficient and kept the capability to inflict serious losses with its day fighters and night fighters, as well as the anti-aircraft guns under its command. From late 1943 to early 1944, the Allies had gained an undisputed air superiority, sufficient to enable them to inflict an unprecedented degree of destruction on the German homeland. For his incompetence, Göring gradually fell from grace, withdrew from direct command of operation into a sybaritic world of drugs, high living and art collecting.

The air war caused many casualties among German civilians (estimated to 600,000) and Allied airmen but it did not at all stop the German war production. Owing to Minister of Armaments Albert Speer's skills—through a policy of rationing and distribution—German industrial production remained astonishingly high till the end of 1944. Factories and industrial sites were scattered, concealed, camouflaged, protected by concrete shelters, located behind bunkers or underground, and heavily defended by Flak artillery. It was the destruction of the transportation system, rather than of factories themselves which eventually defeated the Germans. The main blow was probably the destruction of the Reich's fuel production which further hobbled both the German army and the air force. The loss of the Romanian and Hungarian oil fields and the destruction by bombing of the synthetic-oil plants and refineries in Germany caused such an acute shortage of fuel that a good part of the desperately needed fighter planes had to remain on the ground. There they were not only powerless but destroyed by Allied air attacks. By the time of the Normandy invasion of June 6, 1944, the Allies considered the Luftwaffe to be defeated. Nevertheless the German air force continued to fight. Helped by the shorter ranges now being flown, the Luftwaffe fought grimly in the last months of the war.

The German military situation was critical

at the end of 1944 and desperate in spring 1945, but if the massive Allied bombardments spread fear and discouragement among the German population, they never caused the expected total collapse of morale. The German people stoically went on with their business and—on the whole—obeyed the Nazi regime until the very end.

Late in the war, German technology made revolutionary breakthroughs in military aviation but these technical advances (e.g. jet aircraft, flying bombs, supersonic missiles) were too little, too late and ill-employed. The German aviation industry was not short of talent, but the technical brilliance of its design teams was negated by leaden bureaucracy, corruption, and the personal rivalries of top Nazi leaders. The world's first combat jet fighter, Messerschmitt Me 262, might have won the air war, but Hitler saw it in a bomber's role. The V1 flying bombs and V2 rockets were not used against military objectives but as psychological terror/retaliation weapons against civilians in Belgium and Britain. With the Luftwaffe entirely on the defensive as the western Allies and the Soviets closed in and invaded the Reich itself, its ultimate annihilation was dramatic, leaving the skies open to Allied air forces. The capricious and blundering Hitler and the incompetent and incapable Göring were responsible for the ultimate debacle. During the Battle of the Bulge, in winter 1944–45, the Luftwaffe undertook a finale and desperate offensive which cost it its last meager resources; night bombing attacks against Bastogne, a paradrop and aerial re-supply of German spearheads failed completely. But it was already all over, as Hitler was fast becoming a physical wreck and this poisoned his general outlook. In spite of the dictator's delirious dreams and stubborn hopes, the German air force simply could not continue to sustain its losses. By September 1944, the Luftwaffe received only one-fifth of its minimum fuel requirement. By the end of 1944—due to lack of fuel and shortage of experienced pilots—the depleted Luftwaffe air units were virtually absent from the battles on all fronts. Thus in ten years the Luftwaffe emerged like a phoenix from the funeral pyre of the Treaty of Versailles, reached a peak in 1940 when it looked invincible, only to collapse and die in 1945 at the hands of an Allied air force which had not been shackled by indifferent leadership and which was in the end much more numerous and far better equipped.

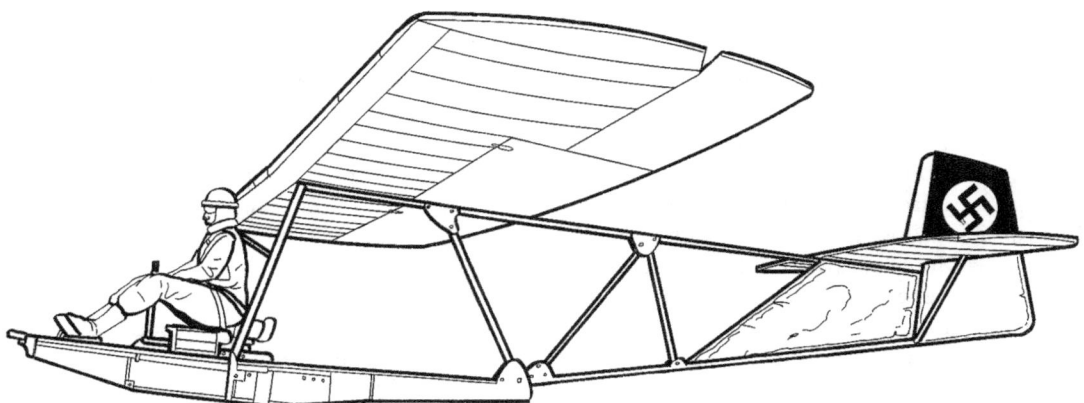

Stamer-Lippisch SG 38 glider. Participation in the Nazi Flyers Corps could eventually lead to a pilot's license, but this was not recognized by the Luftwaffe. An NSFK pilot would still need to complete flight training with the German air force. But there is no doubt that many future Luftwaffe pilots got their interest and basic training from participation in the NSFK. The SG 38 training glider, designed by engineer Alexander Lippisch, was the standard for the basic instruction of Luftwaffe student pilots. It had a total length of 6.28 m (20.604 feet), a wingspan of 10.41 m (34.154 feet), and an empty weight of 110 kg (242 lbs). Maximum speed was 115 km/h (71 mph). The glider had a single seat—so there was no room for a flight instructor.

Lufthansa

The first German civilian airline was founded in November 1909. Named Deutsche Luftschiffahrt AG (DELAG), the company used large dirigible airships designed by count von Zeppelin. After World War I the importance of airships declined, and all lighter-than-air craft disappeared after the catastrophic explosion of the Hindenburg in New York in May 1937. In the 1920s several private commercial airline companies were supported by the Weimar Republic, of which only a few survived the massive inflation and poor economic conditions caused by the 1929 crisis. In January 1926, the government combined two of these, the Deutsche Aero Lloyd (DAL) and the Hugo Junkers Company, to form a national airline company named Deutsche Luft Hansa (DHL). With a monopoly on German air transport, both international and national, and large government subsidy, DHL soon had 162 aircrafts and regularly scheduled service. The company expanded through the late 1920s and early 1930s. It's worth mention that Hitler flew frequently while campaigning throughout Germany, particularly during 1930–1933. Journeying by air was new and modern, but it was not only practical; Hitler's propaganda experts clearly exploited the highly symbolical image of the leader descending from the sky in his modern, all-metal, shining, tri-motor Junker Ju 52. A secret member of the Nazi party, the head of DHL, Erhart Milch, arranged that Hitler and other Nazi leaders never had to pay any airfares. Ironically the company was heavily subsidized by the Weimar Republic which thus unwillingly contributed to the success of its most bitter enemy. After the Nazi's seizure of power in January 1933, DHL was renamed Lufthansa, and the company's growth was helped by a government eager to expand its prestige and spread its influence all over the world. The distinction between civil and military aviation tended to blur, as the Nazi swastika was painted on both combat and civil aircraft, and as civilian airliners were designed with an eye toward military application as bombers. During the war, Lufthansa's air fleet was militarized and served the Nazis, calling into question the company's role in the immoral policies of Hitler's regime. In 1945 all services were discontinued and the company was liquidated. The civilian airline company Lufthansa was re-created in January 1953.

Reich Air Ministry (RLM)

The Reichsluftfahrtministerium (RLM—Reich Air Ministry) was a German organization in charge of development and production of aircraft, primarily for the Luftwaffe, from 1933 to 1945. In typical Third Reich fashion, the RLM was personality driven and formal procedures often did not exist or were purposely ignored while influential Nazi leaders outside the RLM were allowed to interfere with important decisions. As a result, many developments progressed only slowly and erratically during the war.

The RLM was formed in April 1933 with Hermann Göring at its head. In this early phase, the RLM was little more than Göring's personal staff. In May 1933 the RLM was enlarged, consisting of two main *Amter* (departments): the military Luftschutzamt (LA—Air Defense Department) and the civilian Allgemeines Luftamt (LB—General Air Department). Erhard Milch was placed in direct control of the LA, in his function as Staatssekretär der Luftfahrt (Secretary of Aviation).

In September 1933 a reorganization was undertaken to reduce duplication of effort between departments. The primary changes were to move the staffing and technical development organizations out of the LB, and make seven full departments on their own, Air Command Department, General Air Department, Technical Service, Armament Service, Administration Department, Personnel Service, and Logistics Service. By that time the RLM totaled 25,000 personnel. The Reich Air Ministry was housed in a large building located in the Wilhelmstrasse in central Berlin, built on Hermann Göring's order between 1935 and 1936. Designed by architect Ernst Sagebiel in typical Nazi style, it was one of the few major public buildings to escape serious damage during the Allied bombing offensive in 1944 and during the final battle of Berlin in April 1945. As a result it was occupied by the government of the DDR (German Democratic Republic) in 1949, housing the Council of Ministers.

With the excellent personal relations between Göring and Hitler, the RLM had good political support; Göring, however, staffed the RLM with friends who spent more time and effort trying to rise up the organizational chart than they did working at their jobs. In a country and a regime which prided themselves on a logical and methodical approach to problem-solving, the relationship between the individual aviation designers and manufacturers and also between them and the military authorities and the RLM looked like tribal warfare. That projects were initiated, evaluated and developed is a source of wonder as there was no logic or method in evidence. The problem became particularly acute between 1939 and 1942, when the organization had grown so large that Göring was no longer able to maintain control. This period was marked by an inability to deliver desperately needed new aircraft designs, as well as continued shortages of aircraft and engines. Confusion was somewhat increased by Hitler himself who took a great personal interest in aircraft design. His maniacal devotion to minutiae led him to interfere in the procurement programs of all armed services. The Führer often intervened in deliberations, or sent orders or suggestions. On the whole, Hitler's ideas were limited. His technical knowledge was broad, but his military interests were narrowly restricted to traditional weapons and limited by his own experience of World War I trench warfare. He had little feeling for innovations and new developments, such as radar, the atom bomb, jet fighters and rockets. Hitler's interference sometimes delayed or obscured other important matters, and often antagonized staff.

In 1943, Hitler's architect, Albert Speer, took over from Milch, and things immediately improved. Given Hitler's complete blessing, he was able to cut through the rigid hierarchy and could make needed changes almost overnight. By that time Siegfried Knemeyer (who wanted to develop jet-powered aircraft) took over from Ernst Udet as chief of technical air armaments at the RLM and thus had considerable influence. Aircraft production shot up, and projects that had been hampered for political reasons were finally able to proceed. But this time it was too late, and in the summer of 1944 they were not ready to take on the massive Allied air forces that rained destruction over Germany.

Main Luftwaffe Leaders

Göring

Hermann Göring (1893–1946) was an officer with a distinguished record from World War I, in which he had commanded the prestigious Richthofen squadron and won a reputation as an ace. After the war the embittered Göring made a living as a stunt flier and private pilot in Denmark and Sweden. Back in Germany, he soon became a convinced Nazi, one of Hitler's henchmen, a member of his inner circle, and a political activist who took part in Hitler's failed Beer Hall Putsch of November 1923. Badly wounded during the putsch, he became addicted to the morphine he was given to ease his pain, and for several years drifted in and out of mental institutions. In May 1928 he became a Nazi Reichstag deputy and was elected its president in August 1932. When Hitler came to power in January 1933, Göring was appointed minister of the interior for Prussia. From this power base he quickly established the Nazi system of repression, by creating the Gestapo (Secret State Police) and organizing the first concentration camps. Between 1933 and 1939, and even until the end of the Nazi regime, Reichsmarschall Göring's contradictory personality played a fateful part in the history of Nazism. He took charge of creating the new German air force, was involved in international diplomatic dealings, and, though totally incompetent, directed the German prewar economy. Göring's performance was rewarded by Hitler who created the unique rank of Reichsmarschall for him, and awarded him the Grand Cross of the Iron Cross, the only person ever to receive this medal. But most important, Hitler had designated him as his successor. Owing to Göring's unscrupulous dynamism, the Luftwaffe was the most efficient instrument of air power in the world at the outbreak of World War II.

The German air force actually reflected his strengths but also his weaknesses as a leader. Göring, who by nature was indolent, self-indulgent, and easily bored, had great ambitions, but he lacked the concentration and consistency necessary to maintain the trend of the Luftwaffe's development as the war progressed. There was more than a touch of amateurism in him, which did not compare well with the true professionalism of junior commanders. During World War II, Göring repeatedly made serious errors of judgment, did nothing to solve the Luftwaffe's problems, and whenever he *did* do anything, it created total confusion since he never took the trouble to work through the problems but made his decisions on the basis of impulsive inspirations. To make matters worse, the Reichsmarschall surrounded himself with a collection of young, inexperienced and sycophantic staff officers, and often accepted their overoptimistic reports rather than the more realistic ones submitted by his chief of staff. "No enemy bomber can reach the Ruhr!" declared a boastful Göring before the war, and in another speech he added, *"If an enemy bomber ever flies above Germany, my name is not Hermann Göring; you can then call me Meier!"* Promising results which the Luftwaffe could not deliver (e.g. the reduction of the Dunkirk pocket, victory in the Battle of Britain, the succoring of the Sixth Army at Stalingrad, preventing Allied raids against Germany, and effective retaliation), the bragging Göring gradually lost Hitler's favor. His energy, so unflagging before the war, came only in sporadic bursts. This went hand in hand with an obstinate refusal to recognize reality. He became disillusioned with the war and lost his interest in affairs of state. He neglected his numerous official duties and increasingly took refuge in fantasy, drugs and luxurious idleness or traveling aboard his lavishly equipped private train. Officially Second in the Nazi hierarchy, he cultivated ostentation with unparalleled effrontery, was a scandalous accumulator of art and property by looting, and one of the most brutal and unbridled practitioners of despotism. He was a Falstaffian figure whose gross appetites for money, glory, power and art found their full satisfaction under the cover of Nazi activity. In his sumptuous hunting lodge and estate, Karinhall, north of Berlin, wearing extravagant uniforms and grotesque jewels, surrounded by the stolen art treasures of Europe, the fat, corrupt, arrogant, drug-addicted, megalomaniac and ruthless Göring employed administrators, servants, foresters and huntsmen at public expense, and lived in voluptuous ease while Germany starved. Though Hitler, who could be quite sentimental about his *Alter Kämpfer* (Nazi veterans of the first hour), retained a degree of faith in him, Göring was steadily eclipsed by his rivals for power, particularly Himmler and Bormann. He remained—officially at least— the second man of the Third Reich until Hitler had him arrested for high treason in the last week of his regime in May 1945. Göring was dismissed on account of his having planned to contact western Allied authorities with a view to securing a ceasefire before the Soviets overran Berlin. In his place, Hitler appointed Generaloberst Robert Ritter von Greim as the second (and last) commander-in-chief of the Luftwaffe. At the Nuremberg trial in 1946, weaned from his drug addiction and much thinner, Göring reemerged as the strongest-willed and most arrogant of the defendants. He was sentenced to death and cheated the hangman by committing suicide with a smuggled poison pill on the eve of execution.

Greim

Robert Ritter von Greim (1892–1945), after having served in World War I as a fighter pilot credited with shooting down 28 Allied planes, studied law and became the manager of commercial air training centers. In 1934 he reentered army life and was appointed Luftwaffe Chief of Personnel by Göring in 1939. During the war he distinguished himself as an outstanding pilot and received many medals. Head of 5th *Fliegerkorps* in 1942, he was appointed commander of the air force on the Russian front from 1943 to 1945. On April 23, 1945, he succeeded the disgraced Göring as Luftwaffe commander-in-chief. Together with his mistress Hanna Reitsch, the famous woman test-pilot, he flew to Hitler's bunker in Berlin to receive his new assignment. Von Greim was wounded and Hanna Reitsch managed to land the plane between the flames and the explosions. After a short ceremony and a meeting with Hitler, in spite of their entreaties to remain in the Führersbunker, both were ordered to leave the burning town. They succeeded in escaping and flew to the headquarters of Admiral Karl Dönitz, who had just been promoted by Hitler as his political successor and leader of Germany. Imprisoned at Salzburg, General von Greim committed suicide in May 1945.

Jeschonnek

General Hans Jeschonnek (1899–1943) had served as an infantry officer and later as an airman during World War I. He became chief of the air staff in 1939. With a distinguished military career behind him, he contributed considerable practical knowledge and appreciation of new airplane types. He was a firm believer in the potential of the use of medium-high-speed bombers, and got closely involved in general planning during the victorious period of 1939–1941. A dedicated exponent of tactical air power, his term of office from 1939 to 1943—the vital years—was a time when no deviation was possible. Only too late did he realize his error. In early 1943, when it became apparent that the Luftwaffe was unable to support a war on two fronts and unable to protect Germany, Jeschonnek became highly disillusioned, both by the turn of events and Göring's incompetent leadership. In addition, clashes of personality with Milch made his position precarious. By August 1943, after several severe crises with Milch and Göring, Jeschonnek committed suicide. Against his express wishes, Göring attended the funeral and deposited a wreath from Hitler.

Kesselring

Field Marshal Albrecht Kesselring (1885–1960) had served as general staff officer in World War I, and had remained in the Reichswehr until 1932; he was transferred to the newly created air force in 1935. Appointed chief of air staff in 1936, he was in command of Luftwaffe Air Fleet 2 during the campaign of Poland in September 1939 and during the invasion of Holland in May 1940, when he authorized the bombardment of Warsaw and Rotterdam. During the Battle of Britain, he still commanded *Luftflotte* II. In December 1941, Kesselring was appointed commander in chief South to assist Rommel in the North African campaign, and engaged in operations against the Allies in Libya, Malta and Tunisia. After the German withdrawal from Tunisia, as commander in chief in Italy, he conducted an outstanding campaign against the Allies. Skillfully building and rebuilding his defensive lines, and executing a brilliant retreat in the face of superior odds, he delayed the Allied advance for more than a year. In March 1945, Kesselring took over Field Marshal von Rundstedt's command on the Western Front, but the situation was so hopeless that he was forced to capitulate. At the Nuremberg trial, Kesselring was condemned to death as a war criminal for the bombing of civilian populations, the execution of hostages and massacres perpetrated by his troops in Italy. The sentence was soon commuted to life imprisonment, and finally the highly regarded Kesselring was released because of ill health in October 1952. He died in July 1960.

Milch

During World War I, Erhard Milch (1892–1972) had commanded a fighter squadron, and after the war he held various appointments in industry and in commercial aviation. In 1926 he became chairman of the newly created civilian company Lufthansa, and in this capacity was able to exert considerable influence in the aircraft industry. He also began to organize aircrew training and the development of extensive ground equipment, ostensibly for commercial purposes, but in effect laying the foundation for the future military air force. After the Nazi seizure of power in January 1933, Milch was appointed Göring's secretary of state for air. Under Lufthansa cover, he continued to develop the clandestine air arm until the Luftwaffe was officially created in 1935. From then on, he entrusted eminent technicians from leading industrial firms who played a key role in its development. Highly regarded by Göring for his executive ability and efficiency, his half-Jewish origin did not prevent his rapid promotion, since the Reichsmarschall arranged for his spurious "aryanization" by persuading Milch's Jewish mother to sign a legal document that he was not her child. "I decide who is a Jew!" declared Göring. During the war Milch adopted a more cautious and realistic approach to the Luftwaffe situation than Göring. In particular he unsuccessfully warned of the need to manufacture fighter planes for the defense of Germany instead of bombers for taking the offensive. He also tried to alert Göring to the dangers of American bomber production, but the Reichsmarshall was not inclined to listen. Milch's accessions proved to be right in the end when it was too late, and his actions—judged too defeatist—frequently came into question, especially during the latter part of World War II when the Luftwaffe began to collapse. Milch, who more clearly than most understood the Luftwaffe's true needs, proved unable to improve the deteriorating situation. Relations with Hitler, Göring, and Speer became increasingly strained and Milch's influence gradually decreased. In August 1944 he was obliged to relinquish his posts as secretary of state and director of armaments. At the Nuremberg trial, Erhard Milch was sentenced to life imprisonment as a war criminal deeply committed to Hitler's regime. He was released in June 1954, continued to work undisturbed as an industrial consultant in Düsseldorf and died in January 1972.

Reitsch

Like film director Leni Riefenstahl, Hanna Reitsch (1912–1979) was one of the few women to achieve high status in the male-led Nazi society. She attracted much attention in the 1930s as an unrivaled record glider pilot with daring and skill. An enthusiastic admirer of Hitler, she was appointed a flight captain and the first woman test pilot by General Ernst Udet in 1937. She subsequently performed test flights with all sorts of military airplanes before and during World War II (e.g., Focke-Wulf Fa 61 helicopter, Henschel Hs 293 rocket aircraft, Messerschmitt Me 323 Gigant, and piloted V1 Reichenberg prototype). Miraculously surviving several crashes, she and General von Greim were among Hitler's last visitors in the Führerbunker in Berlin on 26–29 April 1945. Begging to be allowed to die with her idol, she was ordered to leave the encircled city and rally the remaining Nazi air forces to support a rescue operation. After the war she was arrested and remained for fifteen months in American custody, then released in 1946. She published her autobiography in 1951 and continued to be active as record competitor and research pilot. An exceptionally courageous woman and a symbol of physical heroism, she was politically naïve and simple-minded in her enthusiasm for Hitler's personality. The indefatigable Hanna Reitsch died in August 1979.

Richthofen

Wolfram Freiherr von Richthofen (1895–1945) joined the German air force in 1917 and served in the famous Richthofen Squadron led by his cousin Manfred, the Red Baron. During the interbellum he was a member of the Technical Division of the RLM and chief of staff of the Condor Legion in 1936. In May 1940 he successfully led a Luftwaffe formation, and he served on the Russian front in 1941 and 1942. By the end of the war he commanded *Luftflotte* IV in Italy, and he died in July 1945.

Speerle

Hugo Speerle (1885–1953) was a man who had worked his way up from humble origins to become one of the Luftwaffe's highest-ranking officers. An air force pilot in World War I, he held various regimental commands between 1925 and 1933. During the Spanish Civil War (1936–1939) he had been the first commander of the German Condor Legion, and became one of the leading figures in the Luftwaffe. In 1939 he was promoted commander of the Luftwaffe forces in the West. He provided Hitler with astonishing victories in 1939 and 1940, but failed to defeat Great Britain. After commanding the German air force in North Africa in support of Rommel's Afrika Korps, he was put in charge of the anti-invasion air force in

Western Europe in 1944. By the time of the Normandy landing, the German *Luftflotte* III, deployed in the West, was a broken reed. It was compelled to use half-trained pilots, its effectiveness was poor, and it was harried constantly. At the beginning of June 1944, *Luftflotte* III mustered some 400 aircraft operational on paper. They were divided into two main fighters units (*Jagdgeschwader* IV and V) which could be diverted in the event of an Allied landing but whose priority was intercepting Allied bombers bound for Germany. In June, July and August 1944, Speerle's forces, greatly depleted, were no match for the formidable air fleets successfully deployed before, during and after D-Day. Craving luxury and public display, Speerle ran a close second to Göring, and was also his match in corpulence. Speerle was acquitted of all war crimes by the court of Nuremberg and died in April 1953.

Student

Kurt Student (1890–1978), a World War I pilot veteran, helped develop the secret Luftwaffe in the early years, with many responsibilities, particularly in the domain of airborne troops and gliders. In 1938, he was promoted to commander of the newly created Fallschirmjäger (parachute troops). Hermann Göring, an ambitious empire builder like the other members of the Nazi hierarchy, insisted that the airborne troops remain under his personal command. Although he lacked the flamboyant appeal of Erwin Rommel and shunned personal publicity, Kurt Student was rather loved by his troops for his genuine concern for their welfare and his courage on the battlefield. After Hitler turned against airborne forces, Student was mainly engaged in conventional land operations and planning a few special airborne missions such as the abduction of Mussolini in September 1943. In September 1944, Student thwarted the Allied airborne offensive at Arnhem (Operation Market Garden), and for this success was promoted to command Army Group G in Holland, a position he held until the end of World War II. In May 1947, Student was put on trial by the British government for atrocities committed by his forces in Crete in 1941, found guilty, and sentenced to five years' imprisonment.

Udet

Ernst Udet (1896–1941), another World War I fighter-ace veteran, was credited with shooting down 62 enemy planes, and achieved further renown after the war as an audacious stunt flier. A personal friend of Reichsmarschall Hermann Göring, he was appointed director general of equipment, and in this position controlled much of the power formerly invested in Milch. The influential and talented Udet favored speed and maneuverability as a result of his own experience but lacked expertise in the field of long-range bombing and transport. He was greatly responsible for the Luftwaffe's concentration on single-engined fighters such as the Messerschmitt Bf 109, on dive-bombers such as the Junkers Ju 87, and light and medium bombers such as the Messerschmitt Bf 110 and Heinkel He 111, an emphasis which proved successful in the early years of World War II, but which turned out disastrously in the long term. The failure of the Luftwaffe during the Battle of Britain undermined Udet's standing with Hitler and Göring. In November 1941, following a serious quarrel with Göring about the Luftwaffe's shortcomings on the Russian front, Udet committed suicide. For obvious political reasons, the affair was covered up. Udet's death was officially reported as resulting from an aircraft accident.

Wever

The Reichswehr's director of infantry training, Walther Wever (1890–1936) was transferred to the Luftwaffe. A convinced Nazi, an untiring worker, and an able staff officer, he did much to develop the air force, with a particular emphasis on the importance of strategic long-range heavy bombers. In May 1936 Wever died in an air crash, and with him the heavy-bomber program lost its momentum and was never to recover. From then on, long-range bombers only received low priority and Kesselring and Milch's view prevailed, favoring light aircraft but depriving Germany of a heavy bomber fleet.

The German air force was rife with arguments, rivalries, vested interests and envy. As seen above, some personal relationships between the main Luftwaffe leaders were bad, so bad as to end with suicide. Göring lacked the wide organizational experience which Milch had obtained as Lufthansa's chief executive, and since he was uncomfortable in such matters he tended to distrust his deputy's motives, with some reason. He also disliked Udet, who had once thrown him out of the Richthofen Veterans' Association on the ground of falsification of his war record. Milch, for his part, despised Udet's easygoing and bohemian lifestyle. Kesselring disagreed violently with Milch on a number of professional and personal issues and left the Air Ministry for the less-heated atmosphere of an operational command.

There was also a touch of amateurism in these founders of the German air force, a lack of professionalism which inevitably led to the Luftwaffe's defeats and failures. Yet, surprisingly, as a team these leaders produced a balanced air force, capable of both strategic and tactical deployment, at least for the early victorious years of World War II. The Luftwaffe's relationship with the other branches of the Wehrmacht did not always go smoothly, though. The army high command was not enthusiastic about aircraft being added to land forces. They suspected that airmen might be difficult and ready to confuse them with technicalities. Besides, many of them were convinced that the Luftwaffe would not play an important role in any modern war. They predicted that opposing air forces would fight each other and burn themselves out in the sky in the initial clashes, leaving the real battle to their tanks, infantry and artillery. In spite of these difficulties, by 1939 both airmen and ground army leaders had learned to work together in close cooperation, providing Nazi Germany with the weapons, organization and methods for Lightning War, while Führer Adolf Hitler possessed the political will and determination to use them.

Organization

Airpower, in terms of war, was young in the 1930s and 1940s. It was just beyond the adolescent stage. It had no historical tradition, whereas land and sea battles were almost as old as humankind itself. The soldier and the sailor had inherited a wealth of precedent by which they could be taught the rudiments of their trade, but it was very different with aviators. All they knew they had to learn by personal experience, not from textbooks. Considerable misconception existed concerning airpower, its organization, and the use that could be made of it. The interwar period was a time of plenty of theory as to the meaning of airpower, but there was no fully tried practice until the Spanish Civil War. One school argued that an air force should be an integral part of the army and navy—that it should be solely under the control of those two services, staffed and operated by men who were primarily soldiers or sailors. Another school maintained that an air force should be a separate fighting service. Advocates of these opposite views were vociferous in the press, on the public platform, in governments and in top military headquarters. The opinion held by German aviators, supported by Nazi circles, was that the Luftwaffe was to be a centralized and independent airpower, a force called upon to conduct an independent war apart from the army and the navy, a force operating above the army's front, above the coasts and the open sea, above and over the entire land and possessions of the enemy. The air force was regarded as purely and simply a weapon, more flexible than any other, a weapon to be used as a whole. The air force, the army, and the navy each had their separate functions, and each was a complement to the others. Finally as a soldier would best lead an army in battle and a sailor lead a fleet, an aviator should be in charge of the organization of air operations. From the start, the Luftwaffe was thus an independent arm led by the *Oberkommando der Luftwaffe* (OKL) placed under the leadership of Reichsmarschall Hermann Göring. Like the *Oberkommando der Marine* (OKM—navy high command) and the *Oberkommando des Heeres* (OKH—ground force high command), the OKL was subordinate to the *Oberkommando der Wehrmacht* (OKW—supreme head command of the German army) which was ultimately responsible to Hitler for the operational conduct of the three armed branches of the German forces.

Within the Luftwaffe itself, several conceptions existed concerning the organization and the use that would be made of the air force. After disputes and many moves, the opinion that prevailed was that of an airpower which was to be a destructive weapon of tactical offense as an adjunct to an attacking army. This choice proved right as long as the German forces fought short Blitzkrieg wars, but terribly wrong when the war became a worldwide conflict. The organization of the Luftwaffe thus reflected the dominance of its tactical role. The support of large ground armies demanded a corresponding mobility and flexibility, this leading to a unique system based upon the traditional military pattern. The composition of units was movable and extendable, and varied according to the requirement of the campaigns.

Luftgau

The basic administrative organization of the German air force was the *Luftgau* (air district) staffed by a *Generalmajor* (air commodore) and 50 to 150 officers and enlisted men. This was a territorial area command within Germany responsible for training, administration, maintenance, active and passive defense against air attack, operation of signal units, recruitment, mobilization and training of reserve personnel. For example, for supply and logistics, each *Luftgau* maintained vehicles organized in *Nachschubkolonnen* (transport units), including *Kesselwagenkolonnen* (*Kewa*, for shot) which were motorized convoys of tanker-trucks transporting fuel and lubricants. The supply section dealt with requisitions for bombs, fuel and ammunition. The administrative service handled clothing, food, pay, billeting, and other accommodations, including a record office, a photographic section, a medical section and a welfare service. The *Luftgau* commanders received most of their instructions directly from the RLM (Air Ministry). The *Luftgaue* permanently established in Germany were numbered nonconsecutively by Roman numerals, and those in occupied lands were generally designated by their location, for example, *Luftgau* Norwegian (Norway).

Luftflotte

The operational Luftwaffe was organized in multi-role *Luftflotte* (air fleets). A *Luftflotte*, the equivalent of an army group, was a temporary grouping of subordinate formations optimized for relevant operational tasks and capable of expansion or contraction in organizational and geographical terms to suit changing tasks. Originally there were four of them, each covering a part of the national territory. *Luftflotte* I, had its headquarters in Berlin and covered North and East Germany, as well as Poland in 1939, and North Russia after 1941. *Luftflotte* II, headquartered at Brunswick, covered Northwest Germany, the Western front in 1940, Great Britain, and later Central Russia, Italy, North Africa and the Mediterranean. *Luftflotte* III, from Munich, directed operations in Southwest Germany, the Western front in 1939, and parts of Great Britain. *Luftflotte* IV, from Vienna, covered Southeast Germany, Poland in 1939, the Balkans, South Russia, Hungary and Slovakia. During World War II the *Luftflotte* sectors were expanded and three additional air fleets were created. *Luftflotte* V (Oslo) covered Norway, Finland, Northern Russia, and the Arctic front. *Luftflotte* VI (Smolensk) covered Poland, Central Russia, Slovakia, Bohemia-Moravia and Croatia. *Luftflotte* VII/Reich, headquartered at Berlin, was created to deal with the protection of Germany from Allied bombers. Each *Luftflotte* had its own signal services, consisting of three *Luft-Nachrichtenregimenter* (signal regiments) and a branch that administrated the *Fliegerabwehrkanone*, in short *Flak* (anti-aircraft artillery).

Each *Luftflotte* was made up of a number of *Fliegerkorps* (flying corps)—again, formations of varying size and extremely elastic composition—which were responsible for all operational matters, including deployment, air traffic, ordnance and maintenance. A *Fliegerkorps*, numbered nonconsecutively in Roman numerals, could be detached at any time for operations in another *Luftflotte* area, and its make-up was flexible as to number and type of aircraft. A *Jagdkorps* was an operational command, similar to a *Fliegerkorps* but whose function was limited to that of a command. The *Fliegerkorps* were divided into *Fliegerdivision* (Jagddivision for fighter aircrafts). These operational commands were similar to—but of less importance than—a *Fliegerkorps*, and in some cases could be directly subordinate to the *Luftflotte*.

There was also a unit known as the *Lehrdivision* whose primary function was to test the latest types of aircraft, anti-aircraft defenses, and air-signals equipment from a tactical and operational point of view. It was organized into a variety of formations and commands, and its personnel were supposed to have previous combat experience. *Lehr* units were distinct experimental units whose tasks were of a technical nature, such as the testing of prototype aircrafts.

Geschwader

Both divisions and corps were composed of a number of tactical *Geschwader*—groups, each totaling between 90 and 120 aircraft. These were the largest homogeneous units. They were designated as follows:

- *Kampfgeschwader* (KG): level bomber
- *Sturzkampfgeschwader* (Stuka or StG): dive-bomber
- *Kampfschulegeschwader* (KSG): bomber training
- *Zertörergeschwader* (ZG): destroyer (ground attack)
- *Schnellkampfgeschwader* (SKG): fast bomber (single-engined ground attack)
- *Jadggeschwader* (JG): single-engined fighter
- *Nachtjadggeschwader* (NJG): night fighter
- *Lehrgeschwader* (LG): advanced training and demonstration
- *Transportgeschwader* (TG): transport
- *Luftlandegeschwader* (LLG): air-landing (glider).

There were also smaller autonomous *Geschwadern* and *Gruppen* for various roles such as shipborne floatplanes, trials (development and evaluation of German and captured enemy equipment), reconnaissance and observation (land or maritime, short- or long-range), sea-mine detection, maritime search and rescue, meteorology, and night ground attack. A *Geschwader* was usually commanded by an *Oberst* or *Oberstleutnant* known as the *Geschwaderkommodore*, who had a small staff of officers for the adjutant, operations, organization, technical, signal, navigation, meteorological and intelligence branches. *Geschwadern* were identified by Arabic numerals, e.g., *Jadggeschwader* 2 (JG 2), or *Zertörergeschwader* 4 (ZG 4), and *Gruppen* by Roman numerals, e.g., III/JG 2 would be the third group of second fighter *Geschwader* (see also "Aircraft markings" in Part 2). According to tactical needs, *Gruppen* could be transferred from one *Geschwader* to another and then renumbered.

Gruppe

Tactically, each *Geschwader* included three or four *Gruppen* ("wings" with 30 or 40 aircraft). A *Gruppe* was the basic combat unit of the Luftwaffe for both administrative and operational purposes. It was a mobile homogeneous unit which was largely self-contained and which might be detached from its parent *Geschwader*. It was commanded by a major or a captain, known as the *Gruppenkommandeur* who had a small staff, including adjutant, operations officer, technical officer and medical officer. Although all *Gruppen* in a *Geschwader* specialized in similar air tactics and were equipped with the same type of aircraft, the make and model might differ among the *Gruppen*. This variation was most prevalent in fighter *Geschwader*, but also occurred in a bomber group; thus a *Kampfgeschwader* might have one *Gruppe* equipped with the Dornier Do 17, and the other two *Gruppen* with the Heinkel He 111 or the Junkers Ju 88. A *Gruppe* generally occupied one airfield and also had its own air-signal platoon, mechanics and administrative personnel, as well as a *Fliegerhorst-Feuerwehr* (FhFw—fire defense), equipped and trained for firefighting; the fire squads held police status, and were thus officially under the control of the SS and detached from Luftwaffe command.

Each *Gruppe* was divided into three or four

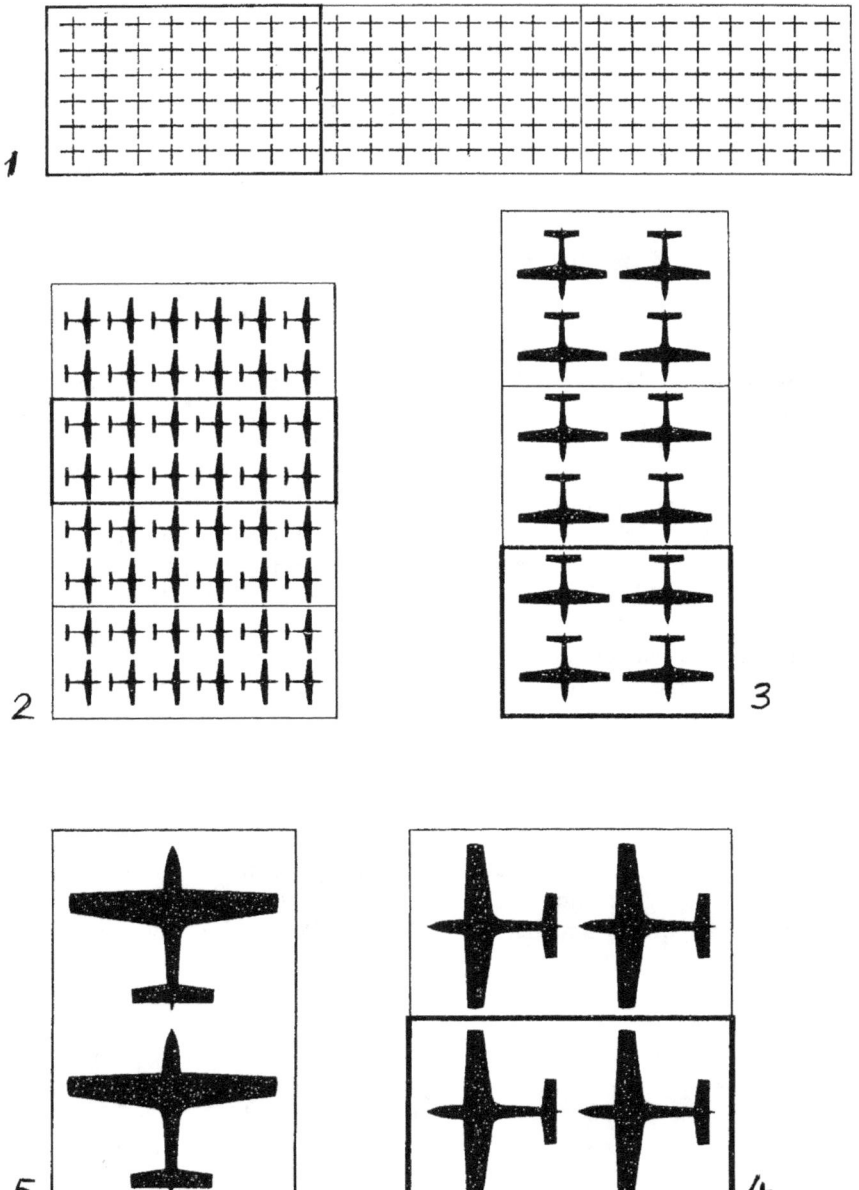

Luftwaffe fighter organization. **1:** Jagdgeschwader *divided into three* Gruppen. **2:** Gruppe *divided into four* Staffeln. **3:** Staffel *divided into three* Schwärme. **4:** Schwarm *divided into two* Rotten. **5:** Rotte *consisting of two fighters.*

Staffeln (squadrons usually counting between twelve and sixteen airplanes, but sometimes as few as five or six). The *Staffel* was the smallest Luftwaffe operational unit, generally commanded by a captain or a lieutenant, known as the *Staffelkapitän*. The *Staffel* generally had its own mobile repair workshop for minor repairs in the dispersal areas. It could be further divided into three *Schwärme* of four or six planes, which in turn were divided into *Ketten* of three aircraft. A *Rotte* was the name given to a pair of fighters, including leader and wingman.

The Luftwaffe's organization was quite flexible, enabling rapid preparedness without the encumbrance of a separate administrative unit. It was well suited for short Blitzkrieg operations, but less adequate to the long-term development of the air force, when more united and better coordinated fighter and bomber commands would have been a decisive asset. The organization and structure of the Luftwaffe had the effect of allowing aircraft and forces to be dispersed at a time when strategic considerations demanded their concentration, as shown by the Battle of Britain, the Russian front and—more particularly—for the defense of the Reich. It should be noted that the Luftwaffe was Hermann Göring's private empire, and that it included other troops apart from the flying ones; it included the huge Flak (anti-aircraft artillery) and ground troops: paratroopers, Luftwaffe field infantry divisions, and the elite Hermann Göring Division, which was expanded to a panzer (tank) and parachute corps. In fact Göring would have done better to place the whole or a part of his ground forces under army command. Until 1943, he refused to do so, partly out of his own pride, and partly because he believed that most of the Heer commanders were ideologically unreliable. In Göring's mind, the Luftwaffe was a Nazi creation and an organization totally devoted to National Socialism, and had to remain so.

Main German Aircraft Manufacturers

The Treaty of Versailles, signed on June 28, 1919, called for a considerable reduction in the size of Germany's army and navy, as well as placing a total ban on military aviation. The German defeat of 1918 had brought about the dismantling of Germany's heavy industry. Prohibition, restriction and industrial dismantling were gradually circumvented, and slowly a small but effective airplane industry was redeveloped to meet the demands for light sports planes and larger civil machines for commercial purposes. Germany, deprived of all aircraft after 1919, was provided with the opportunity to rebuild and develop a completely modern air arm. In 1922 the Allies placed a limit on the size and quantity of civilian aircraft the Germans could build. In the 1920s the glamorous airplane was written about, read about and discussed behind locked doors. Germany gradually became one of the most aviation-minded nations in the world, and General Hans von Seeckt, as chief of the general staff, embarked on a secret policy of building a highly trained and efficient nucleus for a new German army, capable of rapid expansion once the Versailles Treaty restrictions had been swept aside. He discreetly but strongly supported initiative and secret development. His stiff training program emphasized technical and weapons training, coordination of arms, communications and mobility. Seeckt was forced to resign in October 1926 through a combination of domestic and French pressure, but he had done a tremendous job. When Hitler came to power in January 1933, the groundwork for the creation of a modern air force had been more or less completed. The German aircraft industry included many of the companies that were to produce famous World War II machines. Note that *"Werke"* means manufacture. AG, short for *Aktiengesellschaft*, indicates Joint Stock Company; GmbH (*Gesellschaft mit beschränkter Haftpflicht*) means Limited Liability Company; KG (*Kommanditgesellschaft*) denoted Limited Partnership Company.

Ago Flugzeugwerke GmbH

The Aerowerke Gustav Otto company, named after the German aviation pioneer, 1883–1926, was created in 1912 at Oschersleben. It made several designs which were used during World War I. In the early 1930s, the company's initial work was to manufacture aircraft designed by other firms. Ago designed only one aircraft, the ill-fated two-engine light transport Ao 192 Kurier. In late 1936, the small company was taken over by the giant Junkers concern.

Arado Flugzeugwerke GmbH

The Arado company was founded in 1917 with the creation of Werfte Warnemünde der Flugzeugbaus Friedrichshafen. In 1921, the aircraft factory located at Warnemünde was purchased by German engineer Heinrich Lübbe (1884–1940) and was briefly engaged in shipbuilding. In 1924 the company restarted aircraft construction for export, with the opening of a subsidiary, Ikarus in Yugoslavia. Walter Rethel, previously of the Dutch aircraft company Fokker, was appointed head designer. In 1925 the company was renamed Arado Handelsgesellschaft. In March 1933 when the new Nazi government reestablished aviation in Germany, the name Arado Flugzeugwerke GmbH was adopted. Rethel was replaced by a new leader, Walter Blume, formerly of the Albatros company. Arado achieved early prominence as a supplier to the Luftwaffe with its Arado Ar 66, which became one of the standard Luftwaffe trainers. The firm also produced some of the Luftwaffe's first fighter aircraft, the Ar 65 and Ar 68. In 1936, the leadership of the Arado firm refused to join the Nazi Party. As a result the company was nationalized and placed under the direction of the pro-Nazi Erich Serno and Felix Wagenführ.

As World War II broke out, Arado became a manufacturer of great importance, largely in connection with production of aircraft for other companies but also in the development and production of its own models. Two more Arado aircraft rose to prominence, the Ar 96, which became the Luftwaffe's most used trainer, and the Ar 196, a reconnaissance seaplane that became standard equipment on all larger German warships. Unfortunately for Arado, most of their other designs were passed over in favor of stronger products from their competitors. Arado's most celebrated aircraft of the war was the Ar 234, the world's first operational jet-powered bomber. Built too late to have any real effect on the outcome of the conflict, it was nevertheless a sign of things to come. In 1945, the company was liquidated.

Bayerische Flugzeug-Werke

Bayerische Flugzeug-Werke produced a number of airplane prototypes during World War I. After the war, as the Treaty of Versailles forbade the production of warplanes, one branch became the still-famous Bayerische Motoren-Werke (better known as BMW), building motorcycles, cars and aircraft engines. The company was reformed at Augsburg in 1926, taking over the manufacture of the former Bayerische Rumpler-Werke. In 1928, Willy Messerschmitt joined the company as chief engineer and designed the Bf 108 Taifun and the Bf 109, undoubtedly the most famous German fighter of World War II. In July 1938, Bayerische Flugzeug-Werke was renamed Messerschmitt AG (see below).

Blohm & Voss Aircraft Manufacture

On April 5, 1877, Hermann Blohm and Ernst Voss founded the Blohm & Voss Schiffswerft und Maschinenfabrik (shipbuilding and engineering works) on the island of Kuhwerder, near Hamburg. Completely demolished after the end of World War I, Blohm & Voss restarted, designing and building ships and also aircraft for use by both the German state airline, Lufthansa, and later the Luftwaffe. The aviation branch of the company was originally known as Hamburger Flugzeugbau and their early aircraft bore the designation "Ha," later replaced by the prefix "Bv." Particularly noteworthy were the company's large flying boats (e.g., Ha 138, Ha 139, Bv 222 Wiking, Bv 238), as well as ingenious approaches to aircraft building that featured several asymmetrical designs (e.g., Bv 141). The company's main designer and director of development, Dr. Richard Vogt, was credited with no less than 200 different ideas for new aircraft, virtually none of which even was built as a prototype. Blohm & Voss also produced glide bombs (Bv 143, Bv 246 Hagelkorn).

Today Blohm & Voss, along with Howaldtswerke at Kiel and Nordseewerke at Emden, a subsidiary of Thyssen-Krupp Marine Systems. Although Hamburger Flugzeugbau reemerged after the war and now—under different ownership—builds warships both for the Deutsche Marine and for export, as well as oil-drilling equipment and ships for numerous commercial customers, this company has no more ties to the Blohm & Voss shipyards.

Bücker Aircraft Company

Carl Clemens Bücker served as an officer in the German navy during World War I and then spent some years after the war in Sweden where he worked as freelance test pilot before establishing his own aircraft company, Svenska Aero (Saab), in 1921. With the sale of this business at the end of 1932, Bücker returned to his native Germany where he opened a new aircraft factory at Johannisthal a suburb of Berlin, and later at Rangsdorf. Bücker had brought with him a talented Swedish engineer, Anders J. Anderson, and both designers succeeded in creating several superb aircraft: the Bücker Bü 131 Jungmann (1934), the Bü 133 Jungmeister (1936) and the Bü 181 Bestmann (1939). As well as these, the company built designs from several other manufacturers under license, including the Focke-Wulf Fw 44, the DFS 230, and components for the Focke-Wulf Fw 190, Junkers Ju 87, and Henschel Hs 293.

At the end of World War II, the company's premises fell into the Soviet occupation zone and were seized. The company was then broken up.

Darmstadt Akademische Fliegergruppe

This company was established in 1921 by a group of students of the Technical High School of Darmstadt, with the purpose of designing and testing flying machines. They produced a number of sailplanes and, from 1924, a series of advanced light airplanes which held several class records. Work on powered planes ended in 1939.

Deutsche Forschungsinstitut für Segelflug

Established as the Rhön-Rossiten Gesellschaft at Wasserkuppe in 1925, the Deutsche Forschungsinstitut für Segelflug (DFS—German institute for gliding research) received its new name on moving to Darmstadt in 1933. The institute designed and built the successful DFS 230 assault glider, and worked on various projects involving jet propulsion, swept-wing, and delta-wing design under the creative influence of Dr. Alexander Lippisch.

Dornier Aircraft Company

Claudius Honoré Desiré Dornier (1884–1969) was one of the most famous aircraft designers. Founder of Dornier GmbH, his legacy remains in several Luftwaffe aircraft named after him. Claudius Dornier was born in Bavaria. Deeply interested in science, he graduated in 1907 from the Technical University. He first worked as engineer at the Nagel Engineering Company in Karlsruhe, and he joined the airship-building company Zeppelin at Friedrichshaven in 1910. A brilliant engineer, he was soon appointed as Count Zeppelin's personal scientific advisor. In this position Dornier began experimental research and in 1911 he began designing all-metal aircraft and flying boats. Some of his designs of warplanes were used in World War I for Germany. After the First World War, the manufacture transferred to Manzel near Friedrichshaven. In 1922 the company became Dornier Metallbauten GmbH and since the Manzel works were too small, it moved to Altenrhein in Switzerland, adding a branch in Italy known as SMCA-Dornier, at Marina di Pisa. During this period Dornier again started building seaplanes, and he designed the Dornier Do X, at the time the world's largest aircraft. Costing more than it was worth, the use of the Do X was abandoned.

In 1932 production was reestablished in Germany as Dornier-Werke GmbH. Dornier's extensive flying-boat experience gave him a wealth of knowledge, and the company continued to produce flying boats and conventional passenger aircraft during the 1930s. These designs were critical in establishing the international reputation of Germany's aviation industry. Many of Dornier's designs were exported or licensed for foreign manufacture, and Japan was a major customer. During World War II the Dornier Company went back to designing war aircraft. Making use of forced labor, the Company produced several seaplanes used by the Luftwaffe. Dornier's most significant design before and during World War II was the Do 17 and its derivatives, which represented a zenith in Dornier's influence, providing the Luftwaffe with a bomber and later a night fighter. Dornier was a rather conservative designer who would have nothing to do with jet propulsion. However he innovated by developing the fastest piston-engine fighter of the war, the twin-engine Do 335, with its powerplants in a single axis. Dornier was not only a great designer, a skillful manager and a gifted entrepreneur but also an astute politician who not only survived but prospered despite the hardships of Germany's defeat in World War I, the restrictions of the Versailles Treaty, the world economic crisis of 1930, the predatory mismanagement of the Nazi era and the second German defeat in 1945. After World War II, aircraft production was again forbidden in Germany, and Dornier relocated to Spain (as Oficinas Técnicas Dornier) and then to Switzerland where the firm provided aeronautic consultancy services until once again returning to Germany in 1954. Claudius Dornier quickly reestablished himself with highly successful small STOL transports, such as the Do 27 and Do 28 Skyservant. In 1974, the Alpha Jet was developed, in a joint venture with French aircraft manufacturers Dassault-Breguet, as a new, standard NATO trainer. In 1985 Lindauer Dornier GmbH was created, spinning off textile machinery subdivisions. In 1996 the majority of Dornier was acquired by Fairchild Aircraft, forming Fairchild-Dornier. Today the Dornier company also makes medical equipment, such as a lithotripter to treat kidney stones.

ERLA-Maschinenwerke GmbH

This small and virtually unknown company, established in 1933, designed a single-seat monoplane, the unsuccessful Type Erla 5. From 1934 until the end of World War II the company produced assemblies for other military types, namely Arado Ar 65 and Ar 68, Heinkel He 51 and Messerschmitt Bf 109.

Fieseler Aircraft Company

The Fieseler Flugzeugbau was founded after World War I by the German fighter-ace veteran and aerobatics champion, Gerhard Fieseler (1896–1987). After World War I, Fieseler ran a printing company in Eschweiler, but in 1926 he went back to aviation. He became a flight instructor with the Raab-Katzenstein Aircraft Company in Kassel and an accomplished stunt pilot. In 1928, he designed his own stunt plane, the Fieseler F1, built by Raab-Katzenstein. He also designed the Raab-Katzenstein RK-26 *Tigerschwalbe* aircraft in the late 1920s which was sold to a Swedish company called AB Svenska Järnvägverkstaderna (ASJA), which built 25 of the type for the Swedish air force in the beginning of 1930s.

In 1930, Raab-Katzenstein was bankrupt, and Fieseler decided to strike out on his own. Using money he had been saving from his aerobatics, he bought the Segelflugzeugbau Kassel (sailplane factory) and renamed it Fieseler Flugzeugbau. Although he continued with some sailplane manufacturing, in 1932 he set up to start manufacturing sports planes of his own design. In one of these aircraft, he went on to win the inaugural World Aerobatic Championship in Paris in 1934, taking home a prize of 100,000 French francs, which he invested into the company. A Nazi Party member, Fieseler won contracts to license-build military aircraft for the new Luftwaffe in 1935. Real success came the following year, when he won a design contest for a STOL observation plane that he then went on to produce as the Fieseler Fi 156 Storch. Another important contribution to the Luftwaffe and Hitler's regime was the Fi 103 flying-bomb, better known as the V-1 Buzz Bomb. Following World War II, Fieseler spent some time in U.S. custody. When he was released, he reopened part of this factory and spent some years building automotive components. He also published an autobiography, *Meine Bahn am Himmel* (My Road in the Sky). Gerhart Fieseler died in Kassel, aged 91.

Flettner Aircraft Company

Anton Flettner (1885–1962) attended the Fulda State Teachers College in Germany. When he was teaching mathematics and physics in a high school in Frankfurt, he began to develop ideas leading to his work for Germany in World War I. During the war he developed what was perhaps his best-known invention. Called Flettner's control, it was a modern device to lift or lower a plane's nose. Flettner also invented tank improvements for Germany. After World War I he was named managing director of the Institute for Aero and Hydro Dynamics in Amsterdam. In the 1920s, he pioneered the helicopter concept and developed vertical rotor propulsion. In 1931, he created his own company, the Anton Flettner Aircraft Corporation in Berlin, and from then on to 1945, developed and built helicopters, a number of which were used by Hitler's forces in World War II.

Focke-Achgelis GmbH

Formed by Heinrich Focke, formerly of Focke-Wulf, and aerobatic pilot Gerd Achgelis, this company specialized in helicopter design.

Focke-Wulf Aircraft Company

The Focke-Wulf Flugzeugbau AG company was founded in Bremen on October 23, 1923, as Bremer Flugzeugbau AG by Henrich Focke, Georg Wulf and Dr. Werner Neumann. Almost immediately, they renamed it Focke-Wulf Flugzeugbau AG. Initially it produced several commercially unsuccessful aircraft, typically with thick wings mounted high over bulky fuselages. Test piloting one of these, Georg Wulf died on September 29, 1927. In 1931, under government pressure, Focke-Wulf merged with Albatros-Flugzeugwerke of Berlin. The resourceful engineer and test pilot Kurt Tank from Albatros became head of the technical department. Kurt Tank became the driving force in the Focke-Wulf company, and immediately started work on the Fw 44 Stieglitz, the company's first commercially successful design, launched in 1934, and the Focke-Wulf Fw 61, the first fully controllable helicopter in 1936. In 1937 shareholders ousted Heinrich Focke, and he founded, with Gerd Achgelis, the Focke Achgelis Company to specialize in helicopter development. Meanwhile Kurt Tank had designed and produced the passenger-carrying Fw 200 *Kondor*.

The most important aircraft produced in quantity from early 1941 to 1945 by the Focke-Wulf Company was, without doubt, the Fw 190 *Würger* (Shrike) a mainstay single-seat fighter for the Luftwaffe during World War II. After the war, Focke-Wulf was not allowed to continue production for several years. Kurt Tank, like many other German technicians, continued his professional life in Latin America. So did Professor Heinrich Focke who designed light helicopters in the 1960s for the Brazilian Departemento de Aeronaves, the research branch of the Instituto de Pesquisa e Desenvolvimento (IDP). Restricted plane production was permitted again in Germany in 1951, and the reborn Focke-Wulf Company began to make gliders. Production of motorized planes started again in 1955, with the manufacture of trainer aircraft for the postwar German military. In 1961, Focke-Wulf, Weserflug and Hamburger Flugzeugbau joined forces in the Entwicklungsring Nord (ERNO) to develop rockets. Focke-Wulf formally merged with Weserflug in 1964, becoming Vereinigte Flugtechnische Werke (VFW).

Gothaer Waggonfabrik

Gothaer Waggonfabrik (Gotha or GWF) was a German manufacturer of rolling stock, established in the late nineteenth century at Warnemünde. During the two world wars, the company expanded into aircraft building.

In World War I, Gotha was the manufacturer of a highly successful series of bombers based on a 1914 design by Oskar Ursinus. From 1917, these aircraft were capable of carrying out strategic bombing missions over England, the first heavier-than-air aircraft used in this role. Several dozen of these bombers were built in a number of subtypes. While Germany was prohibited from aircraft manufacture by the Treaty of Versailles, Gotha returned to its railway endeavors, but went back to aviation with the rise of the Nazi government and the abandonment of the Versailles Treaty's restrictions.

Gotha's main contribution to the new Luftwaffe was the Gotha Go 145 trainer, of which some 9,500 were built. The firm also produced the Gotha Go 242 assault glider. Perhaps the most famous Gotha product of World War II, however, was an aircraft that never actually entered service, the Horten Ho 229. This was an exotic, jet-powered, flying-wing fighter aircraft designed by the Horten brothers, who lacked the facilities to mass-produce it. Following the war, Gotha once again returned to its original purpose, building trams and light rail vehicles in the former East Germany.

Heinkel Aircraft Company

Heinkel Flugzeugwerke was founded by and named after Ernst Heinkel (1888–1958). The company originated from the Hansa und Brandenburgische Flugzeugwerke in which Ernst Heinkel had been previously been chief designer. The Heinkel Company was established at Warnemünde in 1922 when the restrictions on German aviation imposed by the Treaty of Versailles were relaxed. The company's first great success was the design of the Heinkel He 70 Blitz high-speed mail-plane and airliner for Deutsche Lufthansa in 1932. The type broke a number of air-speed records for its class. Heinkel's most important designers at this point were the twin Günter brothers, Siegfried and Walter, and Heinrich Hertel (1902–1982).

The Heinkel Company is most closely associated with the He 111, which became a mainstay of the Luftwaffe. Heinkel also provided the Luftwaffe's heaviest operational bomber, the Heinkel He 177, although this was never deployed in significant numbers. Heinkel was less successful in selling fighter designs. Before the war, the Heinkel He 112 had been rejected in favor of the Messerschmitt Bf 109, and Heinkel's attempt to top Messerschmitt's design with the Heinkel He 100 failed due to political interference within the Reichsluftfahrtministerium (RLM—Reich Aviation Ministry). The company also provided the Luftwaffe with an outstanding night fighter, the Heinkel He 219, which also suffered from politics and was produced only in limited numbers.

From 1941 until the end of the war, the company was merged with engineer Wolf Hirth's manufacture (prewar producer of sailplanes who also made wooden sub-assemblies for Messerschmitt) to form Heinkel-Hirth, giving the company the capability of manufacturing its own power plants. The company also had a branch, known as Heinkel-Strahlbetrieb (HeS), located at Rostock and Stuttgart-Zuffenhausen, for the development and production of jet engines.

Indeed the Heinkel name was also behind pioneering work in jet-engine and rocket development. In 1939, the Heinkel He 176 and Heinkel He 178 became the first aircraft to fly under liquid-fuel rocket and turbojet power respectively, and Heinkel was the first to develop a jet fighter to prototype stage, the Heinkel He 280. This latter aircraft never reached production, however, since the RLM wanted Heinkel to concentrate on bomber production and instead promoted the development of the rival Messerschmitt Me 262. Very late in the war, a Heinkel jet fighter finally took to the air as the Heinkel He 162 *Volksjäger* (People's Fighter) but it had barely entered service at the time of Germany's surrender.

Following the war, Heinkel was prohibited from manufacturing aircraft and instead built bicycles, motorscooters and the Heinkel microcar. The company eventually returned to aircraft in the mid 1950s, license-building F-104 Starfighters for the West German Luftwaffe. In 1965, the company was absorbed by Vereinigte Flugtechnische Werke (VFW), which was in turn absorbed by Messerschmitt-Bölkow-Blohm in 1980.

Henschel Aircraft Company

Georg Christian Carl Henschel founded the Henschel Aircraft Company in 1810 at Kassel. Followed by his son Karl-Anton, the Henschel company started manufacturing railroad material, and became one of the largest locomotive manufacturers in Germany by the beginning of the twentieth century. Early in 1935 Henschel made a reputation in building tanks, designing and manufacturing the prewar Panzer I. During World War II Henschel was involved in large-scale production of the PzKpw III, and the Tiger I from 1941. Henschel was the primary manufacturer of the Panzer VI.

Henschel and Chief Designer Erwin Adlers also designed aircraft (the most important being the Hs123, Hs 126 and Hs 129) and experimental guided missiles (e.g., Schmetterling, Henschel Hs 293 glide bomb, Henschel Hs 294 anti-shipping glide bomb). During 1945, the company's factories were one of the most important bomber targets in the war, and were destroyed nearly completely.

Manufacturing began again in 1948. In 1964 the company took over Rheinische Stahlwerke and became Rheinstahl Henschel AG; in 1976, Thyssen Henschel; and ABB Henschel AG in 1990.

In 1996 the company became ABB Daimler Benz Transportation Adtranz. The company was subsequently acquired in 2002 by Bombardier (Canada). The Kassel facility still exists and today is one of the world's largest manufacturers of locomotives.

Horten

The Horten brothers conducted flying-wing experiments, built a series of tailless high-performance gliders, and jet-powered wing-only aircrafts. As they lacked production facilities, their designs were developed with the Gothaer Waggonfabrik (see above).

Junkers Aircraft Company

Hugo Junkers was born on February 3, 1859, in a small town named Rheydt near Monchengladbach. After high school and engineering studies, Junkers joined the Deutsche Continental Gasgesellschaft in November 1888. In 1890, Junkers founded an experimental laboratory for gas engines, and in October 1892 created his own company at Dessau. In 1906, Junkers was confronted with aircraft aerodynamic design questions for the first time, and in 1908 he produced the first all-metal aircraft.

With the outbreak of World War I, Junkers continued research work at Dessau, and in late 1915 the Junkers J1 was designed. This was followed two years later by another design, in collaboration with the Dutch designer Anthony Fokker, resulting in the creation of Junkers-Fokker-Werke in October 1917. Conflicts of personality caused Fokker and Junkers to separate in 1918. After the war the newly created Junkers Flugzeugwerke AG became the new nucleus for further Junkers aviation activities. In the 1920s, the company was badly shaken by several financial crises. Nonetheless, convinced that all-metal structure was the ultimate answer to successful aircraft, Junkers designed the large transport Junkers G38 which flew first in 1929. This was followed by the development of new designs leading to the successful and famous Junkers Ju 52. Junkers also ran an engine factory, and in 1923 this was separated out to form its own company, Junkers Motorenbau GmbH, or Jumo. That same year Avions Metalicos Junkers was founded in Madrid to provide facilities for the construction of Junkers airplanes in Spain.

After Hitler took over political control in Germany in January 1933, the Junkers consortium suffered a final crisis. Under Nazi pressure, Hugo Junkers—in open opposition to Hitler—was forced to abandon all his patent rights and sell off the majority of his shares to the German government. In 1934 Junkers was put under arrest at his private home at Bayrischzell, and his health declined. Junkers died on his 76th birthday, February 3, 1935. From then on, the huge Junkers Company was nationalized, placed under the leadership of the ruthless Dr. Heinz Koppenburg from the steel industry, and became one of the most prominent German aircraft manufacturers. With factories built in Germany, France, and Czechoslovakia, the state-owned Junkers consortium produced famous World War II planes such as the Ju 52, the Ju 87, the Ju 88 and many others.

After the war, aircraft production ended, and with the absorption of a small aero-engine plant by the Messerschmitt group in 1975, the name Junkers disappeared entirely.

Klemm Leichtflugzeugbau

The Klemm Light Aircraft Company, located at Boblinggen, was founded and led by Dr. Hans Klemm (1885–1961), an eminent pioneer in the development of light aircraft. The company originated from the Daimler Motorengesellschaft Werke from 1910 which built several aircraft for the German air force in World War I. In 1919, production ceased at the main works and the Daimler-Werke AG continued to design experimental gliders. In December 1926 this company was taken over by Hans Klemm and became Klemm Leichtflugzeugbau GmbH. Klemm concentrated on light and economical aircraft design. His main contribution to the Luftwaffe was the design of two, small low-wing monoplanes used as trainer and liaison airplane. Production of Klemm light aircraft ended in November 1957.

Messerschmitt Aircraft Company

Born in 1898, Willy Emil Messerschmitt was the son of a wine merchant. As a young boy he became obsessed with aviation after seeing a Zeppelin airship. The young Messerschmitt helped the German gliding pioneer Friedrich Harth and it was Harth who arranged for Messerschmitt to work with him at a military flying school during the First World War. Harth and Messerschmitt together designed several gliders in the late 1920s. In the early 1930s, Messerschmitt designed a series of simple single-engined transport aircraft that were cheap to operate. These enabled Messerschmitt to build up his Bavarian Aircraft Works at Augsburg, the Bayerische Flugzeugwerke, hence the prefix "Bf" for the aircraft originally produced there. In 1931 his company was forced into bankruptcy when Lufthansa refused to take any more of its aircraft. The company started up again in 1933 after agreements had been reached with the creditors.

Willy Messerschmitt had an enemy at the highest level in the person of Erhard Milch, head of German civil aviation and ardent Nazi. Milch blamed Messerschmitt for the death of a friend in the crash of a Messerschmitt M20 transport plane, and he made sure that Messerschmitt got no government work. It was also Milch who had, as head of Lufthansa, forced bankruptcy on Messerschmitt in 1931.

In 1933 Hitler came to power and German rearmament started. This gave Milch even greater power and it might have been expected that Messerschmitt would suffer the same humiliation as another of Milch's enemies: Hugo Junkers. However Messerschmitt had cultivated friends in high places. Rudolph Hess the deputy head of the Nazi Party was one; Theo Croneiss, a World War I fighter pilot and associate of Hermann Göring, was another.

In 1934, Messerschmitt, helped by Robert Lusser who had joined the company in 1933 after working at Klemm and Heinkel, designed the Bf 108 Taifun, a remarkable four-seat touring aircraft. When the contest to find a new fighter for the Luftwaffe was announced in 1935, Messerschmitt realized that this was his big chance. The result was the revolutionary Bf 109. By this time Milch's power to influence the choosing of new equipment for the Luftwaffe had been greatly diminished by the appointment of Ernst Udet. Messerschmitt gained worldwide recognition for the Bf 109 design and it went on to be produced in greater numbers than any other single-seat aircraft in aviation history. Willy Messerschmitt gave the Luftwaffe exactly the weapon that was needed to secure the aerial dominance of Europe in 1939–1941. The Bf 109 stayed in production until the very end of the war.

Before and during World War II, Messerschmitt went on to design many other aircraft, for example, the twin-engined, two-seat heavy fighter Bf 110, the giant glider Me 321, and, undoubtedly his finest achievement, the twin-jet Me 262, a design years ahead of its time. Several Messerschmitt projects were failures however, including the long-range bomber Me 264, the rocket-powered fighter Me 163 Komet, and others.

After the war Messerschmitt was arrested and tried for having allowed the use of slave labor in his factories. He was in prison for two years. When released he set to work rebuilding his business. Not allowed to make aircraft in Germany, one of his products was the Messerschmitt Bubble Car. He managed to do some aircraft design for Hispano in Spain, including work on the HA 200 jet trainer. In August 1956 the company, reconstituted under the name Flugzeug-Union Süd with Heinkel, built Fouga Magister under license and later took part in developing programs for Fiat G-91, Lockheed F-104, Transsall C-160 and Bell UH-1D. It also helped in the design of the HA-300 supersonic jet fighter for Egypt in the mid–1960s. The Messerschmitt concern shared in the postwar success of Germany and is now part of the massive Messerschmitt-Bölkow-Blohm concern formed in May 1969 at Munich, which manufactures parts for several important projects, including the European Airbus and the Tornado aircraft.

Udet U-12 Flamingo. The two-seat biplane aerobatic trainer U-12 had a length of 7.47 m, a height of 2.80 m, a span of 9.96 m, a wing area of 24 square meters, and an empty weight of 525 kg. Powered by a Sh 11 piston radial engine, it had a maximum speed of 140 km/h and a range of 450 km.

Willy Messerschmitt retired in 1970 and died in 1978.

Siebel Flugzeugewerke

Established and led by Friedrich Wilhelm Siebel (1891–1954) in 1937 at Halle, the Siebel company's contribution to the Luftwaffe was the production of standard military types and its own design, the Si 204 light-reconnaissance airplane. After the war the Siebelwerke-ATG GmbH was created and the new company produced the Si 222 Super-Hummel and the three-seat Si 308. It was for merged in 1968 with Messerschmitt-Bölkow GmbH.

Skoda-Kauba Aircraft Company

The Czech Skoda-Kauba Aircraft Company was established by the Nazis in 1942. Controlled by the RLM and placed under the leadership of engineer Otto Kauba, it was actually the Czech firm Avia, from Cakovice near Prague, which had been integrated into the Skoda manufacture. Working for the Germans, the company designed several light airplanes as well as experimental jet-powered types.

Udet Flugzeugbau GmbH

Ernst Udet, a German ace of World War I and later a prominent leader of the Luftwaffe, lent his name to this company which was established near Munich in 1921 by an American engineer named William Pohl from Milwaukee. The company produced several types, namely the single-seat lightplane U-1; the cabin monoplane U-5; the parasol-winged single-seat U-7 *Kolibri*; the small airliner U-8; the 11-seat, high-wing transport U-11 *Kondor*, and, most successful of all, the two-seat, open-cockpit, wooden biplane Udet U-12 Flamingo, intended as a trainer. Udet left the growing company in 1925. The Flamingo production continued, and the aircraft served in many roles, notably as a trainer with German civil flying clubs and as clandestine Luftwaffe pilot training centers before 1935. By the end of 1925, the Udet Company was one of the largest aircraft manufacturers, but because of disagreements at management level, and in spite of the Flamingo's success, the firm could not be saved from financial disaster. Negotiations with the Ministry of Transport and the Bavarian State led to the establishment of a new company (Bayerische Flugzeugwerke AG, later taken over by Messerschmitt) to take over control.

Werfte Warnemünde

Established in early 1917 as a subsidiary of Flugzeugbau Friedrichshafen, Werfte Warnemünde became known as Arado Flugzeugwerke after 1933 (see above).

Weser Flugzeugbau GmbH

The Weser Flugzeugbau GmbH originated from the Rohrbach Metal Flugzeugbau GmbH founded in 1922 by Dr. Adolf Rohrbach. The latter was formed in Copenhagen, Denmark, to avoid the limitations imposed on aviation construction by the Treaty of Versailles. In April 1934, Weser Flugzeugbau GmbH took over the company, and Dr. Rohrbach became technical director of Weser. Weser undertook contract manufacture during World War II for other firms. It also developed its own experimental convertiplane, the Weser P 1003/1.

Zeppelin Werke Lindau GmbH

Ferdinand, Count of Zeppelin (1838–1917) was the designer of large metal-framed dirigible airships which were used during World War I as long-range bombers. From 1928 to 1937, Zeppelin airships were used to carry passengers and freight on trans-Atlantic crossings. The Zeppelin aircraft company, established under the patronage of Count Zeppelin, with Claudius Dornier as chief designer, produced multi-engined flying-boats, biplanes and two-seat monoplane seaplanes. In 1922 the Zeppelin Werke Lindau GmbH was renamed Dornier GmbH (see above).

Nomenclature

Between 1919 and 1930, most major German aircraft manufacturers used sequential numbering systems to designate their models, with various types of prefixes. This led to many numbers being duplicated. In 1930, the *Heereswaffenamt* (Bureau of Army Weapons), together with other institutions and the aircraft industry, devised a system of allocating a unique number to every German aircraft design. Prefixes were standardized, and were to consist of two letters designating the manufacturing company. When the Nazis came to power in early 1933, the newly formed RLM took over and refined this aircraft designation system.

The following list includes the commonly used manufacturers' and designers' prefix letters encountered in this book.

- **Al** Albatros Flugzeugwerke GmbH
- **Ao** Ago Flugzeugwerke GmbH (taken over by Junkers in 1936)
- **Ar** Arado Flugzeugwerke GmbH
- **As** Argus-Motoren GmbH
- **Ba** Bachem-Werke GmbH
- **Bf** Bayerische Flugzeugwerke AG (Messerschmitt); changed to Me in 1938
- **BMW** Bayerisch Motorwerke
- **Bü** Bücker Flugzeugbau GmbH
- **Bv** Blohm & Voss, Abteilung Flugzeugbau; originally Ha
- **DFS** Deutsche Forschungsanstalt für Segelflug
- **Do** Dornier Werke GmbH
- **Fa** Focke-Achgelis GmbH
- **Fh** Flugzeugbau Halle GmbH (Siebel); changed to Si in 1936
- **Fi** Gerhard Fieseler Werke GmbH
- **Fl** Anton Flettner GmbH
- **Fw** Focke-Wulf Flugzeugbau GmbH

- **Go** Gothaer Waggonfabrik AG
- **Ha** Hamburger Flugzeugbau GmbH (Blohm & Voss); changed to Bv in 1937
- **He** Ernst Heinkel AG
- **HM** Heinkel-Hirth Flugmotoren
- **Ho** Reimar und Walter Horten
- **Hs** Henschel Flugzeugwerke AG
- **Hü** Ulrich Hütter
- **Ju** Junkers Flugzeug-und-Motorenwerke AG
- **Ka** Albert Kalkert (designer at Gothaer Waggonfabrik AG)
- **Kl** Hans Klemm Leichtflugzeugbau
- **Li** Alexander Lippisch (designer at DFS and Messerschmitt AG)
- **Me** Messerschmitt AG; originally Bf
- **Si** Siebel Flugzeugwerke KG; originally Fh
- **So** Heinz Sombold
- **Sk** Skoda-Kauba Flugzeugbau
- **Ta** Kurt Tank (chief designer at Focke-Wulf Flugzeugbau GmbH)
- **We** Weser Flugzeugbau
- **ZMe** Luftschiffbau Zeppelin GmbH, Abteilung Flugzeugbau/Messerschmitt
- **ZSo** Luftschiffbau Zeppelin GmbH, Abteilung Flugzeugbau/SNCASO

After February 1935, each individual prototype airplane was given the suffix "V" (for *Versuchs*, meaning prototype) and a unique identification number. Once accepted by the Luftwaffe, major variants of the same aircraft were given suffixes alphabetically with capital letters. Minor variants were denoted with numerical suffixes, beginning with -0 for evaluation versions. More minor variants still were given a lower-case alphabetical suffix. The suffix *Trop* (for tropical) was applied to airplanes modified to operate in hot and dusty climates. Manufacturers also built developments of successful existing models, and to reflect the lineage, the new types were numbered in increments of 100 above the number of the basic model (e.g., Messerschmitt 109, 209 and 309 or Junkers Ju 88, 188, 288, 388 and 488). In some cases, the two-letter designation was changed to indicate the designer or the developing team rather than the original manufacturer; for example, the former *Bf* (Bayerisch Flugzeugwerke) was changed to *Me* (Messerschmitt). Some late Focke-Wulf aircraft were prefixed *Ta* after designer Kurt Tank.

American methods of mass production were never adopted and German aircraft would continue to require more labor hours and more skilled labor than their U.S. equivalents. German aircraft manufacturers did their best to overhaul the labor-intensive production methods, but they never fully overcame traditional working practices or the culture prevailing in the German aviation business. For example Henschel had eleven different types of countersunk rivets on the same aircraft. Productivity was hampered even more severely by constant changes to the designs dictated by the RLM. The outbreak of World War II failed to shake German industry into high gear. Indeed Hitler switched production priorities to the army and navy during 1940, reducing aircraft production across the board. Even the belated mobilization of industry achieved by Minister Albert Speer did not make the best of the civilian industrial sector. Under the lackadaisical Hermann Göring and tragically miscast Ernst Udet, German aircraft were subject to continuous interference by various interested parties. Besides, the use of slave labor in the aircraft industry proved to be counterproductive. An underfed, mistreated, and unskilled forced laborer is, of course, always less productive than a well-fed, normally paid and well-motivated free worker.

Propaganda

German propaganda was a very important psychological weapon created and directed by Joseph Goebbels (1897–1945). It was enormously successful and played a central role in the nazification of Germany before and after the seizure of power by Hitler. Goebbels's principle was that an oft-repeated lie eventually would be believed, and manipulation and deception, shameless lies, misquotes, pseudo-scientific "proofs," historical falsification, forgery, intellectual fraud, false promises, and, above all, exploitation of emotion were used for indoctrination purposes in all aspects of German daily life, including the armed forces, criminal justice, religion, press and education. These ruthless methods were successful in Germany and were later applied in all occupied Europe. Nazi propaganda promised peace, order and prosperity in a "purified" continent under German rule.

In the Luftwaffe, emphasis was placed on its supposed invulnerability, in order to impress the Allies, but also to conceal defeats suffered, to discourage occupied nations, and to maintain and boost the morale of the German people. In practice, the propaganda displayed regarding the Luftwaffe made use of all of Goebbels's methods: hoaxing, lies and manipulation. *Propagandakompanien* (PK) were created, composed of journalists and reporters who did not participate in combat, but who wrote articles, made photographs and shot films of military events and on military topics. Such writings and images were published in the numerous strictly censored magazines and newspapers. They only showed political, cultural, social or sporting events glorifying the Nazi regime during the period 1933–1939. During the war and until 1945, the emphasis was on the achievements on the home front and on the Nazi victories on the battlefields. From before the war, the German Ministry of Propaganda disseminated a magazine specializing in the Luftwaffe called *der Adler* (The Eagle), not just in German but also in other languages, including French, and of several countries which were allied with Germany or under German control. While the U.S. remained officially neutral (from September 1939 until December 1941), the propaganda magazine was also published in English.

Postwar German Brain Drain

German designers had some revolutionary aircraft on their drawing boards, and the victorious Allies undertook several operations to benefit from German know-how. After May 1945, they were able to harvest advanced technical efforts, as many German aircraft had been abandoned after being deliberately wrecked for the most part. Operation Paperclip, for example, was the main U.S. effort to obtain technical specimens, data, or the design personnel themselves and discreetly "evacuate" them to the United States. Documents were quickly analyzed by the Americans and much German wartime technology was incorporated into postwar U.S. military aircraft. Similar attempts were made by the U.K., the USSR and France. Many aircraft designers were captured by the Red Army and sent to the USSR to design and build potential fighters and bombers for the Soviet air forces. The German knowledge base benefited the development of most postwar jet aircrafts. The early U.S. and Soviet space programs also employed German hardware and were staffed with many German scientists and engineers, the most famous of whom was Wernher von Braun, subsequently the head of the design team of the American Saturn V moon rocket.

Among the designers sent to Russia was Dr. Hans Wocke, the man who designed the world's first forward-swept-wing jet bomber, Junkers Ju 287. Yet neither this nor any other aircraft designed by the Germans would ever be accepted into the Soviet army or navy air forces, since the Germans themselves were technically prisoners and were denied access to the latest facilities for designing and perfecting modern warplanes. Most of the captured designers were allowed to return to either West or East Germany by the end of 1953.

A Few Figures

At the outbreak of World War II, during the Polish campaign in September 1939, the Luftwaffe had a total of 1,356 aircraft—210 fighters (both Messerschmitt Bf 109 and Bf 110), 249 dive-bombers (both Junkers Ju 87 and Henschel Hs 123) and 897 medium bombers (Dornier Do 17 and Heinkel He 11). Two hundred eight-five aircraft were lost.

For the invasion of Denmark and Norway in April 1940, the Luftwaffe committed some 80 aircraft, including fighters, bombers, transport airplanes and seaplanes.

For the attack against the Netherlands and

France in May–June 1940, the German air force achieved its peak in terms of professionalism and strength, mustering 1,264 fighters and 1,482 bombers of all type. In August 1940, at the start of the Battle of Britain, the Luftwaffe had 734 Messerschmitt Bf 109s, 268 Messerschmitt Bf 110s, 336 dive-bombers (Junkers Ju 87s), and 949 medium bombers (Heinkel He 111, Dornier 17 and Junkers Ju 88). Of this total of 2,287, the German air force's losses were 663 fighters and 691 bombers by mid–September 1940. At the same time, the RAF's losses amounted to about 800 fighters.

For the Balkan operation against Yugoslavia and Greece in the spring of 1941, the Luftwaffe, still a major tactical force, was able to commit some 1,100 warplanes. For the invasion of the Soviet Union in June 1941, the Luftwaffe initially committed 2,770 aircraft. For the Kursk offensive in the summer of 1943, the Luftwaffe massed 1,700 warplanes. When the Allies landed in Normandy on June 6, 1944, the German air force was able to fly only 319 sorties. A final effort was made in early January 1945, when 750 aircraft were grouped to support the Ardennes offensive.

In 1939, factories delivered about 217 bombers and 133 fighters per month; by mid–1941 these had increased to 336 and 244, respectively. From November 1941 deliveries increased from 12,400 aircraft to 15,000 airplanes in 1942 and 24,800 in 1943. Production peaked in 1944 when 40,600 aircraft were delivered. By this time, however, it was not aircraft that were required, but the men to fly them and the fuel to keep them in the air. By the end of 1944, when Allied bombers were free to roam at will over Germany, the Luftwaffe was a pale shadow of its former self, which had never been the force that Nazi propaganda claimed.

At the end of the European war in May 1945, over 97,000 members of the Luftwaffe were recorded as dead, missing or wounded.

The most-produced German aircraft of World War II was the Messerschmitt Bf 109 (about 35,000), followed by the Focke-Wulf Fw 190 (about 20,000). Both the Junkers Ju 88 and Messerschmitt Bf 110 had a production run of about 15,000. About 6,000 Junkers Ju 87 dive-bombers, and 7,300 Heinkel He 111 bombers were produced.

2

Basic Technical Data

Basic Flight Data

An airplane in flight is acted on by four forces. *Weight* or *gravity*, the downward-acting force, and *drag*, the backward-acting force (or retarding resistance of air and wind) are two natural forces inherent in anything lifted from the earth and moved through the air. Gravity and drag are opposed by two artificially created forces used to overcome the forces of nature and enable an aircraft to fly. *Lift*, the upward-acting force provided by the design of flying or lifting aerodynamic surfaces (popularly called wings), overcomes gravity. *Thrust* is the forward-acting force opposing drag, which is provided by a mechanism generating energy (engine). When cruising in straight-and-level unaccelerated flight (coordinated flight at a constant altitude and heading), lift equals weight and thrust equals drag. Any inequality between lift and weight will result in the airplane climbing or descending. Any inequality between thrust and drag result in change in speed (acceleration or deceleration).

Piston Engines

Most of the engines used in German World War II aircraft were sound, reliable and capable of considerable further refinements. The main German aircraft engine manufacturers were key to the construction and development of the Luftwaffe.

Argus Motoren (As), based in Berlin, produced "low power" engines for light aircraft and the pulse-jet engine used on the V1 flying bomb.

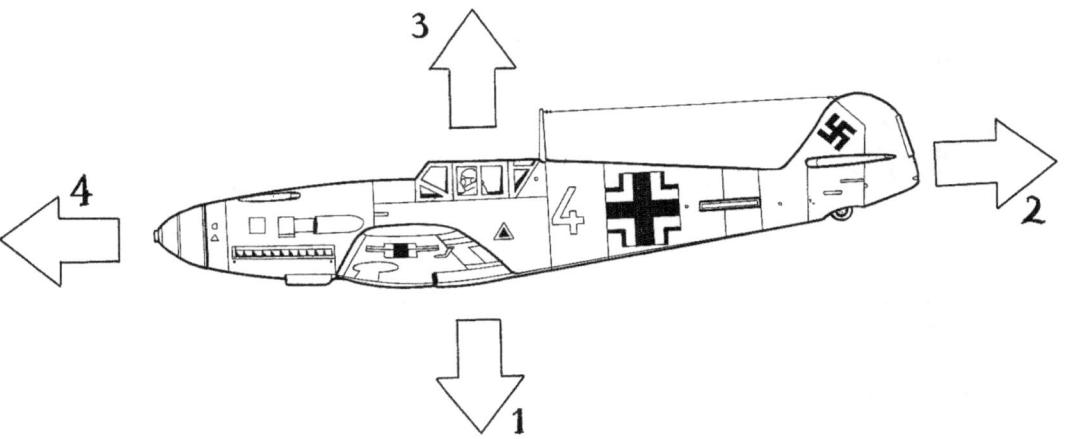

Forces acting on an aircraft. 1: Gravity. 2: Drag. 3: Lift. 4: Thrust.

Bayerische Motorenwerke (BMW), in Munich, was founded by Matthew Ruak; the company was renowned for its motorbikes and other vehicles, but also for its design and construction of aircraft engines, such as the BMW 801 piston and the jet engine BMW 003, as well as rocket-based weapons. The company has admitted to employing between 25,000 to 30,000 slave laborers during World War II; these were prisoners of war and inmates from concentration camps.

Daimler-Benz (DB), in Stuttgart, was formed in 1926 by merging two companies which were pioneers in automobile manufacturing: the Carl Benz company (founded in 1883), and the Gottlieb Daimler company (created in 1890). After 1933, the Daimler-Benz company was closely associated with the Nazi regime. It expanded rapidly and made huge profits by producing not only tanks, cars and trucks, but also submarines and aircraft engines.

Heinkel-Hirth (HeS), based in Benningen, was formed in 1941 by the nationalization of the Helmut Hirth Motoren Company which was merged with Heinkel Aircraft Company; the most prominent designer was Hans von Ohain who developed a series of piston and jet engines.

Junkers Motoren (Jumo) was formed in 1923 as a separate firm from Junkers Aircraft. Jumo had several factories all over Germany and produced piston engines (e.g., Jumo 210, 211 and 213) and jet engines (e.g., Jumo 004, the first jet engine to be considered production quality and used to power the Messerschmitt Me 262).

There were several main classes of engine used by the Luftwaffe. The most conventional were the BMW 132 (derived from the American Pratt & Whitney Hornet) and Bramo Fafnir air-cooled radials. Another category included the V-type gasoline engines. The BMW VI had its output raised from 620/660 hp to 725/750 hp by increasing the compression ratio. In 1934, Daimler-Benz and Junkers had developed much more powerful inverted-V engines, such as the DB 600 and the Jumo 210, both giving over 700 hp—the former soon reaching 900 hp. By 1937, development was fast proceeding on two later inverted-V engines, the DB 601 and Jumo 211, both in the 1,000 hp class, with superchargers and ice-free, direct fuel injection. Both were destined to play an all-important role in the coming conflict. By 1942, German engines were marching forward almost too boldly and interminable problems were encountered. There were so many new designs and concepts that there had to be a ruthless pruning of more than forty engine projects. Work was concentrated on a few major types. The Daimler-Benz DB 601 had yielded to the faster Jumo 213. The excellent new BMW 801, the 14-cylinder air-cooled radial fitted to the Focke-Wulf Fw 190, had been put into production in various forms for several important bombers, such as the Dornier Do 217 and Junkers Ju 88.

A piston engine, also known as reciprocating engine, is a device that utilizes one or more piston in order to convert pressure into a rotating movement. It works with pistons located inside a cylinder, into which a fuel (gasoline, a petroleum-based liquid) and air mixture is introduced by valves and then ignited by a spark plug. The hot gases expand, creating energy that pushes the piston away. The linear movement of the piston is converted to a circular movement via a connecting rod and a crankshaft. The burned gases leave the engine via valves and exhaust pipes. The more cylinders an engine has, the more power it develops, so it is common for such engines to be classified by the number and alignment of cylinders. Named by James Watt in 1782, the unit used for listing the rate of power application of an internal combustion engine is horse power ("hp," for short).

A fairing called a cowling usually encloses an engine. Part of the engine system, the fuel tank covers the functions of filling, storage, gauging, venting and feeding fuel to the engine through a pump. Placement of fuel tanks depended on the aircraft design; some were located in engine nacelles, others in wings or in the fuselage. For increased range, additional jettisonable fuel tanks could be carried externally under the wings or the fuselage.

In-line engine

Before the introduction of jet engine there were basically two sorts of piston engines.

2. Basic Technical Data

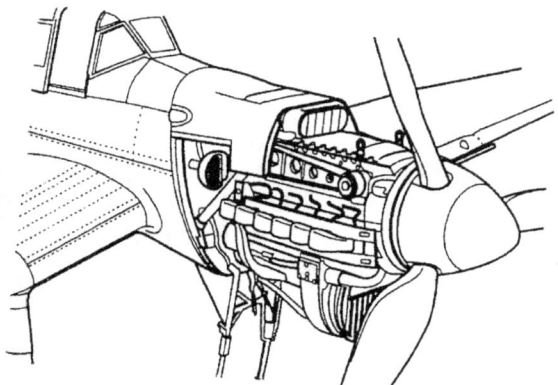

In-line engine (Junkers Ju 87-G)

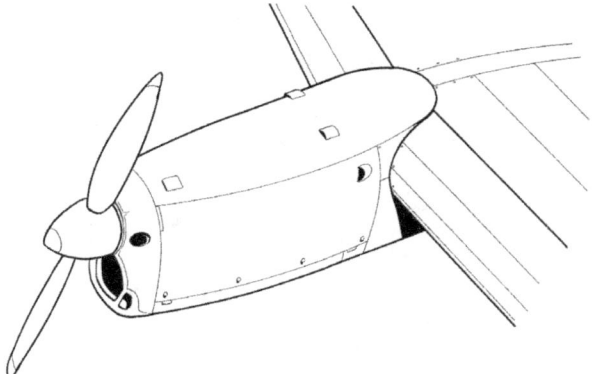

In-line engine. This Argus As 410A-1 twelve-cylinder, inverted-V, air-cooled engine driving a two-blade, controllable-pitch Argus propeller, powered many types of aircraft, for example, the Focke-Wulf Fw 189 A-1.

The in-line engine, as the name suggests, is composed of cylinders placed in a row or bank. It comes in two basic arrangements.

The *straight in-line engine*, in which all cylinders are aligned in a row one after another, is easy to build in a single metal casting; it provides smooth running, is comparatively narrow in volume but at the cost of great engine length.

The *V in-line engine* consists of two banks of horizontally opposed cylinders attached to a single and common crankshaft. The cylinders are usually positioned at either 90 or 60 degree angles from each other; they thus appear to be like letter "V" when viewed along the line of the crankshaft. The V arrangement reduces overall length and weight; it also uses a short and strong crankshaft, and thus tolerates high rotational speeds and high torsional stresses.

Both straight and V in-line engines generally require a cooling fluid to remove heat or complicated baffles to route cooling air, as the rear-most cylinders receive little airflow. Liquid-cooled engines were complicated, costly and vulnerable in battle.

Radial engine

A *radial engine* is a configuration of internal combustion engine, in which the cylinders are mounted equidistant around the circumference of a circular crankcase, in other words arranged pointing out from a central crankshaft like the spokes on a wheel. Cylinders and crankcase are fixed and the crankshaft rotates; but in the case of a radial rotary engine, the crankshaft is fixed and cylinders and crankcase rotate around it. For aircraft use, the radial engine has several advantages over the in-line engine. With all of the cylinders at the front, it is easy to cool them with natural airflow, and air-cooling saves a considerable amount of complexity and also reduces weight. A radial engine is also far more resistant to damage, an important asset for military aircrafts. If the block cracks on an in-line engine that entire cylinder bank loses power, but the same situation on a radial often only makes that individual cylinder stop

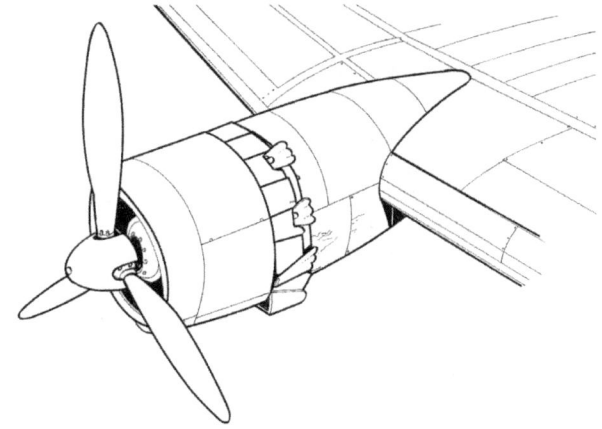

Radial engine. This is a 1,200 hp BMW-Bramo Fafnir 323R-2 nine-cylinder, air-cooled radial engine, powering a Focke-Wulf Fw 299 Condor.

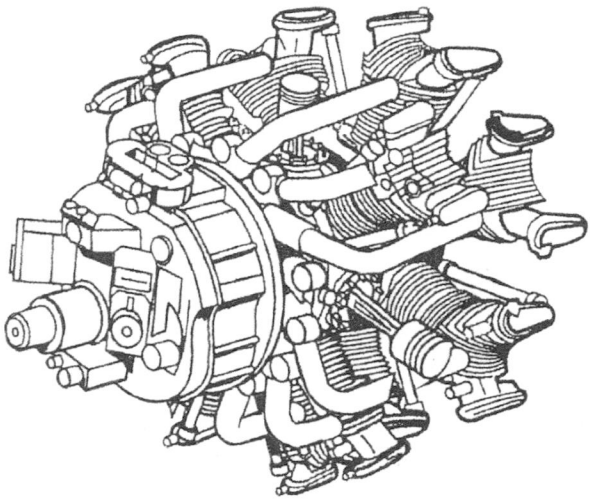

Radial engine (cowl removed).

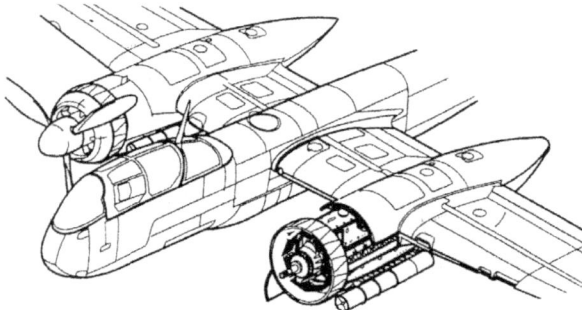

Daimler-Benz DB 603 G engine (Heinkel He 219 A Uhu)

working. The radial design also has disadvantages. One is that a supply of compressed air and feeding fuel has to be piped around the entire engine, whereas in the in-line only one or two pipes are needed, each feeding an entire cylinder bank. Another disadvantage is that the frontal area of a radial is always large, with poor aerodynamics and thus greater drag.

The debate about the merits of the in-line versus the radial engine continued throughout the 1930s and during World War II, with both types widely used.

Diesel engine

Invented by Rudolf Diesel in 1892, this type of internal combustion engine is a compression ignition engine in which the fuel is ignited by high temperature created by compression of the air/fuel mixture, rather than by a separate spark plug. The heavy-oil diesel engine has several advantages: good reliability (namely less risk of catching fire), high durability and low fuel consumption. Diesel fuel is cheaper than gasoline, it is a form of light oil, but the engine can usually operate a variety of different heavy fuels, including crude oil. The main disadvantage is the very sturdy construction needed; the diesel engine is generally heavy and bulky and this generates a severe penalty on an aircraft's weight and speed. For this reason diesel engines played only a small role and were not widely used by German designers before and during World War II. They were mainly mounted to power huge airships like the Zeppelin series, or large flying boats such as the Bv 138, Ha 139 and Bv 222 built by Blohm & Voss, as well as Do 18 and Do 26 produced by Dornier, in which the demand for sturdiness and reliability was more important than weight and speed.

Propeller

The linear movement of the pistons in the cylinders is converted to a circular movement via a connecting rod and a crankshaft, which drives an airscrew, popularly known as a propeller. The propeller, an essential element for flight with a piston engine, consists of two or more blades connected together by a hub, serving to attach the blades to the engine shaft. When the engine rotates the propeller, the blades act as a rotating wing that produces a force generating a difference in pressure between the forward and rear surfaces of the airfoil-shaped blade, and this provides lift or thrust that moves the aircraft forward. Because the velocity of the blade increases from hub to tip, the blade is twisted, providing the most efficient angle of attack at each point along its length. Most German propellers pulled the aircraft through the air (*tractor propeller* placed at the front), but in a number of designs the propeller was placed at the rear of the aircraft; this arrangement was called a *pusher propeller*. The term "pusher" is in fact inaccurate but accepted to describe a propeller mounted

2. Basic Technical Data

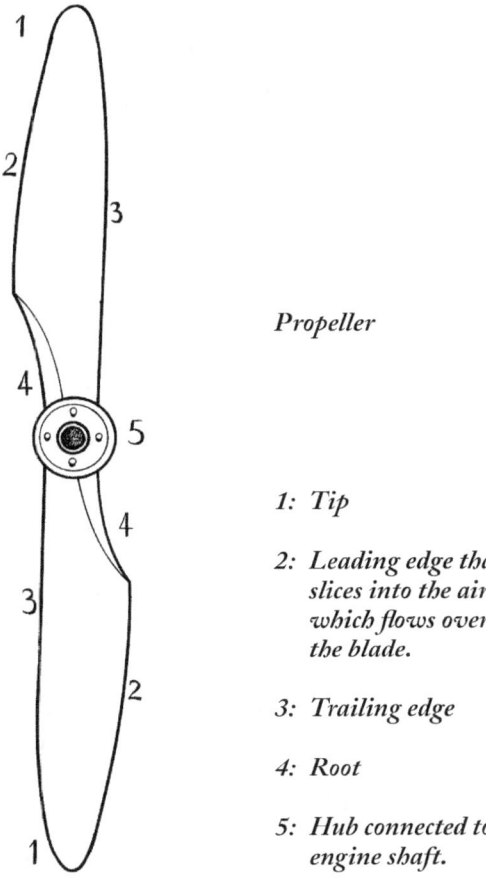

Propeller

1: *Tip*

2: *Leading edge that slices into the air which flows over the blade.*

3: *Trailing edge*

4: *Root*

5: *Hub connected to engine shaft.*

behind an engine; actually it acts aerodynamically as a tractor in action as it pulls the aircraft forward. Very often the propeller hub is covered by a streamlined fairing called a spinner; this could be painted in bright color or feature a spiral marking to help Luftwaffe crews distinguish friend from foe in the confusing maelstrom of air combat. In an autogyro or helicopter, the horizontal rotating-wing assembly, comprising hub and blades is called a rotor.

Jet Engines

A jet engine works according to a simple principle, based on Newton's third law of motion: "To every action there is an equal and opposite reaction." A jet engine produces a forward thrust from the consequent reaction. Air is sucked in the engine and compressed. Fuel is added and the air/fuel mix is ignited, causing a rapid extension of the gases, which are expelled through the engine outlet, thus providing thrust and pushing the aircraft forward. This was a theoretical possibility as early as the early 1900s, owing to the work of pioneers such as René Lorin and Konstantin Tsiolkovsky. The jet engine became a practical reality in the late 1930s. Laws of physics imposed a speed limit about 500 mph on a piston-engined aircraft, and a good alternative was offered by the turbojet engine. This promised to deliver much higher thrust-to-weight ratios, but ran at high temperatures, making it difficult to control. Besides, alloys such as chromium and nickel—absolutely necessary to build a jet engine—were extremely expensive.

With the shadow of war came the inevitable boost to airplane manufacturers, and certainly Germany provided the trigger with its massive rearmament program commenced in 1935. Although designers were hard at work on jet propulsion, the results of their labors were varied. The technological advances were great, but it was piston-engined aircraft that fought World War II.

The basic scheme of jet power had several variations, the purpose being to accelerate and discharge a fast-moving jet of exhaust gases to generate high-velocity forward thrust.

A *ram-jet engine* is the lightest and simplest jet engine. Usually given the necessary high initial velocity by rocket boosters or catapult, it was used mainly for long-distance, high-altitude purposes. In its most primitive form, the ram-jet engine had no moving parts, and resembled a stove pipe into which air was rammed by an inlet diffuser; a spray of fuel was added and ignited, and hot gases were burned

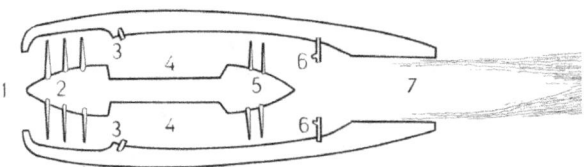

Schematic showing how jet engine basically works. 1: Air intake. 2: Compressor. 3: Fuel injector. 4: Combustion chamber. 5: Turbine. 6: Afterburner. 7: Nozzle.

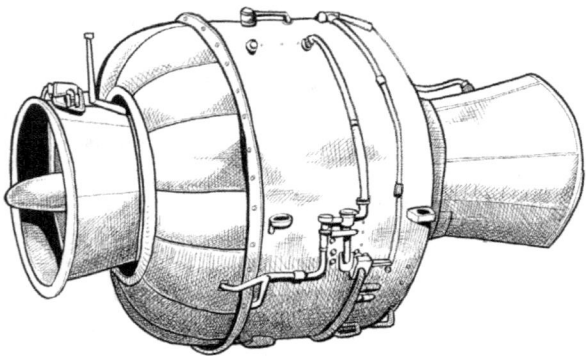

Heinkel HeS 3-B turbojet engine. Designed by engineer Hans Pabst von Ohain, the HeS 3-B developed 340 kg of thrust and was used to power the first jet aircraft, Heinkel He 178 V1, that flew in August 1939.

in the combustion chamber or burner. The expansion of hot gases after fuel injection and combustion accelerates the exhaust air to a velocity higher than that at the inlet and creates energy expelled at the other end of the tube (nozzle) and thus positive push or thrust.

A *pulse-jet engine* (developed by German engineer Paul Schmidt from the ram-jet in the 1930s) worked with the same principle, but operated using a two-part cycle. Ram-jet and pulse-jet engines do not start working until the plane has a speed of about 200 mph, so a launching device has to be provided for take-off. During World War II this consisted of either launching from a parent aircraft, assistance by additional rocket engine, or catapult. Once there was enough air pressure, the valves in the air intake opened, letting air in. This was then mixed with fuel and ignited. The resulting explosion closed the valves and burning exhaust gases exited at high velocity to the rear, creating thrust in bursts as the process was automatically repeated.

The *turbojet engine* is the basic engine of the jet age. It is the largest and most complicated jet engine composed of inlet, compressor, combustor (or burner), turbine and nozzle. The inlet or air intake (which can consists of fans) sucks air into the engine. The compressor draws in and pressurizes large amount of air (thus increasing its pressure) which is forced into the combustor. In the combustor, high pressure air is mixed with a highly flammable fuel; this is injected, ignited, and combusted, producing very hot gases which expand rapidly rearward and pass through the turbine wheels; a part of their energy is used to power the compressor (as the turbine is connected to the compressor by an axle). The exhaust gases exit at the rear of the engine giving the aircraft its forward push or thrust. For additional thrust, an afterburner or augmenter can be added. Extra fuel is introduced into the hot exhaust and burned, with a resultant increase of up to 50 percent in engine power by way of even higher velocity and more push. Finally the gases exit rearward via a nozzle whose shape increases velocity of gases and generates more thrust.

A *turboprop engine* used the power and thrust from a jet engine to turn a propeller. As in a turbojet, hot gases flowing through the engine rotate a turbine wheel that drives the compres-

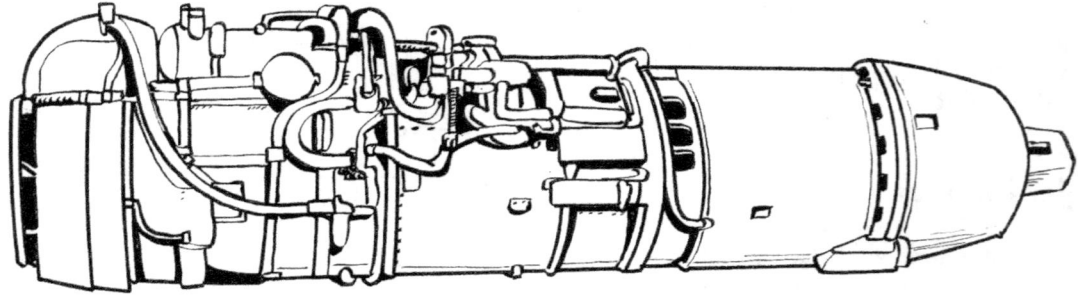

BMW 003 E-2 axial-flow turbojet engine (cowling removed). This jet engine, which powered the Heinkel He 162 Salamander, developed a maximum of 2,082 lbs of static thrust for short periods and 1,7764 lbs for take-off.

sor. The gases then pass through another turbine, called a power turbine. This is coupled to the shaft which drives the propeller through gear connections, and the rotating propeller provides thrust. The turbopropeller engine attracted much attention in the late 1940s and early 1950s, but lost out because the jet engine was faster.

Rocket Engine

Like the jet engine, the rocket engine works by jet propulsion, producing a forward thrust by the reaction to a backward stream of accelerated gases. But when a jet engine accelerates the air it takes in, a World War II German rocket engine produced gases by spontaneous combustion of several chemical solid or liquid fuels. A-Stoff was liquid oxygen. C-Stoff was a mixture of 30 percent hydrazine hydrate, 57 percent methanol, and 13 percent water. GM-1 was nitrous oxide boost. M-Stoff was methanol. MW-50 was a mixture of 50 percent methanol with 50 percent water. R-Stoff or Tonka 250 was a mixture of 50 percent xylidine F with 50 percent triethylamine. S-Stoff or Salbeik was a mixture of 96 percent potassium nitrate and 4 percent chloride. SV-Stoff or Salbei was 98.2 percent nitric acid and .2 percent sulfuric acid. T-Stoff was a solution of 80 percent hydrogen peroxide and 20 percent a stabilizing chemical. Z-Stoff C was calcium permanganate. Z-Stoff N was sodium permanganate solution as catalyst. The expending burning gases produced by combustion were

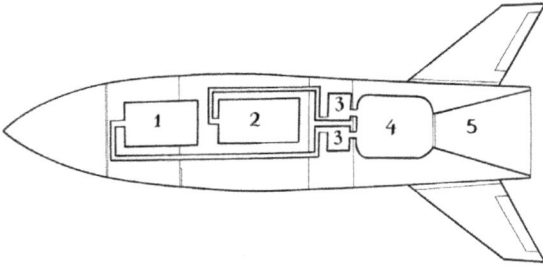

Schematic showing how a rocket engine works. 1: Fuel (for example, hydrazine or kerosene). 2: Oxidizer (for example, nitrogen tetroxide). 3: Pump. 4: Combustion chamber. 5: Nozzle.

allowed to escape at high speed through a back-facing nozzle, thus creating a considerable thrust. The precise shape of the opening or nozzle was important; it had a throat which maintained the pressure in the combustion chamber and a cone-shaped expansion chamber which reduced turbulence and produced a stream of efficiently directed gases. Both provided a smooth, continual expansion and acceleration of the gases, maximizing the propulsive efficiency. To augment the take-off power of an aircraft's engine, solid or liquid rockets could be used: JATO (Jet-Assisted Take Off) or RATO (Rocket Assisted Take Off).

Basic Aircraft Terms

Fuselage

The fuselage is the main body structure of an aircraft, holding crew, passenger, cargo, etc., and holding all the pieces together. It is, of course, always hollow to reduce weight, and often streamlined—that is, given a shape causing the minimum aerodynamic drag. As in ships, port is the left-hand side when facing forward, and starboard is the right-hand side. The fuselage is always designed with enough strength to withstand torques, which are turning or twisting forces acting on an object, and causing it to rotate. In the 1930s and 1940s, four main types of fuselages were constructed. The box-truss structure used linked elements, often triangular ones. A geodesic construction was composed of multiple flat-strip stringers forming a basket-like appearance. A monocoque was a structure in which the outer skin carried the primary stresses and was free of internal bracing. A semi-monocoque was composed of a series of forms held in position on a rigid structure, joined with lightweight longitudinal elements called stringers. Monocoque fuselages and semi-monocoque were referred to as "stressed skin," as all or a portion of the load was taken by the surface covering. In the case of a "flying wing," there is no separate fuselage, instead what would be the fuselage is a thickening portion of the wing structure. "Some aircraft had a twin fuselage (two fuselages and a connecting structure between them), others had a single fuselage between two wings; the components of the latter that support the tail surfaces are called twin booms.

Tail

The empennage, also called tail assembly or simply tail, includes a rudder, fin, tailplane and part of the fuselage to which these are attached. The tailplane, or horizontal stabilizer, is a small lifting surface located behind the main lifting surface (wing). It serves three purposes: equilibrium, stability and control. The most commonly used and conventional tail arrangement includes a rudder (control surface for yaw or horizontal axis) attached to the fixed fin or vertical stabilizer. Another common lay-out was the twin-tail, an empennage formed of a double fin and rudder. Occasionally experimental and unconventional configurations were designed. The V-tail, also called butterfly tail, has a fin replaced by two surfaces set in a V-shaped configuration. A T-tail has the tailplane mounted on top of the fin (e.g., the Blohm & Voss P 197-01 or Messerschmitt *Zerstörer* II). A tailless aircraft is very often a monoplane with a short fuselage deprived of tailplane but fitted with a fixed fin and rudder (e.g. Messerschmitt Me 163); it is thus different from a "flying wing" which may have only small fin and rudder on the trailing edge of the wing.

Wings

An aircraft does not have wings like a pigeon or a duck or an eagle, but instead "lifting surfaces" also called airfoils. The appellation "wing" has however entered into everyday usage. Airfoils are shaped with smooth surfaces; these are curved, helping to push the air over the top more quickly than it goes under the wing, so the air pressure above is less than below. This produces lift (an upward force greater than the weight of the airplane). A monoplane is a fixed-wing aircraft with a single set of wings, i.e., one wing on each side; a biplane had two sets of wings mounted one above another, and a triplane three. An aircraft which has its single wing mounted high on the fuselage is a high-wing monoplane; a

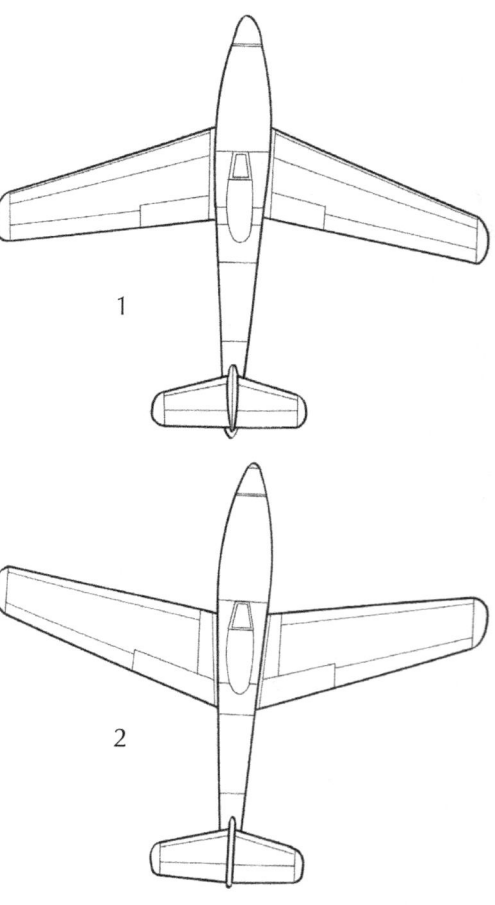

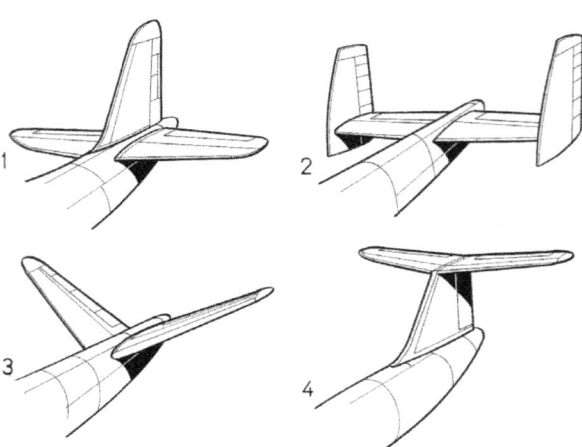

Tail unit configuration. 1: Conventional. 2: Twin rudder. 3: V-tail. 4: T-tail.

Above and opposite: Wing configuration. 1: Back sweep. 2: Forward sweep. 3: Delta. 4: Flying wing.

low-wing being thus mounted low on the fuselage; a mid-wing placed in a mid-position on the fuselage; and a parasol monoplane has its single wing mounted on struts above the fuselage. The root is that part of the wing that is attached to the fuselage. The span is the distance from tip to tip of the wing or tailplane. The edge of an airfoil (shape of a wing or blade as seen in cross-section) which first meets the airstream in normal flight is called the leading edge; the rear edge of the wing is called the trailing edge. The chord is the distance from the leading edge to trailing edge of a wing.

Wings, particularly in the case of divebomber, could be fitted with airbrakes. These were drag-inducing surfaces hinged under the wings. Deployed in flight and extended broadside-on to the airflow, these enabled very steep dives—almost 90 degrees—without reaching excessive speeds. A swept wing is a wing of which the angle between the leading-edge and the center line of the fuselage is less than 90 degrees. This configuration, which increases roll stability, has become almost-universal on modern aircraft. Some German designers also experimented with forward sweep (e.g., Junkers Ju 287 jet bomber, Heinkel He P 1076,

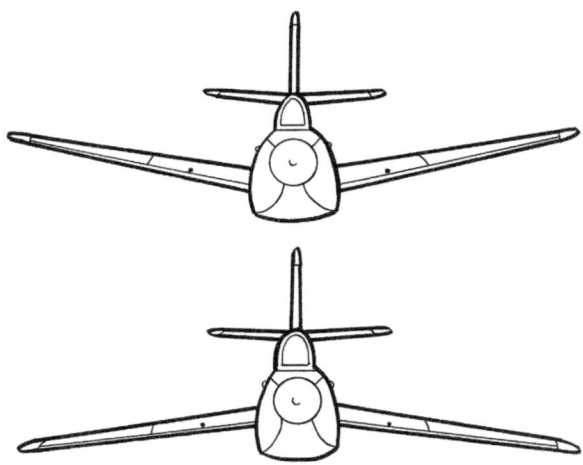

Wing angles. Top: Dihedral. Bottom: Anhedral.

and Blohm & Voss P 209-02); this layout provides good agility and maneuverability, the air flowing from wingtip to wing root.

Dihedral is the upward angle from the horizontal wing from root to tip, as viewed from the front of an aircraft; this confers stability in the roll axis. Anhedral (or negative dihedral) wings are downward angled wings, providing good maneuverability. A delta wing is a wing that has the shape of Greek letter D (an isosceles triangle), the trailing edge forming the base of the triangle. A Variable-geometry wings are a set of wings, which, fully extended, gives the best low-speed performance for take-off and landing, but can be swept in flight to an optimum position for cruising at high speed. A canard design has movable elevators mounted ahead of the main wings, and provides a completely different form of maneuverability than is inherent with a conventional configuration.

Cockpit

The cockpit is a compartment, originally open to the air, for accommodation of the crew or pilot. It contains instrumentation and controls enabling the pilot to fly the aircraft. At a time when no on-board computers existed, these included many devices, for example, master switch, throttle (which sets the desired engine power level by controlling volume of fuel/air mixture delivered to the cylinders), a stick or control wheel (to move the flight

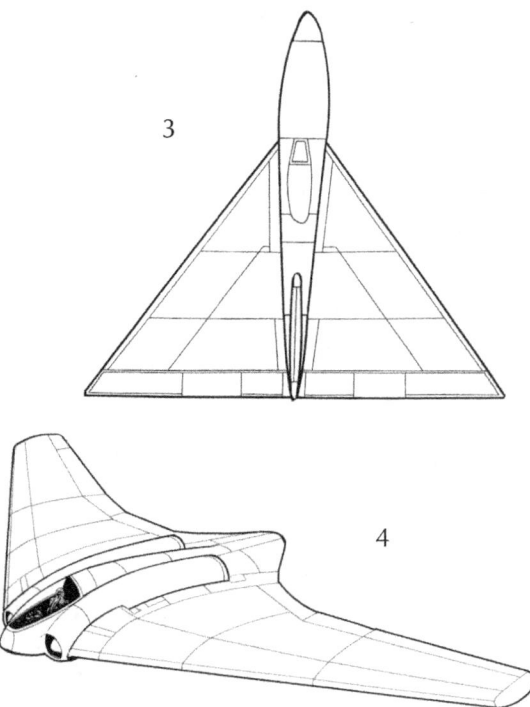

surfaces), pitch control (adjusting propeller pitch), mixture control or "leaning" (which sets the amount of fuel added to the intake airflow as air pressure declines at higher altitude), ignition switch (activates magnetos which generate voltage for spark in cylinder), tachometer (indicating engine speed in revolutions per minute, RPM), oil temperature and pressure gauge, fuel quantity gauge, fuel select valve, and altimeter (indicating altitude). A pitot tube was generally placed on a wing for measuring fluid flow velocity, which determined the

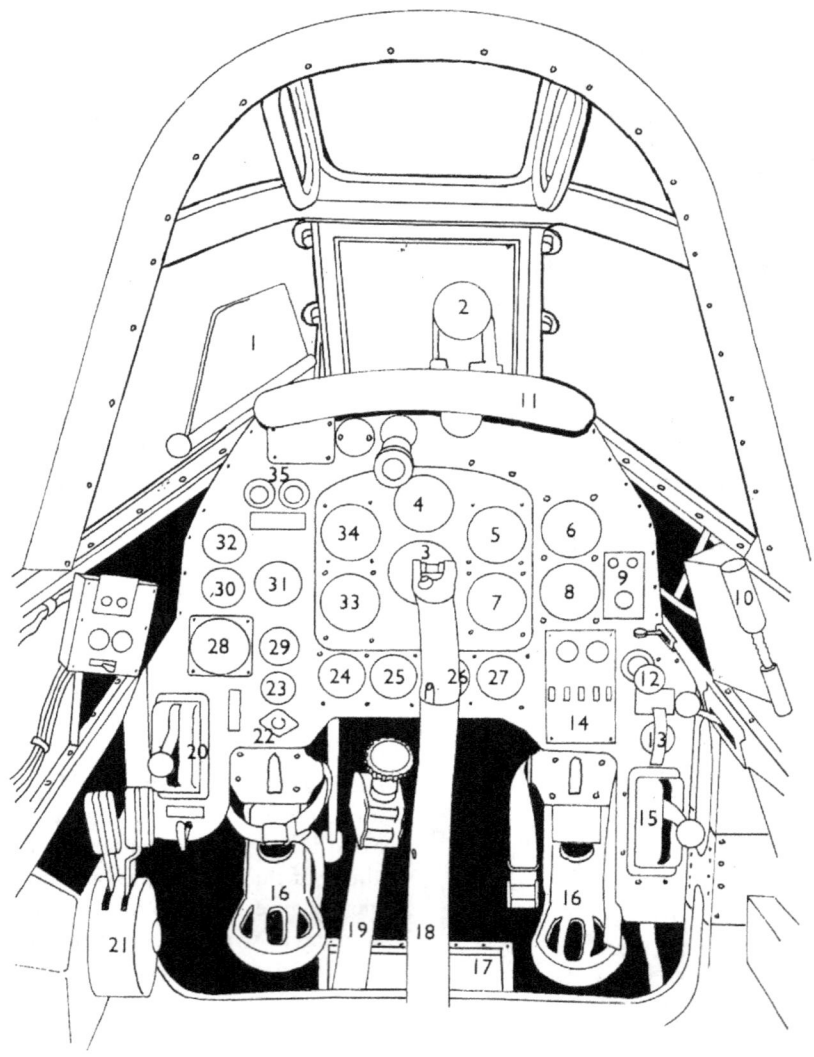

Cockpit of Junkers Ju 87 B2 "Stuka." 1: Visual dive indicator. 2: Gun sight. 3: Artificial horizon. 4: Compass repeater. 5: Speedometer. 6: Boost pressure. 7: Altimeter. 8: Rev counter. 9: Flap indicator. 10: Intercom connection. 11: Crash pad. 12: Manual engine pump. 13: Engine priming pump. 14: Electrical panel (radio). 15: Oil cooler flap control. 16: Rudder bar pedal. 17: Target view window. 18: Control column. 19: Target view window-flap control. 20: Fuel-metering hand-priming pump. 21: Throttle. 22: Starter switch. 23: Main electrical switch. 24: Coolant temperature. 25: Fuel contents. 26: Oil temperature. 27: Oil contents. 28: Compass. 29: Oil pressure gauge. 30: Clock. 31: Dive preset indicator. 32: Fuel pressure gauge. 33: Radio altimeter. 34: Rate-of-climb indicator. 35: Water cooler flap indicator.

speed of the aircraft (named after the inventor Henri Pitot).

Early airplanes had an open cockpit fitted with a simple transparent windshield to give the airman some protection from the airstream in flight. In the late 1930s, the streamlined, closed, glazed, and eventually armored cockpit appeared, offering much more protection and comfort to the pilot, and reducing drag. The positioning of the cockpit was governed by the need to give the crew all-around vision. Conventionally that was on top of the fuselage or in the aircraft's glazed nose as was the case in many German bombers; this "greenhouse" arrangement made of Perspex allowed a good visibility but also ensured that the crew would be very close to any accident, notably an emergency belly landing, and offered no protection to the crew. The concentration of the crew in a glazed nose, particularly evident in the Heinkel He 111, Junkers Ju 88, and Dornier Do 17 and derivates, was thought to offer the psychological advantage of mutual support and interoperability (the isolation of tail and belly gunners in certain RAF and American heavy bombers was notorious), and had the additional advantage of reducing demands on airframe, size, thus reducing weight. However the crew compartment in a German bomber was often terribly cramped and operations revealed that it increased the vulnerability of the crew to fire, and demanded that the crew members move from one firing position to another to engage attackers.

One unconventional positioning of the cockpit was in a nacelle placed on a wing, in the case of asymmetric design (e.g., Blohm & Voss Bv 141) and another unconventional location was at the rear of the fuselage. Late in the war some aircraft were fitted with automatic emergency ejection seats, the modern-looking cockpit with a bubble canopy allowing all-around visibility was introduced, and a pressurized cockpits were developed for high-altitude flight. Cabin pressurization was done by active pumping; air pressure was increased inside the cockpit, and this was required at high altitude, as natural atmospheric pressure was too low to enable a pilot to absorb sufficient oxygen, leading to altitude sickness, loss of consciousness and hypoxia. In World War II German aircraft, pilots were seated in their cockpits, but in some experimental airplanes, they were placed in the prone position, lying on their stomachs. This unusual position was: less tiring for pilots on a long flight; it offered good visibility to the front and downward; crash survival odds were increased; the cockpit and fuselage could be designed smaller and slimmer, increasing aerodynamics and reducing drag; and pilots could endure greater G-force at high speed.

Each Luftwaffe airman was, of course, issued parachute.

The demands of modern warfare made increased protection of the aircrew necessary, and engines and accessory equipment gained protection in the form of armored plates. The armor protection in German aircraft varied in thickness from 4 to 20 mm. The total armor weight per plane could vary from 100 pounds or less in some light reconnaissance types to over 1,000 pounds for heavy attack planes and bombers.

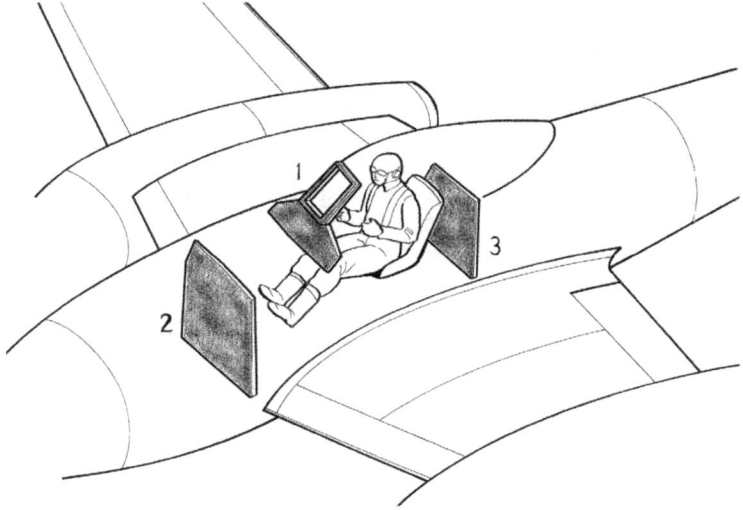

Schematic armor, Messerschmitt Me 262. 1: Bullet-resisting glass screen (90 mm) and frontal armor (15 mm). 2: Frontal armored plate (15 mm). 3: Rear armored plate (15 mm).

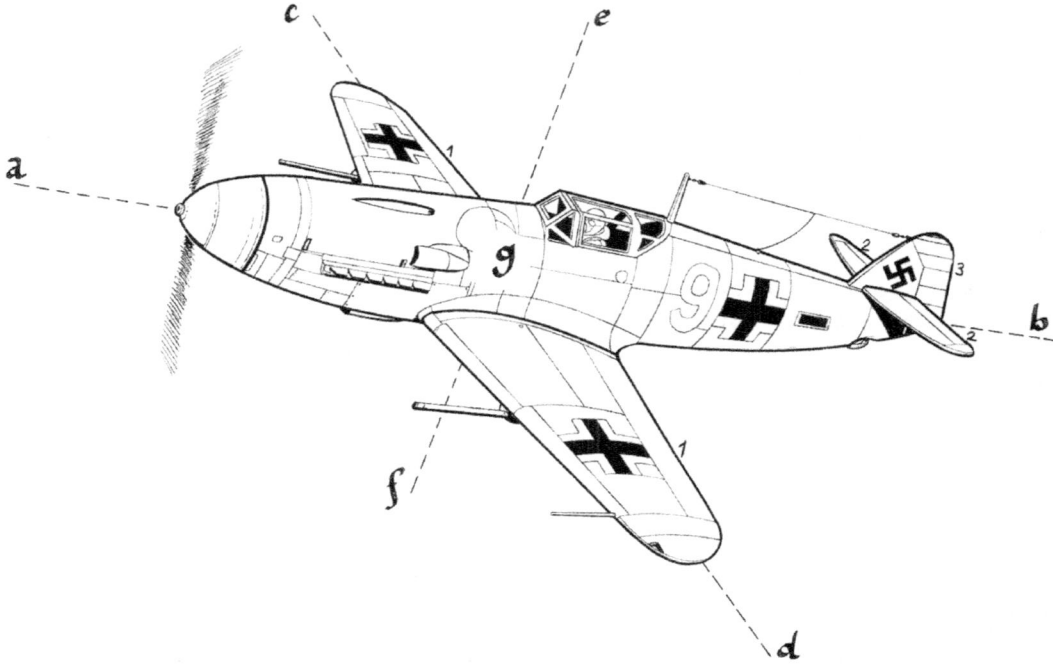

Axis of rotation. **ab**: *Axis of roll (longitudinal).* **cd**: *Axis of pitch (lateral).* **ef**: *Axis of yaw (vertical).* **g**: *Center of gravity.* 1: *Aileron.* 2: *Elevator.* 3: *Rudder.*

Controls

An aircraft can move about three axes, roll, pitch and yaw, which intersect at the center of gravity, each one being always perpendicular to the other two. Moving an aircraft about the three axes is done by movable flight-control surfaces hinged to fixed surfaces. In the 1930s and 1940s this system consisted of rods and cables connected to each other and to the control wheel (or stick) operated, lowered or raised, by the pilot in the cockpit.

The longitudinal axis is the imaginary line extending lengthwise through the fuselage, from nose to tail. Motion about this line is *roll* and is produced by movement of the ailerons placed at the trailing edges of the wings.

The lateral axis is the imaginary line extending crosswise from wingtip to wingtip. Motion about the lateral axis is *pitch* and is produced by movement of the elevators placed at the rear of the horizontal tail assembly.

The vertical axis is the imaginary line which passes vertically through the center of gravity of the airplane. Motion about the vertical axis is *yaw* and is provided by movement (often by means of a pedal) of the rudder placed at the rear of the fin, the vertical tail assembly.

In addition, some aircraft were provided with *trim tabs*, small, adjustable, hinged surfaces placed on the trailing edge of ailerons, elevators and rudder. These labor-saving devices enabled the pilot to release manual pressure on the primary controls.

Landing gear

Landing gear or undercarriage is a structure (consisting very often of wheels or of a wheel assembly, but sometimes of float, ski or skid) that support an aircraft when taxiing and stationary, and on take-off and landing; it is often fitted with shock absorber and brakes. Early aircraft had fixed landing gears. In the late 1930s the retractable undercarriage was developed that much helped to decrease drag, as the wheels retracted behind doors which closed flush with the fuselage. Basically there were two types of undercarriage used by German designers before and during World War II. The *taildragger* consisted of two main wheels

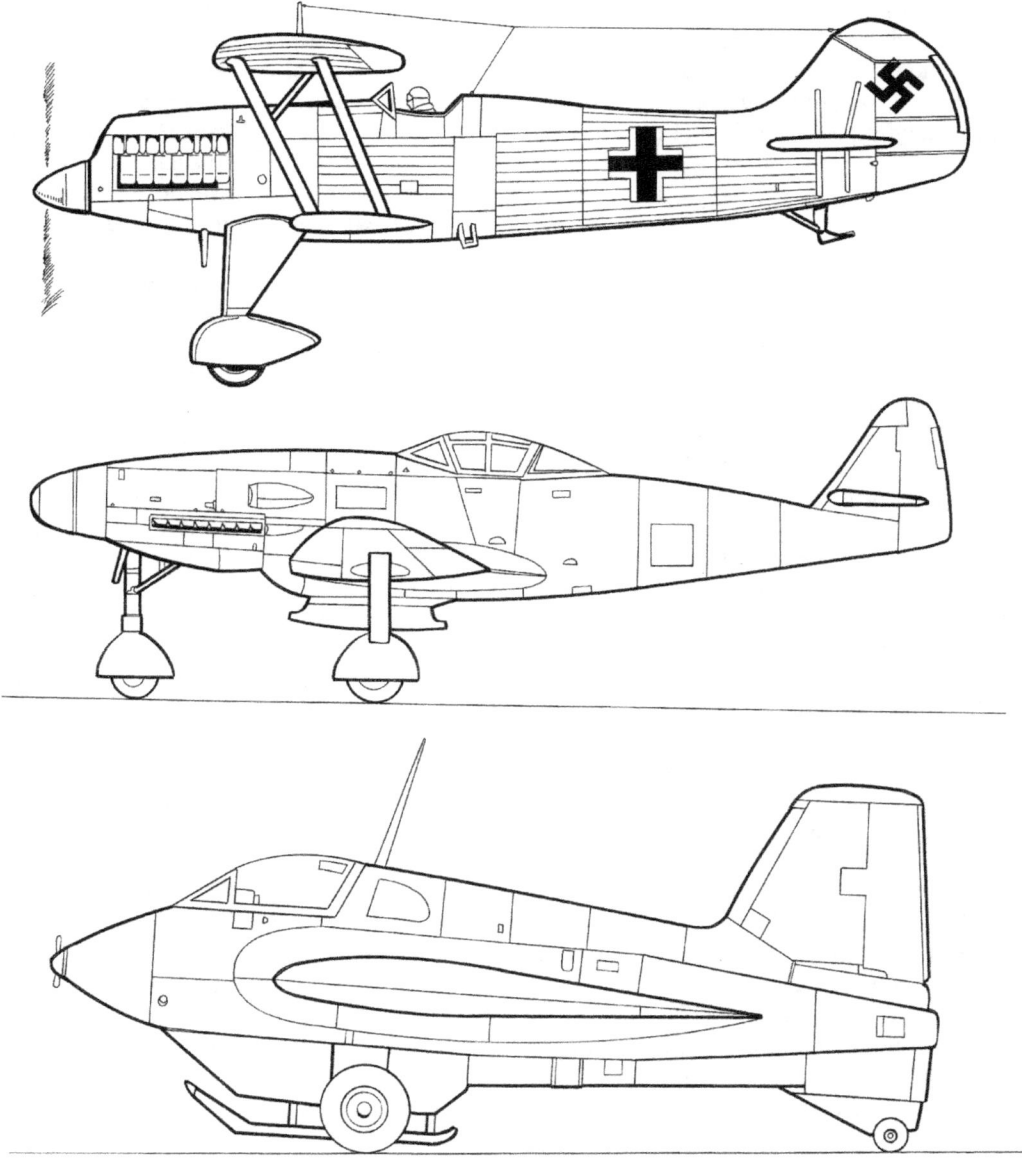

Landing gear. Top: Fixed landing gear (Heinkel He 51). Middle: Tricycle landing gear (Messerschmitt Me 309). Bottom: Jettisonable trolley and skid (Messerschmitt Me 163 Komet).

placed toward the front or under the wing of the aircraft and a single smaller wheel or skid at the rear. This arrangement, putting the nose up, had the disadvantage that by taxiing and take-off, there was a blind spot ahead of the aircraft, a space not seen by the pilot. The *tricycle* undercarriage, that appeared during the war, partly solved this problem. It consisted of two main wheels and a third, smaller, steerable wheel in the nose, thus leaving the fuselage parallel to the ground and offering a better view ahead. All modern aircraft are now provided with a tricycle.

Exceptionally an aircraft could be fitted with a *jettisonable undercarriage*. This consisted of a *Startwagen* (wheeled trolley) which was dropped after take-off, and landing was done on one or more retractable or fixed ventral skids. This arrangement helped improve streamlining, and did away with the use of a complex device, thus saving weight, space and drag in the airplane, but there was a serious disadvantage: landing on a skid could be a very risky affair.

Camouflage

The subject of Luftwaffe airplane camouflage is of great complexity, and sometimes confusing. Although orders and schemes were issued by the RLM, it is often difficult to state which was correct and standard, and which was not, as manufacturers and RLM described colors differently, as applied colors reacted to different weather and altitude, as paint was of different viscosity and quality, and as frontline modifications, adaptations and improvisations were numerous. Thus only a few generalities and the main guidelines are described below.

Aircraft camouflage was not something new in 1935. Already during World War I, efforts had been made to paint flying machines with motley colors and dazzling patterns. A particularly interesting experiment was the four-engine Linke Hoffman R1 bomber which was covered with transparent Cellon in an attempt to make it invisible in the sky. In the period of formation and growth, 1935–1937, Luftwaffe aircraft were not really camouflaged. Bright colors, such as red, yellow and blue, were combined with more neutral colors, such as light blue, white, silver, black and gray, more for a esthetic and decorative purpose than for camouflage. Camouflage on German aircraft appeared during the Spanish Civil War. The color adapted for the Condor Legion craft varied. Some planes were painted pale gray with pale blue undersides; some were overpainted with dark green and brown, in angular segmented patterns.

From 1938, as the threat of war increased, and during World War II, airplane camouflage became of paramount importance. Aircraft were delivered from the production line in more or less standardized colors which were later adapted or modified in the field. Directives were issued from the RLM, but these were often loosely interpreted at the unit level. In Europe, the undersurface of the plane was very often light blue as an imitation of the sky, so that the aircraft might not be spotted from the ground, notably by anti-aircraft artillery. The upper surface was usually dark green or dark blue with a lighter shade of green applied in large, angular, straight-edged patches to give the characteristic "splinter" camouflage. A greenish-gray shade was widely used for painting interior surfaces such as cockpits, wheel-wells, bomb-bays etc. More or less complex patterns were designed and added to break up the aircraft's outline, shadow and shine. According to local environment, the upper surface could receive various patterns of mottling shades of green, brown, grayish blue or white, and light gray "cloudy" overspray. Light gray and light blue tones were often applied to the sides of the aircraft, fuselage, and fin and rudder, so that with machines flying at the same altitude as enemy planes, the German aircraft would blend in with the cloudy horizon. Some aircraft had thin, wavy lines, others wide bands, large blotches, small dots, broad patches, plant-like shapes or puzzle patterns. The complex camouflage of the upper surface had several purposes. It was designed to hide the aircraft on the ground. Indeed an airplane can function only when in motion, and becomes useless and vulnerable when resting on the ground. Therefore airfields have to be defended from air and ground attacks, protected from sabotage and spying activity, and airplanes on the ground must be dispersed and made invisible from the sky. In the air, camouflage helped to merge the plane with the ground when flying lower than an enemy. Engine cowling, propeller boss, wingtip, and fin and rudder—particularly for fighters—could sometimes be painted in white, bright red or yellow for quick and easy friend-and-foe recognition in the confusion of dogfight and aerial combat. For the same purpose insignia and markings were not overpainted. Camouflage, however, had some disadvantages, one of which was additional weight; this could amount to hundreds of pounds and extra weight reduced range, speed and payload. Another disadvantage was the effort needed to adapt to surroundings and time of year. In-

Camouflaged Messerschmitt Bf 109

Heinkel 111 P-2 **Kampfgeschwader** *55 night camouflage during Battle of Britain 1940.*

deed, as World War II expanded to new theaters of operation, different colors had to be applied in order to adapt to specific environments, and the main variations depended on geographical factors.

In North Africa, the undersurface often retained its light-blue sky color, while the uppersurface was predominantly desert-sand yellow, with a light spray of green or red-brown to take away the bright effect of the yellow. A common scheme was sand yellow sprayed with sandy brown, or overlaid by olive green blotches, patches or stripes. Weathering was obviously a major factor in the North African theater and caused endless differences in appearance.

On the Russian front, in winter, the adopted color was white to hide airplanes against the snow-covered steppe. The matte white used in Russia was a water-soluble paint which rapidly weathered, allowing streaks of the basic camouflage to appear in lesser or greater degree. The density of the color was varied, enabling the original camouflage to show through. The exact appearance depended on care of finish and degree of weathering. The Russian front produced more examples of nonstandard color schemes than any other campaign in which the Luftwaffe was involved. During the summer months the southern areas of the vast Russian land enjoy a semitropical climate. Some new color combinations came into being, as various patterns of light gray, light blue, sand yellow, light green or light brown were added. Other spraying styles included a high density pattern of small gray flecks, and a pattern of more sharply defined "holly-leaf" patches. Units on the field produced the greatest variety of finishes, varying from pristine white through delicate spray-gun squiggles to crudely hand-brushed streaks and blotches, or "snakeskin" or "crazy paving" patterns. Mottling was often spotting a dark color on a light background. Units operating in the extreme north of Europe also produced imaginative variations using dark gray with curling, pale blue, wavy lines—the so-called "wave-mirror" effect.

Night bombers and night fighters were often totally painted in black, sometimes with various motley patterns of light gray or light brown. Some were light blue, though, with small dark blue spots or intricate wavy lines. Light colors had the effect of becoming diffuse in darkness, whereas an airplane painted completely in black threw conspicuous shadows at dusk or on moonlit nights.

Seaplanes and long-range reconnaissance aircraft operating in the Atlantic and North Sea generally had their undersurfaces painted in light blue or pale gray, while the upper surfaces were an imitation of the color of the sea, ranging from dark gray or dark green to dark blue.

Central control over color schemes and markings was weak and ill-coordinated. Guidelines, regulations and charts were set out for the manner and type of camouflage to be used in the field, but in practice these regulations seemed to have been either interpreted in different ways, amended to suit local tastes and conditions, or quite simply ignored. That individual units would vary the appearance of their aircraft could be explained by special concealment needs, but also by the simple dislike of the front-line combatant for niggling and minutely detailed instructions emanating from distant bureaucratic administrators. By 1943, as war progressed, economic measures had to be taken. Use was made of captured Allied paint stocks in theaters where these were available. In direct contrast with the Allies, the Luftwaffe became less and less rigid in the application of centrally contrived camouflage colors and patterns. Losses were heavy, some units were disbanded and reformed two or even three times. Dark green became commonplace, and camouflage was simplified to shorten production. Proper colors and stocks were less available, and decreased in quality, due to the deteriorating conditions prevailing in Germany. Paint was in short supply and on occasion there was no time to apply carefully worked-out schemes. Individual efforts with varying degrees of skill and local improvisations under a wide range of circumstances were evident. The paint jobs ranged from excellent to poor depending on how rushed the men were, the quality and availability of paint, and craftsmanship of the artist. This was particularly true during the latter days of the war. From late 1944 onward, with the fluid state of the war and the collapse of the Luftwaffe, it is not possible to say what was and what was not standard. It was a time of confusion and retreat, hasty reinforcement from other theaters of war, disintegration of lines of communication, and lack of supplies. The burden of control and administration passed further and further down the command chain until individual units were obliged to fend for themselves. The result was that aircrafts were painted with whatever came to hand. There were dark green, dark blue, gray and dark yellow aircraft on all collapsing fronts, with all types of green and brown camouflage patterns.

Camouflage painting was not a cure-all. Alone, it could not be relied on to do more than render an airplane obscure, making it hard for an enemy observer to locate it and confusing the observer as to the location of vulnerable areas. Nor could it conceal a flying machine. However, camouflage painting was a valuable supplement to other camouflage measures. Added to good sitting, dispersion, camouflage discipline, and the use of nets and drapes, it increased the benefits derived from these measures. Together, and intelligently used, they provided a high degree of concealment for any airplane on the ground.

It should be noted that, in spite of camouflage and secrecy, it was very rare for a new German aircraft to enter service without the Allies already knowing a good deal about it and having a reasonable clear picture of its capability. After the outbreak of World War II, the British Air Intelligence was expanded and developed swiftly, pulling in resources and data from every avenue open to it, especially after the U.S. entry into the war against Germany in December 1941. Data and information about Luftwaffe aircraft were provided by reports from Allies crews engaged in combat; articles published in the neutral press; attachés and diplomats in neutral countries; reports from resistance spies and informants; captured documents as well as shot down, crashed and captured aircrafts; and interrogations of downed German airmen, prisoners of war, and captured civilian technicians and engineeers. An important source of information was provided by a special air service, known as the Photo-Reconnaissance Unit (PRU), equipped with fast aircraft, taking pictures which were later examined and interpreted by highly skilled (and often intuitive) personnel.

Aircraft Markings

Markings were used so that aircraft could be identified. Just like camouflage, the subject of Luftwaffe airplane markings is complex and rather confusing. When one observes markings used on German aircraft, one is immediately struck by the number of variations from 1935 to 1945. This section merely gives a general outline of markings intended to be applied.

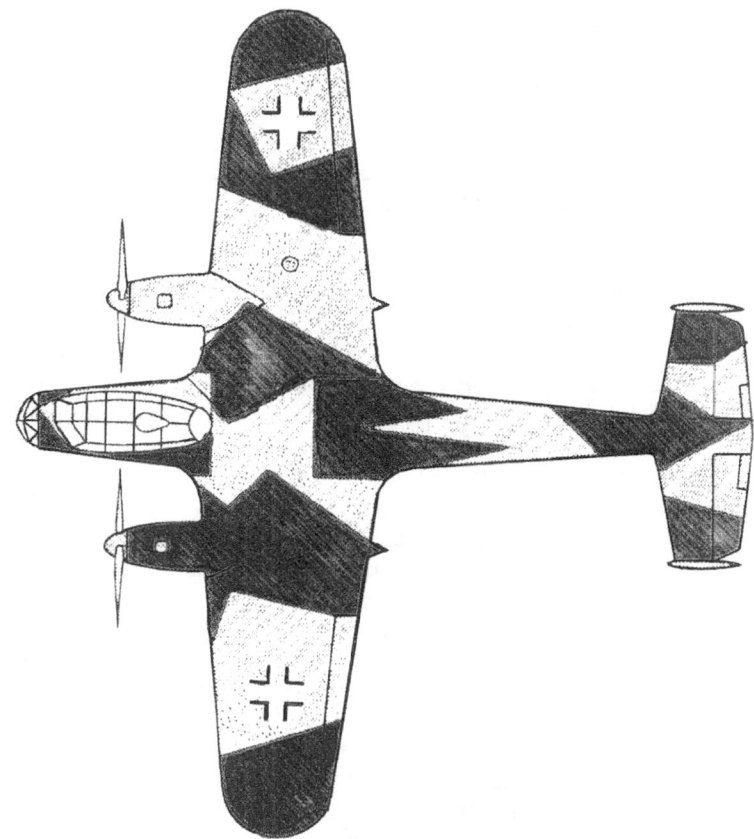

Camouflage scheme (Dornier Do 215 B)

National markings

From 1933 to 1935, Germany did not officially possess an air force, but the nazification of the civilian airfleet was evident by a replica of the Nazi flag painted on both sides of aircraft fins. This consisted of a bright red band with a white circle in which there was a black *Hakenkreuz* (swastika), very often standing on one point to emphasize an impression of dynamism and movement. In early 1936, a series of changes came into force. These included the application of the *Balkenkreuz* (national cross), a Greek cross with four arms of equal length. This was black with white outline similar to that used on German tanks. The *Balkenkreuz* was placed on both sides of an aircraft's fuselage at midpoint between the wing and tail

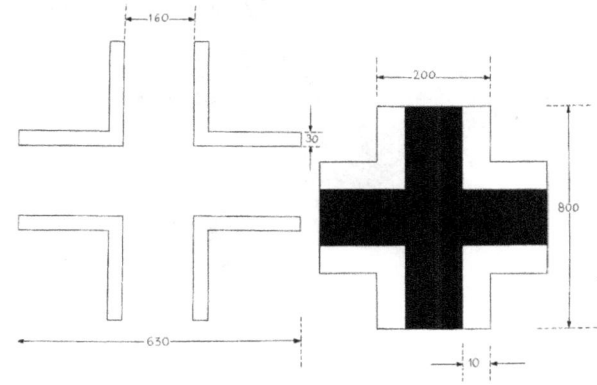

Balkenkreuz *(measurements in millimeters)*

units. It was also painted on the wings, both on upper and undersurface. This emphasized the importance of identifying friend and foe in a campaign where close cooperation between ground-attack aircraft and dive bombers and the assaulting armored forces was a fundamental feature of the *Blitzkrieg*.

The aircraft of the German Legion Condor that took part in the Spanish Civil War were repainted, as Germany was not officially at war against the Spanish Republic. Instead of *Balkenkreuz* and *Hakenkreuz*, they carried a white Andrea's cross in a black circle on both sides of the fuselage, while fins and rudders had a black Andrea's cross on a white background. The conspicuous red/white/black swastika painted on fins and rudders was discarded and replaced in late 1938 by a simple black swastika, often with a thin white outline. In the case of ambulance airplanes, the black and white *Balkenkreuz* was replaced by a red cross on a circular white background. Later in the war, there were several variations on the *Balkenkreuz* theme. For camouflage purposes, the cross was often merely outlined in white or black with the center left in the basic color.

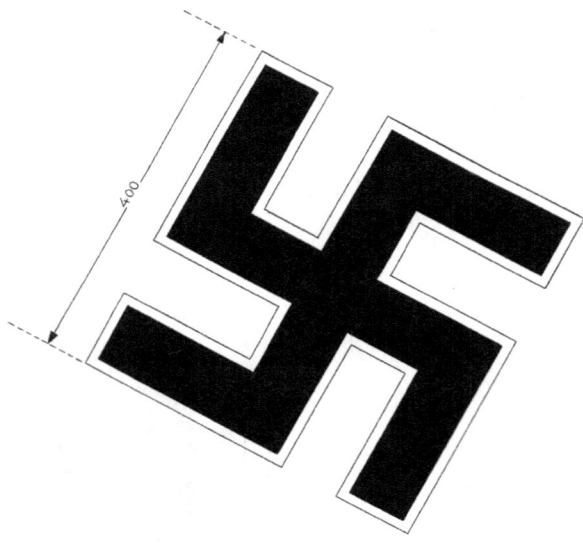

Swastika (measurement in millimeters)

Tactical markings

Tactical markings enabled a unit commander to quickly call up one of his aircraft by radio and pick it out more easily above the battlefield. Before the official creation of the Luftwaffe in 1935, German airplanes had no tactical markings but a civilian registration, generally a letter D for *Deutschand* (Germany) and a sequence of three of four letters. After 1935 identification marks were introduced, consisting of a combination of three letters and an Arabic numeral applied on the fuselage, in conjunction with the *Balkenkreuz*, the cross dividing the four symbols. These codes were painted in such as way that they would be readable if the aircraft was passing over the observer from front to back. These markings represented the plane's *Geschwader*, *Gruppe* and *Staffel*. The expansion of the German air force in the years preceding the war required some administrative changes, particularly when the *Luftflotten* (air fleets) were created in 1939. Single-engine fighter units had their own marking system, showing unit and tactical seniority. These used chevrons to indicate the rank of the pilot; bars, points or cross to indicate the *Gruppe*; a numeral showing the *Geschwader* to which the *Gruppe* belonged; and sometimes a horizontal black line ran entirely around the fuselage indicating a staff pilot. A *Geschwader* commander, for example, was indicated by two chevrons and a vertical bar; a *Gruppe* commander by two chevrons; a *Gruppe* technical officer by a chevron and a small circle. Colors were also applied to indicate the *Geschwader*; they were also designated by their abbreviation followed by an Arabic numeral: e.g. KG 77, NJG 26, ZG 110. *Staffeln* in the *Geschwader* were numbered consecutively in Arabic numerals; the first, second, and third *Staffeln* constituted *Gruppe* I; the fourth, fifth and sixth *Staffeln*, *Gruppe* II; and the seventh, eighth and ninth *Staffeln*, *Gruppe* III. Where a fourth or fifth *Gruppe* existed, the *Staffeln* were numbered 10, 11, and 13 or 13, 14 and 15 respectively. In unit designations, the *Gruppe* numeral was omitted whenever the *Staffel* number was displayed. Thus the fourth *Staffel* of *Kampfgeschwader* 77 was known as 4/KG 77 and no other reference to its position in *Gruppe* II of KG 77 was necessary. *Gruppen* attached to a *Geschwader* were numbered in Roman numerals; thus I/KG 77 and II/KG 77 were the first and second *Gruppen* of the medium-range bomber *Geschwader* 77.

Training aircraft were indicated by letter S for *Schule* (school), a numeral indicating *Luftkreis*, a letter identifying the school, and the aircraft's registration numeral within the school. There were, however, many exceptions to the rules, and systems were partially changed, becoming complicated. As World War II progressed, the application of the rules became somewhat more lax, and interpretation at the unit level varied widely from front to front and year to year, resulting in a complex and confusing "system" without uniformity, markings being omitted, some obscure or rarely seen, others added or placed in unofficial positions. *Geschwader* designations could then consist of three digits, and a system of colors was introduced to indicate *Staffeln* and *Gruppen*. There were many variations on the theme, some being in solid or outlined form, or red, yellow, white or black according to the plane background color. In 1941, colored tail bands were added according to theater of operation, and often wingtips and cowling were painted in the same color. In mid–1944, a more complicated system of colored tail bands was introduced for fighter units in the defense of the Reich, adding to the confusing situation already existing. At unit level, however, the tendency was toward smaller and less conspicuous application of the tactical numbers, and in many cases they were simply omitted.

Next to each of the airplane's filler points, there was a small yellow triangle pointing upward, bearing indications referring to the octane rating of the fuel. Luftwaffe vehicles were marked with an identification plate bearing the prefix WL (Wehrmacht Luftwaffe).

Unit and individual emblems

Individual pilots and those belonging to an established unit had "honor titles," crests and

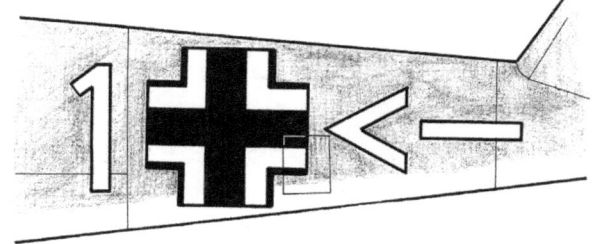

Marking on a Messerschmitt Bf 109 F-4/B 10 Jabo JG2 France c. 1942 (flown by a **Staffelkapitän***).*

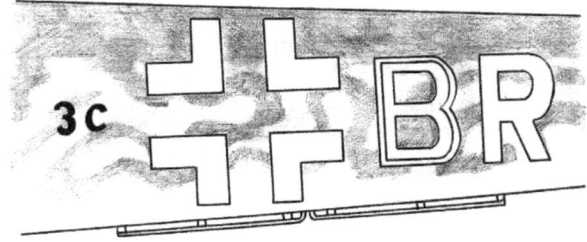

Markings on a Messerschmitt Bf 110 G-4 of 7./NJ G4 in Northwest Germany c. 1943.

Emblems on aircrafts. Left: III/JG 2 (third group of fighter squadron 2). Right: IV/JG 51 (fourth group of fighter squadron 51).

emblems. This practice, started by prominent flyers and units of World War I, such as the famous "Red Baron," Manfred von Richthofen, was revived in the Luftwaffe, and awarded, for example, to fighter JG 132. The fighter *Geschwader* JG 26 was titled *Leo Schlageter*, after a Nazi activist, an early "martyr" of the cause shot down by the French in 1923. Another example is JG 134, which was named *Horst Wessel* after the Nazi Party's gutter poet,

Marking on a Junkers Ju 87 B-2/Trop pf III/St.G1 in Libya 1941.

Rudder of Oberleutnant Hans-Joachim Marseille's Bf 109F. The rudder of the airplane of the **Staffelkäpitan** *of 3/JG 27 displayed his score in June 1942 in North Africa. Marseille was killed on September 30, 1942, with a score of 158.*

and distinguished by its brown, the color of the early Nazi and *Sturm Abteilung* (SA, Storm Trooper) uniforms.

Insignia were of great variety. Directly inspired by classical heraldry, they represented the arms of the city or cities with which the pilot or units were associated, or were individual devices with geometrical forms including colored triangles and diamonds. Pseudo-heraldic signs such as birds (eagle, owl and raven), and other animals (shark, lion, cat, horse, fox, unicorn, even Walt Disney's Mickey Mouse) were frequently used. Some crests were obviously directed at a particular target. Example of this type were the cliffs of Dover, an axe cleaving John Bull's hat, or a dog performing on a puddle-shaped map of England. Numerous other examples were observed, using various aggressive combinations and martial themes, for example, lightning, a falling bomb, a flying devil, and Death with its scythe. The shark's mouth insignia with menacing teeth was also used; it displayed unit heraldry, suggesting personal flamboyance and enhancement of aggressive spirit. It was painted, for example, on Messerschmitt Bf 109C of 2/JG 71, Junkers Ju 87 B-1 Stuka of 2/StG 77, Messerschmitt Bf 110 C of II/ZG 76 (Haifisch *Gruppe*) and even on Gotha Go 242 gliders. Individual, personal or unit good-luck symbols were sometimes used. Crests, insignia and emblems were usually placed on both sides of the cowling near the cockpit or on the aircraft's nose. The kill tally was proudly exhibited in the form of small stars or bars, generally painted on the aircraft rudder. Art and decoration painted on aircraft in the form of pin-ups, fictional or cartoon heroes, lucky or aggressive symbols, animals, and patriotic motifs were often disapproved or frowned upon by military authorities, but they were often tolerated as they benefited morale, expressed individual pride, offered relief from uniform military anonymity, comforted by recalling home, and were believed to work as fetishes against enemy action.

Aircraft Armament

Machine guns and light, quick-firing cannons, owing to their high rate of fire, relative low weight and limited encumbrance, lend themselves to use on aircrafts. One or more crew members could control great firepower. The Germans started World War II with only a few types of aircraft armament, in order to standardize manufacture and achieve large-scale production. As the war progressed, improvements became necessary, and many changes and additions were made, increasing the rate of fire, muzzle velocity, punch, and caliber. Aircraft armament was thus extremely varied and evolved as World War II was in progress, ranging from simple machine guns to sophisticated automatic cannons, air-to-air rockets, and even extravagantly heavy recoilless pieces.

Maschinengewehr MG 15

Widely used in German World War II aircraft, the MG 15 machine gun was developed by the Rheinmetall-Borsig weapon company in 1932. It had a caliber of 7.92 mm (0.32 in), a length of 1,334 mm (52.5 in), a weight of 12.7 kg (28 lbs), and a rate of fire of about 850 rounds per minute. The ammunition was the 7.92 × 57 mm Mauser bullet that weighed 25 grams. The weapon was fed by a *Gurttrommel* (round saddle drum) with 75 rounds; in full

2. Basic Technical Data

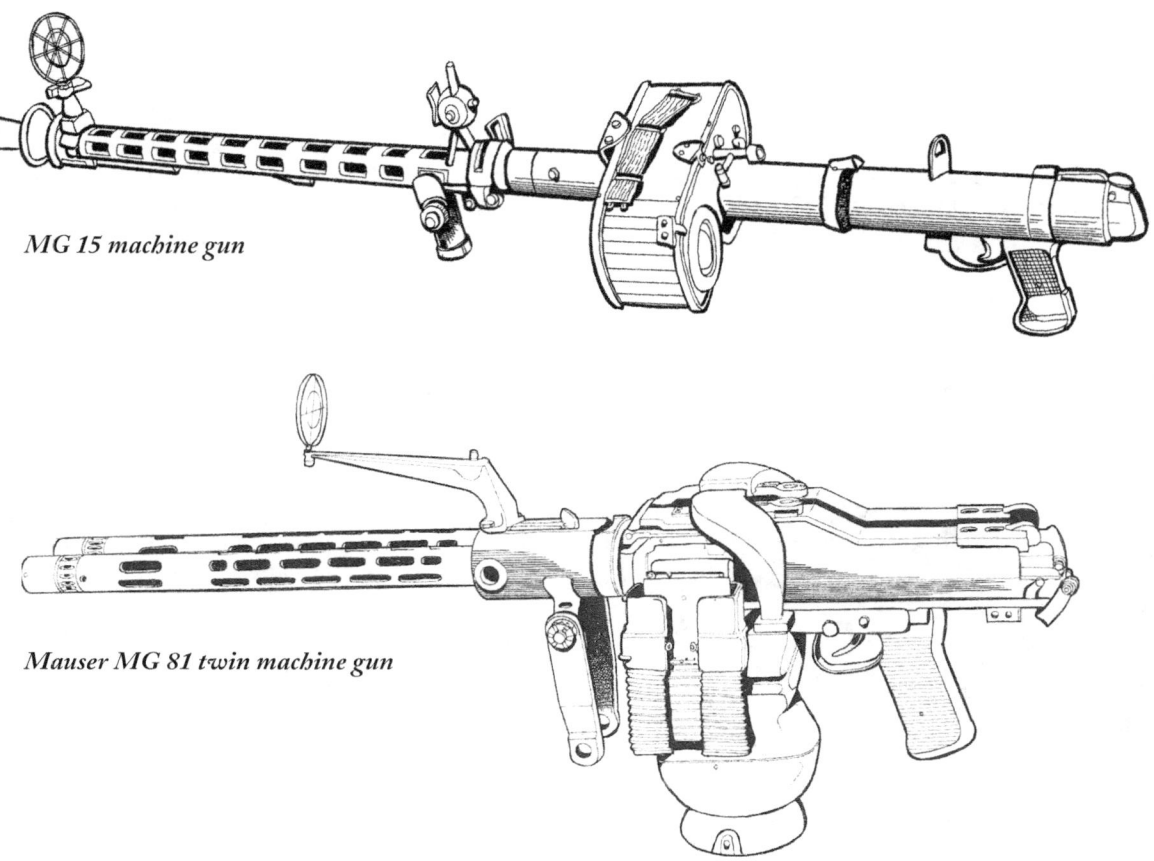

MG 15 machine gun

Mauser MG 81 twin machine gun

automatic fire the gunner had to change the magazine after five seconds, as the rate of fire was 1,250 rpm. A license-built version, known as Type 98, was used in Japanese Army aircraft.

Mauser MG 81

The gas-recoiled twin MG 81 Mauser machine gun weighed 13 lb 14 oz, it had a length of 35 inches, a muzzle velocity of 2,800 ft/sec, and a rate of fire of 1,300 rounds per minute. As with most aircraft-mounted machine guns, the MG 81 was fitted with a canvas empty-round collection chute leading to a collector box.

MG 131 machine gun

The MG 131 was a 13-mm machine gun designed in 1938 by the Rheinmetall-Borsig Company. Manufactured from 1940 to 1945, it was designed for use at fixed or flexible, single or twin mountings in Luftwaffe aircraft. It fired electrically primed ammunition, and was belt-fed. The weapon weighed 16.6 kg, had a length of 1.17 m, a muzzle velocity of 750 m/s, a rate of fire of 900 rounds per minute, and an effective range of 1,800 m (2,200 yd).

MG 151/15 machine cannon

Designed by Mauser and manufactured by Rheinmetall, the MG 151/15 was well constructed, and gave an excellent performance. With a caliber of 15 mm (0.591 in), it had an overall length of 75½ inches, a weight of 84 lbs 1 oz (including electric control), a muzzle velocity of 950 m/s, and a rate of fire of about 700 rounds per minute. The automatic cannon was recoil-operated by muzzle blast and the system of feed was by disintegrating metal-link belt. The MG 151/15 was generally mounted in the nose, for example, on the

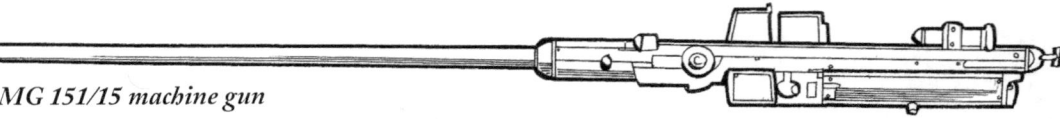

MG 151/15 machine gun

Heinkel He 115, Junkers Ju 88 (night fighter version), Dornier Do 217, and Henschel Hs 129.

Maschinenkanone MK 108/30

Designed by Rheinmetall-Borsig in 1940 as a private venture, MK 108 military development started after 1942. Entering service in October 1943 in Luftwaffe aircraft such as the Bf 110 G-2 and the Bf 109 G-6, the automatic cannon was blow-back operated, belt-fed, and electrically ignited. It was simple to manufacture, easy to maintain, very effective, reliable and compact in size; its weight was 58 kg (127.9 lbs) and its barrel was short. Its total length was 1,057 mm (3 ft 5.6 in). The weapon had a good punch, with a rate of fire of about 650 rounds per minute. It was reported that, on average, just four hits with high-explosive or incendiary ammunition could bring down a heavy bomber such as a B-17 Flying Fortress or a B-24 Liberator, and that a single hit could destroy a fighter. Its distinctive heavy pounding sound and high rate of fire gave it the nickname "pneumatic hammer" among Allied aircrews. The MK 108's main shortcoming was its low velocity of 500 m/s (1,640 ft/sec); this resulted in its projectile trajectory dropping considerably after a comparatively short range. This made its effective firing range short and aiming a challenge, and the pilot had to use careful timing to fire at precisely the right moment. The Mk 108 was used on many Luftwaffe fighters, for example on the Messerschmitt Bf 109, Focke-Wulf Fw 190, and Messerschmitt Me 262. It was also employed for *Schräge Musik* configuration (aiming upward at an oblique angle).

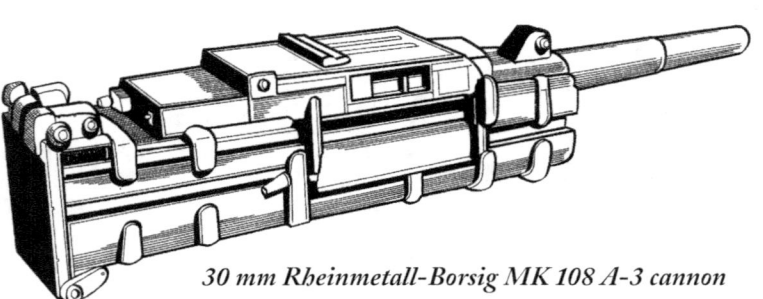

30 mm Rheinmetall-Borsig MK 108 A-3 cannon

Maschinenkanone MK 103

The gas-operated automatic cannon MK 103 had a caliber of 30 mm, weighed 146 kg, and fired at 420 rounds per minute, with a low muzzle velocity of 860 m/sec. It used high-explosive, incendiary and armor-piercing rounds, each weighing 330 gram (11 oz). The MK 103 was principally mounted in a few Focke-Wulf Fw 190 (wings), in some variants of the Messerschmitt Me 262 (nose), in the Ta 152 C3 (above engine cowl), in some Dornier

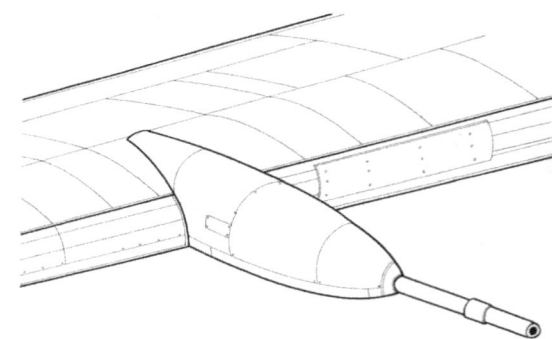

MK 103 cannon (here mounted on starboard wing of a Dornier Do 335 B-5)

Do 335s (above engine and wings), and a few Messerschmitt Bf 109 K fighter (above engine).

Anti-tank cannon BK 3.7 cm

This *Bordkanone* (aircraft-mounted gun) was derived from the 3.7 cm Flak 18 anti-aircraft gun. Designed by Rheinmetall-Borsig and Solothurn, it had a caliber of 37 mm (1.457 in), a practical rate of fire of 80 rounds

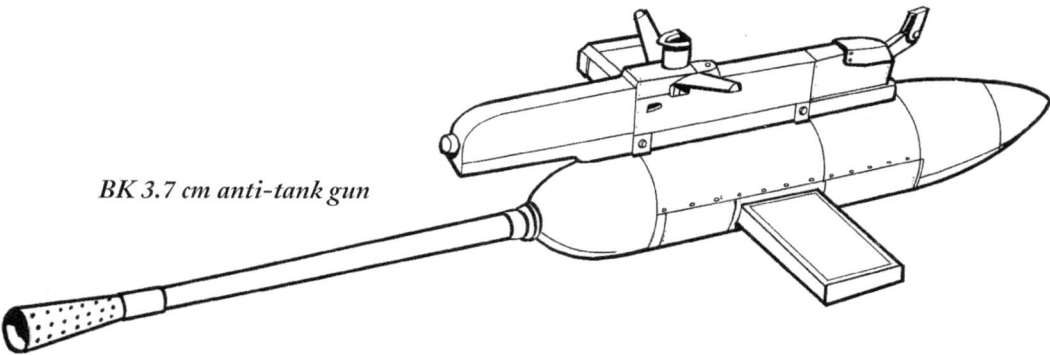

BK 3.7 cm anti-tank gun

per minute, and muzzle velocity of 820 m/s (2690 ft/sec). The BK 3.7 cm, adapted for use as an airborne anti-tank gun, was mounted in pairs, each one attached under the wing of, for example, the Junkers Ju 87G.

Maschinenkanone MK 112/55

The MK 112/55 mm machine cannon weighed 271 kg (597 lbs), and it had a length of 2 m (6 ft 6 in), a rate of fire of 300 rounds per minute and a muzzle velocity of 600 m/ second (1,969 ft/sec). It was either mounted in nose, or wing root for firing forward, or placed in a central fuselage, paired for *Schräge Musik* upward oblique firing. One short burst at close range was often enough to severely damage or even bring down a heavy four-engined Allied bomber.

R4M Rocket

Produced by the Rheinmetall Company, the Rakete 4 Minenkopf (R4M) air-to-air rocket, nicknamed *Orkan* (Hurricane), was developed to deal with Allied heavy bombers. The projectile was composed of a simple steel (later cardboard) tube with eight flip-out fins for stabilization. It was 82 cm (32.2 in) in length and 5.5 cm (2.16 in) in diameter. It was powered by a diglycol, solid-fuel, fast-burning rocket propellant. It mounted a 0.50 kg (1.1l b) warhead, either high-explosive for anti-aircraft use or armor-piercing against tanks. It was usually used in a battery of twelve or twenty-four, mounted and fired from a wooden launch rail attached under wing. The projectiles were unguided and aimed by a cockpit gunsight.

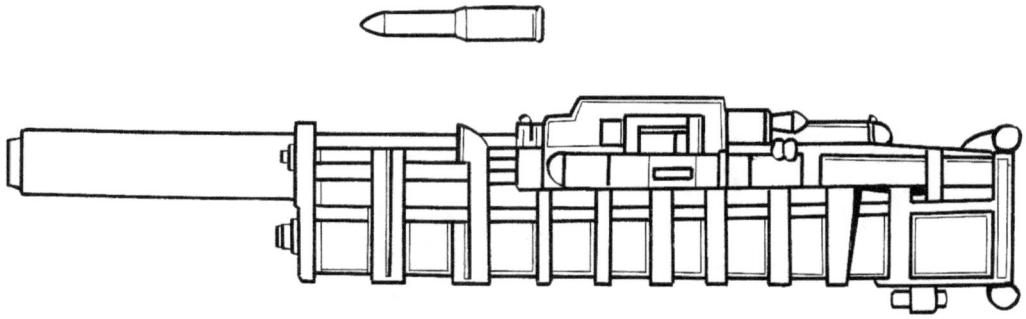

Left side view MK 112/55 mm machine cannon

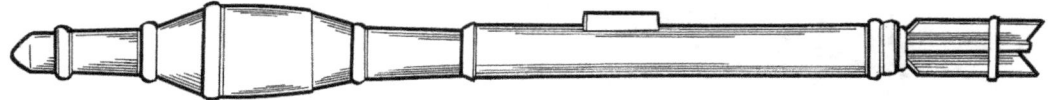

R4M Rocket

They were provided with enough fuel to be fired effectively from 1,000 m, thus beyond the range of bombers' defensive weapons. The rockets were serially fired in four salvos of six missiles each, at intervals of 0.07 seconds, from a range of about 600 m to 1,000 m and at a speed of 1,700 ft/s. One single hit often meant a kill, but it was not an easy task to take accurate aim on a target which was taking evasive action. Simple and easy to manufacture, the R4M was used operationally only for a brief period just before the end of World War II.

SG 500 Jagdfaust

The SG 500 was an airborne rocket especially designed to shoot down heavy Allied bombers. The experimental weapon was to be mounted in two racks of five projectiles, one under each wing root. The rocket featured an optical sensor, which reacted to light and shadow produced by the intended target, but it could not make out any difference between friend or foe. The *Jagdfaust* could also be mounted vertically in order to fire upward (e.g., on Messerschmitt Me 163). The end of the war prevented any wide-scale development of the SG 500, but the rocket system is credited with having shot down one American four-engined B-17.

Anti-tank 7.5 cm Pak cannon

Derived from the standard infantry 7.5 cm Pak, this anti-tank gun was mounted, for example, under the fuselage of a Henschel Hs 129. It is believed that some eighty Hs 129s were converted for use as tank busters. With a modified muzzle brake, a special aircraft mounting and an in-bodied magazine containing twelve rounds, this weapon system was tested with success against Russian tanks at the battle of Kursk in mid–1943. Coming too late and on a too-limited scale, it failed to have any impact on the Eastern front.

Gerät 104

Designed by Rheinmetall, the Gerät 104 was a 35-cm recoilless cannon mounted under the fuselage of a bomber, Dornier Do 217. It was intended to fire a single anti-shipping explosive shell weighing 650 kg. A similar project, known as Münchhausen, was a 54-cm recoilless cannon mounted in the belly of a Junkers Ju 87. Neither of these projects were developed.

Henschel Hs 123 B-3 tank buster armed with 7.5 cm Pak gun

Position of weapons

Early mono- or biplanes could have weapons firing forward between the spinning blades, owing to a synchronized gear. Ventral or dorsal (rearward) firing was done from open hatches, often fitted with a windshield or a transparent fairing to give the gunner some protection from the airstream while in flight. Modern monoplane fighters mounted weapons either in the wings, on the nose, on the sides of the fuselage, above engine cowling or in the engine, firing through the center of the propeller boss.

Bombers were not intended—nor designed—to actively engage in combat with other aircraft. Large and slow, they were always at a disadvantage, but particularly when attacked by fast and agile interceptor fighters. They had to be escorted by a number of fighters. It was also widely accepted that to have any hope of survival in enemy airspace, a bomber would be fitted with defensive weapons. Machine guns were mounted either in rear cockpits, in ventral or dorsal nacelles (or open hatches with windshields), in side-windows, or concentrated in the bomber's glazed nose.

The best method to defend a bomber was to have one or more power-driven gun turrets, not a mere windshield, but a precise aiming device, complete with sighting system, plenty of ammo, and operator controls. The disadvantages of adding a gun turret were the considerable high cost involved and the significant penalty in weight and drag. At the start of World War II, if Britain and the U.S. had large two- or four-engined strategic bombers, each

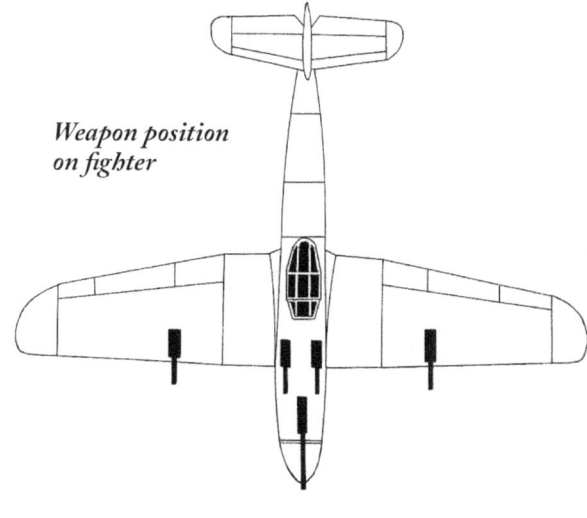

Weapon position on fighter

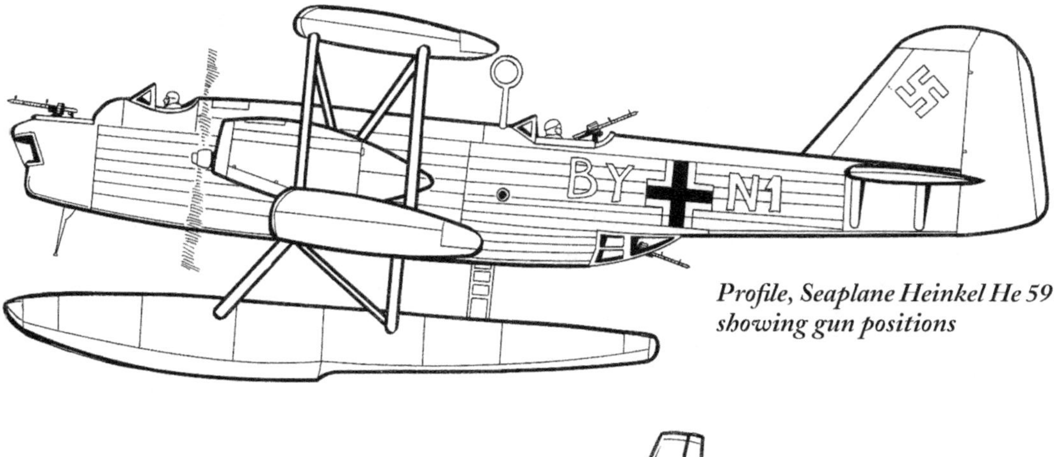

Profile, Seaplane Heinkel He 59 showing gun positions

View of bomber Junkers Ju 290 showing gun positions

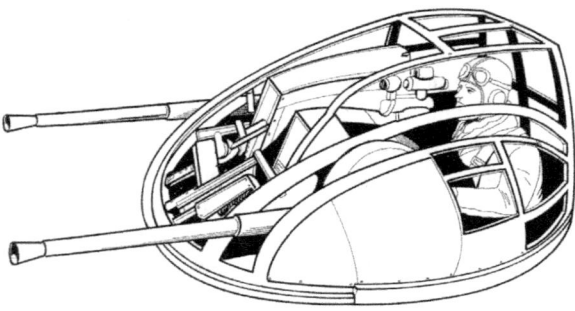

Twin 20-mm cannon mounted on power-driven turret

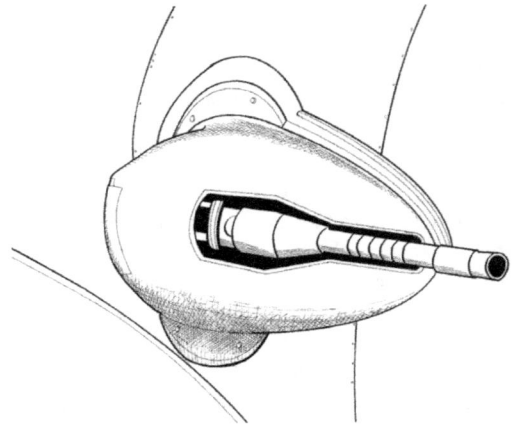

Remotely controlled rear-firing 13-mm MG 131 (on Me 210 and Me 410). This barbette was complicated and rather ineffective in combat, as firing was inaccurate.

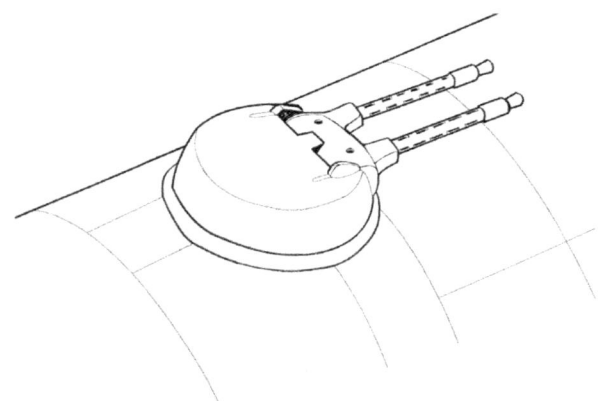

Remote control dorsal turret (B-1 Stand). The unmanned armored turret, here shown on a Heinkel He 177 Greif, was armed with twin 13-mm MG 131 machine guns.

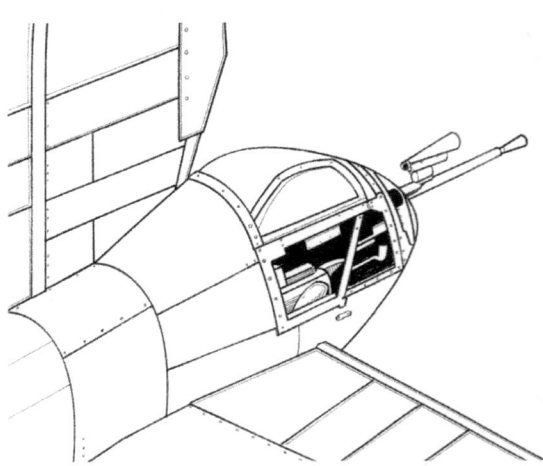

Manned tail turret. The H-Stand (tail turret), here shown on a Heinkel He 177 Greif, was armed with one Gimbal-mounted 20-mm MG 151 cannon with coned gunsight. The gunner was protected by 18-mm-thick armor.

with several gun turrets (e.g., Armstrong Whirworth Whitley, Vickers Wellington, Avro Manchester and Lancaster, Short Stirling, Halifax, Boeing B-17), the Luftwaffe clung to the belief that their fast two-engined tactical bombers could be adequately defended by several hand-held machine guns. Misled by the ease with which their medium aircraft had operated in the opening phase of World War II, the German aviation authorities realized the limitations of hand-held and hand-loaded machine guns during the Battle of Britain—particularly their limited range, their lack of punch and the very short fire (a few seconds) provided by the 75-round drums. As the war proceeded, the Luftwaffe developed several types of accurate multiple belt-fed machine guns and light, fast-firing board cannons in armored, power-driven turrets. One domain in which the Germans did much pioneering work was in remotely controlled barbettes (unmanned gun positions). These were lighter than the conventional manned turret and offered less drag, and it was possible for a gunner at a single sighting station to control several barbettes and bring several weapons to bear on a single target. A forward-firing weapon position was coded A-Stand; a fuselage dorsal weapon posi-

Machine gun MG 404 in turret on Dornier Do 24

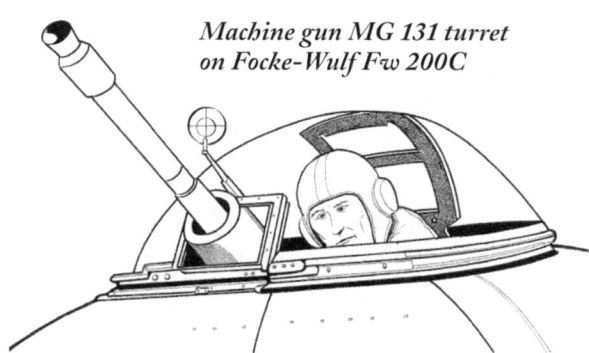
Machine gun MG 131 turret on Focke-Wulf Fw 200C

tion was B-stand; a fuselage ventral position was C-Stand—or "Bola," short for Bodemlafette ("bottom" mount in the form of a somewhat round movable basket); and a tail weapon position was termed H-Stand.

Schräge Musik

Another German innovation in the domain of positioning aircraft weapons was *Schräge Musik* (jazz music, literally "slanting music"), the code name given to the installation of one, two or four upward-firing cannons mounted with an angle of 65 degrees on the back of night fighters. This allowed them to approach and attack British night bombers from beneath, where they were basically invisible, instead of risking a shoot-out with an alert rear-gunner. The crew of the attacking aircraft would aim for a bomber's wings (not for the fuselage), in order to avoid detonating its bomb payload and being themselves hit by exploding debris. They fired non-tracer ammunition, to prevent being spotted. Exploiting airborne radar, stealth, and Allied bomber's blind spots, an attack by a *Schräge Musik*–equipped fighter was typically a complete surprise to the bomber crew, who would only realize a fighter was close by when one of its wings or engines would burst into flame. Developed by Ober-

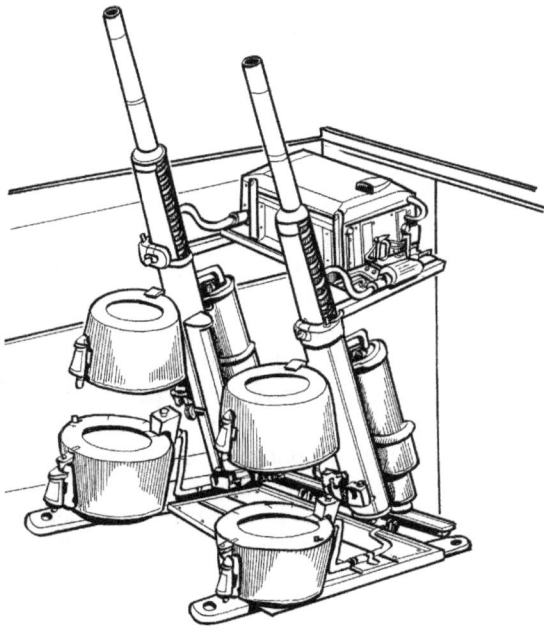
Pair of Oerlikon MG/FF 20-mm cannon in Schräge Musik *mount. The Swiss-made MG/FF had a caliber of 20 mm, a rate of fire of 450 rpm, a muzzle velocity of 820 m/s, and a maximum range of 2,000 m. Ammunition feed was by a 60-round drum magazine placed on the top of the gun.*

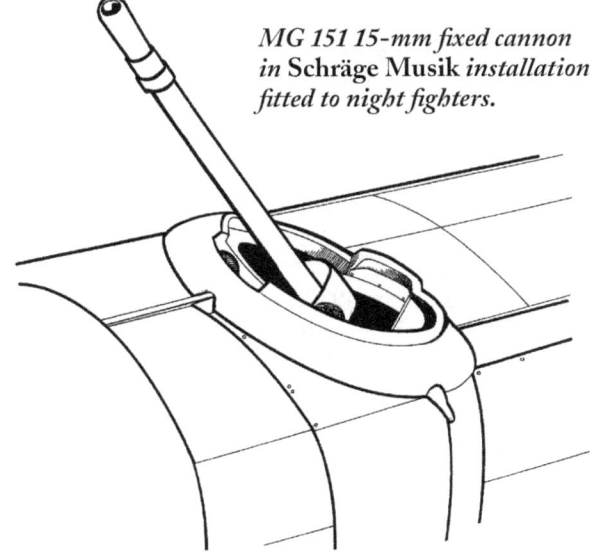
MG 151 15-mm fixed cannon in Schräge Musik *installation fitted to night fighters.*

leutnant Rudolf Schönert in 1942, *Schräge Musik* was first used operationally in August 1943, and wide-scale adoption followed in late 1943. For several months after its introduction, the weapon system was a nasty secret that puzzled the Allies. In 1944, a third of all German night fighters carried upward-firing guns. Had it not been for the ever-increasing abilities of the British anti-radar efforts and the introduction of new aircraft designs, *Schräge Musik*—particularly carried by the formidable Heinkel He 219 night fighter—would have seriously depleted the forces of RAF Bomber Command.

Airborne Radio and Radar

The importance of a comprehensive and efficient air-signal service in aerial warfare is obvious. The transmission of all orders, observations and communications was done by wireless radio, an absolute necessity for the successful conduct of air operations. Radio provided reliable communication and new and accurate navigational systems and bad-weather landing aids. German airborne radio equipment included *Funkgerät* (FuG), composed of transmitters and receivers; *Peilgerät* (PeG), or navigational equipment; and *Notsender* (NS), or emergency transmitter. Aerial warfare, whether the aircraft were bombers, fighters, or other types, was (and still is) a much more individualistic matter than is war on sea or land. Flying crews had to be highly trained and able to absorb all the details of a mission given to them in their briefing. A lot of detailed organization was necessary before any aerial operation. A little time before take-off, last-minute instructions (regarding matters such as change in the weather) could be most important.

During the 1930s, scientists in Britain and Germany were working on newly developed electronic aids to navigation, but because of the different objectives of the two countries, one defensive and the other offensive, development followed two opposite directions. Thus, while the British gave priority to developing a defensive system of radar, the Germans concentrated on building up radio aids for bombing. The German systems which emerged were based on the Lorenz beam. This was basically slightly overlapping radio beams broadcast by ground stations, transmitting Morse dots and dashes. Where the signals interlocked, an aircraft received a steady note by means of a computer; any deviation either way resulted in a changed signal, thus even an inexperienced pilot could follow a predetermined course.

The simplest of these methods was the intersecting *Knickebein* ("Crooked Leg," codenamed "Headache" by the British) which employed two Lorenz beams, one to hold the bomber on course right up to the target, while the second crossed the first at the point where the bombs should be dropped. Knickebein was used in the early stages of the German night-bombing offensive against England, and proved to be fairly effective. When it was jammed, another system was developed. *X-Gerät* (X-Device), was more accurate, as it employed four Lorenz radio beams (each named for a river: Weser, Rhine, Oder and Elbe), and each on a different frequency: one held the aircraft on course to the target while the other three crossed it at intervals, giving a warning of approach, the last signal making an electrical contact that automatically released the bombs. As good as X-Device was, British efforts to jam it were successful. A final system, Y-Gerät "Wotan," consisted of a single, accurate beam directing the bomber to its target.

The disadvantage of the Lorenz beam was that it could be jammed or even deflected so that the German bombers sometimes unwittingly dropped their deadly projectiles at sea or in open country without even knowing they had missed their target. Some bombers even landed at RAF bases, believing they were back in Germany. Another disadvantage of radio navigation was that the approach to a target greatly simplified the organization of the defense because all bombers followed one another along a defined lane which could be patrolled by fighters or barraged by anti-aircraft artillery. In the end, German faith in electronics was completely shattered and navigational aid was abandoned.

The term "radar" (an acronym for "radio detection and ranging") was coined in the

United States and was soon universally adopted. In German, though, radar is called *Funkmeßgerät* (FumG in short). Radar is a detection method based on broadcast of strong and short radio impulses. Waves are reflected if they meet a solid metal flying or navigating body. By measuring the time from the departure of the impulse until the return of the echo, one may calculate the distance between the radar station and the target. Radar thus detects and determines with precision the existence and position of a target. Radar equipment used during World War II were complex, bulky and cumbersome instruments compared to modern devices. Not always totally reliable, it included a powerful generator using very high frequency microwaves, a highly sensitive receiver catching back-echoing beams, sophisticated devices translating radio waves into visual flashing form on a screen, scanners, primitive computers, and various precise calculating instruments, as well as large antennas. Nevertheless, radar, which had been in almost an embryonic state at the start of World War II, developed as a more-or-less reliable detection system, often providing observers with a map of the sky above them. It also developed as a navigational aid, providing aircrews with a map of the terrain below, which was—in theory but not always in practice—unaffected by clouds or darkness.

The German night-fighter branch was headed by Oberst Joseph Kammhuber, who for years waged a fierce struggle in the night above the German skies. War in the air became an immensely sophisticated exercise in tactical and technical ingenuity in which the professional fighting men were at least as dependant on the expertise of scientists as they were on their own skills to carry out their task. Air war was waged by small groups of highly trained fighting men operating complex weapons systems developed by specialized technologists and scientists, and under the leadership of commanders exercising control at very long distance.

Originally limited to bulky ground-to-air equipment, technology evolved as World War II proceeded, and miniaturization enabled the use of airborne radar fitted to night fighters. Waves were sent off and received back by means of a bulky aerial which in some cases could slow a night fighter as much as 50 km/h. The British introduced countermeasures— such as "window" aluminum stripes jamming German radar, and night-fighter hunters, such as the De Haviland Mosquito—to each new Luftwaffe radar system which appeared. In turn the Germans frantically developed new devices such as *Spanner-Auflage* (trouser press), an infrared searchlight designed to expose exhaust gases in the wake of a distant bomber.

The Germans had several radar systems, produced by highly specialized manufacturers, such as GEMA, Telefunken, Lorenz and Siemens. *Radar Lichtenstein BC*, developed by Telefunken in 1941, operated on a frequency of 490 MHz with a 620 mm wavelength. It required four double pairs of dipole antennae bristling from the aircraft's nose. It had a search arc of 24 degrees and a range of between 3,000 and 5,500 m depending on conditions. Provided with three scopes for azimuth, ranging and elevation, the radar was, however, far from user-friendly, and even experienced operators often had to rely upon ground control to vector them into the right area.

Radar 220 Lichtenstein SN2 was an improved and more accurate model developed in 1943, operating on long waves of about 90 MHz. Working through the distinctive "stag's antlers" aerial, the SN2 was only slightly affected by the RAF's "window" countermeasure. *Radar Flensburg*, developed by Siemens, was introduced in mid–1944 using wing-mounted dipole antennae, and was sensitive to frequencies 170–220 MHz. *Radar 218 Neptun* was introduced in 1944 by Siemens; it used frequencies 158 to 187 MHz and had a range of 120 to 500 km. *Radar 240 Berlin*, introduced in April 1945, used a 9 cm wavelength.

These devices were mounted on a few special night-fighter designs. The Messerschmitt Bf 110 remained the primary Luftwaffe night fighter until 1944; the aircraft (G version) proved able to take the addition of radar, a third crewman to operate it, and heavy armament. Other night fighters included the Heinkel He 219, and modifications of existing designs of Me 220 and Me 410 variants, Dornier Do 217 E and N, Junkers Ju 88 G-7 and Ju 188.

Airborne radio and radar were used in cooperation with ground radar stations: early warning sets (Freya, Mammut or Wassermann) for long-range detection, Würzburg Riese for aircraft interception control; and Würzburg, used for short range and height finding. Other types of equipment distinguished between friendly and hostile airplanes. On the basis of information from these various sources, hostile aircraft were plotted in a central headquarters. Proper warning then was given and defensive fighters were put in the air to intercept attackers. Information on the course and expected target of the bombers was passed by radio to the airborne interceptors until contact was made.

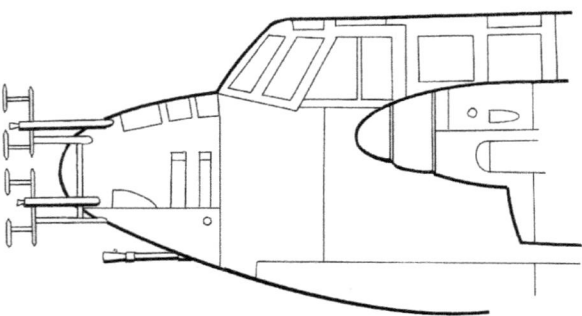

Dornier Do 217 N-2 night interceptor with FuG Hohentwiel search radar mounted in the nose.

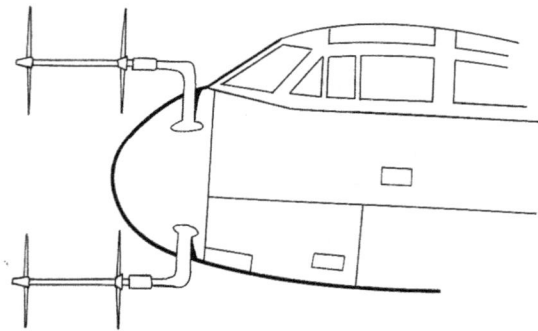

Antenna of radar FuG 220 Lichtenstein SN-2 mounted in nose of Heinkel He 219.

Air-to-Ground Projectiles

Bombs

Aerial bombs are unpowered missiles dropped from aircraft toward a ground target. The first use of an air-dropped bomb was carried out by the Italians in their 1911 war for Libya. Used with success in the First World War, bombs proliferated in World War II, with designs for various purposes, including containers filled with leaflets for propaganda purposes. Explosive bombs were used for general purpose, fragmentation, demolition by heavy blast, or armor piercing. The German *Sprengbombe Cylindrisch* (SC, cylindric general-purpose bombs) were designed for maximum blast effect and came in 50 kg, 100 kg, 250 kg—the most intensively used, and 500 kg. The heaviest German free-fall bomb was the SC 2000 HE; filled with Tinalin high explosive and weighing 1,953 kg (4,306 lbs) it had a length of 3.44 m (11 ft 3.4 in), and a diameter of 0.66 m (2 ft 2 in). Chemical bombs were used for delivering poison gas, a smoke screen or incendiary material. Pyrotechnic bombs were used as flares or target indicators.

Bombs were usually of streamlined shape, and fitted with stabilizing fins, fuses and an arming device to set the fuse. By the end of the war the Germans used complete aircraft as projectiles, filled with high explosive and directed by radio control or abandoned to dive onto the target. This weapon system, known as *Mistel* (Mistletoe), was composed of a piggyback combination of two planes, a manned fighter carried on top of a bomber/projectile.

Bombs (and artillery shells) were identified by a color code. Basically, SC (high explosive) was yellow; SD (semi-armor-piercing) red; and PC (armor piercing) blue. For example, the NG 50 Smoke Bomb had a field gray body with a white nose; it could have four white vertical stripes or two white bands painted on the body. The two-kilogram incendiary bomb B2 E1 Z weighed 4½ pounds, the diameter was 2 inches and the overall length was 20.7 inches. It was filled with TNT or amatol in addition to thermite, and the body color was aluminum or light green.

Many bombs were given a name. For example, the armor-piercing, thick-walled type SD 1400 was called "Fritz"; the somewhat smaller SD 1000 "Essau." The high explosive SC 1000 was "Hermann," and the SC 1800 was "Satan." Electrically charged impact fuses were fitted

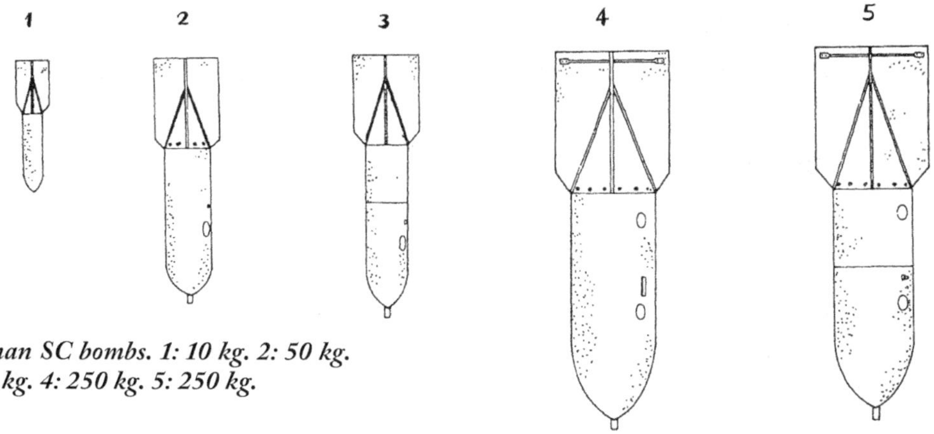

2. Basic Technical Data

German SC bombs. 1: 10 kg. 2: 50 kg. 3: 50 kg. 4: 250 kg. 5: 250 kg.

Mistel 2 (Junkers Ju 88 G-1 with Focke-Wulf Fw 190 A-6). In this configuration the rebuilt Junkers Ju 88 itself was a projectile.

with charging plungers above the main fuse body with its tumbler switch. Below this lay the flash pellet, Penthrite, wax and picric acid to complete the whole, although variations were incorporated. The type 17 clockwork delayed action; the type 50, with a trembler switch fuse, acted as a booby trap; the ZUS 40 was set beneath the normal fuse in such a way that the extraction of one made "safe" activated the other concealed beneath it.

Bombs were often carried in an enclosed

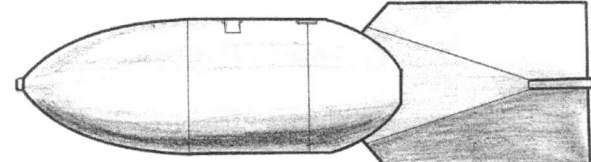

German 250 kg high-explosive bomb. The bomb had an overall length of 64.5 in, a body length of 42 in, an overall width of 18 in, and a body diameter of 14.5 in.

bomb bay placed under the fuselage, or carried in racks attached under the fuselage or under the wings from H- or T-shaped lugs. Anything attached under fuselage and wings (either bombs or additional fuel tanks) reduced speed by adding drag. Bombs were loaded in the airplane by using a trolley and a jack.

The ordinary method of dropping bombs from aircraft was as much a matter of luck as of skill. A projectile dropped from an aircraft continues on the same course as the plane, while dropping toward the ground. Unless the bomber is exactly in line with the target, the bomb will miss to either side. In addition, since the aircraft would be traveling at several kilometers per minute, estimation of the target's distance was crucial. The wind, which might vary at lower levels and come in gusts, would also affect the fall of the bomb. An aircraft moves slightly crabwise in wind, so that it is useless for the pilot to aim the nose of his machine at the target. The corrections to a bombing run had to be made rapidly and deftly, often with anti-aircraft shells bursting all around the bomber, or while under attack from enemy fighters; any evasive action by bank or sideslip meant that either the bombing run had to be made again or that the bombs would miss the targets. Gradually, level bombers were therefore fitted with a bomb sight, a device assisting in the task of accurately dropping bombs on a ground target. Originally as simple as a set of crosshairs or markers arranged transversely, operated by a bombardier lying prone on his stomach, the device became more sophisticated, enabling correction for various factors that affected the ballistic trajectory of the dropped projectile, including altitude, speed and heading of aircraft, strength of the wind, and aerodynamic properties of specific types of bomb. In spite of such advanced devices (e.g., the Lofte 7 D tachometric bomb sight), at least in the early years of World War II, level bombing remained a crude weapon, suitable for large targets but not always sufficiently accurate for pinpoint targets such as strong points, ships and bridges. For accurate bombing, a new aircraft appeared in the late 1930s, the dive-bomber (in German *Sturzkampfflugzeug* or *Stuka*, for short).

Torpedo

Named after a genus of fish that stuns its prey by means of naturally produced electric shocks, the self-propelled torpedo was invented around 1867 by the British naval engineer Robert Whitehead. It was a revolutionary low-cost weapon as it enabled its deployers to attack, damage, cripple or possibly sink a capital warship. Basically a typical World War II torpedo was composed of a tube containing a high explosive warhead detonated on contact by a primer, a pre-programmed gyroscope and a small rudder which controlled its course, and an electric motor fed by battery to power a screw (including generally two contra-rotating propellers) by which it was moved through the water to the target. The torpedo was launched by compressed air from a tube fitted in a submarine or a special torpedo boat, but it could also be dropped from an aircraft. Although requiring a dangerous, close approach, and though accurate aiming was difficult, aircraft armed with torpedoes were dangerous opponents.

German nuclear bomb

As for the fear of a German atom bomb, which had given Washington and London much worry, that was without foundation. In spite of quantum mechanics research and experimentation carried out as early as 1932 by the German nuclear physicist Werner Heisenberg, in 1938 by Lise Meitner, Otto Hahn, and Fritz Strassmann (who showed that atoms of uranium could be split), and in 1940 by Professor Bothe in Heidelberg, German nuclear scientists could not match the purposeful

Torpedo

organization and dynamic drive of the U.S. Manhattan Project which led to practical application in Hiroshima and Nagasaki in August 1945. Lacking experience, raw materials, funds and facilities, German scientists also lacked official support, partly due to ideological reasons. Hitler occasionally referred to nuclear physics as "Jewish" physics, and was not inclined to encourage research in that field. Atomic weapon research made little progress in Nazi Germany due to Hitler's lack of interest in it and Himmler's practice of arresting the nuclear scientists for suspected disloyalty or pulling them off to work on some of his pet nonsensical "scientific" experiments which the Reichsführer SS deemed more important. Eventually, Albert Speer, Hitler's architect and minister of armaments, set up a research project charged with constructing a nuclear reactor, but he was convinced that the project had a very low likelihood of success. It was soon clear that it would take some time before Germany would be able to have an atom bomb, even if the reactor worked. Two atomic piles were eventually built, one near Hechingen, the other near Erfurt, both using deuterium as their moderator. Neither actually achieved a chain reaction, largely because they were too small. By that time, late 1944, the infrastructure of German industry was becoming increasingly chaotic. Such small supplies of uranium ore as were available—from a small field in Belgium and another in Bohemia—were running low, and thanks to a successful bombing raid by the RAF on the deuterium production plant in Norway, that was in short supply too. The program was already dead in its infancy, and one might even say that it was stillborn.

Investigations by teams of Allied experts disclosed that by May 1945 the Germans were still far away from the discovery of how to initiate a nuclear chain reaction. It was one of the ironies of fate that the development of the atomic bomb in the United States owed so much to two scientists who had been exiled because of race from the Nazi and fascist dictatorships: Einstein from Germany and Fermi from Italy. Before the end of 1944 the American and British governments learned, to their great relief, that Nazi Germany would not have a nuclear weapon in time to win the war.

Missiles

The adoption of the machine gun (later of the automatic cannon) had made air-to-air combat feasible, but by the end of World War II, it had come close to causing a stand-off. By then it had become clear that a better weapon was needed for air-to-air combat. Because Allied bombers flew so close together, much consideration was given to the concept of bombing them. A new method emerged, consisting of a rocket-propelled flying bomb, soon known as an air-to-air missile, that could be directed to its target from a plane which stayed outside the lethal area. Broadly speaking, a missile is an unmanned self-propelled airborne craft which carries a destructive load. It may be remotely guided or direct itself to a preselected target, but whatever its specific purpose might be, it consists of an airframe (with or without wings and fins) housing a motor, control system, guidance system and warhead. By the end of the war the Germans had developed glide and radio-guided bombs. The former remained gravity-fall weapons but small fins and rudders affixed to them made it possible to feed in small degrees of correction to what would otherwise have been a free-fall ballistic trajectory. The latter were powered and guided by more or less sophisticated systems which ensured that they would hit the correct target, but radio and radar guidance was still in its infancy in 1945. The few air-launched missiles that were built and used operationally by the Germans were spectacular but they had no significant impact on the war. Had the German glide and guided missiles been ready earlier, they might well have influenced the course of the war.

Henschel Hs 293

The Hs 293 was an anti-shipping, rocket-boosted, glide blast-bomb in the form of a miniature aircraft. The Hs 293 was built up from the nose and body sections of a SC 500 thin-walled bomb, with an elongated rear sec-

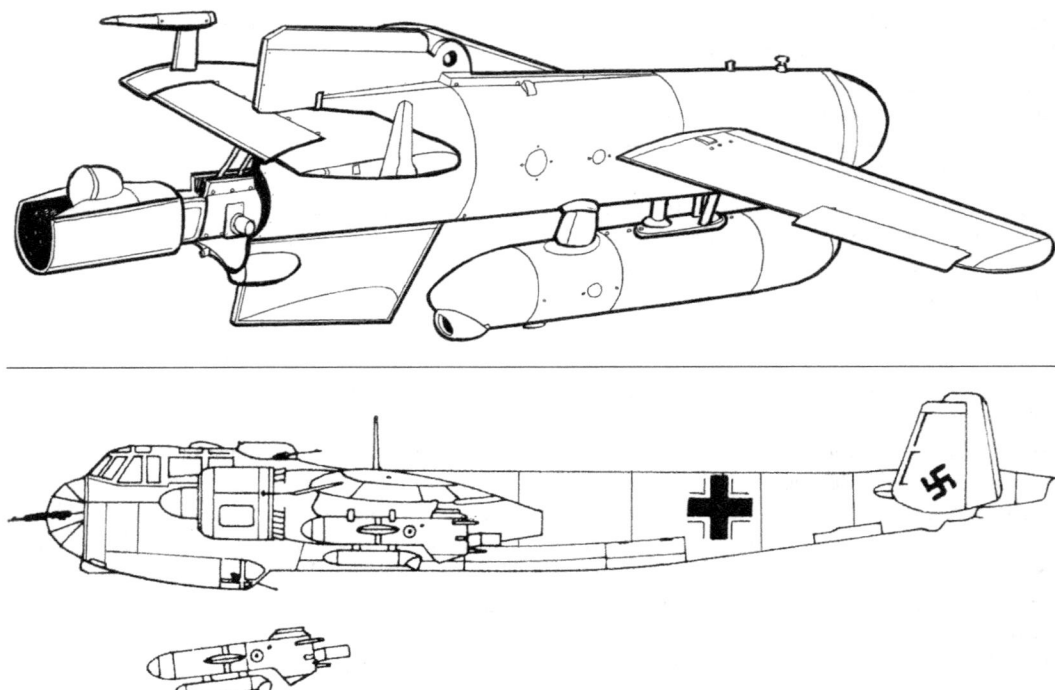

Top: Henschel Hs 293. Bottom: Hs 293 released from Dornier Do 217E-2.

tion tapering in the vertical plane, which extended above and below the body to form fins which carried the guidance system. Short symmetrical wings with ailerons were added, as well as a tailplane. The bomb had a span of 10 ft 2.8 in, a length of 10 ft 5.2 in, and a total weight of 1,730 lbs. Designed to be released from a bomber (e.g., a Dornier Do 217, or a FW 200 Condor), it was radio-controlled by a crew member of the parent airplane who operated a joy-stick controller, the movement of which fed the appropriate up-down/left-right impulses to a radio transmitter which in turn relayed them to the missile. The rocket motor, mounted beneath the fuselage, was a liquid-propellant Walter 109-507B using T-Stoff and Z-Stoff stored in pressurized tanks. The engine gave only 600 kg (1,300 lbs) of thrust for only 10 seconds, but that was enough to propel the bomb well ahead of the parent aircraft to a point where the aimer could see and direct it. The Hs 293 carried 550 pounds of Trialen armor-piercing explosive detonated by an impact fuse placed in the nose. A version of the basic weapon, with an extended nose containing a television camera, was developed as Hs 293D. Another variant, the Hs 293 F, had a delta wing and no tail. It is unclear how many Hs 293 of all types were manufactured, but it was probably about 1,500. Some became operational in August 1943 and were used with success in the Bay of Biscay against Allied warships, with hits on HMS *Egret* and several others.

There was a variant, the Henschel Hs 294, with streamlined fuselage, which was a rocket-propelled anti-ship missile with a long tapered nose cone, containing a 646-kg (1,445-lb) explosive charge and a second rocket unit. The wings and the rear fuselage were mounted so that they could break away on hitting the water, and the bomb (actually a torpedo) would run through the water, and strike the ship below the waterline where it was at its most vulnerable.

Blohm & Voss Bv 246

The Blohm & Voss Bv 246 *Hagelkorn* (Hailstone), designed in late 1943, was a pure glide

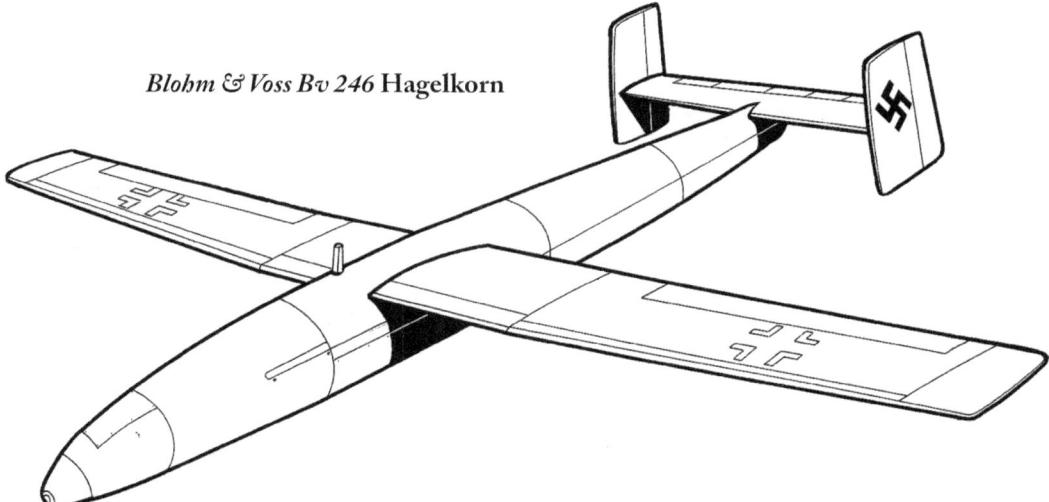

Blohm & Voss Bv 246 Hagelkorn

bomb, intended to attack Allied radio stations transmitting navigational signals to RAF bombers by homing in on their very signals. It was launched at a distance from a carrier at an altitude of about 10,500 m (34,450 ft), and left to glide to the target with a range of 210 km (130 miles). The Bv 246 had a clean, aerodynamic, cigar-shaped fuselage with a cruciform empennage incorporating a vertical control surface, and high aspect-ratio wings. It had a total length of 3.53 m (11 ft 7 in) and a span of 6.4 m (21 ft). With a total weight of 730 kg (1,600 lbs) of which 435 kg (960 lbs) were explosive contained in the nose, *Hagelkorn* was light enough to be carried by a Focke-Wulf Fw 190. Due to the success of the V1 flying bomb, the Bv 246 *Hagelkorn* program was cancelled in February 1944, but revived in early 1945 to use the *Radieschen* (Radish) ultrashort-wave homing device. The slightly modified *Hagelkorn* was tested, and some 1,000 units were built, but they were never used operationally.

Fritz-X

As World War II proceeded, the basic flaw of the dive-bombing principle appeared clearly: dive bombers were uncomfortably vulnerable to effective fighter aircraft and concentrated anti-aircraft fire. Soon thoughts turned to the development of a bomb which could be guided in flight. Also known as FX-1 400, Fritz-X was a guided glide bomb intended to replace ordinary bomb. It was a 1,400 kg armor-piercing bomb particularly designed as anti-ship weapon. The free-fall bomb was not powered but released from a parent aircraft and left to glide with speed accelerating under the force of gravity. It was fitted with small cruciform wings and a tail unit containing the guidance mechanism. It was controlled after launch by an observer in a parent airplane via a radio link. Fritz-X was developed in 1939, and became operational only in 1943. Its most notable success was the sinking of the Italian battleship *Roma* in September 1943. Other successes achieved by Fritz-X were serious damages inflicted to the American cruisers USS *Savannah* and USS *Philadelphia*, to HMS *Uganda*, HMS *Spartan*, destroyer HMS *Janus*,

Guided bomb Fritz-X

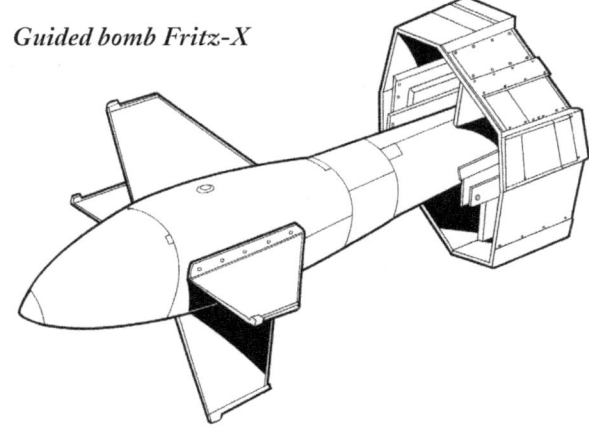

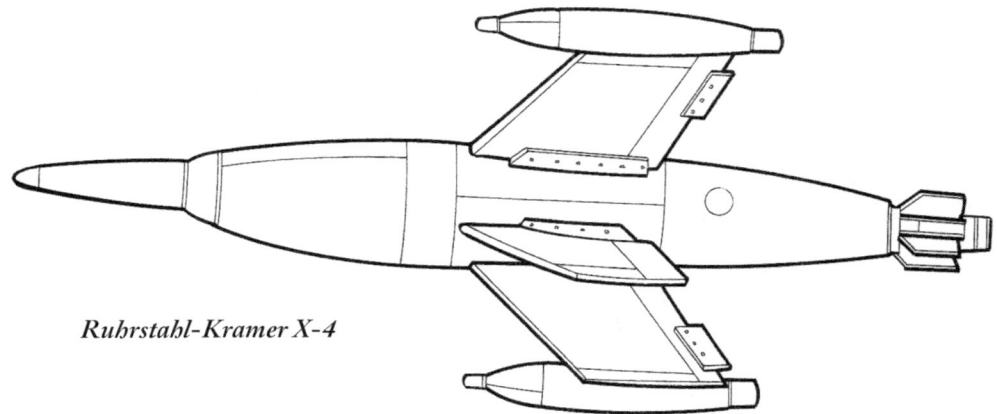

Ruhrstahl-Kramer X-4

and battleship HMS *Warspite*. In spite of its success, Fritz-X was abandoned due to the high loss rate among the bombers equipped to deliver it; because of the need for relative slow speed over the target, launching planes were particularly vulnerable to interception and Flak fire.

Ruhrstahl-Kramer X-4

The X-4, designed in 1943 by the steel-making company Ruhrstahl AG, was a small, fin-stabilized, air-to-air, wire-guided missile intended to equip fighters to knock down Allied bombers. The missile had two sets of four fins, one set swept back at an acute angle with parallel chord width roughly halfway back from the nose; the other, offset by 45 degrees and carrying the moveable spoilers, was at the tail. It had a total weight of 60 kg (132 lbs), of which 20 kg (44 lbs) were explosive contained in the warhead placed in the nose. It had a span of 0.57 m (1 ft 11 in), and a length of 1.90 m (6 ft 3 in). After release from a parent aircraft, the liquid bipropellant rocket engine was started. The engine burning

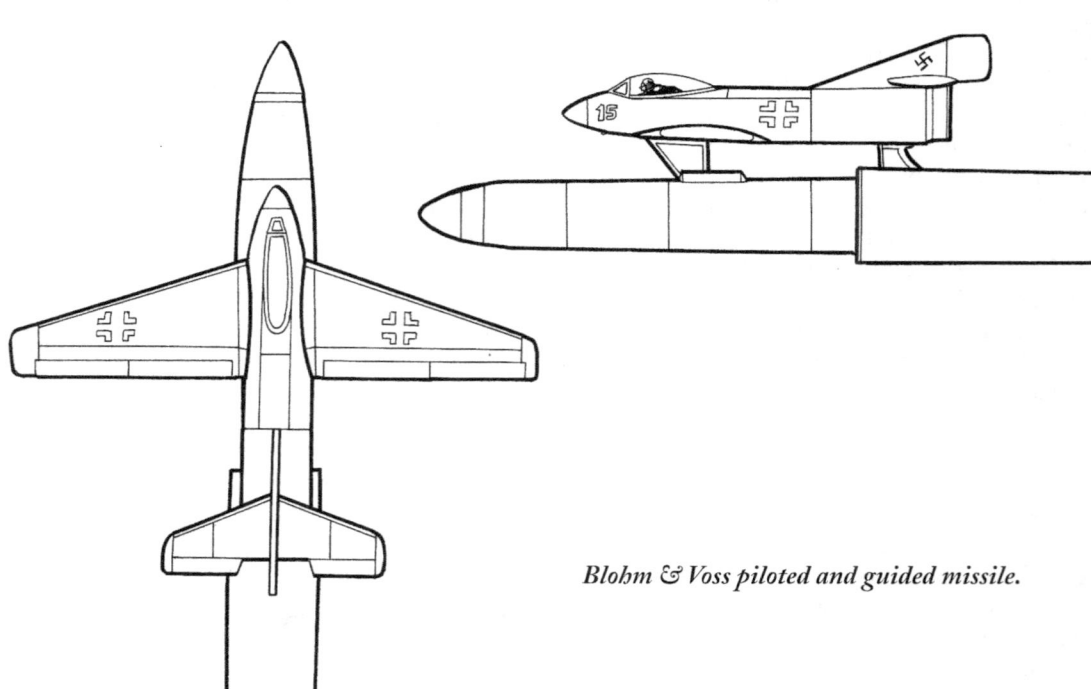

Blohm & Voss piloted and guided missile.

time was 33 seconds and the missile had a speed of 972 km/h (603.6 mph), or, according to other sources, 1,152 km/h (716 mph). The X-4 was guided toward its target from a parent aircraft via electronic signals sent through wires that spun out of the blisters located on two of the missile's four wing tips. Range was about 6 km (3.7 miles)—the length of the guidance wire—and thus well beyond the range of Allied bombers' defensive machine guns. The destruction by Allied air bombing of the BMW plant where the rocket engine was produced ensured that the X-4 was not ready in time to see combat action. Yet it is recognized that the X-4 was the first wire-guided air-to-air missile. Wire-guided missiles remain common, even today (e.g., the French SS-11 and SS-12 anti-tank missiles and the European MILAN anti-aircraft rocket), because they are comparatively cheap to produce and not vulnerable to electronic jamming countermeasures.

Blohm & Voss guided missile

This combination included a two-engined carrier Dornier Do 217 bomber, a rocket-powered missile filled with explosive and a small, manned, rocket-powered guiding aircraft. The Do 217 bomber was intended to bring the weapon in the vicinity of the target, then the bomb and the small aircraft were released. The pilot (who lay in a prone position in the small aircraft) would then locate the target and release the projectile in a ballistic trajectory. He would then ignite his own ramjet for a safe return to his base. This scheme never went any further than the planning stage.

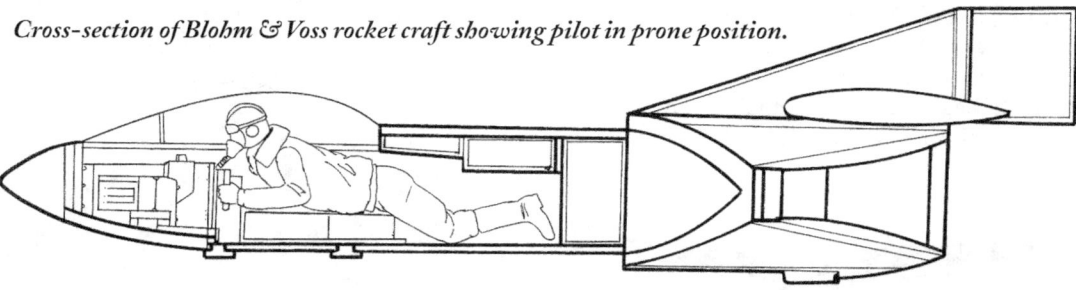

Cross-section of Blohm & Voss rocket craft showing pilot in prone position.

3

Regalia and Uniforms

Regalia

Luftwaffe emblem

The emblem of the German air force, a variant of the Wehrmacht's *Hohenzeichen* (national emblem), represented an eagle in flying position with upswept tail, clutching a swastika in its talons. The emblem (both in metal or textile form) was worn on the upper right breast of the uniform, displayed at the front |of all headgear, and stenciled on the left side of the standard steel helmet model of 1935.

Luftwaffe emblem

Luftwaffe flag

Flags

The Luftwaffe flag was composed of a piece of hand-woven silk measuring 126 cm square. The cloth was bordered on three sides with a 5-cm-wide fringe made of double strands of twisted silver threads. The fourth side was nailed to a black, polished wooden staff whose end was surmounted by an aluminum Lutwaffe eagle with swastika. The cloth was gold-yellow for flying units, technical and aerial warfare schools. It was bright red for the anti-aircraft artillery units and schools. And it was gold-brown for signals formations and schools. In the center of the flag was a white disc with an edge overlaid with an embroidered garland of silver-colored oak leaves and acorns. In the middle of the circle was a black Iron Cross with a silver edge. From the four corners extended four white tapering black-edged wedges. Lying on the central axis of each wedge was a small silver-edged black swastika. The verso of the flag was similar, but instead of an Iron Cross, there was a silver Luftwaffe emblem, an eagle in flight with swastika. The flag was displayed on parades dictated by the annual calendar of the Nazi regime, notably on 30 January (seizure of power in 1933), on 20 April (Hitler's birthday in 1889), on 21 April (the Day of the Luftwaffe), and on 29 August (the Day of the *Wehrmacht*). The ceremonial oath of allegiance to Hitler, taken personally by every Luftwaffe member, was sworn on the flag. Sometimes the Luftwaffe colors were also positioned at the edge of a runway, presumably with the intention of inspiring aircrews when taking off on their missions.

The Legion Condor, send by Hitler to assist General Franco's nationalist army in the Spanish Civil War, was mainly a force provided by Luftwaffe volunteers who had their own flag which displayed several distinctive features. The cloth was smaller (52 cm × 53 cm), it was bright red, and the wedges were yellow-gold. In the center of there was a black Iron Cross with a Luftwaffe eagle; in the lower right corner there were the silver initials LC for Legion Condor. The verso of the flag included three horizontal bands of red, yellow-gold, and red. The center displayed the arms of Spain introduced by Franco in 1938.

For ceremonies, commemorations and parades, flag and standard bearers wore the M35 steel helmet, and the standard grayish-blue service dress with gray gloves, shirt and tie. They had a brown leather bandolier fitted with a cup in which to rest the base of the flagpole; around the neck they wore a moon-shaped metal gorget.

Medals

Hitler, like every commander of every army through history, considered that a lot could be achieved with medals and awards spurring human vanity. The Luftwaffe (and the other branches of the German military) placed much emphasis on the morale-increasing effect of various decorations and awards, the numbers of which were very large. Much of the paperwork of the Wehrmacht was concerned with the awarding of various types of medals, decorations and badges. Luftwaffe, Marine and Heer personnel prized these honors highly, and wore them on their field uniforms, even in combat. Marksmanship awards were worn in the form of fourragers (lanyards) across the right breast.

Iron Cross (2nd Class). The Iron Cross, created in 1813, was reinstituted in 1870. Forbidden after World War I, it was reinstituted in 1939. The Iron Cross 2nd Class was awarded for exceptional front-line bravery. On the first day of award it was worn in the second buttonhole and after that the ribbon only was worn. The inside was black, the outside was white and red. In full dress, the cross was worn above the breast pocket suspended from its ribbon.

Luftwaffe medals fell into two main categories, medals for bravery and campaign medals. Medals for bravery were awarded for outstanding front-line behavior, for acts of great gallantry and valor, to men who had performed exceptionally on the field. The most decorated and most publicized among the glamorous pilots were the *Experte* (aces). By Lufwaffe standards, an ace was a pilot who had achieved five or more aerial victories. The Luftwaffe counted no less than 5,000 of them in World War II. It has been suggested that Luftwaffe pilots were able to score so high for a number of reasons. They had learned their skills during the Spanish Civil War. They were operating largely over their own territory—thus allowing the recovery of airmen who had taken to their parachute. They flew many more missions than their opponents—there was no tour system in the Luftwaffe. And over the Russian front they were faced by a virtually limitless number of targets. Whether these reasons are founded or not is open to dispute. Aggressive pilots were sometimes said to be "medal chasing" or "glamour-seeking showmen" by their more cautious colleagues. The top Luftwaffe fighter-aces were Erich Hartmann (nicknamed the Black Devil of the Ukraine, credited with 352 aerial victories in 1,400 sorties), Gerhard Barkhorn (301 kills in 1,104 sorties), Günther Rall (275), Otto Kittel (267), Walther Novotny (250 kills in only 583 sorties), Wilhelm Batz (237 kills in only 455 sorties), Heinrich Bär (220), Hans Joachim Marseille (with 158 Allied aircrafts shot down in 482 sorties), Werner Mölders (115), and Adolf Galland (104). The German successes are put in perspective by the fact that the highest-scoring British pilot was M. T. J. Pattle (at least 40 and possibly 51

Ground Assault Badge. The Ground Assault Badge was awarded to all ground combat formations of the Luftwaffe who were eligible for an Army Assault Badge.

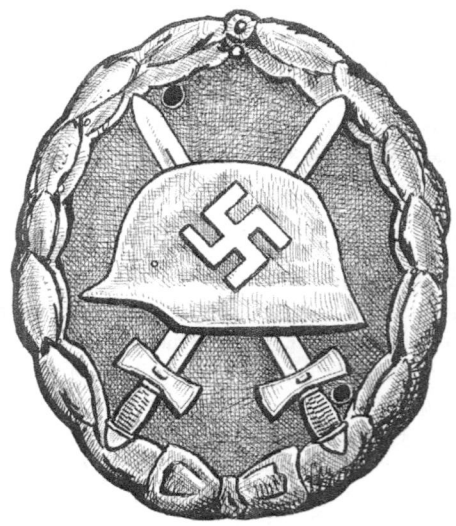

Verwundeten Abzeichen *(Wound Badge)*. *The Wound Badge, reinstituted by Hitler in May 1939 for German volunteers wounded in the Spanish Civil War 1936–1939, was awarded during World War II in three classes: gilt for five or more wounds, for total disablement or permanent blindness; silver for three or four wounds, or for the loss of a hand, foot or eye, or for deafness; black for one or two wounds. The Wound Badge, worn on the left breast without ribbon, was similar to that of World War I but with a swastika added to the steel helmet.*

kills), the highest-scoring American ace was Richard I. Bong (40), and the highest-scoring Russian ace was Ivan N. Kozhedub (62).

Tank killer and ground-attack pilots were also regarded as *Experten*. Top aces in this category were Hartmut Vogt (125 tanks destroyed), Alois Wosnitza (104), Jakob Jenster (100), Anton Korol (100), Wilhelm Joswig (88), Max Diepold (87), Wilhelm Noller (86), Hans Ludwig (85), Heinz Edhofer (84), Kurt Plenzat (80), Siefried Fischer (80), Kurt Lau (80), and Rudolf-Heinz Ruffer (80). Germany's most decorated Stuka airman was Hans-Ulrich Rüdel who flew all his 2,350 combat missions in the Junkers Ju 87. Starting the war as a *Leutnant* (Second Lieutenant), he finished an *Oberst* (Colonel) awarded the Knight's Cross with oak leaves, swords, and diamonds in gold, the highest decoration

Observer Badge. Instituted in March 1936, the Observer Badge was awarded after two month's nonoperational flying service or for five sorties.

Flak Kampf Abzeichen. *The Luftwaffe's Anti-Aircraft Medal, officially instituted in January 1941, was designed by the Berlin artist Wilhelm Ernst Peeckhaus. It was 55 mm long and 45 mm wide. Awarded to all ranks for individual acts of merit, or for shooting down five Allied airplanes, it was later awarded on a point basis: two points for each aircraft, with a total of sixteen points needed to obtain the medal. The medal was worn on the tunic's right breast pocket.*

Ex-Airmen Commemorative Badge. Instituted in 1936, the Ex-Airmen Commemorative Badge was awarded to all former fighting Luftwaffe personnel who had been honorably discharged from aircrew duties.

awarded in Hitler's regime; he was the only man to receive it. Rüdel was credited for 9 aerial victories, the sinking of the Russian battleship *Marat* (as well as a cruiser, a destroyer and 70 landing crafts), and the destruction of 519 tanks and huge numbers of artillery pieces and various vehicles. Such was his reputation that Stalin placed a 100,000-ruble price on his head.

Mission clasp. Worn on the left breast, the mission clasp was awarded to day fighters, heavy fighters and ground attackers. After October 1942, the clasp, decorated with a black garland, was awarded to night interceptors.

Campaign medals were awarded without reference to a soldier's performance but merely in recognition of the fact that a man had been involved in a specific campaign. They could be allotted in bulk to combat units, whether or not the personnel were individually deserving of such decorations. These campaign rewards for "just being there" also took the form of cuff-titles consisting of a cloth band worn on the right lower sleeve. They illustrated great combats such as Spanien (Spain in 1936), Afrika (Africa in 1941), or Kreta (Crete in 1942), for instance.

Mission metal claps (*Frontflugsprangen*) were also awarded to aircrews. Pinned on the chest, they were made of bronze, silver or gold according to the number of sorties.

Specialty badges

There also existed a number of qualification and proficiency badges, generally worn on the lower left sleeve of the tunic. A specialist badge was a gray-blue cloth disc; it carried a letter (often Gothic) or a symbol made of machine-embroidered light-gray thread indicating a trade or a specialty—for example,

Luftwaffe dagger. The model 1937 officer dagger had a total length of 387 mm.

Luftwaffe belt buckle

motor transport, radio-operator, medical personnel, armorer, range finder, and many others. Qualification awards also came in the form of metal clasps pinned on the chest, for qualified aircrew specialists, including pilot, observer, wireless operator, gunner and so on.

Luftwaffe Ranks

The ranks and grades of Luftwaffe personnel are rather difficult to equate. A *Geschwader*, for example, was commanded by a *Kommodore*, a *Gruppe* by a *Kommandeur*, and a *Staffel* by a *Staffelkapitän*. However, these were appointments, not ranks, within the Luftwaffe. Usually, the *Kommodore* would hold the rank of *Oberstleutnant* (Lieutenant-Colonel) or, exceptionally, an *Oberst* (Colonel), even a *Leutnant* (Second Lieutenant) could find himself commanding a *Staffel* because of heavy casualties. The following list of ranks has USAF (and RAF) equivalents. There were no such equivalents for *Reichsmarschall und Oberbefehlshaber der Luftwaffe*—Hermann Göring's title.

Senior Officers

Generalfeldmarschall: General, Five-star (Marshal of the RAF)
Generaloberst: General, Four-star (Air Field Marshal)
General der Flieger: Lieutenant General (Air Marshal)
Generalleutnant: Major General (Air Vice-Marshal)
Generalmajor: Brigadier General (Air Commodore)

Commissioned Officers

Oberst: Colonel (Group Captain)
Oberstleutnant: Lieutenant Colonel (Wing Commander)
Major: Major (Squadron Leader)
Hauptmann: Captain (Flight Lieutenant)
Oberleutnant: First Lieutenant (Flying Officer)
Leutnant: Second Lieutenant (Pilot Officer)

Officer Candidates

Oberfähnrich: Officer Cadet (Leading Cadet)
Fahnenjunker-Oberfeldwebel: Officer Cadet
Oberfeldwebel: Officer Cadet
Fahnrich: Officer Cadet
Fahnenjunker-Feldwebel: Officer Cadet

Noncommissioned Officers

Hauptfeldwebel*: no equivalent
Stabsfeldwebel: Warrant Officer (Warrant Officer)
Oberfeldwebel: Master Sergeant (Flight Sergeant)
Feldwebel: Technical Sergeant (Sergeant)
Unterfeldwebel: no equivalent
Unteroffizier: Staff Sergeant (Corporal)
Hauptgefreiter: Sergeant (no equivalent)

Enlisted ranks

Obergefreiter: Corporal (Leading Aircraftman)
Gefreiter: Private First Class (Aircraftman First Class)
Flieger: Private (Airman Second Class)

Ranks were indicated by insignia, including colored tunic collar patches, shoulder straps, and symbols worn on the right sleeve.

Each branch of the Luftwaffe had a *Waffenfarbe* (arm of service color); this was displayed in piping and rank badge background. For example, the color bright red was for Flak artillery; light brown for air signals; black for RLM members; rose for pioneers and engineers; gold-yellow for aircrews, ground technical units, and paratroopers; dark blue for medical personnel; light green for airfield security police; dark green for administrative personnel; carmine red for general staff; orange-red for retired officers; bordeaux red for military justice officers; and white for generals and the Hermann Göring Division.

The Luftwaffe, a high-tech arm, employed *Sonderführer* (auxiliary leaders). These were persons who were posted to do an officer's duty, not because of their military qualifica-

---

*The term *Hauptfeldwebel*, colloquially called "*Spiess*," was not a rank but the label for the NCO administrative head of a company or corresponding unit (*Staffel*, Flak battery, etc.). His rank could be anything from *Unteroffizier* to the various *Feldwebel*.

Oberleutnant *(First Lieutenant)*

Oberstleutnant *(Lieutenant-Colonel)*

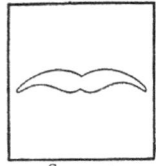
Sergeant

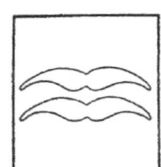
Staff sergeant

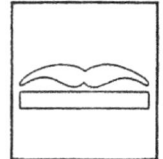
Second lieutenant

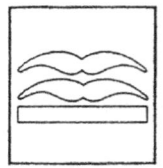
First lieutenant

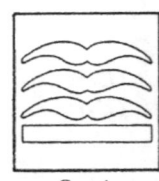
Captain

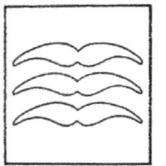
Technical sergeant

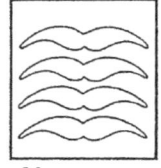
Master sergeant

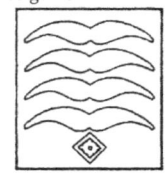
Warrant officer

Aircrew and paratrooper rank badges. These were worn on both sleeves of upper arm of the flying suit. The symbol was white with the appropriate arm of service color background.

tions but because of their professional ability (e.g., administrators, meteorologists, interpreters, reporters and journalists, doctors, industrial managers, engineers, designers and other specialist trades). *Sonderführer* were usually issued standard Luftwaffe officer uniforms and given ranks as Lieutenant, Captain, Colonel and Major, but they commanded no unit,

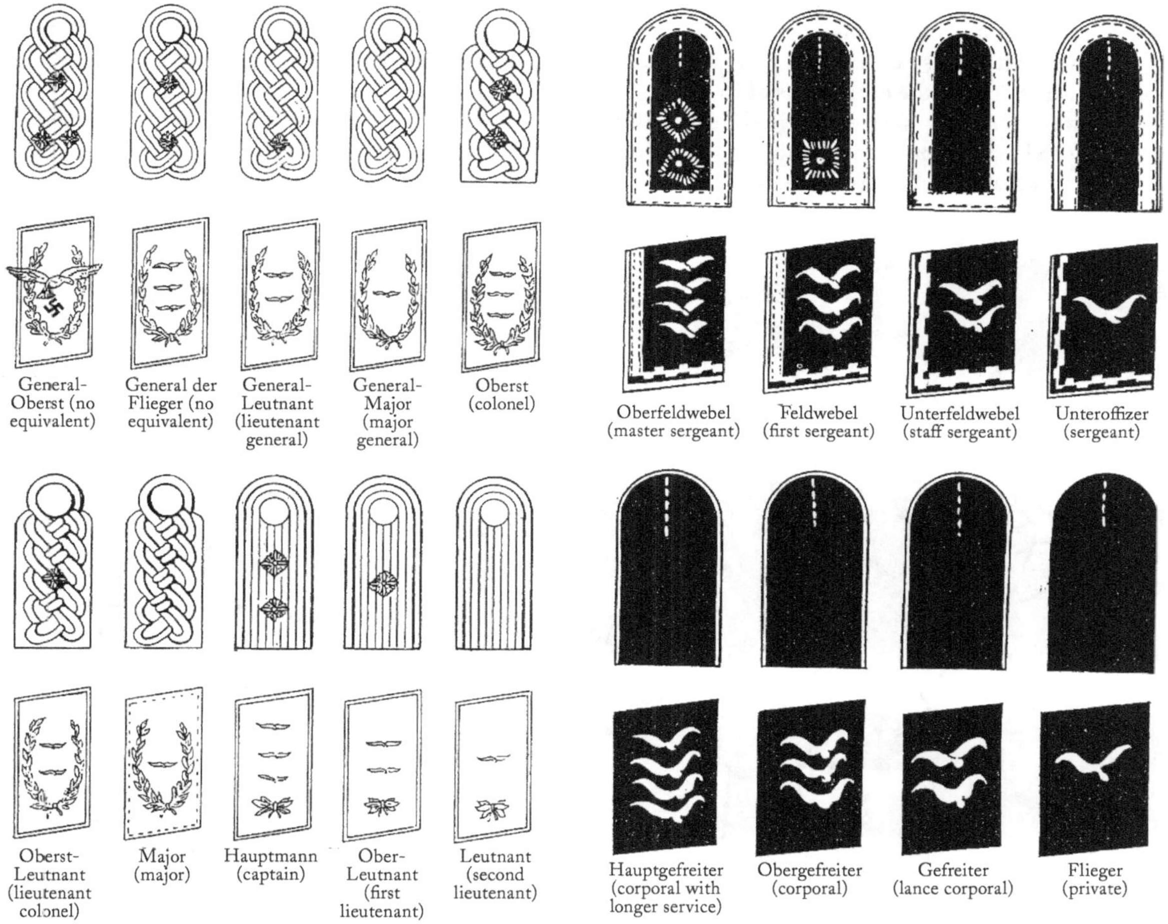

Luftwaffe rank insignia. Ranks were displayed on **Achselklappen** *(shoulder strap) and* **Kragenspiegel** *(collar patch) with piping and background in appropriate* **Waffenfarbe** *(arm of service color).*

only led in the area of their job, they did not hold commission and they were not always armed.

Uniforms and Flight Equipment

After 1935, the Luftwaffe was rapidly transformed from an experimental and largely clandestine department into an important fighting branch of the German army. Airmen—like members of the *Panzer-*

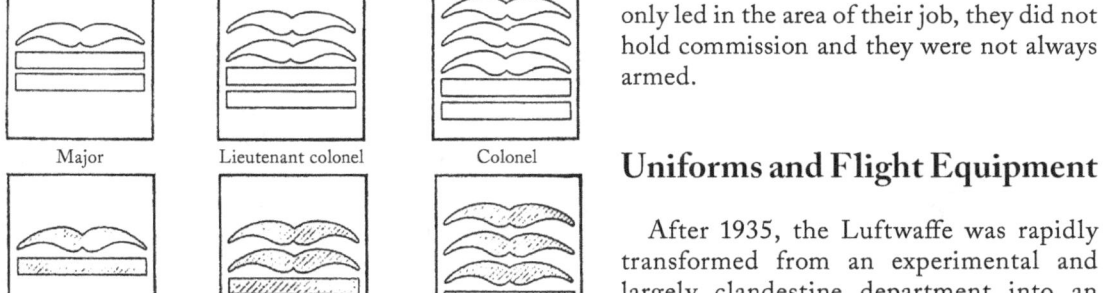

waffe (armored troops)— were newcomers with only a few traditions when the Luftwaffe and the Panzerwaffe were created in 1935. Special uniforms were designed for airmen and these were a slight departure from the standard-issue military uniform in use by that time by the German forces. Intended to be practical yet also to convey the elite status of the Luftwaffe, they were distinctive, original and striking, both in style and color, combining functionality and a rather smart appearance.

German Luftwaffe uniforms were basically grayish-blue but that varied and underwent a number of changes made necessary by the increasing diversity of climate and terrain in which the troops fought and by the variety of tactical requirements to which they were subjected. Also, the unexpected prolongation of the war into 1942 and the effective blockade brought upon Germany resulted in shortage of raw materials; therefore a need to simplify and use poorer-quality cloth arose by 1943. By 1944–45, all attempts to maintain quality had gone overboard. The only goal was to meet the

Above, left: **Fliegerbluse.** *Above, right: Service uniform. The stiff* **Schirmmütze** *cap,* **Waffenrock** *tunic, riding breeches and boots are worn here by a Lieutenant.*

3. Regalia and Uniforms

Mantel

needs of the military machine with whatever was available in the best way possible.

Service dress

The gray-blue *Tuchrock* (tunic), designed for everyday wear in 1935, had four pleated pockets, turn-back cuffs, and open collar. It was of fine quality and cut for officers. It was worn with straight or baggy gray-blue trousers for enlisted men, and with riding breeches for officers. Slightly modified in November 1938, the tunic was then called *Waffenrock* (service tunic). The most distinctive item of the Luftwaffe uniform was the *Fliegerbluse* (flyer's blouse). Originally designed for aircrews, this highly popular item became standard wear for all Luftwaffe personnel. It was a short, close-fitting blouse, without external pockets, with buttons concealed by a fly front, and with a convertible collar which could be either fully fastened or open.

For cold season, all ranks were issued with a warm *Mantel* (overcoat); this was mid-calf in length, double-breasted, with a large collar, two rows of six buttons, slanted hip pockets and turn-back cuffs. The overcoat was worn over the service tunic by soldiers, NCOs and all other ranks alike, with only detail differences to account for rank and insignia.

Headgear

Officers, NCOs and administrative personnel wore a *Schirmmütze*, a stiff (or unstiffened) wool or canvas peaked service cap. Of various quality in cloth and finish, this was worn with service dress, parade dress and walking-out uniform.

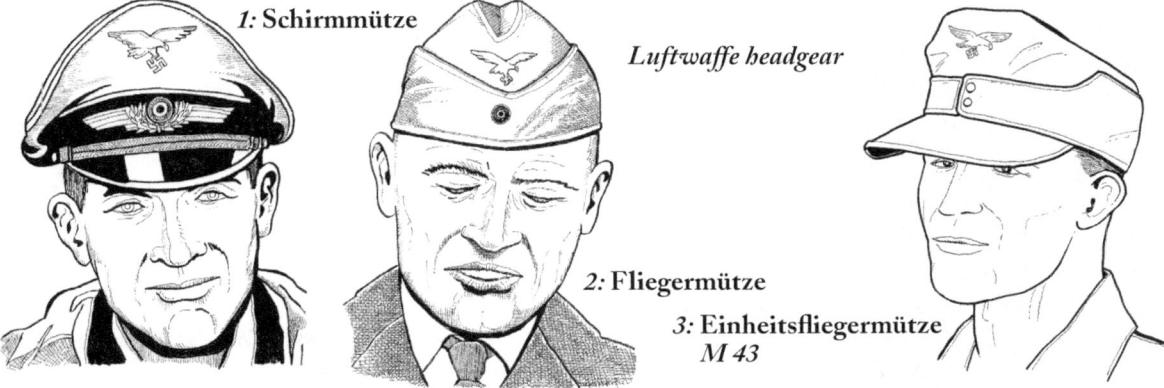

Luftwaffe headgear

1: Schirmmütze
2: Fliegermütze
3: Einheitsfliegermütze M 43

All ranks from private to general wore a very popular *Fliegermütze* (visorless cap). This was a garrison cap made of grayish-blue material. It existed in various styles, finishes and qualities. Some were designed to allow the sides to be pulled down and buttoned around the wearer's ears.

In June 1943, a new, standard, soft-peaked field cap—called *Einheitsfliegermütze*—was introduced. It was based closely on the style of peaked cap worn by mountain troops and Afrika Korps soldiers. It was very convenient and popular, subsequently it became the most widely worn type of headgear for active service personnel. The standard cap had a rather large, protruding, semi-stiff peak. It was made of canvas for warm climates and wool for cold. The latter had sides which could be folded down and buttoned under the chin in cold weather.

Footwear

Trousers were tucked into three-quarter-length, black, strong leather *Marschstiefel* (boots or jackboots), with hob nails, heel irons, toeplates and studded soles. The boot's finish was either pebbled or smooth. Officers and generals usually wore high leather riding boots with adjustable straps, sometimes with attached spurs for parade. From late 1943 however, material shortages forced a change and the issue of jackboots ceased. Leather had become a precious commodity for industrial use and frequently, in place of boots, short, black, lace-up ankle shoes were issued, and these were worn with old-fashioned puttees, canvas leggings, anklets or gaiters fastened by buckles. These cheap items of footwear were derisively called *Rückmarsch* (retreat) boots.

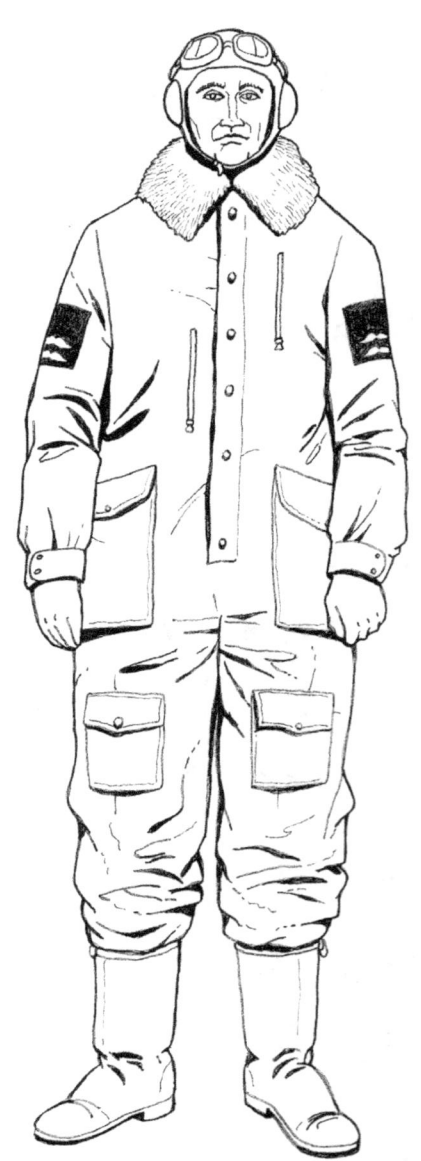

Unterfeldwebel *1939. This NCO wears a light-brown, one-piece flight overall.*

Marching boots

3. Regalia and Uniforms

Aircrew flight dress and equipment

Flight personnel actually constituted a very small branch of the Luftwaffe, numbering no more than about 50,000 men in 1939. This number included highly regarded combat pilots—a tiny, much-publicized minority of fighter "aces," but also many pilots of less glamorous craft (e.g., seaplanes, gliders, transport, liaison and trainer aircraft), as well as flying crewmen, such as observers, gunners, bombardiers, radio and radar operators.

Aircrews wore the standard Luftwaffe service uniform over which was donned a light-brown *Fliegerschutzanzug* (one-piece flight

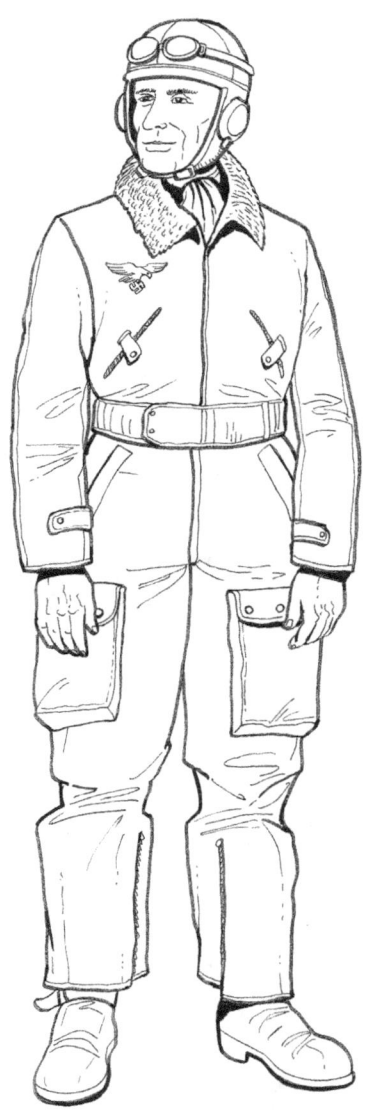

One-piece flight suit c. 1940. The depicted airman wears the light-brown, thick KW 1/33 winter suit with knee pockets, fur collar, double-button cuffs, and buttoned front with double flap for better insulation. Headgear is the LKp S 100 soft helmet with goggles. The man is equipped with a 30-I seat parachute with snap-hook fittings.

Two-piece flight suit c. 1942. This dark-blue uniform included a LKp N101 helmet, a short jacket with fur collar, large trousers with thigh pockets and zips to ease the wearing of the heavy flight boots.

suit) with zip-up pockets. The overall was available in summer and winter weights, and for flight over land or sea. When necessary (e.g., for high altitude or cold weather) it could be electrically heated. In fighter aircraft, where cockpit space was limited, pilots wore a lightweight suit of woven synthetic-silk twill. After April 1941, the overall was replaced by a two-piece flight suit, including a simple jacket and trousers with voluminous pockets for rescue equipment and survival items (e.g., emergency rations, medical kit, and flares). This too existed in summer and winter weights, and for flight over land or sea. Flying suits were completed with various types of thick, heavy gloves with press-stud or buckle-fastened straps, some electrically heated. Pilots of fighter aircraft—particularly famous "aces"—adopted non-issue practical flight uniforms, generally purchased at individual expense. These included elegant flyers' tunics with riding breeches, blouses with fur collar, expensive all-leather suits, and short leather jackets (some copied or even captured RAF and USAF items), all with different cut, fastenings, collar, pockets, quality, appearance and color.

Unteroffizier (NCO) c. 1941. The depicted NCO is wearing the yellow, semi-rigid **Schwimweste** *(life vest) model 10-75A.*

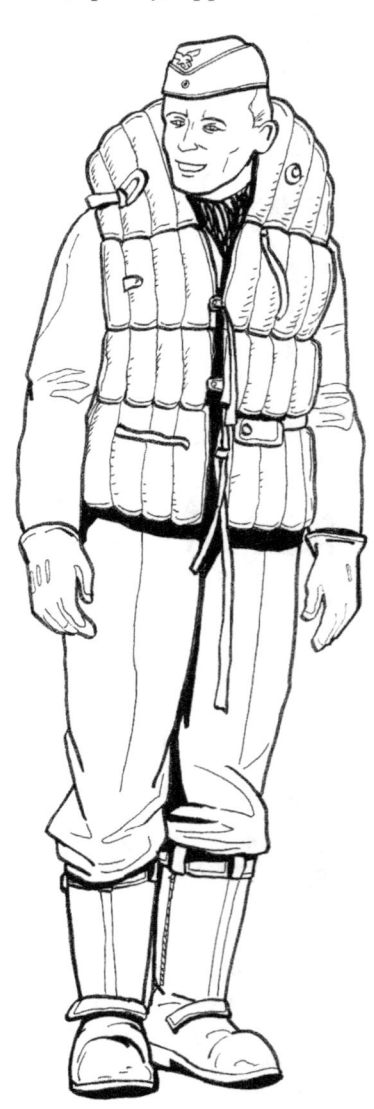

Life vest

These were worn only for operational actions; for ceremonies and off-base daily life, the official parade uniform, standard military walking-out suit and service dress were worn.

Footwear for aircrews consisted of fur-lined boots of stout leather with rubber heel and sole. They had full-length steel zips at the inner and outer calf to ease fitting over several layers of clothing, were fastened by buckled straps, and, when necessary, worn with electrically heated socks.

Headgear consisted of a leather or linen flight helmet, in both summer and winter weights, generally fitted with radio earphone (set within rigid leather side panels) and throat microphone, all furnished with plugs and wires for connecting to the board equipment. The soft helmet offered no protection against shocks, flying debris and enemy projectiles, so in 1941 a special aircrew helmet was issued, known as SSK 90. This was made of leather-covered

Pilot with inflatable life vest, c. 1942.

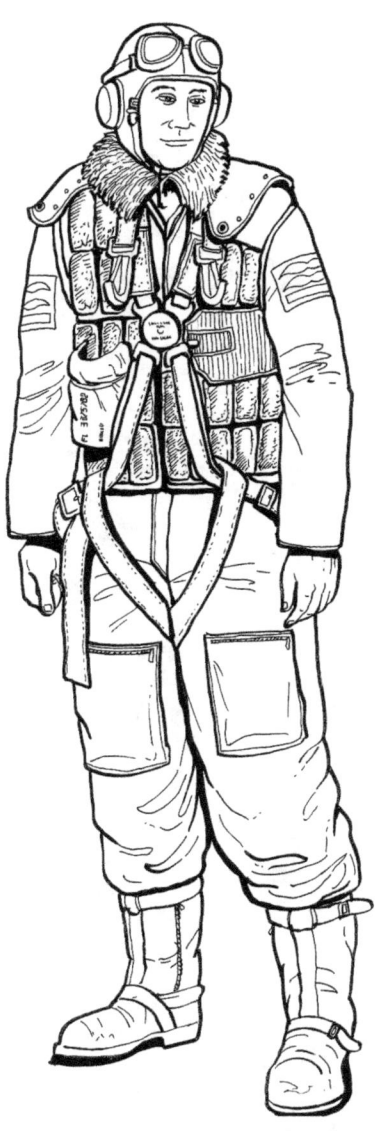

Oberleutnant, *c. 1942. This flying officer wears the chest-type parachute harness and kapok 10-76 B1 life vest with dye-marker pack attached, as well as Auer M295 goggles over the LKp W 101 flight helmet.*

steel plates and its shape resembled that worn by the German paratroopers; rather cumbersome and of limited protection, it was soon discarded. Another crash helmet was designed in late 1944. It was made of leather-covered steel plates, had extra lining layers, double chin strap, and padded comb extending around the top and front. Produced in limited number, this item, known as a "jet helmet," was only used by a few test pilots flying early jet aircraft with experimental, primitive ejection seats. It was, however, a pioneering effort against impact and shock, and had implications for the protection of jet-flying crews after 1945.

Fighter pilot, c. late 1944. The man wears a softened **Schirmmütze** *and a leather suit, including jacket and trousers. By 1944 and early 1945, Luftwaffe fighter pilots wore numerous different uniforms, and operated mostly above Germany in hopeless defensive actions against Allied bombers. Rapid identification to local inhabitants (sometimes seeking revenge upon downed Allied airmen) was thus a necessity. For that purpose our pilot wears a yellow armband carrying the Luftwaffe eagle and the label "German Air Force."*

Hauptmann, *c. 1943. This captain, pilot of a fighter aircraft, wears a blue shirt, a privately purchased brown leather jacket, blue riding breeches and heavy zip-up flight boots.*

All aircrews were equipped with various types of *Windschutzbrillen* (goggles) with curved lenses enabling optimal vision. Some were tinted against snow glare, searchlight and sunlight. For high-altitude flying, crews were issued with a *Höhenatemmaske* (oxygen mask) composed of a rubber facepiece (secured to the helmet by two or three elastic or sprung straps), and a ribbed rubber hose connecting to the board system. Airmen were also provided with survival aids. Those operating above sea were issued with a *Schwimmweste* (life vest); these were yellow or bright red to assist rescue operations. The model 10-75A from 1940, derived from a navy design, was made of cotton canvas filled with kapok with a semi-rigid structure. Cumbersome and not totally effective, it was soon replaced by other models (e.g., type SWp 734 or 10-30A), which were more compact, made of soft, proofed cotton duck, pneumatically inflated, and activated by a small compressed air cylinder or a rubber mouth-inflation tube. They also had one-, two-, three- or four-man dinghies stowed in the airplane. The inflatable canoe was equipped with paddles, emergency rations, a medical kit, and possibly one or more kapok-filled sleeping bags. Recognition equipment included a mirror, a dye-marker pouch, a signal flag, a smoke marker, and a flare pistol.

All airmen were equipped with a parachute, either of seat, back, or chest type. The canopy had an average diameter of 7.32 m held by white synthetic weaves, giving an average descent rate of 6.5 m per second. The harness featured webbing risers from the shoulders which kept the center of gravity high for a safe landing. The airman also had a knife to cut himself free of entangled parachute risers and shroud lines.

Each man had a wrist compass and each crew had durable, plasticized-linen navigation maps of the area where they operated. Most of them were armed with a pistol held in a leather holster fixed on the waist-belt.

Oxygen mask

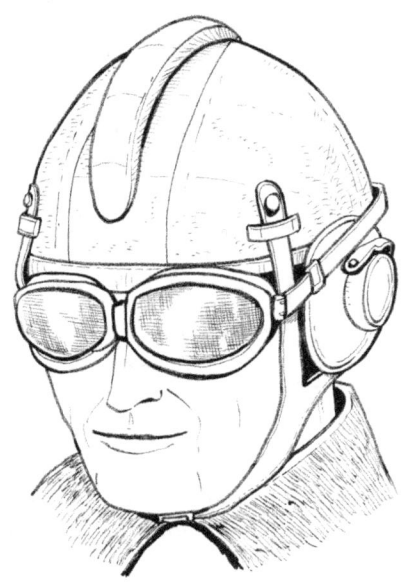

Armored "jet" flight helmet (1945)

Work clothing

To each *Geschwader* were attached *Fliegerhorstkompanien* (Technical Companies) which were divided into *Züge* (platoons, singular: *Zug*) placed under the leadership of an *Oberwerkmeister* (line chief). The precise number of technical personnel assigned varied widely according to aircraft type and quantity. These technicians included airframe, engine and safety equipment fitters, armorers, and instrument and radio mechanics. They were supported by a *Werkstattzug* (workshop) with engine fitters, sheet-metal workers, painters, harness repairers, carpenters, electricians and technical storekeepers. The ground crews handled overhauls and major repairs, and were responsible for maintenance of motor vehicles, for bomb, ammunition, fuel and other supply stores, and for equipment stores and the armory. These technical personnel were generally drawn from civil engineering backgrounds or had trained in aircraft factories. A high proportion were career NCOs, some with previously failed aircraft training. These unsung heroes made up qualified technical teams working in difficult conditions, particularly in hostile environments such as the North African desert or the Russian steppe. When the tide turned in 1943, there was an increasing shortage of everything, and they had to work under even harder conditions and under increasing pressure to keep the Luftwaffe air-

Mechanic. This "Blacky" wears the model 1937 denim, one-piece, lined work overall. He is preparing to paint an aircraft with a spray device.

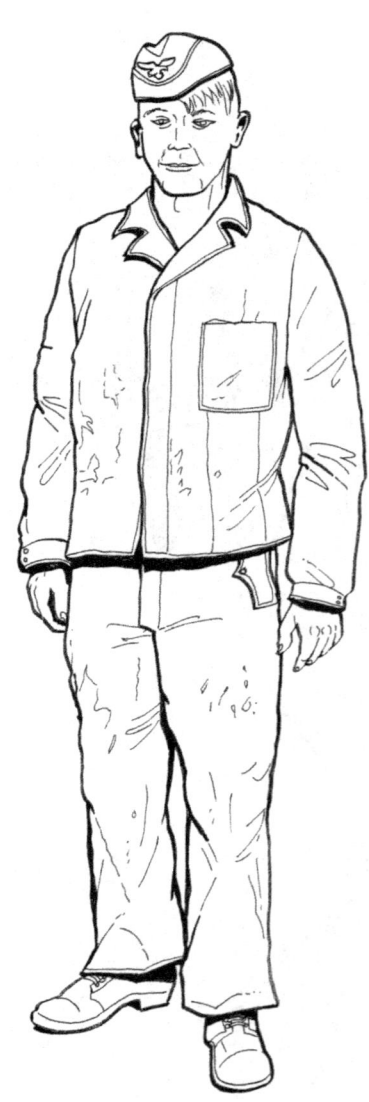

Drillichanzug. *The effectiveness of the Luftwaffe put a heavy responsibility on the fitters and riggers of the ground crews. They needed to be entirely reliable, and able to work at high speed and often in primitive conditions.*

worthy. The ground crews were indispensable to the efficiency of the air force; without their service nothing could be achieved. Their endurance, skill, and patience, although different, was in the equal of that of the aircrews. They often enjoyed a close relationship with their fellow airmen who affectionately nicknamed them *Schwarze* (Blackies) because of their general-issue black overalls. Actually the Blackies were issued with various work clothes, overalls, and a *Drillichanzug* (fatigue suit). This latter uniform, made of strong denim material, was white/light-gray, black or dark blue. It consisted of a shapeless buttoned jacket with internal pocket, adjustable cuffs and a turn-down collar. The trousers were made of the same material, simple cut with two side pockets. The suit was easily washable and used extensively for fatigue duty, work, instruction, training maneuvers, weapon cleaning and engine maintenance. After 1940, large stocks of fatigues and work suits were captured from defeated European nations and used in the Luftwaffe.

Tropical uniform

The Luftwaffe forces engaged with the Afrika Korps in Northern Africa were issued a variety of lightweight clothing appropriate for desert warfare conditions. Originally the tropical uniform was composed of a olive-green/sand-yellow, four-pocketed field tunic. This

Airman, North Africa, c. 1941

Tropical uniform

was worn with a shirt (with short or long sleeves), drill shorts, knee-length stockings and canvas-topped lace-up boots. Alternatively, there were straight-cut long trousers in khaki drill which were worn full length, gathered in at the ankle into normal army boots or khaki-brown canvas boots. Colors tended to vary quite considerably as the bleaching effect of the sun was severe; after a period of service they faded to lighter shades of brown and green; in many cases they ended up the color of the natural fabric. At night the desert can be very cold and Luftwaffe men wore the standard greatcoat manufactured from a dark-blue material.

Headgear varied with the period. At the early stage in 1941, a special tropical cork helmet was often worn, called *Tropische Kopfbedeckung*. Covered with khaki cotton or greenish felt, it proved cumbersome and of dubious value. The men discarded this item of uniform after a few months and reverted to standard, canvas, light peaked caps.

In practice, the wearing of unorthodox and sometimes, non-military articles of clothing accorded more to personal choice and comfort

Desert dress

Oberstleutnant Geschaderkommodore, *in North Africa, 1942. The Wing Commander wears a forage cap; a short-sleeved shirt; tan, single-pocket, light flight trousers; and thick-soled, lace-up boots.*

rather than to fixed rules and official regulations. Campaigning in open, broad and empty desert was the tactician's paradise but the quartermaster's hell, in which logistics and above all supply of ammunition, water and fuel were always vital. Front-line soldiers suffered most from the lack of supplies. One should also not forget that heat, thirst, sandstorms, flies and dysentery were almost worse than the war, greater enemies than all the armies in the world. Due to the specificities of desert warfare, the wearing of official apparel and the strict observance of military regulations were largely a matter between enlisted men and their commanding officers. The scarcity of water also encouraged the growing of beards.

Tropical dress was practical, comfortable and versatile. Introduced for use in North Africa, it was later often found in other theaters of the war and became the standard summer dress for all warm climes. Combined with various parts of the European service uniform, it was worn by Luftwaffe units in southern Russia, in the Balkans, in Italy and even during the Battle of Normandy in June and July 1944.

Winter uniforms

During the first winter on the Russian front (1941–42) German soldiers adopted every kind of improvisation in order to survive in the extreme cold, using fur, leather, cloth, wool and even straw before several sorts of wind-and waterproof, warm *Windblusen* (mountain-style anoraks) and suitable winter-weight combat suits were issued. For example, the *Winterwaffenrock* (winter suit) was first issued on the Russian front in winter 1942–43 as a result of the bitter experience of the previous winter. Designed specifically to combat the severe sub-zero weather conditions encountered on the Eastern front, the smock and overtrousers were made of two thick layers of windproof and waterproof cloth with a woolen lining; the double-breasted smock was fitted with a detachable hood. The winter suit was generally worn over the field-service uniform, and was reversible: all white on one side and camouflaged on the other.

Some fortunate units got white quilted winter parkas or warm sheepskin coats, fur-lined greatcoats with fur collars, but these luxuries were in short supply. Many soldiers in need wore a mixture of regular army issues and captured Russian military or civilian clothes or sheepskins, making them sometimes look like tramps or shabby scavengers. Winter headgear consisted of Russian-styled *Pelzmützen* (fur-covered caps) with ear, neck and front flaps faced with field-gray cloth and rabbit-fur which could be tied down under the wearer's neck and chin. Another form of cold-weather head-dress was the toque, a kind of cowl, a wrap-around woolen scarf. There was also a close-fitting reversible hood, protecting neck and shoulders. Apart from these official hats,

Winter suit

many other improvisations and unofficial combinations of woolen knitted caps, fur-covered hats, close-fitting and brimless caps, and civilian mufflers and scarves were used.

Winter footwear was also introduced to suit the sub-zero weather conditions encountered on the Eastern front. Copied from a Russian model called *valenki*, these consisted of compressed or molded felt combined with a leather or wooden sole to make big overboots. A variant design of Russian origin was made from thick layers of plaited straw. In both cases, valenki and overboots were large enough to be worn over the regular marching boots. They were in limited number, however, and issued temporarily to soldiers assigned to sentry duty, for example. Some men in noncombat conditions also wore the traditional wooden clogs and some officers were issued special insulated boots made of felt and leather. Various kinds of leather or woolen gloves, padded mittens and gauntlets completed the winter suit.

Musicians

The singing of marching songs with bellicose lyrics by powerful, virile choirs was part

Schneeanzug, *winter suit with hood, quilted parka and straw boots*

Luftwaffe drummer

of German military training. Military bands and orchestras were constituted to accompany parades and meetings but also as entertainment. Luftwaffe musicians wore the standard walking-out uniform with insignia and piping of the units they belonged to, with the addition of special, elaborate, parade shoulder straps called *Schwalbennester* (swallows' nests) decorated with cording, a lyre and stars indicating rank. The swallows' nests were made of aluminum braid on a white wool base; they were removable and attached to the shoulder by small hooks. Musicians were divided in three groups: fife-and-drum musicians; buglers; and bandsmen and trumpeters. They were considered as specialists with special ranks such as *Spielmann* (Bandsman), *Musikerschütze* (Musician), *Obermusikmeister* (Lieutenant), *Stabsmusikmeister* (Captain), *Musikinspizent* (Inspector of Music/Colonel).

Uniforms of Luftwaffe Ground Forces

Hermann Göring, in accordance with the private empire building that was so fundamental to the Nazi regime, had gathered into his Luftwaffe many associated units. The German air force did not solely operate aircrafts. Like Heinrich Himmler who had organized the private Nazi Waffen SS, Göring would also have his own private ground army. Next to airmen, technical and ground personnel, administrative services staff, and signals troops, the air force encroached upon the *Heer* (ground forces) as it had a number of ground fighting troops, including Flak artillerymen, infantry field divisions, parachute divisions, and one armored division. It also had its transport, pioneer and construction units, and auxiliaries, both male and female. Altogether the Luftwaffe amounted to about 20 percent of Germany's total armed personnel. It should also be noted that the Luftwaffe ran POW camps (as depicted in the sixties CBS sitcom *Hogan's Heroes*, created by Bernard Fein and Albert S. Ruddy).

Flak Artillery

The Flak (short for *FliegerAbwehrKanone*) was created during World War I and was served by the regular artillery ground force. Forbidden by the Treaty of Versailles, the Flak was reconstituted after the Nazi takeover in 1933. In June 1935, it passed under Luftwaffe command, and from then on its members wore the air force grayish-blue uniform, though retain-

Luftwaffe artillery **Hauptmann** *(Captain). This Flak artillery captain wears the standard air force blue-gray uniform composed of steel helmet, flying blouse, trousers and marching boots. On the service waistbelt he carries a pistol in its holster, and a model M1935 leather report/map case.*

ing the artillery's bright red piping. The Flak, a high-tech arm equipped with sophisticated detection means (radar, acoustic devices, and searchlights) and armed with numerous and reliable light and heavy guns, was an important branch of the Luftwaffe. In 1939, the air defense had 6,500 light guns and 2,450 medium and heavy guns. Served by 571,000 men, it represented 35 percent of the German air force in 1941. In June 1944, the time of maximum strength, the total was 30,463 light guns and 15,087 medium and heavy guns. As World War II proceeded, the decline of German airpower meant that Flak defense became more and more important. The well-organized, voluminous and effective anti-aircraft artillery made a major contribution to the defense of Germany. From May to August 1943, the Flak damaged 1,594 Allied aircraft and destroyed 88. In May-June 1944, they damaged 7,920 aircraft and destroyed 286. The Flak artillery was also engaged in direct fire on the ground, (particularly in an anti-tank role) with great effect. Flak artillerymen wore the standard Luftwaffe uniforms, often with the addition of army clothing and equipment.

Flak artilleryman

Flak gunner in winter dress. This gunner wears the warm **schwere Winteranzug** *(thick winter suit) with detachable hood, thick gloves, and felt-topped winter boots.*

Paratroopers

Developed by General Kurt Student, the German *Fallschirmjäger* (paratroopers) were a small elite force that played a substantial role during World War II. Using both gliders and parachutes, the carefully selected and highly trained German airborne units achieved some remarkable successes in Belgium and Holland in 1940. The casualties suffered at the landing in Crete the following year, though the landing led to the capture of the Greek island, were judged too costly by Hitler for him to permit a repetition. Paradoxically, as the likelihood of another large-scale airborne operation receded, the parachute forces expanded, earning a reputation as formidable fighters as they attracted a steady flow of young volunteers of the highest caliber from throughout the German air force, army and Hitler Youth. Until the end of the war, the much-respected German parachute forces grew to ten divisions which were used as elite infantry assault troops. They took part in many major operations, notably in Leningrad, Tunisia, Sicily, and Italy (Monte Cassino) in 1943, and Normandy (Carantan) in summer 1944.

In 1939–1941, *Fallschirmjäger* wore the standard blue/gray, short, double-breasted *Fliegerbluse* and baggy trousers, over which they wore a sort of canvas coverall, a gray-green smock just over knee-length, with zippered-breast pockets, nicknamed *Knockensack* (bone-bag) by the troops. It could be fastened up around the top of the wearer's legs to prevent the parachute harness from fouling when jumping. Special gloves and rubber elbow and knee protection were also worn to absorb the shock of

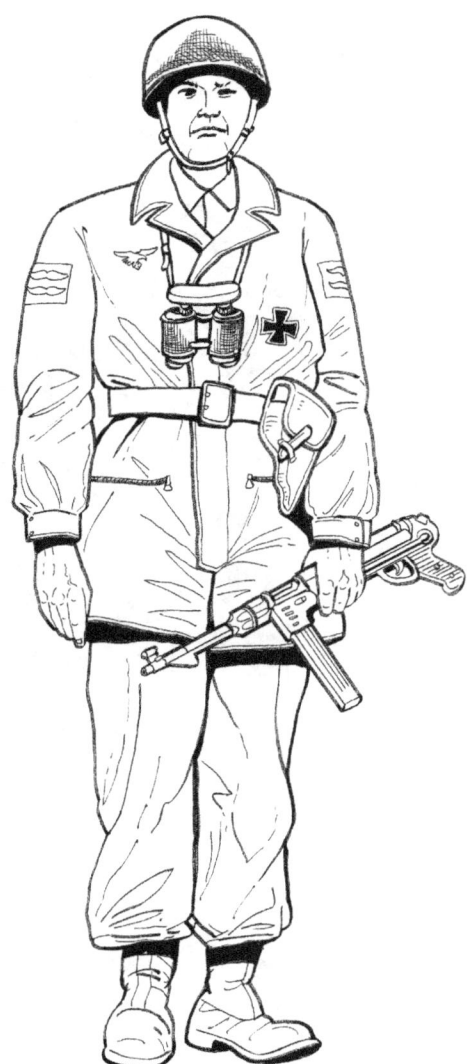

Unterfeldwebel Fallschirmjäger *(NCO), c. 1940. The man wears the para steel helmet, early gray-green jump smock, Luftwaffe trousers and jump boots.*

Fallschirmjägershelm *(Paratrooper helmet). The helmet was fitted with a reinforced padding, chin harness and back straps. Decorated with a Luftwaffe eagle decal on the left side, it was later fitted with a camouflage canvas cover or netting.*

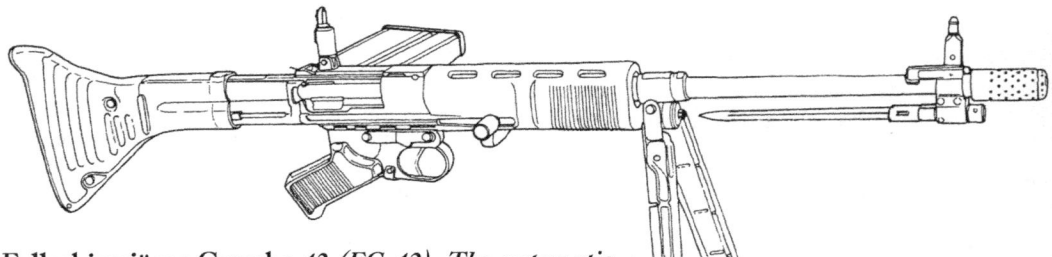

Fallschirmjäger Gewehr *42 (FG 42)*. *The automatic Fallschirmjager Gewehr model 1942 (FG 42) — designed and produced for the Luftwaffe — was intended to give paratroopers the extra firepower that they needed when operating in small detached groups. The FG 42 was actually the first of what are now called assault rifles. It was an all-metal rifle fitted with a folding bipod to steady it, weighing 4.5 kg, shooting a 7.92-mm Kar. 98 rifle cartridge, and capable of single-shot or fully automatic action, with a rate of fire of 750 rounds per minute. The bullets were contained in a 20-round detachable magazine feeding from the left side. The remarkable FG 42 was a light, advanced and superior weapon but very expensive and time-consuming to make. By 1943 Germany could not afford to spend much time in rifle manufacture because quantity was the order of the day. Only 7,000 were produced and the FG 42 was never issued in sufficient number to replace other service weapons, thus it never made any impact on the conduct or outcome of the war.*

landing. Paratroopers were issued a special lightweight and compact jump helmet without visor and ear and neck guards. Until 1941, they wore special, strong, laced jump boots, and later various footwear, including Army jackboots and heavy shoes with gaiters. Although the jump smock (that later was made of camouflaged cloth) was used throughout the war, the deployment of *Fallschirmjäger* troops to the North African and Eastern fronts demanded changes in their uniform to suit the climate of the theater. Tropical jackets and trousers, based on the Luftwaffe standard uniforms, as well as shirts and shorts were introduced, manufactured from lightweight tan material. When German airborne troops were deployed in the East they were issued with army-style protective winter clothing, including reversible, hooded, snow-white-camou-

Paratrooper, Italy, 1944. The man wears the standard helmet with camo cover, a lightweight camouflage jump smock, and general-issue hobnail ankle boots. He is equipped with standard infantry webbing and is armed with a Mauser rifle.

flaged, padded parkas with thick trousers. They were also issued with toque and ear protectors which were worn under the steel helmet.

Their equipment was standard infantry but the gas mask was carried in a soft canvas case designed to prevent injury to the wearer on landing from an air drop. Paratroopers often carried additional rifle ammunition in cloth bandoliers hung around the neck, consisting of several compartments for rifle clips.

Luftwaffe Field Divisions

Luftwaffe Felddivisionen (LwFD, field divisions of the air force) were composed of Luftwaffe ground personnel who were drafted to serve as infantrymen. They originated from ad hoc defense units raised in late 1941 on the Russian front, from airbase volunteer personnel and other rear-echelon units, to defend Luftwaffe installations (e.g., airfields, fuel

Anti-partisan war badge. The **Bandenkampfabzeichen** *(anti-partisan badge), instituted by Reichsführer SS Heinrich Himmler in January 1944, was awarded in three grades: bronze finish for 20 days active operational service, silver for fifty days and gold finish for 100 days of campaigning. It represented a sword bearing a runic solar wheel crushing a writhing, five-headed hydra.*

Luftwaffe Field Division NCO. The depicted **Oberwachtmeister** *wears the regular blue/gray Luftwaffe uniform under a camouflaged smock. The three-quarter-length, five-button smock was specially designed in 1943 for the LwFD, and it became the most distinctive piece of their uniform. The camouflage of the smock is in "splinter" patterns. By 1944, the expensive leather marching boots were often replaced by what were derisively called "retreat" boots—cheap ankle boots and canvas gaiters.*

dumps, supply depots, and Flak batteries) against partisans who harassed the Germans behind their lines. As the fighting proceeded in Russia longer than expected after an appalling winter, the German army desperately needed replacements. The Luftwaffe units were expanded to brigade and regiment size, known as *Feldregimenter der Luftwaffe* (FR der Lw, Air Force Field Regiments), and engaged in anti-partisan duty and soon as a normal infantry force on the front, notably at the sieges of Demyansk and Kohlm. Göring was asked in early 1942 by Hitler to comb out 50,000 personnel who could be spared from air force duties. By providing the dictator with 100,000 men instead, and by promising to create a powerful infantry force, Göring sought to reverse his political decline. Raised from Luftwaffe surplus ground staff, regiments (later expanding to ten Luftwaffe Field Divisions, LwFD) were hastily created, deployed to help hold the line on the Russian front, and used as

Private, Luftwaffe Field Division c. 1943

LwFD private c. 1944. This private wears a mixture of Heer (Army tunic model 1936) and air force dress, Luftwaffe M43 field cap and captured Italian leaf-green, brown and yellow camouflage trousers. Equipment is army standard and the weapon is an MP 40.

anti-partisan task forces behind the front in 1942 and 1943. Understrength and poorly armed, with inadequate numbers of trained officers and experienced NCOs, lacking efficient administrative and logistics services, deprived of significant reconnaissance, transport, and heavy support, the LwFDs had different fortunes. In the end, Göring's attempt to establish a private army along the lines of the Waffen SS was a total failure. By the end of 1943, Göring reluctantly placed his LwFDs under Heer command. The Luftwaffe Field Divisions, reorganized by the army, were used as occupying forces in the western static defenses (Atlantic Wall) in France, Belgium, Holland, Denmark and Norway in 1944. Some units also saw combat in the Mediterranean theater in Greece and Italy. The LwFDs met their end on the Russian front in late 1944 to early 1945. Twenty-two of them had been raised and, on the whole, they had been of limited military value and had made little operational impact on the battlefields. The LwFDs proved a disaster to Nazi Germany's war effort, tens of thousands of soldiers paying for Göring's ego with their lives.

a Prussian motorized *Polizeigruppe Wecke* (paramilitary police militia) established in February 1933 by Göring (then secretary of interior), the unit continually expanded before and during the war. In 1935 the detachment grew to regimental size (named Regiment General Göring), and consisted primarily of Flak and searchlight batteries with a motorcycle company and a ceremonial guard battalion. From a regiment it grew to a powerful, elite infantry combat unit (soon brigade and later armored division), built on a core of former paratroopers with 5,000 Luftwaffe conscripts to bulk it

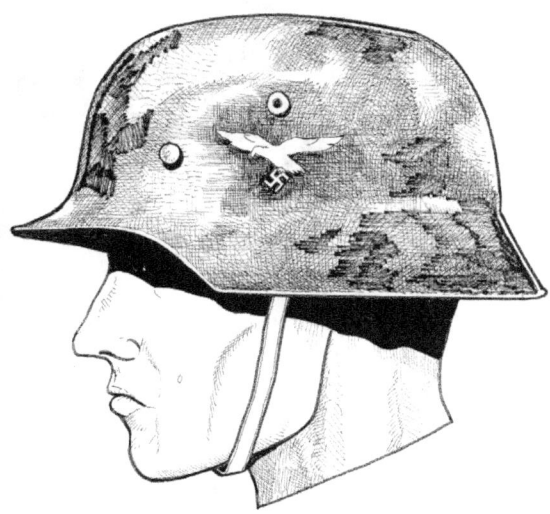

Luftwaffe steel helmet type 1935

Division Hermann Göring

In contrast to the sad story of the Luftwaffe Field Divisions, the Hermann Göring Division had a good reputation. Originating from

NCO General Göring Regiment 1940

out. Remaining a Luftwaffe unit, its ethos, spirit and combativeness were close to those of the Waffen SS. Well-equipped, powerfully armed, and competently led, the H. Göring Division won a reputation as an excellent fighting formation in North Africa in 1942, Sicily in 1943, and—enlarged into a two-division corps—on the Eastern front for the rest of the war.

From 1933 to 1935 the men of the police group wore "police green" uniforms. From 1936 to 1940 the soldiers of the Regiment General Göring wore various Luftwaffe and army uniforms. From 1943 to 1945, Waffen SS camouflaged smocks and LwFD tunics were issued to soldiers of the HG Division. The previously described tropical uniform was worn in Northern Africa in 1942-43 and various winter clothing worn on the Russian front in 1944-45. When the HG Division was expanded to armored formation, crews of armored vehicles wore the black Panzer uniform. Equipment, headgear, weapons, artillery, vehicles and tanks were the same as those used by the Heer and

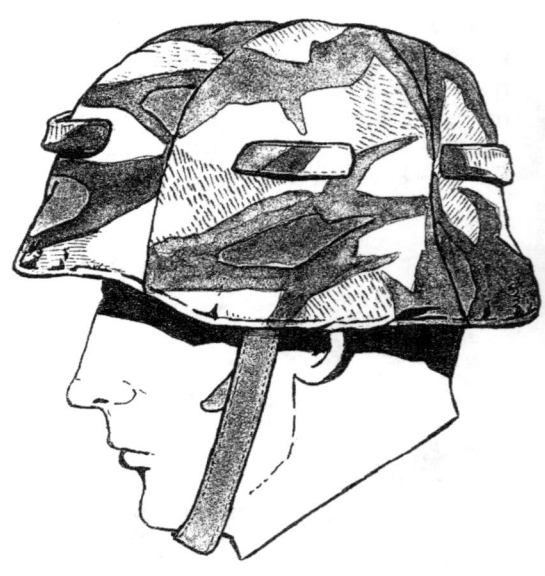

M35 steel helmet with model 1943 camouflage cloth

Tank crew HG Division. The two-piece Panzer uniform consisted of a jacket and trousers worn with shirt and tie. It was very practical, being especially designed for men having to operate in a confined space, and having to easily climb in and jump out of the vehicle. The Panzer **Feldjacke** *was a short, hip-length, double-breasted, tight-fitting jacket, without external pockets and with no external features which would snag inside the tank. It had a deep fall collar and broad lapels decorated with collar piping. The collar patches were the most eye-catching feature since they displayed a white metal* **Totenkopf** *(death's head). The Panzer uniform had a summer version, in reed-green denim, strong, light and easily washable. Crews operating self-propelled guns wore the same uniforms but they were gray instead of black. Above: Death's head worn by armored troops on the collar patches.*

Waffen SS. But all through the war the original Luftwaffe diving eagle emblem was retained, as well as typical Luftwaffe rank badges displayed on white collar patches (with appropriate *Waffenfarbe*). In addition the elite character of the HG Division was emphasized by a black cuff title generally worn on the lower right sleeve carrying the label "Hermann Göring" in silver letters.

Obergefreiter *HG Division 1945. This corporal wears a cheap, grayish, four-pocketed field blouse with matching trousers and "retreat" ankle boots with canvas gaiters. He is armed with a pistol and a Panzerfaust 30 single-shot, anti-tank rocket launcher.*

Grenadier Hermann Göring Division c. 1943

Luftwaffe Feldgendarmerie

Ground combat units of the Luftwaffe (LwFD, paratroopers and Division Hermann Göring) included small detachments of *Feldgendarmerie* (Military Police) whose main task was to maintain order and security among the forces. Military police were also responsible for control duties in ports and airfields, administrative control of aliens, patrol duties, collecting and evacuating prisoners of war, hunting and rounding up of deserters, and also regulating and directing road traffic. A branch of the military policemen—called *Wachtruppen*—was concerned with the guarding of headquarters and senior officers in the field. The Luftwaffe military police were self-contained detachments under the command of air-force divisions. They were organized into battalions of three companies, each company made up of three platoons, generally transported in trucks, cars and motorcycles for rapid movement. They wore the standard Luftwaffe uniforms, often with the addition of a cuff title bearing the legend "*Feldgendarmerie*." On duty, their most characteristic feature was the

Military policeman. The depicted MP wears the standard M35 steel helmet, a **Schutzmantel** *(a long, double-breasted, waterproof rubberized greatcoat for motorcycle riding), and a gorget around his neck, and he is armed with an MP 40 submachine gun.*

HG Division policeman. This **Obergefreiter** *of the Hermann Göring Division wears a standard M35 steel helmet with goggles, an Army four-pocketed tunic with HG and* **Feldgendarmerie** *cuffbands, and the Luftwaffe* **Feldgendarmerie** *gorget.*

Ringkragen (gorget), a metal plate in the form of a half moon positioned just below the collar on the breast and held by a chain; the gorget was lettered "Feldgendarmerie" and decorated with embossed buttons and an eagle/swastika emblem. The letters, buttons and emblem were finished with luminous paint so that they were easily visible in the dark.

NSKK Transportregiment *Luftwaffe*

The *Nationalsozialisches Kraftfahrkorps* (NSKK National-Socialist Motorized Corps), founded in 1934, was a branch of the Nazi Party (NSDAP). It was a paramilitary motorized organization which drove and maintained the party vehicles before the war, promoted information about automobiles, and organized rallies, races, etc. along strict Nazi lines. During the war the NSKK oversaw the transportation of supplies and the training of recruits for the German army's motorized and armored units.

The Battle of Britain, which began in summer 1940, saw the creation of a new NSKK branch. Air force command had to be reorganized, squadrons retrained and refitted. Before the air offensive could be launched, substantial ground installation, technical services and stocks of fuel and bombs had to be moved from the Reich. By that time French, Dutch and Belgian airfields had to be extended, improved and made suitable for German bombers. During the battle, large quantities of ammunition and supplies had to be delivered to the forward airfields in northern France and Belgium. For this purpose a special branch of the NSKK was created, known as the *NSKK Transportregiment Luftwaffe* (air force transport regiment). This unit grew to brigade and then divisional strength and it was redesignated in July 1943 *NSKK Transportgruppe Luftwaffe* (Air force transport division) placed under the leadership of *Obergruppenführer* (Lieutenant-General) Graf von Bayer-Ehrenberg. Later in the war, the *NSKK Transportgruppe Luftwaffe* was expanded and deployed on all World War II fronts to supply airfields.

As many German nationals were drafted in combat formations, foreigners were allowed and encouraged to join the Transport Group Luftwaffe. They could enlist as drivers and mechanics on short-term contracts or for the duration of the war as *NSKK Freiwillige* (volunteers). About 3,000 Flemish, 1,000 Walloons (mainly coming from the Belgium pro-Nazi parties AGRA and Rex), 4,000 Dutch (from the pro-Nazi party NSB) and 2,000 Frenchmen (from various pro-Nazi parties) were recruited.

NSKK **Obersturmmann** *(Corporal). This corporal driver wears the standard gray-blue Luftwaffe uniform with distinctive NSKK badges. Top right: NSKK badge. Bottom right: NSKK driver badge.*

Members of the NSKK-Luftwaffe generally wore the basic air force light-blue/gray uniform composed of a short jacket, trousers and boots, but they had black-sided hats with the NSKK eagle on the left, as well as a sleeve which also displayed the NSKK diamond. On the cuff was the title with the number and *"NSKK Transport Regiment."* On duty, members of the NSKK wore various fatigue overalls, working suits, and the previously described *Drillichanzug* (fatigue uniform).

Luftwaffe vehicles carried a registration plate with the prefix WL (short for Wehrmacht Luftwaffe).

OT Einsatz *Luftwaffe*

The *Organisation Todt* (OT) was a German public construction company developed by the Nazi regime. The OT was created and headed by engineer Fritz Todt from 1938 to 1942, and led by Hitler's architect, Albert Speer, from 1942 to 1945. It was a conglomerate of building companies which built the prewar German motorways, the bunkers of the Westwall (Siegfried Line) and Hitler's concrete headquarters. During the war, the OT became a huge paramilitary body. Its tasks became various, carried out by slave labor, and all connected to the war effort: building, reparation and establishment of roads, support to Army engineers and pioneers. The organization established an electric power grid, took over the exploitation of sources of raw materials (e.g., the extraction of oil) restarted factories and transported looted strategic products to the Reich. The OT also managed farms in occupied countries, supervising harvests, and constructed harbor facilities, dams, and dikes in marshy districts. It ran ammunition, vehicle and tank factories. It also built most bunkers constructed by the Germans in World War II, notably the Atlantic Wall, fortified lines in Russia and Italy, as well as huge U-Boat bunkers on the French

Engineer, **Organisation Todt.** *A current issue was the Nazi red brassard with a black swastika in a white disc worn on the left arm.*

Atlantic coast. Göring was of course jealous of Speer's prerogative and influence, and used every opportunity to undermine his position. He managed to submit a part of the OT to air force control. Known as *OT Einsatz Luftwaffe*, this construction branch of Göring's private empire built and repaired airfields in northern France during the Battle of Britain in 1940, Flak bunkers, fortifications and installations, as well as concrete sites for V1 flying bombs and V2 rockets in 1944. At local level the Luftwaffe had a *Bauleitung* (construction service) which was charged to carry out construction, maintenance and repair of airfield installations, such as buildings, runways, dispersal areas, defense works, camouflage, and lighting systems.

Youth Auxiliaries

As the demand for able-bodied men increased during the war, the Luftwaffe had to

Right: Luftschutz *helmet M38. Worn in action by nonmilitary personnel (e.g., firemen, Red Cross workers, rescue teams, and police squads) or Army-affiliated personnel (e.g. Flak auxiliaries), the round, domed "Luftschutz" helmet had air vents on each side, a large visor and neck guard.*

Organisation Todt *worker wearing fatigue suit*

Young man serving in fire brigade

HJ-Flakhelfer, *1944. Many young men and boys of the Hitler Youth served as Luftwaffe* **Flakhelfer** *(anti-aircraft artillery auxiliaries). They wore the basic air force light-blue/grayish uniform (left) and the greatcoat with steel helmet (right).*

rely increasingly on young members of the *Hitler Jugend* (HJ—Hitler Youth), boys aged 14–18, and young men from the *Reichsarbeitdienst* (RAD—German Labor Service) who were recruited to serve in a wide variety of auxiliary military roles. Many of them served in the *Heimat Flak* (Home Anti-aircraft Artillery). The young auxiliaries manned guns, searchlights, and altitude-prediction and sound-detection equipment.

Women auxiliaries

The German air force also employed *Helferinnen* (women auxiliaries) who served in communications, and did administrative and clerical duties. Women up to 45 years old and girls from the *Bund Deutsche Mädel* (BdM, the female branch of the Hitler Youth, aged 14–18) served in several air force-controlled branches: *Flugmeldedienst* (Aircraft Reporting Service), *Luftnachrichten* (Air Signal), *Luftschutzwarndienst* (LSW Air Raid Warning Service), Staff Service and Anti-Aircraft Artillery. They were employed as clerical workers, telephone workers, canteen and kitchen staff, and cleaners, but also in more specific military roles, operating in the field with binoculars, searchlights and sound-locating devices; they detected and identified enemy bombers and reported their findings to the Flak units. Women and schoolgirls thus greatly contributed in releasing men for front-line duties. They never served in a combat capacity (such as tank driver, pilot, or sniper) but operated searlights and Flak guns in the homefront. In the autumn of 1944, at peak strength, there were some 128,700 women serving in the German air force.

The basic uniform of the female Luftwaffe auxiliaries consisted of a blue-gray *Fliegermutze* (standard side cap); a blue-gray, single-breasted jacket with the standard Luftwaffe eagle/swastika displayed on the right breast; a straight, blue-gray, knee-length skirt with

3. Regalia and Uniforms

Left: *Flak* **Helferin**, *c. 1944.* This young woman of the Luftwaffe anti-aircraft artillery wears a functional uniform suitable for outdoors. The helmet (painted in grayish blue) is the standard M35; the gray-blue, three-quarter-length tunic has patch pockets and integral cloth belt. She wears gray/blue, long, loose, ski-styled trousers and ankle boots. **Right: Helferin**, *c. 1943.* This Luftnachrichtenhelferin *(Luftwaffe signal auxiliary)* wears the standard blue-gray service dress with the air force "diving" eagle, specialty badge (qualified radio operator) and a sleeve chevron of rank.

single pleat; a blue-gray shirt, often worn with a black tie; blue-gray stockings and black shoes. Rank insignia were displayed on the lower sleeves and trades badges were worn on the upper right sleeves. In situations where skirt and jacket were not practical (e.g., in the field), women auxiliaries were issued various types of service tunics, trousers, and they wore M43 *Einheitsfliegermutze* (soft-peaked field caps) or standard M35 steel helmets or Luftschutz M38 helmets; warm, double-breasted greatcoats (when needed and when available by the end of the war); and heavy, black-laced shoes.

4

Bombers

During World War I, it was realized that if the enemy could be spied on from the sky for reconnaissance purposes, then one could as well profitably drop explosives in the form of bombs on such a target. It became clear that an air force which enjoyed command of the air over the battlefield might act not only as the eyes of the commanders, but also as a substitute or at least as a complement for the artillery. Thus there evolved three major types of combat aircraft—reconnaissance, scout or fighter, and bomber (an aircraft specially designed to attack ground targets primarily by dropping bombs). The scope of the bomber was considerably enlarged, namely by the Italians, Germans and British who had ambitions in the field of long-range offensive operations with large strategic bombers whose task was to damage their enemy's war effort by attacking the home front: supply bases, manufacturers, shipyards and cities themselves. German heavy bombers of World War I included, for example, the Gotha series bombers, the two-engined Friedrichshaven GIII, and Allgemeine Elektrizität Gesellschaft AEG G IV, and the four-engine Zeppelin Staaken R VI. The giant British long-range bomber, the twin-engined Handley Page, could have reached Berlin from advance bases in France if the war had not come to an end just as plans for its use were complete.

After the war, in the 1920s and 1930s, as aircraft increased in range, speed, reliability and armament, bombers could make battlefield deployment and movement impossible or at least dangerous and costly for the enemy. Bomber aircraft were soon recognized as having an important role in modern warfare, and new generations of bombers appeared with diversified and specialized roles.

German World War II bombers were first and foremost aggressive weapons, and they reflected the fundamental role of the Luftwaffe: tactical ground support. Therefore these airplanes were designed primarily to fit this task. As such they were successful, but their failure became only too evident when they were required to perform other roles, for example strategic bombing. The Luftwaffe bomb-carriers existed in two main types: relatively small but highly powered, well-armed, and maneuverable ground-attack aircraft (including shallow dive bombers) and medium bombers with a relatively short range, capable of delivering medium-sized bomb loads while at the same time being fast enough to elude enemy fighter interceptors. Both types had range and payload that did not allow them to assume a worthwhile long-range strategic role. They were especially designed to meet the requirements of a short and aggressive *Blitzkrieg*—lightning war. *Blitzkrieg* tactics, a journalist's descriptive term, was influenced by the trench warfare of World War I. The concept, drawn up by German military planners of the 1930s, was to bring rapid mobility to the battlefield. Tanks were concentrated into an offensive phalanx, supported by squadrons of bombers as flying artillery, and when driven against a defended line at a weak spot, they cracked it and then swept on to spread confusion in their wake. The tactics called for close cooperation between air and ground forces, and rested on surprise, concentration of force, and speed—speed of attack, speed of communication by radio, speed to exploit opportunities for advance.

Dive Bombers and Ground Attackers

Dive bombers and ground attackers were (and the latter still are) aircraft designed to operate in direct support of ground forces such as infantry and tanks.

Dive bombers, the principal German weapon of aggression, played a vital role in the victorious German campaigns of 1939–1941, as the Blitzkrieg doctrine involved close integration of tactical air power and mechanized army units on the ground. The combination of Panzer mobility and Stuka firepower seemed to be unstoppable, and enabled the German ground force to hold the initiative—at least as long as the Luftwaffe possessed air superiority over the battlefield.

A dive bomber was an aircraft that flew nearly vertically at the target in the same direction the bomb would go, released it close to the target at high speed, and then pulled away to safety. This form of attack, which did not require any sophisticated precision-aiming equipment, could accurately hit a relatively small and/or moving target (e.g., a bridge or a ship) with relative ease, and limited the exposure and effectiveness of enemy anti-aircraft fire. Indeed a dive bomber approached its target in such a way that anti-aircraft fire against it was handicapped. The normal level bomber's

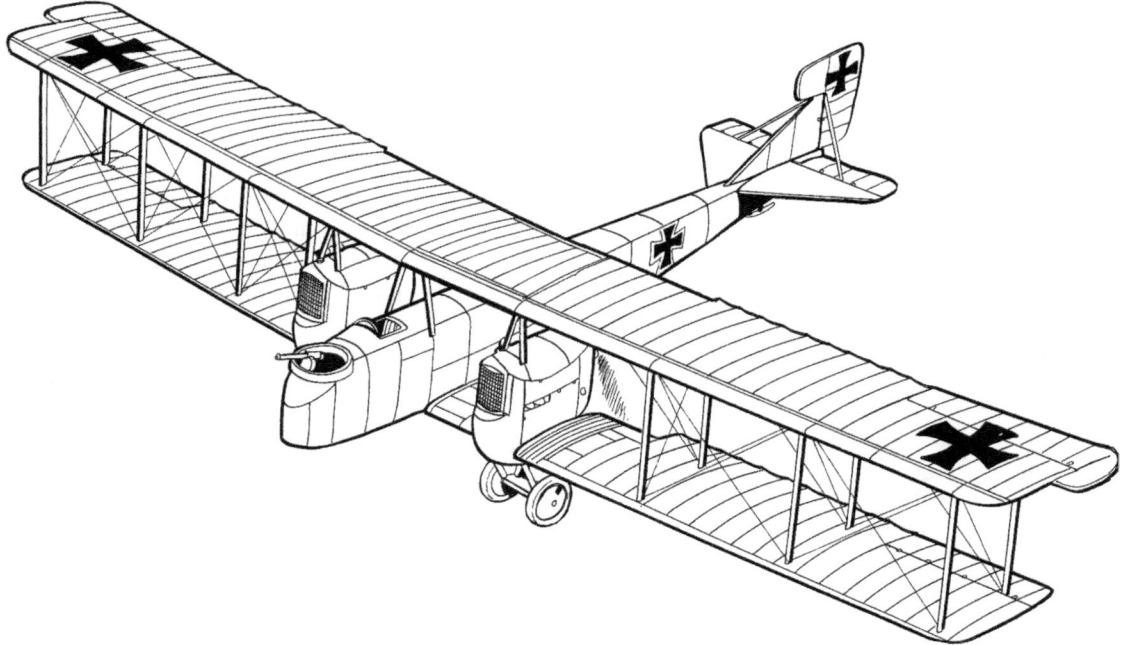

Gotha G4 heavy bomber. The G4 long-range bomber, designed in 1915, was produced by Gothaer Waggonfabrik AG, Luftverkehr GmbH, and Siemens Schuckert Werke GmbH. It had a crew of three, including pilot, rear gunner, and front gunner/bomb aimer. It was powered by two Mercedes-Benz D IVA six-cylinder, water-cooled, in-line engines (each developing 260 hp) in "pusher" arrangement. The aircraft had a maximum speed of 87.5 mph and a range of 522 miles. It was a large biplane with a span of 77 ft 10 in, a length of 38 ft 11 in, and an empty weight of 5,280 lbs. It could carry a bomb load of 1,100 lbs and was armed with two Parabellum machine guns manually operated from nose and rear. Some 230 units were produced. Entering service in March 1916, they carried out a number of daylight raids against England.

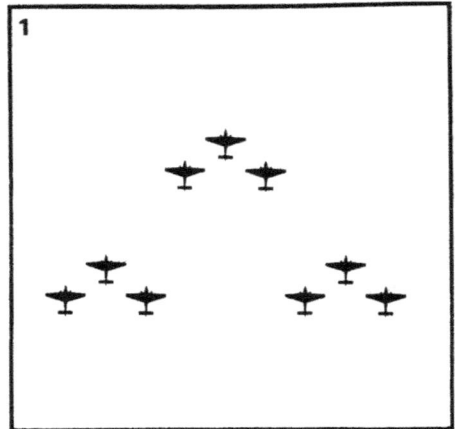

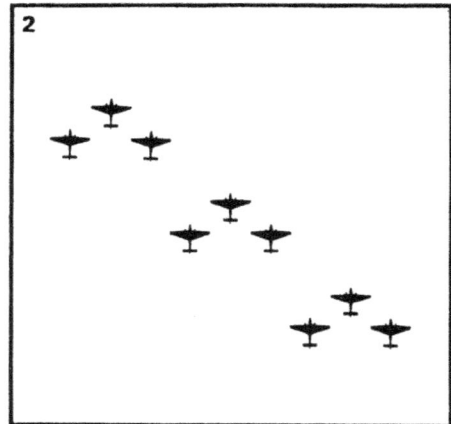

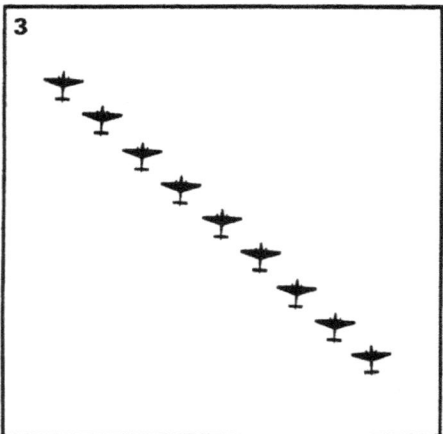

straight flight could be predicted by an enemy gunner, the dive bomber on the other hand circled to spot its target and peeled off at an unpredictable angle. When diving, it lost height so rapidly that it could escape anti-aircraft barrage more quickly than a craft flying level. The dive bomber also had a considerable morale effect on ground troops until they got well used to it. The use of dive bomber was thus tactical rather than strategic, operating at the front of the battle rather than against targets deeper in the enemy's rear. With airplanes growing in speed, strength and load capability in the early 1930s, the valuable technique of dive bombing attracted much attention.

In Germany in the late 1930s, dive bombing was developed by Ernst Udet who advocated the use of the so-called *Sturkampfflugzeug* (for short, *Stuka*—dive bomber) in order to allow the newborn Luftwaffe to operate in a tactical and ground-support role. The dive bomber caused a minor revolution: all the movements of the German land forces were timed, coordinated and planned in conjunction with the air weapon. It could be called up by ground forces in a moment of emergency, and immediately appreciated by the hard-pressed soldier below. The dive bomber, however, also produced an obsession with tactical support, resulting in the stipulation of fatal requirements; for example the Junker Ju 88 had to have dive-bombing capacity, and therefore had to be fitted with heavy air brakes which reduced its performance. It was also idiocy to require of the four-engined Heinkel He 177 that it should dive. Besides, when facing a formidable fighter in opposition, the dive bomber suffered catastrophic losses. After the pendulum of fortune swung back following the battles at Stalingrad and El Alamein, the Luftwaffe no longer had it in its power to dispute Allied superiority in the skies over the German army. After World War II, the dive-bomber class quickly disappeared. One of the reasons was the improvement of anti-aircraft artillery which

Stuka dive attack. The Stuka approach usually went like this: 1: The Ju 87 Stuka **Staffel** *flies to its target in three* **Ketten** *in V formation. 2: As they approach their objective, the formation changes to triple* **Ketten** *in echelon to starboard which enables the pilots to move easily into the third step. 3: The dive bombers in stepped-up echelon singly to starboard are ready to peel off, one after the other, on a near-vertical dive.*

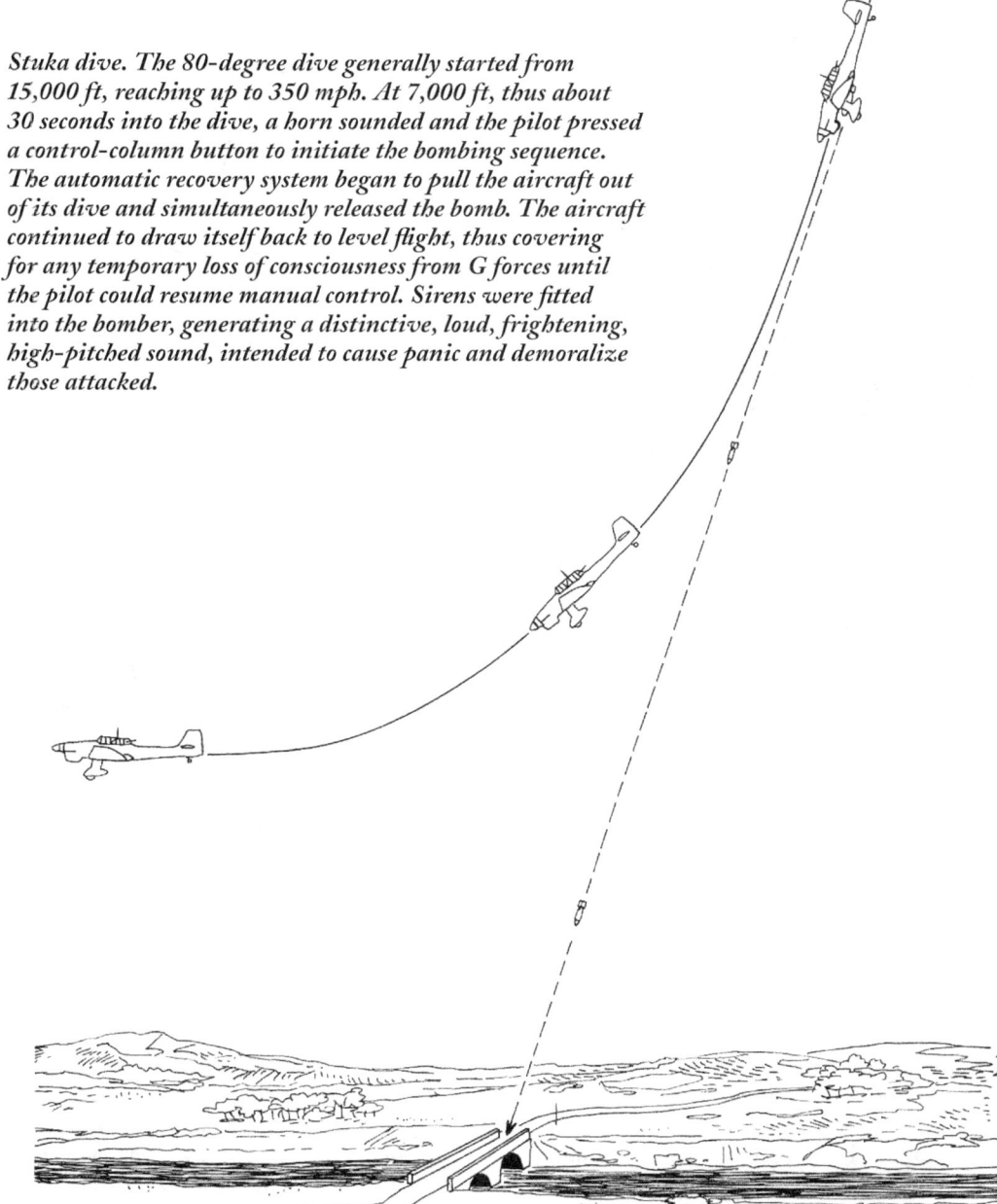

Stuka dive. The 80-degree dive generally started from 15,000 ft, reaching up to 350 mph. At 7,000 ft, thus about 30 seconds into the dive, a horn sounded and the pilot pressed a control-column button to initiate the bombing sequence. The automatic recovery system began to pull the aircraft out of its dive and simultaneously released the bomb. The aircraft continued to draw itself back to level flight, thus covering for any temporary loss of consciousness from G forces until the pilot could resume manual control. Sirens were fitted into the bomber, generating a distinctive, loud, frightening, high-pitched sound, intended to cause panic and demoralize those attacked.

had become effective against the low-flying and vulnerable dive bomber. At the same time the quality of various computing bombsights allowed for better accuracy from smaller dive angles and could be fitted to almost any airplane.

The most famous World War II German dive bomber was the mass-produced, gull-winged, monoplane, two-seat Junkers Ju 87. This airplane became the epitome of Blitzkrieg in the first years of the war, and gained a great reputation because it had freedom to operate without interference or opposition. The Ju 87 was not the only German dive bomber and, of course, other Stukas existed.

Heinkel He 50

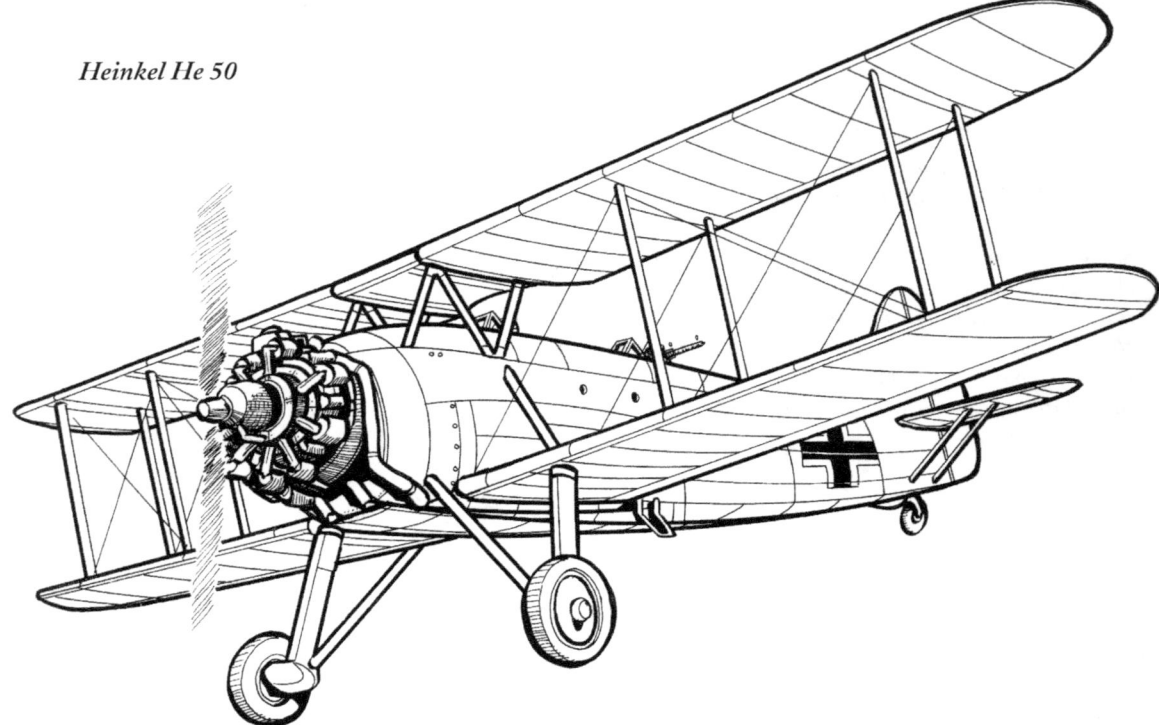

Ground attack is the use of aircraft to provide close support to troops in the battlefield. The effectiveness of air attack on ground targets, in term of destructiveness and lethality, was considerably less than might be expected from the quantity of firepower that can be mounted on a relatively small aircraft. This was due in large part to the inaccuracy inherent in finding and attacking a target while passing over it at great speed and in the relative instability of the aircraft as a weapon platform, in comparison with ground-based weapons. Nonetheless, aircraft demonstrated that they could have an important role in supporting troops when artillery support was limited or could not reach targets effectively. Ground-attack aircraft also had a tremendous influence on ground troops' morale—a very negative effect upon troops being attacked and a positive one on those being supported. Ground attackers (called *Zerstörer* in German—destroyers) were organized into *Schlachtgeschwader* (battle or attack groups) with distinctive, low-altitude missions and tasks. For example, they could spot and attack targets from above, weaken enemy defenses, support hard-pressed friendly troops, destroy enemy supply dumps, help repulse an offensive, and add to the general demoralization of the retreating enemy. These advantages justified the design and employment before and during World War II of specialist battlefield-support aircraft such as the mass-produced Messerschmitt Bf 110. From the start, the Luftwaffe was strongly geared toward tactical strike support of ground forces. Such an emphasis suited Hitler who saw his conquests being achieved quickly using concentrated ground and air forces on the battlefield. For such tactics, complete mastery of the air was a requirement. In the early campaigns, the skies were swept clear of opposition by sudden attacks on enemy airfields followed by destruction in the air of aircraft which had escaped. Without such freedom from enemy fighter interception, dive bombers and ground attackers were vulnerable. With the advent of appreciable Allied fighter strength, dive bombing and ground attack in daytime could continue only in areas where the enemy lacked fighter strength. By the end of the war, when Germany was forced to a defensive strategy, Stukas and *Zerstörer*, which were regarded primarily as offensive and tactical weapons, were relegated to limited sorties, chiefly at night.

Heinkel He 50

The He 50, intended to be a dive bomber and reconnaissance aircraft, was designed in 1931 originally to meet an order from the Japanese navy. It had a crew of two, pilot and observer/rear gunner. A sturdy, two-bay biplane made of wood and metal, it had a span of 11.5 m (37 ft 9 in), a length of 9.6 m (31 ft 6 in), and an empty weight of 1,600 kg (3.528 lbs). Powered by one 650-hp Bramo 322B SAM 9-cylinder, air-cooled, radial engine, it had a speed of 235 km/h (146 mph), and a range of 600 km (373 miles). *Bramo* was short for Brandenburgische Motorwerke (Brandenburg Engine Works). The He 50 was armed with one fixed 7.92-mm MG 17 machine gun firing forward, and one 7.92-mm MG 15 machine gun aimed by the observer. A bomb load of 250 kg (551 lbs) was carried. Demonstrated to the Defense Ministry in 1932, the aircraft was adopted. In all, some 90 units were built, a few survivors seeing active service on the Eastern front as late as 1943.

Arado Ar 81

First flown in the spring of 1936, the biplane dive bomber Ar 81 had a crew of two, pilot and rear gunner. It had a length of 11.5 m (37 ft 9 in), a span of 11 m (36 ft), and an empty weight of 1,925 kg (4.244 lbs). Powered by one 640-hp Junkers Motorenbau (Jumo) 210Ca inverted-V, 12-cylinder, water-cooled engine, it had a speed of 344 km/h (214 mph), and a range of 692 km (430 miles). Carrying a bomb load of 250 kg (550 lbs) and armed with one fixed 7.92-mm MG 17 machine gun firing forward and one 7.92-mm MG 15 on flexible mounting in rear cockpit, the Ar 81 was superior in performance to the Junkers Ju 87, but the fact that it was a biplane made its production seem a retrograde step. So the "modern" monoplane Ju 87 was chosen, and the Ar 81 design was abandoned after three prototypes had been built.

Blohm & Voss Ha 137

The dive bomber Blohm & Voss Ha 137 was designed in 1935 by Richard Vogt, who had been working for a decade with Kawasaki and was looking to return to Germany. The single-seat, low-wing, cantilever monoplane aircraft had a length of 9.46 m (31 ft), a span of 11.15 m (36 ft 7 in) and an empty weight of 1,814 kg (4,000 lbs). The all-metal design used fixed, faired landing gear, so in order to reduce their length, and thus the drag, the wings featured a sharp, reverse-gull bend at about ¼ span.

The wheels were mounted on two shock absorbers each, so the fairing around the gear was large enough to allow the mounting of a 7.92-mm MG 17 machine gun for testing, and a 20-mm MG FF cannon if required. Two additional MG 17 machine guns were mounted

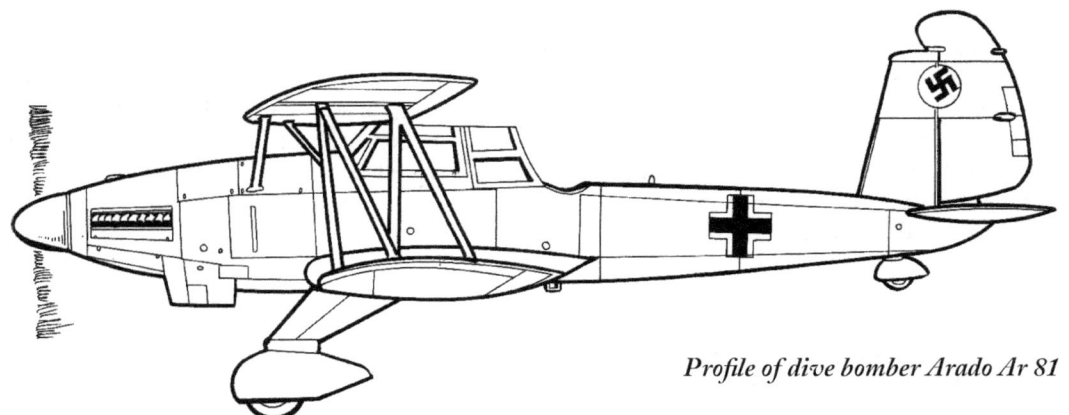

Profile of dive bomber Arado Ar 81

Dive bomber Blohm & Voss Ha 137 V5

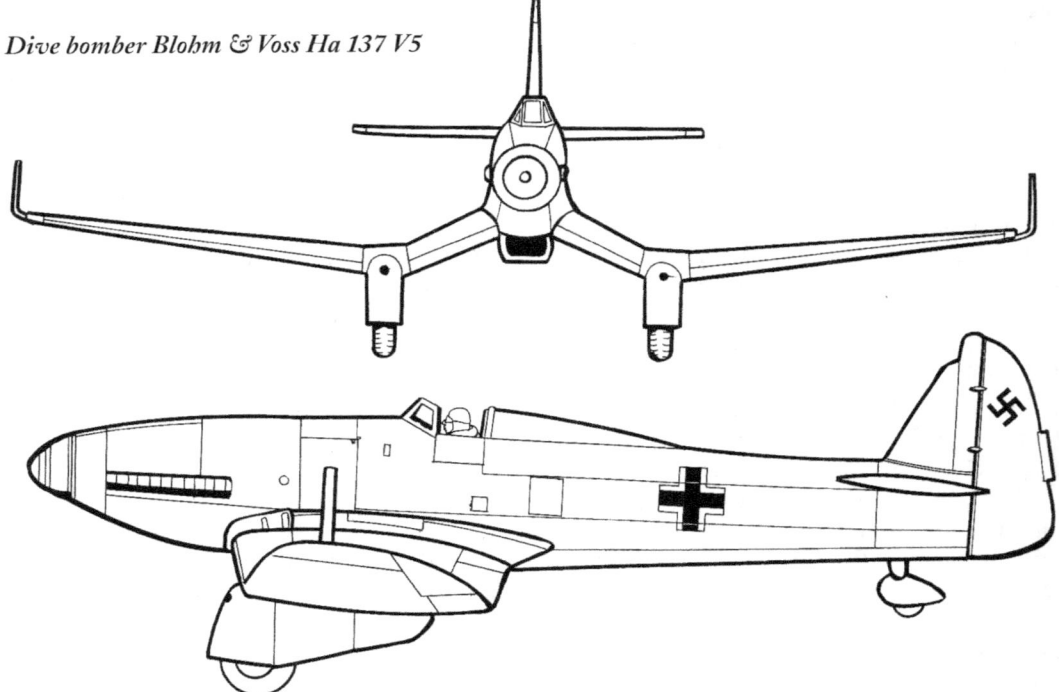

in the fuselage decking above the engine cowl. Four 50-kg (110-lb) bombs were carried on underwing racks. The dive bomber was originally powered by one BMW XV engine, then by a 650hp Pratt & Whitney Hornet, licensed for production in Germany as the BMW 132. Three prototypes were built and the Ha 137-V1 first flew in April 1935, followed the next month by prototype V2. It quickly became apparent that the Hornet engine was so large that the visibility during diving was greatly affected. Fitted with a 610hp Jumo 210 engine, three new Ha 137 prototypes were built and tested. The aircraft was sturdy and well-designed; it would probably have been a tough and maneuverable close-support fighter/dive bomber. It had a speed of 330 km/h (205 mph) and a range of 580 km (360 miles) but the Reichsluftfahrministerium (RLM—State Ministry of Aviation) chose the two-seat Junkers Ju 87 as standard Luftwaffe Stuka. The Ha 137 was thus excluded, and the project was dropped in 1936. The existing planes were maintained in flying condition as testbeds for experimental tasks, e.g., test firing of air-to-air rockets. There was a plan to produce a naval seaplane version of the design, known as Projekt 11. However the additional weight of the floats dramatically reduced performances and made the design untenable.

Fieseler Fi 98

The little single-seat biplane Fi 98 was another unsuccessful competitor in the RLM's interim dive-bomber program. The aircraft had a length of 7.4 m (24 ft 3.5 in), a span of 11.5 m (37 ft 9 in), and an empty weight of 1,450 kg (3.197 lbs). It was powered by a 650-hp BMW 132A-3 9-cylinder radial engine and had a maximum speed of 295 km/h (183 mph) and a range of 470 km (292 miles). The Fi 98 was armed with two 7.92-mm MG 17 machine guns firing forward and could carry four 50-kg (110-lb) bombs. The rival Henschel Hs 123 was favored and although two Fi 98 prototypes were ordered, only the first was completed.

Henschel Hs 123

The single-seat dive bomber/ground support Hs 123 was designed in 1933, and entered Luftwaffe service in 1936. Powered by a 880-

hp BMW 132 Dc nine-cylinder radial engine, it had a maximum speed of 345 km/h (214 mph) and a range of 850 km (530 miles). The biplane had an empty weight of 1,504 kg (3,316 lbs), a length of 8.3 m (27 ft 4 in), a height of 3.2 m (10 ft 6.5 in) and a wingspan of 10.5 m (34 ft 5.5 in). Its armament was two 7.92-mm Rheinmetall MG 17 machine guns located in the nose between the engine and the open cockpit. Four 50-kg (110-lb) bombs were carried in racks under the lower wing. About 265 units were produced, of which most were version Hs 123 A-1. A batch was sold to China in 1938 and some were sent with the German

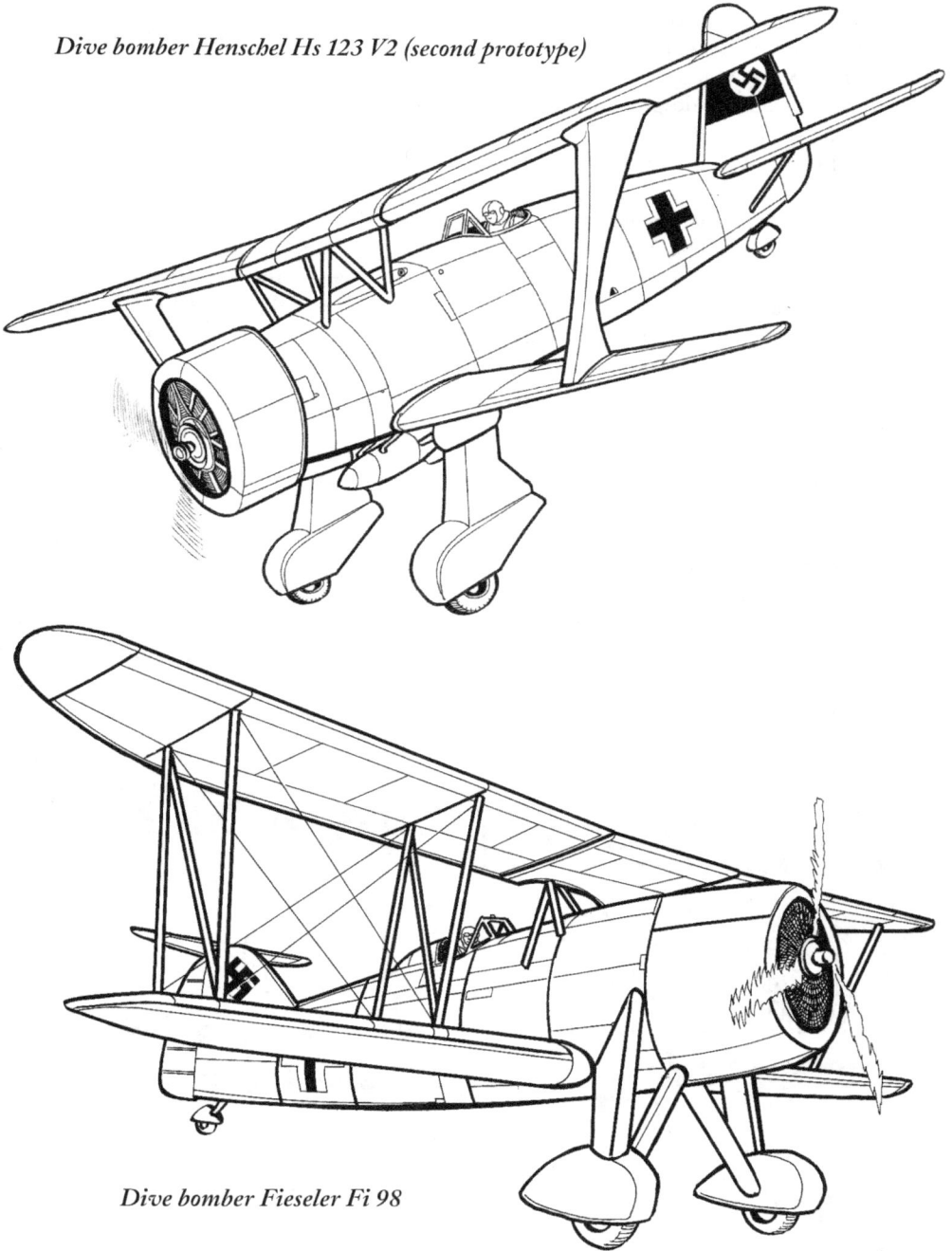

Dive bomber Henschel Hs 123 V2 (second prototype)

Dive bomber Fieseler Fi 98

Legion Condor to fight in the Spanish Civil War between 1936 and 1939. At the outbreak of World War II, the Henschel Hs 123 was replaced by the legendary Junkers Ju 87 in the Stuka role, but—although outdated—it remained the last operational biplane used by the Luftwaffe, apart from some trainers and floatplanes. It was used with great success in a close-support role during the campaign of Poland in 1939, and in Holland and France in 1940. The Hs 123 was able to give strafe and bomb with great accuracy despite the lack of any radio link. It could survive a lot of anti-aircraft punishment, and by virtue of careful setting of the propeller speed, it could produce a demoralizing screaming noise. Although representing a class of aircraft generally regarded as obsolete, the trim little biplane continued front-line service, especially on the Russian front. Such was its value that it was suggested that the aircraft should return to production in 1943. The suggestion was declined, but the existing Hs 123s continued in combat service until mid–1944 when all of them were destroyed in operation. For an old-fashioned biplane with fixed landing gear and open cockpit to be serving with frontline units in 1944 must seem anachronistic, but the Henschel Hs 123 established a good reputation for its maneuverability, reliability, sturdiness, robustness, and ability to operate in conditions that modern, sophisticated aircraft found too harsh to withstand.

Heinkel He 70

The Heinkel He 70 was a reconnaissance/bomber aircraft with a crew of two or three. Designed and first flown in 1932, it was in Luftwaffe service from 1934 to 1938. Its length was 12 m (39 ft 4.5 in), its wingspan was 14.80 m (48 ft 6.75 in), its height was 3.1 m (10 ft 2 in) and its weight (empty) 2,360 kg (5,203 lbs). The powerplant was a 750-hp BMW VI 7-3 V-12, water-cooled engine. Its Maximum speed was 360 km/h (224 mph) and its range was 900 km (559 miles). Its armament consisted of one 7.92-mm MG 15 machine gun aimed by observer from rear cockpit, and six 50-kg (110-lb) or twenty-four 10-kg (22 lbs) bombs could be carried.

Before becoming a Luftwaffe combat aircraft, the Heinkel He 70 Blitz was designed in the early 1930s to serve as a fast mail plane for the civilian commercial company *Deutsche Luft Hansa* (DLH German State Airline). Although useful, it had a relatively short commercial career before it was replaced by types which could carry more passengers. As a combat aircraft it was not a great success and it rapidly became outdated. Nevertheless, the He 70 was a brilliant design for its day, setting no fewer than eight world records for speed by the beginning of 1933. The main characteristics of its revolutionary design were its elliptical wing and its small, rounded control surfaces, designed by the Günther brothers. The He 70

Dive bomber Henschel Hs 123 A1 (1935)

is known mainly as the direct ancestor to the famous Heinkel He 111 which used its distinctive oval wings and streamlined fuselage in a twin-engine configuration. The He 70 was imported to Japan for study and inspired the Aichi D3A (Val) carrier-launched light bomber. This plane, too, shared the He 70's distinctive, low-mounted oval wings and was only one of several collaborations between Heinkel and the Japanese aviation industry. In all, 306 Heinkel He 70s were produced and some continued on in Spanish service until the early 1950s. A fast, reconnaissance, export version, powered with one 910-hp WM-K-14 radial engine, known as Heinkel He 170, was delivered to Hungary, and saw service in the Hungarian Air Force in early World War II. A more powerful version, the Heinkel He 270, never went further than the prototype stage.

Heinkel He 118

The two-seat dive bomber He 118 had a length of 11.8 m (38 ft 9 in), a span of 15.09 m (49 ft 6.5 in), and an empty weight of 2,700 kg (5,952 lbs). First flown in late 1935 with a British Rolls-Royce Buzzard engine, the following prototypes were powered by a 910-hp Daimler-Benz DB 600C inverted-V-12, liquid-cooled engine. The aircraft had a maximum speed of 395 km/h (245 mph) and a range of 1,050 km (652 miles). Armed with two MG 17 machine guns mounted in the wings, and one MG 15 machine gun in rear cockpit, it could carry a bomb load of 500 kg (1,102 lbs). In spite of its modern appearance, the all-metal monoplane with retractable landing gear failed to attract the RLM's attention. Only a few He 118s were built, some of which were used by the Heinkel company to test the HeS 3A turbojet engine in 1939.

Junkers Ju 87

In early 1935, the *Technisches Amt* of the RLM gave Arado, Heinkel, and Junkers specifications for a new dive-bomber and tasked them each with designing and building a prototype. Within three months the Ju 87 V1 was undergoing test flight at Dessau. Thus was born the two-seat dive bomber and close-support Ju 87, which became one of the most

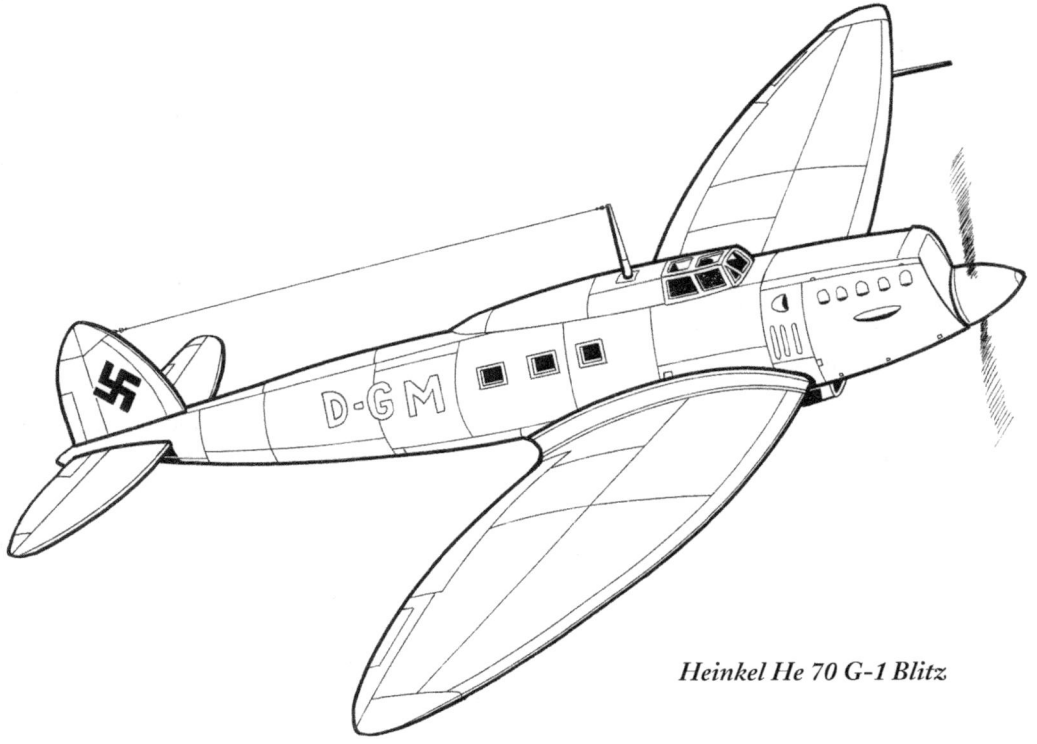

Heinkel He 70 G-1 Blitz

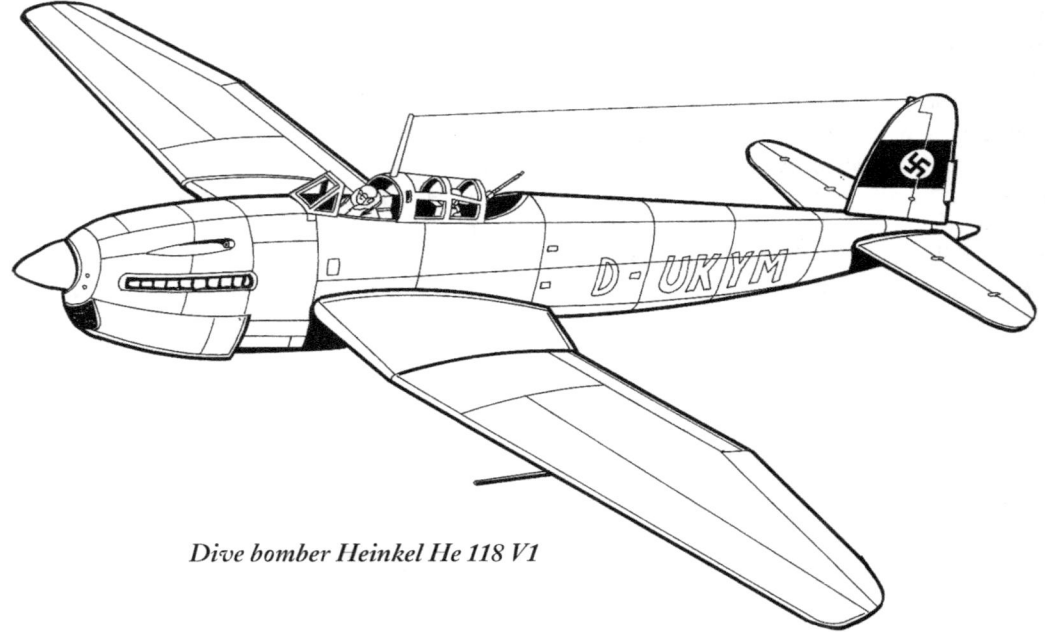

Dive bomber Heinkel He 118 V1

famous warplanes of history, and perhaps the most potent symbol of the Luftwaffe in the victorious period 1939–40. The first Ju 87 V-1 Stuka flew in 1935, and after much development the Ju 87 A-1 was delivered in numbers from April 1937. It was an odd-looking machine resembling a bird of prey, with swept-forward, "trousered" fixed landing gear like talons. Tested with success during the Spanish Civil War, the much-improved Ju 87 B became the epitome of *Blitzkrieg* in the victorious period 1939–1941. In its heyday, the Ju 87 was the dive bomber without rival—a vital component of *Blitzkrieg*, second only to the *Panzer*. The destructive and psychological impact of the "Stuka" was enormous. Demonstrating amazing pinpoint accuracy of less than 30 yards, they opened the way for the Panzer divisions, supported infantry assaults, blasted the enemy's front-line defenses, destroyed communications, prevented counterattacks, and—vividly remembered by all—attacked hapless columns of refugees and retreating troops whose panic paralyzed morale, and further hindered all efforts to mount a cohesive defense. The Ju 87 B was powered by a 1,100-hp Junkers Jumo 211 12-cylinder inverted-V liquid-cooled engine; it had a typical speed of 390 km/h (242 mph) and a range of 600 km (373 miles). It had W-form cranked wing with a span of 13.8 m (45 ft 3 in), a length of 11.1 m (36 ft 5 in), a height of 3.9 m (12 ft 9 in), and an empty weight of 2,750 kg (6.080 lb). It had a high cockpit canopy for a crew of two (pilot and observer/rear gunner), a square tail and fixed, "spatted" undercarriage. The aircraft was armed with two fixed 7.92-mm MG 17 machine guns mounted in the wings, and one flexible-mounted 7.92-mm MG 15 (later a twin 7.92-mm MG 81Z) machine gun manually aimed by the observer in the rear cockpit. It could carry four 50-kg (110-lb) bombs on wing racks, and one 500-kg (1,102-lb) bomb on centerline; these were carried on pivoting arms, and at the bottom of the screaming dive, these swung the bomb clear of the three-bladed propeller. The aircraft was sturdily designed to stand up to enormous stresses generated by repeated 6-G pull-outs from vertical dives. It had an automatic device (almost an autopilot) to ensure proper pull-out from the very steep dive, in case the pilot would black out and otherwise lose control. It had air brakes in the form of hinged plates under the wings to keep the speed down when diving, allowing the pilot more time to aim. Sirens were installed to strike even greater terror into those attacked.

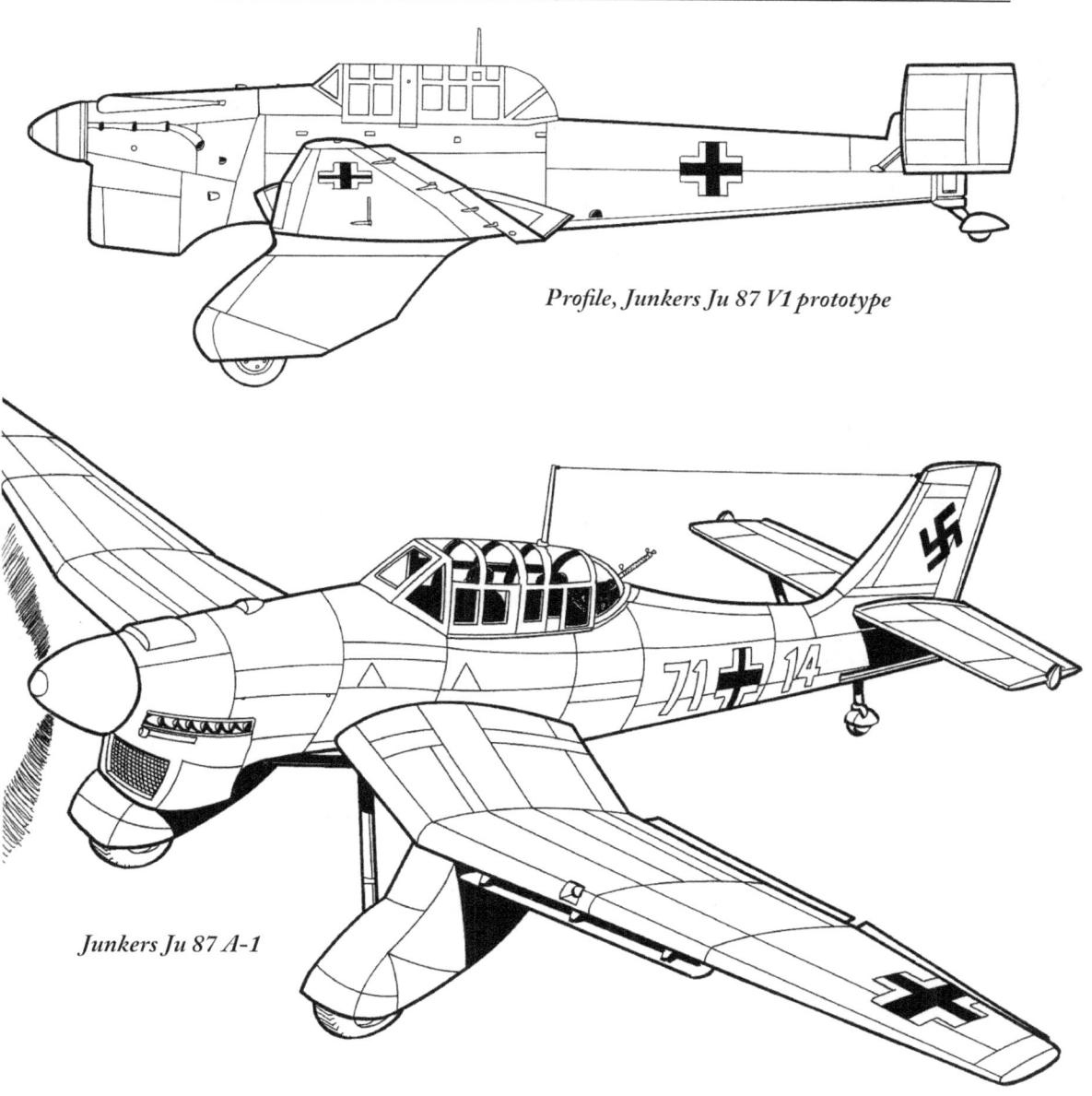

Profile, Junkers Ju 87 V1 prototype

Junkers Ju 87 A-1

Though a relatively slow airplane, the vulnerability of the Ju 87 was not an issue as long as the sky was free of enemy fighters. During the Battle of Britain in summer 1940, when first facing the top-class fighter Spitfire, the Ju 87 proved to be an easy target and soon had to be withdrawn to areas where the Axis still enjoyed some air superiority. Despite popular belief, the aircraft, although obsolete and much too slow by 1940, was not phased out after its disastrous commitment in the Battle of Britain. Still effective, it continued to see service in all theaters of operation. In fact, there was no plane to replace it, though several were intended, like the Junkers Ju 187 and the Messerschmitt Me 210 (the latter never overcame design faults). Due to its poor speed and light defensive armament, the Ju 87 was particularly vulnerable to fighter opposition, but where the Luftwaffe enjoyed complete control of the air it was still useful. In 1941 the "Stuka" wrought havoc on British ships in the Mediterranean and North African fronts. In 1942–43, its main work was close

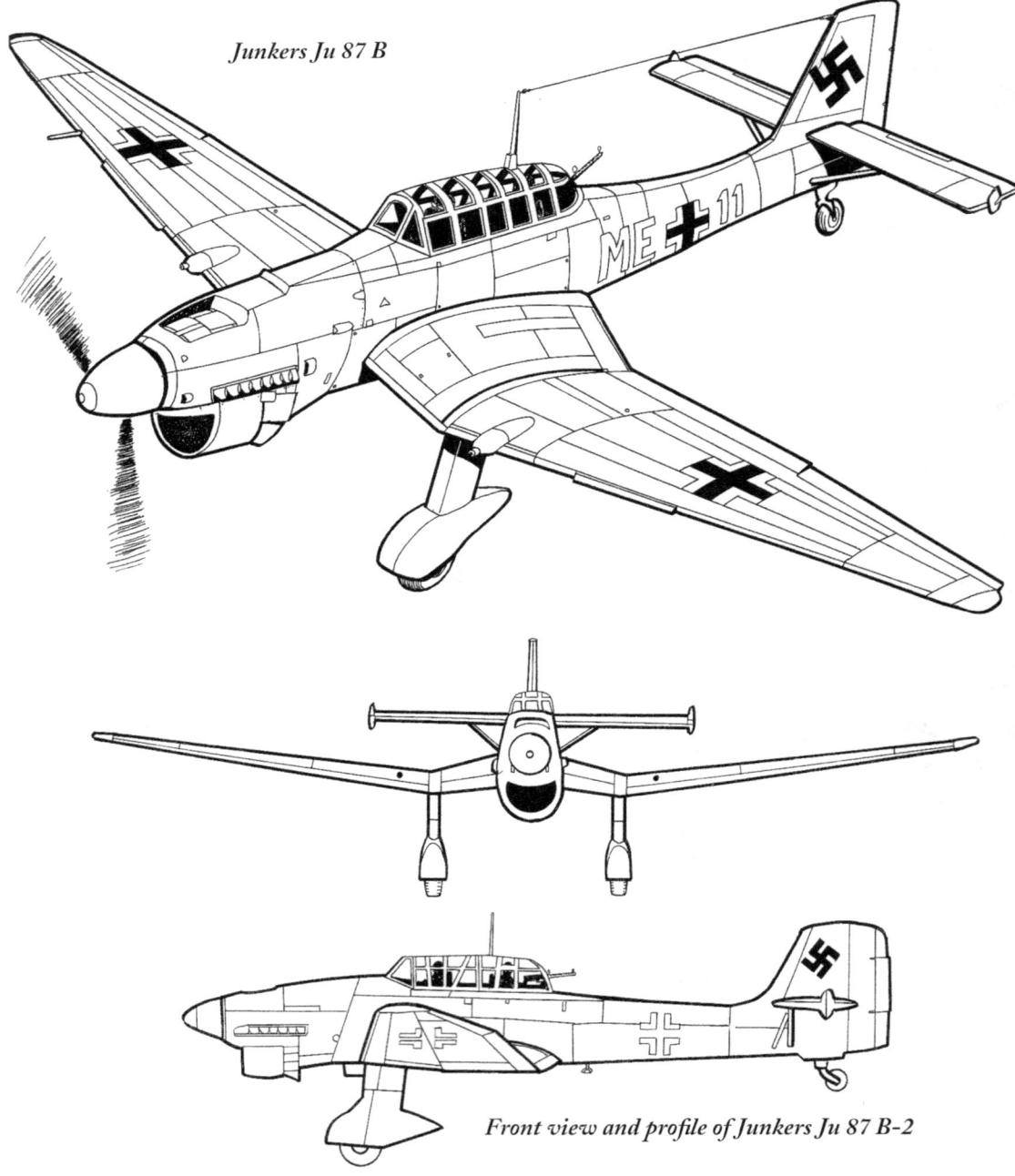

Junkers Ju 87 B

Front view and profile of Junkers Ju 87 B-2

support on the Russian front, restricted when possible to night operations with large, flame-damping exhaust pipes. The very characteristic wheel spats (mudguards) were often removed to facilitate operation away from mud- or snow-covered airfields. It was not until mid-1943 that the Stukas were seriously menaced by a new generation of Soviet fighters. The Ju 87, which should have been phased out of service long before it was, was never replaced. It was produced in several versions, but the whole program was totally unplanned. Output was always being tapered off, only to be suddenly boosted to meet urgent demands.

The JU 87 B model was fitted with a variety of conversion sets including better radio, armor, skis, and many other improvements; it could also be used as a glider tug, and there was a "tropical" subtype with engine fitted with sand filter for use in Northern Africa; however, due to difficulty of maintenance in desert conditions, the Ju 87 B Trop's engine had a life of sixty to seventy hours flying, compared to the 200 encountered in normal European conditions. The T-version (*Trager*—carrier) was a proposal for a carrier-borne conversion intended for the aircraft carrier *Graf Zepellin*; this modified Ju 87 B-1, intended to carry torpedoes, featured folding wings to save storage space, a deck-landing hook placed at the tail, and detachable landing gear for eventual ditching in the sea. Only a few converted Ju 87Ts were made, as the one and only German aircraft carrier was never completed. The R-variant was basically a Ju 87 B version with facilities for fitting external wing-drop fuel tanks enabling a range of 1,000 km (620 miles). The improved D-version had a slightly more aerodynamic fuselage with a refined engine cowling, and redesigned cockpit line; it could carry an increased bomb load, had a greater range, and could mount various weapons, notably two underwing WB 81 containers each housing six MG 81 guns. The Ju 87-G, a modified D-variant, was a formidable tank buster which achieved astounding success. It was armed with two 37-mm Flak 18 (BK 3.7 cm) cannons mounted under the wings, which could penetrate the armor of a tank, but the weight and drag caused by the guns further reduced the airplane's already marginal performances. The Ju 87 H was a dual-control trainer. Various models served with the Italian, Slovakian, Romanian and Hungarian air forces. Junkers Ju 87s, although of a totally outmoded design, were built until 1944 by Junkers and subcontracted to Weser Flugzeugbau, and components were manufactured by SNCASO in France. After 1943, they were progressively replaced by the Focke-Wulf Fw 190, Messerschmitt Me 410, and Henschel Hs 129. Production halted in September 1944 but many remained in use until the end of the war, after a total of about 5,700 units had been built.

Junkers Ju 87 G

Junkers Ju 187

The Ju 187 was an attempt made to modernize the venerable Junkers Ju 87 which, by the time of the Battle of Britain in 1940, had displayed disastrous shortcomings. The new Ju 187 kept some of the features of the earlier Ju 87, notably full-metal construction, dive brakes, and gull wings, but it was faster, better armed and better armored. It was powered by one Jumo 213A 12-cylinder, liquid-cooled engine which developed 1,750 horsepower at take-off. The Ju 187 had two particular features: it was fitted with a retractable landing gear and a very novel reversible vertical tail. This most unusual feature could be moved 180 degrees in flight, thus clearing the field of fire for the remote-controlled rear-top turret, armed with one 151/20 20-mm cannon and one MG 131 13-mm machine gun. The bomb load consisted of one 500-kg (1102-lb) bomb attached under the fuselage, and two 50-kg (110-lb) bombs on racks under each wing on either side of the landing-gear bulges. Wind-tunnel models and a full-sized mock-up were built, but the design was soon abandoned. The projected performance of the new Ju 187 was not that much of an improvement from the old Ju 87. Besides, fast fighter-bombers (e.g., the Focke-Wulf Fw 190F series) could fulfill the task of dive bombers as well as, even better than this highly specialized aircraft.

Focke-Wulf Fw 57

The Fw 57 was a prototype fighter bomber built in 1936 as a RLM requirement for a *Kampfzerstörer* (bomber destroyer), a tactical multi-role fighter/bomber. Focke-Wulf submitted the Fw 57, Messerschmitt submitted the Bf 110 and Henschel produced the Hs 124. The Fw 57 was larger than its two competitors but suffered from overweight and poor handling. In the end, the Messerschmitt Bf 110 proved to be the winner. The Focke-Wulf Fw 57 never saw production, and only three prototypes, V1, V2 and V3, were completed during 1936. "V" was short for *Versuchs* (experimental prototype). All further research into the Fw 57 was abandoned and dropped shortly thereafter. The Focke-Wulf Fw 57 had a crew of three (pilot, navigator, and rear-gunner), a length of 16.57 m (54 ft 4⅓ in), a wingspan of 25 m (82 ft), a height of 4.08 m (13 ft 5¼ in), a wing area of 73.5 square m (791.17 square ft), and an empty weight of 6,800 kg (14.991 lbs). Powerplant was two Daimler-Benz DB 600A inverted-V-12 (each developing 910 hp), maximum speed was 404 km/h (251 mph), and service ceiling was 9,100 m (29,855 ft). The proposed armament was three 20-mm MG FF cannons (two mounted in the nose and one in a Mauser electric dorsal turret operated by the rear-gunner). Six 100-kg (220-lb) bombs could be carried.

Henschel Hs 124

Designed in late 1934, the Hs 124 was intended to be a Luftwaffe fast ground attacker/light bomber for reconnaissance and close support. The aircraft was all-metal, had a crew of three (pilot, navigator, and rear-gunner), and had a span of 18.19 m (59 ft 8.5 in), a length

Junkers Ju 187

4. Bombers

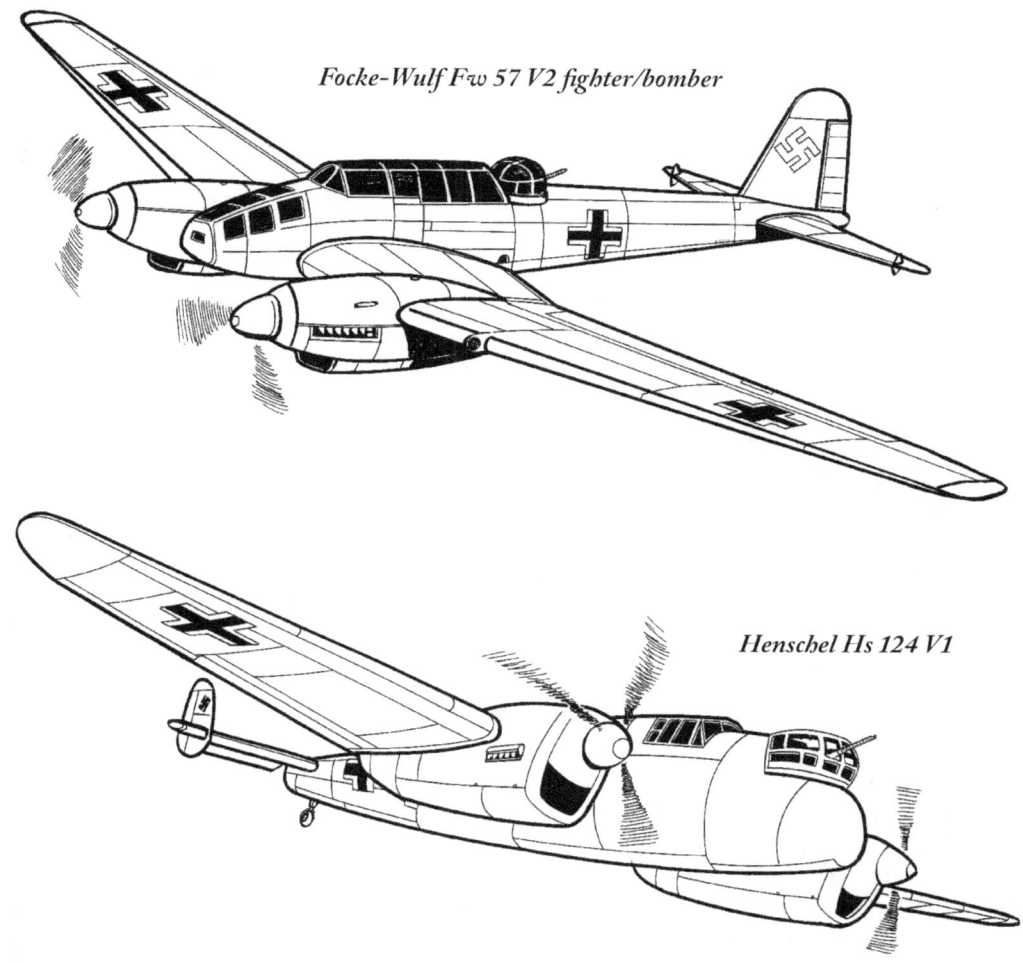

Focke-Wulf Fw 57 V2 fighter/bomber

Henschel Hs 124 V1

of 14.50 m (47 ft 6.7 in), and an empty weight of 4,240 kg (9,347 lbs). Only three units were built, flying in spring 1936. The experimental prototype V1 was powered by two 640-hp Jumo 210C inverted-V, 12-cylinder engines, and the other two (V2 and V3) by two 880-hp BMW 132DC 9-cylinder radial engines. Maximum speed was 440 km/h (273 mph) and maximum range was 4,200 km (2,610 miles). Prototype V1 had a dummy nose machine-gun turret, and V2 a blunt, glazed nose. The project was not further developed, as the Luftwaffe chose the Messerschmitt Bf 110 for its standard heavy fighter/light bomber.

Messerschmitt Bf 110

Designed in 1934 by Willy Messerschmitt's Bayerische Flugzeugwerke (Bf), the first Bf 110 V1 prototype flew in May 1936. An aircraft of very mixed fortune, the wartime-production Bf 110C joined the German air force in early 1939. The strategic fighter was intended to perform as a heavily armed escort fighter to accompany bombers deep into enemy territory, blasting a path through all opposition, and raiding deep into enemy heartland. Seen as offering a multi-role capability, and complementing their primary force of single-engined light fighters, the heavily armed twin-engined Bf 110 raised considerable enthusiasm and high expectations. Special *Zerstörer* (destroyer) wings were formed, and regarded so highly that most of the best fighter pilots were posted to them. The two-seat, twin-engined monoplane Bf 110 had a span of 16.25 m (53 ft 5 in), a length of 12.1 m (39 ft 8.5 in), a height of 3.5 m (11 ft 6 in) and an empty weight of 4,500 kg (9,920

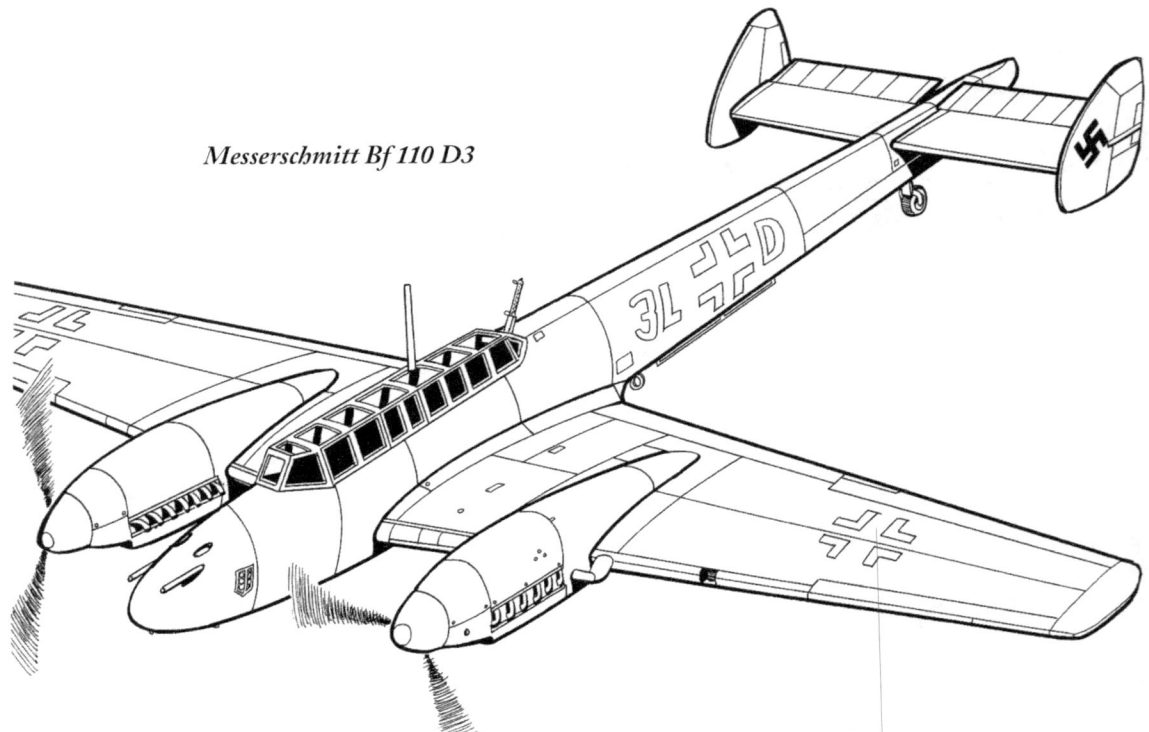

Messerschmitt Bf 110 D3

lbs). Powered by two 1,100-hp Daimler-Benz DB 610A engines, it had a speed of 562 km/h (349 mph), and a range of 850 km (528 miles) but this could be significantly increased to 700 miles by jettisoning underwing fuel tanks. Armament was formidable, including two forward-firing 20-mm Oerlikon MGFF cannons (placed in ventral position), four forward-firing Rheinmetall 7.92-mm MG 17 machine guns (fixed in the nose), and one 7.92-mm MG 15 manually aimed in rear cockpit. Four 250-kg (551-lb) bombs could be carried in underwing racks.

Right before the war a photograph appeared in the German press, showing the new Messerschmitt bomber Me 210 Jaguar; this was an elaborate hoax (in fact a Bf 110 with a glazed nose photographically superimposed) to fool the British and the French. Too late to be tested in the Spanish Civil War, the Messerschmitt Bf 110 met its requirements and, despite unimpressive maneuverability, performed extremely well in the close-support role in the Polish, Norwegian, Dutch and French campaigns. The Battle of Britain, however, proved a turning point in the Messerschmitt Bf 110 heavy fighter's career. Lacking a powerful rear defensive armament, agility and acceleration ability to cope with the opposing fast, agile and modern single-engine British fighters, it proved itself almost as vulnerable to Spitfires and Hurricanes as were the bombers it was suppose to protect. Suffering heavy losses, the result was that the escort Bf 110s themselves had to be escorted by Bf 109 fighters. As a long-range fighter/light bomber, the Bf 110 was a flop. Despite this setback and its ultimate failure in its originally intended role, the Messerschmitt Bf 110s continued to serve in all theaters. Improved D and E versions with many improved sub-types performed in various roles in 1941 and 1942, in less dangerous skies in the Balkans, North Africa and Russia, including ground and shipping attacks, light bomber runs, glider tug work, and long-range reconnaissance. By 1942, production was scheduled to end, and the aging Bf 110 was supposed to be replaced by the new Messerschmitt Me 210. The failure of the latter led to the Bf 110 being reinstated (G version) and modified well beyond its original design. Though outdated in 1943, the Bf 110 G was

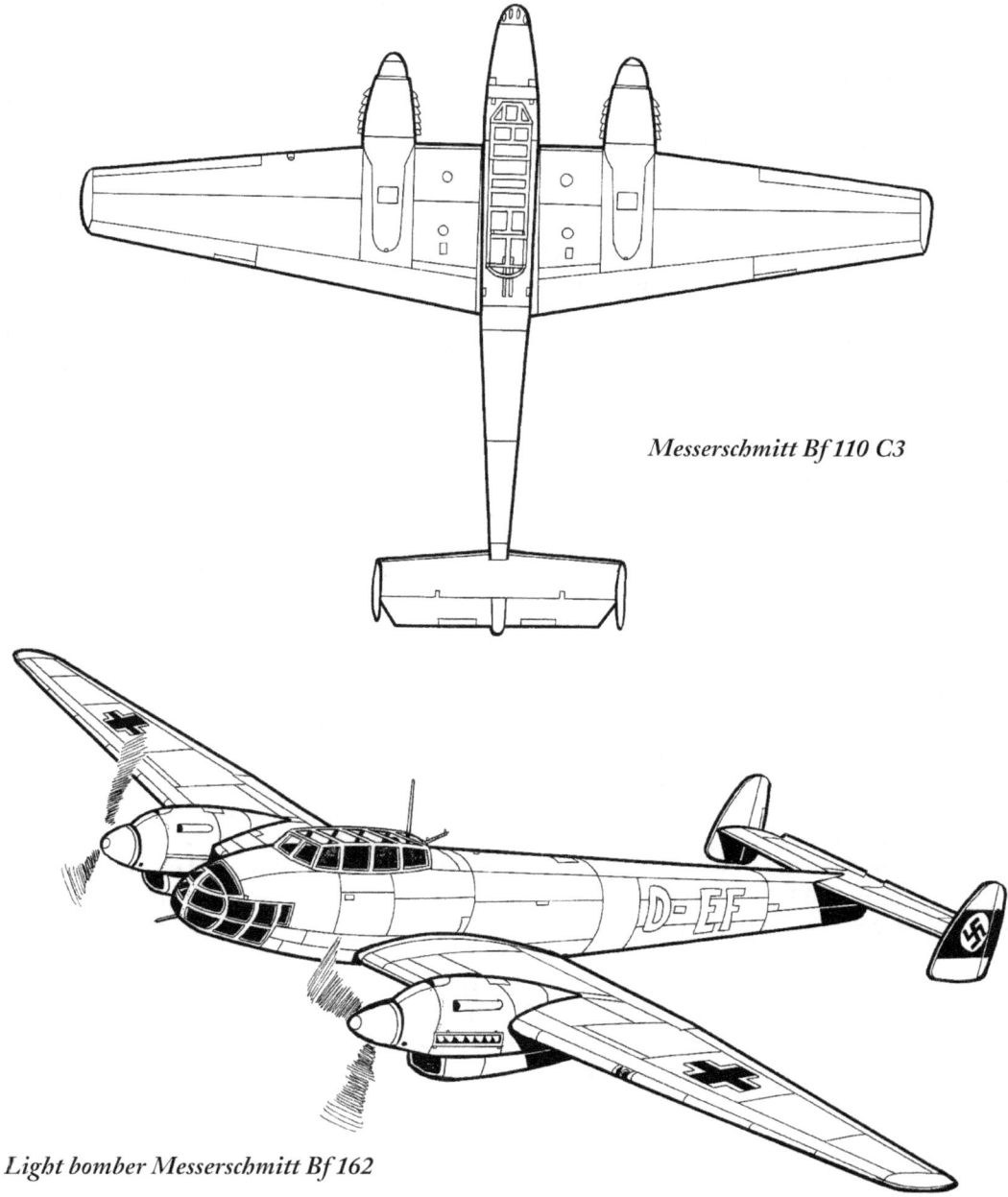

Messerschmitt Bf 110 C3

Light bomber Messerschmitt Bf 162

built in larger numbers than all other versions combined. The type found its true niche in the defensive role in which its heavy armament, long range, and ability to carry airborne radar made the Bf 110 useful again. Away from opposition fighters, its destroyer capabilities could work once more. Mainly used as night fighter, the improved G version was powered by two 1,475-hp Daimler-Benz DB B engines, and fitted with flame dampers on the exhausts. Mounting Lichtenstein radar, heavy MG 151 oblique-firing *Schräge Musik* guns (and eventually 21-cm rocket tubes), the Bf 110 achieved remarkable successes as much as a night fight as day interceptor. That was to change when the Bf 110's nemesis, long-range escort single-engine fighters (P-47 or P 51 for example), returned to the scene. By March 1944, due to heavy losses, the Bf 110 was forced to withdraw from the daylight air war above Germany. A final version (Bf 110 H ground attacker) was produced in February 1945, after a total of 6,050 of all types had been manufactured.

Messerschmitt Bf 161 and Bf 162

These two aircraft, derived from the mass-produced Messerschmitt Bf 110, were quite similar, with only a slightly different glazed nose arrangement. The Bf 161 was intended to be a reconnaissance airplane and the Bf 162 a fast light bomber/ground attacker. They were powered with two 986-hp Daimler-Benz DB 601 A inverted-V-12 liquid-cooled engines; they had a maximum speed of 480 km/h (298 mph) and a range of 780 km (485 miles). Span was 17.16 m (56 ft 3.5 in), length was 12.75 m (41 ft 10 in), and empty weight was 4,400 kg (9,700 lbs). They had a crew of three. Proposed armament consisted of two MG 15 machine guns. The Bf 162 could carry ten 50-kg (110-lb) bombs and eventually two additional 250-kg (551-lb) bombs. First flown in 1937, they never made it, as the RLM preferred the Junkers Ju 88 because of the high production pressure on Messerschmitt (Bf 109 and Bf 110). Material for these airplanes were used in the Bf 110 production. Only three test prototypes were made in 1937 and 1938. Bf 162 prototype V1 was scrapped after trials. V2 and V3 were eventually later used for research.

Messerschmitt Me 210 and Me 410

Submitted to the RLM in mid-1937 as a more powerful and more versatile replacement to the Bf 110, the Messerschmitt Me 210 seemed on paper to be an extremely useful aircraft. It had a crew of two (pilot and observer sitting back-to-back), a length of 12.22 m (40 ft 3 in), a span of 16.4 m (53 ft 7.7 in), a height of 4.3 m (14 ft) and an empty weight of 5,440 kg (12,000 lbs). It was powered by two Daimler-Benz DB 603A 12-cylinder liquid-cooled inverted-V engines, each developing 1,850 hp, and had a maximum speed of 620 km/h (385 mph) and a range of 2,400 km (1,491 miles). Armament was various but basically included four forward-firing 20-mm MG 151 cannons, and two 13-mm MG 131 in remotely-controlled barbettes (blisters) firing aft; these rear-firing barbettes, operated by the radio operator/observer, were complicated to use, and rather ineffective and inaccurate in combat. Two 500-kg (1,102-lb) bombs were carried in external wing racks or internal bomb bay in a specialized version. Dive brakes permitted the airplane to be used as a dive-bomber. The Me 210 was a product of Göring's misplaced faith in the *Zerstörer* concept. An order for 1,000 units was placed before the project even left the drawing board. The first Me 210 (then fitted with twin fins) flew in September 1939, but the type proved extremely disappointing, unstable and subject to structural failure. In spite of several notably good points, it did not prove as successful as hoped. It was however used on the Russian and Mediterranean fronts in the fighter/bomber and reconnaissance role. After many accidents at an unacceptable rate, production was stopped in April 1942 after 550 units were manufactured. The Me 210's failure represented a considerable financial loss to the firm, and caused much tension between Willy

Messerschmitt Me 210 A-1

Messerschmitt and Hitler who threatened to put the company under state control. The fiasco resulted in pressure for Willy Messerschmitt to resign from the position as chairman and managing director. Despite these problems, development work continued, as the Messerschmitt Company had become the largest aircraft builder in Germany and could survive the flop of the Me 210.

After complete redesign, the Me 210 re-emerged in 1943 as the Me 410 *Hornisse* (hornet). Although quite similar in appearance to the Me 210, the Me 410 incorporated many modifications, namely adapted tailfin and lengthened fuselage, overcoming the Me 210's longitudinal stability problems, and two Daimler-Benz DB 603G 12-cylinder, liquid-cooled engines, each developing 1,900 hp. The result was a greatly improved aircraft. The Me 410, engaged in operational service in May 1943, achieved more success than its predecessor and served in a reconnaissance role (then fitted with cameras), and with various armaments as torpedo attacker, glide-bomb carrier, intruder, bomber/destroyer, and night fighter.

The Me 410, in spite of technical innovation and powerful armament, was never a pronounced success, and production stopped in 1944, after over 1,160 units were produced. After the Allied landing in Normandy in June 1944, all Messerschmitt Me 410s were withdrawn from combat operation.

Messerschmitt Me 329

Following the failure of the Me 210 heavy fighter aircraft (which, as seen above, was upgraded to the Me 410 by lengthening the fuselage and adding more powerful engines), a search was begun on a new design for a twin-engine heavy fighter. Professor Alexander Lippisch began work on his Li P 10, and at the same time Dr. Hermann Wurster independently developed the 329. After both submitted their ideas, Willy Messerschmitt asked to have a performance comparison drawn up between the Li P 10, Me 329 and Me 410. There were high hopes for the tailless Me 329, and some of the roles envisioned were heavy fighter, escort fighter, night fighter, dive bomber, fighter/

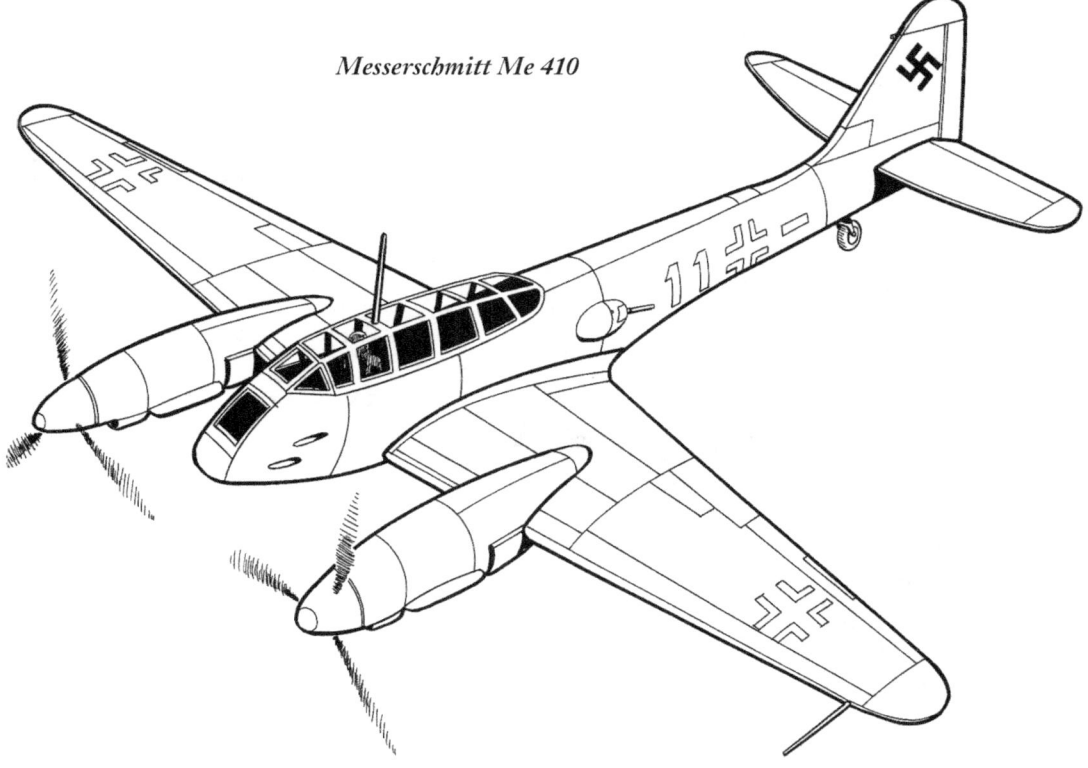

Messerschmitt Me 410

bomber, and reconnaissance role. The Me 329 was to be constructed mainly of wood. This would save on strategic materials and keep the weight low. As many components of the Me 410 were to be used as possible to save time on factory retooling. The large-area wing was swept back at approximately 26 degrees, it had a span of 17.5 m (57 ft 6 in) and a wing area of 55 square m (592 square ft). The purpose of the swept wing (one in which the angle between the wing leading-edge and the centerline of the rear fuselage forms an angle of less than 90 degrees) was to delay the drag rise caused by the formation of shock waves, thus enabling the plane to be flown at high speed without the onset of buffeting. Two Daimler-Benz DB 603 G or Jumo 213 piston engines were mounted in the rear of the wings, each driving a 3.4-meter (11.2-ft) three-bladed propeller in "pusher" arrangement. The aircraft had a range of 4,450 km (2,765 miles) and a maximum speed of 792 km/h (492 mph). The fuselage had a length of 7.7 m (25 ft 4 in), and a height of 4.74 m (15 ft 6 in). A single large fin and rudder was mounted at the rear. The main landing gear retracted forward, and the twin-wheeled front gear retracted to the rear. A two-man crew sat under an extensively glazed cockpit, with the pilot and navigator/rear gunner sitting in a staggered, side-by-side arrangement. The Messerschmitt Me 329's armament would have consisted of four MG 151/20 20-mm cannon mounted in the nose, and two MK 103 30-mm cannon in the wing roots. A single defensive MG 151/20-20mm cannon was located in a remote-controlled barbette in the tail, which was aimed via a periscope system from the cockpit. A bomb load of 2,400 kg (5,291 lbs) could be carried in an internal bomb bay or underwing racks. Although a wooden mockup was built to check the placement of various components, production was not pursued due to the long development time for such a novel design. Besides, the Messerschmitt Me 410 was already in use in many different roles, with the upgrade additions from the Me 210. It is reported that one prototype, the Me 329 V1, was completed as an unarmed glider, and test flown at the Rechlin Test Center in early 1945.

Messerschmitt Me 265/ Lippisch Li P 10

The Messerschmitt Me 265, also known as Lippisch Li P 10, was designed in late 1942 as another alternative to the failed Messerschmitt Me 210. The aircraft was a tailless swept-wing *Zerstörer* with a crew of two, sitting back-to-back. It used the cockpit and several parts of

Messerschmitt Me 329

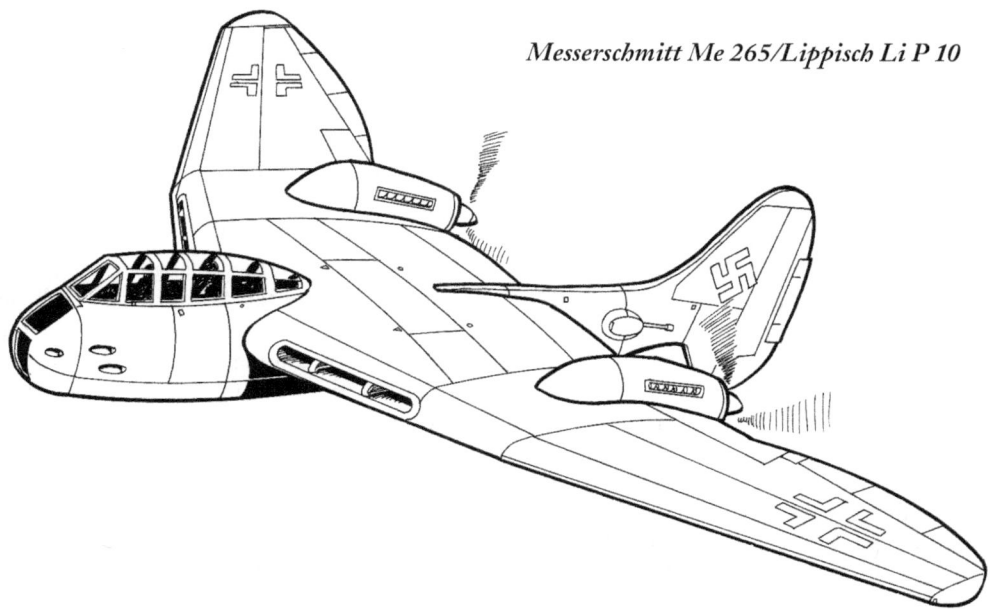

Messerschmitt Me 265/Lippisch Li P 10

the fuselage of the Me 210. Length was 10 m (32 ft 10 in), height was 3.80 m (12 ft 6 in). The delta wing was totally rebuilt with a backsweep, a span of 17.40 m (57 ft 1 in) and a flying area of 45 square meters (484.38 square ft). The aircraft was powered by two Daimler-Benz DB 603 liquid-cooled, 12-cylinder piston engines (each developing 1,750 hp) and each driving one three-bladed propeller in pusher arrangement. A maximum speed of 675 km/h (419 mph) was estimated. Armament included various cannons and machine guns mounted in the nose and two rear-firing, barbette-located, remote-controlled machine guns (similar to the Me 210). A bomb bay was placed under the fuselage. When Messerschmitt started to develop the improved Me 410, the Me 265/Li P 10 became redundant and development was stopped.

Henschel Hs 129

Designed by Henschel's engineer Friedrich Nicolaus, the Hs 129 was first flown in early 1939. The triangular-section fuselage had a length of 9.75 m (31 ft 11.7 in), a height of 3.25 m (10 ft 8 in), and the wings had a span of 14.2 m (46 ft 7 in). The aircraft was heavily armored and had an empty weight of 4,060 kg (8,940 lbs). Originally it was powered by two 495-hp Argus As 410A-1 air-cooled, inverted-V, 12-cylinder engines. The first production having proved severely underpowered, the Luftwaffe rejected it. Henschel persevered with the project and designer Nicolaus completely revised it. The next batch of Hs 129 B was fitted with captured French 690-hp Gnome-Rhône 14M 04/05 14-cylinder, two-row, air-cooled radial engines. This was an improvement but the Hs 129 B tended to suffer from underpower throughout its combat service life. It entered Luftwaffe service in 1941 as a single-seat close-support and ground-attack aircraft. Typical speed was 408 km/h (253 mph) and maximum range was 880 km (547 miles). The single pilot sat in a small, cramped, armored cockpit behind a 3-inch-thick windscreen with inadequate field of vision. If pilots were not overwhelmed by its design, performance, maneuverability and engine reliability, they were grateful for the Hs's 129 sturdiness and wide range of weapons. Armament was indeed very powerful and varied with the sub-types. The Hs 129 R1 was armed with two 7.92-mm MG 17 machine guns and two 20-mm MG 151 cannons, plus two 110-lb bombs. The Hs 129 R2 was armed with two 30-mm MK 101 cannons. The Hs 129 R3 had four MG 17 machine guns. The bomber version Hs 129 R4 carried a 551-lb bomb. The reconnaissance version Hs 129 R5 was equipped with a camera. The Hs 129 B2 was armed with various machine guns and cannons. There was also a *Panzerknacker* (tank buster) version, armed with a 75-mm *Bordkanone* (BK fixed-aircraft cannon) with muzzle about eight feet ahead of the nose. Conceived as a tank-killing warplane, the Hs 129 was so heavy and underpowered that performance was disappointing. A total of about 841 units was built, and most of these saw service on the Russian front, a few being briefly engaged in the North African campaign. Certain faults blighted the Hs 129's career, notably problems with serviceability, lack of power and poor visibility, but it did achieve limited success in the antitank role, owing to its firepower and sturdiness. The zenith of the Hs 129's career came during Operation Zitadelle, the large-scale offensive at Kursk in 1943 when it accounted for a large number of destroyed Russian armored vehicles. The limited number built and the fact that the aging Junkers Ju 87 "Stuka" (G version) was developed for the antitank role clearly suggests the failure of the Henschel Hs 129. It was a pity, however, that the Luftwaffe planners failed to fully appreciate the Hs 129's importance, and therefore did not place enough stress upon its development.

Arado Ar 240

The Arado Ar 240 was a twin-engine, multi-role *Zerstörer*/heavy fighter/light bomber aircraft developed as the response to a 1938 request for a much more capable second-generation heavy fighter to replace the Messerschmitt Bf 110. Designed by Arado's technical director Walter Blume, it had a crew of two, a length of 12.8 m (42 ft), a wingspan of 13.33 m (43 ft 9 in), a height of 3.95 m (13 ft), and an empty weight of 6,200 kg (13,669 lb). The two-engine aircraft was powered by various engines (the most used being Daimler-Benz DB 603 G inverted-V-12 liquid-cooled). Maximum speed was 618 km/h (384 mph) and range was about 2,000 km (1,240 miles). Armament included two fixed 7.92-mm MG 17 and two remote-control barbettes, each with two 7.92-mm MG 81 machine guns. A bomb load of 1,000 kg could be carried. The Ar 240 featured numerous advanced features, such as traveling flaps which offered excellent low-speed lift performance, a pressurized cock-

Henschel Hs 129 B2

Arado Ar 240

pit which dramatically lowered pilot fatigue for any flight above about 4,500m (15,000 ft), a technically advanced remote-control defensive gun system, and fuel cells in the wings which were provided with a newly developed self-sealing system that used thinner tank liners, allowing for more fuel storage. The Ar 240 made its first flight in May 1940 but immediately proved to have terrible handling in all three axes, and also tended to overheat during taxiing. Problems with the design hampered development and the Arado Ar 240 remained only in prototype phase. Two units entered service during 1941, flying reconnaissance missions over England, successfully avoiding interception due to their high speed. The project was eventually canceled in early 1942 in favor of the Messerschmitt Me 210, with the existing airframes used for a variety of test purposes at the Arado factory.

There was a redesigned variant made in late 1942, the Arado Ar 440 (also known as E 564 Scorpion), designed by Walter Blume. This had a single, vertical, high-mounted fin and rudder and was powered by two Daimler-Benz DB 614 engines. The Ar 440 *Schnellbomber* showed promising test results but was rejected in the 1944 production program in favor of Dornier's "push-pull" Do 335. Like the Ar 240, the Ar 440 was not developed, and Allied air intelligence commented in August 1944, "Thank the German Luftwaffe for not having accepted this aircraft."

Focke-Wulf Fw 187 Falke

The heavy fighter/*Zerstörer* Fw 187 *Falke* (Falcon) made its first flight in May 1937, having been designed without an RLM specification. Powered by two Junkers Jumo 210 inverted-V-12, liquid-cooled, 680-hp engines, it had a maximum speed of 525 km/h (326 mph). It had a span of 15.30 m (50 ft 2.5 in), a length of 11 m (36 ft 5 in), and an empty weight of 3,700 kg (11,023 lbs). Its armament consisted of four 7.92-mm MG 17 machine guns placed in the nose and two 20-mm MG FF cannons positioned under the nose. Fast, maneuverable and hard-hitting, the *Falke* was operated by a single pilot. It was a nice machine that could have been the basis for a series of multi-role aircraft. Probably because it was too short to accommodate rear armament, because its cabin was so small and narrow, and because of difficulty in getting engines, it did not attract attention. Instead, the Messerschmitt Bf 110 was chosen by the RLM to fulfill the role of Luftwaffe standard heavy

Focke-Wulf Fw 187 Falke

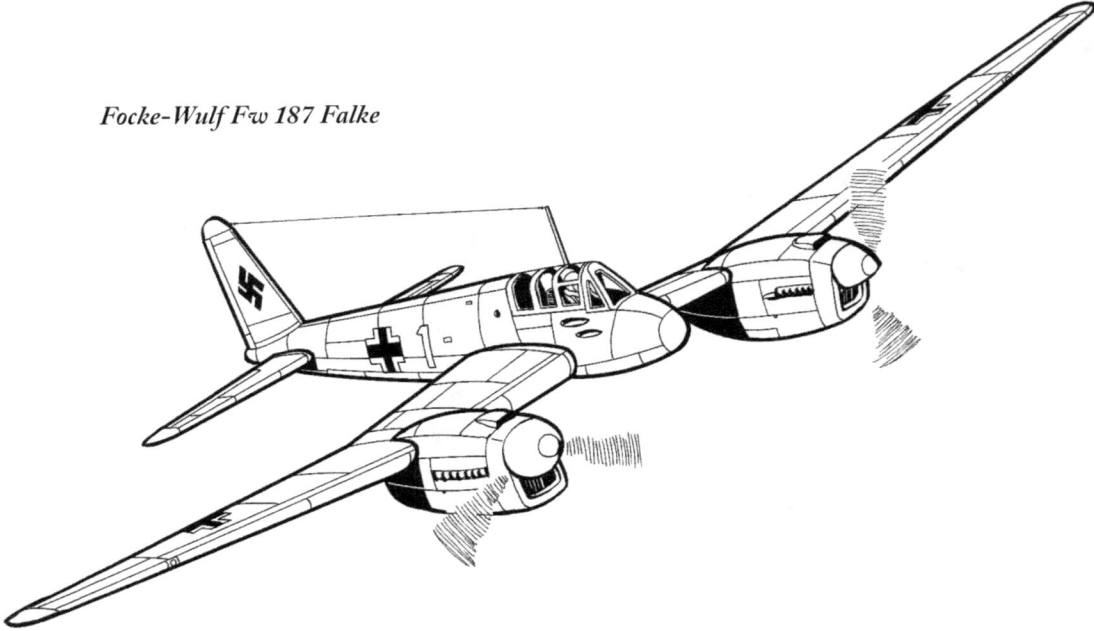

fighter/*Zerstörer*. Only three Fw 187s were manufactured, though some sources say twelve were produced. They were engaged in the war in Norway in the winter of 1940-41 and performed rather well. They were later used by the Focke-Wulf Company to defend its Bremen plants from Allied attacks, but their further fate remains unknown.

Unconventional Stuka and *Zerstörer*

Arado E 500

Designed in 1936 as a heavy fighter/ground attacker, the Arado E 500 had a short gondola-like fuselage and two Daimler-Benz DB 603 engines mounted on twin nacelle/tailbooms. The aircraft, for which no data is available, was to be operated by a crew of four (pilot, co-pilot/observer, and two gunners), and was to be armed with two turrets. The upper dorsal turret was manned by a gunner operating two 20-mm Rh LB 202 cannons. The ventral

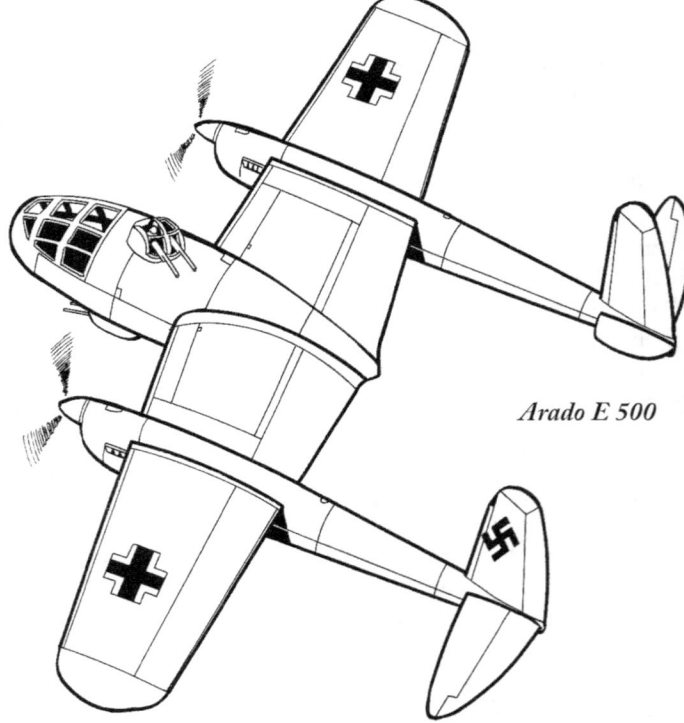

Arado E 500

turret had the same guns and was to be operated by another gunner from a prone position using a periscope for aiming. A full-size mock-up was built, but the design was soon abandoned.

Arado Ar E 530

The Arado Ar E 530 was a design for a single-seat, fast light bomber/ground attacker. It had a twin fuselage with a length of 14.15 m (46 ft 5.5 in) and a wingspan of 16.25 m (53 ft 4.2 in). The single pilot sat in a pressurized cockpit placed in the port fuselage. The aircraft was powered by two Daimler-Benz DB 603 G 12-cylinder engines and was intended to have a speed of 770 km/h (648 mph). Owing to its speed, it was expected not to be intercepted and thus featured no defensive armament. A bomb load of 500 kg (1,100 lbs) was to be carried in a rack placed under the center wing section. Offering no appreciable advantage over existing models, the E 530 design was not continued.

Hütter Hü 136

Conceived by the glider designers Ulrich and Wolfgang Hütter right before the start of World War II, the Hü 136 was intended to be a *Sturzbomber* (*Stubo*, for short—dive bomber). Two versions were designed by the brothers.

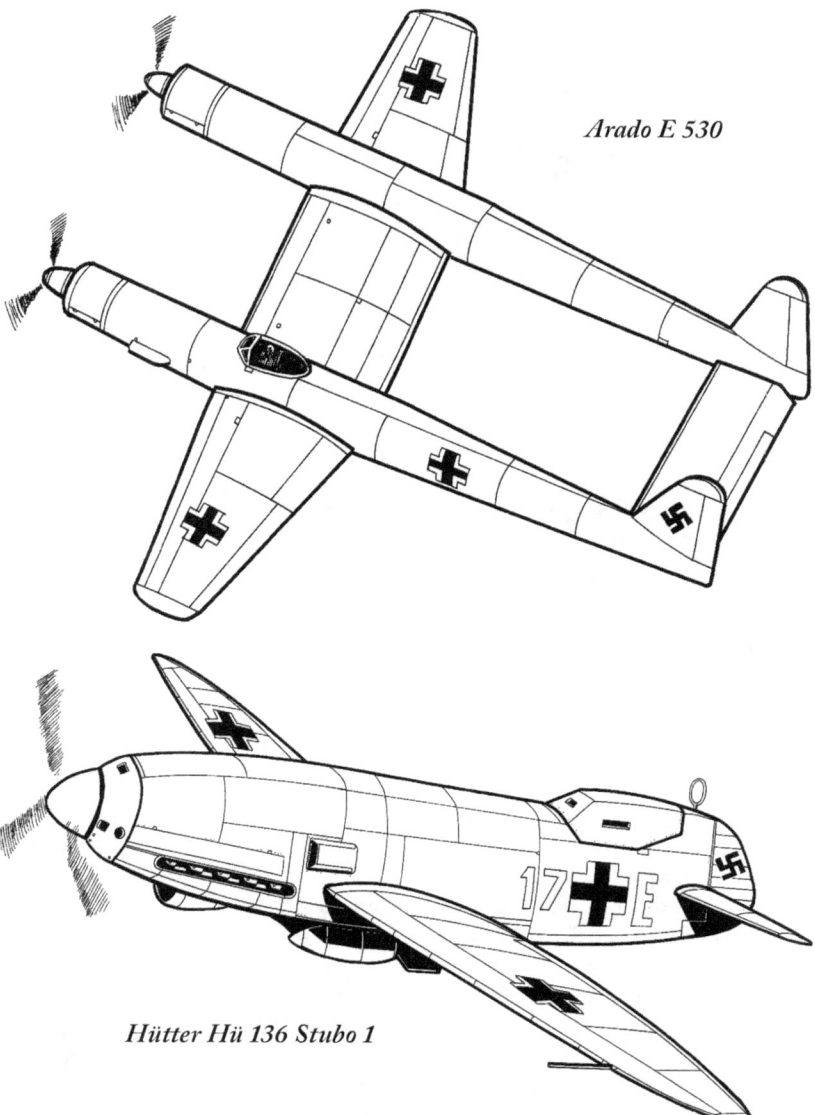

Arado E 530

Hütter Hü 136 Stubo 1

Stubo 1 had a stressed airframe and armored fuselage with a length of 7.2 m (23 ft 8 in), and small, low and elliptical-shaped wings with a span of 6.5 m (21 ft 4 in). The pilot sat in a small, heavily armored cockpit fitted with only small slits, located at the rear of the fuselage right in front of a single fin and rudder. For the sake of saving weight, the Hü 136 was not fitted with a proper landing gear. The aircraft took off on a jettisonable trolley, and landed on a belly skid after the propeller was detached and dropped by parachute for later reuse. Strabo 1 was powered by a single 1200-hp Daimler-Benz DB601 in-line piston engine, with a maximum speed of 560 km/h (348 mph) and a range of 2,000 km (1,242 miles). The aircraft was to be armed with forward-firing machine guns placed above the engine cowling, and would carry one 500-kg (1,102-lb) bomb placed on a rack under the fuselage.

Stubo 2 had exactly the same features but the fuselage was lengthened to accommodate an internal bomb bay for a bomb load of 1,000 kg (2,205 lbs). The Hütter dive-bomber did

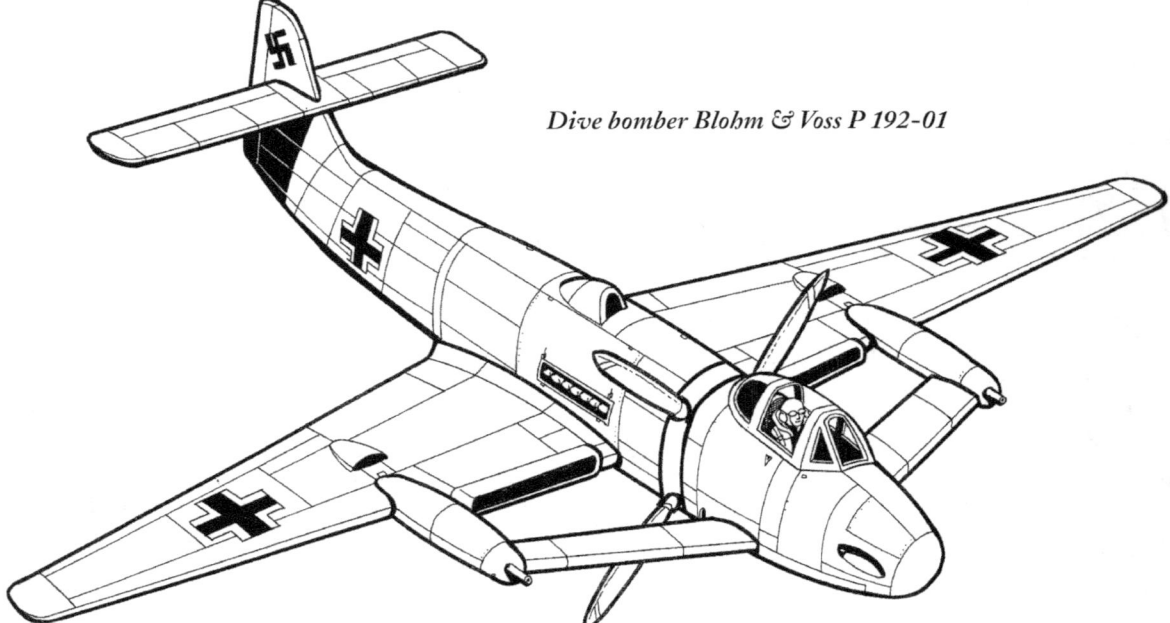

Dive bomber Blohm & Voss P 192-01

not reach the specifications set down by the RLM. The aircraft was rejected, and never materialized further than the design board.

Blohm & Voss P 192-01

The project P 192-01 for a dive bomber had a length of 11.7 m (42 ft 8.2 in) and a span of 11.7 m (42 ft 8.2 in). The single pilot sat in a cockpit placed at the front and supported by two booms projecting from the wing leading edge. The most unusual feature was the propellers placed right behind the cockpit, powered by a Daimler-Benz DB 603 G engine located at mid-fuselage. The dive bomber would carry a bomb load of 500 kg (1,100 lb) and was to be armed with two MG 151/20 20-mm cannons located in the nose and two MG 151/20 20-mm cannons placed in the twin booms which supported the nose. This odd design never made it off the drawing board.

Blohm & Voss Bv P 170

This odd, three-engine fast bomber was designed by Dr. Richard Vogt in 1942. It was powered by three BMW 801D radial engines, one located on the front of the fuselage, and the other two mounted on wingtip gondolas, each with a single vertical fin and rudder placed at the rear. The two outside engines rotated in opposite directions to help cancel out excessive torque. The airplane was operated by two airmen, pilot and radio-operator/observer, who sat in a cockpit located in the extreme rear of the center fuselage. The landing gear consisted of three retractable wheeled legs placed just aft of each engine and a taildragger placed at the back of the central fuselage. Maximum speed would have been 820 km/h (472 mph), maximum operating ceiling 11,650 m (38,222 ft) and range 2,000 km (1,243 miles). The aircraft was meant to carry a bomb load of 2,000 kg (4,400 lbs) in underwing mountings. Owing to the impressively high maximum speed, it was acknowledged that the aircraft could not be intercepted so no defensive armament was planned.

Blohm & Voss P 193-01

The Project 193-01 was a design for a ground attack/dive bomber. This aircraft had a span of 11.4 m (37 ft 5.2 in), and a length of 10.3 m (33 ft 9.8 in). The wing had a straight leading edge and tapered trailing edge. The aircraft would have been powered by one Jumo 213A piston engine driving a pusher propeller

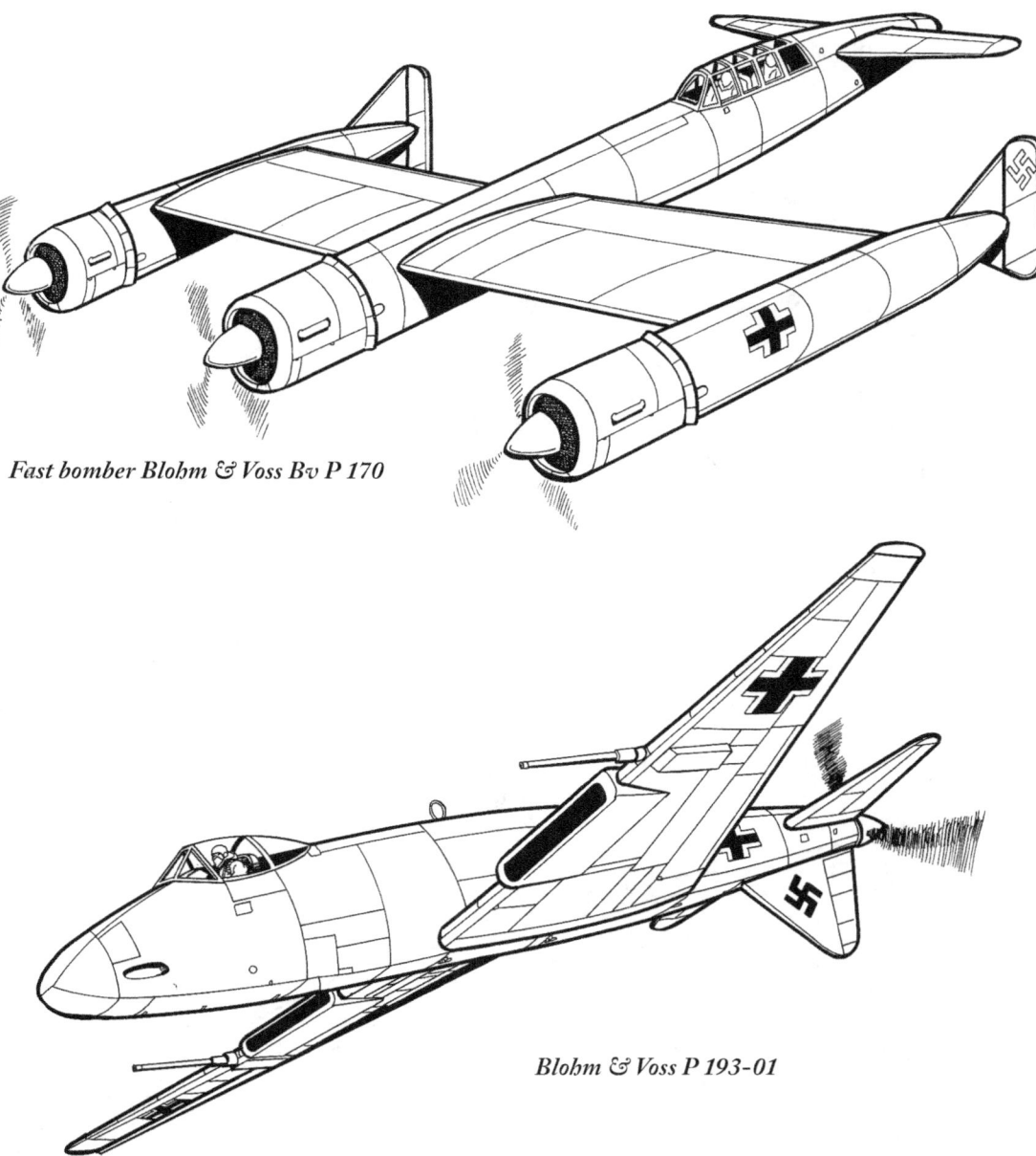

Fast bomber Blohm & Voss Bv P 170

Blohm & Voss P 193-01

(placed at the rear) via a long shaft. A single fin and rudder was mounted beneath the fuselage to provide the rear propeller with protection and ground clearance during landing and take-off. Maximum speed would have been 570 km/h (354 mph). Projected armament included two MK 103 30-mm cannons in the wings and two MG 151/20 20-mm cannons on the nose sides. The Bv P 193-01 was intended to carry a 1,000-kg (2,200-lb) bomb load.

Junkers Ju EF 112

Designed in December 1942, the Ju EF 112 was to be a ground attack/dive bomber aircraft. (The initial EF stands for *Erprobungs-flugzeug*—test aircraft.) It was composed of a fuselage and two booms attached to the bottom of the wing surfaces containing the tail assembly. Length was 10.7 m (35 ft 1 in), span was 12.8 m (42 ft) and height was 4.1 m (13 ft 6 in). The aircraft was powered by two 1.460-

Dive bomber Blohm & Voss Bv P 193-01

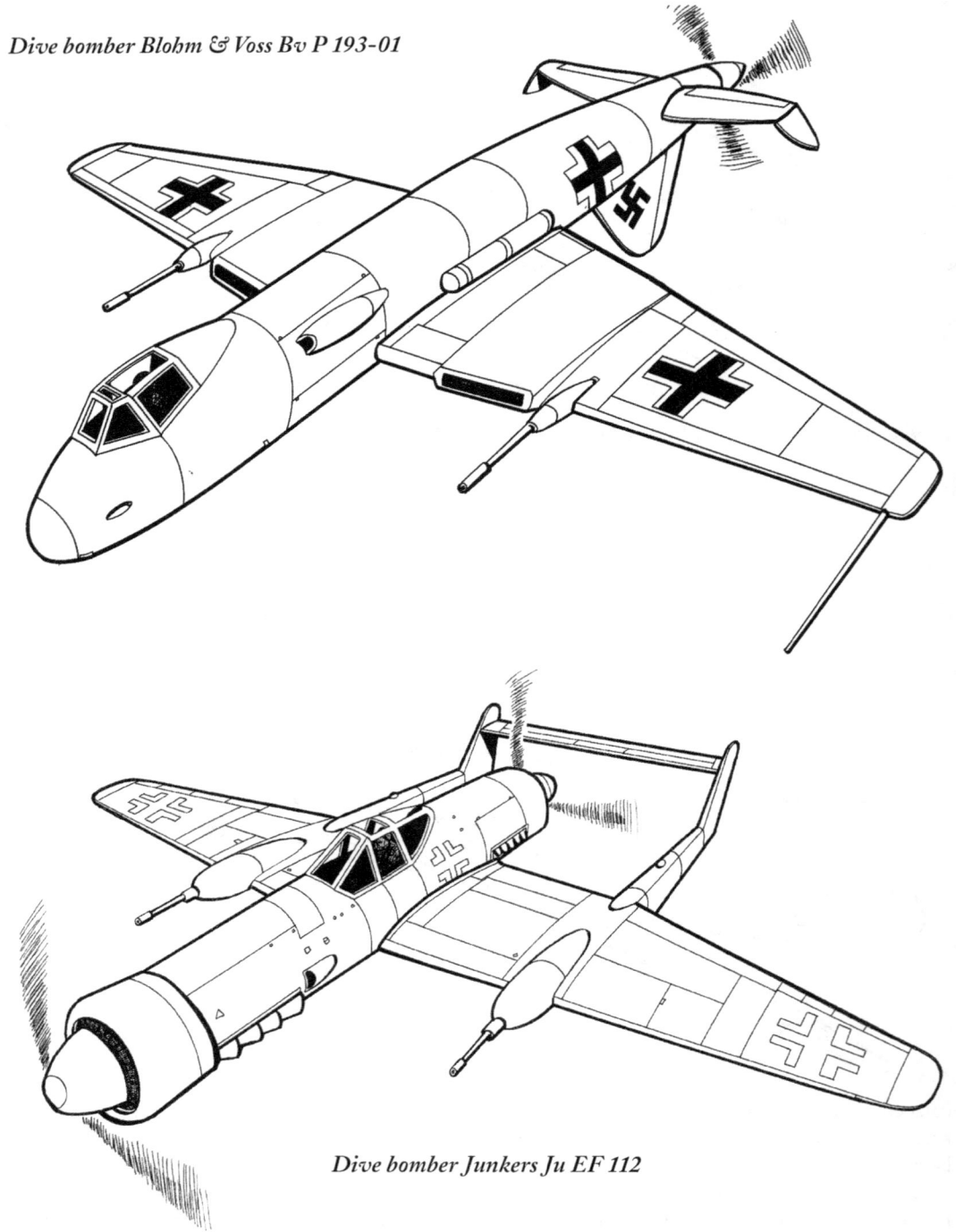

Dive bomber Junkers Ju EF 112

hp Daimler-Benz DB 603G piston engines, one in the nose pulling and one at the rear pushing. Speed was to be 760 km/h (472 mph). The single pilot sat in a cockpit between the two engines. Armament would have included two forward-firing MK 103 30-mm cannons mounted in the booms, and there was a provision for four R-100 air-to-air rockets. A maximum bomb load of 500 kg (1,102 lbs) could have been carried as well. The project

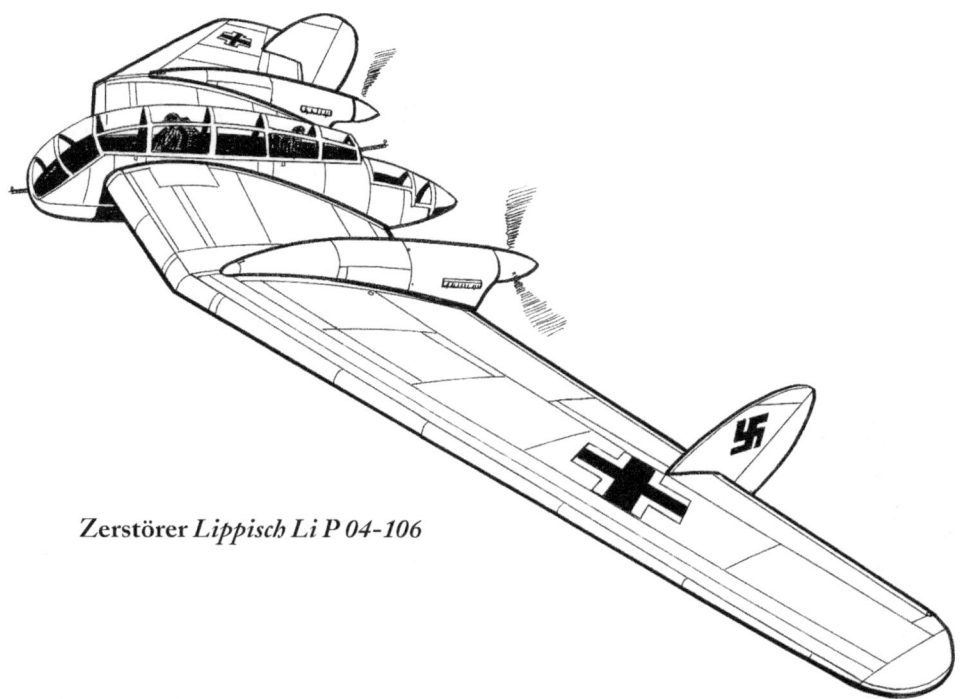

Zerstörer *Lippisch Li P 04-106*

failed to attract the RLM's attention and the Ju EF 112 never materialized.

Lippisch Li P 04-106

Designed in December 1939 by engineers Rentel and Lippisch who had just begun his activities at the Messerschmitt Company, the Li P 04-106 was a light bomber/ground attack aircraft with a flying-wing layout. The futuristic flying-wing configuration—a plane without fuselage and tail units—was given some thought in the late 1930s. It was believed that without lifting surfaces other than the wing itself, aerodynamics could enhanced and weight reduced. However as the flying wing had to provide flight stability and control, it required constraints, and the expected gain in drag and weight was often partially or totally impaired due to design compromises needed to provide stability and control. The Li P 04-106 had a span of 16 m (52 ft 6 in), with two different swept-back sections. The short fuselage had a length of 5.83 m (19 ft 1 in), and housed a glazed cockpit at the front for the crew of two, pilot and radio-operator/rear-gunner. On the trailing edge of the wings there were two small rudders. A long telescopic-extension tailwheel protected the propellers from damage at take-off and landing. Power was provided by two Daimler-Benz 601 E piston engines (1,200-hp each), each driving a pusher propeller. In order to get a good balance with the center of gravity, the engines were mounted far forward in the wings. The curious machine would have had a speed of 510 km/h (316 mph). It would have been armed with four fixed MG 151 machine guns placed in the sides of the fuselage for front fire, and two MG 131 machine guns aimed by the observer/radio-operator for rear fire. Intended to replace the Messerschmitt Bf 110 in the role of *Zerstörer*, the Li P 04-106 never passed the initial design stage.

Lippisch Li P 09

The Messerschmitt/Lippisch Li P 09 existed in two versions: heavy fighter (designed in 1941) and ground attacker/light bomber (designed in 1942). The light-bomber version was operated by a single pilot sitting in a glazed cockpit canopy placed at the front. It had a wingspan of 11.60 m (38 ft 1 in), a length of 7.10 m (23 ft 4 in) and a height of 3.25 m

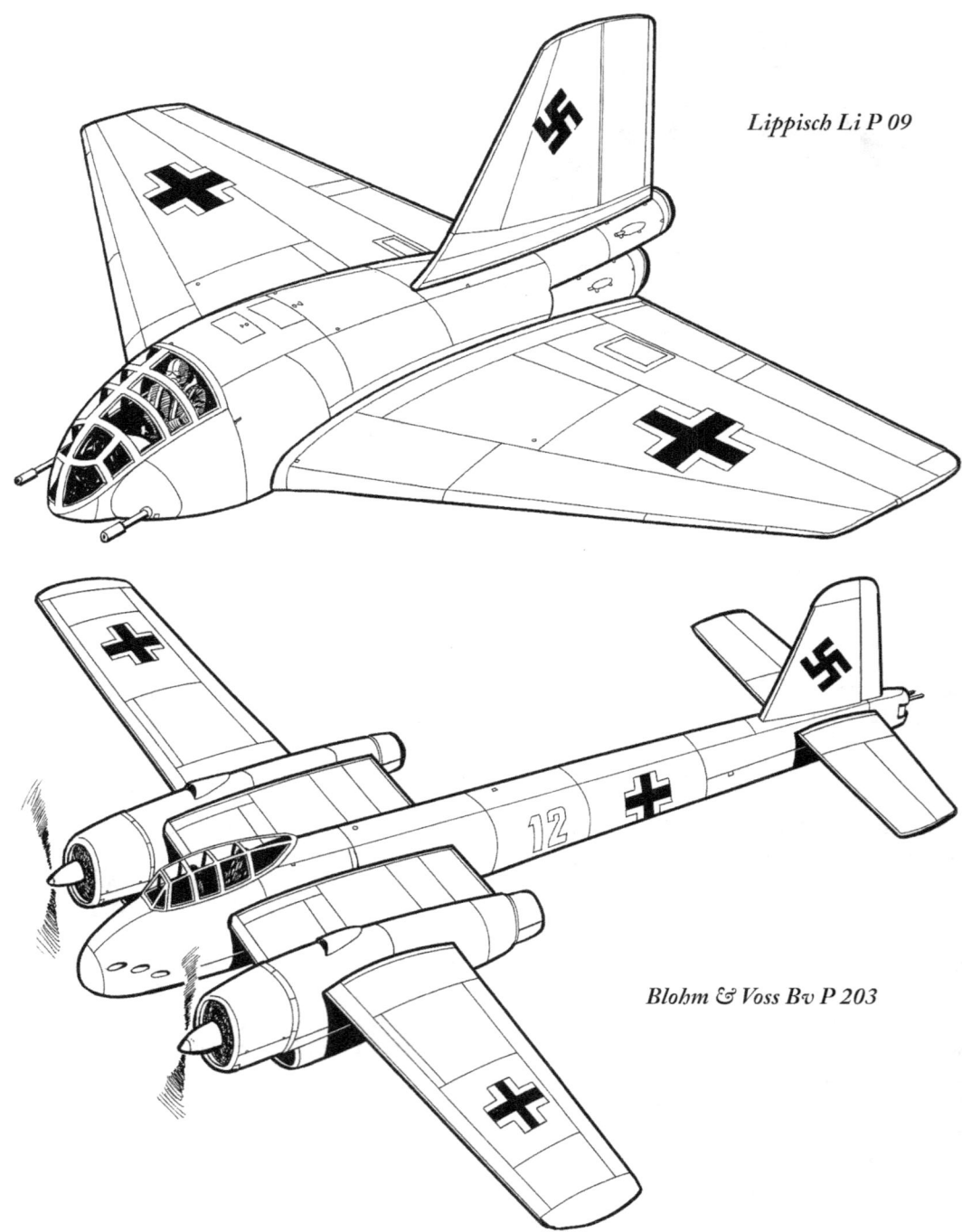

Lippisch Li P 09

Blohm & Voss Bv P 203

(10 ft 8 in). The landing gear featured two skids retracting into the fuselage, and a tailwheel. The aircraft was powered by two 1.500-kp (kilogram pond) thrust HKW 509 rocket engines (some sources assert two Jumo 004A turbojets), with a maximum speed of about 850 km/h, a range of 3,000 km, and a ceiling of 12,000 m. A 1,000-kg (2.200-lb) bomb was carried in an internal bomb bay placed under the fuselage. Armament would have consisted of four MG 151/20 machine guns; a pair mounted in the nose beneath the cockpit for

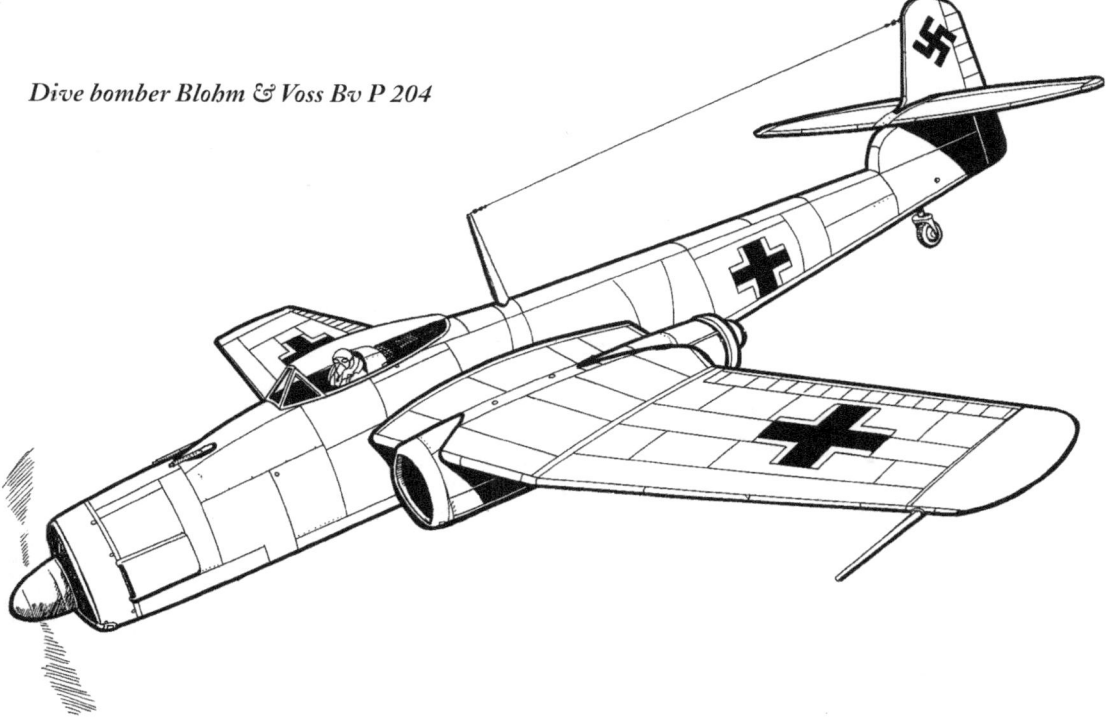

Dive bomber Blohm & Voss Bv P 204

forward fire, and another periscope-operated pair located in the tail for rear fire.

There was a different version, known as Lippisch Li P 10-108, designed by engineers Alexander Lippisch and Hermann Wurster in May 1942. This single-seat, tailless, swept-wing light bomber could carry a bomb load of 1,000 kg, and was powered by a Daimler-Benz DB 606 piston engine which drove a four-bladed propeller in push arrangement.

Bohm & Voss Bv P 203

The Bv P 203, if it had been completed, would have been a powerful and fast general-purpose, long-range heavy fighter/ground attacker. The aircraft had a length of 16.6 m (54 ft 6 in), and a straight and unswept wing with a span of 19.95 m (65 ft 6 in). The main wheels of the tricycle landing gear were housed in a thick section with increased chord between the two engine nacelles. The P 203 was to be powered by four engines: two BMW 801 TJ engines with turbo superchargers were placed at the forward end of the nacelles, and two He S011 jet engines (or two Jumo 004) were mounted in the rear of the nacelles, with air intakes located beneath the nacelles. A maximum speed of 920 km/h (571 mph) was envisioned. The aircraft was to be heavily armed with two MG 131 13-mm machine guns, two MG 151/15 15-mm machine guns, and two MK 103 30-mm cannons, all firing forward and mounted in the nose. In addition there was a remotely-controlled twin MG 131 13-mm machine gun mounted in the tail, firing to the rear. A bomb load of 1,000 kg (2,220 lbs) would have been carried in external racks.

Blohm & Voss Bv P 204

The Bv Project 204, designed by Dr. Richard Vogt, had a conventional landing gear and tail unit, but presented an asymmetric layout as it had a dual propulsion. The single-seat airplane had a BMW 801 D radial piston engine driving a propeller located in the nose and a turbojet engine (either a Jumo 003A or Heinkel He S011) placed beneath the port wing. The Bv P 204 had a span of 14.33 m (47 ft 02 in) and a length of 12.6 m (41 ft 4.1 in) and

Blohm & Voss Bv 237 (Stuka)

would have had a speed of 760 km/h (472 mph). Armament would have consisted of two MG 151 MK 103 30-mm cannons with provision for two additional MK 103 30-mm cannons. The aircraft could have carried under the fuselage either a bomb load of 1,000 kg (2,200 lbs) or a Bv 246 *Hagelkorn* (Hailstone) winged glide bomb. The project Bv P 204 never materialized.

Blohm & Voss BV 237

The Blohm & Voss Bv 237 ground attack and dive bomber was another asymmetric aircraft conceived by Dr. Richard Vogt, who designed the Bv 178, the Bv 179 fighter (see Part 5), and the Bv 141 tactical reconnaissance aircraft (see Part 9). According to Vogt, the unconventional, asymmetric layout presented the following advantages: good visibility for the crew, good weapon concentration, good bomb load and easy access to bomb bay, good low-level speed, and good climbing speed, and the aircraft was also cheap to build and maintain. The Bv 237 was designed to become the Luftwaffe's replacement for the aging Junkers Ju 87 Stuka (dive bomber). The fuselage had a length of 10.75 m (35 ft 3 in), and a height of 3.3 m (10 ft 10 in). It was of a lightweight, simple construction with a round cross-section throughout. The single BMW 801D air-cooled, 14-cylinder, double radial engine was mounted in the fuselage front. The aircraft was to have a maximum speed of 579 km/h (360 mph) and a range of 2,000 km (1,243 miles). The wing was mounted low, and was completely of metal construction; span was 14.46 m (47 ft 5 in) and wing area 42 square m (452 square ft). The tail unit was also asymmetric, with a strut providing support under the left horizontal tail. The landing gear was retractable. The one-man cockpit was located to the right of the main fuselage, was armor plated, and its nose housed the weapons. Armament would have consisted of two fixed forward-firing MG 151 and two rear firing MG 131 cannons. The normal bomb load was a single 500-kg (1,102-lb) bomb, carried beneath the cockpit. An additional 500 kg of bombs could have been carried in racks under the wings. Maximum loaded weight was 6,685 kg (14,738 lbs). Additional versions were planned, including one with a two-seat cockpit, and a provision was even made for a single Jumo 004 jet

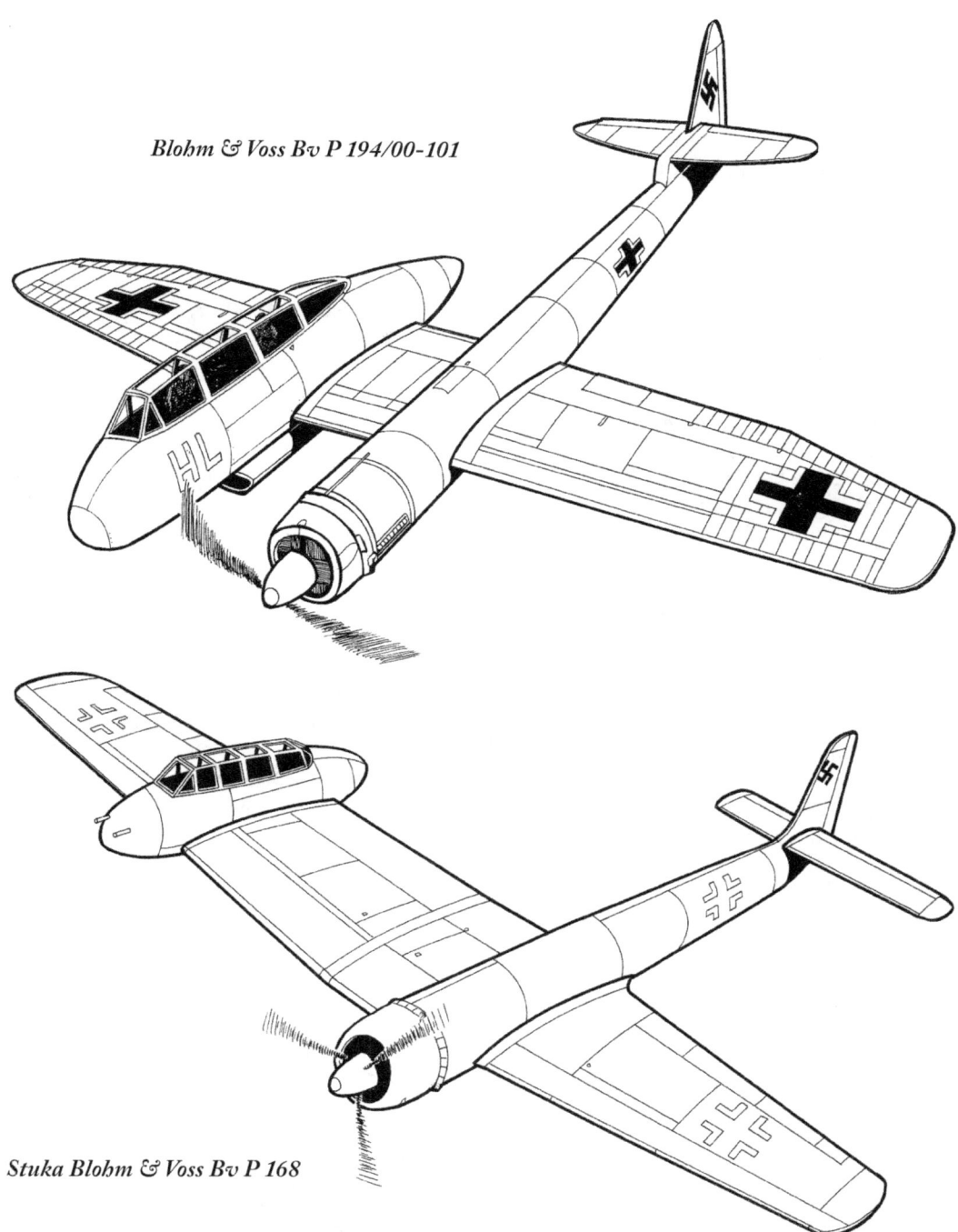

Blohm & Voss Bv P 194/00-101

Stuka Blohm & Voss Bv P 168

engine to be mounted beneath the wing between the fuselage and cockpit. Although a wooden mock-up was constructed, the unusual and dubious asymmetric design was not accepted, as the Bv 237 showed no marked performance improvement over the Junkers Ju 87 Stuka. There was a variant, known as Blohm & Voss Bv P 194/00-101 with a crew of two, intended for multi-role use, including heavy fighter, dive bomber, reconnaissance and ground attacker/destroyer aircraft.

Blohm & Voss Bv P 168

The Bv P 168 was another asymmetric design for a Stuka. The crew of two (pilot and observer) sat in a nacelle positioned on the right wing. The aircraft had a span of 15 m and a length of 12.45 m. It would have been armed with two 13-mm MG 131 guns and would have been able to carry a bomb load of 500 kg.

Heinkel He P 1065/IIC

Rather similar to the Blohm & Voss design, the Heinkel He P 1065 had an asymmetrical layout, with the crew sitting in a nacelle on the right wing. The aircraft, intended to be a fast light bomber, had a span of 20.4 m, and a length of 19.5 m. Powered by one BMW 803 (3,500-hp) engine, it was to have a maximum speed of 520 km/h. Planned defensive armament included two MG 151/20 cannons and one MG 131 cannon, all mounted in the nacelle for rear firing. The He P 1065 would have carried a bomb load of 1,000 kg.

Blohm & Voss/Isacson Zerstörer

Little is known about this odd, asymmetrical *Zerstörer* (ground attacker/long-range fighter/light bomber) from 1944. Who designed it remain unclear, some sources attributing it to Dr. Richard Vogt of the Blohm & Voss Company (who had made several asymmetrical designs, including the Bv 141 and Bv P111), others mentioning the Swedish engineer Sigurd Isacson. The aircraft was to be powered by two in-line tandem engines (presumably DB 613) in push/pull arrangement. It had a wingspan of 16 m, a length of 13 m, a weight (loaded) of 9,000 kg, a maximum speed of 770 km/h, a range of 1,800 km, and a service ceiling of 10,700 m. Armament would have consisted of two 20-mm cannons placed in the fuselage nose, six 13-mm machine guns integrated in the wings, and a bomb load of 1,500 kg. The crew would have included two airmen located in lying positions, the pilot on his belly and the radio-navigator on his back.

Henschel Hs P 87

This project was Henschel's design for a *Schnellbomber* (Fast Bomber) to be powered by a single 2200-hp Daimler Benz DB 610 engine placed at the rear, driving a pusher propeller. Like the Focke-Wulf Fw 42 from 1933, an *Entenbauform* (canard) design was used, with the tailplane having movable elevators mounted ahead of the main lifting surface.

Schnellbomber Heinkel He P 1065/IIC

4. *Bombers* 141

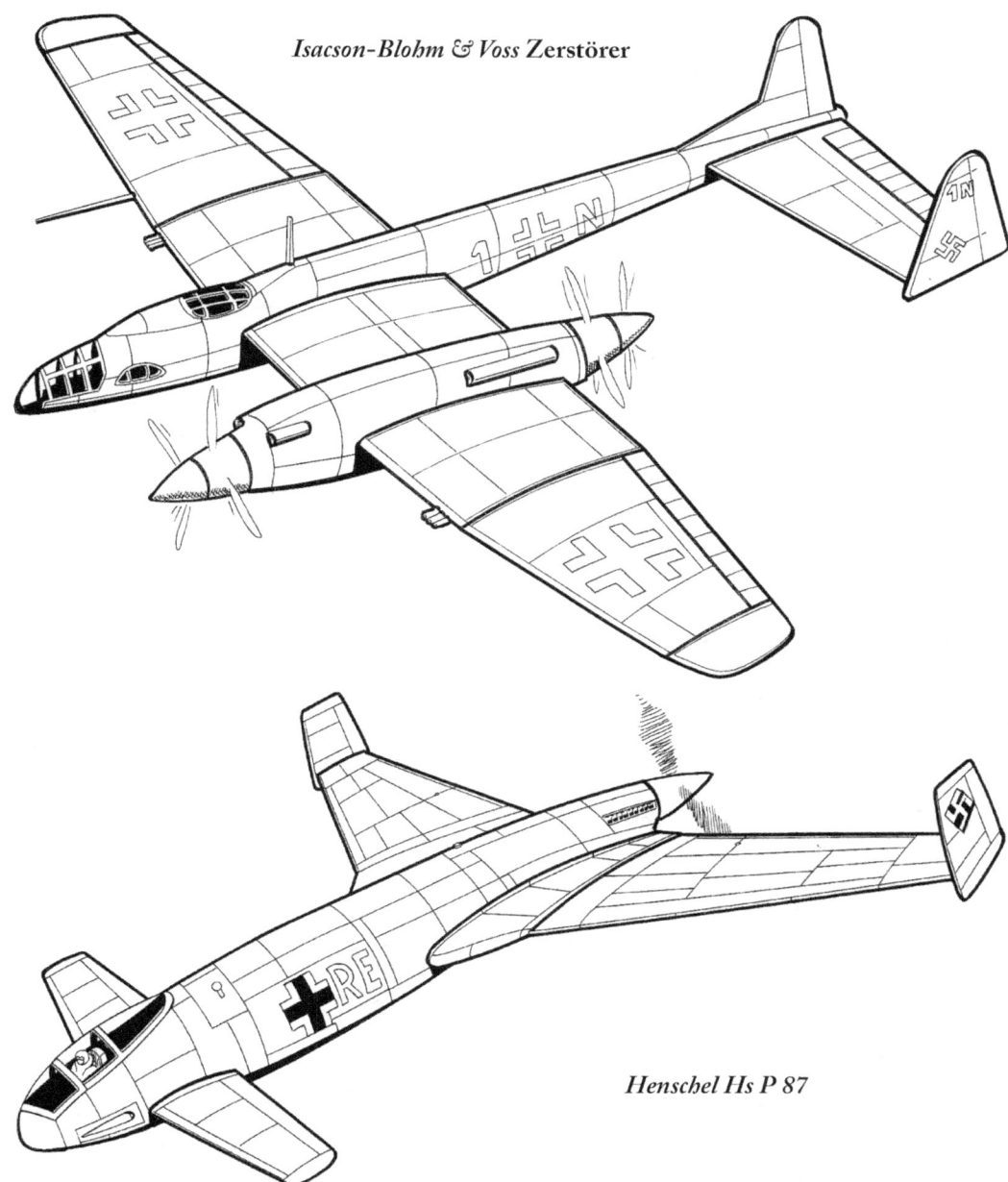

Isacson-Blohm & Voss Zerstörer

Henschel Hs P 87

The advantage was that the aircraft was stable, as the layout reduced lift-induced drag; but the disadvantage was that the wing efficiency was reduced, as it was difficult to apply flaps to the wing. Vertical fins were located at the wingtips. The cockpit was in the forward fuselage with accommodations for a crew of three or four. Length was 12.15 m (39 ft 10.7 in) and planned maximum speed was 750 km/h (466 mph). The prototype construction was not begun, and the further development of tail-first aircraft was not pursued due to lengthy development time and design cost. The project thus never left the drawing board.

Lippisch Li P 13

Designed in December 1942 by Josef Hubert (Lippisch's aerodynamics expert working for the Messerschmitt Company), the Li P 13

Lippisch Li P 13

was a project for a single-seat tailless *Schnellbomber*. The aircraft was planned to have a length of 9.40 m (30 ft 10 in), and large wings featuring compound sweep on the leading and trailing edges, with a span of 12.80 m (42 ft). It was to be powered by two Daimler-Benz DB 605 B piston engines placed fore and aft of the cockpit driving tractor and pusher propellers. A maximum speed of 750 km/h was estimated. In order to provide ground clearance for the two propellers, the machine was fitted with a long retractable landing gear bringing height—with wheels down—to 5.10 m (16 ft 9 in). Armament and bomb-load data are not available.

Lippisch-Messerschmitt Bomber Glider

Who designed this bomb-carrying glider remains uncertain. Some sources attribute it to the DFS (German Research Institute for Sailplane Flight). The single-seat, delta-winged glider with cruciform tail unit had a span of 4.28 m and a length of 7.25 m. The glider, carrying a 1,000 kg bomb attached to its belly, was to take off and be flown down behind a mother aircraft. In the vicinity of the target, the glider would be released and go in a steep attack dive. After bomb release the pilot would dive away to safety, then initiate compressed-air equipment placed behind the cockpit, releasing a balloon that would be inflated, thereby slowing down the aircraft to the point where the pilot could jump out and get back to the ground via parachute. The curious project never materialized.

Medium Bombers

During the early 1930s, before the Luftwaffe officially existed, a great deal of emphasis was placed upon the bomber as a war-winning weapon. This was primarily caused by a strong belief that a fast, maneuverable bomber could easily outfly existing fighters, but this was also a logical preference given the restrictions imposed upon Germany by the Treaty of Versailles from 1919. After all a bomber could be disguised as a civilian airliner whereas a fighter was obvious to all. Thus when it was decided to create an air force, German aviation authorities naturally turned toward designs offering protection from prying Allied eyes, and followed existing trends toward small, fast aircraft, which were, of necessity, almost exclusively twin-engined. Dive bombers and ground attackers remained Germany's principal close-support air weapon during World War II, while interdiction tasks (bombing of commu-

Lippisch-Messerschmitt bomber glider

nications, assembly areas, troop concentrations and airfields, isolating the battlefield and preventing reinforcements from reaching the front) were carried out by a level bomber fleet of medium (generally two-engined) aircraft such as the Dornier Do 17, Heinkel He 111 and later Junkers Ju 88. The Luftwaffe did not stress strategic long-range bombing, the emphasis being on dive bombers, ground attackers and tactical medium bombers. It approached World War II with good equipment and carefully conceived policies, yet it remained an air force exclusively designed for short *Blitzkrieg* wars.

The Luftwaffe authorities strongly believed that fast medium bombers would get through enemy defense and would wreak havoc on a vast scale. Events showed that this assumption was, if not false, at least greatly overestimated. The trim Dornier Do 17, the broad-winged Heinkel He 111 and the high-performance Junkers Ju 88 were all extremely advanced by the standards of the late 1930s when they were designed. They were faster than the single-seat fighters of that era and (so the argument went) therefore did not need much defensive armament. In mid–1940, the over-optimistic Hermann Göring declared: "My Luftwaffe is invincible. Just look at its achievements in Poland and France! Can one conceive of a war machine in history which has contributed so much towards such total victories as these?" German medium bombers, however, showed themselves to be anything but invincible, particularly during the Battle of Britain. The inadequacy of the Luftwaffe bomber force for strategic and long-range operations was never corrected and as World War II proceeded their main employment was as close support, a function which progressively declined as the Luftwaffe more and more lost its previous superiority to the growing air forces of the Allies. By 1944, relatively few bomber units remained operational. They were then unable to go on the offensive, except occasionally and with limited scope, and they were engaged in a limited number of missions, including level bombing from medium height in dusk and nighttime attacks by small formations, nighttime mining of coastal waters and estuaries, occasional torpedo attacks on shipping, and miscellaneous minor offensive activities.

The design of medium bombers was such that all that could be done was a succession of modifications. Most of the German bomber effort during World War II went into develop-

Focke-Wulf Fw 42

ing and improving the four major prewar types already in service: the already described Junkers Ju 87 "Stuka," the Dornier Do 17, the Heinkel He 111, and the Junkers Ju 88. A persistent emphasis thus existed upon proven prewar designs, and very little (if any) provision was made for a second generation of aircraft. Basic airframe designs tended to remain unchanged, and subtypes incorporating different engines and weapons proliferated. This, among other things, contributed to Germany's eventual defeat in the air.

Focke-Wulf Fw 42

One of the most unusual bombers ever designed, the Focke-Wulf Fw 42 was a twin-engine aircraft with main wing placed at the rear and tailplane at the front. Designed in 1932, the aircraft was planned with a retractable landing gear, a crew of six, a span of 25 m (82 ft), a length of 17.7 m (58 ft 1 in), a height (at cockpit) of 2.35 m (7 ft 9 in), and an empty weight of 5,600 kg (12,346 lbs). Defensive armament included two machine-gun posts, one in the nose, the other in the tail. A bomb load of 1,000 kg (2,205 lbs) could be carried. The Fw 42 was to be powered by two 750-hp BMW V1 12-cylinder engines, and it would have had a maximum speed of 310 km/h (193 mph) and a range of 1,200 km (746 miles). A full-size mock-up was built and, although good results were reported from wind-tunnel tests, no contract was issued, and all work on this curious "canard" design was abandoned.

Messerschmitt M22

Designed in the early 1930s, the biplane, two-engined, three-seat M22 had a length of 13.6 m, a height of 5.17 m, a span of 17 m, a wing area of 63.2 square meters, and an empty weight of, 2,900 kg. It was powered by two Siemens Jupiter VI engines with three-bladed wooden propellers, and had a maximum speed of 220 km/h, a cruising speed of 185 km/h, and a range of 500 km. It was planned to carry a bomb load of 500 kg, and defended by two machine guns, one placed in the front, and another in a dorsal position. During a test flight in October 1930, the aircraft crashed, killing test pilot Eberhard Mohnike. As a result the design was abandoned.

4. Bombers 145

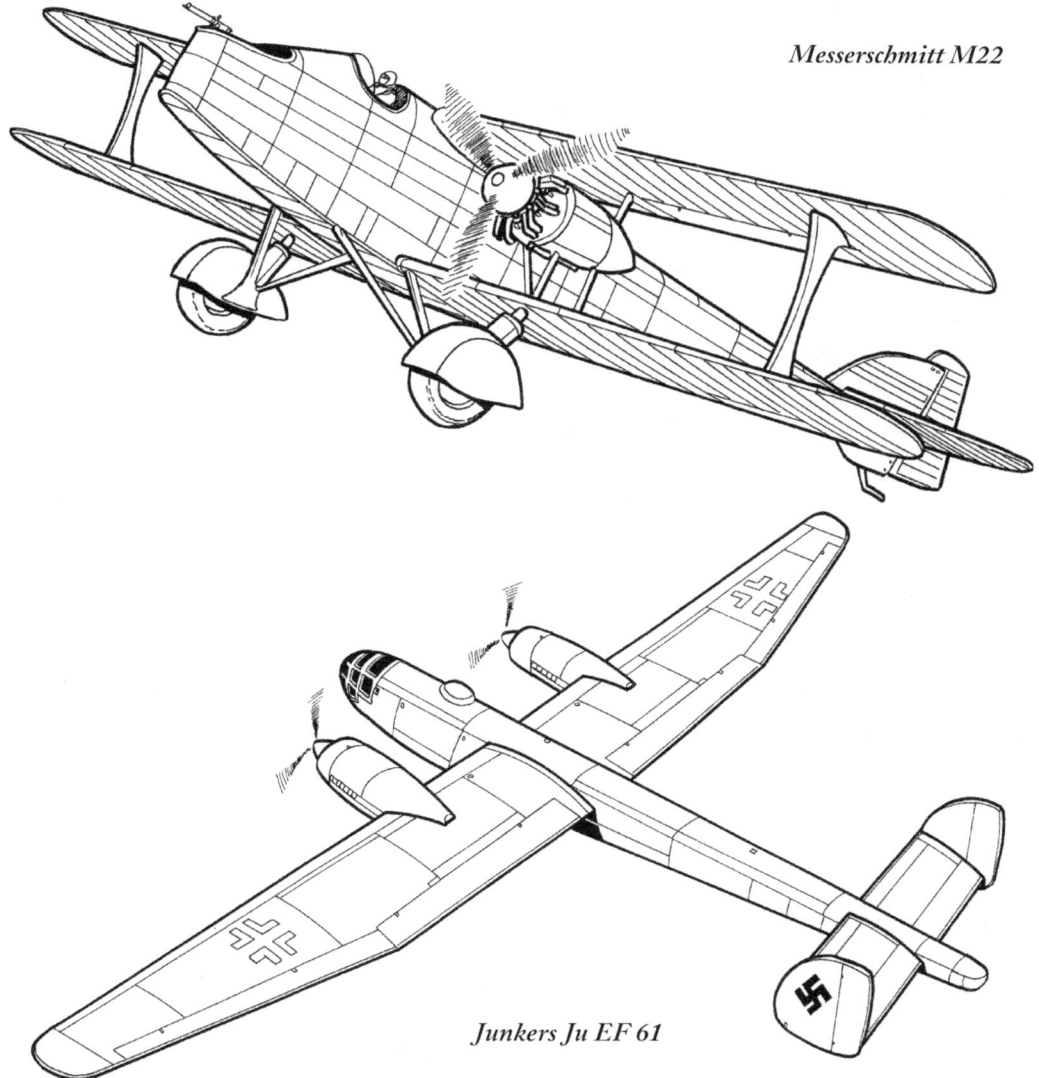

Messerschmitt M22

Junkers Ju EF 61

Junkers Ju EF 61

The Junkers Ju *Entwicklungsflugzeug* 61 (EF development aircraft) was a project for a *Höhenschnellbomber* (high-altitude fast bomber). Designed in March 1936, the aircraft was powered by two Daimler-Benz DB 600A inverted V-12, liquid-cooled engines, each developing 950 hp. It was intended to have a range of 2,000 km, a maximum speed of 350 km/h (217 mph), and a maximum ceiling of 15 km (49,300 ft). It had a span of 27 m (88 ft 7 in), a length of 14.34 m (47 ft 0.75 in), and could carry a bomb load of 800 kg. Two prototypes were built. In March 1937, the first Ju EF 61 E1 (V1) made a flight to a height of 3,500 m, but became uncontrollable forcing the crew to bail out by parachute. In December 1937, the second prototype Ju EF 61 E2 (V2) made a flight that ended in a crash. After this failure, further development of the machine was abandoned, but the design led to the development of the high-altitude reconnaissance and bomber Junkers Ju 86 P-1 and P-2.

Junkers Ju 86

The Junkers Ju 86 was originally a two-engine, monoplane, civilian airliner designed in the early 1930s, later turned into a German

Luftwaffe bomber. The civilian model Ju 86B could carry ten passengers; two were delivered to Swissair and five to Lufthansa.

The early model Ju 86-D1 (1936) had two 600-hp Jumo 205C-4 diesel engines, but in the later Ju 86E these were replaced with 800-hp BMW 132F gas engines. Some were sold to Sweden, South Africa, Chile, Portugal, Japan, Hungary, Bolivia, Hungary, and Spain. The Ju 86K was an export model, also built under license in Sweden with 905-hp Bristol Mercury XIX engines, and stayed in service with the Swedish Air Force until 1956.

The bomber saw active combat service in the Spanish Civil War, where it proved inferior to the Heinkel He 111. It was again used in the 1939 invasion of Poland, but retired soon after. In January 1940 the Luftwaffe tested the prototype Ju 86P that had a longer wing span, two-man crew in pressurized cabin, a noise-reducing apparatus that made the aircraft entirely inaudible at extreme heights, and was powered by two Jumo 207A1 turbocharged diesel engines. The Ju 86P could fly at heights of 12,000 m (39,000 ft), where it was safe from enemy fighters.

Satisfied with the newer version, the Luftwaffe ordered that some forty older-model bombers be converted to Ju 86P-1 high-altitude bombers and Ju 86P-2 photo reconnaissance aircraft. These operated successfully for some years over Britain, the Soviet Union and North Africa. In August 1942 a modified Spitfire V shot one down over Egypt; when two more were lost, Ju 86Ps were withdrawn from service in 1943. Junkers was continually experimenting with new methods to increase altitude, and developed the Ju 86R with even larger wings and newer engines that could have flown higher yet—up to 16,000 m (52,500 ft)—but production was limited to prototypes. General characteristics and data varied with the types, but on the whole the aircraft had an average wingspan of 32 m (105 ft), a length of 16.46 m (54 ft), a height of 4.7 m (15 ft 5 in), a wing area of 82 square m (883 square ft), an empty weight of 6,700 kg (14,800 lb), and a gross weight of 11,530 kg (25,420 lb). The bomber had defensive armaments including three MG15 and could carry a 1,000-kg (2,200-lb) bomb load. When powered by two Junkers Jumo 207 B-3/V diesel engines, maximum speed was 420 km/h (260 mph) above 9,150 m (30,000 ft), rate of climb was 280

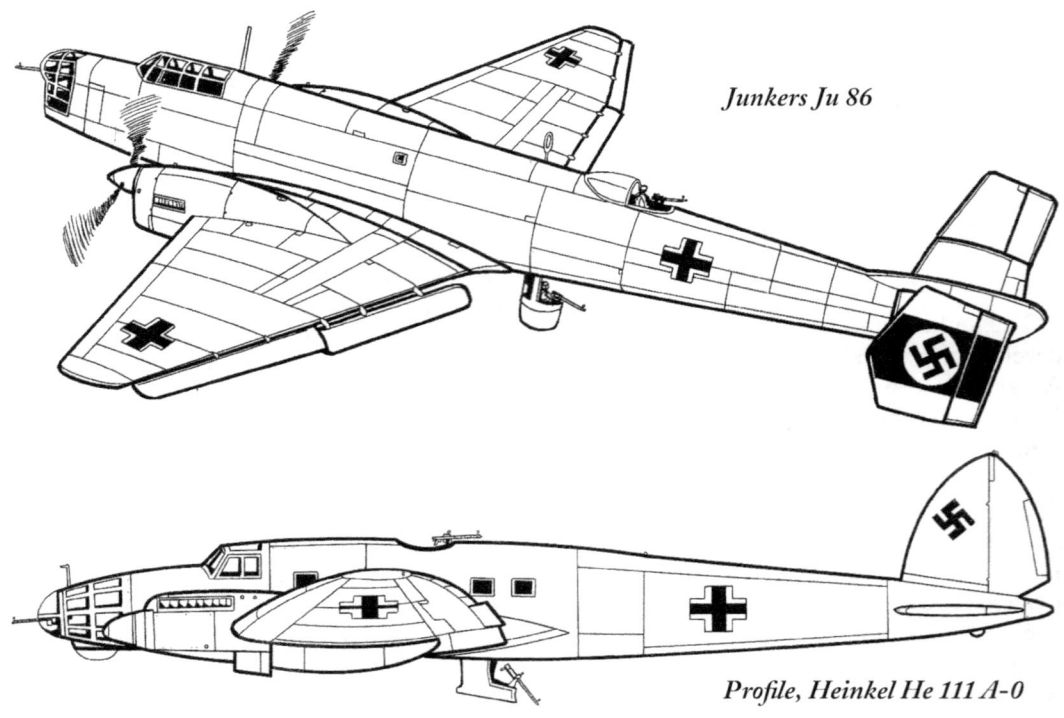

Junkers Ju 86

Profile, Heinkel He 111 A-0

m/min (900 ft/min), service ceiling was 13,000 m (42,650 ft), and maximum range was 1,580 km (980 miles).

Heinkel He 111

The Heinkel He 111 remained throughout World War II one of the primary offensive weapons of the Luftwaffe's *Kampfgeschwader* (medium bomber units). Derived from the passenger carrier Heinkel He 70, the He 111 prototype was designed in 1934 by the Günter brothers as an unconvincingly disguised commercial transport, in fact as a twin-engined bomber for the then clandestine Luftwaffe. In 1935 the He 111A was produced and it made a name for itself as a fast civil airliner. This was followed by the more powerful military He 111B which was successfully tested in combat conditions during the Spanish Civil War in 1936. Several improved versions, C, D, E, F, and G finally led to the P version with redesigned, fully glazed nose and broad, straight-tapered wings which characterized the whole range of wartime series. In 1939 the standard H version appeared, nicknamed "Spade" by aircrews, which became the most important, successful and most-built He 111. By that time the He 111 formed about three-quarters of the Luftwaffe's twin-engine bomber force. The aircraft was operated by a crew of five: pilot; observer/bombardier; radio operator/gunner; engineer/gunner; and gunner. It was powered by two 1,200-hp Junkers Jumo 211D 12-cylinder, inverted-V, liquid-cooled engines, and had a typical speed of 415 km/h (259 mph), and—with full load of bombs—a range of 1,200 km (745 miles). Span was 22.60 m (74 ft 1.7 in), length was 16.40 m (53 ft 9.5 in), height was 4 m (13 ft 2 in), and empty weight was 7,720 kg (17.000 lbs). Armament consisted of 7.92-mm Rheinmetall MG 15 machine guns on manual

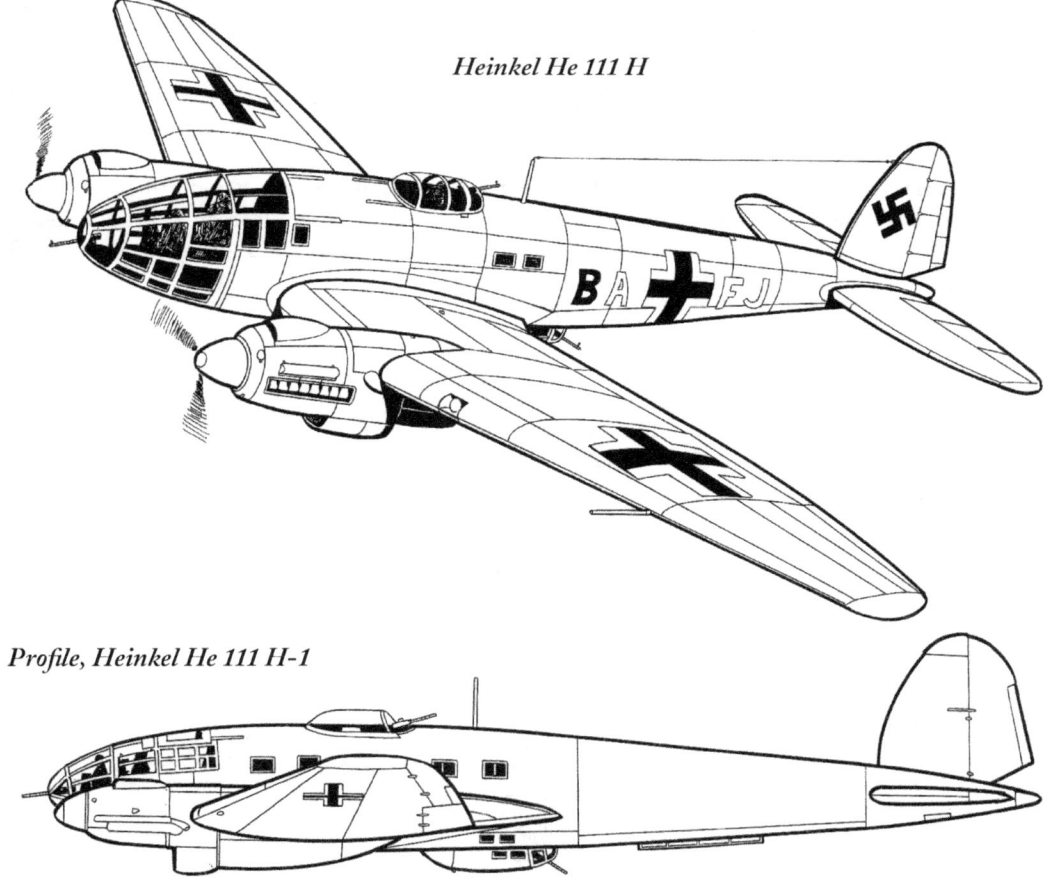

Heinkel He 111 H

Profile, Heinkel He 111 H-1

mounting in nosecap, open dorsal position, ventral gondola, waist windows, and sometimes a fixed MG 17 mounted in the tail. The Heinkel He 111 H carried a bomb load up to 2,000 kg (4,414 lbs) in a bomb bay in the center fuselage. The bombs were stored nose-up in vertical cells in the fuselage. Icing was a massive problem with the He 111, and crews would not fly in high-altitude cloud formations; the service ceiling of the aircraft was 8,500 m. Rocket-assisted take-off could be used in order to reduce runway length by about 60 percent. The Heinkel 111, originally a civil-transport aircraft, had a para transport version with a capacity of 16 men who jumped out via a ventral hatch; two 800-kg (1,764-lb) supply containers with arms and ammunition for the paratroopers were carried in external racks.

Like the Junkers Ju 87 dive bomber, the He 111 performed extremely well in the opening phase of World War II, but was recognized as terribly inadequate during the Battle of Britain. By mid-1940, the He 111 still formed the backbone of the Luftwaffe, but it was evident that it had become obsolete. Indeed the fast aircraft of 1937 had become a lumbering, poorly armed bomber, extremely vulnerable to modern fighters. In response Heinkel added extra machine guns and armor, and tried to improve both altitude and speed, but to no avail. Coupled with incessant growth in equipment and armor, the result was only further deteriorating performance. The short-sightedness of the RLM was shown by the fact that they made no use of available replacements. Instead the obsolete and waddling He 111 was built in ever greater number until the end of the war, as it was easy to manufacture, economical in manpower and material, could absorb a great deal of enemy fire, and remained reasonably effective on the less demanding Russian front. The Heinkel 111 served on all fronts as medium bomber, but from mid-1943 its role was less important. It remained in service and was used for more specialized missions, including as torpedo bomber, barrage-balloon cable-cutter, magnetic-mine exploder, V1 missile carrier, and transport aircraft. The He 111 was also used as glider tug. Undoubtedly the most spectacular conversion was the special He 111 Z (*Zwilling*—twin), designed in 1942 for the purpose of towing the enormous Messerschmitt 321 glider; this consisted of two He 111s joined by a common center wing carrying a fifth engine (see Part 8).

The Heinkel He 111 was manufactured by the Ernst Heinkel Works at Marienehe and Oranienburg, but also by Norddeutsche Dornierwerke in Wismar, Allgemeine Transportgesellschaft in Leipzig, Arado in Babelsberg, and many factories in Romania. Production of the He 111 stopped in 1944 after about 7,000

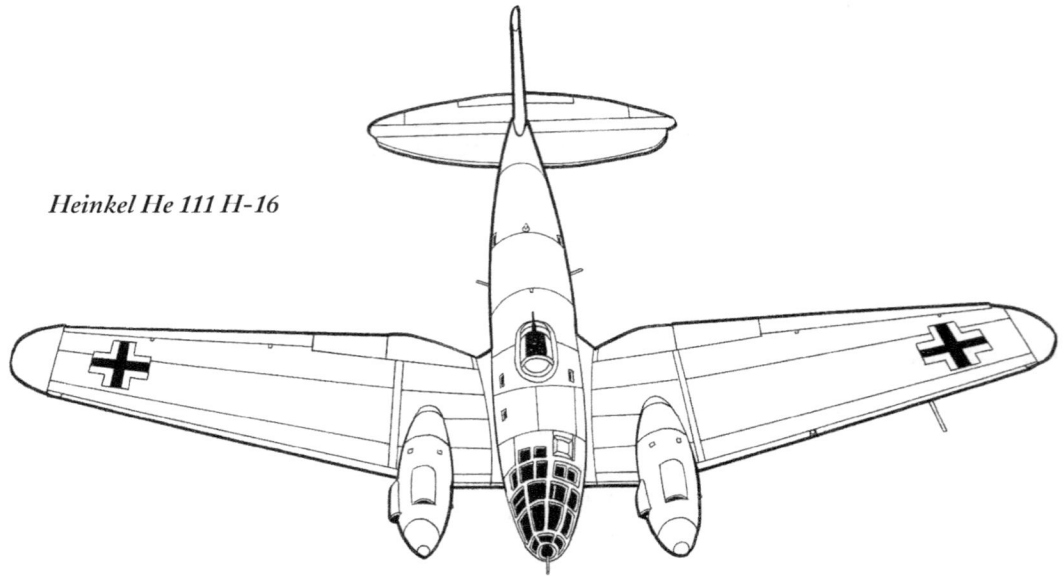

Heinkel He 111 H-16

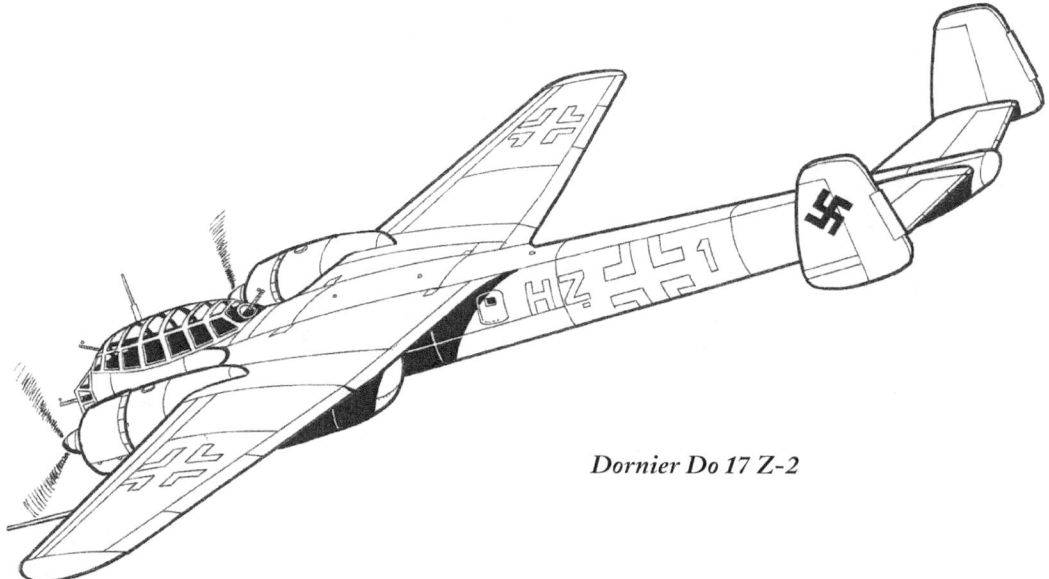

Dornier Do 17 Z-2

units were built for the German air force. Production continued after World War II in Spain until 1956.

Dornier Do 17

Originally designed in 1934 as a six-passenger, high-speed transport or mail plane, the Dornier Do 17 was turned into a medium bomber in mid–1935. Several versions were produced, and in 1937 the Do 17 F was operating with success in the Spanish Civil War with the Condor Legion. The later Do 17 S introduced a completely new front with much deeper, all-glazed nose cockpit. Such a change had been evident from the inadequate defensive armament of the earlier models. At the outbreak of World War II, the improved Do 17 Z version performed very well. Known to the British as the "Flying Pencil" for its slim fuselage, the Do 17 Z was operated by a crew of four, including pilot, observer/bomb aimer/gunner, radio operator/gunner, and gunner. It had a span of 18 m (59 ft), a length of 15.79 m (51 ft 9.6 in), a height of 4.56 m (14 ft 11.5 in), and an empty weight of 5,210 kg (11,484 lbs). Powered by two 1,000-hp Bramo Fafnir 323P 9-cylinder radial engines, it had a maximum speed of 425 km/h (263 mph) and a range of 1,160 km (721 miles). Armament generally included four or six 7.92-mm Rheinmetall MG 15 machine guns located in the front, under and at the rear of the glazed nose. A bomb load of 1,000 kg (2,205 lbs) could be carried. Between late 1939 and the summer of 1940, about 535 Do 17 Z bomber and reconnaissance machines were produced. Fast and maneuverable, especially at low level and by the *Blitzkrieg* standards of 1939 and 1940, the popular and reliable airplane played a substantial part in the initial German victories. Although it could absorb much punishment, the Do 17 Z proved to be disastrously vulnerable to modern British fighters during the Battle of Britain. The model was subsequently engaged on the Russian front in the spring of 1941. By 1942 the Do 17 Z was regarded as outdated and withdrawn from combat bombing missions. From then on it was only used as reconnaissance aircraft, glider tug, and for battlefield supply dropping.

Dornier Do 215

The Do 215 was basically an export version of the Do 17 Z. It had the same appearance and dimensions, but greater power (owing to two Daimler-Benz 601 engines) and thus slightly higher performance. Originally ordered by Yugoslavia and Sweden at the outbreak of World War II in September 1939, the Nazi authorities embargoed export, and the

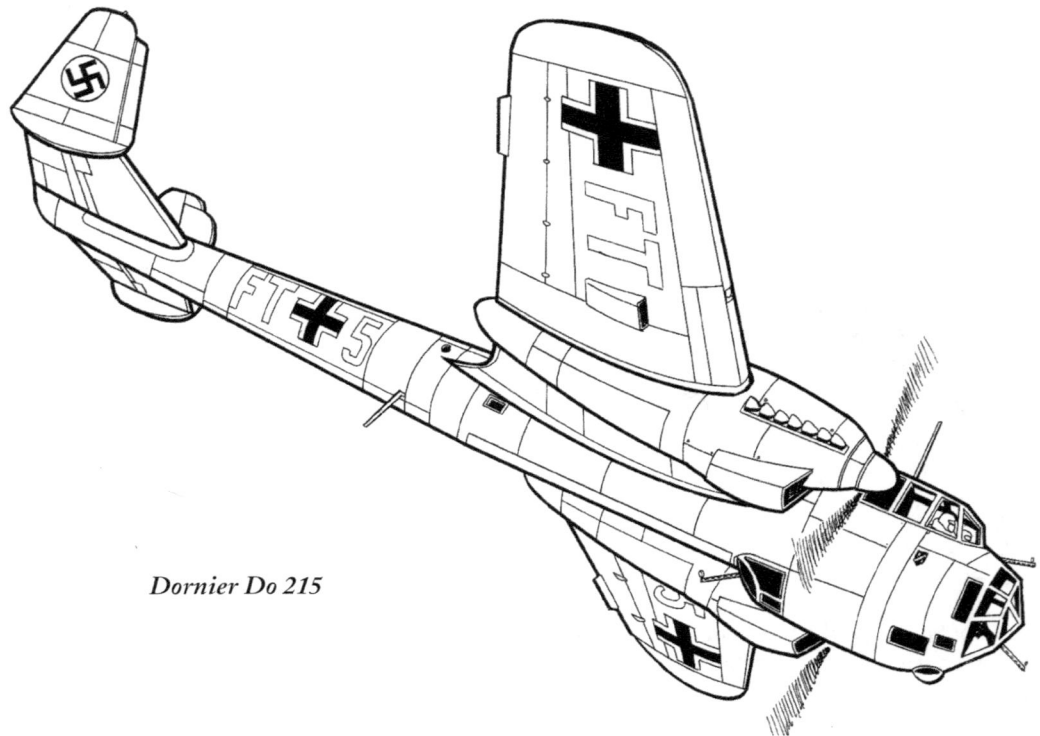

Dornier Do 215

aircraft were converted according to Luftwaffe requirements, and entered operational service under the designation of Dornier 215. Owing to its speed, versatility, maneuverability and good flying characteristics, the Do 215 was used in several roles. The Do 215 B-4 was used in 1940 in the intruder role, armed with two nose-mounted 20-mm MG FF cannons and four 7.92-mm NG 17 machine guns. The aircraft was also employed in reconnaissance and a ground-attack role. As a night fighter it was equipped with FuG 202 Lichtenstein radar. By 1942, the night interceptor Dornier 215 was replaced by the Junkers Ju 88 and Messerschmitt Bf 110, and from then on it was relegated to test flying of new equipment.

Dornier Do 217

First flown in August 1938, the multipurpose Do 217 looked like an enlarged and strengthened derivative of the Do 17. Although externally rather similar to the Do 17, the scaled-up Dornier Do 217 was actually an entirely new design. After teething problems with engines and streamlining of the fuselage, the Do 217 became a great Luftwaffe all-rounder, much popular with crews. First production version was the Do 217 E which was equipped with two BMW 801A radial engines and entered Luftwaffe service in the reconnaissance role in late 1940 and as a bomber in March 1941. The Do 217 blossomed out into a prolific family including several subtypes. The E-5 version was designed to carry the Henschel 293 stand-off radio-controlled bomb. The modified Do 217 H was an experimental high-altitude bomber with DB 601 engines, and a bomb load of 4,000 kg (8,818 lbs). Versions J-1 and J-2 were designs for a night-fighter role, with powerful armament and FuG 202 Lichtenstein BC radar mounted in a solid nose. The Do 217 K had a completely redesigned bulbous glazed nose, increasing room for the crew and enabling the placing of additional defensive weapons. The K-1 was designed to carry a torpedo, and the K-2 (with extended wing span) was intended to carry the Fritz X 1400 radio-controlled stand-off bomb. Both subtypes were used in an anti-shipping role, and a successful attack was carried out in September 1943 when the Italian battleship

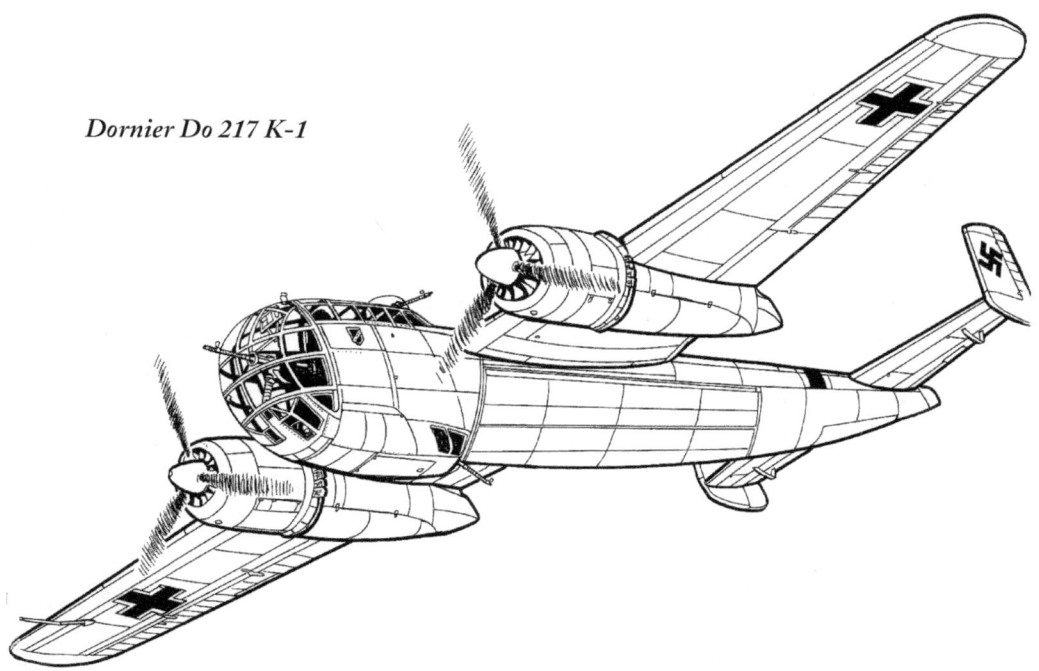

Dornier Do 217 K-1

Roma was sunk and the *Italia* badly damaged. The Do 217 M-1 was powered by two DB 603A in-line engines, and was used as night fighter with some success under the designation Do 217 N. Dimensions, weight, powerplant and thus performance were slightly different according to the various versions, but on average the Do 217 had a span of 19 m (62 ft 4 in), a length of 17.3 m (56 ft 9.2 in), a speed between 515 km/h (320 mph) and 557 km/h (348 mph), and a typical range of about 2,100 km (1,300 miles). Defensive armament varied, but later versions typically included one 15-mm MG 141/15 cannon and one MG 15 machine gun in the nose, two MG 15s in the side windows and two 13-mm MG 131 heavy machine guns in the dorsal turret and rear ventral position. The crew also differed from one version to another, comprising three, four or five airmen. A typical bomb load of 4,000 kg (8,818 lbs) could be carried. A total of 1,730 units in eleven variants of the Do 217 was produced, and nearly all of them saw a great deal of front-line action.

The pressurized high-altitude Dornier Do 217 P series had fantastic performance that would have put them out of reach of any Allied fighters had they been put into service in time. From 1943, the Dornier designers devoted much effort to develop a yet further improved version, known as Do 317, which never went into service.

Henschel Hs 127

The Henschel Hs 127 was a bomber aircraft that was designed in response to a 1935 RLM (Reichsluftfahrtministerium) request for a fast, tactical medium bomber. Junkers, Focke-Wulf, Messerschmitt and Henschel all submitted designs. According to RLM specifications, the plane was to be able to maintain a speed of 500 km/h (313 mph) for 30 minutes, take off to a height of 20 meters (65 ft) in not more than 750 meters (2,460 ft), and carry one defensive machine gun and 500–800 kg (1,100–1,760 lbs) of bombs. The crew was to consist of a pilot, a bombardier/navigator and a gunner. Focke-Wulf soon withdrew from participation and three projects were presented: the future Hs 127, the Junkers Ju 88 and the Messerschmitt Bf 162. Prototypes were ordered of all three, with new Daimler-Benz DB 600 engines to be installed on all planes. The maiden flight of the Hs 127 V1 was at the end of 1937. Only two unarmed prototypes were built of this low-wing monoplane with monocoque fuselage. Its two-spar wing had an all-metal covering and was equipped with flaps. Its retractable gear had shock-absorbers to facilitate operations from poor airstrips. All three crew members sat in the nose. The plane was smaller and lighter than the Junkers Ju 88—it had a span of about 18 m (59 ft), a length of 12 m (39 ft) and a very good top speed of 565 km/h (353 mph)—but the Ju 88 was chosen because of its bigger bomb load. In May 1938, the contract for the Henschel Hs 127 development was canceled by the RLM and a third prototype was not finished.

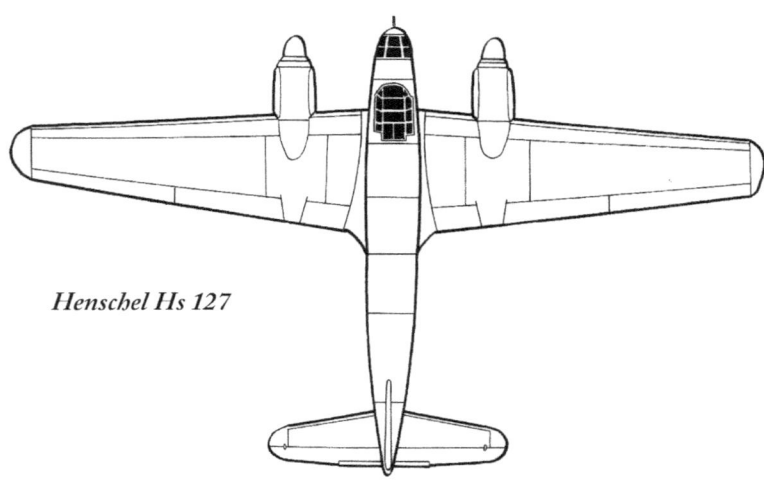

Henschel Hs 127

Junkers Ju 88

The Junkers Ju 88, one of the most versatile combat airplanes of all time, was the most important bomber used by the Luftwaffe throughout World War 2. The first prototype, a civil venture with an eye to military application, flew in December 1936 and won several speed records which attracted RLM's attention. Greatly altered and improved with the objective of increasing both speed and bomb load, the Ju 88A entered service with the Luftwaffe in late 1939 in the tactical medium-range bomber role.

With a typical speed of 485 km/h (300 mph), the Ju 88 was easily faster than the other chief types of German tactical bomber, the Dornier Do 17 and the Heinkel He 111. Combining an average bomb load of 2,000 kg (4,409 lbs), a typical range of about 1,610 km (1,000 miles), great strength, robust airframe, good maneuverability and agility, the development of the Ju 88 exemplifies the effect of the Luftwaffe's demand for optimization in the tactical bombing role. The most numerous and most widely used Ju 88 A-4 was operated by a crew of four, all placed in the glazed cockpit: pilot; bomb-aimer (sometime doubling as a second pilot and also operating a forward-firing 7.92-mm machine gun); engineer (also manning one or two rearward-firing upper machine guns); and radio operator (ready to squeeze into the gondola to man the rearward-firing belly machine gun). The aircraft had a span of 20.13 m (65 ft 10.5 in), a length of 14.4 m (47 ft 2.5 in), a height of 4.85 m (15 ft 11 in) and an empty weight of 8,000 kg (17,637 lbs). It was powered by two 1.340-hp Junkers Jumo 211J 12-cylinder, inverted-V, liquid-cooled engines. Like the He 111 and the Do 17, it had some failings, namely the concentration of the crew in the forward fuselage in glazed nose cockpit, and its limited defensive armaments which were based on manually operated single machine guns rather than turreted weapons. Junkers had to squeeze extra defensive machine guns and later light cannons into the already crowded cockpit. However, crews held the Ju 88 in high regard; when proficient hands were at the controls, results were often impressive. The aircraft was manufactured by Junkers Flugzeug und Motorwerke AG (led by the industrialist Heinz Koppenburg), dispersed among fourteen plants with subcontract or assembly by Siebel, ATG, Opel, Volkswagen and various French aircraft building companies. Originally designed as a specialized high-speed medium bomber, the Ju 88 proved suited for virtually every type of combat mission. Indeed the excellent performances combined with good combat maneuverability led inevitably to its use in other roles. Junkers Ju 88s existed in numerous versions—A, B, C, D, G, H, P, S

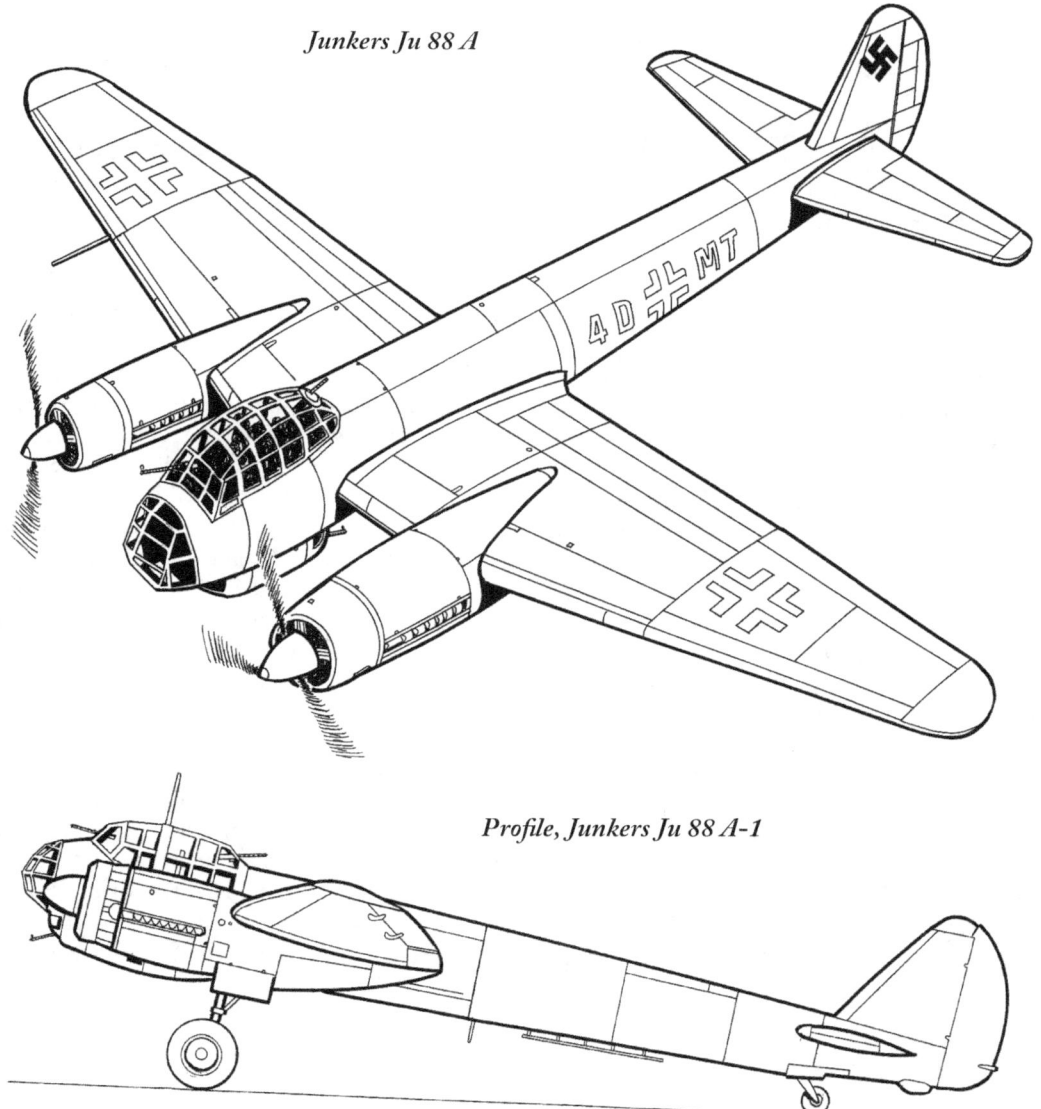

Junkers Ju 88 A

Profile, Junkers Ju 88 A-1

and T—most of them based on the A-4, but each with several subtypes undergoing constant improvements. They served on every World War II front in almost every role, with different engines and a wide variety of weapons, including as dual-controlled trainer, balloon cable-cutter, heavy fighter, bomber with various load capacities, tropical bomber, night fighter, reconnaissance aircraft, anti-shipping attacker and torpedo bomber, dive bomber, intruder, ground support craft, tank buster, mine layer, and finally as the lower half of the *Mistel* composite aircraft. As the war proceeded, the Junkers Ju 88 even supplanted the Heinkel He 111, which was increasingly used as a transport. The Junkers engineers tried to improve the design by developing a faster and more streamlined Ju 88, known as Ju 188. Further follow-up designs Ju 288, Ju 388 and Ju 488 were unsuccessful and full production never got under way, so the old Ju 88 was never replaced. About 15,000 units were produced until 1945, of which over 9,000 were bomber variants, more than all other bomber types combined.

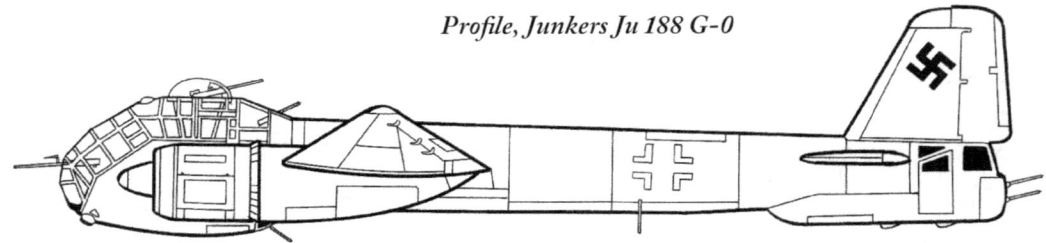

Profile, Junkers Ju 188 G-0

Junkers Ju 188

The medium bomber Ju 188 was a private venture by the Junkers company to upgrade the aging Ju 88. Intended as an interim replacement, the Ju 188 had a redesigned nose, better defensive armament, more streamlined fuselage, increased wing span, efficient pointed wings and large, squarish tail. The forward crew compartment was more spacious than that of the Ju 88, and seems to have been fitted with an emergency exit. The Ju 188 made its first flight in early 1940 but went into production only by mid-1943, after protracted development. It was operated by a crew of four: pilot; observer/bomb aimer; radio operator/gunner; and radar operator/gunner. Length was 14.7 m (49 ft 1 in), span was 22 m (72 ft 2 in), height was 4.9 m (16 ft 1 in) and empty weight was 9,900 kg (21,825 lbs). Powered by two BMW 801D-2 14-cylinder, air-cooled radial engines, each developing 1,700 hp, the aircraft had a speed of 420 km/h (325 mph) and a range of 2,480 km (1,550 miles). Take-off could be assisted with rocket boosters. Defensive armament featured one 20-mm MG 151 cannon in nose, two 13-mm MG 131 machine guns, one in dorsal turret, one in rear cockpit, and twin 7.92-mm MG 81 Z machine guns firing aft below the fuselage. Some versions had a tail turret armed with twin MG 131 machine guns. The Ju 188 existed in several versions for different roles, including bomber with a 1,500-kg (3,300-lb) bomb load; the aircraft had a new system of electrically operated bomb doors, which simultaneously fused the bombs, making it impossible to drop the payload unfused. Other roles included torpedo bomber; night fighter equipped with radar; and close-support craft with 50-mm BK-5 cannon. Over 50 percent of the Ju 188s manufactured were high-altitude reconnaissance versions. In spite of its excellent qualities, the outstanding Ju 188 was never to replace the Ju 88. Some 1,076 units were produced, seeing action in Europe, the Mediterranean Sea and Russian

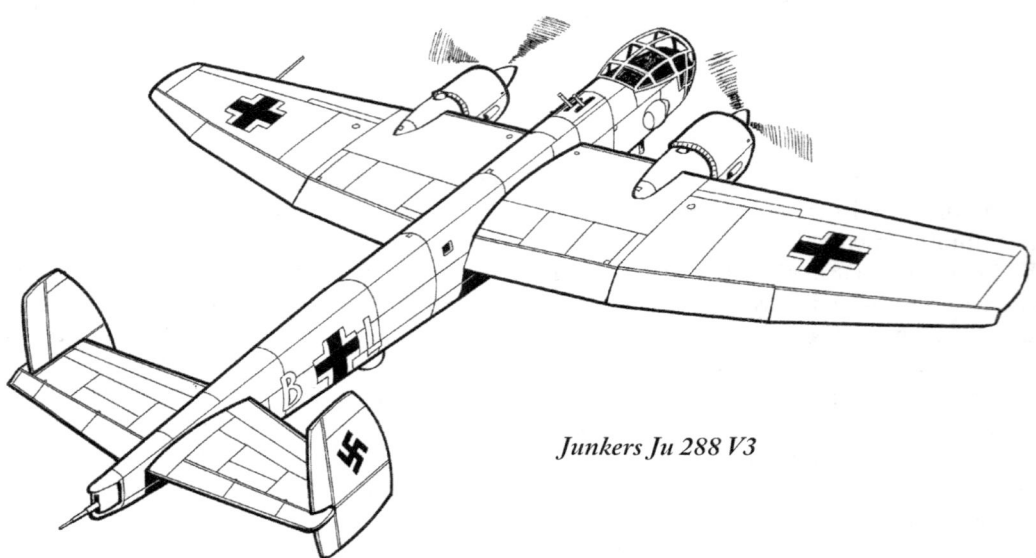

Junkers Ju 288 V3

front, but they did not make a significant impact on the war.

Junkers Ju 288

The Ju 288 medium bomber was designed in 1940 by the Junkers Company to meet the demands of the so-called high-speed, long-range Bomber B program launched by the RLM. The aircraft, an improved version of the famous Junkers Ju 88, had a crew of three, including pilot, observer/bomb aimer, and radio operator/gunner, sitting in a pressurized, glazed-nose cockpit for high-altitude flight. It had a span of 18.30 m (60 ft), and a length of 15.90 m (52 ft 2 in). It was powered by two 2,500-hp Junkers Jumo 222 A-1/B-1 24-cylinder, liquid-cooled radial engines, and had a maximum speed of 670 km/h (416 mph) and a range of 3,600 km (2,237 miles). It was armed with two 13-mm MG 131 machine guns in remotely controlled turrets, one forward dorsal, and one aft ventral. A bomb load of 3,000 kg (6,614 lbs) could be carried. Essentially another derivative of the Ju 88 layout, the Junkers Ju 288 differed in that its snake's-head nose and tail fin and rudder configuration bore little resemblance to the other Ju 88 variants. The maiden flight of Ju 288 prototype V1 was originally scheduled for October 1940, and series production was planned to begin in early 1942, but development met serious troubles. The Jumo engines failed to live up to expectation, and flight trials were delayed until mid-1942. Even then the first prototype flew with BMW engines, a change that confused the test evaluation process even further. Besides, a shortage of strategic materials and a fear that production would adversely affect the manufacture of other current aircraft eventually led Junkers to cancel its full development in late 1942. In June 1943 the whole Bomber B program was canceled as it consumed too many resources and would have interfered with production of proven (but obsolete) aircrafts. This left the Luftwaffe with a complete absence of a modern bomber, and also with no realistic facility in the strategic role. In the end, the sophisticated Ju 288 program proved a failure. Of a total of 22 Ju 288 prototypes built, seventeen crashed during flight tests.

Junkers Ju 388

Following the unfortunate abandonment of the Ju 288 program, Junkers, in spite of obvious problems, continued development of high-altitude variants of the Ju 88. The Ju 388 was

Junkers Ju 388L

another attempt to create a fast high-altitude bomber (K version), night and all-weather interceptor (J version), and reconnaissance aircraft (L version). Based on the Junkers Ju 188 design, it had a crew of three, including pilot, observer/gunner, and gunner sitting in a pressurized cockpit. Armament was one remotely operated turret armed with two 13-mm MG 131 machine guns. The interceptor version was armed with two MG 151 cannons in a *Schräge Musik* oblique installation in the rear fuselage, and equipped with a FuG 218 Neptun radar with a fourth crew member. The bomber version could carry a bomb load of 3,000 kg (6,614 lbs). Although the Junkers Company devoted much engineering effort to the project, the Ju 388 never reached production status and only forty-seven high-altitude reconnaissance L versions reached the Luftwaffe. The Ju 388 L was powered by two 1,890-hp BMW 801 TJ 14-cylinder, air-cooled radial engines (a few by two 1,750-hp Junkers Jumo 213E inverted-V-12, liquid-cooled engines), and had a speed of 655 km/h (407 mph), and a range of 2,950 km (1,838 miles). Span was 22 m (72 ft 2 in), length was 15.20 m (49 ft 10.5 in), and empty weight was 10,345 kg (22,810 lbs).

The whole series of Junkers Ju 188, Ju 288, and Ju 388 were evidence of the increasingly urgent need to make up for the absence of properly conceived new designs by wringing the utmost development out of the obsolescent types with which the German air force started the war.

Henschel Hs 130

The Hs 130 was a two-engined, high-altitude reconnaissance and bomber aircraft. A development of the Hs 128 high-altitude research aircraft, the Hs 130A first flew in November 1940, and was used to test engines, turbochargers, remote-control cameras, and other experimental devices. The aircraft had a span of 29 m (95 ft 1.7 in), a length of 14.95 m (49 ft 0.5 in), and a weight (fully loaded) of 11,680 kg (25,750 lbs). Maximum speed was between 470 km/h (292 mph) and 610 km/h (379 mph) and range was between 2,230 km (1,385 miles) and 3,000 km (1,860 miles), depending on engines used. The final development of the Hs 130 was the E model which took to the air in September 1942. The Hs 130E was intend to flight test the new BMW 018 jet engine, when the only complete example was destroyed in an air raid in late 1944. No other engines were finished by the time the war ended.

Focke-Wulf Fw 191

The Focke-Wulf Fw 191, designed to a July 1939 Luftwaffe specification for a high-perfor-

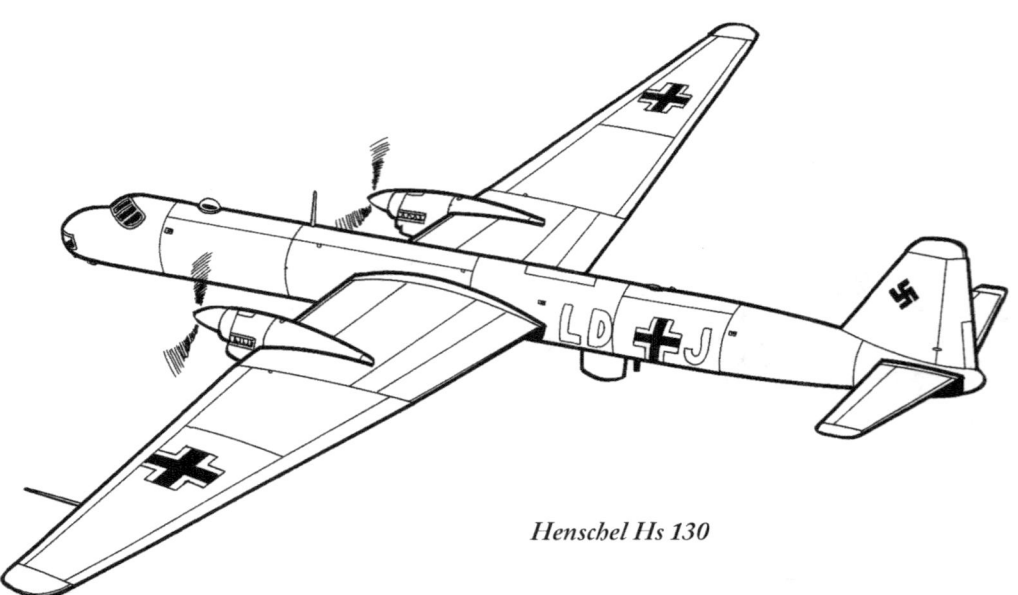

Henschel Hs 130

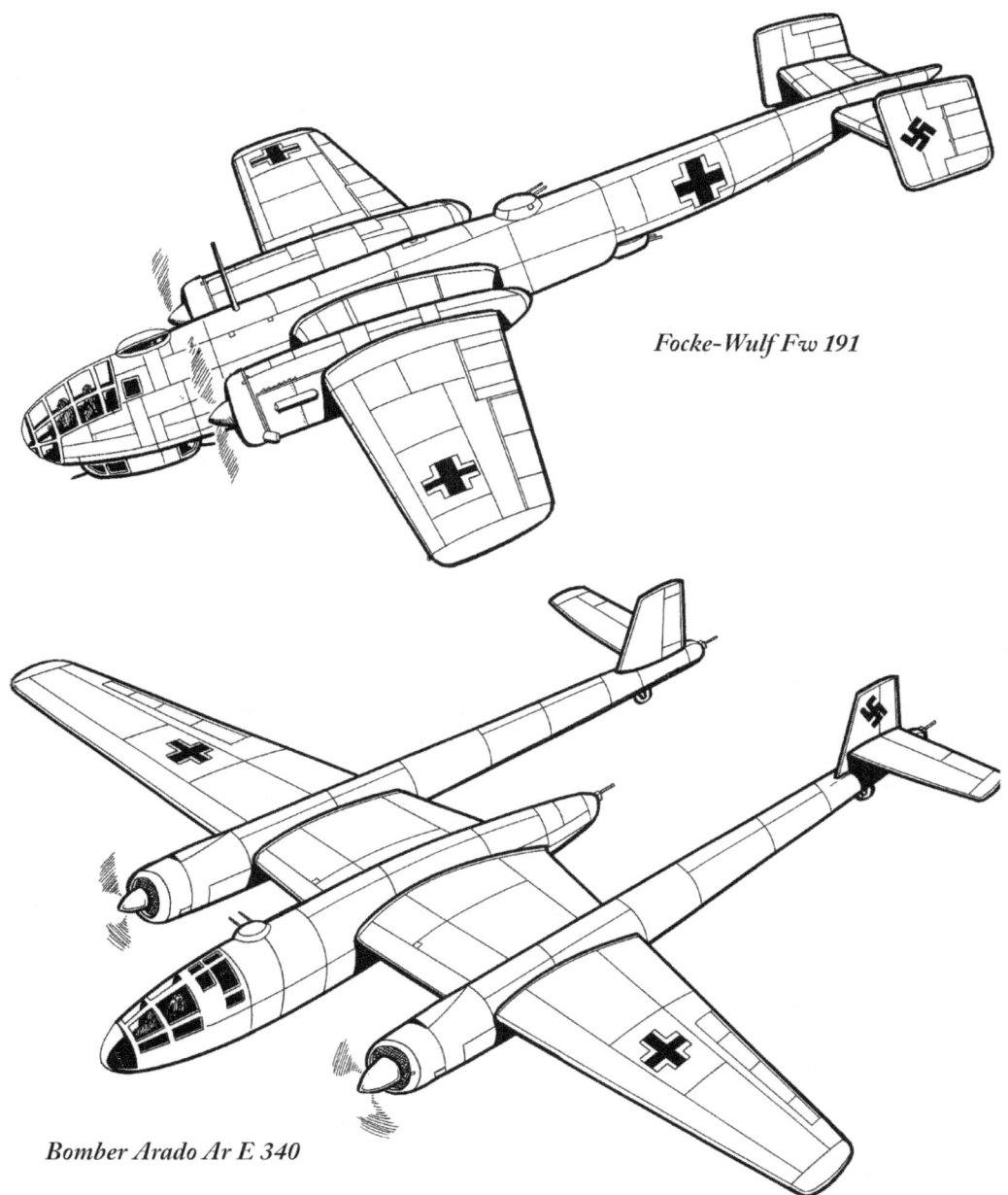

Focke-Wulf Fw 191

Bomber Arado Ar E 340

mance medium bomber (the so-called Bomber B program), was intended to have the performance ability to bomb any target in Britain from bases in France and Norway. A maximum speed of 620 km/h (385 mph), and a range of 3,600 km (2,237 miles) were planned. The Fw 191 made its first flight in early 1942, but the 2,500-horsepower (1.9 MW) Junkers Jumo 222 engines, which would have powered it, proved troublesome. The project was finally abandoned in 1943 after the building of only three prototypes. The aircraft had a length of 18.45 m (60 ft 6 in), a wingspan of 25 m (82 ft), a height of 4.80 m (15 ft 9 in), a wing area of 70.5 square m (759 square ft), and an empty weight of 11,970 kg (26,389 lbs). The crew included four airmen (pilot, observer, engineer and radio operator) placed in a glazed-nose cockpit pressurized for high-altitude operations. The armament would have consisted of

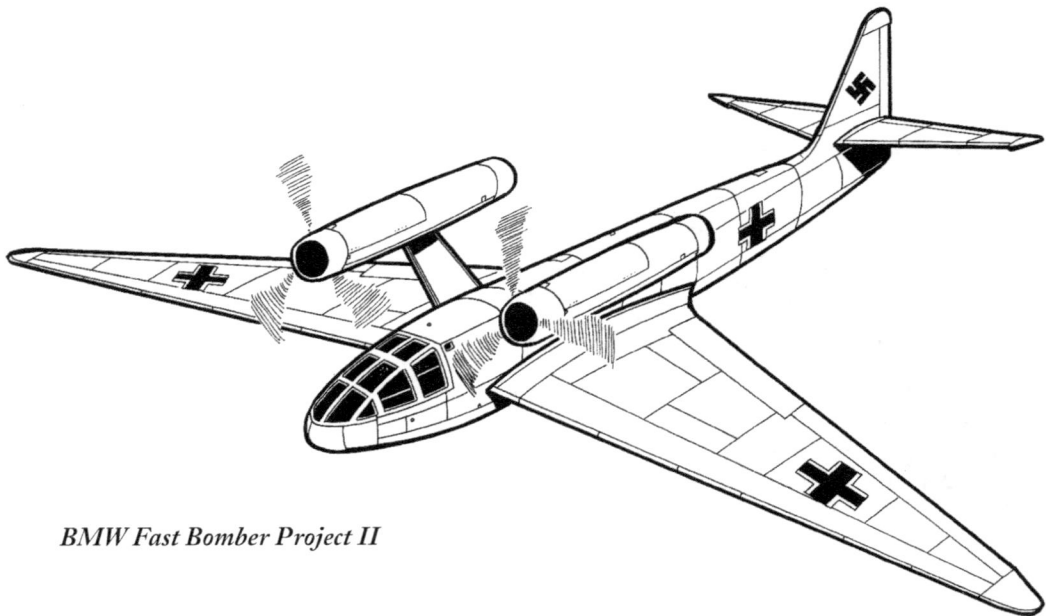

BMW Fast Bomber Project II

one MG 151 in a chin turret, twin MG 151 in a remotely controlled dorsal turret, twin MG 151 in a remotely controlled ventral turret, a tail turret with one or two machine guns, and remotely controlled weapons in the rear of the engine nacelles. The aircraft was fitted with an internal bomb bay with a capacity of 3,000 kg (6,624 lbs), and additional bombs or torpedoes could be carried on external racks between the fuselage and the engine nacelles. An enlarged version for a long-range strategic bomber with four engines, known as Focke-Wulf Fw 191 C, never passed the design stage.

Arado Ar E 340

The Arado Ar E 340 was intended to replace the Junkers Ju 88 and the Dornier Do 217 by 1943. Designed in 1939, this medium bomber was composed of a central fuselage with glazed and pressurized cockpit for the crew of four, with two booms mounting two Jumo 222 engines and the retractable landing gear. The airplane had a span of 23 m (75 ft 4.8 in), a length of 18.65 m (61ft 2.3 in) and would have had a speed of 625 km/h (388 mph). Armament was to consist of two rear-firing MG151 20-mm guns placed in both boom tails, and two EDL 13-mm cannons placed in remote-controlled small turrets, one below the fuselage and the other mounted behind the cockpit. The experimental Ar E 340 never made it further than the drawing board, as the project was canceled.

BMW Fast Bomber Project II

Rather little is known about this odd design by Bayerische Motorenwerke (BMW) for a *Schnellbomber*. It had a length of 21.5 m (70 ft 6.5 in), and wings swept forward 45 degrees with a span of 35.7 m (117 ft 1.5 in). Curiously the two BMW 028 turboprop engines were mounted on arms above the fuselage. The aircraft would have had a crew of two sitting in a pressurized, glazed cockpit at the front. Two cannons were to be fixed for firing rearward. This design never left the drawing board.

Mistel Composite

Mistel (Mistletoe) was a generic term adopted for an attack weapon system comprising two aircraft. An unmanned bomber, filled with explosives, was guided toward a target by a manned fighter attached via struts to its top. The fighter pilot released the bomber and either left it to dive down or steered it by radio-control onto the target, and then withdrew to

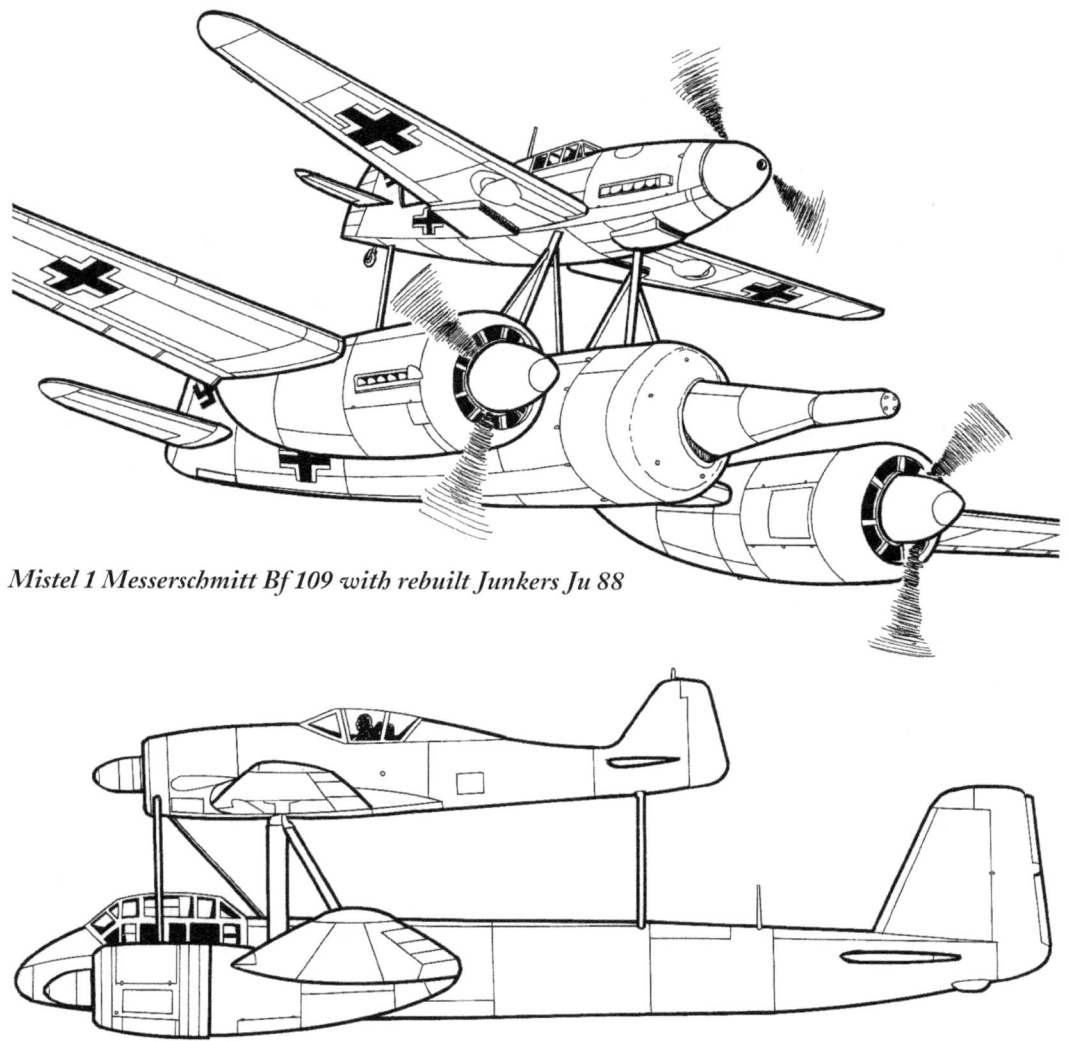

Mistel 1 Messerschmitt Bf 109 with rebuilt Junkers Ju 88

Mistel S 2 Junkers Ju-88 G1 with Focke-Wulf Fw 190 A-8

safety—at least that was the theory. The concept was initiated in 1941 by Siegfried Holzbauer, test pilot of the Junkers Company. This scheme was ignored until July 1943 when a conversion was made, joining a pilotless Junkers Ju 88 bomber and a manned Messerschmitt 109 fighter. Several prototypes followed, and tests made against a discarded battleship and concrete fortifications were encouraging. It should be noted that the concept had already been developed as early as 1938 by a certain Major R. Mayo, when Imperial Airways flew small floatplane Mercury Short S 20 on top of a larger flying boat, the Maia Short S 21. At that time this commercial civilian endeavor was more curiosity than practical idea.

The German Mistel military conversions required substantial systems and structural changes to both bomber and fighter. For example, the lower aircraft was stripped of interior fittings, which were replaced with fuel and explosive; the upper aircraft had duplicate controls for the lower bomber, and modifications were carried out to save weight; notably the fighter's wing-guns were removed. The upper aircraft was attached by several struts placed on the top of the bomber's fuselage. Control cables were strapped to them and plugged into

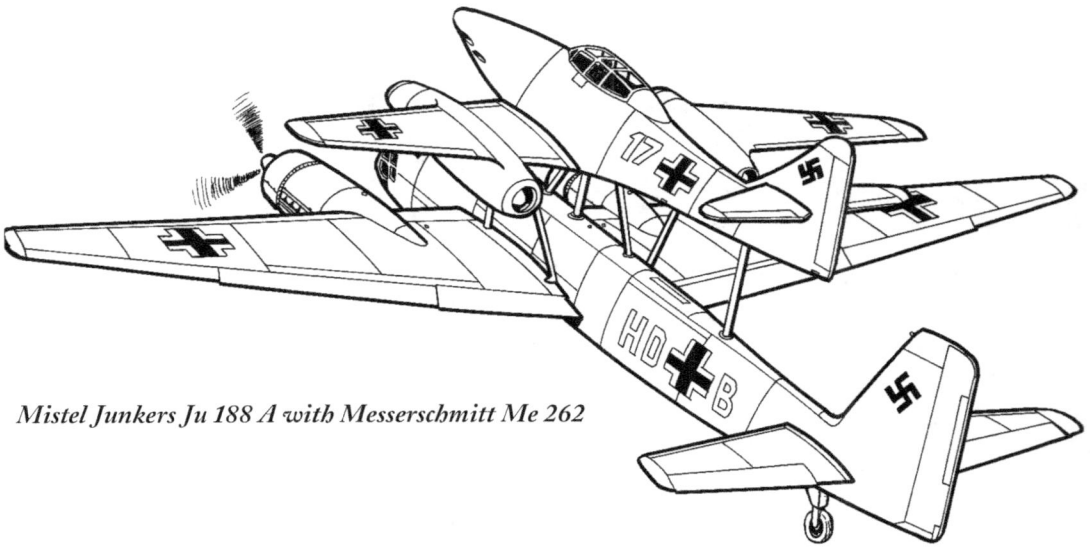

Mistel Junkers Ju 188 A with Messerschmitt Me 262

the underside of the fighter. The rear strut buckled first when releasing the Mistel, giving the fighter a "nose-up" attitude; the electrically detonated explosive ball joints then detonated, releasing the fighter. Conversions were developed and carried out by the Junkers, DFS, Patin and Askania companies. There were a number of possible Mistel combinations. The training schemes Mistel S1, codenamed "Beethoven," was composed of a Junkers Ju 88 A-4 with a Messerschmitt Bf 109F; Mistel S2, a Ju 88G-1 bomber with a Focke-Wulf Fw190A-8; and Mistel S3A with a Ju 88A-6 and a Fw 190A-6. The first operational version was Mistel 1, composed of a Messerschmitt Bf 109F guiding a totally rebuilt Ju 88A-4 whose glazed cockpit was removed and replaced with a large 3,800-kg high-explosive (or hollow charge) warhead with a distinctive solid bulkhead fitted with a long extended-contact fuse; the impact fuse was intended to detonate the charge. The penetrative force was exceptionally high, with the capacity to inflict considerable damage to a large installation, destroy a bridge, or even sink a capital ship with one hit.

Other combinations were built. Mistel 2 included a fighter Focke-Wulf Fw 190-A-6 guiding a rebuilt Junkers Ju 88G-1 with a front warhead. Mistel 3C was composed of a fighter Focke-Wulf Fw 190-A-8 on top of a rebuilt Junkers Ju 88H-4 with nose warhead and enlarged fuselage. Other combination included a Klemm 34 carried by a DFS 230 glider and a Focke-Wulf Fw 56 with a DFS 230 glider.

There were also similar projects using jet airplanes. A combination of two Messerschmitt Me 262 jet fighters was planned; the unmanned component was full of explosives, with cockpit canopy being faired over. Mistel 5 included a Heinkel He 162 Salamander jet fighter combined either with an unmanned Heinkel He 177 *Greif* filled with explosives, or an Arado Ar E 377 flying bomb. The Arado Ar E 377 was an unmanned glide-winged bomb with a circular fuselage made of wood. It had a length of 10.9 m (35 ft 9 in), and a span of 14.4 m (47 ft 3 in). The bomb carried 2,000 kg (4,408 lbs) of high explosive in the nose and 500 kg (1,202 lbs) of incendiary liquid. The Ar E 377 was carried under the fuselage and launched from an Arado Ar 234C or from a Heinkel He 162, and could be guided onto the target by remote control. Take-off of carrier and bomb was done with a large rocket-propelled five-wheel jettisonable trolley. It was planned to motorize the glide bomb (in that case designated Ar E 377A) with two BMW 003 jet engines to be launched from a Heinkel He 162. A piloted version for suicide attack was also envisioned but never built.

Over 250 Mistel combinations were planned, a few of them built. Of these only a few saw combat service and were used to attack tacti-

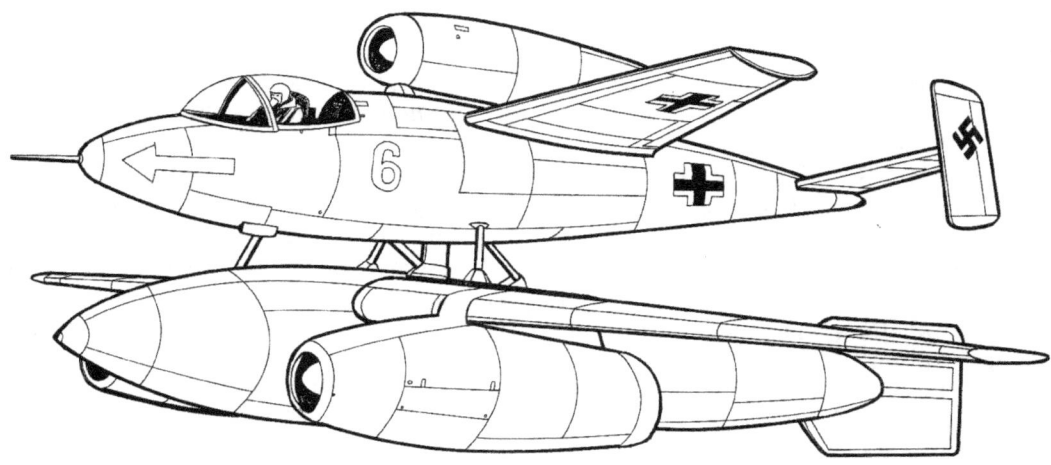

Mistel Heinkel He 162 A with Arado E 377A flying bomb

cal targets such as a bridges and ships. Initial attacks in May 1944 were unsuccessfully conducted at night against Allied shipping. Mistel 1—flown by 2/KG 101 headed by Hauptmann Horst Rudat—made a sortie during the invasion of Normandy in June 1944 but, as far as it is known, failed to sink any Allied battleship. Plans were made for a mass raid on the Royal Navy fleet base of Scapa Flow in December 1944. Some sixty Mistel combinations were to fly from Denmark to make a night attack. The mission was canceled, officially due to bad weather. In the spring of 1945 several attacks were launched against river crossings and bridgeheads. As with most of the Nazis' last-ditch schemes, the Mistel combination made no significant impact on the outcome of the war.

Long-Range Heavy Bombers

Airpower was the subject of conflicting theories and considerable misconception in the twenty years following the end of World War I. Of these, that put forward by the Italian General Guilio Douhet (1869–1930) in his book *Il Dominio dell'Aria* (The Command of the Air), published in 1921, received most attention. What Douhet recommended was strategic bombing. He recognized the airplane as the offensive weapon par excellence because of its independence from the ground and its superior speed. Convinced that no defense against bombers could be possible, he advocated violent, surprise air attacks on an opponent's vulnerable civilian population. Large air fleets of long-range bombers would attack enemy cities, ports, dams, oil stores, railway junctions, industrial and power plants, commercial and distribution centers, with a rain of high explosives, gas and incendiary bombs until the enemy's morale cracked. The damage inflicted would be psychological as well as physical, and conventional ground troops would simply have the task of mopping up. Douhet's theory was shared by Hugh Montague Trenchard, chief of the British Air Staff, and by William Mitchell of the U.S. Army Air Service, who spoke of air attacks that would destroy the cities, factories and food supplies of an enemy, demoralizing its civilian population, and thus shattering its will to fight. These theorists of presumed horrors of aerial assault bombing were preoccupied with the consideration of the bomber and failed to credit the fighter as an effective method of defense and underestimated the potential of anti-aircraft artillery. Douhet and Mitchell's gloomy predictions over the extent of civilian demoralization through air raids failed to come true, they overestimated the effect of offensive bombing, and many of their theories were found wanting at the Battle of Britain in 1940. Although air superiority was shown to be an absolute necessity for success, the air arm alone could not win a war. The long-range strategic bomber was simply a means of delivering a load of bombs with reasonable accuracy at a great range, but it suffered from the disadvantage that it was vulnerable.

In the mid-1930s, Generalleutnant Walter Wever, the Luftwaffe's first chief of staff, was the most persistent advocate of a German long-range strategic fleet composed of big bombers with large loads, like the ones being developed in Britain and the United States during World War II. Largely because of Wever, the RLM *Technisch Amt* (technical section of the state ministry of aviation) issued specifications for four-engine heavy bombers. Several aircraft companies, including Dornier and Junkers, were competitors for the contract. Prototypes were designed resulting, in a few models with potential (e.g., Dornier Do 19 and Junkers Ju 89) but when Generalleutnant Wever died in 1936 in an airplane crash, the heavy-bomber program lost its momentum and was not to recover. It is ironic that despite the emphasis laid upon the long-range bomber before World War II, the Luftwaffe failed to develop any practicable heavy craft. The death of Wever ensured that the protagonists of the tactical ideal would dominate. Albert Kesselring, Wever's successor, argued that large strategic bombers would involve far too high a cost, and strongly believed that what Germany required was more fighter-bombers and tactical medium bombers. The seal was set upon the development of large strategic bombers, and priority was then given to a large fleet of short-range bombers which performed extremely well during the early stage of World War II. Hitler never asked how big the Luftwaffe bombers were but how many there were of them. His penchant for quantity rather than quality was to have a serious long-term effect on Germany's ability to wage a protracted war. When the Luftwaffe was given its first heavy blow over the skies of England in 1940, the error of not having heavy bombers became apparent. The deficiency was never corrected, and by then it was too late anyway to develop the bombers required. The lack of an efficient, strategic, long-range, heavy-bomber fleet was one of the Luftwaffe's most serious shortcomings. The concept of a strategic heavy bomber, however, was never ruled out, particularly when war broke out between the Reich and the United States in December 1941, when the Luftwaffe found itself without the means of attacking its new and remote enemy. Certain individuals at the RLM contemplated the possibility of bombing the Eastern coast of the United States. Specifications were issued, programs were launched and various projects were envisioned, but technical specifications were so dominated by tactical requirements that they came to nothing. Until the end of the war the Luftwaffe never had a real effective fleet of long-range heavy bombers adequately equipped for a strategic role such as the American B-17 Flying Fortress or B-24 Liberator or the British Avro Lancaster. When Germany was forced to the defensive in 1943 onward, when the Allies gained air supremacy, it is doubtful whether German long-range bombers, even if they had been produced in large number, would have made a significant difference in the outcome of World War II.

Dornier Do 11

During the late 1920s, the German Dornier Metallbauten set up a subsidiary at Altenrhein in Switzerland to build heavy aircraft expressly forbidden under the terms of the Versailles Treaty. The Do P had four engines, the Do Y three, and the Do F was a large twin. All were described as freighters, but their suitability as bombers was obvious. In late 1932 it was boldly decided to put the Dornier Do F into production at the German factory at Friedrichshafen, the designation being changed to Do 11. The first customer was the German State Railways which under the cover of a freight service actually enabled the embryonic Luftwaffe to begin training future bomber crews. The Do 11 had a slim, light-alloy fuselage with a length of 18.79 m (61 ft 8 in), and high-mounted metal wing with fabric covering, with a span of 28 m (91 ft 10.3 in). It was fitted with a retractable landing gear whose vertical main legs were laboriously cranked inward along the inner wing until the large wheels lay flat inside the nacelles; giving much trouble, the landing gear was soon permanently locked down. The aircraft was powered

Dornier Do 11

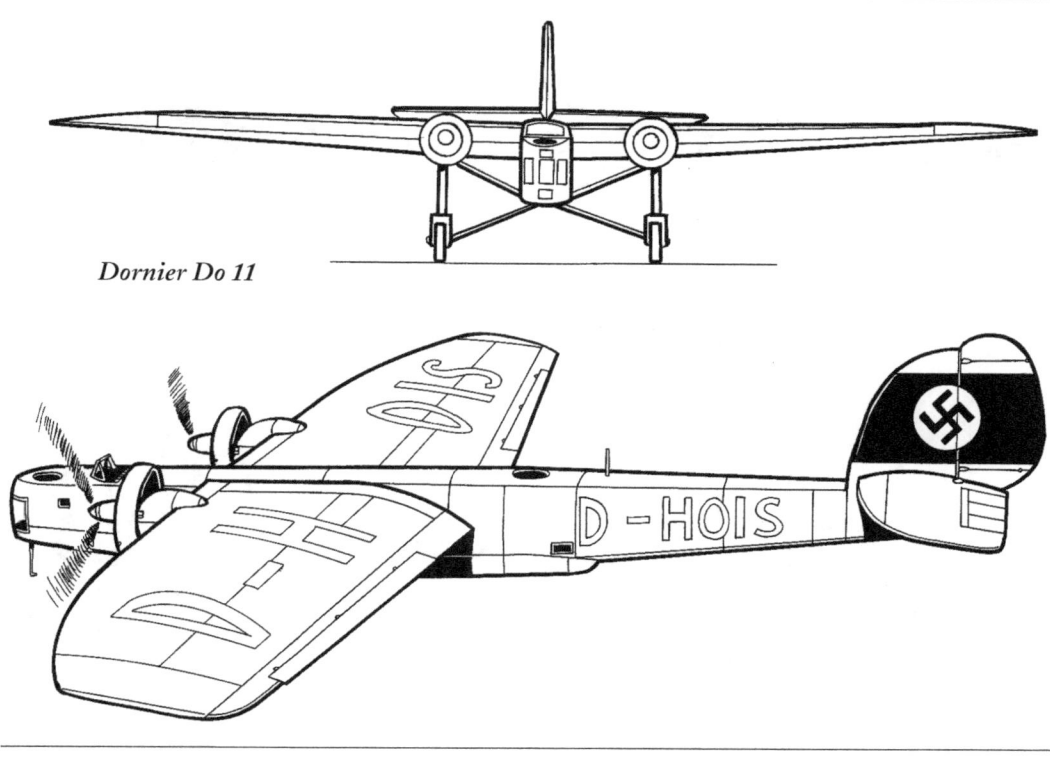

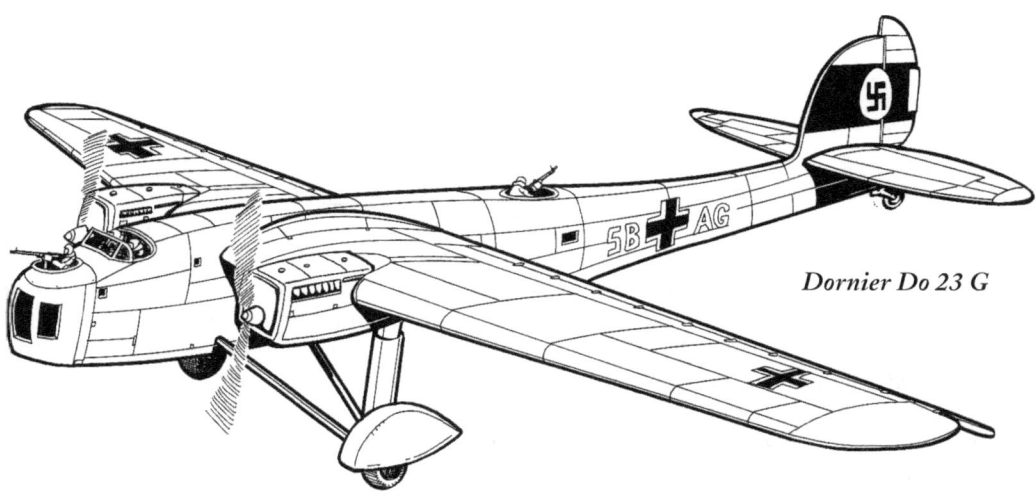

Dornier Do 23 G

by two Siemens Sh 22B 9-cylinder, air-cooled radial engines (developing 630 hp). Cruise speed was 225 km/h (140 mph), and maximum range was 960 km (596 miles). It carried a bomb load of 1,000 kg (2,205 lbs) in an internal bomb bay. Defensive armament included three manually aimed 7.92-mm MG 15 machine guns placed in nose, dorsal and ventral positions. By the end of 1934 there were about 77 units produced, operating in by-now overt military flying schools. As accidents were frequent, the unpopular Dornier Do 11 was gradually replaced by other aircraft.

Dornier Do 23

The heavy bomber Dornier Do 23 corrected many of the faults that had plagued the earlier Do 11 but remained a mediocre performer. The aircraft had a crew of four, a wingspan of 25.5

Heavy bomber Dornier Do 23

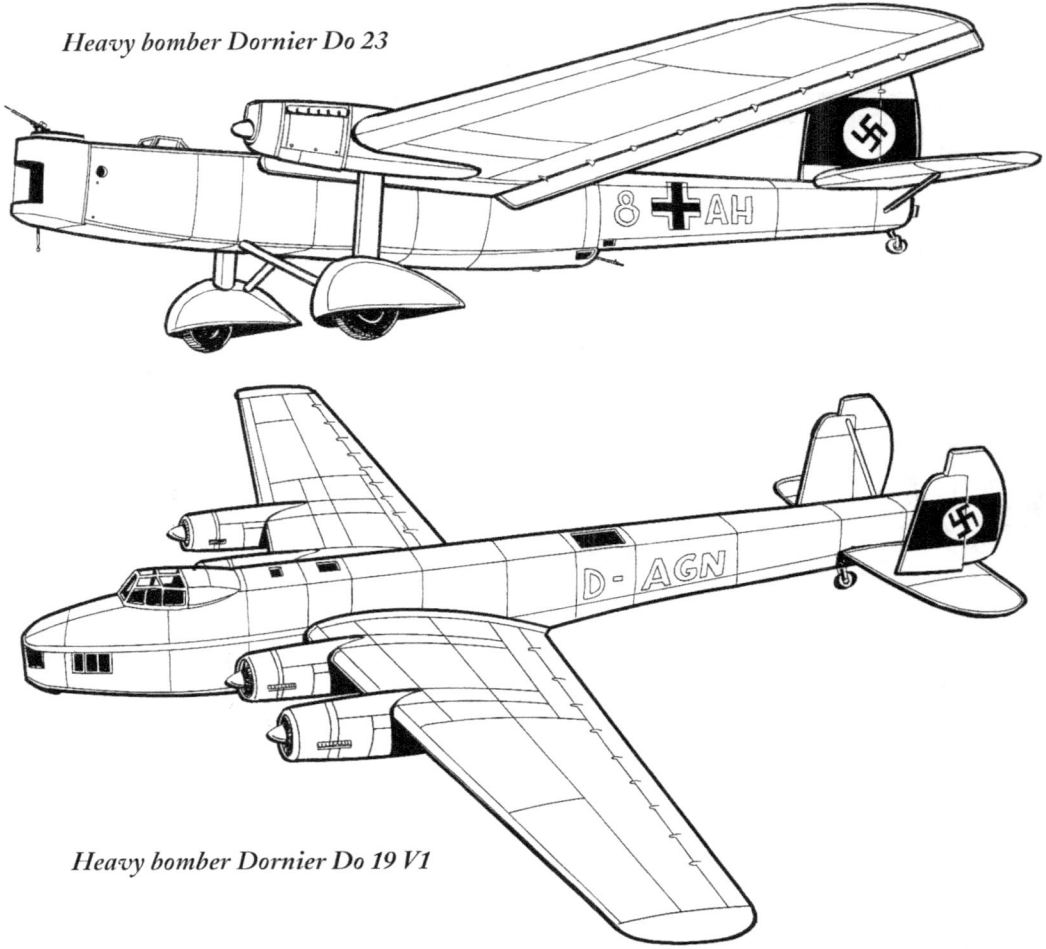

Heavy bomber Dornier Do 19 V1

m (83 ft 8 in), a length of 18.8 m (61 ft 8 in), a height of 5.4 m (17 ft 8 in), and an empty weight of 5,600 kg (12,346 lbs). The most-developed G-version was powered by two 750-hp BMW VIU liquid-cooled (ethylene-glycol) piston engines. Maximum speed was 259 km/h (161 mph), and range was about 1,352 km (840 miles). A bomb load of 1,000 kg (2,205 lbs) was carried in an internal bomb bay, the projectiles being housed in vertical cells in the fuselage. Designed in 1933, thus at a time when Germany was still officially forbidden to have a military air force, no attempt was made to disguise the function of the bomber: the fuselage had a glazed nose for visual aiming of the bomb, and defensive armament included three manually aimed 7.92-mm MG 15 machine guns in nose, mid-upper dorsal, and rear ventral positions. By late 1935, 210 units had been delivered and used by bomber squadrons. Although the Dornier Do 23 played a major part in the formation of the Luftwaffe, it was not much better than its disappointing predecessors. The aircraft was phased out of service in the German Luftwaffe by the late 1930s, replaced by superior designs such as the Heinkel He 111. It did go on to see action in World War II in the Czech branch of the Luftwaffe and continued to be used until the end of the war in utility tasks, training, trials and research roles.

Dornier Do 19

The Dornier Do 19 was an intriguing possibility that, for several reasons, never panned out. The Dornier Do 19 was a mid-wing cantilever design, and was mostly metal in con-

4. Bombers

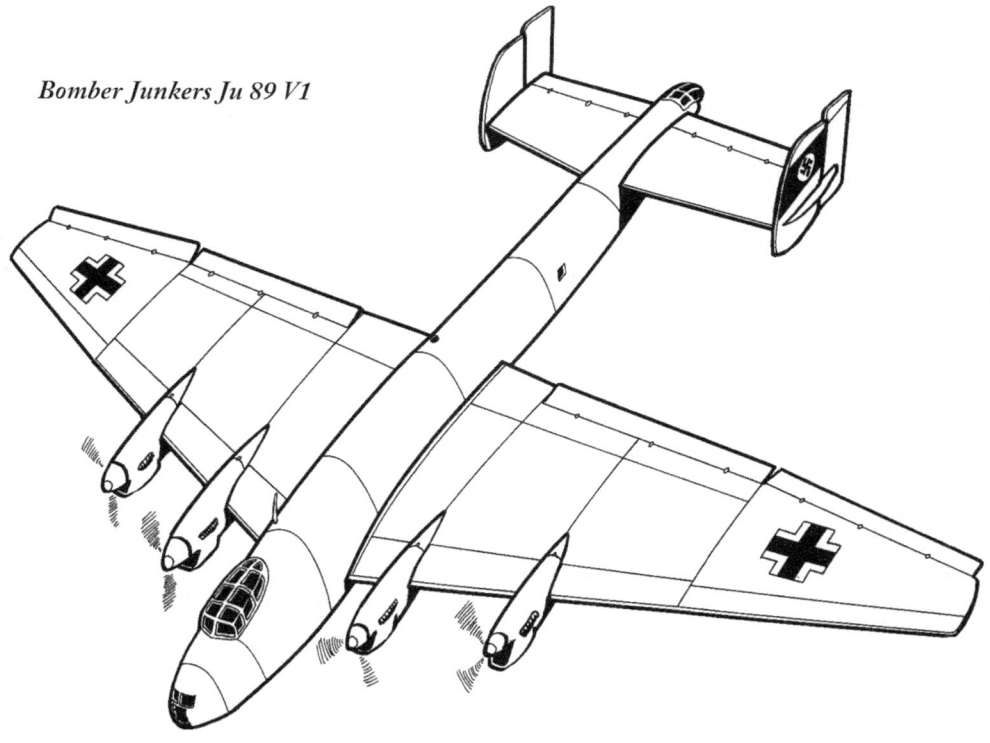

Bomber Junkers Ju 89 V1

struction. It had a rectangular-section fuselage and a tail unit with braced twin fins and rudders. Empty weight was 11,850 kg (25,125 lb), span was 35 m (114 ft 10 in), length was 25.45m (83 ft 6 in), height was 5.77m (18 ft 11), and wing area was 162 square m (1,743.81 square ft). It also had retractable landing gear, including the tailwheel. The powerplant was four Bramo 332H-2 radial engines, that were mounted in nacelles at the leading edges of the wings. Maximum speed at sea level was 315 km/h (196 mph), service ceiling was 5,600m (18,370 ft), and range was 1,600 km (994 miles). Armament included two 7.92-mm (0.31-in) MG 15 machine guns, in nose and tail positions; and two 20-mm cannon (one each in two-man operated ventral and dorsal turrets). A bomb load of 1,600 kg (3,527 lbs) was carried in internal bays. The aircraft was to have a crew of nine, which would have consisted of a pilot, copilot, navigator, bombardier, radio operator and five gunners. The V1 prototype flew in October 1936, but the death of General Walther Wever, the strategic-minded chief of staff, prevented its further development. The program was canceled and V2 and V3 prototypes were scrapped. The original V1 became a transport in 1938. The Dornier Do 19 was a promising design that could have yielded a useful long-range bomber and desperately needed experience in a field where the Luftwaffe failed to shine.

Junkers Ju 89

The Junkers Ju 89 was intended to be a Luftwaffe *Langstrecken-Großbomber* (long-range heavy bomber), and its development was spurred by General Walter Wever. Designed by a Junkers team under leadership of Engineer Ernst Zindel, the large and impressive four-engine aircraft made its first flight in December 1936. It had a smooth, duralumin-skin fuselage with a length of 26.40 m (86 ft 11.3 in), low-mounted, double-flapped wings with a span of 53.25 m (115 ft 8.5 in) and an empty weight of 17,000 kg (34,480 lbs). It was fitted with a modern, retractable, hydraulic landing gear, and was operated by a crew of nine. Armament was to include two 20-mm cannons mounted in dorsal and ventral turrets and front and rear MG 15 machine guns. A load of sixteen 100-kg (220-lb) bombs was to be carried. Only two units were built. Prototype V1 was powered by four inverted-V-12 engines, and V2 by four Jumo 211A engines. Average speed was 390 km/h (242 mph) and typical range was 2,000 kg (1,242 miles) giving the machine the popular nickname of Uralbomber. After Wever's death the long-range heavy bomber program was canceled in April 1937, and the much promising and capable Junkers Ju 89 was never further developed.

Focke-Wulf Fw 200 Condor

The Focke-Wulf Fw 200 Condor was a long-range maritime reconnaissance/bomber aircraft. Built under Lufthansa specification and with Wilhelm Bansemir as project director, it was designed in partnership with the Focke-Wulf Company and Blohm & Voss/Hamburger Flugzeugbau in 1937, as a long-range civil airliner for the Lufthansa Company. It made headlines with its spectacular flights to distant cities. It was the very first airplane to fly nonstop between Berlin and New York—on August 10, 1938 in 24 hours and 56 minutes. The return trip took only 19 hours and 47 minutes on August 13, 1938. An all-metal, four-engine monoplane, it was capable of carrying 25 passengers up to 3,000 km. It was built in three versions (Fw 200A, B, and C). The Model A was a purely civilian plane used by Lufthansa, DDL in Denmark, and Syndicato Condor in Brazil.

The military version originated from a requirement of the Japanese navy, which ordered five Fw 200s in 1939, through the airline Dai-Nippon. Intended for use as long-range patrol aircraft over the Pacific Ocean, the Condors were not delivered. When World War II broke out, existing airliners were militarized and fulfilled this role in the Atlantic. The Fw 200B and Fw 200C models were used as long-range bombers, reconnaissance craft, and troop and VIP transport planes. Adolf Hitler used his own Fw 200V-1 model. His personal seat in the cabin was equipped with back-armor plating and an automatic parachute with downward throws. This plane was named *Immelmann III*. To adapt the airliner for wartime, hard points were added on the wings for bomb racks, the fuselage was extended and strengthened to create more space, and front, aft and dorsal gun positions were added. Wingspan was 30.8 m (107 ft 9 in), length was 23.4 m (76 ft 11 in) and weight (empty) was 12,951 kg (29,550 lbs). The landing gear was composed of two forward-retracting legs, each fitted with twin main wheels, and a forward-retracting tail wheel. The crew was generally made up of six to eight airmen. Defensive armament included one backward dorsal turret, armed with one 15-mm MG 151 machine gun; one hydraulically operated turret placed on top of the fuselage behind the cockpit, armed with a 7.92-mm MG 15 machine gun; two 7.92-mm MG 15 machine guns placed in a ventral gondola; and two beam windows each armed with a 13-mm MG 131 machine gun. A bomb load of 2,100kg (4,626 lbs) was carried in the ventral gondola and in racks located beneath the outer wings. In spite of its prewar record breaking, the Condor had modest performances, and was basically more a commercial airliner than a military aircraft. It was powered by four 1,200-hp BMW-Bramo Fafnir 323R-2 9-cylinder radial engines. Maximum speed was 360 km/h (224 mph), and range with standard fuel was 3,550 km (2,206 miles). The Condor could fly for fourteen hours, but it also had notable deficiencies. Relatively lightly constructed, the airplane was inadequate for low-level flying over the ocean in which continuous turbulence put too much stress on the airframe. Evasive maneuvers had to be carried out with extreme precaution otherwise wings could break. The airplane suffered from structural weakness and sometimes came apart, either the fuselage or the wing breaking, especially on take-off and landing. The bomb load was much less than that of military-purpose-designed aircraft, such as the Junkers Ju 88 or the Heinkel He 111. Serviceability of the Fw 200 was to remain low throughout its operational career. Yet the Fw 200 remained a thorn in the Allies' side until near the end of the war. Particularly in the period 1941–1943, Condors exerted an effect on Allied Atlantic shipping, and were called—in Winston Churchill's words—the "scourge of the Atlantic." As backup and scout for the German U-Boat, Fw 200 aircraft were used for bombing stragglers and

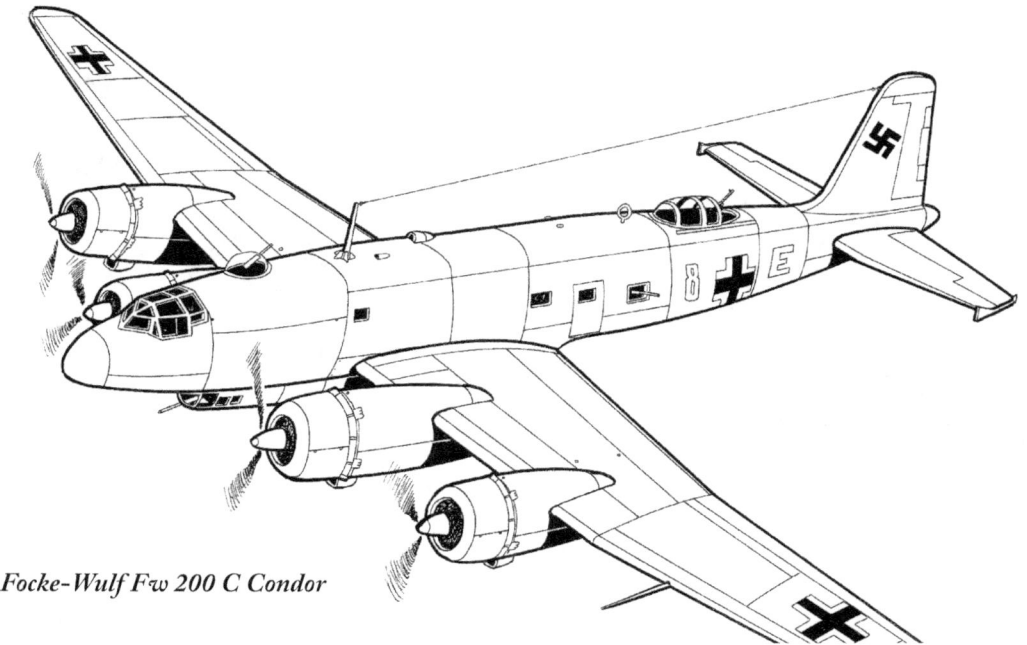

Focke-Wulf Fw 200 C Condor

for reconnaissance. For example, the Condors of I/KG40, based at Cognac and Bordeaux-Mérignac (France), sunk about 90,000 tons of Allied ships and cargo. Their most notable victim was the 42,000-ton liner *Empress of Britain*. They could fly a giant loop over the North Atlantic Ocean convoy routes to their northern bases in Norway. When they found a target they were used as orbiting beacons, and by transmitting continuously they provided course data both to the German navy high command and to submarines, which could home in on their transmissions. At the same time they were used to report on weather conditions encountered during their long-range operations, giving valuable data by radio to weather stations. When Allied merchant ships were armed with anti-aircraft quick-firing guns, this made low-and-slow attack by the Condor a hazardous affair, and surviving Fw 200s were withdrawn from combat service and relegated to a transport role, notably flying supplies into the Russian front in 1943. Some 276 units were built, and served from 1940 to 1945.

Junkers Ju 290

The Junkers Ju 290 was a direct development from the Junkers Ju 90 airliner, versions of which had been evaluated for military purposes (see Part 8). By mid 1942, two prototypes were militarized and accepted into service, and the type was ordered into production. These two (Ju 290A-0), plus the first five production aircraft (Ju 290A-1), were completed as heavy transports, equipped with loading ramps in their tails and defensive gun turrets. Some of these aircraft participated in the Stalingrad airlift in December 1942. Production lines were set up at the Letov factory in Prague for the combat versions of the aircraft, commencing with the Ju 290A-2, which carried a search radar for its patrol role. Minor changes in armament distinguished the A-3 and A-4, leading to the definitive A-5 variant. The aircraft was operated by a crew of nine. Length was 28.64 m (93 ft 11 in), wingspan was 42 m (137 ft 9 in), wing area was 203 square m (2,191 square ft), height was 6.83 m (22 ft 5 in), and empty weight was 33,005 kg (72,611 lbs). The Ju 290 was powered by four 6,920-hp BMW 801G/H, its maximum speed was 440 km/h (273 mph), its range was 6,150 km (3,843 miles), and service ceiling was 6,000 m (19,680 ft).

Armament included two 20-mm MG 151/20 guns in dorsal turrets, one 20-mm MG 151/20 in tail, two MG 151/20 at waist, one MG 151/20 in gondola, and two 13-mm MG 131 in

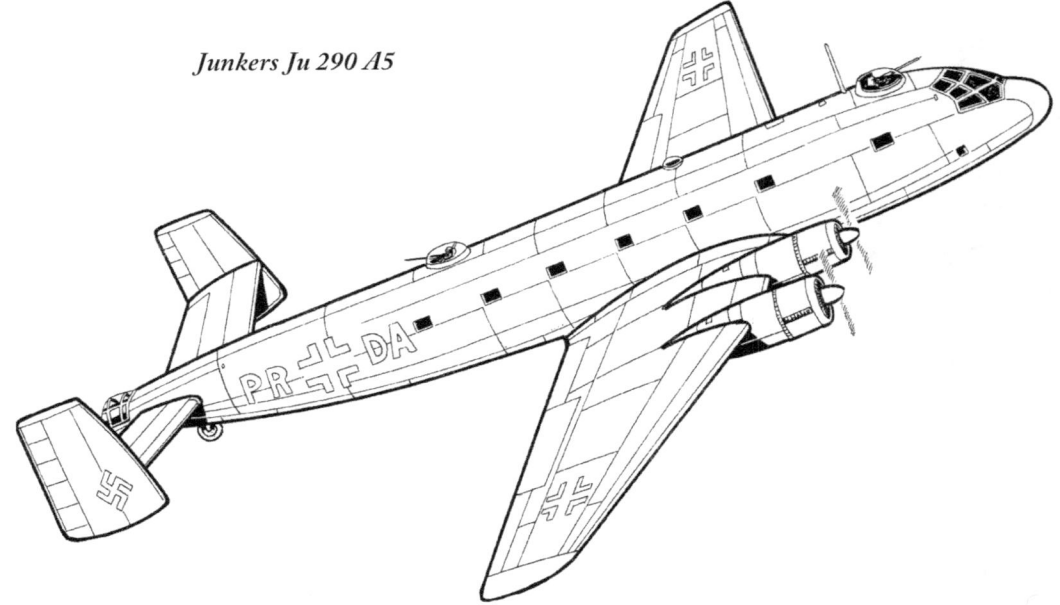

Junkers Ju 290 A5

gondola. Some were fitted with a Radar FuG 200 Hohentwiel. From late 1943, Junkers Ju 290 A5s began to replace the Focke-Wulf Fw 200 Condor in spotting targets for the U-boats operating in the North Atlantic Ocean; typical was 1/FAGr 5 (long-range reconnaissance squadron) based at Mont-de-Marsan, southern France, used for this task. The Ju 290 was well-equipped for its role, but shortages meant that it could not be built in quantity. As Germany lost access to the ocean, their role soon evaporated. It is also believed that at least one Ju 290 made a transatlantic flight to New York City and took photographs of likely targets. A total of forty-eight Ju 290s were delivered. By October 1944, all production of this aircraft was stopped, but a number of Ju 290s survived the war. At least two were evaluated by the Allies, and one or more found their way to Spain. One was operated for some years after the war by the Spanish Air Force. One final Ju 290 was built by the Russians after the war, utilizing parts intended for the Ju 290B high-altitude prototype. It was completed as an airliner, designated Letov L 290 Orel.

Junkers Ju 390

The long-range bomber and reconnaissance Ju 390 was an enlarged version of the Ju 290. Designed by engineer Heinz Kraft, the aircraft had a fuselage length of 34.2 m (112 ft 2 in), a span of 50.30 m (165 ft 1 in), a height of 6.89 m (22 ft 7 in), and an empty weight of 36,900 kg (81,350 lbs). It was powered by no less than six 1,970-hp BMW 801E 18-cylinder, two-row radial engines, had a maximum speed of 505 km/h (314 mph). In mid–1942, prototypes V1 (transport with tail section that could be lifted hydraulically) and V3 (maritime reconnaissance) were ordered but not produced. A heavy-bomber version flew in August 1943. This could carry about 10,000 kg (22,046 lbs) of bombs to a range of 8,000 km (4,971 miles). Another prototype flew in October 1943 with FuG 200 Hohentwiel radar. It could have carried four heavy bombs, each weighing 1,800 kg (3,968 lbs) or various missiles (e.g., Hs 293, Hs 294 or FX 1400) for offensive anti-shipping attacks. Defensive armaments would have included eight 20-mm MG 151 guns in nose and tail turrets, and eight 13-mm MG 131 guns in fore and aft turrets and in ventral barbette. Trials were conducted with the use of four parachutes fastened to the end of the fuselage that opened on landing and thus reduced the length of runway required. The Ju 390 had a maximum range of 9,700 km (6,027 miles), but with additional fuel tanks this could be increased to 18,000 km. A Ju 390 of *Fernauf-*

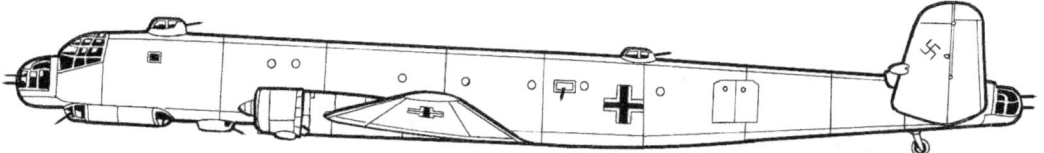

Profile, heavy bomber Junkers Ju 390

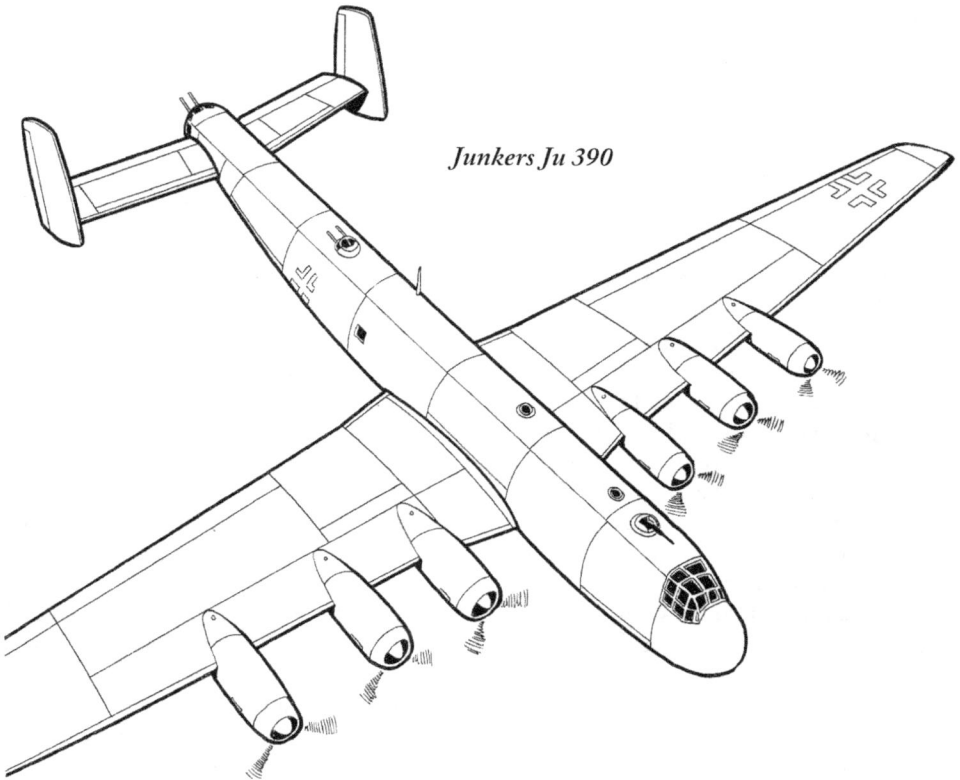

Junkers Ju 390

klarungsgruppe 5, based at Mont-de-Marsan, demonstrated 32-hour endurance, and flew within twelve miles of the U.S. coast just north of New York City. Late in the war, a test pilot flew a Ju 390 nonstop from Germany to Japan over the polar route, and Hans Baur (Hitler's personal pilot) had proposed to fly the Führer out of Berlin in April 1945. Baur spoke of Manchukuo (now part of China) as Hitler's ultimate destination. A transhemispheric flight might well have been aeronautically feasible, but politically it just would not have been Hitler's style.

There was also a planned twin version, known as Ju 390 Z (*Zwilling*—"twin") consisting of two Ju 390 fuselages joined together by a center wing section, increasing span to 60 meters, powered by eight BMW 109-801D engines. The formidable and ambitious Junkers Ju 390 series was never completed. The RLM ordered a halt in development in May 1944, switching virtually all aircraft production to the emergency fighter program.

Blohm & Voss Bv P 184

Designed by Dr. Richard Vogt, the P 184 was intended to become either a long-range reconnaissance airplane or a long-range bomber. The all-metal Bv P 184 had a length of 17 m (56 ft 9 in), long untapered wings with a span of 35.8 m (117 ft 5 in), and a wing area of 82

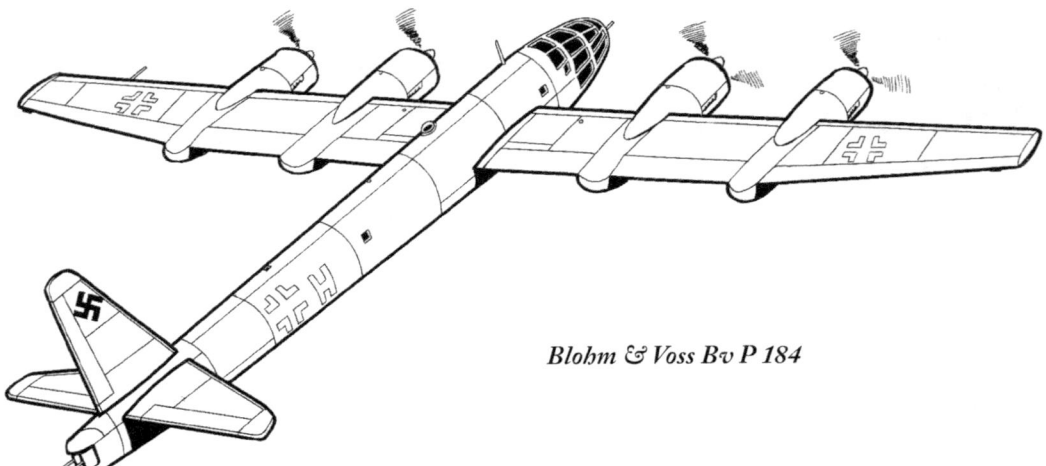

Blohm & Voss Bv P 184

square m (882.6 square ft). It was powered by four 1,600-hp BMW 801-E radial engines, and had a maximum speed of 500 km/h (311 mph) and a range of 7,500 km (4,688 miles). The crew of five sat in a glazed cockpit in the nose. Defensive armament included a remote-controlled turret in the tail armed with two MG 131 machine guns, and one MK 103 30-mm cannon mounted in the nose. The bomber version would have carried a bomb load of 4,000 kg (8,800 lbs) stored in a bomb bay. The reconnaissance version was to be equipped with cameras. The Bv P 184 never went further than the initial design stage.

Messerschmitt Me 264

The large, four-engined, long-range bomber/maritime patrol Me 264 made its first flight in December 1942. Operated by a crew of five or six, it had a length of 20.9 m (68 ft 7 in), a wingspan of 43 m (141 ft), a height of 4.3 m (14 ft), a wing area of 127.8 square m (1.376 square ft), and an empty weight of 21,150 kg (46,630 lbs). It was powered by four BMW 801G/H piston engines, and had a maximum speed of 560 km/h (350 mph). It was an all-metal, high-wing, four-engine heavy bomber of classic construction. The fuselage was round in cross-section and had a crew cabin in a glazed nose, strikingly similar to the American Boeing B-29. The wing had a slightly swept leading edge and a straight rear edge. The tailplane had double tail fins. The undercarriage was a retractable tricycle gear, with quite large-diameter wheels. The aircraft carried very little armor and few guns in order to save weight and thus increase fuel capacity and range. Armament consisted of four 13-mm MG 131 machine guns, and two 20-mm MG 151 cannons. It could carry a bomb load of 3,000 kg (6,600 lbs). Intended to replace the Fw 200 Condor, the Messerschmitt Me 264 could fly for up to eleven hours nonstop. It was thus supposed to be capable of flying from Germany to New York City and back, whence its nickname of *Amerika Bomber*, although it is highly doubtful that this would have been achieved with a meaningful payload, if at all. In order to provide comfort for the crew on the proposed long-range missions, the Me 264 featured bunk beds, lavatories, and a small galley, complete with hotplates. Due to a shortage of resources, the program never developed. Only one prototype was made and trials showed numerous minor faults, and handling in fully loaded conditions was found to be difficult. It is possible, but not confirmed with certainty, that the Me 264 made a flight to Japan and back in 1944. Further effort on the Me 264 was abandoned to allow Messerschmitt to concentrate on fighter production and because another design, the Junkers Ju 390, had been selected in its place as a maritime long-range reconnaissance plane. On September 23, 1944, work on the Me 264 project was officially canceled. It is reported that the one and only existing Me 264 was

4. Bombers

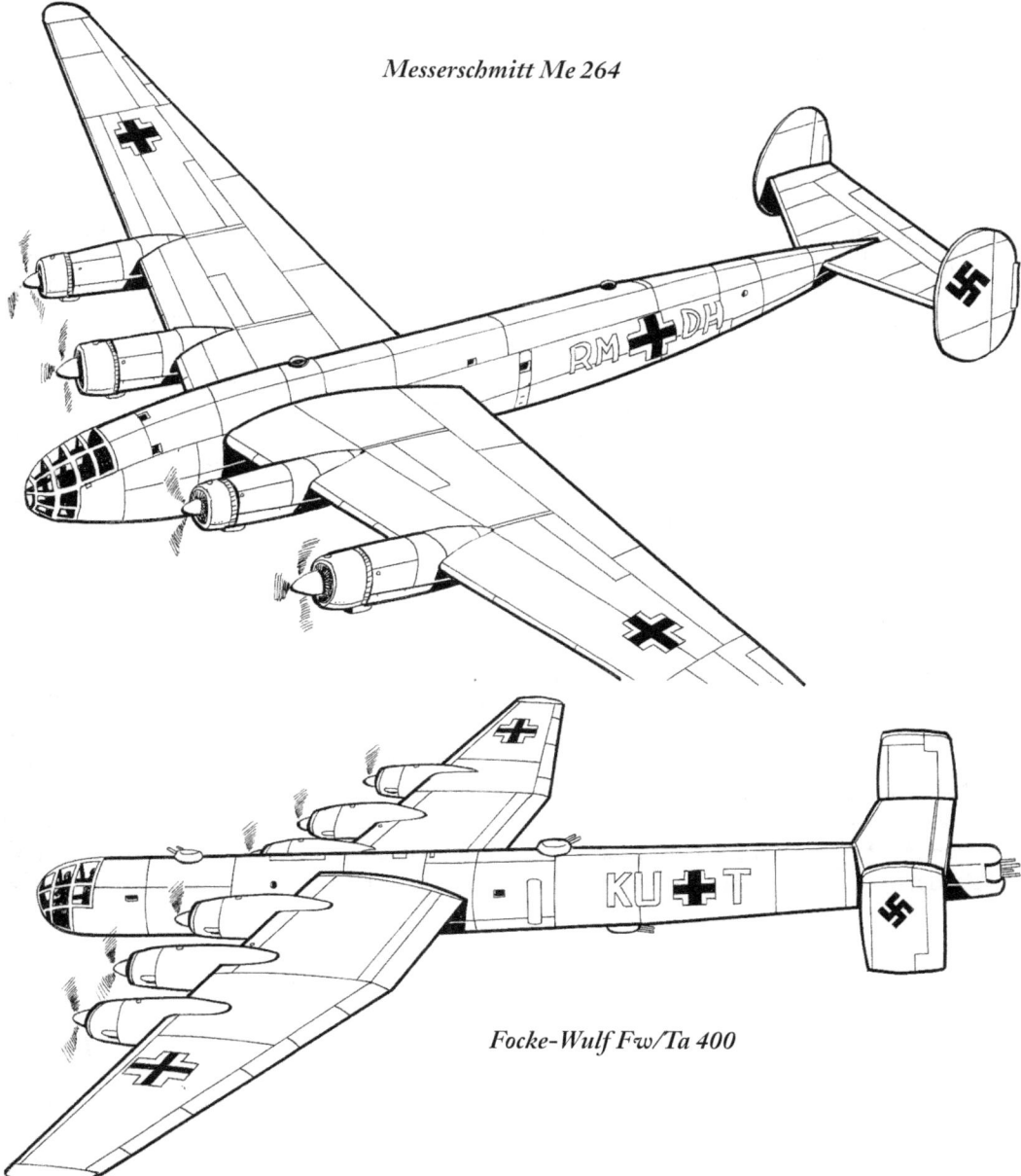

Messerschmitt Me 264

Focke-Wulf Fw/Ta 400

destroyed during an Allied air raid on Memmingen.

Focke-Wulf Fw/Ta 400

The Fw/Ta 400 was designed by engineer Kurt Tank (whence the prefix "Ta") in 1943 as a heavy bomber, long-range reconnaissance craft, and submarine-support aircraft. This ambitious program was designed by a team of French engineers and technicians, and developed by a number of French, German and Italian companies located at Chatillon-sous-Bayeux near Paris. The Fw/Ta 400 had a length of 29.4 m (96 ft 5 in) with twin fin and rudder tail unit. The shoulder-mounted wing had a span of 42 m (137 ft 10 in). The aircraft was powered by six BMW 801D radial engines (each providing 1,700 hp), and a plan existed to mount two additional Jumo 004 jet engines beneath the outermost radial piston engines. Its speed would then have been 720 km/h (447 mph). With thirty-two fuel tanks for a total of 27,000 liters (7,133 gallons), the Fw/Ta 400 was intended to have a range of 4,800 km (2,981 miles). A retractable tricycle undercarriage was planned, consisting of a single nose wheel and four main wheels. The bomber was to be operated by a crew of nine. Its defensive armament was to include one remote-controlled turret armed with two MG 151 20-mm cannons placed beneath the fuselage, two remote-controlled turrets each with two MG 151 20-mm cannons on the upper fuselage, and a remote-controlled turret armed with four MG 151 20-mm cannons in the tail. A bomb load of 10,000 kg (22,000 lbs) was to be carried. This formidable bomber did not go further than wind tunnel model research.

Focke-Wulf Fw 261

The Fw 261 was intended to be a heavy bomber or a maritime reconnaissance craft or submarine support aircraft. It was to be powered by four BMW 80 ID radial engines (each providing 1,600 hp), and had a maximum speed of 560 km/h (348 mph), a maximum range of 9,000 km (5,593 miles), and a flight endurance of 22 hours. The outer two engine nacelles extended to the rear with tailplane with fin and rudder. Total length was 26.78 m (87 ft 10 in), height was 6.35 m (20 ft 10 in), and empty weight was 26,760 kg (58,995 lbs). The shoulder-mounted wing had a span of 40 m (131 ft 3 in), and a wing area of 187 square m (2.010 square ft). The aircraft was to be fitted with a tricycle landing gear and heavily armed, including two twin MK 108 30-mm cannons in a remote-controlled turret below the cockpit, two HD 151Z cannons in remote-controlled turrets (one in dorsal, the other in ventral position), and four MK 108 30-mm cannons in remote-controlled tail turret; to clear the field of fire, the tailplane was not connected to the two tail booms. The project was not developed.

Junkers Ju 488

Using an assortment of parts of the Ju 88, Ju 188, Ju 288 and Ju 388, the Ju 488 was intended to be a four-engine strategic heavy bomber. Designed in early 1944, it had a length of 22.23 m (76 ft 3 in), a span of 31.27 m (102 ft 8 in) and an empty weight of 21,000 kg (46,297 lbs). The aircraft was powered by four 1,890-hp BMW 801TJ radial engines and had a maximum speed of 690 km/h (429 mph) and a maximum range of 3,400 km (2,113 miles). Two prototypes were built at the Laté-

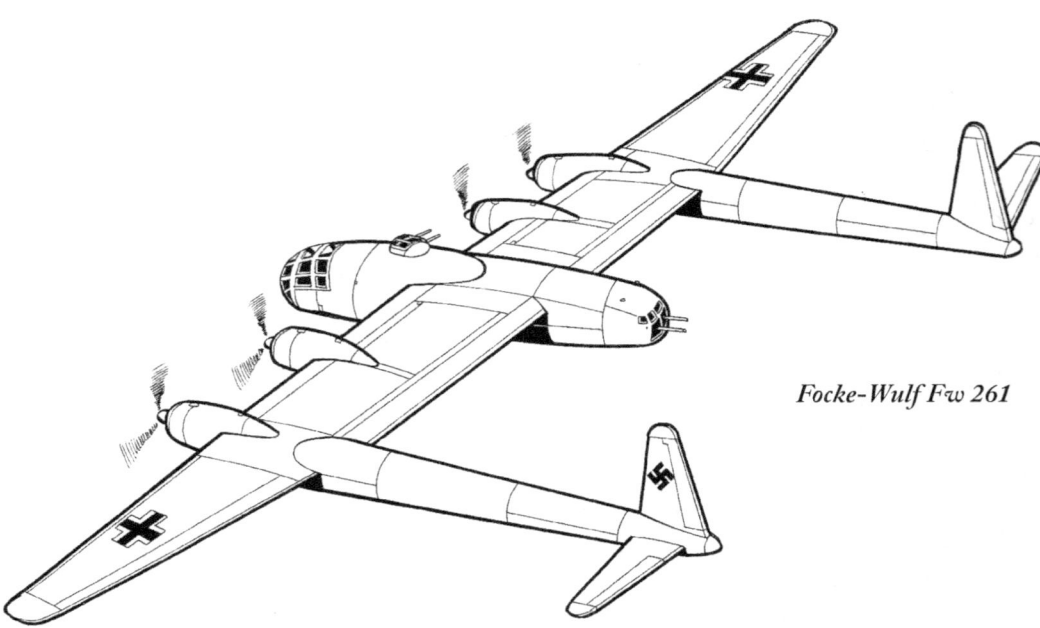

Focke-Wulf Fw 261

4. Bombers

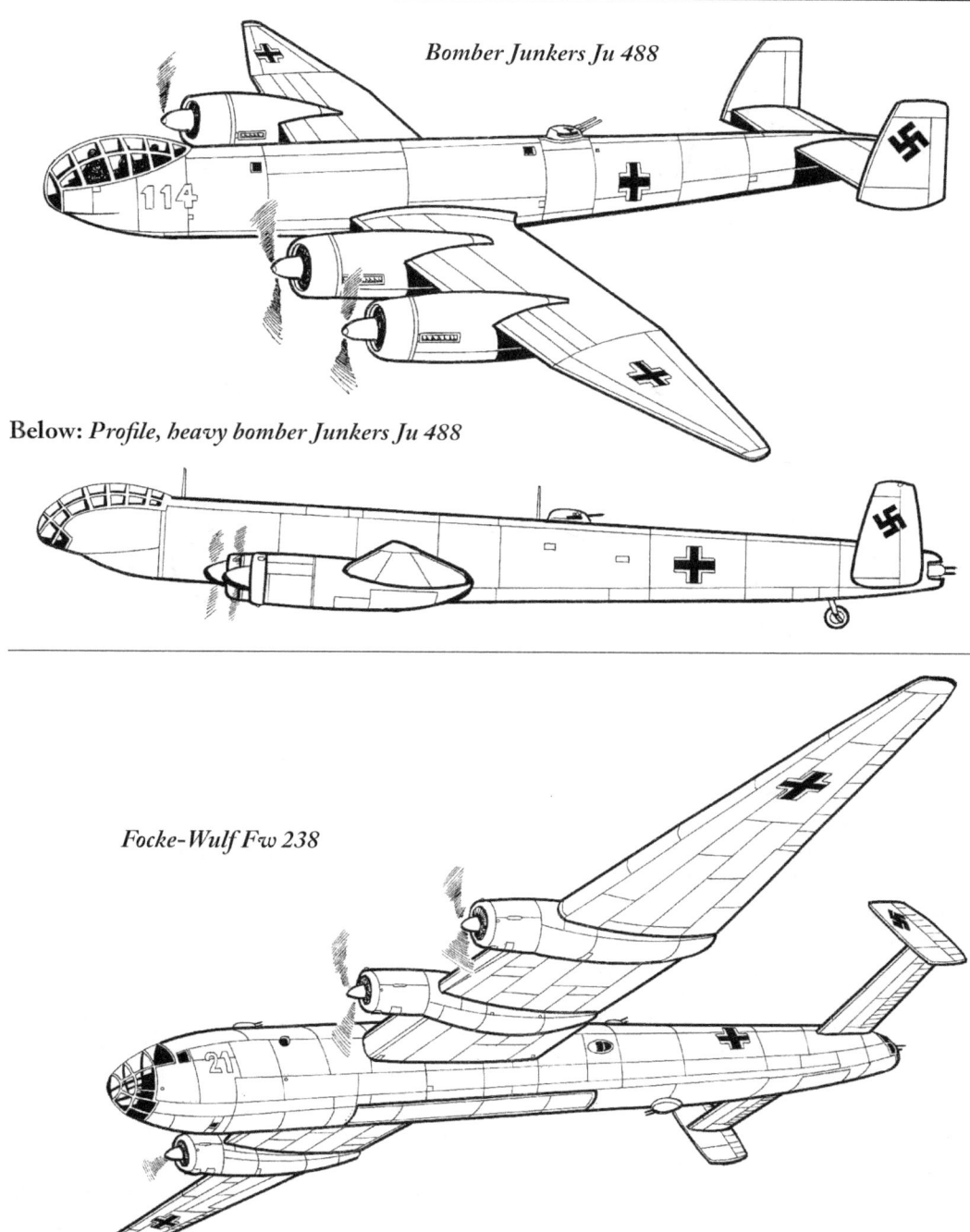

Bomber Junkers Ju 488

Below: *Profile, heavy bomber Junkers Ju 488*

Focke-Wulf Fw 238

coère Aircraft Manufacturer in Toulouse (France). In July 1944, the aircraft were nearly completed when they were destroyed by a raid by French resistance saboteurs. Development of the impressive Ju 488 was abandoned in November 1944.

Focke-Wulf Fw 238

The Fw 238 was designed as a strategic bomber with a range of 15,000 km (9,321 miles). The aircraft, made of wood, had an empty weight of 55,620 kg (12,262 lbs), a

Heinkel He 177 Greif

length of 35.3 m (115 ft 9 in), a span of 52 m (170 ft 7 in) and a wing area of 290 square m (312.5 square ft). It was powered by four 3,900-hp BMW 303 piston engines. Speed was 500 km/h (311 mph) and endurance was 29 hours. A bomb load of 5,000 kg (11,023 lbs) could be carried. Defensive armament included four remote-controlled turrets each armed with two MG 151/20 20-mm guns, two dorsal mounted on top of the fuselage, the third in ventral position, and a fourth one in the tail. There was an enlarged variant, known as Fw 238 C with six DB 603 engines, and a smaller version of the aircraft, known as Fw 239H. None were built, as all long-range bomber designs were cancelled in February 1943.

Heinkel He 177 Greif

Arguably the largest bomber built by the Germans, the ill-fated He 177 *Greif* (Griffin) suffered many flaws and turned into one of the Luftwaffe's biggest failures, comparing service use to the amount of resources invested. The aircraft, designed by engineer Siegfried Günter of Ernst Heinkel Aircraft Company, made its first flight in November 1939. It incorporated many advanced innovations, and came near to satisfying the requirements of a strategic bomber. But as teething troubles and technical problems were never overcome, a large number of test pilots were killed and the aircraft had a dismal development record and an inauspicious career. A significant problem that plagued the program from the beginning was a ludicrous requirement that this extremely large aircraft be capable of dive bombing. Idiocy it was, and that ensured that the Luftwaffe never had an effective long-range heavy bomber. This combined with the attempt to reduce drag by coupling the engines, while theoretically sound, proved to be impossible in practice. Seventy-five percent of the initial production batches of A1 prototypes crashed and a good percentage of the 35 A-0 pre-production airframes were lost due to crashes or in-flight fires. Due to this disturbing propensity to catch fire, the He 177 was dubbed "the flying firework." It was not entirely clear why this problem existed: Heinkel blamed oil leaks in the engines, other engineers pointing out

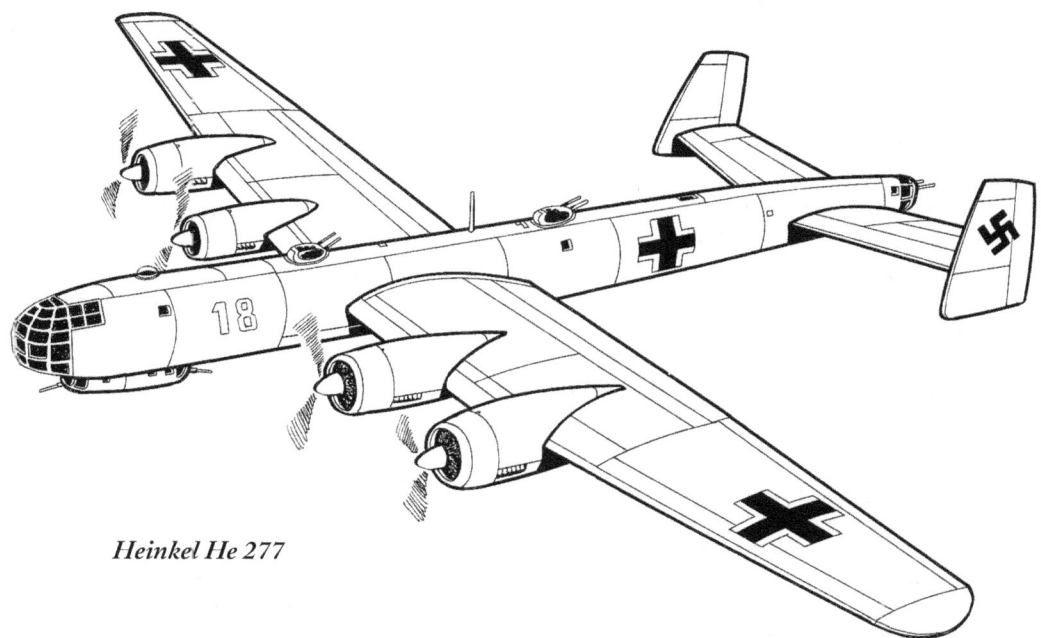
Heinkel He 277

cooling issues. The A-0s were followed by type A3 using DB engines, and A4, intended to be a high-altitude project. The major production was the He 177 A5. This had a span of 31.44 m (103 ft 2 in), a length of 22 m (72 ft 2 in), a height of 6.4 m (21 ft), and an empty weight of 16,800 kg (37,038 lbs). The He 177 A5 was powered by two 2,950-hp Daimler-Benz DB 610A-1/B1 engines, each including two close-coupled, inverted-V-12, liquid-cooled engines geared to one 4-bladed propeller. Maximum speed was 472 km/h (295 mph) and range was about 5,000 km (3,107 miles). The airplane had a crew of six, including pilot, copilot, observer/radio operator, bomb aimer/nose gunner, dorsal gunner, and tail gunner. Armament included one 7.92-mm MG 81J manually aimed in nose, one 20-mm MG 151 manually aimed at front of ventral gondola, one or two 13-mm MG 131 guns in forward dorsal turret, one MG 131 in rear dorsal turret, one MG 151 manually aimed in tail and two MG 81 or one MG 131 manually aimed at the rear of the ventral gondola. The He 177 could carry an internal bomb load of 6,000 kg (13,600 lbs). It was also adapted to carry Henschel 293 and Fritz X guided missiles, FX 1400 parachute mines, or torpedoes. Its design faults were such that only a few ever became operational and their

results were poor. In late May 1944, the aircraft was used in combat and achieved notable but limited successes on the Russian front; when everything worked, the He 177 was an excellent four-engine long-range bomber. Total production was about 1,000 units, of which some 700 served on the eastern front, using 50-mm and 75-mm guns for tank-busting, while a few brave aircrews ineffectually bombed England.

The He 177 proved to be such a big problem that Göring forbid Heinkel to develop another version, though Heinkel did anyway, the result being the He 277.

Heinkel He 277

The He 277, intended to be a heavy bomber, long-range reconnaissance craft and anti-shipping aircraft, was an enlarged version of the He 177. It was secretly developed by Ernst Heinkel. In May 1943, the designer, ignoring Göring's interdiction, informed Hitler that the He 277 could meet the demand for a new bomber, and the dictator encouraged him to go on. The He 277 prototype V1 made its first flight in late 1943, followed by a more advanced version, V2, in February 1944. Other designs (V3, B-5, B-6, and B-7) were also planned. The aircraft had a span of 31.44 m

(103 ft 2 in), a length of 22.15 m (72 ft 8 in), a height of 6.66 m (21 ft 10 in), and an empty weight of 21,800 kg (48,067 lbs). To solve the engine-fire problem of the He 177, the 1,850-hp Daimler-Benz DB 603A inverted-V-12 (or Jumo 213F) engines were separated into four units. Maximum speed was 570 km (354 mph) and range was 7,200 km (4,474 miles). The aircraft was planned to be heavily defended with gun turret and gondola, and would carry a heavy load of bombs and guided missiles. In July 1944 the whole program was cancelled, with Heinkel being ordered to design and build nothing but his proven models.

Heinkel He 274

The He 274 would have been a formidable and outstanding long-range heavy bomber. It was actually a variant of the Heinkel He 177. The main difference was that each engine had its own nacelle on the wing, rather than using a paired engine in which two engines drove a common propeller. This was arranged in order to prevent the He 177's engine problems. As the Heinkel factories were too busy making other aircrafts, the program of the He 274 was assigned in 1941 to the French SAUF-Farmann Company located at Suresnes near Paris. The development went extremely slow and two prototypes V1 and V2 were completed only in July 1944, right before the liberation of Paris. The impressive He 274 was operated by a crew of four, it had a span of 44.20 m (145 ft), a length of 23.80 m (78 ft 2 in), a height of 5.50 m (18 ft), and an empty weight of 21.300 kg (46.964 lbs). It was powered by four 1.850-hp Daimler-Benz DB 603A-2 inverted-V-12 piston engines with turbochargers. Speed was 580 km/h (360 mph) and range 4,250 km (2,640 miles). Planned armament was five MG 131/13 13-mm machine guns, plus one gun in the nose and two in two fuselage turrets. One of the two prototypes made its first flight in December 1945 with French markings and the designation AAS-01A. Their further fate is unknown. Probably they were used for a while by the French Armée de l'Air as high-altitude research planes.

Messerschmitt Me P 08-01

Designed in September 1941 by Alexander Lippisch, the Me P 08-01 was a large flying wing with a span of 50.6 m (166 ft) and a length of 15.35 m (50 ft 4 in). The bomber was powered by four Daimler-Benz DB 614 piston engines mounted on the wing trailing edge in a push arrangement. Maximum speed would have been 645 km/h (401 mph) and range would have been 27,150 km (16,871 miles). The aircraft was intended to fulfill several roles. A long-range bomber would carry a bomb load of 20,000 kg (44,092 lbs). Another version was a long-range maritime patrol craft (armed with torpedo or sea mines), or long-range land reconnaissance aircraft. A third variant would have been a transport aircraft with a payload of 25 tons. Another version would have been used to tow assault gliders. A last variant would have been a gunship armed with four 8.8-cm cannons in an anti-aircraft role. The Me P 08-01 did not progress further than initial design stage.

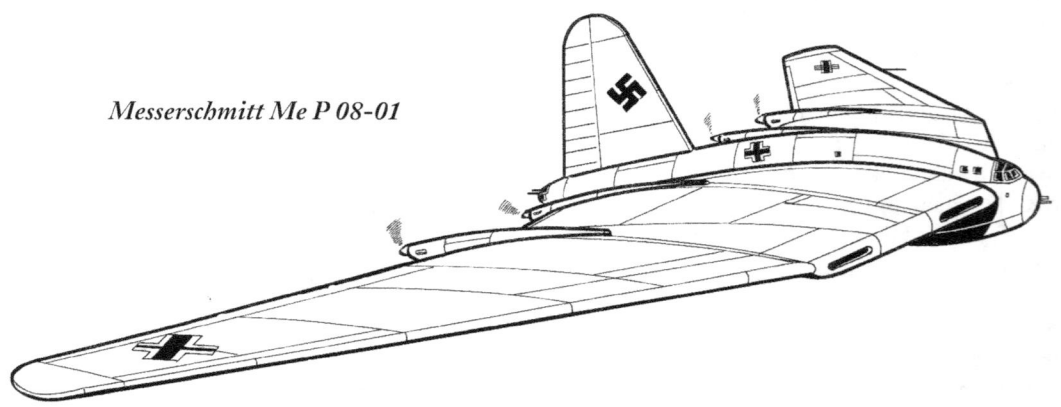

Messerschmitt Me P 08-01

Daimler-Benz carrier aircraft project B and C

This huge and odd aircraft, designed by a team of engineers from Daimler-Benz and Focke-Wulf in 1943, was intended to be a very long-range bomber which would be capable of attacking targets in the United States and Soviet industrial plants behind the Ural Mountains. Attacks were to be carried out in nonstop flight and without recourse to refueling. The aircraft—which was simply referred to as Project B and C—was to be used as a flying launching site for parasite fighters and bombers, thereby significantly increasing their range. The carrier had large and broad wings, with a span of 54 m (177 ft 2 in) and a twin boom layout containing the tail unit, with a total length of 35 m (117 ft 5 in). The aircraft was to be operated by a crew of three or four who sat in a pressurized cockpit placed in the glazed nose. It was powered by six Daimler-Benz DB 9-609E piston engines, four pulling and two pushing, with an unknown estimated speed. It had a high fixed landing gear composed of two nacelles, each with three large wheels; this had a wide track of 24.97 m (82 ft) in order to allow clearance to mount parasite aircrafts beneath the carrier. Total height was 11.20 meters. The Daimler-Benz project B was intended to carry a jet bomber with sharply swept-back wings (much like the Hen-

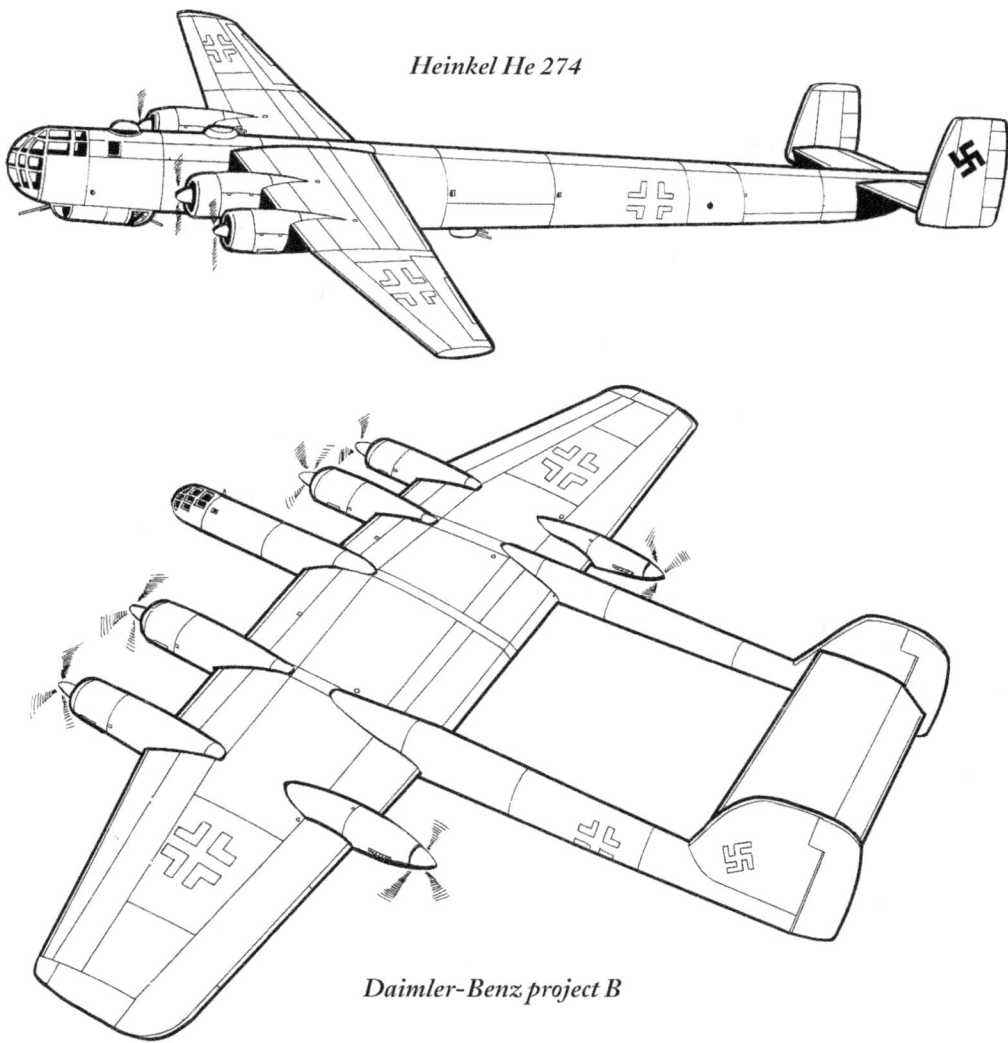

Heinkel He 274

Daimler-Benz project B

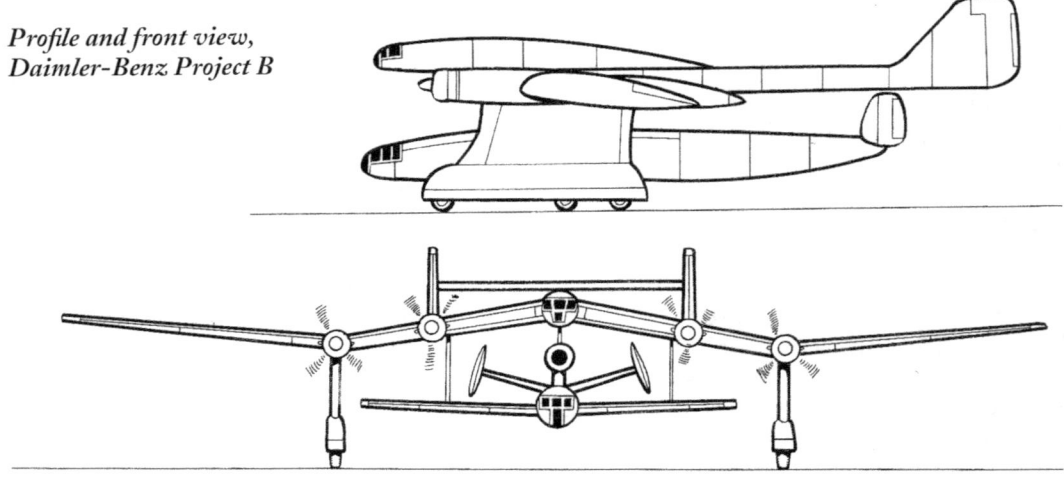

Profile and front view, Daimler-Benz Project B

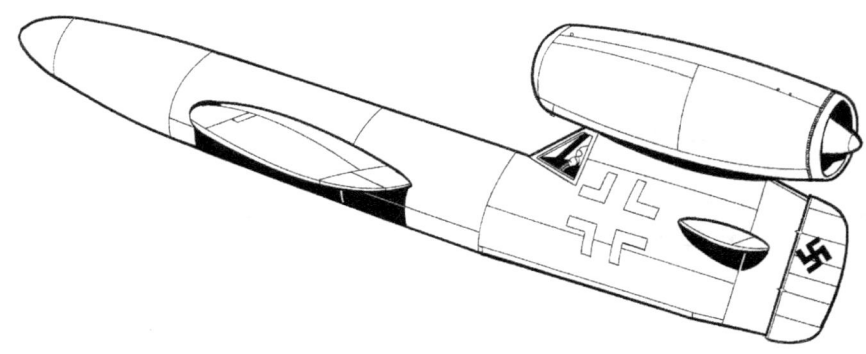

Daimler-Benz parasite fighter (carried by project C). The aircraft had a span of 9 m (26 ft 6.33 in), a length of 12.96 m (42 ft 6.24 in) and a speed of 1,050 km/h (652 mph).

schel Hs 132), powered by a single DB S06 jet engine, with a speed of about 1,000 km/h (621 mph). Operated by a crew of two, the parasite bomber had a span of 22 m (72 ft 2.14 in), a length of 30.75 m (100 ft 10.63 in), and could carry a bomb load of 3,000 kg (6.000 lbs). The general idea was that the larger aircraft carried a parasite toward the target and released it when this was relatively close, thus giving the combination great range as the parasite aircraft did not waste fuel on take-off and during cruise.

The project C, quite similar to project B, was intended to carry six small parasite piloted Daimler-Benz jet interceptors. These aircraft were powered by one BMW 018 or a He S 011 jet engine (mounted either on the bottom aft or top aft of the fuselage). The wings and tailplanes were swept back, and each parasite machine carried in its nose a 2,500-kg (5,500-lb) explosive charge, which was detonated on impact. The parasite aircraft was released by the carrier near the target; the pilot would chose a target, then dive toward it, and when assured of a hit, was to escape using an ejection seat. Although this system was not officially considered a suicide attack, the pilot had only a very tiny chance of survival, due to the speed of his machine and the proximity to the target when ejecting.

No need to say that DB Project B and C never left the drawing board, although it was planned to be built by 1944. Curiously, the carrier/parasite concept was revived in the United States in the mid–1950s when a giant Vultee Boeing B-36 strategic bomber was teamed with a F-84 fighter; the purpose was to launch the fighter when the bomber was threatened by enemy aircraft. Another escort parasite fighter, the McDonnell XF-85, was also designed to be carried in the bomb bay of a B-36 bomber for the same purpose. Sophisticated surface-to-air missiles and advanced jet interceptors rendered the concept totally obsolete, and this dead-end development was abandoned.

Jet Bombers

Already before and during World War II the serious limitations of the conventional piston-engine had been recognized by aviation designers, and the full potential of advanced modern aircraft propulsion became apparent. The promising area of research centered on rocket, turbojet and jet airplanes. Every major belligerent power made some advances in this field, but it was the Germans who made the greatest progress. In spite of enormous practical problems inherent in this futuristic research, they were supreme in the field. Much of the effort expended by German scientists, technicians and engineers was anticipatory and many designs dated from the prewar period. The knowledge that jet reaction was potentially the most efficient of all aircraft propulsion systems had existed for some fifteen years. Germany had a rich heritage of rocket and jet-engine development in the early 1930s which was carried out for its own sake by more or less earnest and well-intentioned pioneers. Fritz von Opel had already experimented with solid-fuel rocket power, Paul Schmidt with pulse jet, and Hans von Ohain with the gas turbine. As early as 1939 Professor Ernst Heinkel had designed a jet-propelled aircraft and Messerschmitt was at the forefront with his far-ahead twin-jet-engined Me 262 Schwalbe in 1944 which narrowly predated the first RAF Gloster Meteor. Hitler, however, was confident of winning the war with the conventional weapons he had developed and massed, weapons which were largely those of World War I, though enormously improved technically.

Heinkel and Messerschmitt were not the only ones to develop jet propulsion. Many other companies made jet designs for both bombers and fighters (see Part 6) — some effective or potentially so, others completely extravagant. In a last frantic effort to halt the Allied bomber fleets, and to bring death and destruction as far as the United States, visionary designs appeared. However, Germany's overall military situation was by 1944-45 so bad that German scientists were unable to exploit their advantages. Besides, technical superiority and scientific achievements before and during the war were often bedeviled by the Nazi administrative muddle. Possessing a lead in many fields, and often gaining a lead where they at first had none, German technologists frequently saw their achievements come to nothing through interservice rivalries and an utter lack of vision at the top. Hitler had only contempt for the intellectual, the expert, and the specialist, and preferred to rely upon his own "creative genius" and his "fanatical will." There was thus a lack of centralized effort in the Nazi program of technological and scientific development, a program characterized not by systematic organization but by chaos.

Higher authorities were slow to realize the potential of technological developments, and technical, requirements were subject to abrupt and frequent vacillations stemming mainly from confusion and conflicting concepts of the use of airpower. Under great pressure, the Germans needed to develop "war-winning weapons." Particularly in the later stage of World War II when Germany had virtually lost the war, there was a proliferation of designs which only wasted time, funds and means. These efforts were conducted without a coherent system, a vast number of prototypes being designed and tested only to be quickly abandoned. Besides, the decision to maintain full-scale production of trusted designs (as the Heinkel 111 and Junkers Ju 88, for example), meant that many revolutionary and potentially useful bombers were never given a chance. In the end the lack of organization proved unproductive and disastrous. Nevertheless, the appearance of jet engines and high-flying pressurized aircraft along with the development of rockets and guided missiles revolutionized air warfare. Without doubt, the numerous German jet and rocket designs acted as progenitor to a wide variety of post–World War II military development. Bearing in mind the primitive state of the technology, German jet aircraft were outstanding pieces of engineering. By the end of the war, the Allies were astounded to discover the advances made by Germany when they examined the spoils of war.

Even if the German jet bombers had been built and made to work in 1945, one wonders what it would all have been for. A paltry ton of high explosives could hardly have a measurable effect on the war. It could never justify the program's staggering cost in money, raw materials, and industrial capacity at a time when the war was lost for Germany. Some writers have suggested that German jet bombers were intended to deliver a nuclear weapon. But the Nazis had no hope of fielding an atom bomb by 1944 or 1945. It would be decades before a Nazi nuclear weapon could have been developed. The German jet bomber and space program is thus best understood as little more than a self-indulgent delusion, one of many that occupied Germany's bunker-bound leadership and self-serving intelligentsia as disaster and defeat overtook the nation they professed to lead.

Messerschmitt Me P 1101

The designation Me P 1101 included several jet proposals intended for various roles such as fighter, interceptor, night fighter, and ground attacker. Using various configurations, the *Zerstörer* (ground attackers) of this series were intended to mount large-caliber weapons for attacking large ground targets such as tanks or fortified positions.

The two-seat Me P 1101/28 had swept mid-wing with a span of 14.30 m, a length of 12.35 m, and a height of 4.40 m. Powered by two jet engines mounted in the wing roots, it was expected to have a maximum speed of 910 km/h.

Designed by Hans Hornung, the Messerschmitt Me P 1101/99 was intended to be a powerful *Zerstörer*. The aircraft had a crew of two sitting side-by-side in a cockpit located at the front fuselage. It had a length of 15.2 m (49 ft 10 in), an empty weight of 12,730 kg (28,065 lbs), and wings swept back at 45 degrees with a span of 15.4 m (50 ft 6 in). It was powered by four Heinkel-Hirth He S011 turbojet engines located in the wing roots, giving a maximum speed of 960 km/h (597 mph). De-

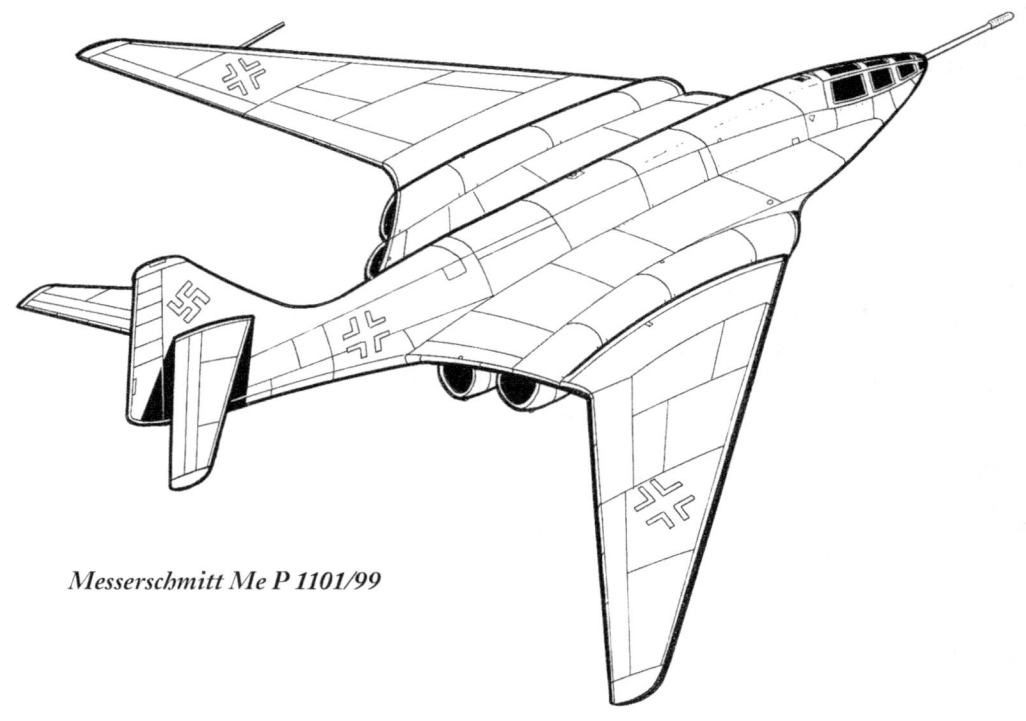

Messerschmitt Me P 1101/99

signed in 1944 by Dr. Hans-Joachim Pabst von Ohain (1911–1998), the He S011 jet engine had a diameter of 1.08 m, a length of 4 m, a weight of 940 kg and developed 2,965 lbs thrust. The Me P1101/99 was to be heavily armed with five MK 112 55-mm machine cannons and one Rheinmetal 7.5-cm Pak 40 anti-tank gun placed in the nose. The Pak 40 had a muzzle velocity of 990 m/sec (3248 ft/sec) and could fire an anti-tank shell of 3.18 kg (7 lbs) to a range of 2 km (2,190 yards). The aircraft, which would have been ready to fly in 1948, never went further than the design stage.

Lippisch Li P 11-92 and Li P 11-105

Quite similar in design to the Li P 09, the tailless two-seat fast bomber Li P 11-92 was designed by the end of 1942. It had wing swept back at 30 degrees with a span of 12.65 m (41 ft 6 in). Its length was 8.14 m (26 ft 9 in). The machine was powered by two Jumo 004A turbojet engines developing 750 kp thrust and two Schmiddings 109-553 RATO auxiliary rocket motors for take-off. Armed with two MG 151/20 guns mounted in wing roots, it could carry a bomb load of 1,000 kg (2,205

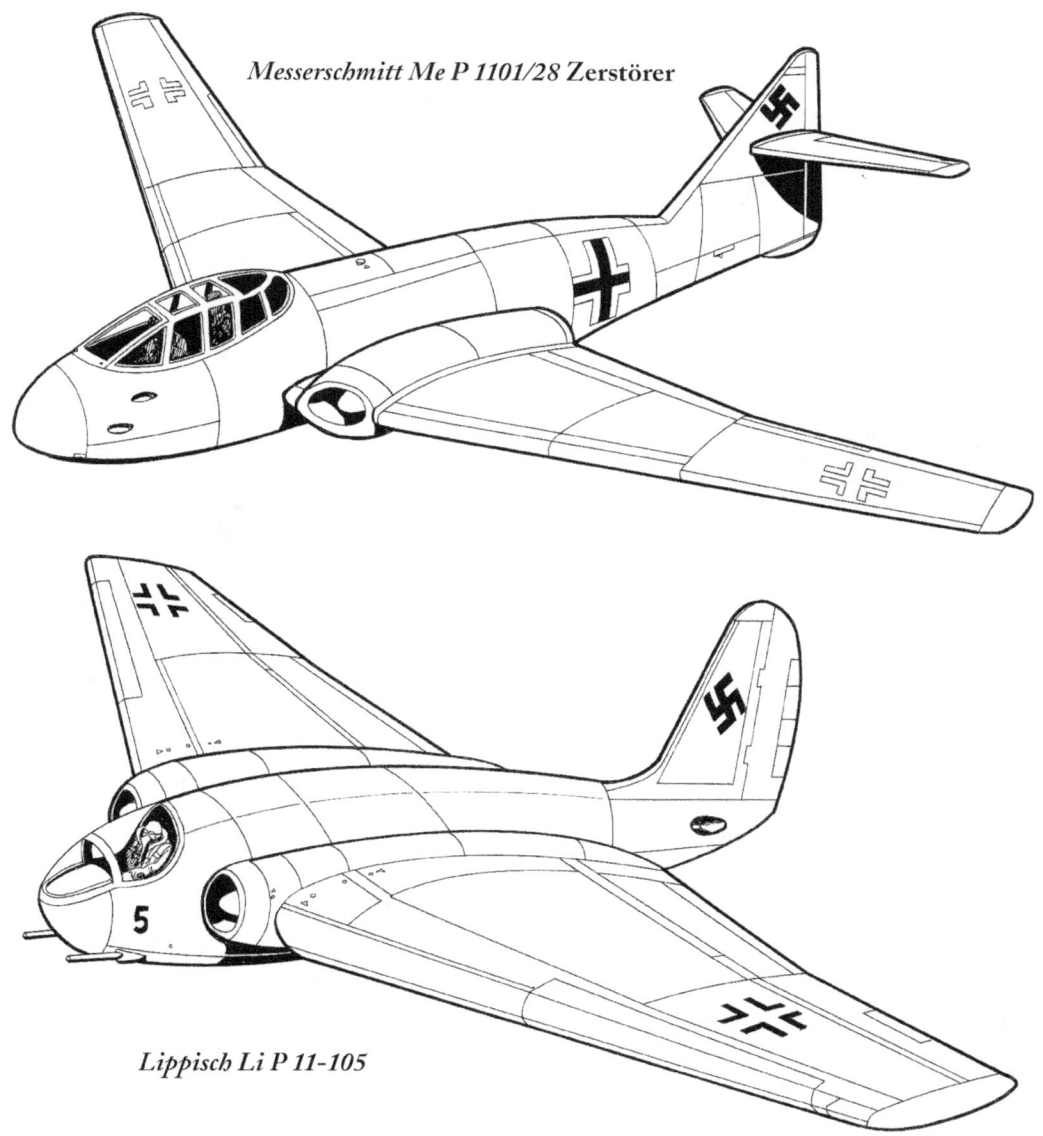

Messerschmitt Me P 1101/28 Zerstörer

Lippisch Li P 11-105

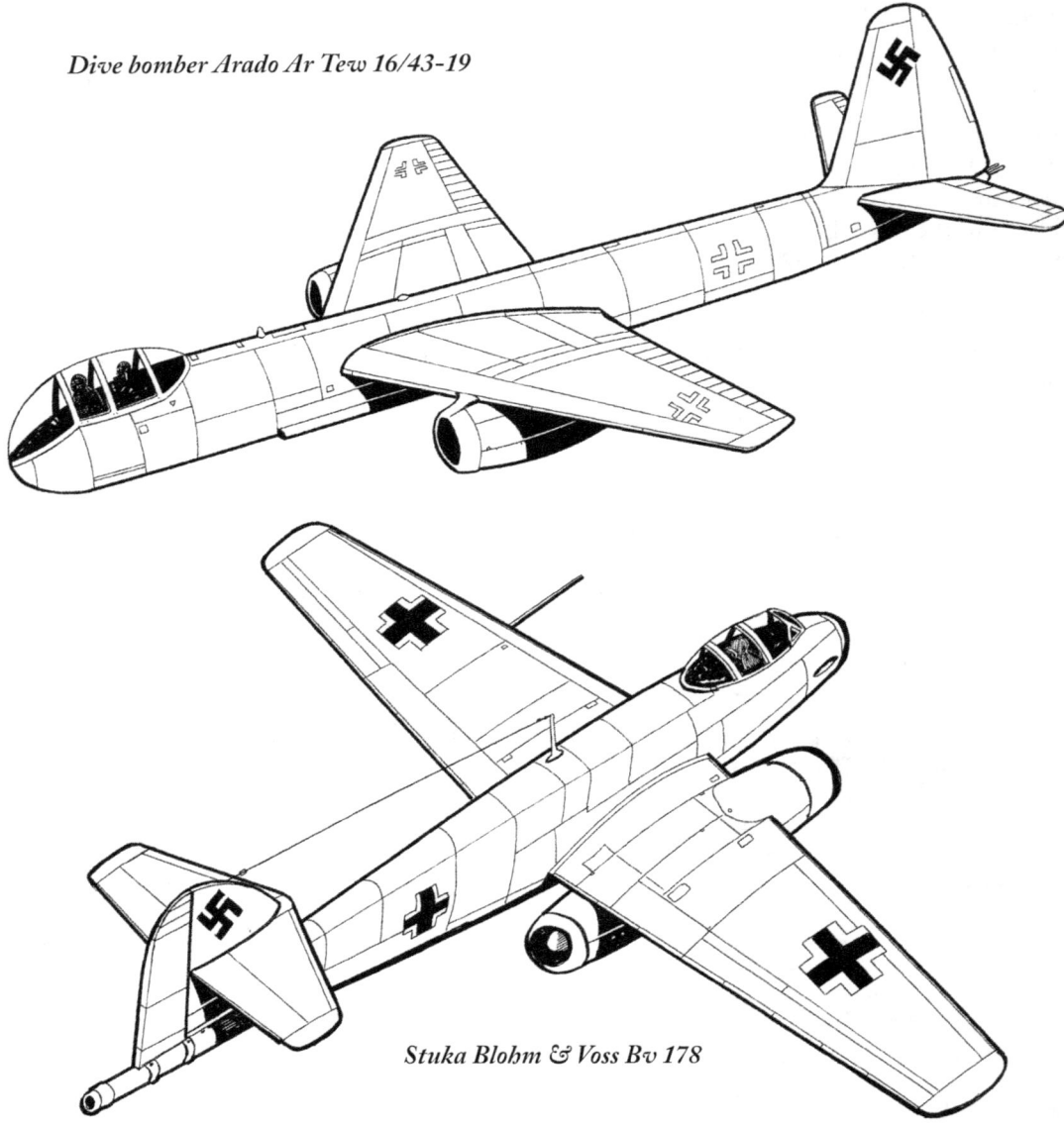

Dive bomber Arado Ar Tew 16/43-19

Stuka Blohm & Voss Bv 178

lbs). A similar fast bomber, designed in December 1942, the single-seat Li P 11-105 had a modified cockpit but otherwise practically the same armament, bomb load, performance and powerplant.

Arado Ar Tew 16/43-19

The multi-role Ar Tew 16/43-19, designed in August 1943, was an all-metal, mid-wing monoplane with a span of 16.2 m (53 ft 2 in) and a length of 18 m (59 ft 1 in). The Ar Tew 16/43-19 was powered by two jet engines mounted under the wings and it was fitted with a retractable tricycle undercarriage. Operated by a crew of two sitting back-to-back, several versions of this aircraft were envisaged. A reconnaissance version was to be equipped with cameras. A high-speed bomber was to carry a bomb load of 2,500 kg (5,512 lbs) or a Hs 295 Fritz X flying bomb. A *Zerstörer* version was to be armed with five cannons firing forward and two firing to the rear. A night fighter and bad-weather version was to be heavily armed with a third crew member operating an on-board radar. The Ar Tew 16/43-

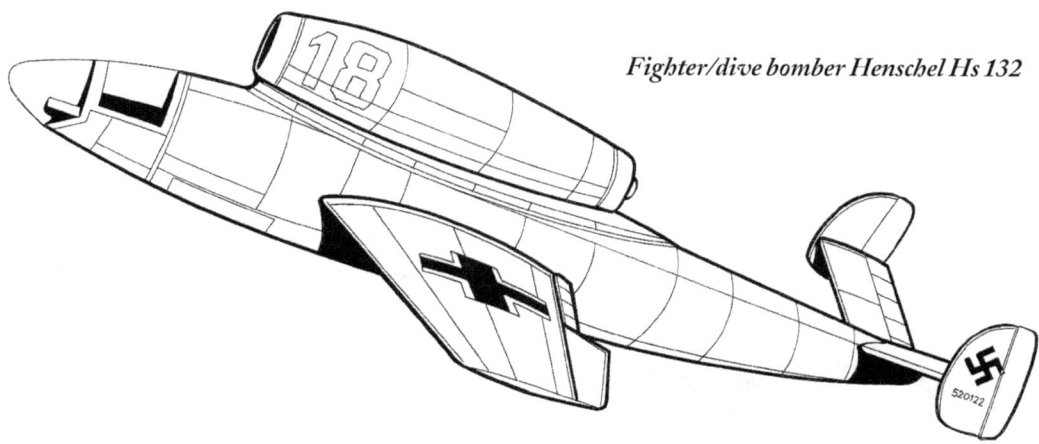

Fighter/dive bomber Henschel Hs 132

19 design had good potential but the project was abandoned when the RLM decided to develop the Messerschmitt 262.

Blohm & Voss Bv P 178

The asymmetrical, single-seat Bv P 178 was powered by a Junkers Jumo 004B turbojet positioned under the wing at starboard. It had a length of 10.8 m (35 ft 5.5 in) and a span of 12 m (39 ft 3 in). The landing gear was retractable and rockets (placed in the tail) would have been used for take-off. Armament would have included two MG 151 15-mm machine guns placed in the nose. One SC 500 or SC 1000 bomb could have been carried in a rack under the fuselage. Although the asymmetrical layout was favored by Blohm & Voss, it was not popular, and the Bv 178 dive bomber did not progress past the initial design stage.

Henschel Hs 132

The jet-powered Henschel Hs 132 was planned in two versions: dive bomber and heavy fighter. The fast dive bomber Hs 132A, powered by a BMW 003 A-1 jet-engine, carried 500 kg (1,102 lbs) of bombs, and had no defensive weapons. The fast fighter/interceptor Hs 132B, powered by one Jumo 004 jet engine, was to be armed with two 20-mm MG 151 cannons. The bomber version had a speed of 700 km/h (435 mph); the fighter version had a speed of 780 km/h (485 mph). In both versions the jet engine was located on top of the fuselage. Wingspan was 7.2 m (23 ft 7.5 in), length was 8.9 m (29 ft 2.5 in), and height was 3 m (9 ft 10 in). The pilot was placed in a prone position, allowing the very aerodynamic profile given to the fuselage and increasing the pilot's tolerance to high-acceleration turns. The Henschel Hs 132 was never completed, as Soviet troops overran the factory when the prototype V1 was nearing flight-testing.

Messerschmitt Zerstörer project II

A second unnamed Messerschmitt *Zerstörer* project became known through a sketch which was published in France after the war. A later well-known drawing suggests that there were two configurations of the same design, although the engine installation and tail design were different; one version had a T-tailplane, with the fin and rudder sharply swept forward. Apparently, it was planned to utilize two He S 011 turbojets which were fed by an air intake located on each side of the fuselage under the wings. To extend its range, plans were made to mount two 300-liter, auxiliary, wingtip fuel tanks. Armament was to be two MK 108 30-mm cannons. The aircraft had a span of 12 m (39 ft 4.8 in) and its length was 12 m (39 ft 4.8 in). This was another futuristic design that never materialized.

Messerschmitt Me 1102/5

Designed in mid–1944, the Messerschmitt Me 1102/5 was a project for a fast, light, jet bomber with a crew of one. It was designed to carry a bomb load of 3,000 kg (6,612 lbs) in a

Messerschmitt Zerstörer II

Messerschmitt Me 1102/5

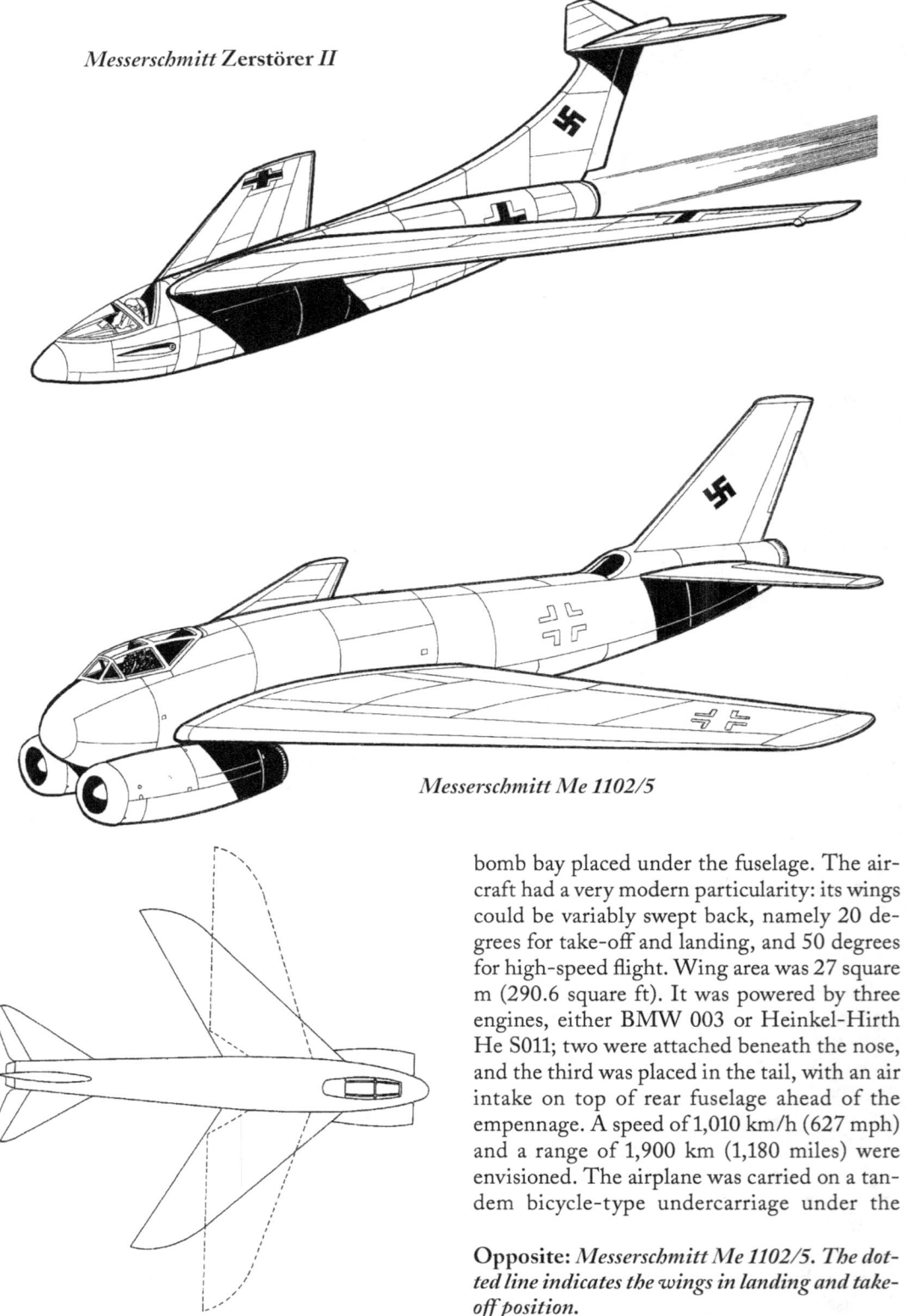

bomb bay placed under the fuselage. The aircraft had a very modern particularity: its wings could be variably swept back, namely 20 degrees for take-off and landing, and 50 degrees for high-speed flight. Wing area was 27 square m (290.6 square ft). It was powered by three engines, either BMW 003 or Heinkel-Hirth He S011; two were attached beneath the nose, and the third was placed in the tail, with an air intake on top of rear fuselage ahead of the empennage. A speed of 1,010 km/h (627 mph) and a range of 1,900 km (1,180 miles) were envisioned. The airplane was carried on a tandem bicycle-type undercarriage under the

Opposite: *Messerschmitt Me 1102/5. The dotted line indicates the wings in landing and take-off position.*

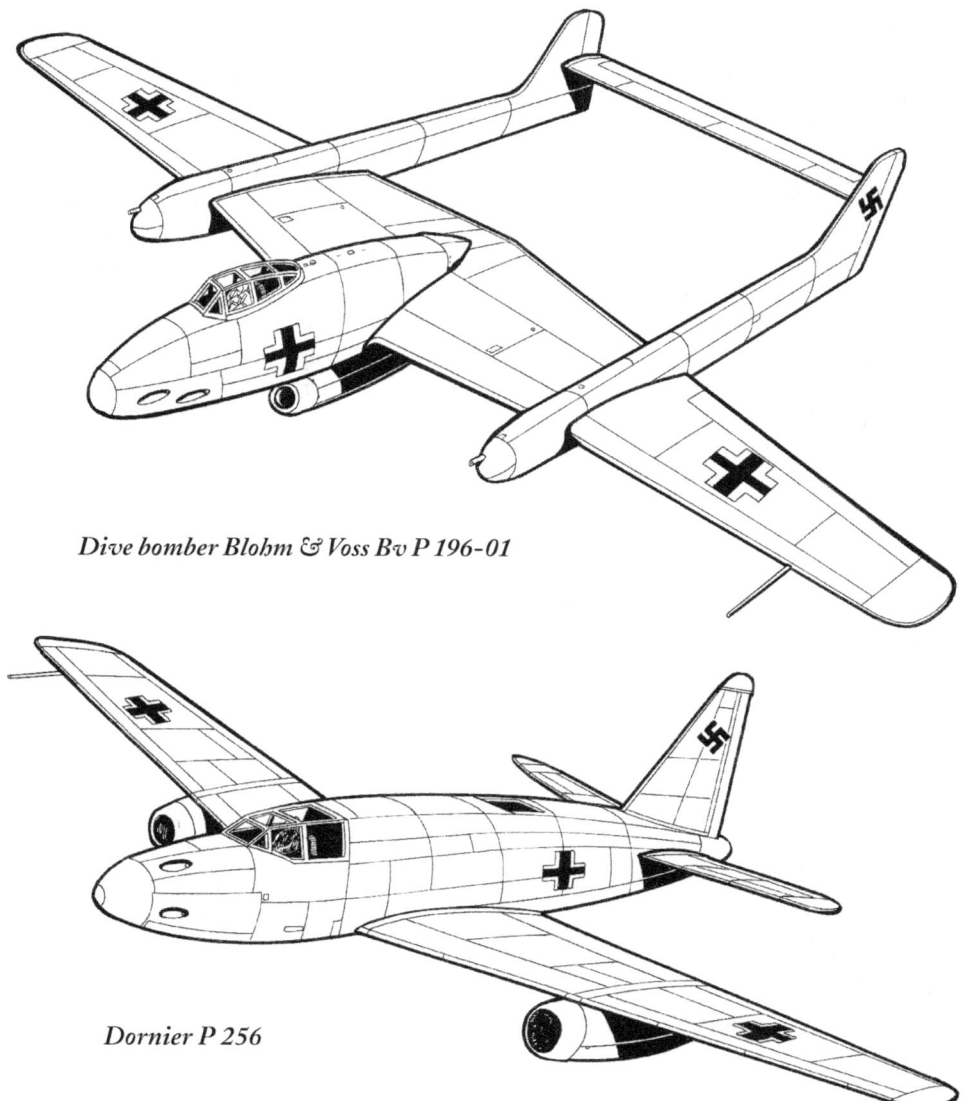

Dive bomber Blohm & Voss Bv P 196-01

Dornier P 256

fuselage, balanced by outrigger wheels beneath the wings. The Me 1102/5 did not reach completion, but documents describing it were seized by American troops at the end of World War II. The Messerschmitt design was without doubt the inspiration for the U.S. Martin XB-51 that first flew in 1949.

Blohm & Voss Bv P 196-01

The single-seat dive bomber Bv P 196 had a twin-boom design. It had a span of 15 m (49 ft 3 in), and a length of 11.7 m (38 ft 5 in). The aircraft was powered by two BMW 003 jet engines placed side by side under the center nacelle on top of which sat the pilot. Located in the nose of the nacelle, weapons included two MG 151/20 20-mm cannons and two MK 103 30-mm cannons. The Bv P 196 could carry two SC 250 bombs placed in two small enclosed bomb bays located in the booms. The project was never developed.

Dornier P 256

The Dornier P 256 was intended to become a heavy (night) fighter, or a light bomber/ground attacker. It had a crew of two, pilot in front and navigator seated in rear fuselage facing aft. It had a length of 13.6 m (44 ft 7.8 in) and a span of 15.45 m (50 ft 8.7 in). Fitted with a standard tricycle landing gear, it was powered by two He S011 jet engines placed beneath the wings and had a maximum speed of 882 km/h (548 mph). The aircraft was armed with four MK 108 30-mm cannons located in the nose, and could carry two bombs of 500 kg (1,100 lbs). The design was never completed.

BMW Schnellbomber *Project I*

A project for a fast long-range bomber was designed by the Bayerische Motorwerke (BMW) in Munich. It had a span of 50.6 m (166 ft) and a fuselage length of 32.5 m (106 ft 7.5 in), with a crew of three sitting in a pressurized, glazed cockpit located in the nose of fuselage. It was a dual-propulsion aircraft powered by two BMW 018 jet engines and two BMW 028 turboprop engines placed above the wing leading edge. With all engines operating, the bomber was expected to have a maximum speed of 850 km/h (528 mph). The wings had a curious layout as they had a short section of forward sweep, then the outer wing swept back. The aircraft could carry a bomb load of 15,000 kg (33,000 lbs) in an internal bay. Its defensive armament included two remote-con-

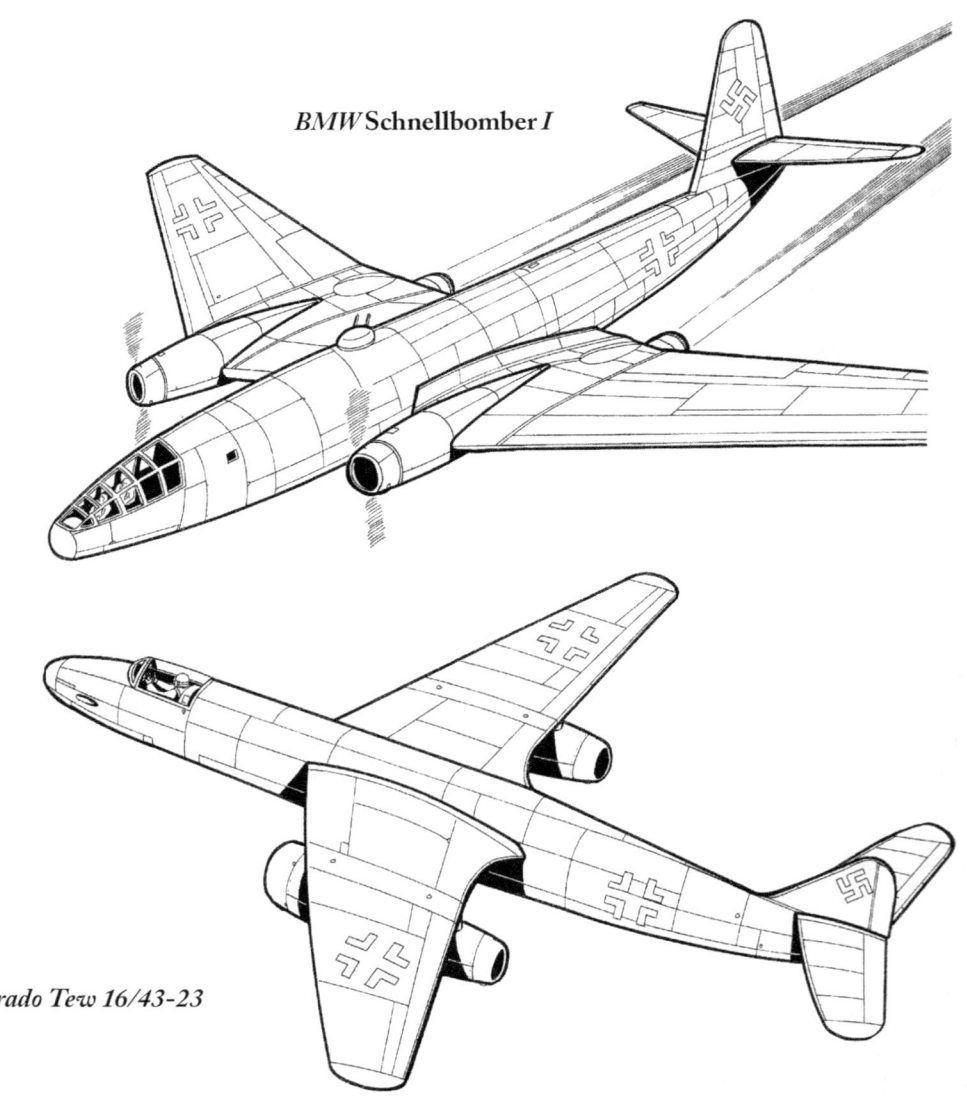

BMW Schnellbomber *I*

Arado Tew 16/43-23

trolled turrets (each armed with two cannons), one on top of the fuselage, the other in ventral position, both aimed by a periscope from the cockpit. The end of World War II prevented any further development of this project.

Arado Ar Tew 16/43-23

Designed in 1943, the Arado Tew 16/43-23 was intended to be an all-metal light bomber/ground attacker. It had a length of 12.2 m (40 ft 1 in), a crew of one, a retractable landing gear, swept-back wings with a span of 10.6 m (34 ft 9 in), and a wing area of 20 square m (215.28 square ft). The aircraft would have been powered by two jet engines placed under the wing, and was to be armed with one MG 151/15 15-mm machine gun and two MG 213/20 20-mm cannons, all mounted in the nose. This project was cancelled when design and production were concentrated on the bomber Arado Ar 234.

Arado Ar 234 Blitz

Designed by engineer Walter Blume as early as 1941, but first flown in July 1943, the Arado Ar 234 Blitz ("Lightning," also known as the *Hecht*—"Pike") was the world's first operational high-performance, jet-engine medium bomber. This came not from one of the major manufacturers, but from a relatively minor company. Prior to the development of the Ar 234 Blitz the Arado company had only ever been involved in the production of light aircraft. Many of them, such as the Ar 196, were produced as floatplanes. In 1940 the RLM issued a specification for a high-speed reconnaissance aircraft to be powered by jet engine. Arado's response was the shoulder-wing monoplane Ar 234 (originally designated E 370). This had a crew of one pilot. The length of the thin fuselage was 12.6 m (41 ft 6 in), wingspan was 14.1 m (46 ft 4 in), height was 4.3 m (14 ft 1 in), wing area was 26.4 square m (284 square ft), and empty weight was 5,200 kg (11,500 lbs). The bomber's design was conventional, neat and simple, but featured several innovations, including automatic pilots, landing-brake parachutes, and ejector seat, that are still used in military aircraft today. It was powered by two Junkers Jumo 004B-1 turbojets. Maximum speed was 742 km/h (461 mph), combat range was 800 km (500 miles), and service ceiling 10,000 m (32,800 ft). Armament included two rearward-firing, 20-mm MG 151 guns, aimed by the pilot through a periscope, but these were not always fitted. Two bombs of 500 kg (1,100 lb) or one of 1,000 kg (2,200 lb) or 1,400 kg (3,180 lb) could be carried.

In the field, the Ar 234 was used almost

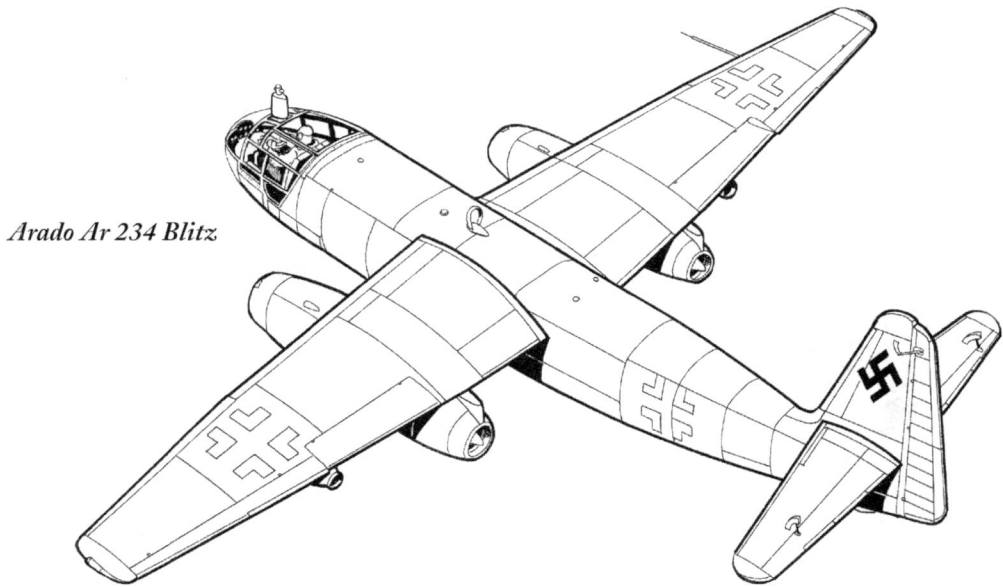

Arado Ar 234 Blitz

entirely in a reconnaissance role, but in its few uses as a bomber—owing to its remarkable speed and high ceiling—it proved to be impossible to intercept. The aircraft, however, lacked fuselage volume for any bomb load, which was therefore carried externally. To reduce weight, early prototypes had no landing gear; they took off on a wheeled trolley, and landed on skids at the end of the flight. Such a landing arrangement was out of the question for operational purposes, so the improved bomber version, Ar 234B, that flew in March 1944, had its fuselage slightly wider to hold a retractable landing gear fitted with two main wheels and nosewheel. It made use of RATO (rocket assisted take-off) and had an added bomb load. Twenty Arado Ar 234 Bs were produced and delivered by the end of June 1944. The only notable use of the plane in the bomber role was during the Ardennes offensive in winter 1944-45, and the most spectacular operational bombing mission was the repeated attacks by Ar 234 B-2s flown by III/KG 76 on the vital Ludendorff Bridge at Remagen in March 1945. The uninterceptable aircraft, though handicapped by fuel shortage, continued to see scattered front-line action for reconnaissance until Germany surrendered on May 8, 1945. There was a planned improved version, known as Arado Ar 234C, powered by four BMW 003A engines. Fifteen prototypes of the Ar 234C were completed before the end of the conflict. Although Hauptmann Diether Lukesch was preparing to form an operational test squadron, the Ar 234C was not developed in time to participate in actual combat operations.

Although a successful design, the small number manufactured, combined with shortage of fuel and lack of experienced airmen, meant that the Ar 234 failed to make any significant impact on the course of the war. The revolutionary bomber simply came too late, and was nowhere near as successful in operational terms as the Messerschmitt Me 262. At the end of World War II some surviving Luftwaffe jets, including several Ar 234s, made their way to Norway to escape capture by the Allies. These were eventually surrendered to the British and three of the Ar 234s were subsequently taken to the United States for evaluation.

Junkers Ju 287

The Ju 287 was intended to provide the Luftwaffe with a fast jet bomber that could avoid interception by outrunning enemy fighters. Designed in early 1943 by engineer Dr. Hans Wocke, the most striking feature was the revolutionary forward-swept wings which provided extra lift at low air speeds, necessary because of the poor responsiveness of early turbojets at the vulnerable times of take-off and

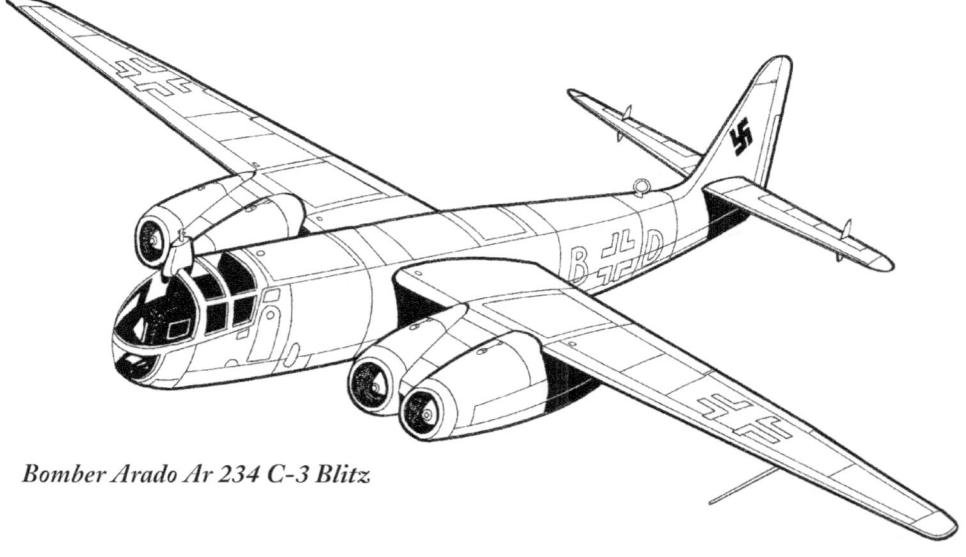

Bomber Arado Ar 234 C-3 Blitz

landing. The first prototype from August 1944 was built from scavenged components from other aircraft: fuselage of a Heinkel He 177, the tail of a Junkers Ju 388, main fixed undercarriage with "spatted" wheels from a Junkers Ju 352 and nose wheels taken from a crashed American B-24 Liberator. The Ju 287 was operated by a crew of two, pilot and copilot/bomber, and was powered by four Junkers Jumo 004 B-1 turbojet engines, two mounted in nacelles on each side of the forward fuselage and two hung under the wings. Maximum speed was 560 km/h (348 mph), range was 1,585 km (985 miles), and service ceiling was 9,400 m (30,000 ft). The forward-swept wings were aerodynamically efficient, but they required an extremely strong main spar, and available materials were not strong enough to withstand the stresses produced in flight. Wingspan was 20.11 m (65 ft 11 in), length was 18.30 m (60 ft), height was 4.70 m (15 ft) and wing area was 61 square m (655 square ft). The production version was to have two 13-mm MG 131 machine guns in a remote-controlled tail turret, and a bomb load of 4,000 kg (8,800lbs) was to be carried. After successful flight tests in August 1944, the Ju 287 demonstrated excellent characteristics, and three pro-

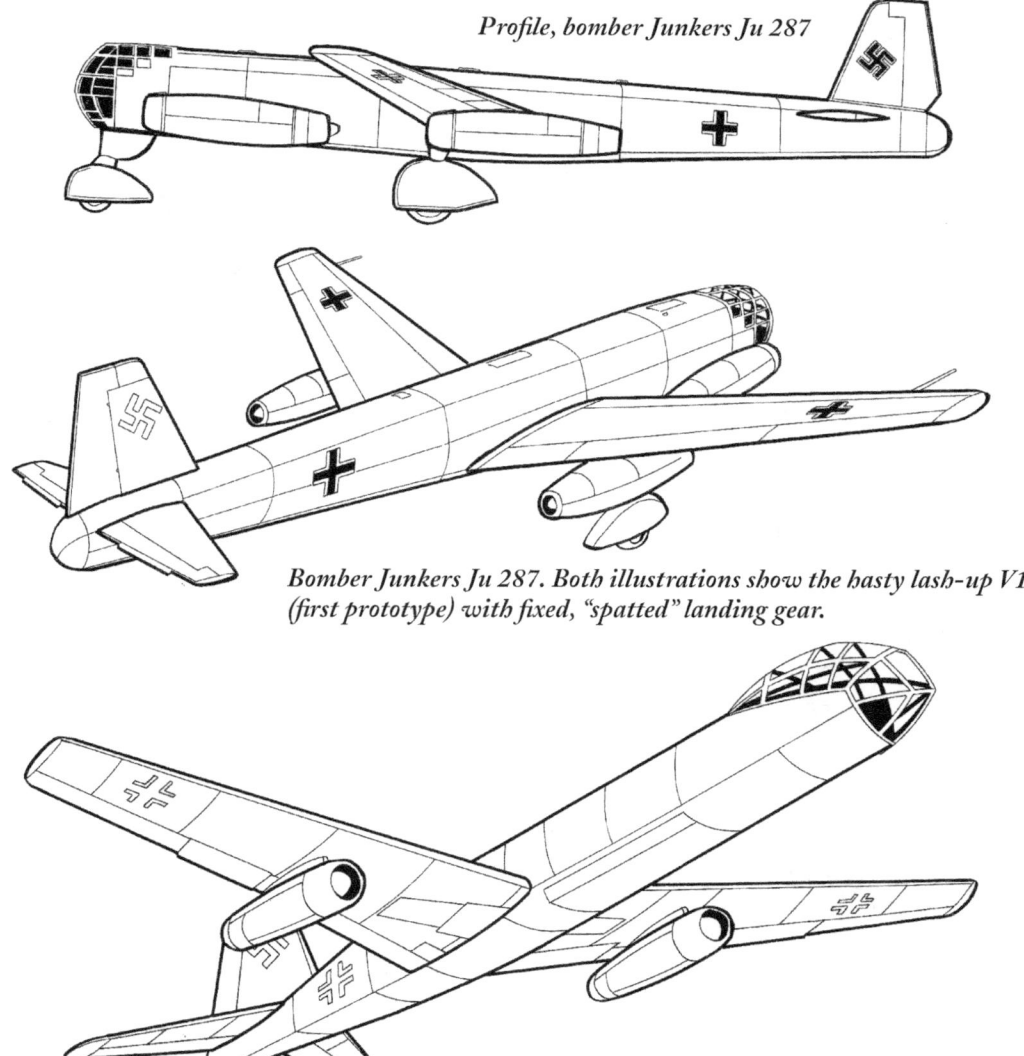

Profile, bomber Junkers Ju 287

Bomber Junkers Ju 287. Both illustrations show the hasty lash-up V1 (first prototype) with fixed, "spatted" landing gear.

EF 125 (Variant Ju 287)

totypes were built with more powerful engines, and improved features including pressurized cockpit (for a crew of 3), retractable landing gear and take-off-assistance rockets. The aircraft never entered mass production, though, as Hitler ordered that all development not concerned with fighters and interceptors be stopped. Besides, the Junkers factory was overrun by the Allies. Two prototypes, as well as Hans Wocke and his staff were taken to the Soviet Union where the development of the Ju 287 (redesignated OKB-1 EF 140) was continued. In 1949, when it became obvious that the project was leading nowhere, work on this odd aircraft was abandoned. There was a planned enlarged version, known as Ju 287 V-2, with six turbojets, three under each wing; this variant had to develop a speed of 800 km/h and has to accommodate up to four tons of bombs.

Messerschmitt P 1108

Designed in February 1945, the long-range bomber project Messerschmitt P 1108 existed

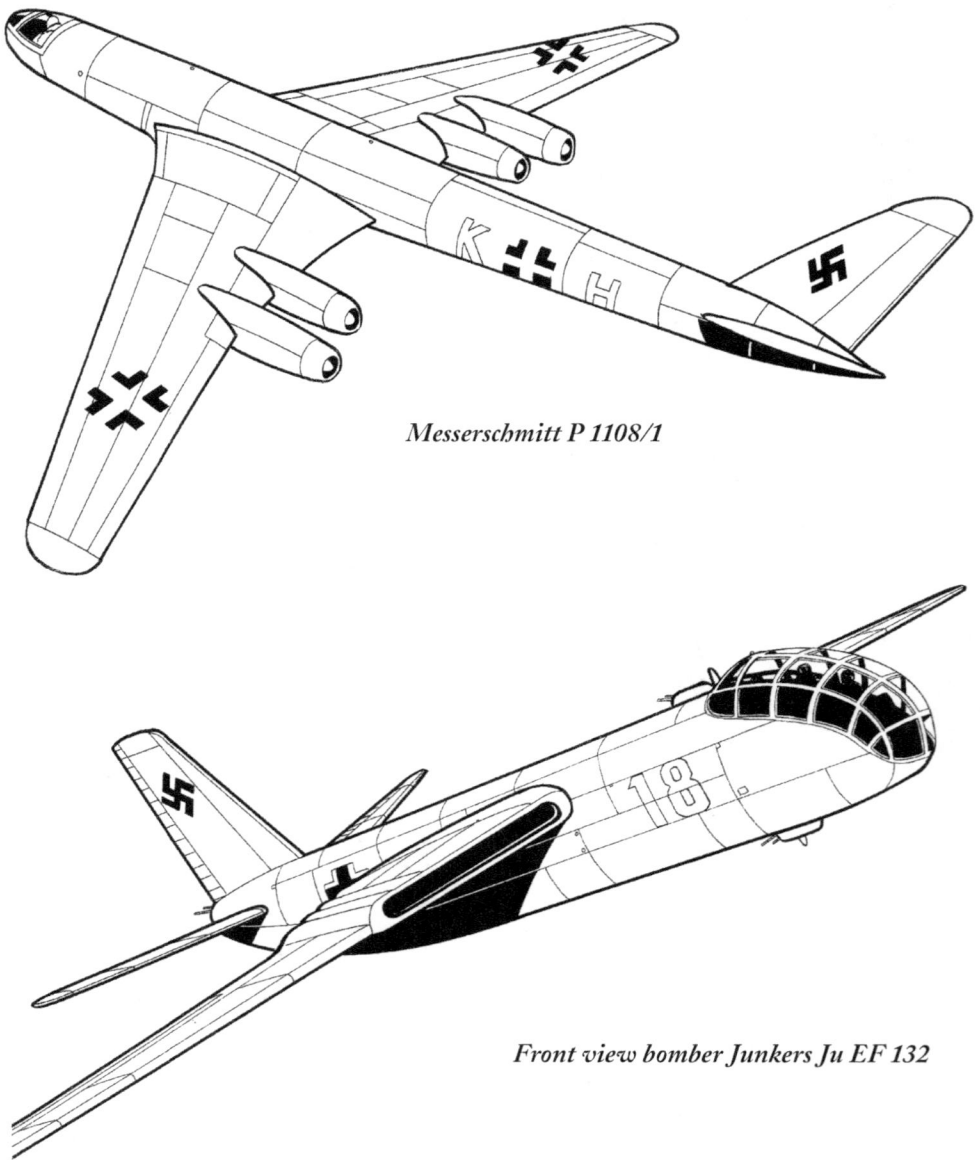

Messerschmitt P 1108/1

Front view bomber Junkers Ju EF 132

in two main versions. The P 1108/1 had a low swept-back wing with a span of 20.12 m (66 ft 1 in) and a length of 18.2 m (59 ft 9 in). It was to be operated by a crew of two sitting in tandem arrangement. The aircraft was powered by four HeS011 jet engines, mounted in paired nacelles embedded in the wing trailing edge, fed by a common air intake on each lower wing surface. It was to have a speed of 850 km/h (528 mph) and a range of 2,000 km (1,243 miles). The P 1108/1 had a retractable tricycle landing gear. It could have carried a bomb load of 1,000 kg (2,200 lbs).

The variant P 1108/2, designed by engineer Alexander Lippisch, was a delta flying wing with single vertical fin and rudder. It had a span of 21.7 m (71 ft 3 in), a length of 12.5 m (41 ft) and a bomb load of 2,500 kg (5,500 lbs).

Junkers EF 132

The Junkers EF 132 was intended to be a long-range jet bomber. Its wingspan was 32.4 m (106 ft 4 in), its length was 30.8 m (101 ft 1 in), its height was 8.4 m (27 ft 7 in), and its wing area was 161 square m (1.733 square ft). Powered by six Jumo 012 jet engines integrated in the wing roots, it had a maximum speed of 930 km/h (578 mph), a cruising speed of 850 km/h (528 mph), and a maximum range of 3,500 km (2,175 miles). The crew of three operated the aircraft in a fully glazed, pressurized cockpit. Armament consisted of twin 20-mm cannons in a remote-controlled turret placed aft of the cockpit; another remote-controlled turret with twin 20-mm cannons was located beneath the fuselage, and a remote-controlled machine gun with two 20-mm cannons was placed in the tail. A load of about 4,000 kg (8,800 lbs) in bombs was carried in a

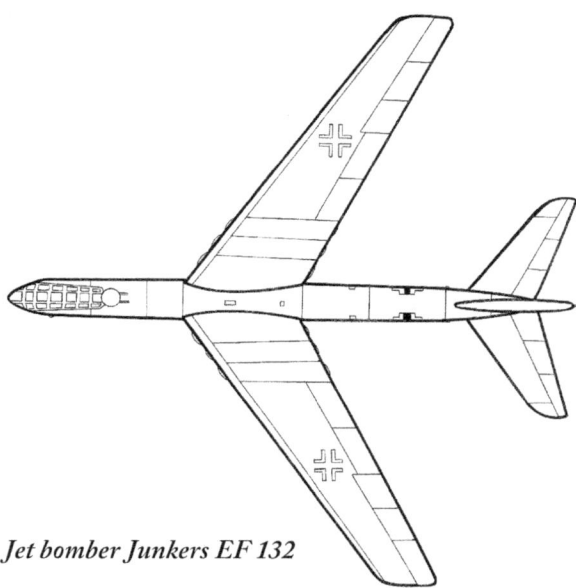

Jet bomber Junkers EF 132

Heinkel He P 1068-01-80

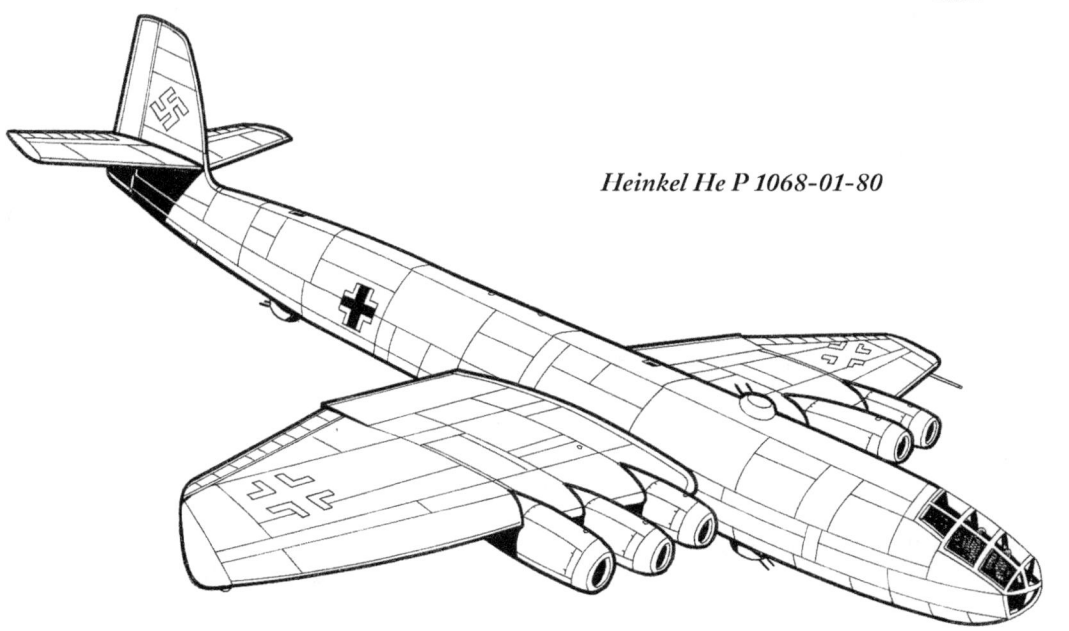

large, closed bomb bay arranged in the fuselage. The Ju EF 132 never went further than the drawing board and the project was cancelled by the end of the war. Work on the aircraft continued in Russia under Soviet supervision, but development was dropped in October 1946.

Heinkel He P 1068-01-80

The Heinkel He P 1068-01-80 project for a long-range strategic bomber was designed in late 1943 by engineer Siegfried Günter. The aircraft was powered by six He S011 or six Jumo 004C turbojet engines placed on the wings. It would have had a speed of 930 km/h (578 mph) and a range of 1,430 km (858 miles). The bomber had a span of 19 m (62 ft 4 in), a length of 20 m (65 ft 7 in), a wing area of 60 square m (654.84 square ft) and an empty weight of 14,800 kg (32,628 lbs). The project was never realized.

Heinkel He P 1068-01-83

The He P 1068-01-83 was a smaller version of the He P 1068-01-80. Slightly different in layout, it had low-mounted wing with a span of 17 m (55 ft 9 in), a length of 17 m (55 ft 9 in), a wing area of 43 square m (462.85 square ft) and an empty weight of 10,760 kg (23,721 lbs). The aircraft had a crew of two sitting in a pressurized, glazed cockpit placed in the nose of the fuselage. Powered by four He S011 turbojet engines placed on the wings, it would have had a speed of 910 km/h (565 mph) and a range of 1,610 km (1,000 miles). The bomber could have carried a bomb load of 2,000 kg (4,409 lbs).

There was a different version known as P 1068-01-84. This had performance, crew, dimensions and capacity similar to the P 1068-01-83, but featured a swept wing at 35 degrees and four He S 011 jet engines placed along the

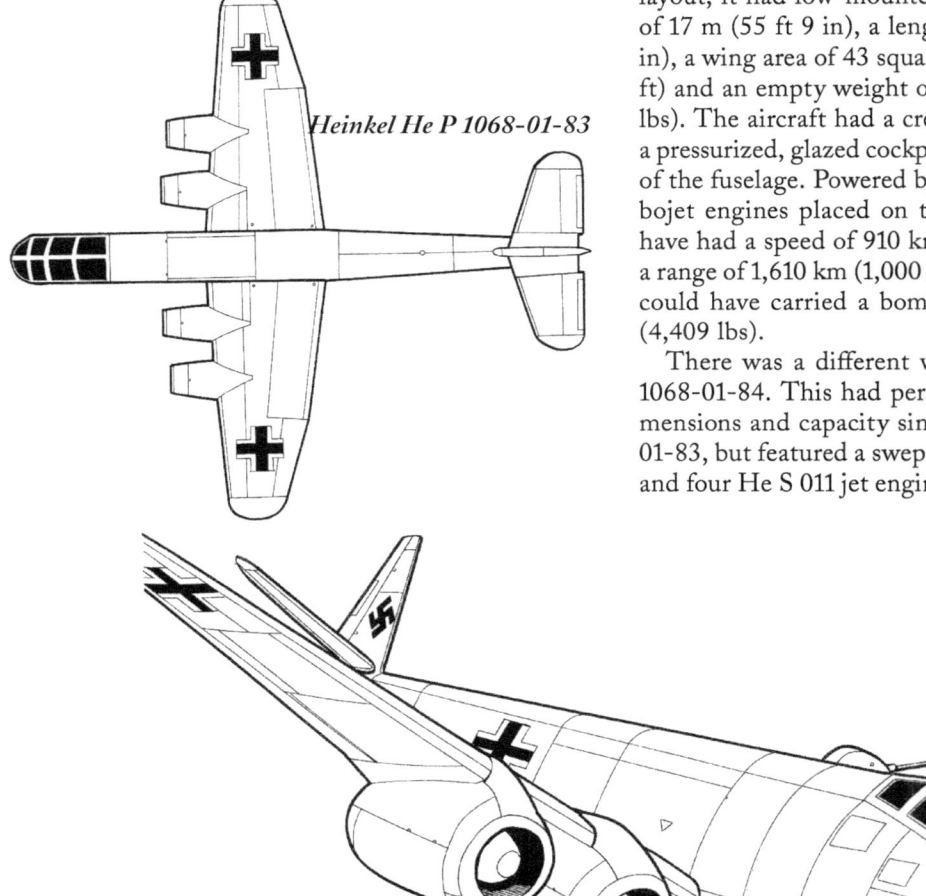

Heinkel He P 1068-01-83

Heinkel He P 1068-01-83 (front view)

fuselage, two in front and below the wings, and two behind and above the wings. These projects, too, never passed the drawing-board stage.

Heinkel He 343

Work on the four-engined jet bomber Heinkel He 343 started in January 1944. The aircraft, also known as *Strabo* 16 (*Strabo* being short for "*Strahlbomber*"—"jet bomber"), had a length of 16.5 m (54 ft 2 in), a height of 5.35 m (17 ft 7 in), and unswept wings mounted mid-fuselage with a wingspan of 18 m (59 ft 1 in) and a wing area of 42.25 square m (454.78 square ft). The Heinkel He 343 would have had an average empty weight of 9,068 kg (19,991 lbs). It was to be powered by four jet engines mounted singly beneath the wings. The design offered a great flexibility as virtually any turbojet could be used, either Jumo 004B, or Jumo 004C, or BMW 003, or He S 011. An average maximum speed of 835 km/h (519 mph) and a range of 10,000 km (32,808 ft) were planned. The crew of two sat in a pressurized, glazed cockpit placed in the nose. Four main versions of the He 343 were planned.

The Heinkel He 343 A-1 was the bomber version, carrying a bomb load ranging between 2,000 kg to 3,000 kg, with 2,000 kg to be carried internally in a bomb bay and 1,000 kg to be carried externally on racks under the wings. The He 343A-1 could also carry a Fritz X radio-controlled bomb, operated by an additional third crew member. Defensive armament included two fixed rear-firing MG 151 20-mm cannons (with 200 rounds each) mounted in the rear fuselage.

The Heinkel He 343 A-2 was intended for a reconnaissance role. This version was quite similar to the He 343A-1, but the bomb bay was replaced by an additional fuel tank with a capacity of 2,400 kg of fuel, which considerably extended the range. The He 343A-2 was equipped with two Rb 75/30 cameras. Defensive armament was the same as the bomber version He 343A-1: two fixed rear-firing MG 151 20-mm cannons mounted in the rear fuselage.

The *He 343A-3* was the first *Zerstörer* (destroyer/ground attack) version. This could carry a bomb load of 2,000 kg (4,409 lbs) and would have been armed with four forward-firing MK 103 30-mm cannons (with 400 rounds each) mounted in the bomb bay, or two forward-firing MK 103 30-mm cannons (with 100 rounds each) and two forward-firing MG 151 20-mm cannons (with 200 rounds each). Defensive armament, like the A-1 and A-2 variants, included two fixed rear-firing MG 151 20-mm cannons (with 200 rounds each) mounted in the rear fuselage.

The He 343 B-1 was the second *Zerstörer* variant which differed from the A-3 in its armament. The two fixed rear-firing guns in the fuselage rear, were to be replaced by a FHL

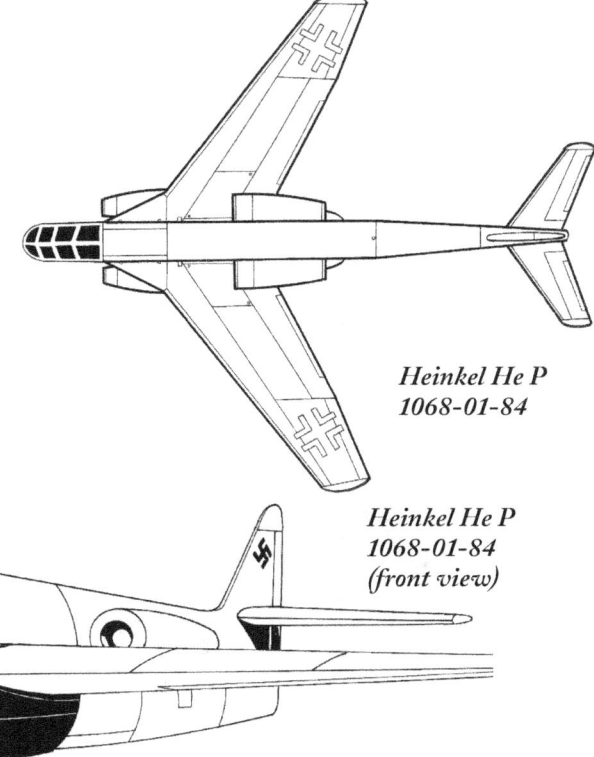

Heinkel He P 1068-01-84

Heinkel He P 1068-01-84 (front view)

151Z remote-controlled turret placed in the extreme rear fuselage. The turret, armed with two MG 151 20-mm cannons, was remotely operated from the cockpit, owing to a rear-facing periscope. The placement of the turret required a tail redesign with a twin fin-and-rudder set-up.

The RLM ordered twenty He 343 airplanes (including prototype and pre-production examples), but there was a fierce competition between Heinkel and Junkers, which at the same time and for the same purpose, designed a formidable four-jet-engined bomber competitor: the Junkers Ju 287 with forward-swept wing. In spite of Professor Ernst Heinkel's effort to promote his He 343, touting its quicker development time, lower material cost and basic simplicity, the He 343 was rejected and the development program was stopped in late 1944.

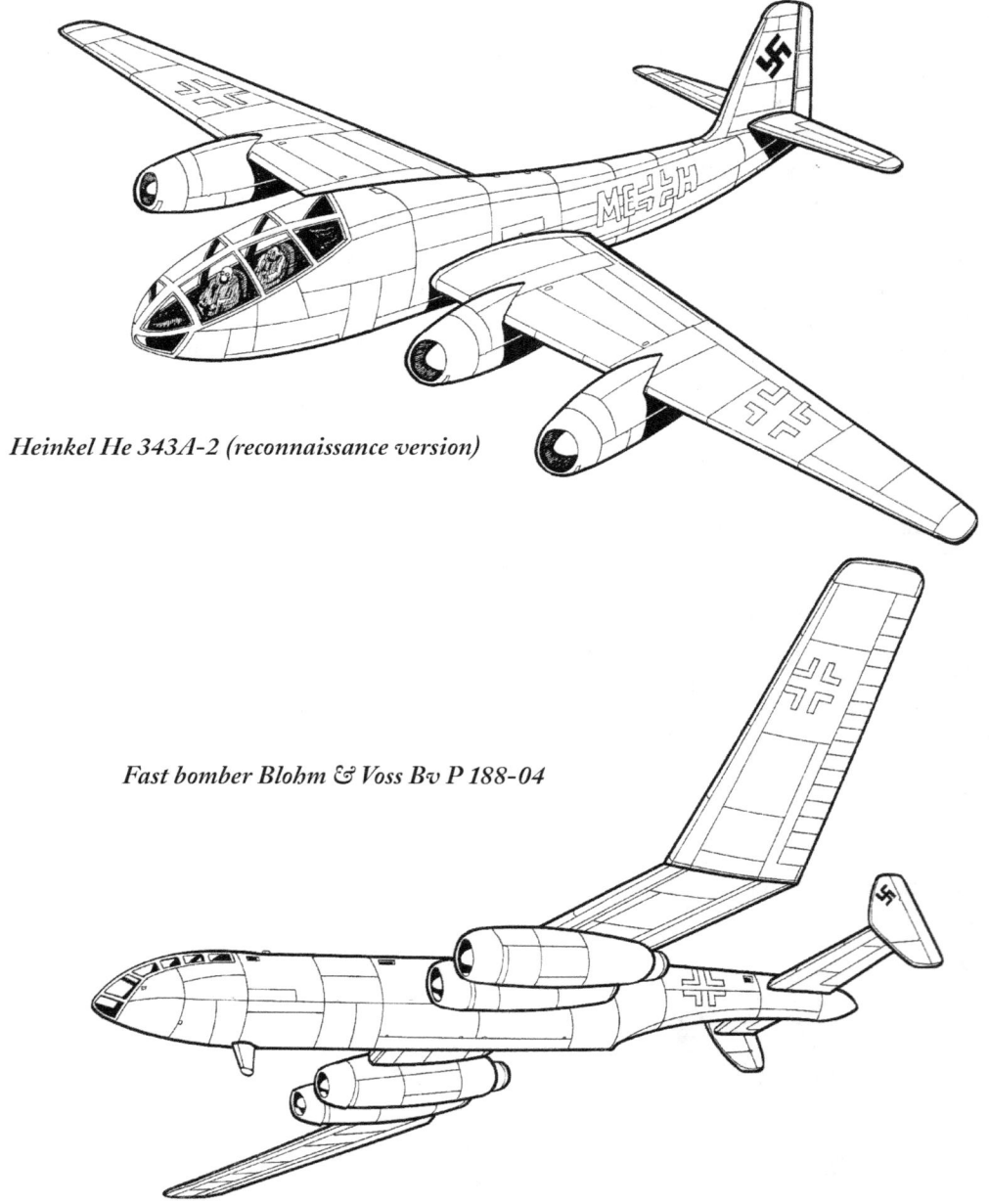

Heinkel He 343A-2 (reconnaissance version)

Fast bomber Blohm & Voss Bv P 188-04

Blohm & Voss Bv P 188

The Blohm & Voss P 188-04 was intended to be a long-range jet bomber. The fuselage had a length of 17.55 m (57 ft 7.5 in) and the tail unit was of a twin fin and rudder design. The most striking and unusual feature was the wing which had a constant 3-degree dihedral and was of a very novel design, featuring both a 20-degree swept-back inner section and then a 20-degree swept-forward in order to give good performance at both low and high speeds; wingspan was 27 m (88 ft 7.8 in). The crew of two sat in the glazed and pressurized cockpit. The aircraft was powered by four Jumo 004C turbojets mounted on nacelles located beneath each wing. Speed was to be 820 km/h (509 mph). Defensive armament included two remote-controlled FDL 131 Z twin 13-mm machine gun turrets. A bomb load of 2,000 kg (4,409 lbs) was to be carried in a bomb bay and externally in racks under the wings. A variant, known as P 188-01, had a single fin-and-rudder tail unit. The bomber project P 188 never passed the design stage.

Henschel Hs P 122

The Hs P122 was a jet bomber projected by the Henschel Company. It had a length of 11.57 m (38 ft) and a large span of 21.32 m (70 ft). The wing was mounted low on the fuselage and was swept back. The machine was to be powered by either two BMW 018 (developing 3,400 kg thrust each) or two He S011 engines (1,300 kg each), slung beneath the moderately swept wings, which would have enabled the bomber to have an impressive ceiling and range. A speed of 1,010 km/h (627 mph), and a range of 2,000 km were planned. Relying upon speed, the bomber was not intended to have any defensive armament, only a bomb load of 1,500 kg (3,300 lbs). The crew was composed of two airmen accommodated in a glazed cockpit at the front of the aircraft. The project did not leave the drawing board.

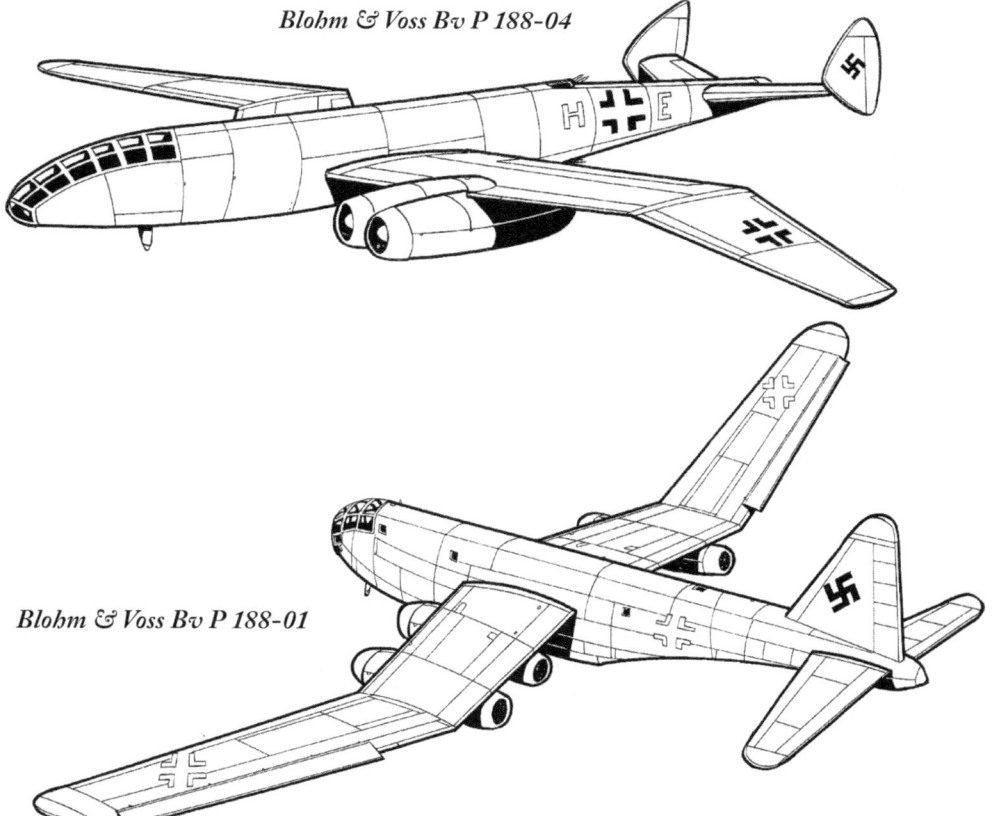

Blohm & Voss Bv P 188-04

Blohm & Voss Bv P 188-01

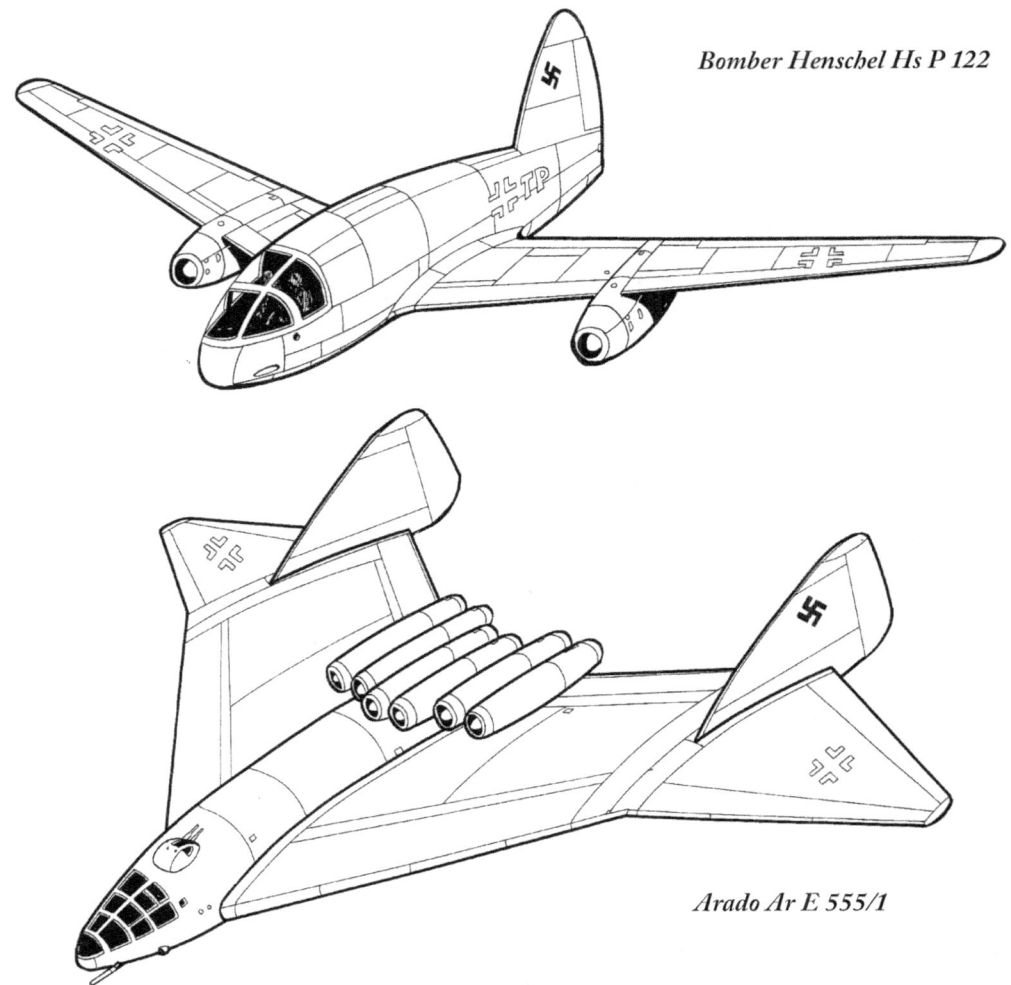

Bomber Henschel Hs P 122

Arado Ar E 555/1

Arado Ar E 555

Designed by engineers Laute, Kosin and Lehmann, the Arado E 555 project was an ambitious program for a series of fifteen delta-wing, long-range, fast jet bombers. The basic design, Arado Ar E 555/1, was constructed entirely of metal—both steel and duraluminum. It had a crew of three sitting in a pressurized cockpit, a span of 21.2 m (69 ft 7 in), and a wing area of 125 square m (1345.5 square ft). The aircraft was powered by six BMW 003 jet engines mounted at the rear upper surface of the delta wing. The aircraft was intended to have a speed of 860 km/h (534 mph) and a maximum range of 4,800 km (2,983 miles). Armament would have included two MK 103 30-mm cannons mounted in the wing roots; one remote-controlled turret (armed with two MG 15/20 20-mm cannons) located behind the cockpit; and one remote-controlled tail turret (armed with two MG 151/20 20-mm guns) placed under the surface of the wing for rear firing. The aircraft was intended to carry a bomb load of 4,000 kg (8,818 lbs).

The other planned versions of the E 555 had a different way of propulsion, slightly different layout and configurations, and a number of jet engines. The Arado E 555/2 was powered by four He S011 jet engines, the E 555/3 by two BMW 018 engines, and the E 555/4 by three BMW 018 engines. The E 555/6 was powered by three BMW 018 jet engines and had a different wing design. The E 555/7 was powered by three BMW 018 engines and its wing were fitted with slightly larger rudders. The E

4. Bombers

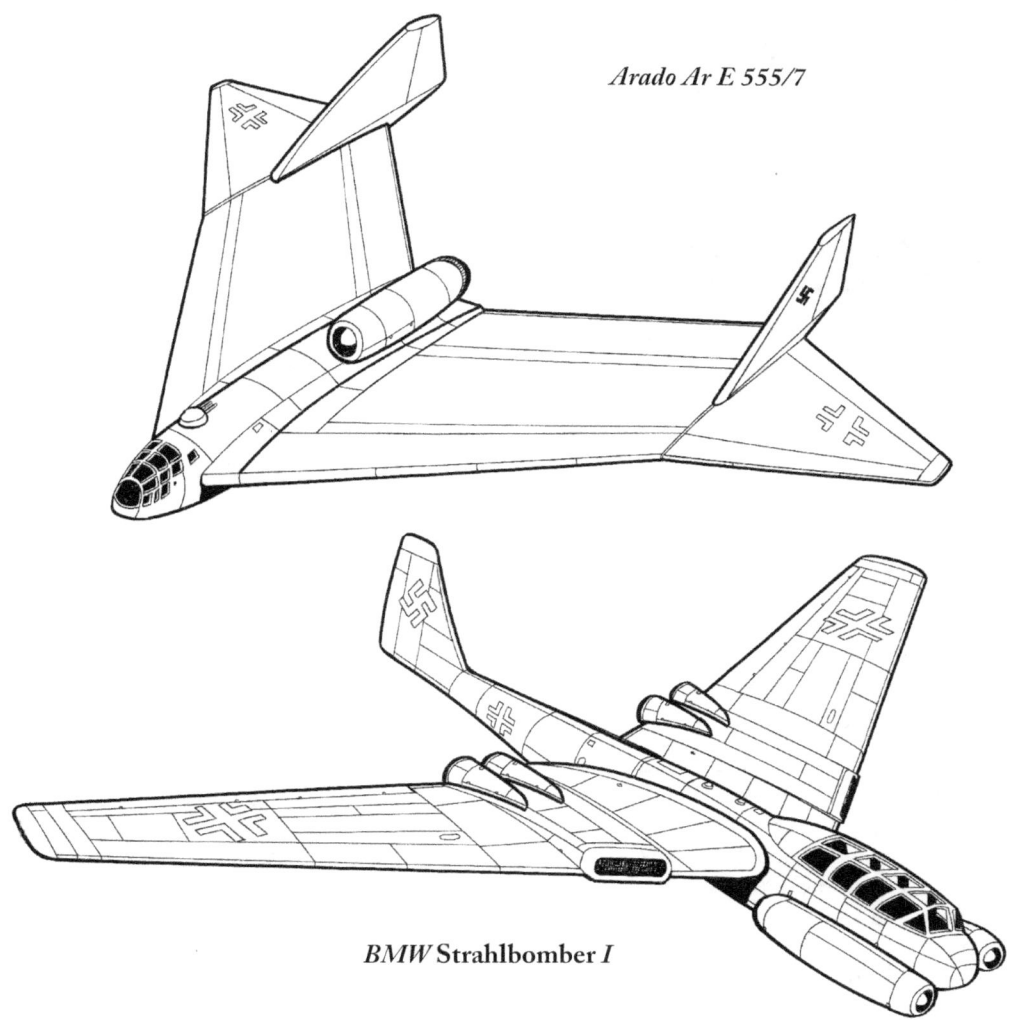

Arado Ar E 555/7

BMW Strahlbomber *I*

555/8a, E 555/8b, E 555/9 and E 555/10 were powered by three BMW 018 jet engines and had various twin-boom layouts holding a tail unit. The E 555/10 was powered by four BMW 018 jet engines, and a fuselage in the shape of a long tail held the tail unit. The unfinished Arado E 555 project program was cancelled in December 1944.

BMW Strahlbomber *1*

A Bayerische Motorenwerke (BMW) project was intended to produce a fast *Strahlbomber* (jet bomber—*Strabo*, for short). The aircraft was powered by no less than six BMW 003 turbojets, two mounted on either side of the forward fuselage, the other four mounted in pairs in the trailing edge of the wing, the latter using a shared air-intake duct. A maximum speed of 820 km/h (510 mph) was expected. The aircraft had a length of 18.5 m (60 ft 8.9 in). It had a span of 26.5 m (87 ft), with swept-back, shoulder-mounted wings. The vertical tail surface was of conventional design, but no horizontal tailplane was used. The crew of two was accommodated in a pressurized cockpit located in the forward fuselage. The BMW Strabo 1 would have been armed with two fixed aft-firing machine cannons in the rear of the fuselage, and would have carried a 4,000-kg (8,800-lb) load of bombs. The BMW Strabo never left the drawing board.

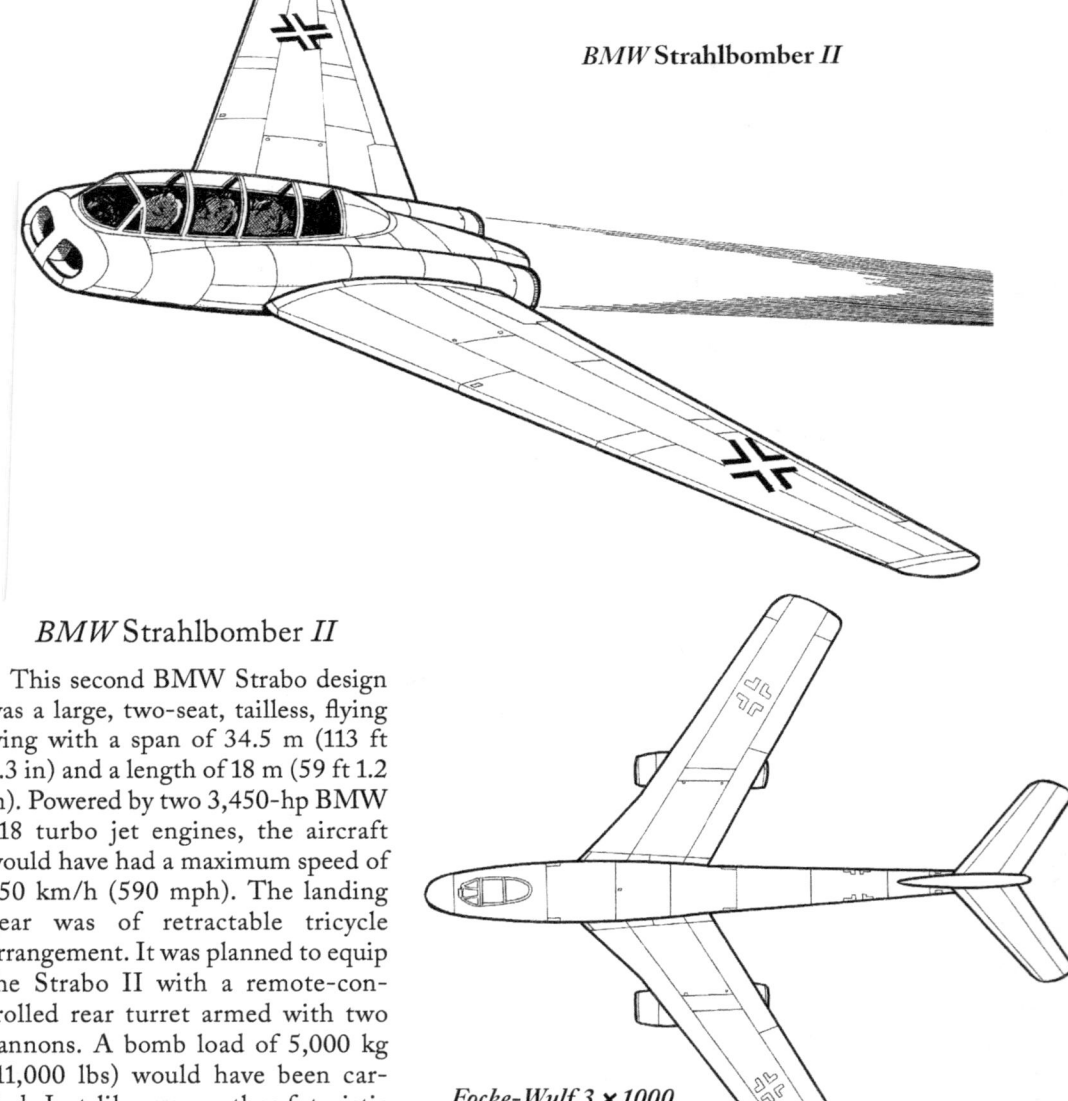

BMW Strahlbomber *II*

Focke-Wulf 3 × 1000 bomber project A

BMW Strahlbomber *II*

This second BMW Strabo design was a large, two-seat, tailless, flying wing with a span of 34.5 m (113 ft 3.3 in) and a length of 18 m (59 ft 1.2 in). Powered by two 3,450-hp BMW 018 turbo jet engines, the aircraft would have had a maximum speed of 950 km/h (590 mph). The landing gear was of retractable tricycle arrangement. It was planned to equip the Strabo II with a remote-controlled rear turret armed with two cannons. A bomb load of 5,000 kg (11,000 lbs) would have been carried. Just like many other futuristic projects, Strabo II never materialized.

Focke-Wulf 1000 × 1000 × 1000 Bomber Project A, B, and C

A Focke-Wulf series of three long-range bombers was intended to carry a bomb load of 1,000 kg (2,201 lbs), at a range of 1,000 km (620 miles) with a speed of 1,000 km/h (620 mph). Designed by engineers H. von Halem and D. Küchemann, models A and C were of conventional configuration. In both cases the fuselage had a length of 14.2 m (46 ft 7 in), and the swept-back wing a span of 12.65 m (41 ft 6 in), with a wing area of 27 square m (290.6 square feet). Both A and C were powered by two Heinkel-Hirth He S011 turbojet engines, each developing 1,300 kg (2,866 lbs) of thrust, with a maximum speed of 1,000 km/h (621 mph) and a range of 2,500 km (1,305 miles), and both could carry a bomb load of 1,000 kg (2,205 lbs) housed in an internal bomb

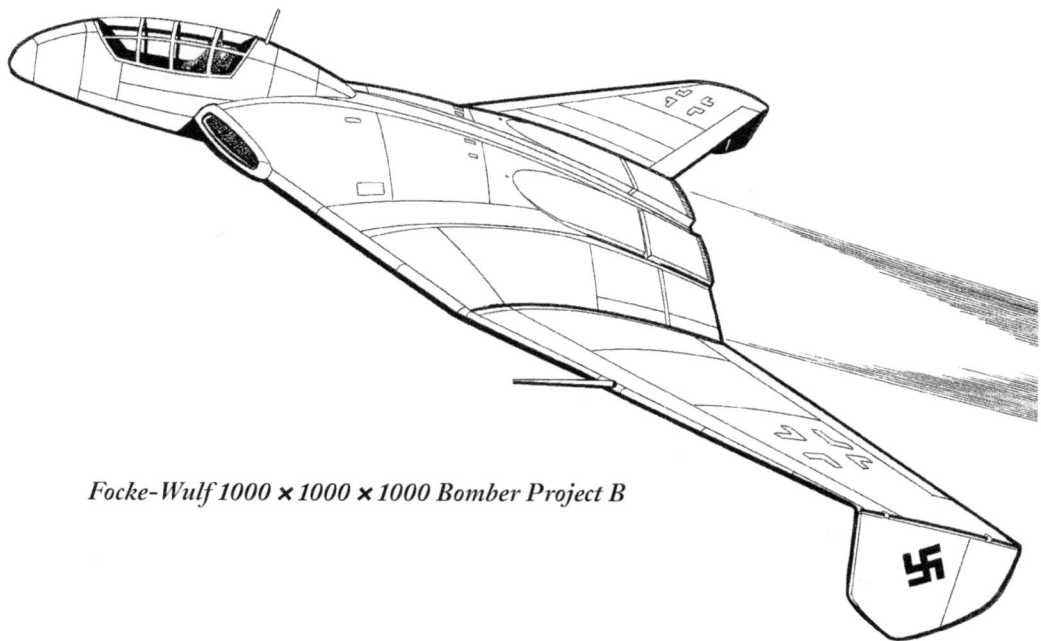

Focke-Wulf 1000 × 1000 × 1000 Bomber Project B

bay. Both had a tricycle undercarriage. The two projects slightly differed in their cockpit arrangement (A was operated by a crew of one, and C by three airmen) and the manner by which the jet engines were mounted under the wings. In the A model these were slung, and in project C on underwing pylons to increase the mass-balance effect; they were also turned out of line to help enhance controllability.

Project B was a flying-wing model with a back-sweep of 35 degrees, a span of 14 m (45 ft 11 in), and a length of 5.8 m (19 ft 1 in). The wingtips were bent down with small rudders, and the retractable landing gear was of tricycle arrangement. The crew of two sat in a pressurized, glazed cockpit placed at the front of the short fuselage. Powered by two Heinkel Hirth He S 011 jet engines placed at the back of the main wing, it would have had a speed of 1,060 km/h (659 mph) and a range of 2,500 km (1,305 miles). The aircraft could have carried a bomb load of 1,000 kg (2.205 lbs) in an internal bomb bay positioned in the center wing. Given the impressive high speed of the series, no defensive armament was considered necessary. Like so many other designs, the 3 × 1000 series project was never realized.

Horten Ho XVIII A and Ho XVIII B

Designed in 1944 by engineers Reimar and Walter Horten, this huge "Amerika Bomber" flying wing was intended to become a fast, strategic heavy bomber, able to fly from Germany to New York and back without refueling. The aircraft had a span of 40 m (131 ft 4 in) and was to be powered by six Junkers Jumo 004B turbojets buried in the fuselage. Maximum speed was to be 900 km/h (559 mph) and range 11,000 km (6,835 miles). To save weight the Ho XVIII A was to be made of wood, and to use a jettisonable landing gear for take-off and skid for landing. The Horten brothers were ordered by Reichsmarschall Hermann Göring to work with other companies to build the aircraft. Junkers and Messerschmitt engineers wanted to change the design, use other engines, place a tricycle landing gear and relocate the bomb bay. The brothers, however, were not happy with the final Ho XVIII A design, so they went about redesigning it, with the redesign known as Horten Ho XVIII B. The new aircraft had a fixed landing gear including two nacelles, each with four wheels. In flight, the wheels were covered by doors to help cut down drag and air resistance. The Ho XVIII B was powered by four He S011

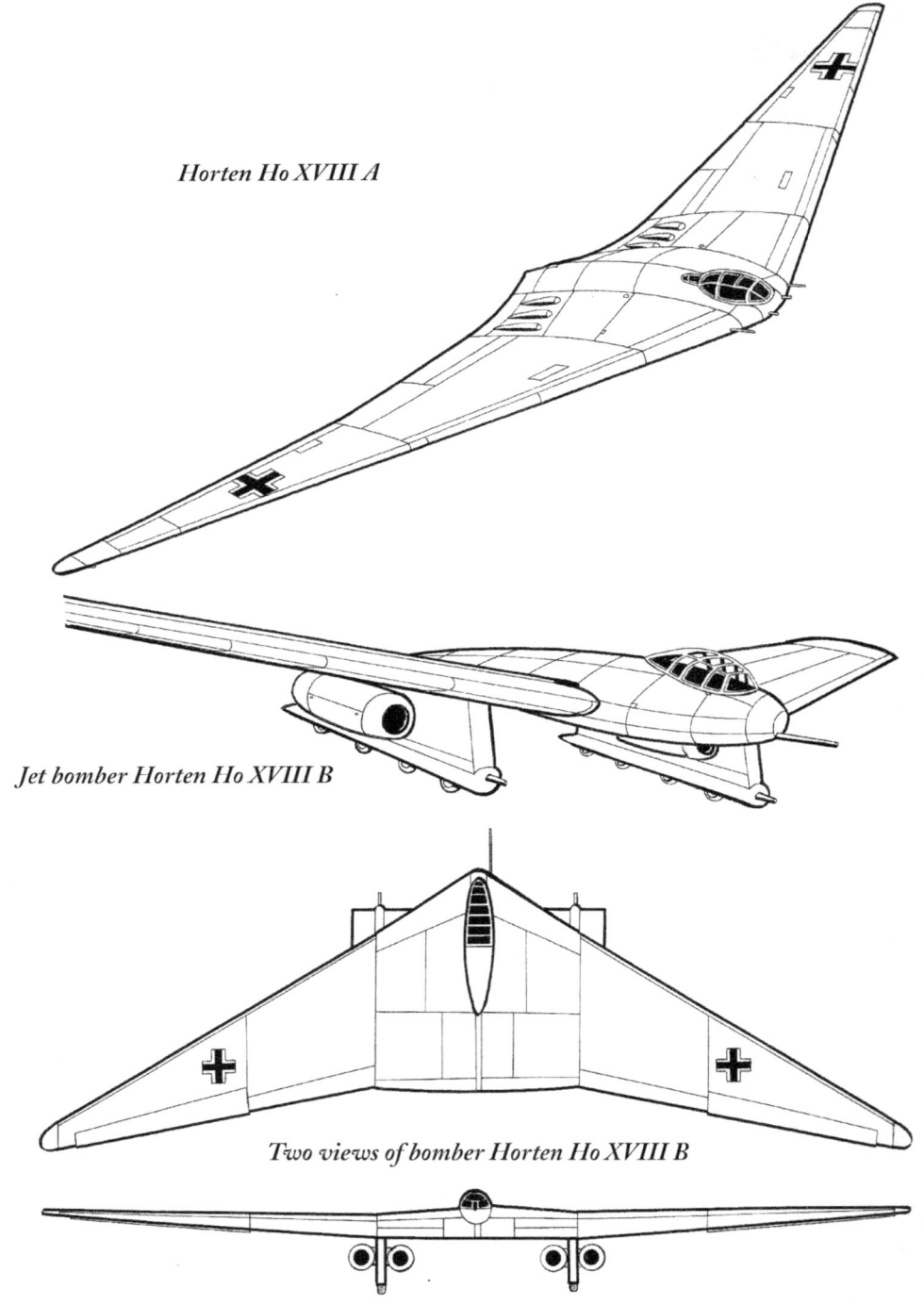

Horten Ho XVIII A

Jet bomber Horten Ho XVIII B

Two views of bomber Horten Ho XVIII B

turbojet engines, positioned in pairs at the side of the large, fixed landing gear. An unknown load of bombs could be carried and defensive armament would have consisted of two MK 108 30-mm cannons mounted below the cockpit. The crew of three sat upright in a pressurized bubble-type cockpit placed at the top of the wing. The end of World War II prevented any further design of this curious and futuristic bomber.

Junkers EF 130

The Junkers EF 130 was also known as DFS 130, as it was a joint design in 1943 by Junkers and the *Deutsche Forschungsanstalt für Segelflug* (DFS—German Institute for Gliding Research). Intended to be a fast, long-range jet bomber, and inspired by the Horten brothers' wing-only design, the EF 130 was designed by the talented engineers Hans Wocke, Ernst Zindel and Heinrich Hertel. The machine consisted of a large flying wing (24 meters in span, with a wing area of 120 square meters) constructed of wood, with metal inner wing and fuselage, with the cockpit at the front for a crew of three. Powered by four BMW-003 turbojet engines mounted side by side above the central trailing wing edge, the aircraft would have had a speed of 1,000 km/h, a range of 6,000 km and a bomb payload of about 3,000 kg. Landing gear was designed to be of a retractable tricycle arrangement. The aircraft's speed was thought to preclude interception, thus no defensive armament was to be fitted.

There was also another larger project,

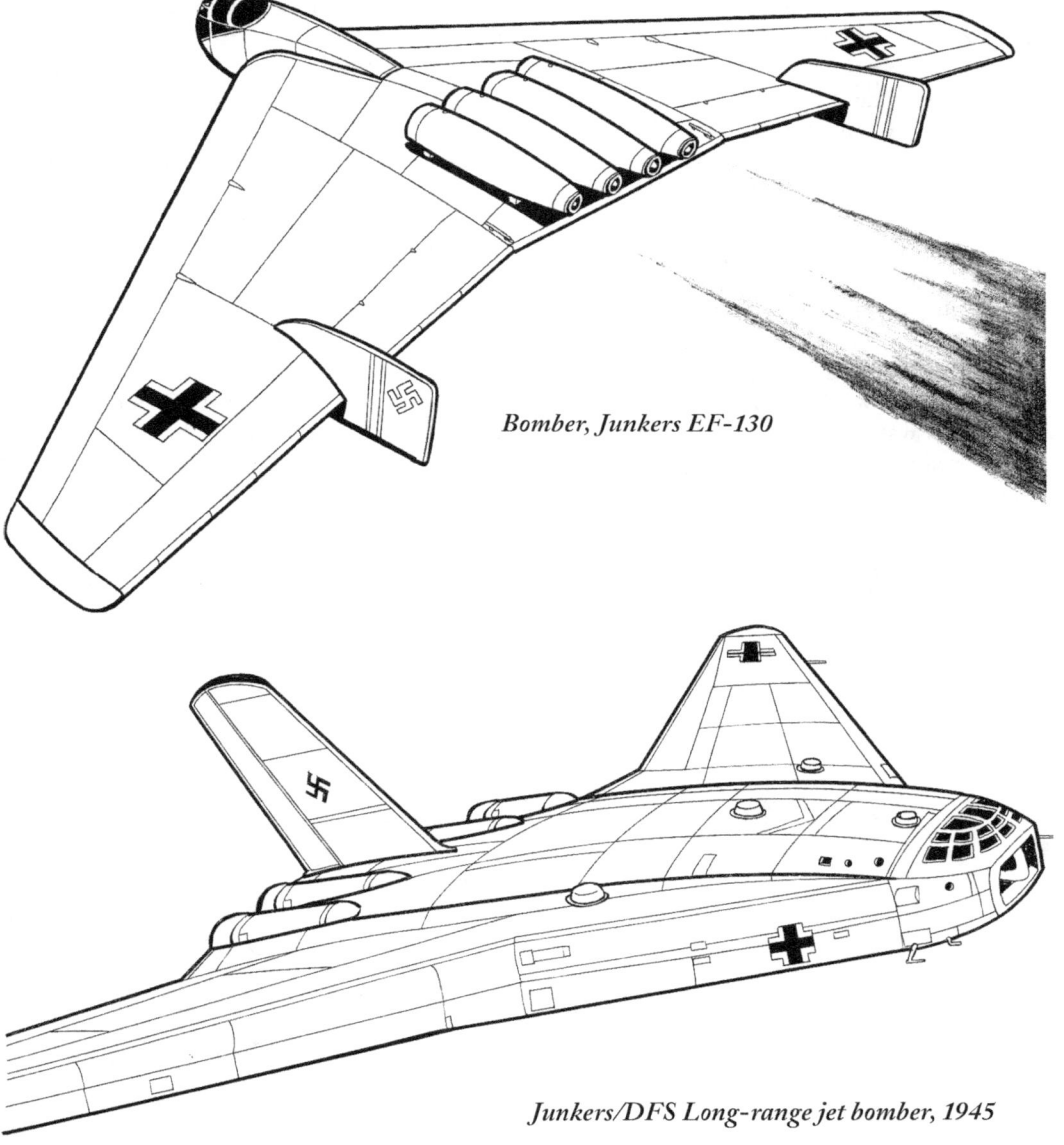

Bomber, Junkers EF-130

Junkers/DFS Long-range jet bomber, 1945

known as EF 130 B, which featured a combination of piston and jet engines.

A similar design for an even larger high-speed transatlantic bomber was created in 1945. Known as a long-range bomber, this was designed by the Ernst Hertel and DFS. This flying-wing aircraft had four Jumo 012 jet engines integrated into the rear wing section. Operated by a crew of eight, it would have had a span of 51.3 m, a speed of 1,000 km/h, a range of 17,000 km, and a bomb payload of 9,000 kg. It seems that this huge flying wing was seen as a postwar, intercontinental civilian passenger and cargo airliner. None of these futuristic projects proceeded beyond the drafting board.

After the war the "wing-only" design was continued—without success—by the American Northrop Company which produced two 4-engined bomber prototypes, known as Northrop YB-35 and YB-49, in 1946.

Sänger orbital bomber "Silbervogel"

This advanced bomber originated from forward-thinking research and experimentation led in the 1930s by Dr. Eugen Albert Sänger who had developed a liquid-fueled rocket engine that was cooled by its own fuel. This engine produced an astounding 3,048 meters/second (10,000 feet/second) exhaust velocity.

In 1935 and 1936, Dr. Sänger was head of the Aerospace Research Institute in Trauen when he secretly began to design a manned, winged vehicle code-named *Amerika Bomber* or *Silbervogel* (Silverbird). The Sänger bomber, designed for supersonic, stratospheric flight, was an extraordinary conception for the late 1930s. It had a span of 15 m (49 ft 2 in) and a length of 27.98 m (91 ft 10 in). The bottom of the planoconvex fuselage was flattened, which helped create lift and earned the Silverbird the nickname of "flat iron." The wings were short, ultra-thin, and knife-edged. A horizontal tail surface was located at the extreme aft end of the fuselage, with a small fin on each end. The fuel was carried in two large tanks, one on each side of the fuselage, running from the wings aft. Oxygen tanks were located one on each side of the fuselage, placed forward of the wings. The futuristic bomber was powered by a Sänger rocket engine of 100 tons of thrust, mounted in the fuselage rear, and by two auxiliary rocket engines. The single pilot sat in a pressurized cockpit in the forward fuselage, protected by jettisonable heat shields. A tricycle undercarriage was fitted for a glided landing. There was a central bomb bay with a capacity of 3,629 kg (8,000 lbs), and owing to the aircraft's tremendous speed, no defensive armament was envisaged. The empty weight was to be approximately 9,979 kg (22,000 lbs).

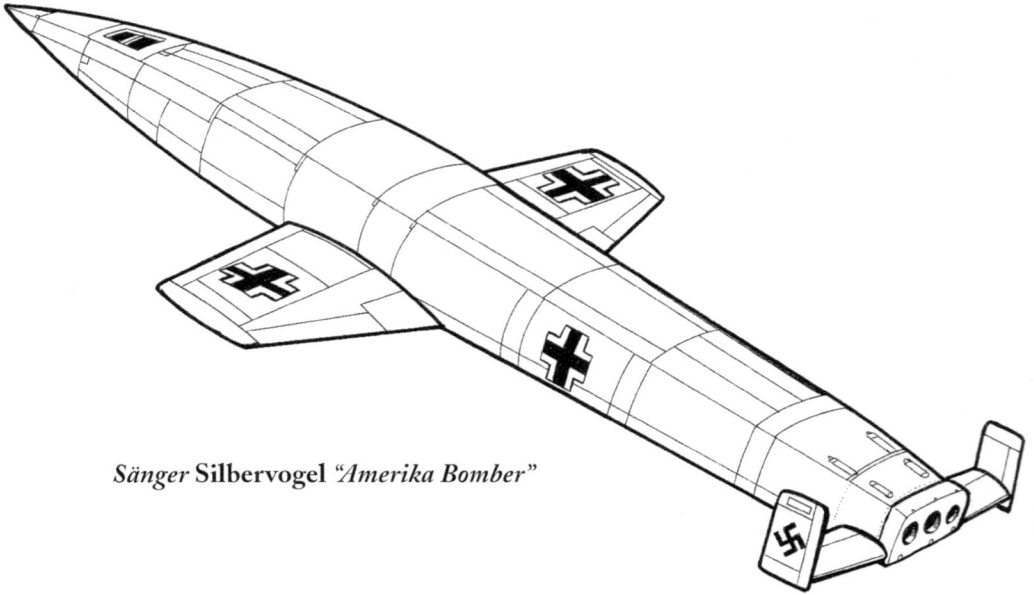

Sänger **Silbervogel** *"Amerika Bomber"*

For launch, the Silverbird was to be propelled down a 3-km (1.9-mile) monorail track by a rocket-powered sled that developed a 600-ton thrust for 11 seconds. After taking off at a 30-degree angle and reaching an altitude of 1.5 km (5,100 ft), a speed of 1,850 km/h (1,149 mph) would be reached. At this point, the main rocket engine would be fired to propel the Silverbird to a maximum speed of 22,100 km/h (13,724 mph) and an altitude of over 145 km (90 miles). Some sources indicate the maximum altitude to be reached as 280 km (174 miles). When the Second World War started, all futuristic programs were canceled due to the need to concentrate on proven conventional combat designs. Dr. Sänger went on to work on ramjet designs for the DFS (German Research Institute for Gliding). After the war, Sänger went to work for the French Air Ministry.

Bomber EMW A4

The futuristic EMW A4 (also known as project A9/A10) was a two-stage, hypersonic, semiballistic, manned bomber with a planned 3,000-mile range. Taking the aerodynamics of the experimental, winged A4b version of the V2 for their starting point, the engineers of Elektro Mechanische Werk (EMW) at Germany's Peenemünde rocket center added a pressurized cockpit, landing gear, flaps, ailerons,

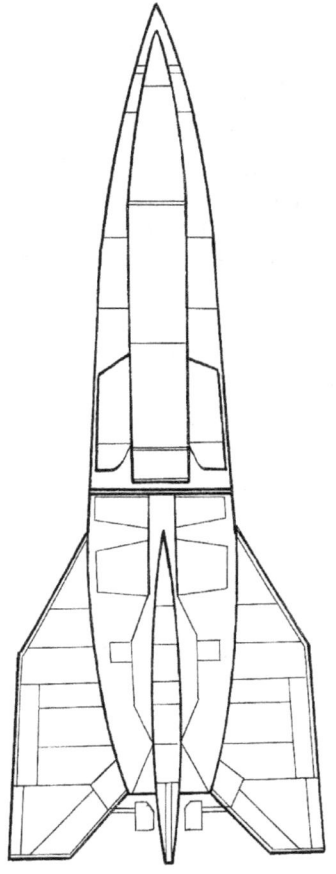

Above: *A-10 booster with A4 rocket. The A-10 was an enlarged A-4 with a 100-ton thrust engine and a 4-ton payload with a 500-km (310-mile) range. The whole spacecraft had a total length of 26 m, and the largest diameter was 4.75 m.*

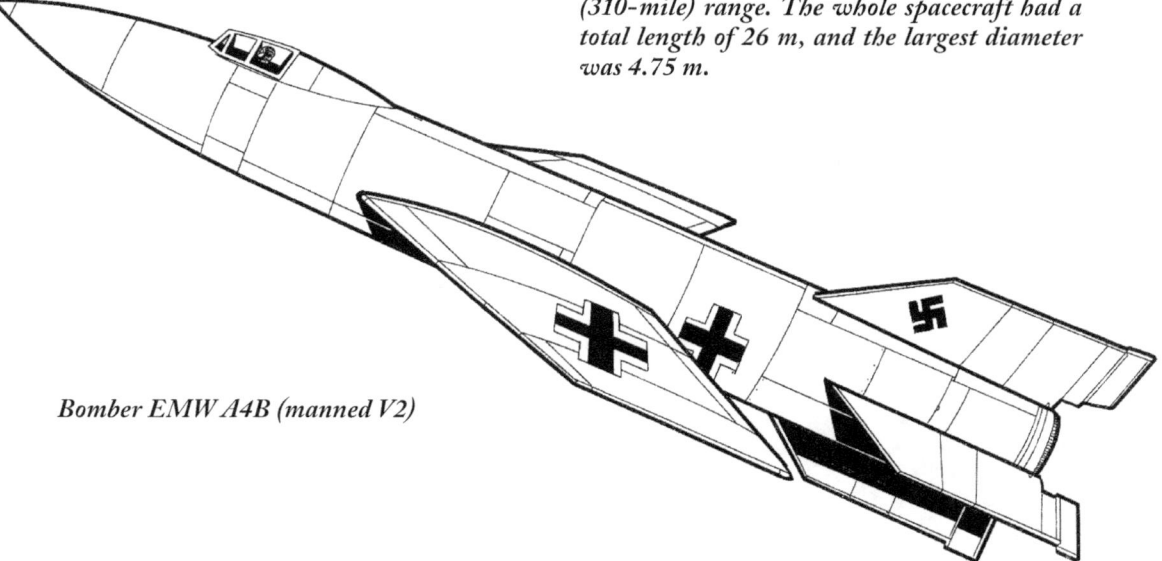

Bomber EMW A4B (manned V2)

elevators, and a turbojet sustainer engine. The aircraft was to be powered by one 55,880-hp EMW rocket engine developed by Elektro Mechanische Werk, and would have had a speed of 9,200 ft/s. It had a span of 11 ft 7 in and a total weight (loaded) of 16,260 kg. It could carry a 1,000-kg bomb, and was operated by a crew of one. It would land in a conventional manner owing to a retractable tricycle landing gear. The manned A-4/V2 was planned to be launched vertically like a rocket. It could also be mounted on a huge, two-stage A-10 booster. The A-10 was the first stage, in essence a V2 rocket grown to monstrous proportions, carrying the A-4 in its nose. After launching vertically from a platform, the A-10 would carry the A-4 into a high stratospheric trajectory and there launch it. Optimistically, it was thought that a range of about 2,800 miles would be achieved. It was only a paper project and no construction work was ever done on this multi-stage, transatlantic bombardment system.

5

Fighters

The fighter aircraft was born during the First World War. Acceptance of aircraft by the military as a useful weapon was slow, and this hesitancy was understandable, as early flying machines were unreliable and capable of lifting only a small payload. Originally planes had low performances, haphazard design and flimsy structures, and for one airplane to shoot down another was unknown in 1914. Airplanes were considered to be the eyes of the ground forces, and confined to the reconnaissance role. Soon the need to destroy or protect observation aircraft led to a seesaw battle in the development of fighting machines. A technical race thus started for air supremacy, and the major combatants sought superiority in speed, ceiling and climb rate, range, strength, versatility, firepower and maneuverability. Fighting air-

Fokker DR1 triplane. Introduced in 1917, this **Dreidecker** *(triplane), designed by engineer Rheinhold Pfalz of Fokker Flugzeugwerke, had a short but spectacular career. The legend that has grown around the machine owes a great deal to its use by the "Red Baron," Manfred von Richthofen. In 1918, 39 DR1 craft were produced.*

planes originated thus as an ancillary aspect of the land battle, as aircraft fought each other for the freedom to carry out their primary task of reconnaissance. A new weapon appeared, the fighter, a comparatively small, fast and maneuverable aircraft, designed primarily for attacking other aircraft, as opposed to a bomber, which was designed to attack ground targets. Fighter aircraft were the primary means by which to gain air superiority. In World War I, the most popular fighters were the French Spad and Nieuport; the Albatros, Halberstadt and Dutch-built Fokker used by the Germans; and the British Camel and De Havilland. These planes had greater speed and were armed with machine guns. With the fighter came a new breed of airmen, the "aces," the prestigious and celebrated sky-knights who shot other airmen down in "dogfights." For the sensation-seeking masses at home, aces were made into national heroes by propaganda on both sides, but their highly publicized chivalric exploits and duels in the sky hardly mattered, at least at the beginning of the war.

German fighter and interceptor development was stopped after the defeat of 1918, and only regained momentum after the Nazi seizure of power in 1933. German military aircraft were developed in earnest after 1935, when the limitations of the Versailles Treaty were repudiated and when the Luftwaffe was officially created. Owing to secret research, experimentation and development carried out from 1920 to 1934, new modern designs appeared, with the task of protecting the homeland from enemy bomber fleets, but also with an eye on future aggressive war. However, fighters were regarded as secondary until the middle of World War II. Indeed, fighter units, considered defensive weapons, were somewhat neglected, and much less numerous than aggressive and offensive bomber units, as Göring strongly believed that his bombers would not need fighter escort in depth, and that there was no major requirement for them in defending the German homeland. In Hitler's personal brand of military philosophy, the fighting of defensive battles was not to be considered. In 1940, out of a total of 10,247 airplanes produced, 3,455 were bombers and ground attackers, and only 2,746 fighters.

When World War II broke out, Luftwaffe fighters were used to clear the air of enemy air weapons, put up a guarding screen, and escort and protect bombers from enemy interception, while the task to locate, harass and interdict ground forces—thus gaining air superiority—was carried out by specialized light planes, dive bombers and ground attackers. Once the enemy was beaten from the sky, fighters could be used to attack ground targets, moving forward, becoming "ground strafers," and a part of the mobile striking arm.

As the development of the war forced Germany to go more and more on the defensive, from 1943 onwards the role played by Luftwaffe fighters became more important, as they were increasingly occupied with the interception of Allied bomber penetration. Therefore their number was increased and tactics were continually revised to meet problems presented by enemy equipment, greater firepower, new defense formations and increased Allied fighter escort. A standard tactic against American daylight bomber groups was a concentrated attack against one particular formation, preferably an outside or laggard one. Effort was made to bring the bombers to loosen their formation and thus lose much of their advantage of combined crossfire. Individual attacks were made from behind and from the direction of the sun if possible, as this partially blinded Allied machine gunners. Single-pass and mass attacks were both employed. Against escort fighters, German interceptor tactics followed whenever possible the usual basic principles of attack from the sun, from above, and from behind. Speed and maneuverability remained, as always, the decisive factors. Tactics were based on the *Rotte* formation of two fighters, with number two protecting his leader, and, always on the alert for opportunities, they would take quick advantage of gaps between successive fighter cover waves. Whenever possible, interceptors made early attacks on enemy escorts to compel them to drop their auxiliary fuel tanks and thus shorten their protective fights. *Wilde Sau* (Wild Boar) was a tactic involving fighters roving at will without radar, intercepting by visual contact in cooperation with German ground anti-aircraft artillery. Initial successes with *Wilde Sau* were soon reversed by heavy and mounting losses and the technique was dropped in March 1944. Against British RAF night penetration, the Luftwaffe developed both single— and twin-engine aircraft, but the latter soon became the basic equipment of the night fighter-force. The Second World War indeed saw the development of night fighting in the sky. From a very imprecise hit-or-miss art using rudimentary equipment in hastily converted airplanes pioneered by Great Britain between 1940 and 1942, German night fighting became a refined science, using highly developed tactics in purpose-built aircraft equipped with sophisticated detection devices (radar) and appropriate weapon systems (e.g. upward-firing cannons). Not surprisingly, with so many RAF heavy bombers operating almost every night over occupied Europe and Nazi Germany during 1942–1945, Luftwaffe ingenuity produced highly efficient night-fighter adaptation of the Messerschmitt Bf 110 and the Junkers Ju 88, and the development of the Heinkel He 219. German night fighters operated in freelance independent hunts or guided by radio from a ground station with target locations determined by airborne radar. They could also carry out night intruder attacks against returning Allied bombers on or near their bases as they prepared to land, as well as strafing strikes against airfields in England.

The German fighters evolved from a simple wooden biplane with fixed landing gear and open cockpit to a modern, high-speed, full-metal monoplane with retracting undercarriage and enclosed cockpit, such as the revolutionary Messerschmitt Bf 109 and later the Focke-Wulf Fw 190, both of which performed extremely well. For a lot of reasons, attempts to produce serious successors to these aircrafts were unsuccessful. Manufacturers had, in fact, potentially successful replacement designs on hand, but efforts to get them into production at the right time were often frustrated until it was too late. By late 1942, with the balance of the air war gradually swinging away from the Luftwaffe, a touch of something close to desperation crept into fighter designs, and unconventional and revolutionary ideas were explored in an attempt to regain air supremacy. Night interception with airborne radar and heavy board weapons as well as jet aircraft were greatly developed, but the full-scale production of trusted designs was maintained, with the result that many revolutionary aircrafts were never given a chance. Such fighters as the Bf 109 and Fw 190 proved to be classics of their time, but they were modified and improved during their service life to a degree well beyond their originally planned life. Matters were made worse by Hitler's overwhelming adherence to the concept of the offensive, so fighters had to be able to deliver significant offensive bomb loads as well.

In spite of tremendous technical advances by the end of World War II, the Luftwaffe lost its original numerical superiority and, due to continually receding front lines and defense of the homeland, new problems were added. As a result, tactics were modified from bold attack to conservation of strength, assuming risks only when decisive results appeared obtainable. Within the limitations of such enforced caution, the Luftwaffe fighter force held to basic concepts such as surprise, concentrated attack and exploitation of the enemy's mistakes. Even so, the fighter force was brought to the point of total collapse. The war in the air was lost not so much through inferior airplanes or lack of aircraft—indeed, owing to Albert Speer's skillful management, production peaked, as it did in almost all sectors of the German industry up to mid 1944—but through increasing lack of fuel. Not only did this force the grounding of many brand new aircraft, but it also increasingly cut into the flying hours of trainee aircrews. That problem was worsened by the growing shortage of instructors, as more and more were required to replace casualties in combat formations. Thus the quality of aircrews vis-à-vis their Allied opponents also declined and further contributed to eventual defeat. In 1945 Hitler sadly questioned—and admitted: "What has gone wrong? The Luftwaffe lies a broken wreck, unable to halt the Allied advance for one hour, let alone one day." What had gone wrong was that from the start the Luftwaffe had been created solely for an offensive tactical role, only equipped for a quick and short Blitzkrieg war, preferably on one front. Although it was the largest air force in the world in 1940, it was substantially weaker than it appeared. Due to the inadequate planning and development of new designs, the German air force's airplanes, in the main, declined in comparison with those of their enemies. The Luftwaffe failed to have any form of strategic force, and its indifferent leaders ignored the warning given by Milch, Kammhuber and others. They only stressed the fighter role when it was too late. The reserves were inadequate, and Germany lacked proper stockpiles of such vital building materials as aluminum and rubber, as well as fuel. Until the end, the absurd and stubborn continuation of its offensive tactics ensured the German air force's death.

Conventional Fighter Designs

Arado Ar 65

The Arado Ar 65, designed in 1931 by engineer Walter Rethel of the Arado Handelsgesellschaft located at Warnemünde, was a biplane, single-seat, day fighter. Produced in contravention of the Versailles Treaty which forbade Germany to produce combat aircraft, it was the first clandestine Luftwaffe warplane to enter service in late 1933. It was powered by a 750-hp BMW VI 7 3 V-12, water-cooled engine with a maximum speed of 300 km/h (186 mph). Its span was 11.20 m (36 ft 9 in), its length was 8.40 m (27 ft 7 in), and its weight (empty) was 1,501 kg (3,329 lbs). Armament consisted of two fixed synchronized 7.92-mm MG 17 machine guns. The Arado Ar 65 (improved version type F) served as a Lufwaffe fighter and then as a trainer until 1940.

Arado Ar 67 and 76

The single-seat fighters Arado Ar 67 (a biplane) and parasol-winged Ar 76 were pro-

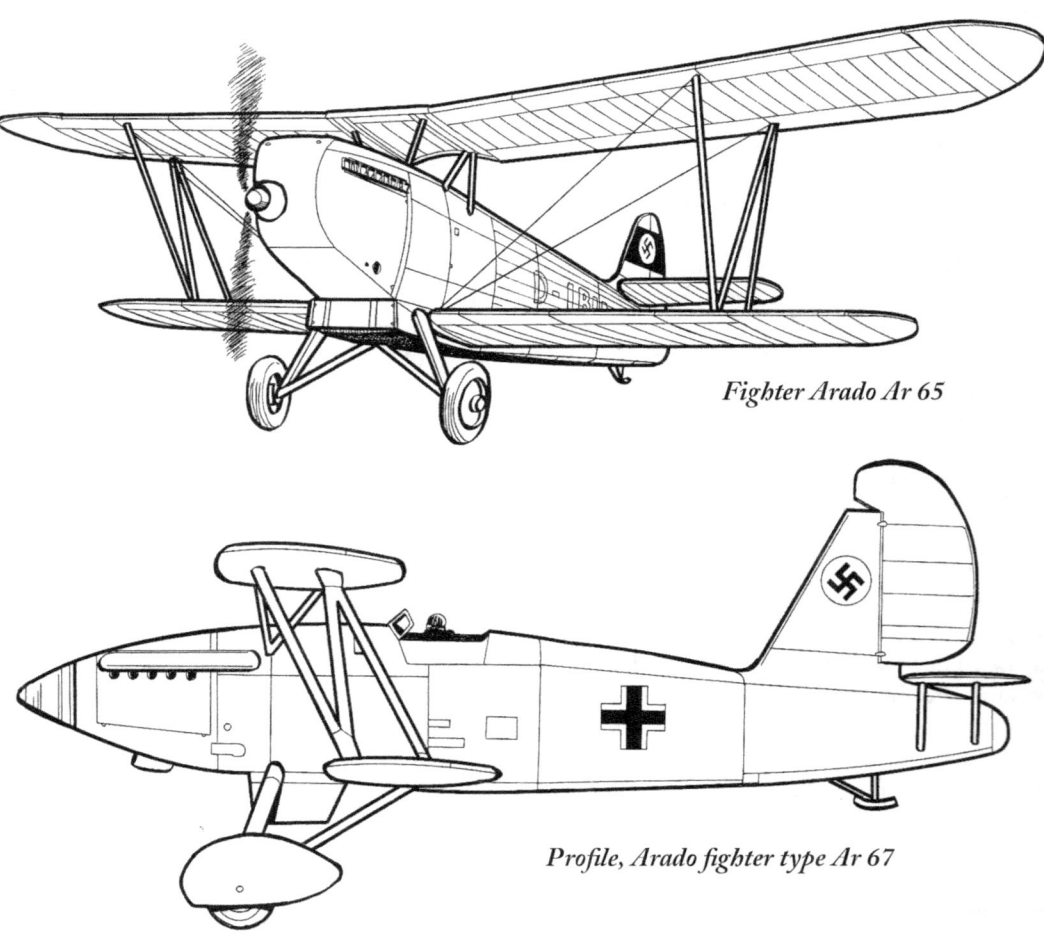

Fighter Arado Ar 65

Profile, Arado fighter type Ar 67

totypes with performances slightly superior to the Ar 65. Designed by engineer Walter Blume of the Arado Handelsgesellschaft with specifications issued by the clandestine Luftwaffe, they offered little advance over other types. Only one Ar 67 was manufactured in late 1933. The Arado Ar 67 had a length of 7.87 m (25 ft 11 in), a span of 9.68 m (31 ft 9 in), and an empty weight of 1,270 kg (2,799 lbs). It was powered by one 525-hp Rolls-Royce Kestrel VI V-12, water-cooled engine, and had a speed of 340 km/h (211 mph). As for the Ar 76, a few prototypes were built and flown in late 1934, and later used as trainers. Production orders for a light home-defense fighter with capability as an advanced trainer went to the later Arado Ar 68 and Focke-Wulfe Fw 56 Stösser.

Heinkel He 51

The single-seat biplane He 51, designed in 1932 by the Ernst Heinkel Aircraft Company, was the first fighter ordered into production for the reborn German air force in 1935. The He 51 had a span of 11 m (36 ft 1 in), and a length of 8.4 m (27 ft 7 in). It was powered by a 750-hp BMW V-12 water-cooled engine; maximum speed was 330 km/h (205 mph) and range was 390 km (242 miles). Total production was about 272 units which existed in several versions; the He 51 A-1 was a single-seat fighter; the He 51 B-2 was a reconnaissance seaplane fitted with floats; and the He 51 C-1 was a ground attacker/light bomber carrying six 10-kg and four 50-kg bombs. Standard armament on all models included two 7.92-

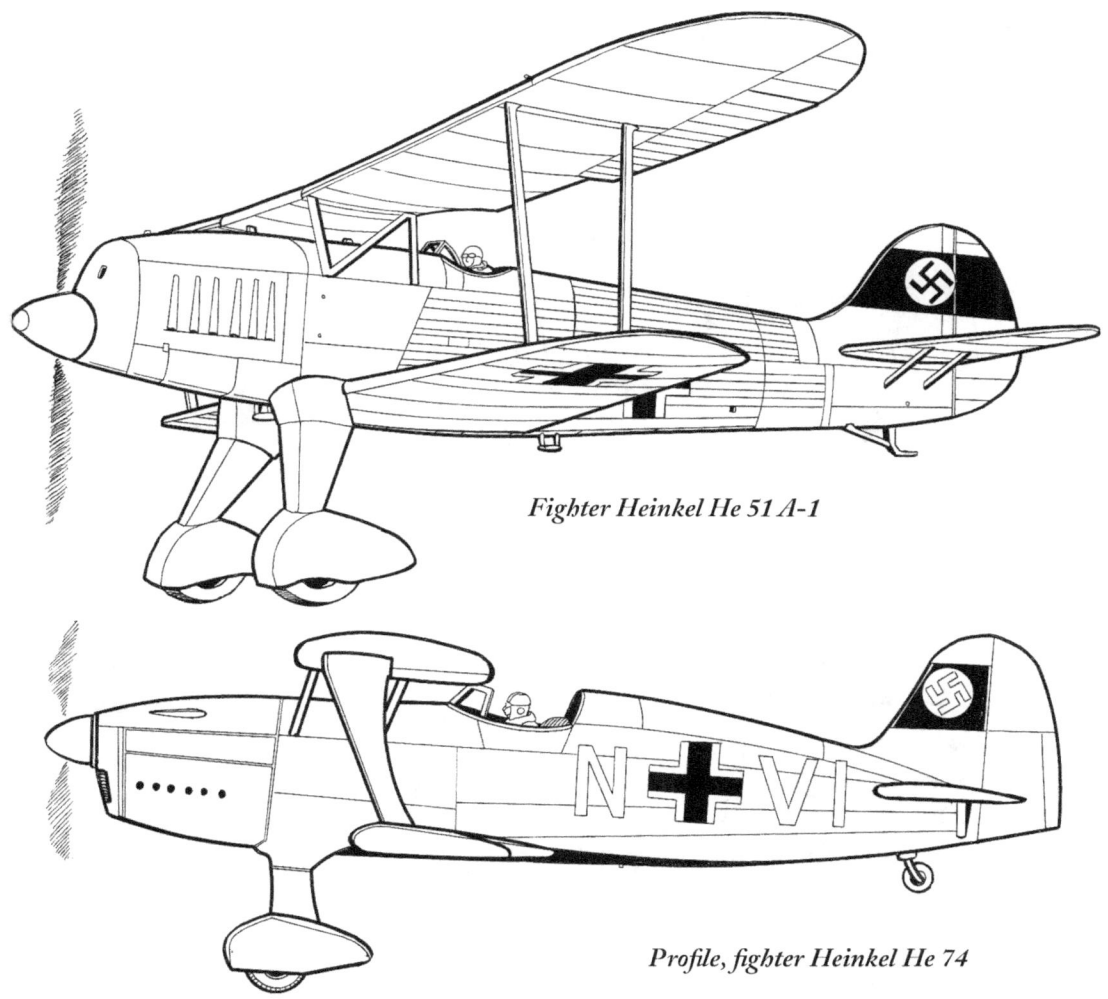

Fighter Heinkel He 51 A-1

Profile, fighter Heinkel He 74

mm Rheinmetall MG 17 guns placed at the front above the engine. In November 1936, thirty-six units, as part of the German Legion Kondor, were engaged to support General Franco in the Spanish Civil War. The He 51 saw further action in the close-support role at the start of World War II in the Polish campaign of September 1939. The aircraft remained in service as a Luftwaffe trainer until 1943.

Heinkel He 74

The biplane He 74 was a scale-down He 51 intended to be a home defense fighter. The single-seat aircraft had a span of 8.15 m (26 ft 9 in), a length of 6.45 m (21 ft 2 in) and an empty weight of 770 kg (1,697 lbs). It was powered by one Argus As 10 C Series 1 eight-cylinder, inverted-V, air-cooled engine, developing 240 hp, and had a maximum speed of 280 km/h (174 mph) and a range of 370 km (230 miles). It was to be armed with one 7.92-mm MG 17 machine gun. Only three prototypes were built, and the He 74 never entered mass production, as the Focke-Wulf 56 was chosen by the Luftwaffe.

Arado Ar 68

The single-seat biplane fighter Arado Ar 68 appeared as prototype in early 1934, and proved to have admirable handling characteristics on its first flight despite the inability to secure a sufficiently powerful engine for the prototype. Eventually a Junkers Jumo 210 was installed, the Ar 68 went into production, and it entered service in 1935 when the newly created Luftwaffe was publicly announced. Later the machine was powered by a 750-hp BMW

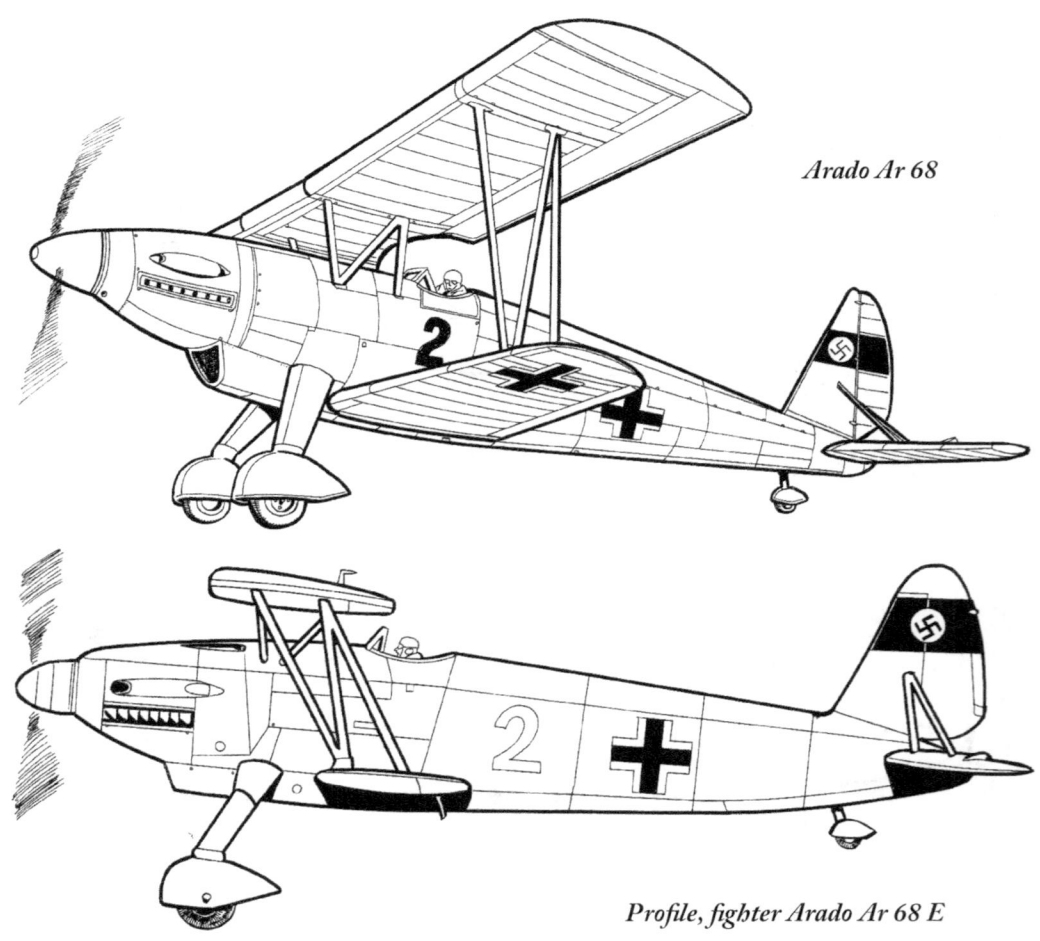

Arado Ar 68

Profile, fighter Arado Ar 68 E

VI V-12-cylinder, liquid-cooled engine giving a maximum speed of 310 km/h (193 mph), and a range of 550 km (342 miles). Span was 11 m (36 ft), length was 9.5 m (31 ft 2 in), height was 3.3 m (10 ft 10 in), and weight (empty) was 1,500 kg (3,307 lbs). Armament included two 7.92-mm MG 17 machine guns placed above the engine. A bomb load of 50 kg (110 lbs) could be carried in a rack located under the fuselage. There existed several models of the Arado Ar 68 with different engines. The Ar 68 V1 (prototype), powered by a 660-hp BMW VI piston engine, made its first flight in 1934. The Ar 68E, powered by a 610-hp Junkers Jumo 210 piston engine, was the first type to enter Luftwaffe service. The Ar 68F and Ar 68 G, powered by a 670-hp BMW VI piston engine, were the most commonly produced. The Ar 68H, powered by an 850-hp, supercharged, BMW 132Da, nine-cylinder, air-cooled radial, only existed as a single prototype with enclosed cockpit.

Designed to replace the Heinkel He 51, the Ar 68 never became an outstanding pre–World War II Luftwaffe aircraft, having lesser performances than its great rivals the Heinkel He 51 and Focke-Wulfe Fw 56 *Stösser*. Several Ar 68 fighters were sent to fight in the Spanish Civil War in 1936 where it soon appeared that they were outclassed by the stumpy, Russian-made Polikarpov I-16. Before World War II the Arado Ar 68 was replaced by the modern fighter Messerschmitt Bf 109, and then relegated to a training role.

Henschel Hs 121 and Henschel Hs 125

The single-seat, high-gull-winged, parasol monoplane Hs 121 was designed in late 1933 by Friedrich Nicolaus. Intended to become a

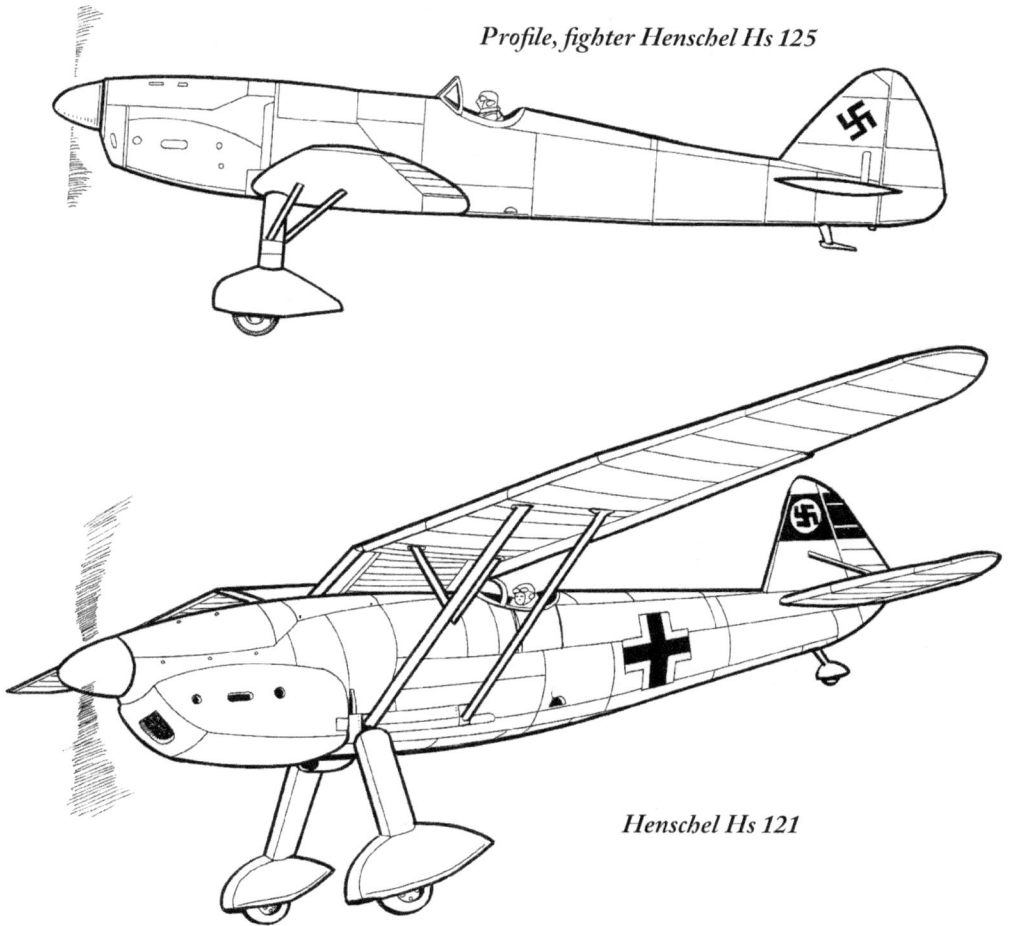

Profile, fighter Henschel Hs 125

Henschel Hs 121

light fighter or a trainer aircraft, it had a span of 10 m (32 ft 10 in), a length of 7.30 m (23 ft 11 in), and an empty weight of 710 kg (1,565 lbs). It was powered by one 240-hp Argus As 10 C inverted-V-8, air-cooled engine and had a maximum speed of 280 km/h (174 mph) and a range of 500 km (311 miles). Two prototypes were built, but after fly test in January 1934, the Hs 121 proved a failure. The project was abandoned, but Nicolaus and his team designed an improved version with low wing, known as Hs 125. Tested in the spring of 1933, the Hs 125 proved a much better aircraft than the Hs 121, and two prototypes were built. The plane never made it, though, as it was the Focke-Wulf Fw 56 that was finally adopted by the Luftwaffe.

Focke-Wulf Fw 56 Stösser

The Fw 56 *Stösser* (Bird of Prey) was the first airplane designed by engineer Kurt Tank for the Focke-Wulf Company. The prototype flew in November 1933. It had a span of 10.50 m (34 ft 5 in), and a length of 7.55 m (25 ft 1 in). Powered by a 240-hp Argus As 10C inverted-V-8, air-cooled engine, it had a maximum speed of 270 km/h (168 mph) and a range of 370 km (230 miles). Aerobatic and robust, the Fw 56 was a light fighter armed with two synchronized MG 17 machine guns, but it was also used as advanced trainer, and eventually as a dive bomber fitted with racks carrying three 10-kg (22-lb) bombs. Some 1,000 units were produced until 1940, serving in the German Luftwaffe and some being sold to the Austrian and Hungarian air forces.

Focke-Wulf Fw 159

The Focke-Wulf Fw 159 was a heavier version of the Fw 56. Designed by engineer Kurt Tank, it included several improvements, such as easy-access maintenance panels, retractable landing gear, enclosed cockpit, and slightly larger dimensions. A more powerful 610-hp

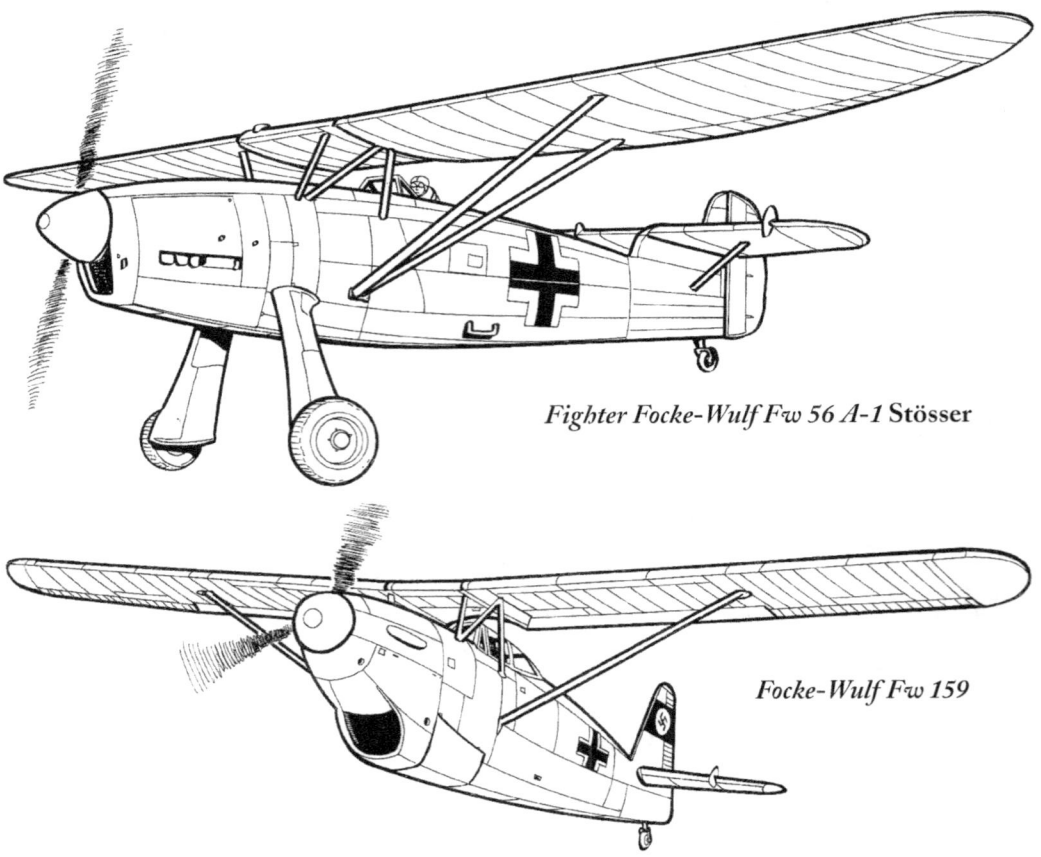

Fighter Focke-Wulf Fw 56 A-1 **Stösser**

Focke-Wulf Fw 159

Junkers Jumo 610A inverted-V-12 engine allowed better performances: maximum speed was 385 km/h (239 mph) and range was 650 km (404 miles). Yet the old-fashioned high-wing layout could not compete with the more modern low-wing design (e.g. Messerschmitt Bf 109), and only three Fw 159s were ever produced.

Dornier Do 22 L

The Dornier Do 22 L was the land version of the Dornier Do 22 torpedo bomber and reconnaissance floatplane (see Part 7).

Arado Ar 80

The Arado Ar 80 was designed by engineer Walter Blume of the Arado Handelsgesellschaft in 1934. The single-seat fighter had inverted gull wings and all-metal fuselage with non-retractable, "spatted" landing gear. It was 10.88 m (35 ft 8 in) in span, 10.30 m (33 ft 9 in) in length, and had a weight (empty) of 1,642 kg (3,620 lbs). Planned armament consisted of two synchronized 7.92-mm MG 17 guns. Only two prototypes were built, both in 1935.

Gotha Go 149

Designed by Albert Kalkert in 1936, the Go 149 was a low-wing cantilever monoplane, intended to be a light fighter/interceptor. Built of metal and plywood, the fuselage was a light monocoque, the cockpit for the single pilot was enclosed, and the undercarriage retracted inward. The aircraft had a length of 7.31 m, a span of 7.8 m, a height of 2.08 m and an empty weight of 830 kg. Powered by an Argus As 410 engine, the Go 149 had a maximum speed of 345 km/h. Armament was planned to include two 7.92-mm MG 17 machine guns mounted in the cowling. The aircraft was not further developed after three prototypes were built.

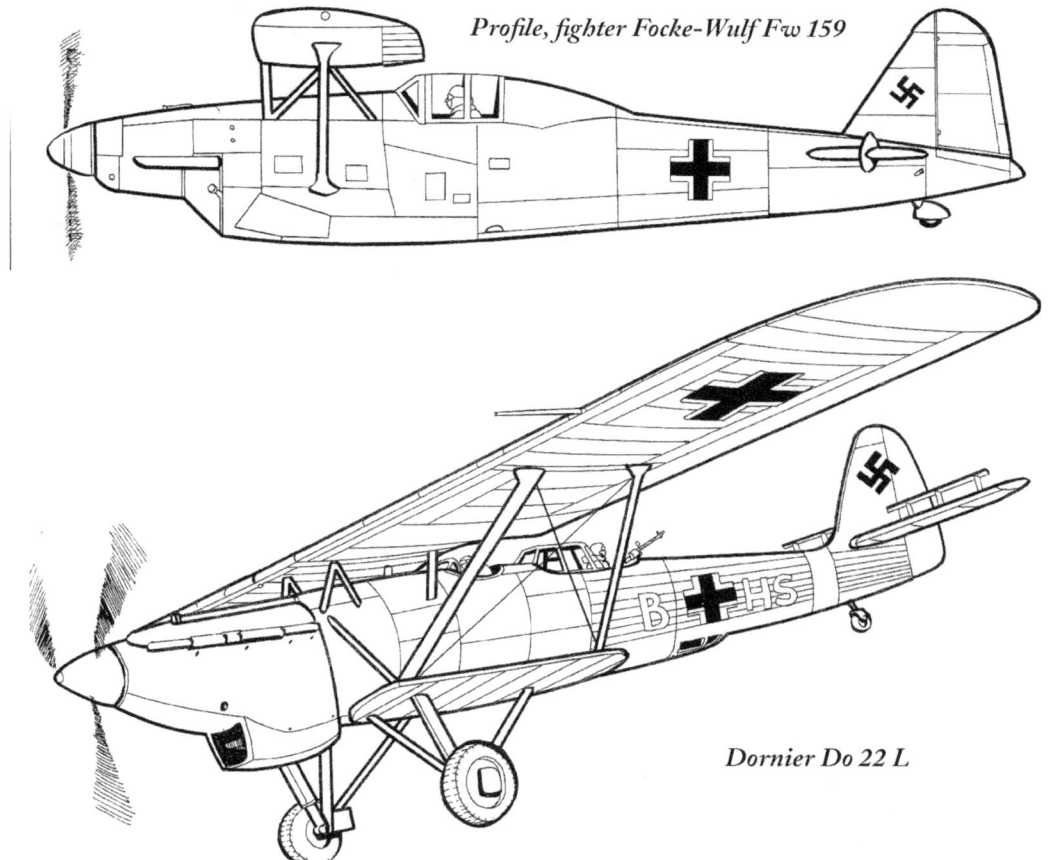

Profile, fighter Focke-Wulf Fw 159

Dornier Do 22 L

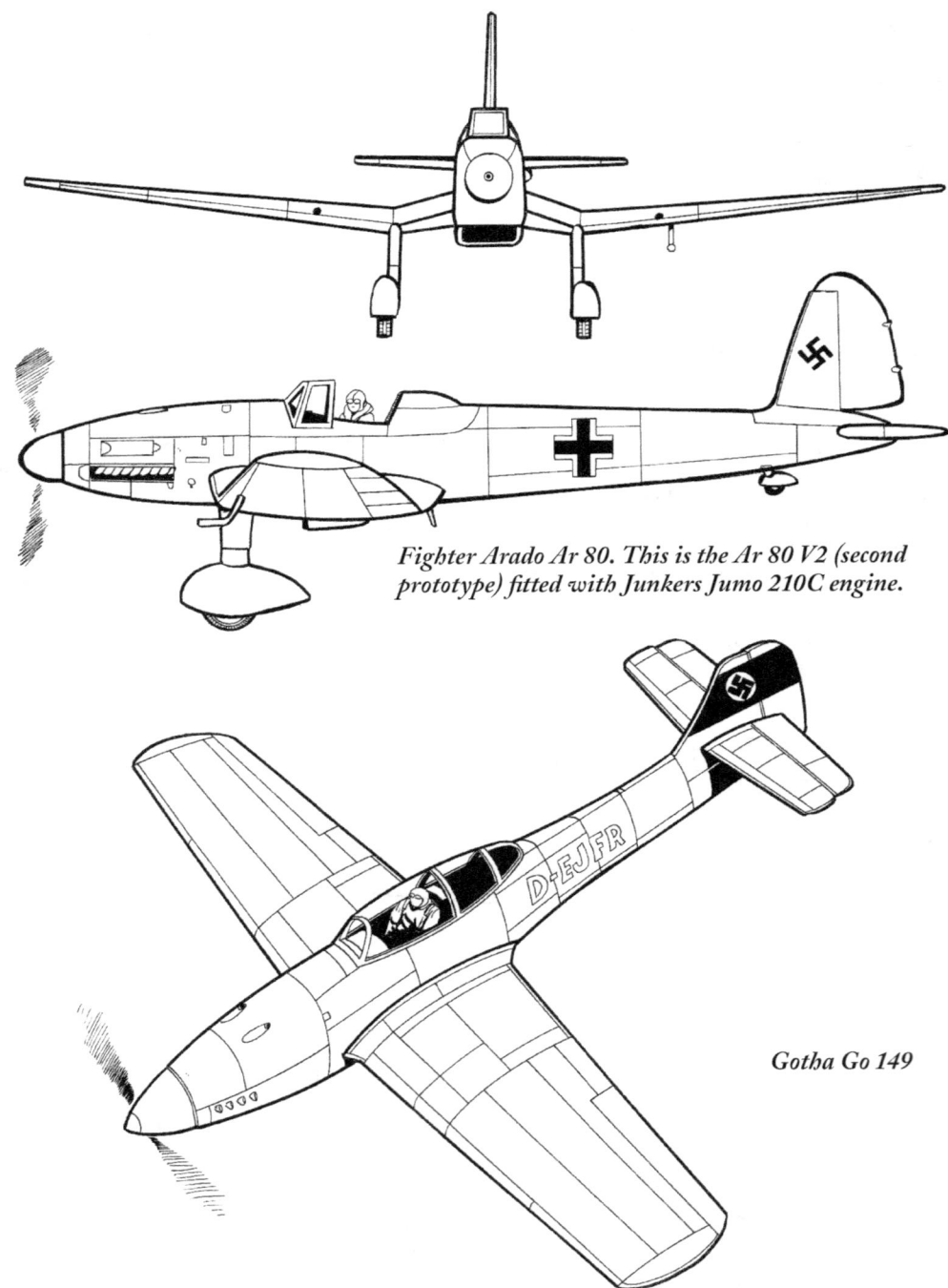

Fighter Arado Ar 80. This is the Ar 80 V2 (second prototype) fitted with Junkers Jumo 210C engine.

Gotha Go 149

Heinkel He 112

The single-seat monoplane Heinkel He 112 competed unsuccessfully against the Messerschmitt Bf 109 to become the Luftwaffe's standard monoplane fighter. Designed by the Günther brothers, the He 112 was basically a scaled-down version of the Heinkel He 70 (see Part 4) and shared its all-metal construction, inverted gull wings, and retractable landing gear. The aircraft, first flown in September 1935, had a span of 9.1 m (29 ft 10 in), a length

Heinkel He 112

of 9.3 m (30 ft 6 in), and an empty weight of 1,620 kg (3,571 lbs). Powered by one 680-hp Junkers Jumo 210Ea inverted-V-12, liquid-cooled engine, it had a maximum speed of 510 km/h (317 mph) and a range of 1,100 km (684 miles). Armament consisted of two 20-mm Oerlikon MG FF cannons mounted in outer wings and two 7.92-mm Rheinmetall MG 17 machine guns in engine cowling. Six 10-kg (22-lb) bombs could be carried in underwing racks for a ground attack role. Intended to replace the aging Arado Ar 68 and Heinkel He 51, the Heinkel He 112 had slightly better performances than the Messerschmitt Bf 109. So when the rival was chosen to become the Luftwaffe standard fighter, Ernst Heinkel was amazed and bitter. The Heinkel He 112 was nonetheless built in small numbers, thirty units being supplied to the Luftwaffe for evaluation. Nineteen were sold to Spain and saw action in the Spanish Civil War. Twenty-eight units were exported to Japan, three to Hungary, and thirty sold to Rumania, this batch being used on the Russian front in 1941.

Another prototype was designed and built by engineer Werner von Braun, known as Heinkel He 112 V-5. This variant of the fighter He 112 was powered by an additional rocket engine. First flown in early 1937, the He 112 V-5 demonstrated the feasibility of rocket power for aircraft.

Heinkel He 100

After losing the production contract for the Luftwaffe's new monoplane fighter to the Messerschmitt Bf 109, Ernst Heinkel proposed an improved version of the He 112. The new design was known as Heinkel He 100. Actually it should have been designated He 113, but since the number 13 was unlucky, this had been dropped. It had a length of 8.2 m (26 ft 11 in), a span of 9.41 m (30 ft 11 in), and an empty weight of 1,810 kg (3,990 lbs). The single-seat aircraft was powered by a 1,175-hp Daimler-Benz DB 601 Aa inverted-V-12, liquid-cooled engine, and had a speed of 670 km/h (416 mph) and a range of 900 km (559 miles). Armament consisted of one 20-mm cannon and two 13-mm machine guns. In March 1939, a prototype He 100, V3, with clipped wing, established a top-speed record at 746 km/h (464 mph). The aircraft's excellent maneuverability made it potentially a good fighter and possibly a fast ground attacker. In spite of its high performance and many ad-

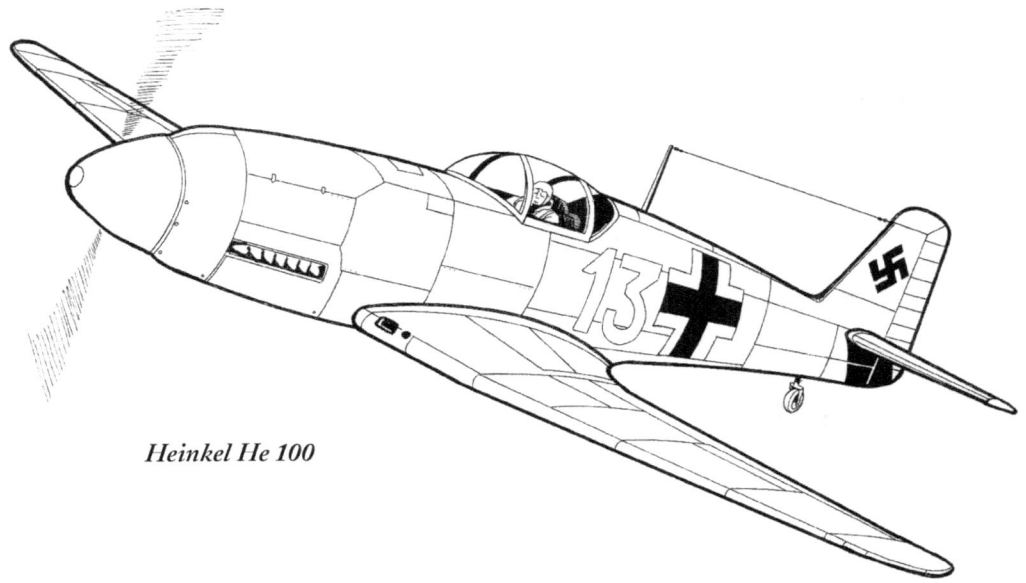

Heinkel He 100

vanced technical features, the He 100 was rejected and never reached mass production. The exact number built is unclear. Some sources state 100; other sources state that six units were sold to Russia (from which came the Lawotschkin, Gorbunow & Gudkow LaGG 3), and three to Japan (developed as Kawasaki Ki 61 Hien). Twelve formed a private fighter group intended to protect the Heinkel factory at Rostock-Marienhe. The aircraft were mainly used as propaganda in 1940, as Goebbels attempted to get Britain to believe that Germany possessed a superfast fighter.

Messerschmitt Bf 109

The single-seat Messerschmitt 109 was prefixed "Bf" because, although designed by Willy Messerschmitt, it was built by the company Bayerishe Flugzeugwerke. Undoubtedly one of the greatest World War II combat aircraft, and a truly great long-lived airplane in aviation history, the slim monoplane made its first flight in September 1935. The last one, manufactured in Spain, was built in 1956. However its introduction in the Luftwaffe, to replace the aging Heinkel He 51 biplane, did not go without trouble because at the time Messerschmitt was a relatively minor company with no track record in military aircraft. The Bf 109 was not given much chance against its vaunted rivals such as Heinkel, Arado or Focke-Wulf, more especially as Willy Messerschmitt and Erhard Milch shared a dislike for each other. After fierce competition, pressure, intrigues, complicated deals and tortuous political moves, the "One-O-Nine" prevailed. The Arado Ar 80, with fixed landing gear, was found too heavy, too slow and lacking agility. The parasol Focke-Wulf Fw 159 was judged too "old-fashioned" and too slow. Only the Heinkel He 112 proved a worthy rival, with better features than the 109, but it was considered too complex and expensive to produce. The Bf 109's success was certainly due to its outstanding aerodynamic qualities, speed, acceleration, maneuverability, high rate of climb and dive, and the fact that it was relatively cheap to build and easy to maintain and service. Production of the Bf 109 started in May 1937 and it became absolutely dominant as the leading fighter of the expanding Luftwaffe, and later other of Germany's allied air forces. There is still controversy as to its relative performance but in the late 1930s the Bf 109 was indeed a pioneering single-engined fighter of the modern type, with a stressed-skin metal construction, cantilever low-wing configuration, enclosed cockpit, retractable undercarriage, flapped wing, provision for heavy armament, and fuel-injected engine.

The early versions B and C performed well with the Legion Condor during the Spanish Civil War, quickly gaining air superiority for Franco's nationalist force. By the outbreak of World War II, the improved version 109 E, nicknamed "Emil," appeared. This had a span of 9.87 m (32 ft 4.5 in), a length of 8.64 m (28 ft 4 in), a height of 2.28 m (7 ft 5.5 in), and an empty weight of 1,900 kg (4,189 lbs). Powered by a 1,100-hp Daimler-Benz 610 A engine, it had a speed of about 570 km/h (354 mph) and a typical range of 700 km (460 miles). Armament was very powerful, including two 7.92-mm Rheinmetall-Borsig MG 17 guns placed above the engine cowling, one 20-mm MG FF cannon firing through the propeller hub, and two 20-mm MG FF cannons in wings.

Like all other Luftwaffe aircraft designed and planned for short Blitzkrieg campaigns, the Bf 109 E performed extremely well in the opening phase of World War II. Its good points were small size, fast and comparatively cheap production, high acceleration, fast climb and dive, and good maneuverability. A classic of the time and synonymous with German airpower, it dominated the skies over Poland, Norway, the Low Countries, and France. The first serious opposition came, however, during the Battle of Britain, when it appeared that the Bf 109 was slightly slower than the Spitfire and that it could be outmaneuvered even by a well-flown Hurricane. The duels between Bf 109s and Spitfires became the stuff of legend, and the duels continued into the late 1940s, when Egyptian Spitfires fought Czech-built Israeli Bf 109s over Palestine. There is still

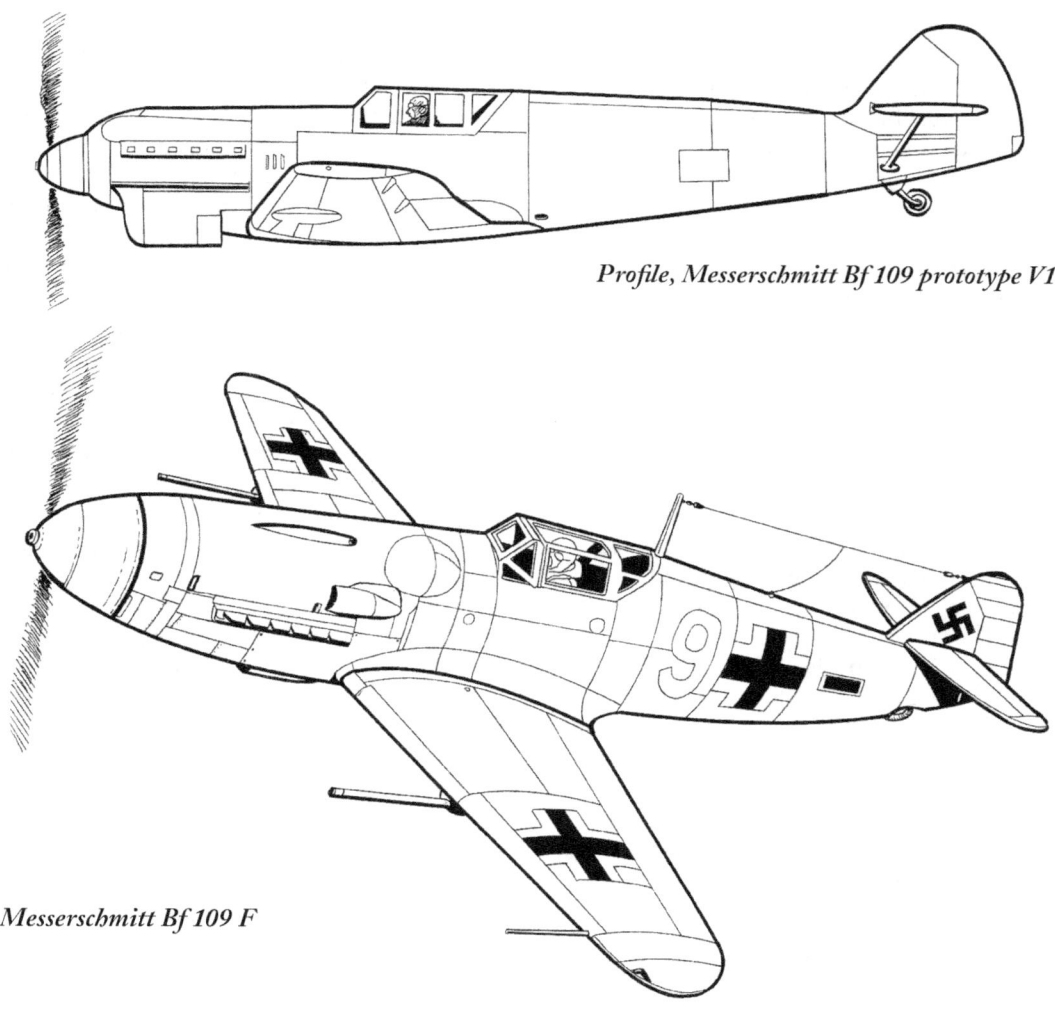

Profile, Messerschmitt Bf 109 prototype V1

Messerschmitt Bf 109 F

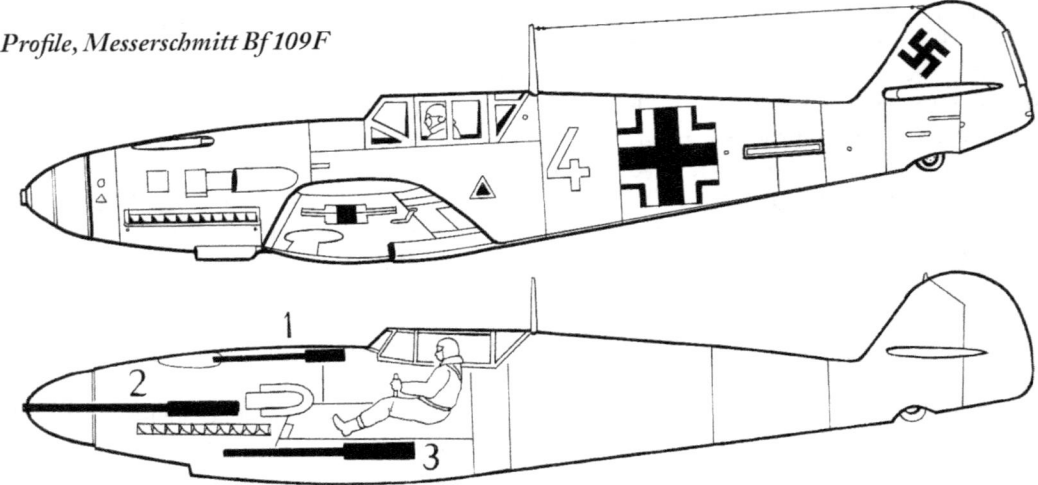

Profile, Messerschmitt Bf 109F

Armament, Messerschmitt Bf 109 G. 1: Two fixed 7.92-mm machine guns on engine cowl. 2: One 20-mm cannon firing through propeller hub. 3: Two 20-mm cannons fixed on each wing.

controversy over which was the superior fighter. By 1940, the Bf 109's heavy armament had proved quite effective, but deficiencies came to light: a cramped cockpit with limited visibility; a short range and endurance; a high landing speed combined with the narrow track undercarriage that retracted outward into the undersurfaces of the wing with poor stability, something that caused many accidents (at take-off too); the tires having a tendency to blow out on a concrete runway; the rather thin wings, which offered little room for the mounting of heavy weapons; and the tight controls, making the 109 rather tiring to fly at full speed. By that time the optimistic Hitler and the RLM did not consider that developing a second generation of fighter was a matter of great urgency as it was believed that Nazi Germany would have secured all her military objectives by 1941 at the latest.

The basic Bf 109 E "Emil" fighter existed in many versions and subtypes. For example, the 109 E-1/B, 109 E-4/B, and 109 E-7 were fighter-bomber versions with a load-carrying capacity of 500 kg. In this role, the Bf 109 was inadequate because of its short range; the aircraft was an inspired fighter design with a very good climbing speed and angle, not a bomber or a dive bomber. The Bf 109 E/T was a proposed *Trager* (carrier fighter). Intended for the never-completed aircraft carrier *Graf Zeppelin*, it featured increased wing area, spoilers on the wing uppersurface, folding wings, catapult spools and arrester hook.

When it became clear that the war would last longer than expected, development of the Bf 109 was accelerated instead of looking for a serious replacement. The E type was followed by the Bf 109 F which entered service in most Luftwaffe fighter units in the spring of 1941. Once teething troubles had been dealt with, the 109F was generally reckoned to have marked the highest point of the Bf 109's development. The F (sometimes known as "Friedrich" or "Franz") was aerodynamically enhanced, had higher performance, and improved handling. The airplane, however, retained its main drawbacks: the narrow landing gear; poor lateral control at high speeds; and the fact that in combat the slats on the wings often opened in tight turns, and while this prevented a stall, it snatched at the ailerons and threw the pilot off his aim. Of course, the Bf 109 was operated by many German top aces such as Erich "Bubi" Hartmann (352 kills) and Hans-Joachim Marseilles (158 kills).

In a constantly changing air war, the Bf 109 proved adaptable enough to accept new powerplants and weapons with a minimum of modification, allowing variants and subtypes such as the 109 F-2/Trop (North African desert fighter), the 109 F-4 bomber, and the

Messerschmitt Bf 109 Z

109 F-5 and F-6 reconnaissance aircraft. Versatility was one of the keys to the aircraft's great success, and one of the reasons why it was so difficult to find a replacement.

In 1942, because of increasing Allied raids over Germany, the Bf 109 G (Gustav) appeared with a powerful 1,475-hp Daimler-Benz DB 605A engine. This was heavier, better armored, and fitted with various weapons, including heavy machine guns, long-range cannons, and rockets with devastating effects. The disadvantage of heavy armament was the penalty of weight and increased drag which slowed the aircraft, reduced maneuverability, and made them even more vulnerable. Subtypes included the desert-adapted Bf 109 G-1/Trop, Bf 109 G-8 and Bf 109 G-10 long-range reconnaissance craft, Bf 109 G-12 (a proposed two-seat trainer), and the Bf 109 G-16 fighter-bomber. By 1943, the Bf 109 G in many variants was a brute to fly and completely outclassed by the improving Allied machines, but it was kept in ever-increasing production as the RLM did not fully estimate available replacements. At a time when the revolutionary two-jet-engined fighter Messerschmitt Me 262 could have been made available in great numbers, the already obsolete 109 G was built in greater quantity than any other model, over 70 percent of the total production being of this version.

The final model, Bf 109 K, a high-altitude version, was somehow improved, with a pressurized cockpit offering better view, new tail, and engine with two-stage, supercharger boost system. It was produced only in modest numbers, and very few reached operational status.

One of the most unusual experiments with the Bf 109 airframe was the Bf 109 Z (*Zwilling*—twin), which consisted of two fuselages connected by means of a common center section and tailplane; the single pilot sat in the port fuselage. The 109 Z, intended to become a heavy fighter/bomber/ground attacker, was to be armed with five 30-mm MK 108 cannons. There was also a project to fit the aircraft with two jet engines (see Part 6). None of these projects were developed. Late in the war, Bf 109s were employed as the upper half of Mistel composite aircraft.

The Bf 109 was manufactured by Messerschmitt, subcontracted to various organizations and built under license by numerous other manufacturers. Parts were also produced by Dornier and numerous dispersed workshops and small plants. The exact number of Bf 109 produced is not clearly known; Bayerishe Flugzeugwerke and Messerschmitt AG (as the company was called after 1938) made about 12,000, and Erla of Leipzig and Wiener Neustadt Flugzeugwerke produced about 13,000; other manufacturers in Czechoslovakia, Spain and Switzerland added about 8,000, making a grand total close to 33,000. Other sources say 30,500 units and even 35,000, but—whatever the true number might be—the 109 was built in greater number than any other World War II warplane (except for the contemporary Russian Yak).

After the war, production of the 109 was continued for several years by the Czech company Avia (known as Avia S-199, some being sold to the new state of Israel), and by Hispano-Aviacion in Spain until 1956.

Messerschmitt Me 209

Messerschmitt's designation Me 209 was actually used for two separate projects during World War II. The first, described below, was a record-setting single-engined race plane for which little or no consideration was given to adaptation for combat. The second, the Me 209-II was a proposal for an enhanced version of the highly successful Messerschmitt Bf 109 which served as the Luftwaffe's primary fighter throughout World War II.

The first Me 209 was in fact a completely new aircraft whose designation was used by Messerschmitt as a propaganda tool. Although the plane was designed only to break speed records, it was hoped that its name would associate it with the Bf 109 already in combat service.

The Me 209 was constructed in 1937 and shared only its Daimler-Benz DB 601 engine with the Bf 109. Willy Messerschmitt designed the small plane with a cockpit placed far back along the fuselage just in front of its unique cross-shaped tail section. Unlike the Bf 109, the Me 209 featured a broad-track undercarriage mounted in the wing section instead of the fuselage. The plane achieved its purpose when test-pilot Fritz Wendel flew it to a new world record speed of almost 756 km/h (470 mph) on April 26, 1939.

The idea of adapting the Me 209 racer to a fighter role gained momentum when, during the Battle of Britain, the Bf 109 failed to gain superiority over RAF Spitfires. The little record setter, however, was not up to the task of air combat. Its wings were almost completely occupied by the engine's liquid cooling system and therefore prohibited conventional installation of armaments. The plane also proved difficult to fly and extremely hard to control on the ground. Nevertheless, the Messerschmitt team made several attempts to improve the aircraft's performance by giving it longer wings and a taller tailplane, and installing two MG 17 guns in the engine cowling. Its various modifications, however, added so much weight that the plane ended up slower than the contemporary Bf 109E.

This first Me 209 project was soon cancelled, and though it never went into widescale production, Messerschmitt's design did make its mark with its impressive speed record, which was not broken by another piston-engined aircraft until August 16, 1969, by Darryl G. Greenmayer's highly modified F8F Bearcat.

The Me 209 V1 was operated by a single pilot, it had a length of 7.24 m (23 ft 9 in) and a wingspan of 7.80 m (25 ft 7 in). The aircraft was powered by one 1,800-hp Daimler-Benz DB 601ARJ engine, and had a maximum speed of 755 km/h (470 mph).

Profile, fighter Messerschmitt Me 209-II

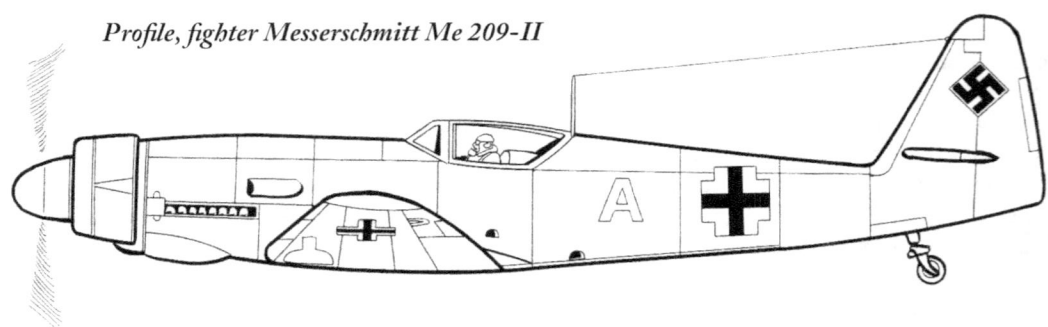

Messerschmitt Me 309

The Me 309 was one of several failed Messerschmitt projects intended to replace the aging Bf 109, the others being the previously described Me 209-I and the Me 209-II. Although it had many advanced features, the Me 309's performance left much to be desired and it suffered from so many problems that the project was cancelled with only four prototypes built.

The Me 309 project began in mid–1940, just as the Bf 109 was having its first encounters with the Spitfire in the Battle of Britain, the first aircraft to match the 109 in speed and performance. Already Messerschmitt anticipated the need for an improved design to replace the Bf 109. The RLM, however, did not feel the same urgency, the project was given a low priority and the design was not finalized until the end of 1941. The new fighter had many novel features, such as tricycle landing gear and a pressurized cockpit which would have given it more comfortable and effective high-altitude performance. The Me 309 had a length of 9.46 m (31 ft), a wingspan of 11.04 m (36 ft 3 in), a height of 3.90 m (12 ft 10 in), a wing area of 16.6 square m (179 square ft), and an empty weight of 3,530 kg (7,766 lbs). Powerplant was one 1,750-hp Daimler-Benz DB 603G engine, maximum speed was 733 km/h (457 mph), range was 1,100 km (686 miles), and service ceiling was 12,000 m (39,360 ft). Armament consisted of two 15-mm MG 151 machine guns, and three 13-mm MG 131 machine guns.

Low government interest in the project delayed completion of the first prototype until spring 1942 and trouble with the nosewheel pushed back the 309's first flight to July. When it did fly, the Me 309's performance was satisfactory but not exemplary. In fact, the Bf 109 G could outturn its intended replacement. With the addition of armaments, the plane's speed decreased to an unacceptable level. In light of its poor performance and the much more promising development of the Focke-Wulf Fw 190D, the Me 309 was cancelled.

Messerschmitt Me 509

After the failure of the Me 309 to replace the Bf 109, the Messerschmitt Company made a new design. The new fighter was to be an all-metal design with a fuselage length of 9.94 m (32 ft 7 in) and a wingspan of 11.27 m (37 ft). The cockpit was placed forward near the nose (for better visibility), the Daimler-Benz 605B 12-cylinder engine was located behind the cockpit and drove a propeller by an extension shaft passing beneath the cockpit, and a tri-

Fighter Messerschmitt Me 309

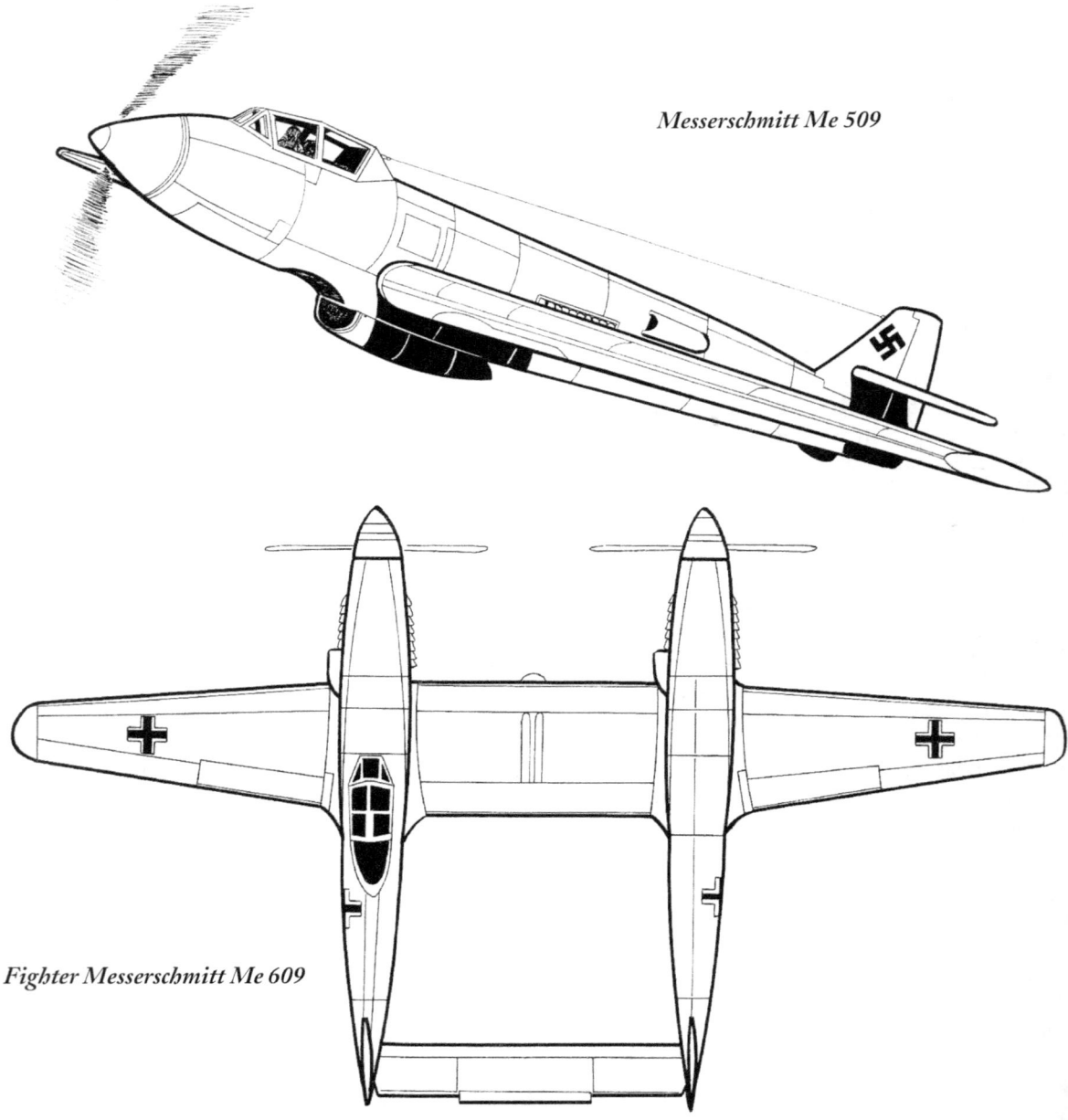

Messerschmitt Me 509

Fighter Messerschmitt Me 609

cycle landing gear was to be used. Armament would probably have consisted of two MG 131 13-mm machine guns and two MG 151 20-mm cannons. The design of the new Me 509 was abandoned in mid-1943, but it seems that the Japanese used some information about the Me 309 and Me 509 to design the Yokosuka R2Y *Keiun*, which was built for the Japanese navy in May 1945.

Messerschmitt Me 609

The Messerschmitt 609, designed in 1941, was intended to be a single-seat *Zerstörer* (destroyer/heavy fighter/ground attacker). It was a *Zwilling* (twin) composed of two Me 309 fuselages joined with a constant-chord center wing section. The pilot sat in a cockpit placed in the port fuselage, with the starboard cockpit canopy being faired over. The short-lived Me 609 had a span of 15.75 m (52 ft 6 in), a length of 9.72 m (31 ft 11 in), and a maximum speed of 760 km/h (472 mph). Two versions were planned; a heavy fighter with four or six MK 108 30-mm cannons, and a light bomber variant with two MK 108 30-mm cannons and a bomb load of 1,000 kg (2,200 lbs) carried beneath the fuselages. As the jet-powered Me 262 could take over both roles for which the Me 609 was designed, the project was not further developed.

Other German twin-fuselage airplanes included the Messerschmitt Me 509 *Zwilling* (2 × Bf 109), the Arado Ar 530 and the Heinkel He 111 *Zwilling* (see part 8). Also worthy of mention is the U.S. North American F-82 twin (composed of two P-51 Mustang fuselages) which was designed in 1944 and used in the Korean War in 1950 as a long-range escort fighter and reconnaissance plane.

Focke-Wulf Fw 190

The Fw 190, one of the most formidable single-seat fighter and ground-attack aircraft of World War II, made its first flight in June 1939 and the first production model, the Fw 190 A-1, began to leave the assembly lines in Bremen and Hamburg late in 1940. Designed by engineer Kurt Tank, the quick, maneuverable and versatile Fw 190 *Würger* (Shrike) was probably the most complete fighter produced during World War II. The aircraft dumbfounded the aviation experts who had believed for so long that a fighter must have an in-line engine if it was to be sleek and fast. Kurt Tank and BMW showed that a properly cowled, bluff-fronted radial engine with air ducted to a cooling fan, could provide sparkling performances and was free from the weight and vulnerability of a liquid-cooling system. Although flown before the outbreak of the war, the Fw 190 was unknown to the Allies; its introduction came as a nasty surprise and caused a major shock to British airmen. First seeing action in the spring of 1941, it was in almost every way superior to the RAF's latest version of the Spitfire, the Mark V-B. The general consensus of opinion was that the airplane was versatile, fast and well-armed, and also a small target. Altogether it gave Allied pilots and designers an inferiority complex. Powered by a BMW 801Dg 18-cylinder, two-row, radial, air-cooled engine developing 1,700 hp, the nimble and agile Fw 190 A had a speed of 653 km/h (408 mph) and a range of about 900 km (560 miles). It was a rather small aircraft, with a span of 10.50 m (34 ft 5.5 in), a length of 8.84 m (29 ft), a height of 3.96 m (13 ft) and an empty weight of 3,200 kg (7,055 lbs). It carried a heavy armament, the usual arrangement being four 20-mm cannons and two machine guns. It had unsurpassed maneuverability, was well-protected, easy to maintain in the field, and had a streamlined cockpit with wide all-round vision, powerful yet well-balanced controls, and a broad-track retractable undercarriage unlike the Messerschmitt Bf 109. The pilot's seat was tilted,

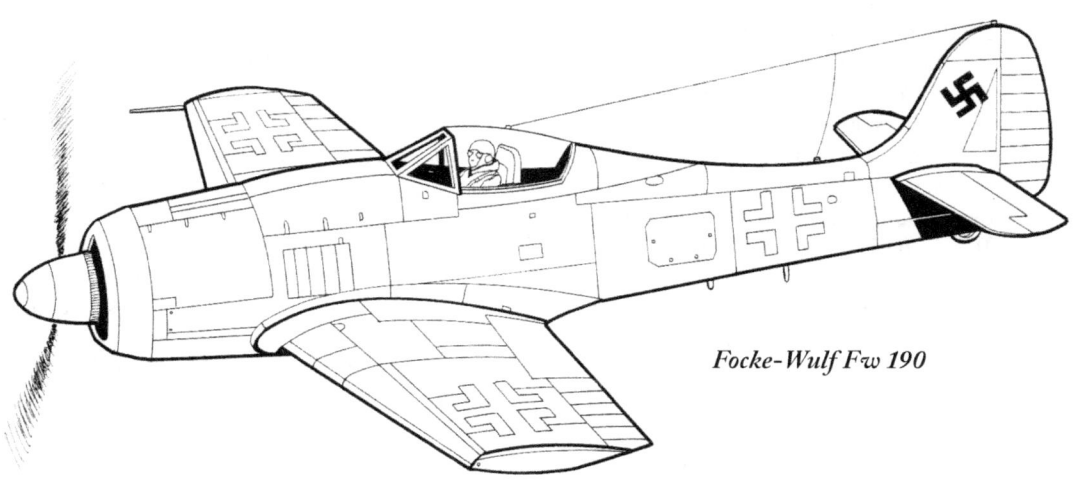

Focke-Wulf Fw 190

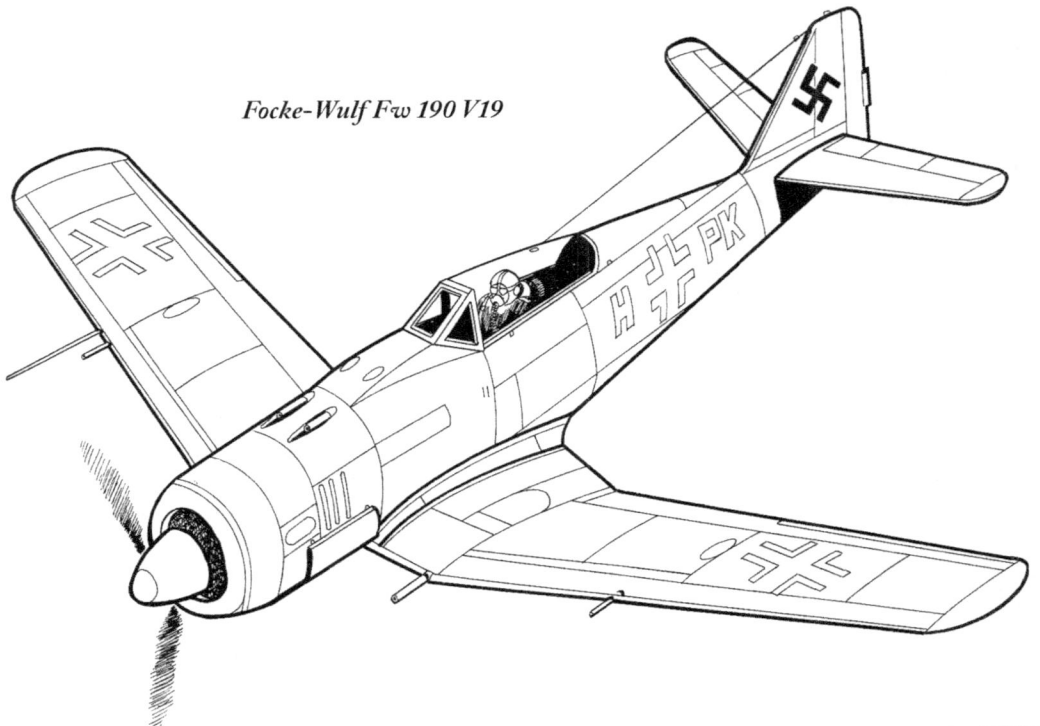

Focke-Wulf Fw 190 V19

helping to prevent mental blackout; the sliding cockpit canopy could be jettisoned for quick bailing out by pressing a button. It was, however, not very easy to fly, as it had a high landing speed. Its best operational height was between 24,000 ft and 16,000 ft, elsewhere its performance was less good. Though it never supplanted the Bf 109, it was made in many different versions by many factories. By the end of 1942, about 2,000 units had been delivered, and most went to dominate the skies on the Eastern front and in North Africa.

Originally designed as a fighter, the Fw 190 was soon adapted for a host of other roles, and new versions appeared, including types with even heavier armament. The Fw 190 A-5/U-13 *Jabo* (fighter-bomber), fitted with two 300-litre jettisonable fuel tanks and carrying one SC 500-kg bomb under the fuselage, and two SC 250-kg bombs in underwing racks, was used for hit-and-run ground-attack raids. A tropical fighter version was fitted with sand-filter engines. In spite of its small size, the Fw A-5/U/14 was able to carry a naval torpedo. There was also a dual-control, two-seat trainer variant, the Fw 190 A-8/U-1. The Fw 190 B fighter had a turbo-boosted BMW radial engine for better high-altitude performance. The subsequent C model series was outstandingly formidable, with a Daimler-Benz DB 603 engine, a four-blade propeller and massive supercharger for improved performance. The Fw 190 F model, with strengthened structure, carried eight 50-kg bombs, rockets and cannons. It entered service in the winter of 1942-43, replacing the vulnerable Junkers Ju 87 in the Stuka and ground attack role. The Fw 190 G *Pulk Zerstörer* could carry rockets and two 21-cm mortars mounted underwing for use against American daylight bombers. There was also a version (Fw 190 V 19) with gull wings, and the Fw 190 was also often used in Mistel composite (see Part 9) as the upper, manned aircraft. Fastest of all versions was the redesigned and enlarged Fw 190D or *Langnase* (Long Nose) high-altitude fighter series powered by a Jumo 213A-1 liquid-cooled line engine, which was much longer than the compact BMW radial of the earlier series. Its speed and maneuverability, coupled with a heavy armament, enabled the Long Nose to dogfight Allied fighters adequately and shoot down bombers. Not surprisingly, many German aces flew the Fw 190, including Gerhard Barkhorn,

Otto Kittel, Walter Nowotny, Hans-Heinrich Rudel, and many others. In late 1943, Hermann Göring personally ordered the formation of *Stürmstaffel* I, a unit made up of volunteers and pilots undergoing disciplinary action; before each mission, pilots signed a declaration stating that they would not return to their base unless they had shot down at least one Allied bomber, and if all else failed they would ram enemy aircraft. The performance advantage enjoyed by the German Fw 190 was finally eclipsed by the arrival of the Russian Lavochkin and Yak, as well as the U.S. North American P-51 Mustang in 1944. By 1945, production of the Fw 190 continued but many of the excellent new aircraft remained on the ground due to lack of fuel. Total Fw 190 production amounted to 16,724 aircraft of all types (some sources indicate 20,000), placing it second only to the Messerschmitt Bf 109 as the most extensively produced Luftwaffe airplane. The Fw 190 was built by the Focke-Wulf Company, with extremely dispersed manufacture and assembly, and partly subcontracted to the French company Brandt-SNCA. Toward the end of the war engineer Kurt Tank designed a final development, known as Focke-Wulf Ta 152, to replace the long nose D series.

Focke-Wulf Ta 152

The Focke-Wulf Ta 152 was a *Höhenjäger* (high-altitude interceptor fighter). It was a development of the Focke-Wulf Fw 190 D "long nose" fighter, but the prefix was changed from "Fw" to "Ta" in honor of Kurt Tank who headed the design team. Designed for high-altitude missions, the Ta 152H boasted excellent performance, using a Jumo 213E engine (a high-altitude version of the Jumo 213A/C used in the FW 190D), a 2-stage, 3-speed supercharger, and the MW 50 methanol-water-mixture engine-boost system. The Ta 152H was among the fastest piston-engined fighters of the war. Speed was 759 km/h at 12,500 m (472 mph at 41,000 ft), and range was 2,000 km (1,240 miles) with additional jettisonable fuel tanks. The aircraft featured a lengthened fuselage and larger tail surface area. Length was 10.82 m (33 ft 11 in), wingspan was 14.82 m (48 ft 6 in), wing area was 23.5 square m (253 square ft), height was 3.36 m (13ft 1 in), and empty weight was 3,920 kg (8,640 lb). The H-model was heavily armed to allow it to deal with the massive Allied bomber formations. The armament consisted of a Rheinmetall-Borsig MK 108 30-mm cannon firing through the propeller hub, and two Mauser

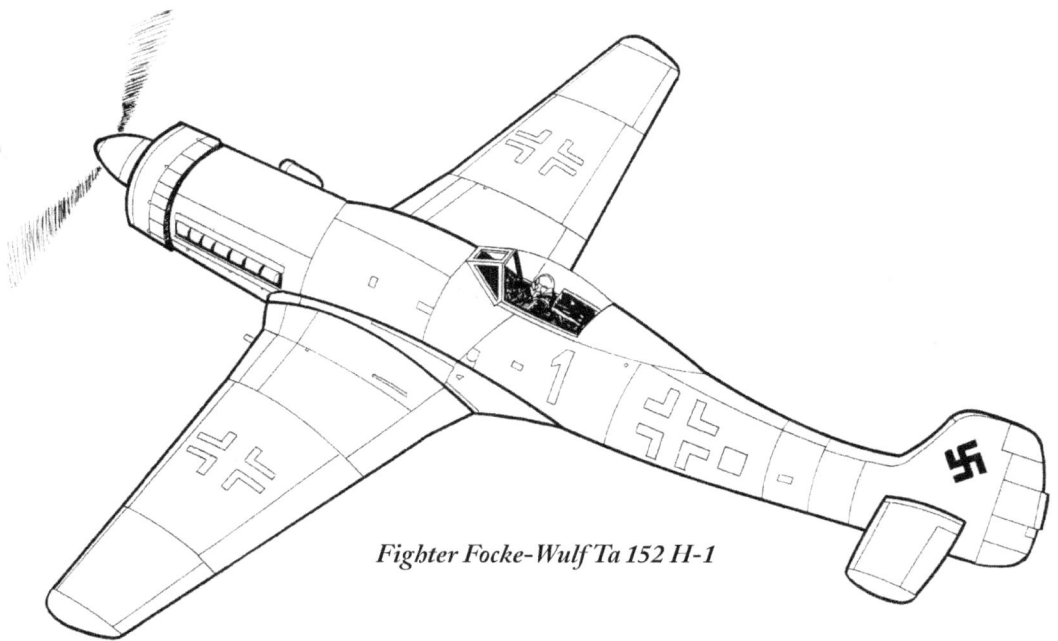

Fighter Focke-Wulf Ta 152 H-1

MG 151/20 20-mm cannons located in the wing roots. The total number of Ta 152 craft produced is not well known, but it should be about 150 aircraft of all types, including prototypes. But for the familiar problems—lack of fuel and trained pilots—the Ta 152 could have posed a real threat for the Allies had it entered service in significant numbers. The first Ta 152 entered service with the Luftwaffe in October 1944, and only 67 production aircraft were delivered. This was too late to allow the Ta 152 to have an impact on the war effort. Of the Ta 152Hs produced, more than half were destroyed by the Allies before they could be delivered to the air force. Of those Ta 152H that flew, most were used in a close-support role and as escorts protecting the Me 262 airfields while the vulnerable jets took off and landed. This was not the role for which they had been intended, but the necessity of supporting the ever-retreating ground troops demanded it. Nonetheless the Ta 152H proved quite successful, and its fighter capabilities were confirmed.

Focke-Wulf fighter project

Focke-Wulf made an unsuccessful attempt to improve the Focke-Wulf 190. The project, using the Fw 190 as basis, was powered by a BMW 802 18-cylinder, twin-row, radial engine or a BMW 802 engine with gas turbine. A speed of 725 km/h (450 mph) was envisaged. The aircraft would have had a span of 12.5 m (41 ft), a length of 11.3 m (37 ft), a height of 3.8 m (12 ft 5 in) and an empty weight of 4,475 kg (9,865 lbs). It is not known what weapons would have been carried, but a bomb load of 500 kg (1,102 lbs) was planned. The project never developed.

Focke-Wulf Ta 154 Moskito

The Focke-Wulf Ta 154 Moskito was a fast night fighter designed by Kurt Tank and produced by Focke-Wulf late in World War II. A competitor to the Heinkel He 219, the Focke-Wulf Ta 154 was intended as the Luftwaffe's response to the British De Havilland Mosquito, and came near to becoming a major combat Luftwaffe airplane. The first prototype, V1, fitted with two Jumo 211F engines, flew on July 1, 1943. The first armed version of the Ta 154 with Lichtenstein radar was the V3, which also was the first to fit the Jumo 211R engines. By June 1944, the Jumo 213 engine was finally arriving in some numbers, and a small batch of Ta 154A-1 craft were completed with these engines. The Ta 154 had a crew of two, a length of 12.55 m (40 ft 3 in), a wing-

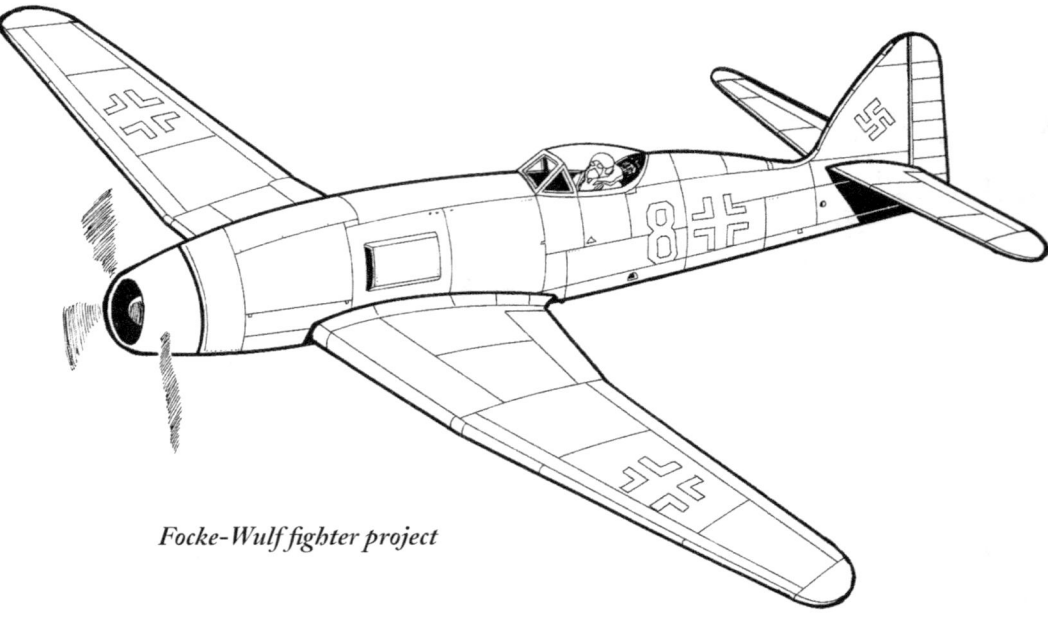

Focke-Wulf fighter project

Focke-Wulf Ta 154 Moskito

span of 16.30 m (52 ft 5 in), a height of 3.60 m (11 ft 4 in), a wing area of 31.40 square m (333.68 square ft), and an empty weight of 6,600 kg (14,550 lbs). It had a maximum speed of 615 km/h (404 mph), a range of 1,400 km (872 miles), and a service ceiling of 9,500 m (31,200 ft). The landing-gear was a tricycle arrangement with steerable nose wheel. Armament included two 20-mm MG 151 cannons, two 30-mm MG 131 nose-mounted cannons, and a MG 131 *Schräge Musik* cannon firing upward at a 60-degree angle. By August 1944, about fifty production versions had been completed, but the aircraft never made it, mostly because a glue of bad quality was used which ate away the wooden parts. Like the British De Havilland Mosquito, the German Focke-Wulf Ta 154 *Moskito* was made of wood. This led to some of the production versions breaking up in mid-air, as the glue was incapable of withstanding the stresses produced in flight. The inability to find an adequate adhesive prevented completion of an order for 250 planes. Some of the planes produced served with *Nachtjagdgeschwader 3* (Night Fighter Group 3), a few were later used as a training aircraft for jet pilots, and some were modified to form the bottom half of Mistel composite aircraft.

Heinkel He 219 Uhu

The He 219—informally called the *Uhu* (Owl)—was potentially the best and most formidable night fighter developed during World War II. Designed as a private venture, Ernst Heinkel first offered the project in August 1940, but the aircraft did not receive the attention it deserved. The German Air Ministry was not interested, Göring and Hitler firmly believing that the war would be won before such an aircraft could be needed. Erhard Milch, who was striving to reduce the number of aircraft types in service, opposed its development. Not until RAF night raids were beginning to build up in intensity in late 1941, was it decided to go ahead with the highly specialized He 219. General Josef Kammhuber used the special powers granted him by Hitler to force the project into service. The prototype flew in November 1942, and proved its worth in actual combat—fortunately, much too late in 1944—as preference continued to be given to existing night fighters (e.g., converted Messerschmitt Bf 110, Junkers Ju 88, and Dornier Do 17 and Do 215). As with many promising aircraft, the He 219 was victim of prejudice, and political wheeling and dealing. Although underpowered, it was extremely

Heinkel He 219

maneuverable, powerfully armed, sufficiently armored, and featured modern features (such as ejection seats, retractable tricycle landing gear, and de-icing, autopilot, and blind-landing aids). The Heinkel He 219 was manufactured at Rostock, Vienna-Schwechat, and Mielec and Buczin in Poland. Only 268 Uhus were completed and used, a small figure given the scale and urgency of its task, and an indication of the confusion in German fighter design by the latter half of the war. In 1943 a few He 219 craft flew in operations with great success, but production was canceled in May 1944. The He 219 existed in several versions (He 219-A-0 to A-7, B and C series) with different roles, engines and weapons. The night-fighter A-series was operated by a crew of two (pilot and radar/operator), it had a length of 15.54 m (50 ft 12 in), a span of 18.5 m (60 ft 8 in), a height of 4.1 m (13 ft 5.5 in), and an empty weight of 11,200 kg (24,692 lbs). It was powered by various engines, generally two 1,900-hp Daimler-Benz DB 603G inverted-V-12, liquid-cooled engines, and had a typical speed of 670 km/h (416 mph) and a range of 2,000 km (1,243 miles). Armament was varied, from two to six 30-mm cannons and two, oblique, upward-firing *Schräge Musik* cannons.

There was a project intended to increase the He 219's performance by fitting a jet engine under the fuselage. Another plan for a fast fighter, known as He 319, was powered by two DB 603 A engines (each developing 1,750 hp) with a span of 20.30 m, and a length of 15.40 m. Another version, the He 419, was a project for a high-altitude machine capable of flying up to 9,200 m.

Blohm & Voss Bv 155

The Blohm & Voss Bv 155 was a high-altitude interceptor aircraft intended to be used by the Luftwaffe against raids by the USAF when the performance estimates of the B-29 Superfortress first started reaching German command in early 1942. The B29 had a maximum speed of around 563 km/h (350 mph) and would attack in a cruise at about 362 km/h (225 mph) at 8,000 to 10,000 m (27,000 to 32,000 ft), an altitude that no German plane could operate at effectively. In the hope of countering attacks by this formidable bomber, the Luftwaffe would need new fighters and new destroyers as soon as possible.

Work on a special high-altitude fighter was started by Messerschmitt, but in 1943 the project was passed to Blohm & Voss. The result was the Bv 155 prototype that made its first test flight in September 1944. The aircraft had a crew of one, a length of 11.9 m (39 ft 4 in), a span of 20.3 m (67 ft), with large radiators mounted in the wings, a wing area of 39 square m (384 square ft), and an empty weight of

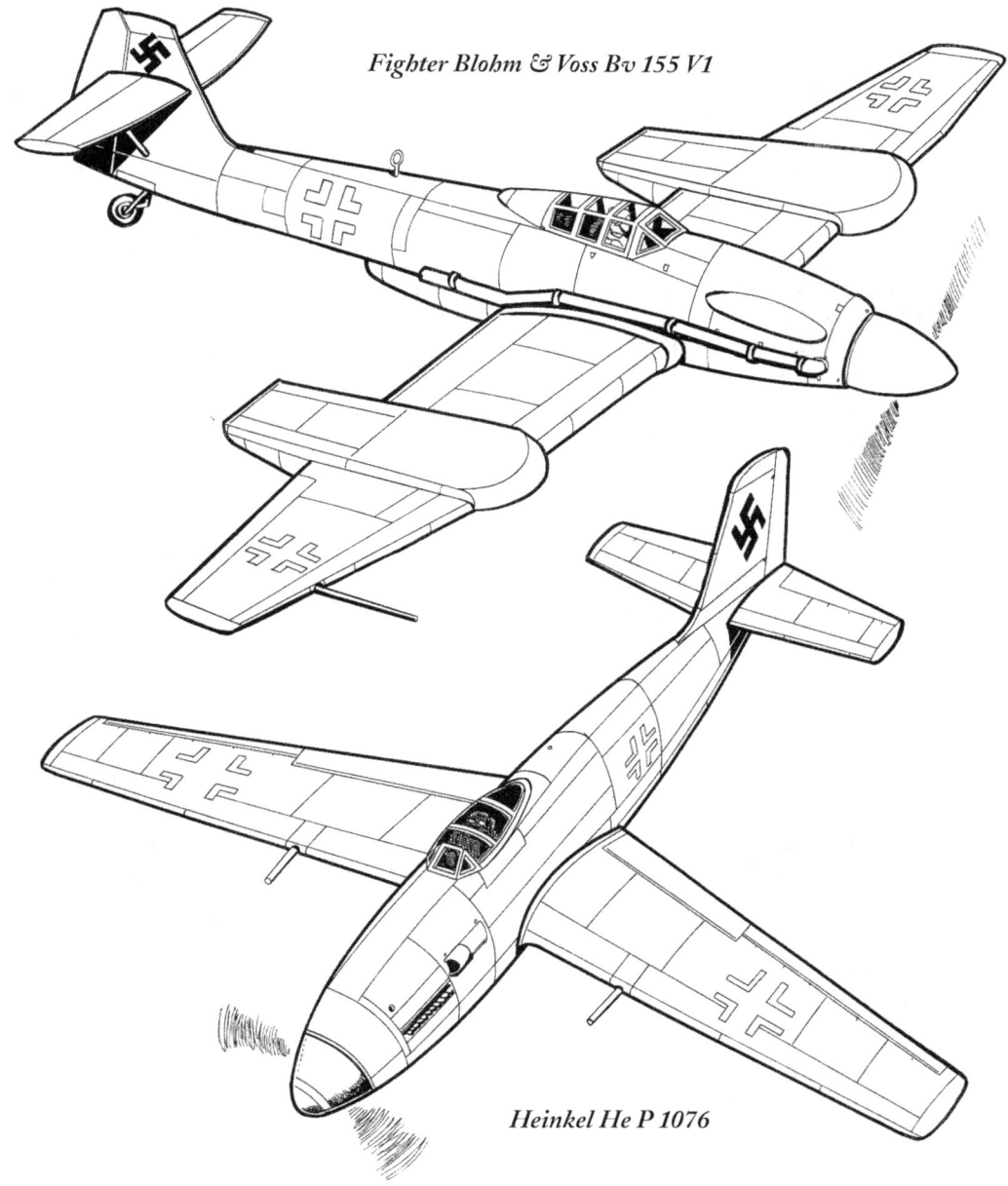

Fighter Blohm & Voss Bv 155 V1

Heinkel He P 1076

4,868 kg (10,734 lbs). Powerplant was one 1,610-hp turbocharged Daimler-Benz DB 603. Maximum speed was 690 km/h (429 mph) at an altitude of 16,000 m (52,493 ft), and range was to be 1,440 km (895 miles). Armament would have included one 30-mm MK 108 cannon and two 20-mm MG 151/20 cannons. The project was interrupted by the capture of the Blohm & Voss factory in Hamburg at the end of World War II, and no Boeing B-29 craft were ever used in Europe, anyway, as the type was concentrated on air attacks on Japan.

Heinkel He P 1076

The He P176 was designed in late 1944 by engineer Siegfried Günther as a fast, high-altitude, single-seat fighter. The fuselage was 9.6 m (31 ft 6 in) in length, and the wings were swept forward at 8 degrees with a span of 11 m (36 ft 1 in). The aircraft was fitted with a pressurized cockpit, conventional retractable landing gear, and an elaborate evaporation cooling system. It would have been powered either by a 2,100-hp Daimler-Benz DB 603M twin supercharger piston engine, or a 2,100-hp Junkers Jumo 213E two-stage, three-speed supercharger piston engine, or a 2,750-hp Daimler-Benz two-stage twin supercharger with integrated heat exchange and contra-rotating three-blade propellers. A speed of 880 km/h (546 mph) was expected. Armament would have consisted of two MK 108 30-mm cannons mounted in the wing, and two MK 103 30-mm cannons positioned in the nose above the engine, firing through the propeller hub. The project was never realized.

Unconventional Designs

Blohm & Voss Bv 179

The asymmetrical Blohm & Voss 179 was a scaled-down version of the dive-bomber Bv 237 (see Part 4). Engineer Vogt of the Blohm & Voss company claimed that there were certain advantages to the asymmetrical design, such as a superior pilot view and ease of construction and maintenance. The Bv 179 had a span of 10.39 m (34 ft 1.4 in) and a length of 8.43 m (27 ft 8.1 in). The fighter Bv 179 had a crew of one sitting in a nacelle placed to the starboard side of the fuselage to which was fitted the single BMW 801 14-cylinder radial piston engine. The aircraft would have had a

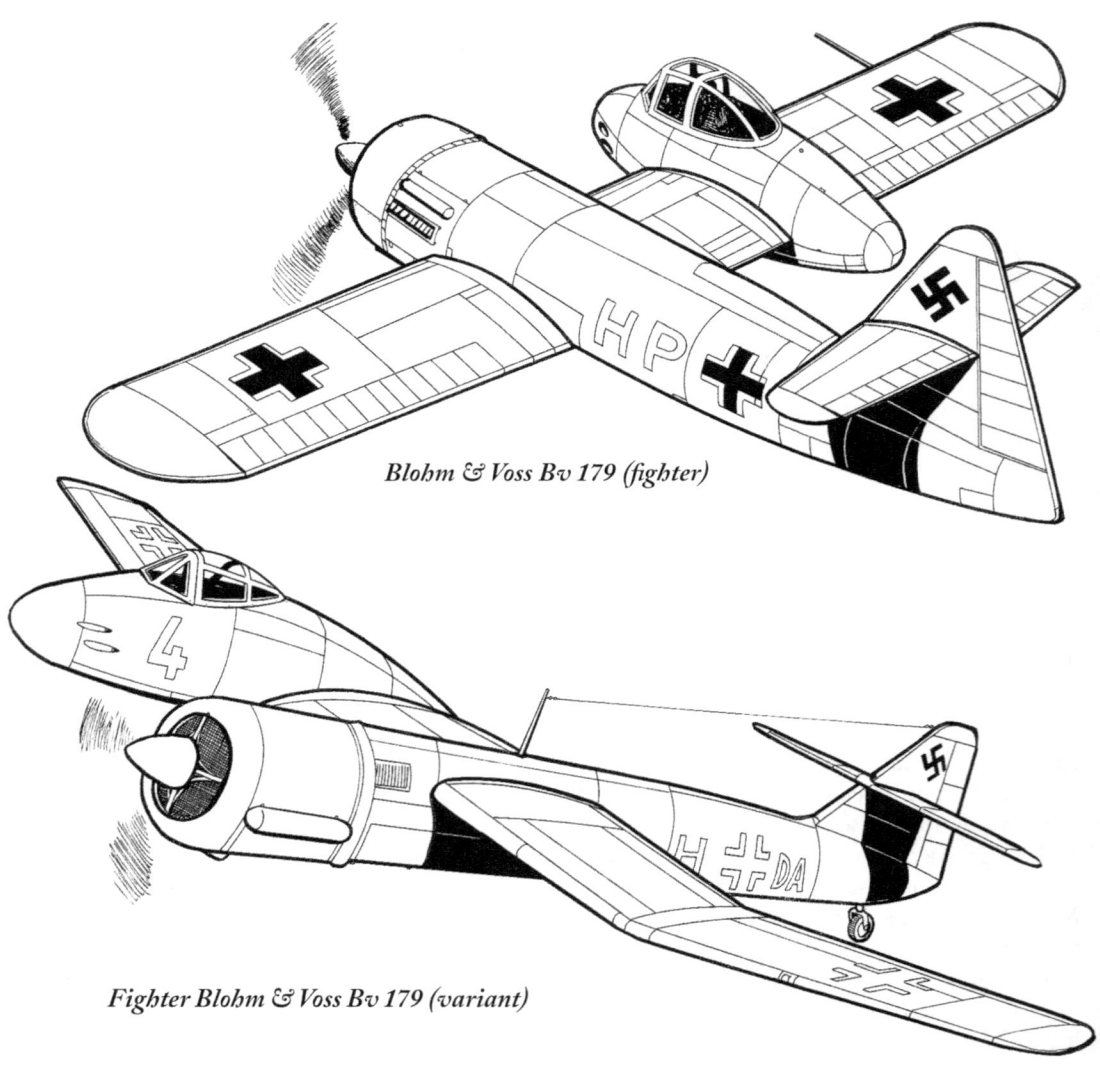

Blohm & Voss Bv 179 (fighter)

Fighter Blohm & Voss Bv 179 (variant)

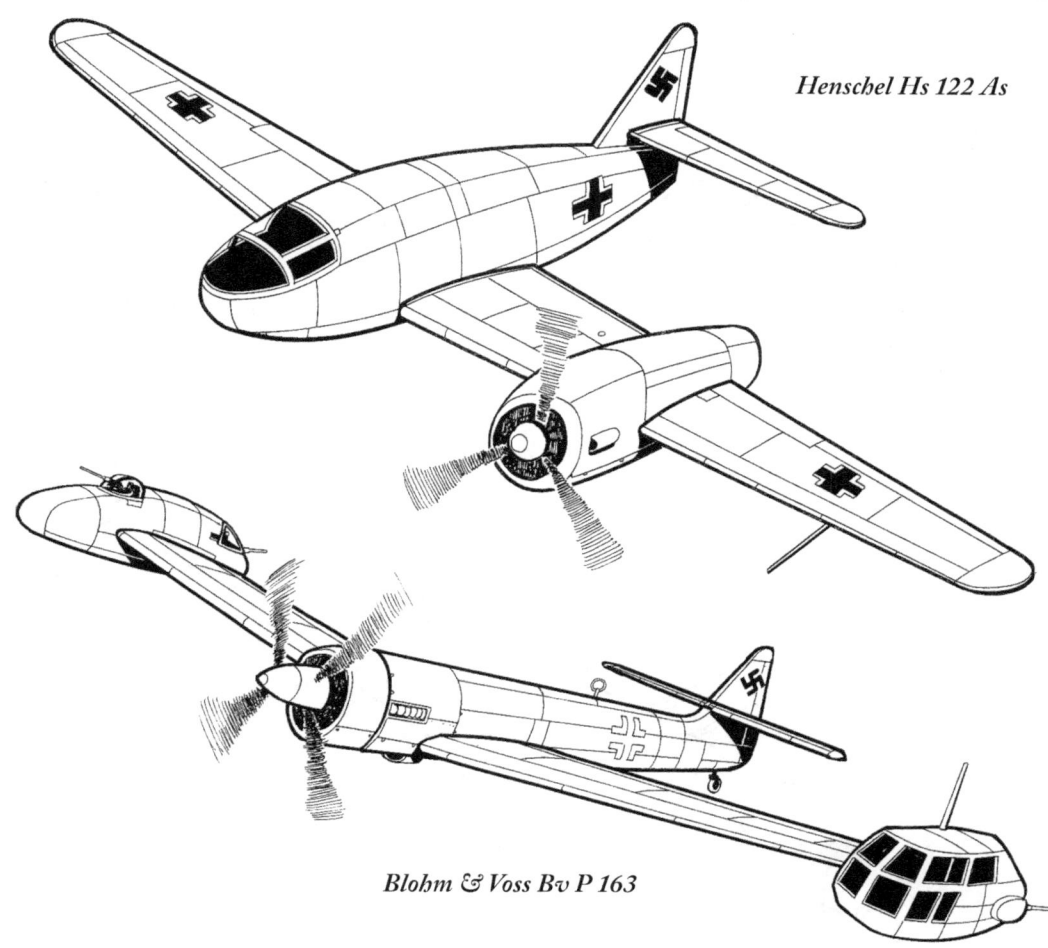

Henschel Hs 122 As

Blohm & Voss Bv P 163

speed of 500 km/h (373 mph). Planned armament included two MG 151/20 20-mm cannons located in the pilot's nacelle nose. A bomb load of 500 kg (1,100 lbs) could have been carried, as well.

Henschel Hs 122

The Hs 122 had a asymmetrical configuration—the engine was placed on the left wing. No data is available for it.

Blohm & Voss Bv P 163

The Bv P 163, intended to be a heavy fighter/light bomber, had a very curious layout. The engine (either one DB 613 or one BMW 803, driving two contra-rotating propellers) was placed at the front of the main central fuselage. The tail unit was quite conventional, but the crew of four was placed in two nacelles located on the tips of the wings. Pilot and navigator/gunner were on the left, and two gunners were placed on the right. This odd design was intended to provide a maximum visibility for the pilot and a 360-degree arc of fire for the gunners. The idea was also to lighten the load distribution by shifting cockpit and armed nacelles out to the wingtips. On the paper it had been calculated that this unconventional configuration would reduce the wake turbulence on the outer part of the wing, that this would have a positive influence on lift, and that the entire fuselage could be used as a fuel tank, allowing a range estimated to 2,255 km. The aircraft would have had a retractable landing gear, a length of 15 m (49 ft 3 in), a span of 20.50 m (67 ft 3.7 in), and a maximum speed of 570 km/h (338 mph). Armament would have consisted of four or six MG 151 15-mm

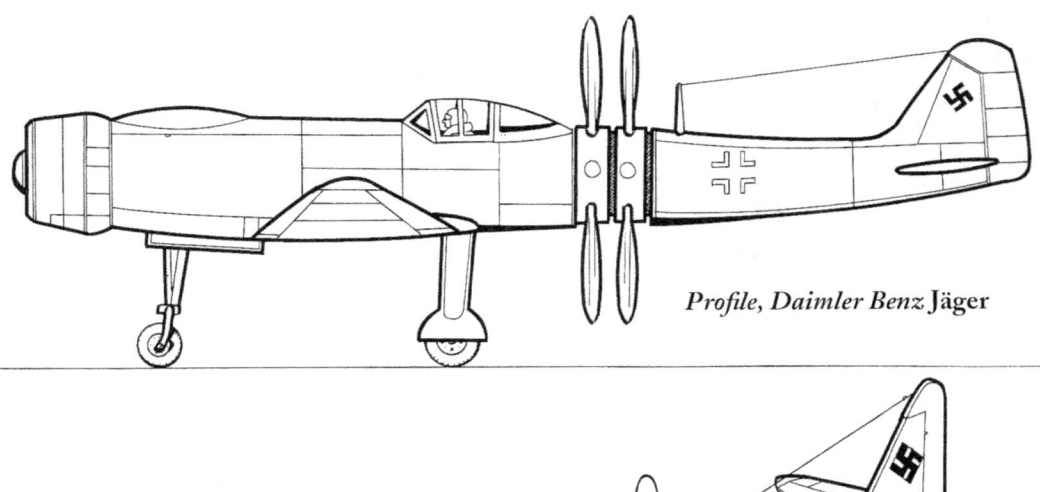

Profile, Daimler Benz Jäger

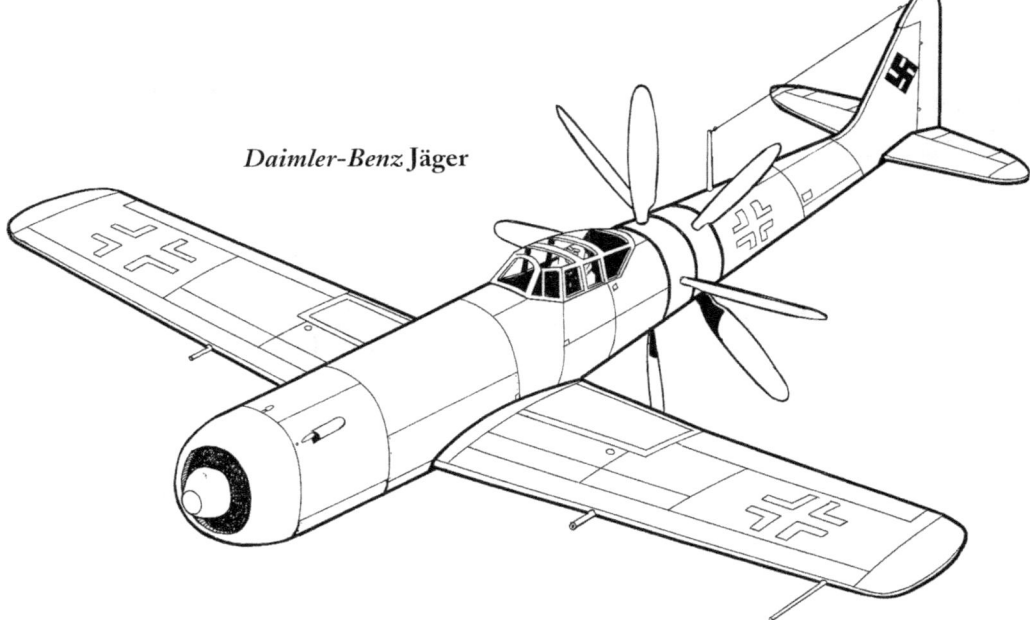

Daimler-Benz Jäger

machine guns. A bomb load of 2,000 kg (4,400 lbs) was to be carried in racks under the wings. This strange aircraft, which was intended to exist in two slightly different versions, never left the initial design stage.

There was also a project for a two-seat Stuka (dive bomber), known as Bv P 165, with only one nacelle (for the crew of two: pilot and observer/rear gunner) placed on the tip of the right wing. This was to have a length of 12.82 m, to be probably powered by a 2,000-hp Junkers Jumo 222 piston engine, and to carry a bomb load of 500 kg.

Daimler Benz DB Jäger

The DB Jäger (Daimler Benz fighter) had basically a conventional design with unswept wings, tail unit with a single fin and rudder piston engine in the fuselage nose with an annular radiator in front, a closed cockpit for the single pilot, and a tricycle landing gear with long legs to keep ground clearance for the propellers. Where the Daimler Benz Jäger differed from all other aircrafts was the extremely unusual propeller placement. These, a pair of four-blade contra-rotating propellers, were located in the fuselage between the cockpit and the tail. Theorical development of the DB fighter started in September 1942 using a 2,700-hp Daimler Benz DB 609 in-line, 16-cylinder, injection-type engine. A mock-up of the forward fuselage was built, as far back as the propeller location, but because delivery of a prototype was scheduled in April 1947, the RLM cancelled the Daimler Benz project in

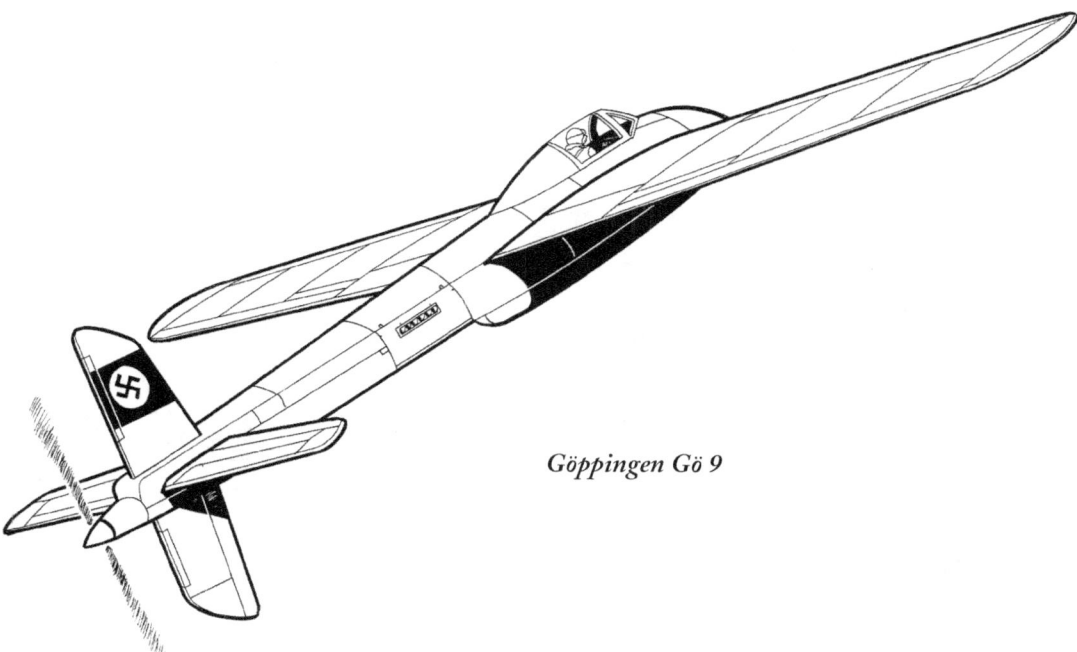

Göppingen Gö 9

May 1943. Unfortunately no dimension, weight, performance and armament data are available for the very odd Daimler Benz Jäger project.

Göppingen Gö 9

The Gö 9 was a small aircraft designed in early 1940 by engineer Ulrich Hütter. The airplane had a span of 7.2 m (23 ft 8 in), a length of 6.8 m (22 ft 4 in) and a weight of 720 kg (1,587 lbs). The most striking feature was the pusher propeller mounted at the rear of the fuselage. The Gö 9 project was soon abandoned but the idea gave birth to a series of push-engined aircraft, notably the Dornier Do 335.

Dornier Do 335 Pfeil

The Dornier Do 335 *Pfeil* (Arrow) was a fast, single-seat, two-engine fighter. Potentially the fastest piston-engined fighter of the era, it was powered by two inverted-V, liquid-cooled Daimler-Benz engines, each developing 1,900 hp, one mounted in the nose and the other in the rear fuselage, driving conventional tractor and tail pusher propellers with a maximum speed of 665 km/h (413 mph) and a range of 2,050 km (1,280 miles). The Do 335 had a wingspan of 13.8 m (45 ft 4 in), a length of 13.7 m (45 ft 6 in), a height of 4 m (16 ft 4 in), and an empty weight of 7,400 kg (16,314 lbs). The aircraft was armed with one 30-mm MK 103 cannon firing through the front propeller hub, and two 15-mm MG 151 cannons mounted above the nose. A bomb load of 500 kg (1,100 lbs) was carried in racks placed under the fuselage in proposed fighter/bomber configuration. The twin-engined Do 335 exhibited most of the maneuverability of a single-engined fighter, and did all right when flying on only one engine; it could even take off with one engine inoperative. The main drawback of the push/pull arrangement was that it required special measures to abandon the plane in an emergency: the rear propeller and upper tail fin would have to be jettisoned, then the canopy blown off, before the pilot could attempt to bail out.

Initially, there was considerable RLM reluctance to the Do 335's development, for the reason that Dornier was a bomber manufacturer. After the company got permission to build it, progress was forthcoming and the machine made its first flight in September 1943. Tests soon revealed the vast potential of the unique, twin-engined, push/pull layout. Production of

Two-seat night fighter Dornier DO 335 A-6 "Pfeil"

Dornier Do 435

90 aircraft started in November 1944. Twenty-eight units were delivered to combat formations, but the war ended before the Do 335 could become fully operational. There was a two-seat, night-fighter version equipped with a radar. There was also a planned twin version of this airplane, known as Dornier Do 634 Z (*Zwilling*), composed of two aircraft linked together by means of a central wing section. There was another planned variant designed in 1944, known as Dornier Do 435, with mixed propulsion; this consisted of a DB 603 LA piston engine driving the front propeller and a He S011 jet engine at the rear; a speed of 830 km/h was anticipated.

5. Fighters 235

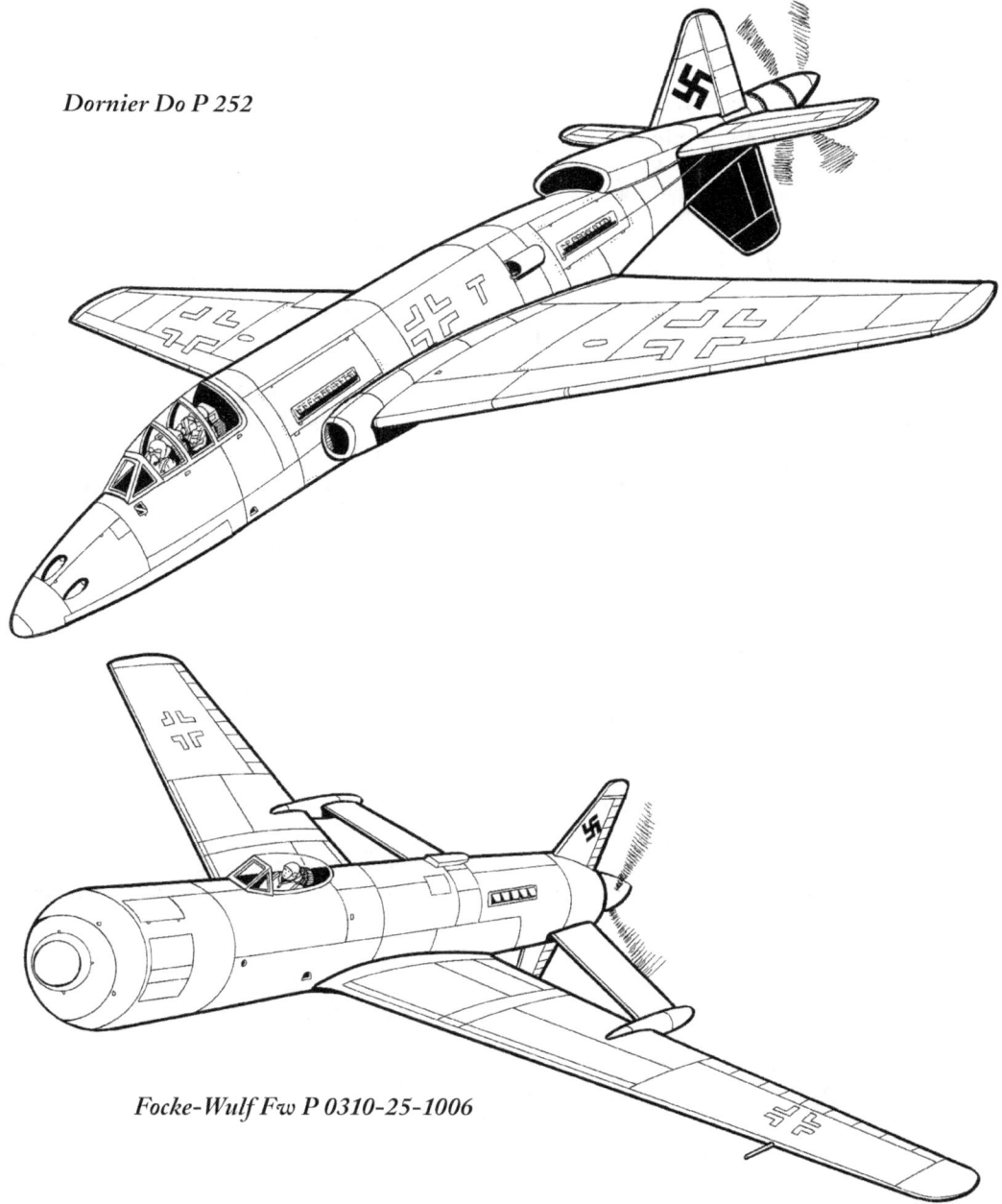

Dornier Do P 252

Focke-Wulf Fw P 0310-25-1006

Dornier Do P 252

Similar in layout to the Do 335, the Dornier Do P 252 was powered by two Junkers Jumo 213J liquid-cooled, 12-cylinder piston engines which drove two contra-rotating pusher propellers located at the large cruciform tail. A maximum speed of 930 km/h (577 mph) was planned. The fuselage had a length of 17.2 m (56 ft 4.8 in). The wings had a span of 15.8 m (51 ft 9.5 in) and were swept back at 22.5 degrees. It was discovered that a swept wing, that is one in which the angle between the wing leading-edge and the centerline of the rear fuselage forms an angle of less than 90 degrees, was able to be flown at above-normal speeds without the onset of buffeting. The aircraft had a crew of two and an empty weight of 8,600 kg (18,959 lbs). Three versions were considered—P252/1, P 252/2 and P 252/3—with various models of airborne search radar (e.g., Type FuG 244 Bremenanlage) and various weapons, consisting of Mk 108 30-mm or MK 213C 30-mm cannons positioned in the nose or in the wing, or a 500-kg bomb load.

Focke-Wulf Fw P 0310-25-1006

This project for a fast high-altitude/bad-weather fighter was designed in October 1944. The single-seat aircraft had a length of 14.2 m (46 ft 7.5 in), and swept-back wings with a span of 16.4 m (53 ft 10.2 in). It was powered by one 4,000-hp Argus As 413 which drove two contra-rotating propellers placed at the rear in a push arrangement. Planned weapons would have included two Mk 103 30-mm cannons and two MG 213 20-mm cannons. The project never left the drawing board.

Focke-Wulf twin boom fighter project

This twin-boom fighter had a length of 13.8 m (45 ft 3.7 in) and its slightly swept-back wings had a span of 13.2 m (43 ft 4.1 in). Operated by a single pilot, it was powered by a 3,900-hp BMW 803 radial engine driving a propeller in a push arrangement. Armament was to be two MK 103 30-mm cannons and two MG 151/20 20-mm cannons. This project, too, never left the drawing board.

Focke-Wulf Fw P 03-10251-13

The Focke-Wulf Fw P 03-10251-13 project, designed in late 1944 by engineers Schüffel and Merkel, was a mixed-propulsion airplane intended for a role as night and all-weather fast fighter. There were three similar versions of the aircraft, known as P 03-10251-13/I, P 03-10251-13/II, and P 03-10251-13/III, the difference being the engine used. The design II, for example, was powered by one piston engine (either a Daimler-Benz DN 603N or Jumo 22 C/D 24 or Argus As 413) placed mid-fuselage, driving a rear push propeller. In addition there were two BMW 003A turbojet engines (either slung under the wings or placed in the wing roots). The Fw P 03-10251-13/II was operated by a crew of three (pilot, navigator and radar operator), it had a length of 16.55 m (54 ft 3.6 in), and it was fitted with a cruciform tail, the lower fin helping to keep the push propeller from striking the ground during take-off and landing. The wings were swept back with a span of 21 m (68 ft 10.8 in). The aircraft was to have a maximum speed of 848 km/h (527 mph), and its endurance could be increased to eight hours with the jet engines shut down and the piston rear engine operating at half throt-

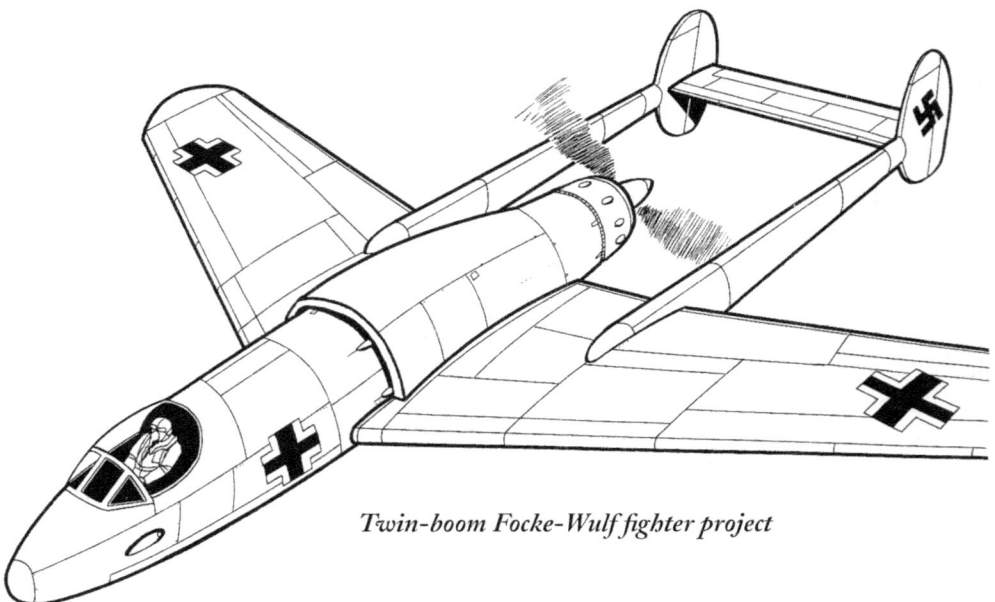

Twin-boom Focke-Wulf fighter project

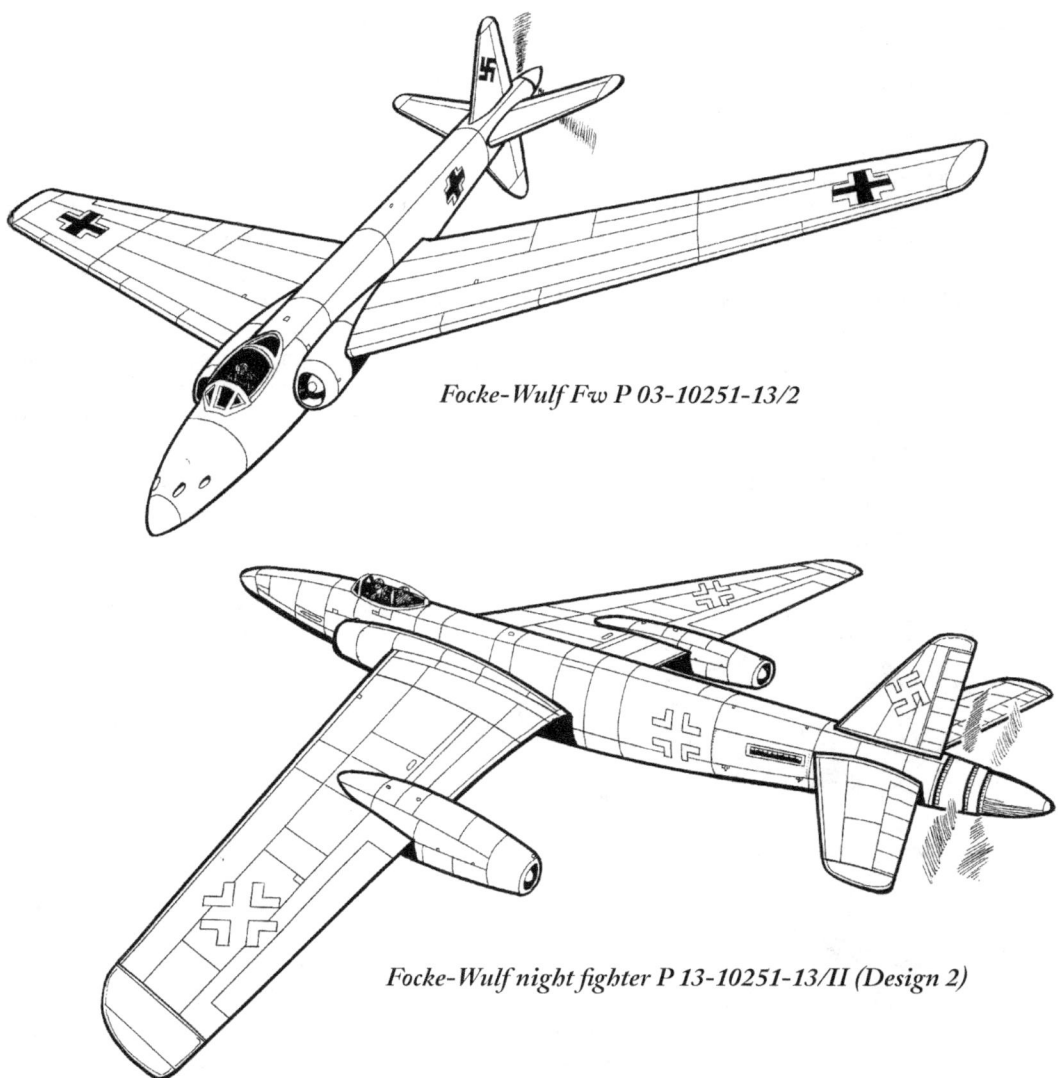

Focke-Wulf Fw P 03-10251-13/2

Focke-Wulf night fighter P 13-10251-13/II (Design 2)

tle. The aircraft was to be armed with four forward-firing cannons (either MK 108 or MK 112) mounted in the nose, and two 500-kg (1,100-lb) bombs could be carried in racks under the wings.

Focke-Wulf P 13-10251-13

The Focke-Wulf P 13-10251-13, intended to be a night and all-weather fighter, was designed by engineers Schüffel and Merkel. Three different versions were proposed for this project. Design 1 was powered by a Daimler Benz DN 603N in-line, push-piston engine, placed mid-fuselage, driving the rear propeller by an extension shaft. Two air intakes were located in the wing roots. Design 1 had a span of 20.4 m (66 ft 11.1 in), a length of 16.65 m (54 ft 7.5 in), and a maximum speed of 816 km/h (507 mph). Designs 2 and 3 had mixed-propulsion, including a pusher-piston engine and two BMW 003A turbojets slung under the wings. Design 2, powered by a Jumo 222 C/D 24 cylinder four-row radial engine and two turbojets, had a span of 21 m (68 ft 10.8 in), a length of 16.55 m (54 ft 3.6 in), and a maximum speed of 848 km/h (527 mph). Design 3, powered by one Argus As 413 in-line engine and two turbojet engines had a span of 22.8 m (74 ft 9.6 in), a length of 18.10 m (59 ft 4.6 in), and a maximum speed of 850 km/h (528 mph). In design 2 and 3, flight times could be increased to eight hours with the jet engines shut down and the rear engine operating at half throttle. All three designs included swept-back wings and cruciform tail unit, the lower tail helping to keep the propeller from striking the ground during take-off and landing. The crew included two airmen (pilot, and navigator/radar operator), who sat together in a pressurized cockpit beneath a bubble canopy. All designs were to be armed with four forward-firing automatic cannons placed in the nose (either MK 108 30-mm, MK 103 30-mm, MK 213 30-mm, or MK 112 55-mm). Two upward-firing oblique MK 108 30-mm cannons (*Schräge Musik*) could also be fitted. In addition, two 500-kg (1,100-lb) bombs could be carried in racks under the wings. None of these designs made it further than the drawing board.

Messerschmitt Me 334

Designed in 1943 by engineer Alexander Lippisch of the Messerschmitt Company, the Me 334 was a small, tailless, single-seat fighter. The aircraft had a fuselage length of 7 m (22 ft 11.8 in), and wings swept back at 23 degrees with a span of 9.3 m (30 ft 6.4 in). Powerplant was a Daimler-benz DB 605 12-cylinder piston engine, placed at the front, which drove a pusher propeller located at the back. There was a vertical lower fin helping to keep the propeller from striking the ground during take-off and landing. Planned armament would have included two MG 131 13-mm machine guns. The Me 334 was never built.

Blohm & Voss Bv P 207/02

The never-completed fighter Bv P 207/02 was to have been powered either by one 4,000-hp Argus As 413 engine or one 1,800-hp Junkers Jumo 213, mounted in the fuselage behind the cockpit, driving a pusher propeller. An air intake was placed under the fuselage, and a tricycle landing gear and a cruciform tail unit were used. Armament would have consisted of two MK 103 30-mm cannons and two MG 151 20-mm cannons, all mounted in the nose.

Blohm & Voss Bv P 207/03

This other design of the BV P 207 single-seat fighter was to have used a single DB 603G (2,000 hp) or one

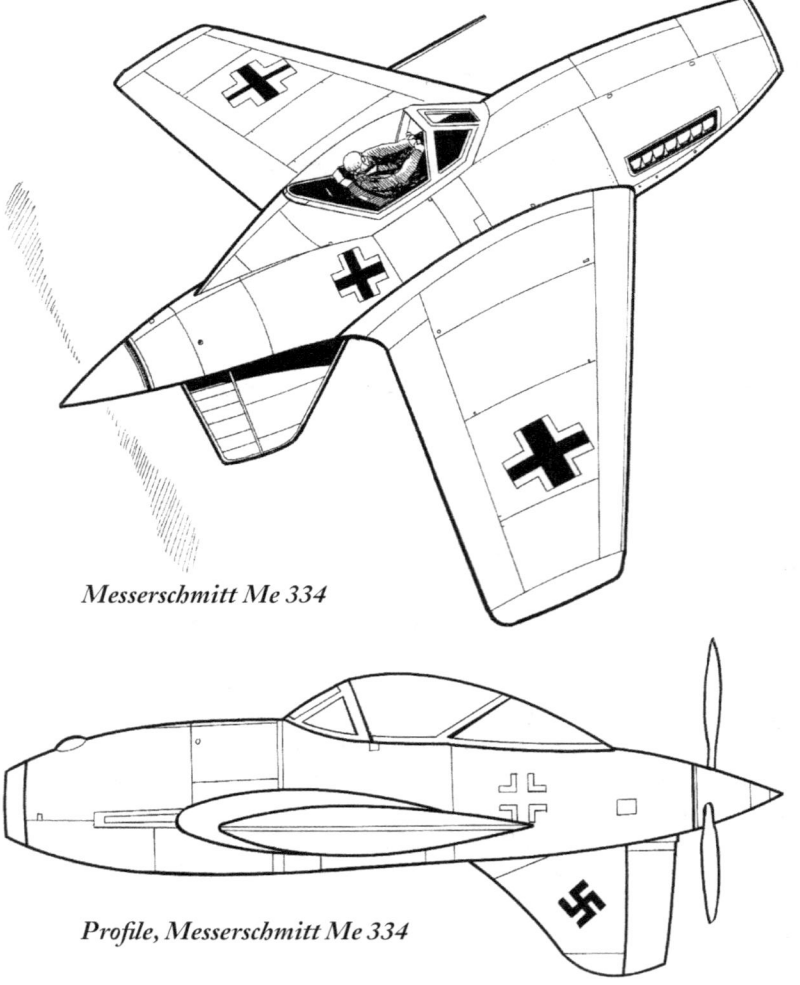

Messerschmitt Me 334

Profile, Messerschmitt Me 334

5. Fighters

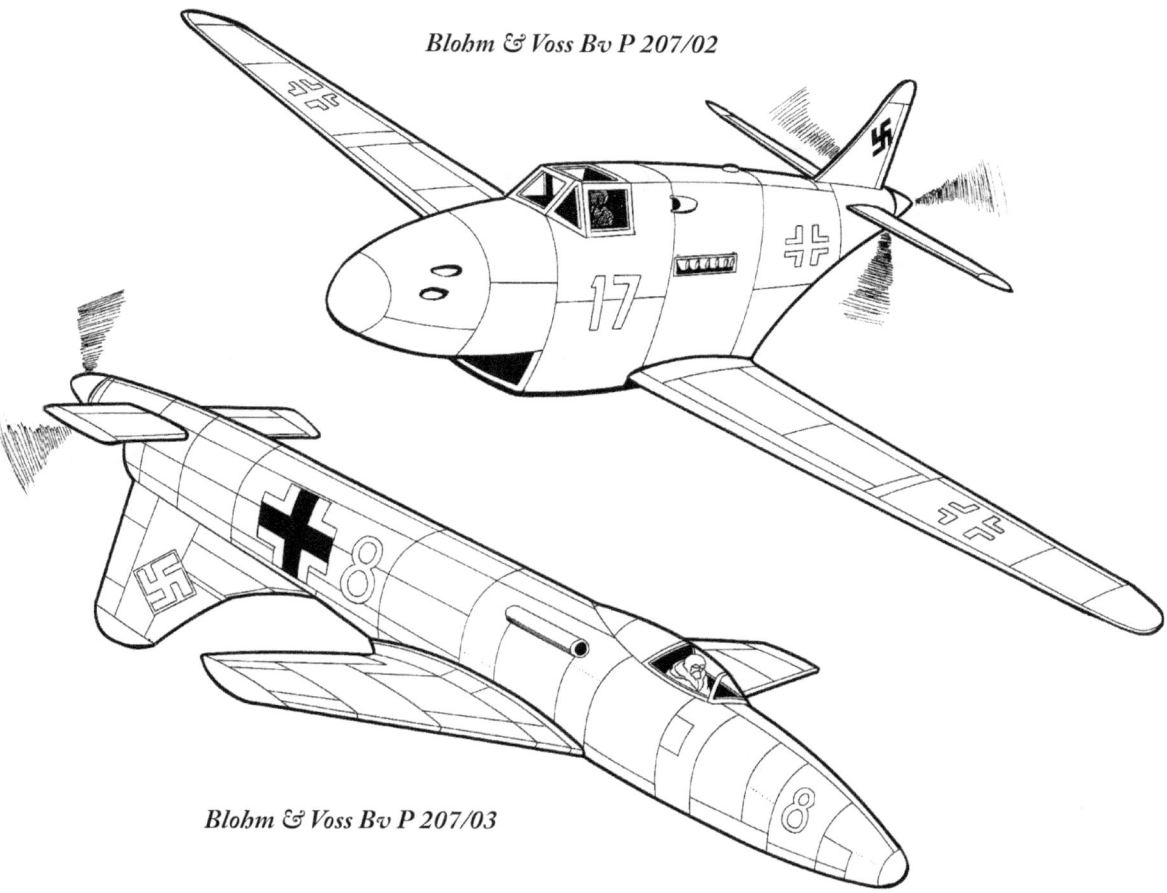

Blohm & Voss Bv P 207/02

Blohm & Voss Bv P 207/03

Argus As 413 (4,000 hp) or Jumo 213 (1,800 hp) located inside the fuselage aft of the cockpit. The radiator had been moved back and buried inside the fuselage, and was fed by an intake located on the starboard side. Span was 9.9 m (32 ft 6.1in) and length was 9.73 m (31 ft 11.4 in). The wing had a slight taper and dihedral (slightly angled). The tail unit was of cruciform design, with the lower tail preventing the propeller from striking the ground at take-off and landing, but the upper fin and rudder were omitted, with only the lower stabilizer retained and enlarged. Armament was to include four MK 108 30-mm cannons. Both Bv P 207/2 and 3 never proceeded past the design stage.

Skoda-Kauba SK V 6

The Skoda-Kauba V6 was one aircraft of a series designed by engineer Otto Kauba who had taken over the Czech company Skoda. The SK V 6 (V stood for *Versuchs*—prototype) was a small, experimental, twin-boom monoplane with fixed landing gear. Operated by a single pilot, it was powered by a 105-hp Hirth HM 504 A engine driving a two-blade propeller in "pusher" arrangement. Test flights were carried out in 1944, and the SK V 6 was modified in order to test control arrangement of the Blohm & Voss P 208 series.

Blohm & Voss Bv P 208-02

The experimental Bv P 208 series was a design for tailless fast fighter using swept wings and a divided tailplane carried on short booms on the outboard edge of the main wing panel. No fin or rudder was necessary because of the anhedral on the tailplane. The Bv P 208-02 had a Jumo 222E engine with air intakes in the wing roots, driving a pusher propeller. It

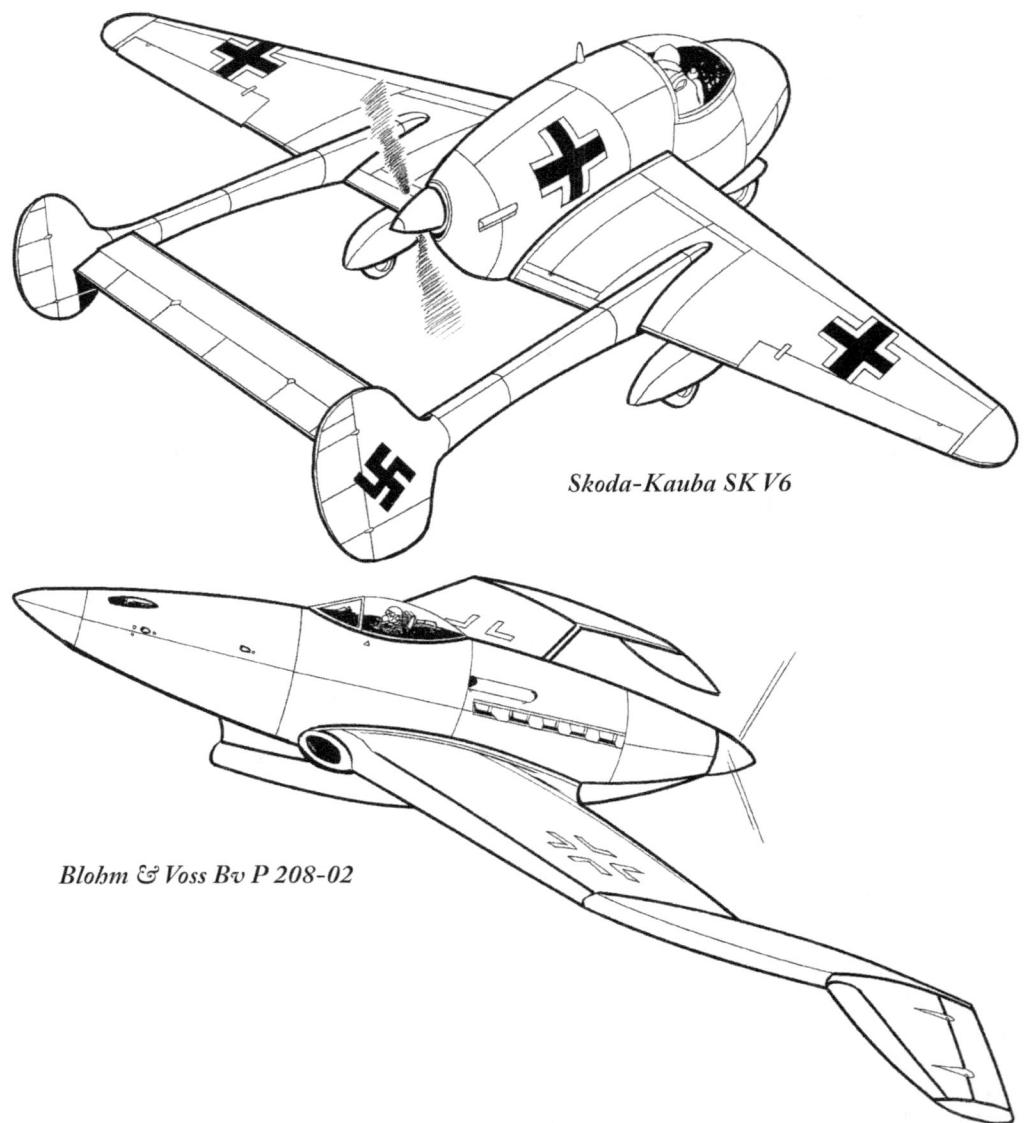

Skoda-Kauba SK V6

Blohm & Voss Bv P 208-02

had a retractable tricycle landing gear, a span of 12 meter, a length of 9.2 meters and an estimated speed of 790 km/h. Projected armament included three MK 108 30-mm cannons.

Blohm & Voss Bv P 208-03

The Bv P 208-03 was the final design. Its total length was 9.2 m (30 ft 2.5 in). A single Daimler Benz 12-cylinder DB 603L engine with a two-stage supercharger (2,100 hp with MW 50 methanol-water injection) was imbedded within the fuselage aft of the cockpit. The engine drove a pusher propeller and was cooled by an air intake mounted beneath the fuselage. Maximum speed was 790 km/h (491 mph). The most striking feature of the P 208 series was the cantilevered wings which had a span of 12.08 m (39 ft 8 in). These were swept back at 30 degrees and were of a constant cross section. Downturned wingtips were connected aft of the main wing trailing edge by small booms, which served the purposes of elevators and rudders. A tricycle undercarriage was used, with the wide-track main wheels retracting into the center section and the nosewheel retracting forward. All armament was in the aircraft's nose, and consisted of three MK 108

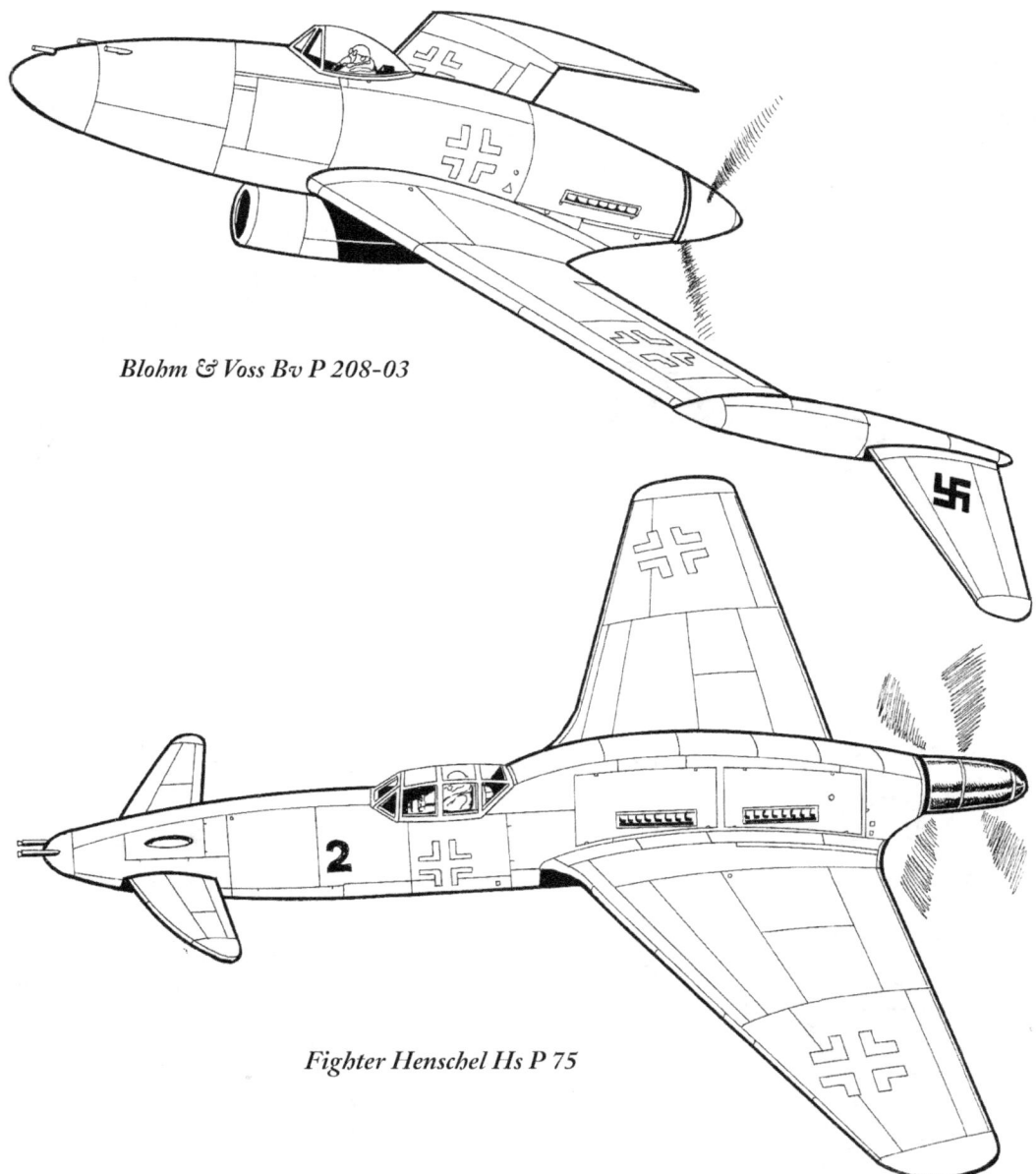

Blohm & Voss Bv P 208-03

Fighter Henschel Hs P 75

30-mm cannon. The Blohm & Voss P 208 series never left the drawing board.

Henschel Hs P 75

Work on the Henschel Hs P 75 design began in 1942. Intended to replace the heavy fighter Messerschmitt Me Bf 110, the Hs P 75 was of "canard" configuration—tail-first design. The main wing was placed at the rear and slightly swept backward. Span was 11.3 m (37 ft 1 in), length was 12.2 m (40 ft) and wing area was 28.4 square m (square 30 ft 5.7 in). The aircraft was powered by two Daimler-Benz DB 605 piston engines joined side by side aft of the cockpit, driving two contra-rotating pusher propellers. Expected speed was 790 km/h (491 mph). The Henschel Hs P 75 had a crew of one. Armament would have included four MK 108 30-mm cannons mounted in the nose. The project P 75 was never realized, but the concept gave birth to two tail-first pro-

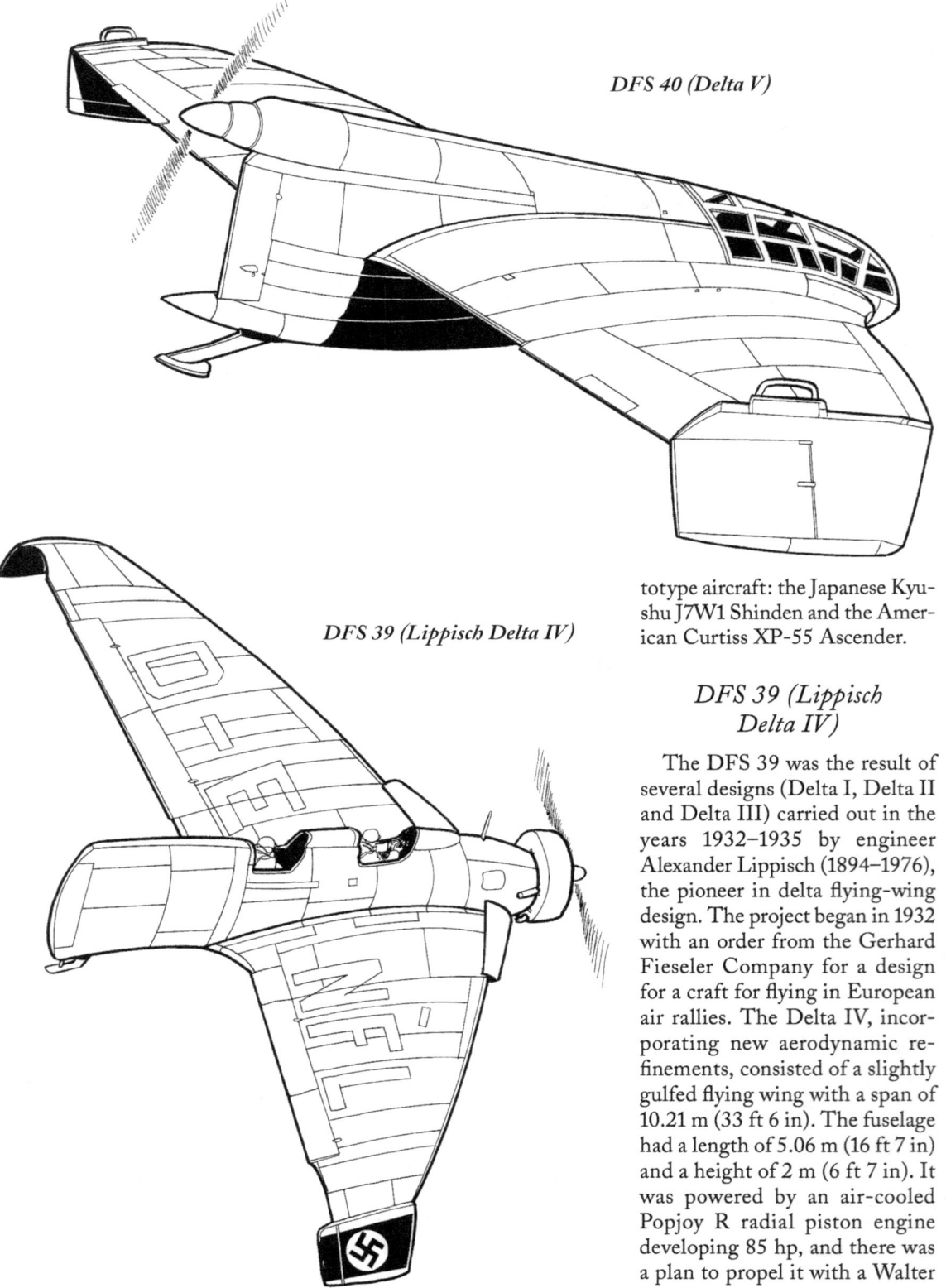

DFS 40 (Delta V)

DFS 39 (Lippisch Delta IV)

totype aircraft: the Japanese Kyushu J7W1 Shinden and the American Curtiss XP-55 Ascender.

DFS 39 (Lippisch Delta IV)

The DFS 39 was the result of several designs (Delta I, Delta II and Delta III) carried out in the years 1932–1935 by engineer Alexander Lippisch (1894–1976), the pioneer in delta flying-wing design. The project began in 1932 with an order from the Gerhard Fieseler Company for a design for a craft for flying in European air rallies. The Delta IV, incorporating new aerodynamic refinements, consisted of a slightly gulfed flying wing with a span of 10.21 m (33 ft 6 in). The fuselage had a length of 5.06 m (16 ft 7 in) and a height of 2 m (6 ft 7 in). It was powered by an air-cooled Popjoy R radial piston engine developing 85 hp, and there was a plan to propel it with a Walter

Payen Pa 22

rocket engine. It had downturned fins fixed on the tips of the wings and a fixed landing gear (two braced wheels and a tail skid). Designed as a sport plane, it had a crew of two placed in open cockpits. The prototype was given the official designation DFS 39 in 1936 after completing intensive testing at the Luftwaffe Flight Testing Center at Rechlin, and was licensed as a two-seater sport aircraft. It proved to be a stable and well-designed aircraft, which attracted the RLM's interest. The Delta IV formed the starting point for a secret scheme designated Project X.

DFS 40 (Delta V) and DFS 194

The Delta V was designed by engineer Lippisch in 1937 as part of the Project X. The DFS 40 was an experimental all-wing aircraft intended to allow comparisons of different versions of tailless aircraft. It was propelled by a 100-hp Argus piston engine located at the back in a "push" arrangement. The aircraft had a span of 12 m (39 ft 4 in), and a length of 5.1 m (16 ft 9 in). It was operated by a single pilot placed in a glazed cockpit at the front. It incorporated futuristic aerodynamic features and was fitted with a retractable landing gear. The DFS 40 was flown for the first time by test pilot Heini Dittmar in 1939. The flight ended with a crash, but the pilot managed to bail out safely.

Next to be completed in Project X was the tailless glider DFS 194 which was powered by rocket booster HWK 203-I. The prototype DFS 194, operated by a single pilot, was flown with success, reaching a speed of 550 km/h. The aircraft attracted the RLM's attention for the development of a high-speed point-defense interceptor. In January 1939, Alexander Lippisch and his team were transferred to Messerschmitt. Research and experiments went on and the Project X/Delta series eventually led to the design of the rocket-powered Messerschmitt Me 163.

Payen Pa 22

Designed by the French engineer Nicolas Payen, a pioneer in the delta-wing configuration, blessed with imagination and energy, this aircraft was designed in 1935 and built in 1939 as a top-speed machine to compete in the Coupe Deutsch de la Meurthe race. The Pa 22 had a large delta wing with a pair of canard wings at the front, a fixed landing gear, and the single-pilot cockpit that was set well back and faired into the tail. It had a span of 4.8 m, a length of 7.48 m, and an empty weight of 560 kg. The aircraft was originally intended to be powered by a ramjet engine, but as this was not available, it was fitted with a 180-hp Regnier R6 piston engine driving a two-bladed propeller. Its speed was 360 km/h and its range was 1,200 km. The Pa 22, still under construction, was captured by the Germans after France's defeat in 1940. A prototype, probably intended to be further developed as a fighter, was built by the Germans, and made its first flight in October 1942. For unknown reasons, the project was discontinued. The Payen Pa 22 was destroyed in 1943 during an Allied air raid.

6

Jet Fighters

Early German jet fighters represented an attempt to use turbojets for propulsion, providing greatly increased speed. Many early jet designs were far from perfect, they resembled their piston-powered counterparts, and their operational lifespans could be measured primarily in hours—at least for the few that were actually built and engaged in front-line actions. Early jet engines were bulky, fragile, and often unreliable. Experiments with jet-propelled aircraft were not a German preserve, they were arrived at virtually simultaneously by the Italians and British, but the Germans had a short lead in advanced aircraft propulsion.

Jet and rocket-powered aircraft were very attractive to the German Air Ministry, for they seemed to offer a realistic possibility of being able to threaten the high-flying Allied heavy bombers which by 1944 were decimating Germany's industrial base. This was particularly true since rocket-propelled aircraft did not require fossil fuel, which was in very short supply, and they could be manufactured cheaply, largely from plywood. Considerable efforts were deployed to develop such new aircraft, but fortunately these achievements came to nothing owing to bad organization and lack of vision at the top. A majority of projects fell by the wayside, some due to lack of time and resources, others because they were flawed, others because they were too fanciful, far-fetched and extravagant. Had the Nazi authorities decided to concentrate on only a few types, they would surely have completed some of them in time. The depressing picture of missed opportunities is further highlighted by the history of German rocket -and jet-powered fighters. The Germans suffered from an excess of projects in development. If designs—both useful and extravagant—proliferated, only a very small number were built and used, and then their deployment came too late in the war to be effective. A typical example of this uncoordinated development is shown by the so-called *Volksjäger* (People's Fighter) program which was launched by the German Air Ministry on September 8, 1944. Due to the rapidly deteriorating war conditions in Germany in the last months of World War II, this scheme ordered the design of a fighter that would use a minimum of strategic materials, be suitable for rapid mass production and have a performance at least equal to the best piston-engined fighters of the time. The People's Fighter was almost a disposable weapon which was to be operated by barely trained personnel. It needed to weigh no more than 2,000 kg (4,410 lbs), have a maximum speed of 750 km/h (457 mph), a minimum endurance of 30 minutes, a take-off distance of 500 m (1,604 ft), and it was to use the BMW 003 turbojet engine. These requirements were issued to Arado, Blohm & Voss, Fieseler, Focke-Wulf, Junkers, Heinkel, Messerschmitt and Siebel. These companies made various designs but only one *Volksjäger* ever got underway: the Heinkel He 162 Salamander. In November 1944, another RLM call was issued for a very simple, rapidly produced small fighter aircraft. This *Miniaturjäger* (Midget Fighter) program was to use the simplest and cheapest powerplant available, and to require the minimum of strategic materials and practically no electrical equipment. The motive power chosen was to be the Argus As 014 pulse jet, and the *Miniaturjäger* was to take off and land conventionally. The plan was to build large numbers of these aircraft, and thus simply overwhelm the enemy bomber formations with their numbers. Only three firms participated in this design competition, Heinkel (with a pulse-jet-powered He 162 airframe), Junkers (with their Ju EF 126 project) and Blohm & Voss (with the Bv P 213). The whole *Miniaturjäger* program was canceled in December 1944.

So desperate was the situation in Germany by the summer of 1944 that individual fighter pilots had taken to ramming Allied bombers. Special units such as IV/JG3 and TI/JG300 were formed as *Sturmgruppen* (assault groups organized by Major Hans-Günter von Kornatzki and Major Erwin Bacsila) with suicidal ramming as an accepted fallback tactic. Using the Focke-Wulf Fw 190A fitted with frontal armor, they had a measure of success: between 7 July 1944 and the end of March 1945, when they ceased to operate, they accounted for the destruction of around 500 Allied bombers, but only ten of them by ramming. In April 1945, *Sonderkommando* (Special Commando) *Elbe* was formed from volunteers; they trained for ten days in ramming tactics, and then went into action. In all, they rammed and downed eight Allied bombers, but at a high cost to themselves: a total of 77 Bf 109s and Fw 190s. If such potentially self-sacrificial *Selbstopfermänner* (Suicide Men) tactics were to be employed, then clearly a much less sophisticated aircraft, using little in the way of strategic materials, could be employed instead of some of the best piston-engined fighters of the entire period, so several manufacturers made rammer designs. It was never the stated intention to require or even ask aircrew to commit suicide in Germany in the way that it was in Japanese kamikaze scheme, and great pains were taken to maintain that the very reverse was actually the case. The *Selbstopfermänner* were expected only to employ their aircraft as weapons in the last resort (though volunteers to the *Sturmgruppen* were required to take an oath that they would indeed do this if necessary), and to make every effort to ensure that the attack left them with the possibility of escape. The possibilities of this happening were remote, and it must be concluded that there was a secret agenda, and that the men concerned knew exactly what they were being called upon to do, and that the disclaimers were there only for public-relations purposes. The contract signed and sworn by the volunteers of the *Sturmgruppen* stipulated that all attacks were to be carried out within the closest possible range of the enemy; that losses suffered during the approach were to be compensated for by immediate closing up on the unit leader; and that the enemy was to be shot down at close range or, if this was unsuccessful, destroyed by ramming.

Jet- and rocket-propelled aircraft possess significant advantages over conventional types. In level flight, dive, speed, and rate of climb, all known, conventional, piston-engine aircraft were generally surpassed by jet-powered machines. Their tactics were based on the use of speed to escape anti-aircraft fire and air interception. But their main asset, high speed, also had the disadvantage of giving pilots very little time to aim and fire when attacking a slow target.

Jet fighters, midget aircraft, ramming aircraft, jet bombers, flying bombs (V1), and ballistic rockets (V2) were Hitler's "secret weapons." In the dictator's mind these were to quickly change the situation, break the domination of the Allies in the German sky, and—used in offensive operations—destroy their cities, causing both civilian and military collapse, and ultimately winning the war. There is no doubt that if produced earlier in sufficient numbers, German jet fighters could have wrested command of the air from the Allies. It is interesting to see that the "military genius" Adolf Hitler, whose strategic skill was so much admired, at least in the opening phase of World War II, was also capable of making crude mistakes. At the same time, it is frightening to contemplate what might have happened had Hitler pushed scientific achievements with fanatic zeal and with all the resources of the Nazi state. Had he marshaled the scientific talent at his disposal, he might have won the war. Unfortunately for Hitler and luckily for the Allies, the importance of the jet fighter was not realized until it was too late to make any difference. The story of "too little, too late" applied to all of Hitler's secret weapons, even to those which were actually built and used, such as the formidable Messerschmitt Me 262. Hitler and Göring had counted on their revolutionary jet fighters driving the Anglo-American air forces from the skies, and well they might have, had the Allied not taken successful countermeasures right on time. The conventional Allied fighter and bomber were no match for the German jets in the air, but few ever got off the ground. The refineries producing the special fuel for them were located, bombed and destroyed, and most of the hopelessly grounded jets were bombed and destroyed on their airfields.

Many German jet designs were outstanding achievements and some of them certainly opened a new dimension of air warfare. Jet designs of 1945 were a far cry from fighters of 1935. Innovations and new technologies, including swept wings, delta-wing layouts, "wing-only" designs, ejector seats, and all-moving tailplanes, were introduced in that period. Knowledge and techniques acquired during the latter part of World War II were the inspiration for the first generation of subsonic rocket- and jet-powered aircraft in the late 1940s and early 1950s, such as the American Bell P-59 Aircobra, McDonnell FH-1 Phantom, Lockheed XP 80A Shooting Star, and North American F-86 A Sabre; the British Gloster Meteor and de Havilland Vampire; the Swedish SAAB 21-R and SAAB 29-F; the French Dassault Mystère IV; and the Russian Berezniak-Isaev Bi-1 and Mikoyan-Gurevich Mig-15 and Mig-17, just to name a few.

Rocket-Powered Aircraft

Heinkel He 176

The He 176 was to be the first aircraft in history to fly using only liquid-fueled rocket power. Design work was begun in late 1936, with detailed engineering drawings being completed around July 1937. Construction of the prototype began at the same time. All design work for the Heinkel He 176 was done in Sonderentwicklung I, a department that was kept isolated from the remainder of the Heinkel factory at Rostock-Marienehe. The main designers of the He 176 were Walter Künzel (project leader/engine installation), Walter Günter (aerodynamics), Adolf Jensen (aerodynamics/flight mechanics), and H. Bosch (loading and stress analysis). The He 176 featured a circular cross-section fuselage with the diameter being barely large enough for a pilot to be seated in a reclining position. The stubby wings, which were really little more than control surfaces, had an elliptical form with a straight leading edge, and featured positive dihedral. Behind the cockpit were located the fuel tanks (methanol and super hydrogen oxide) and the Walter HWK R1 liquid-propellant rocket engine. A tail-dragger-type retractable landing gear was chosen with a fixed-nose wheel added for taxi and towing trials. The extensive cockpit glazing provided an excellent view, and in an emergency the entire forward cockpit section could be jettisoned via an explosive charge, after which a braking parachute enabled the pilot to bail out. The Heinkel He 176 had a wingspan of 4 m (13 ft 1 in), a length of 5.2 m (17 ft 1 in), a height of 1.50 m (4 ft 11 in), a wing area of 5.5 square m (59.2 square ft), and a weight (empty) of 1,570 kg (3,462 lbs). Theorical speed was to be 750 km/h (466 mph) and maximum range was 110 km (68 miles). In July 1938 the He 176 was tested at the large wind tunnel at Göttingen. Although the He 176 program was begun at the Heinkel factory at Rostock-Marienehe, the completed prototype was soon moved to Peenemünde, where better secrecy could be maintained. Tests were conducted, and the first short air hops took place in March 1939 under rocket power. The first official flight of the Heinkel He 176 V1 was on June 20, 1939 flown by *Flugkapitän* Erich Warsitz. On the next day, June 21, the He 176 was demonstrated in front of some of the RLM leaders (including Ernst Udet and Erhard Milch). Udet was not impressed, and prohibited further tests due to the inherent dangers of rocket flight. This ban was twice lifted and twice issued again until July 3, 1939, when another demonstration was arranged at Roggentin for Adolf Hitler

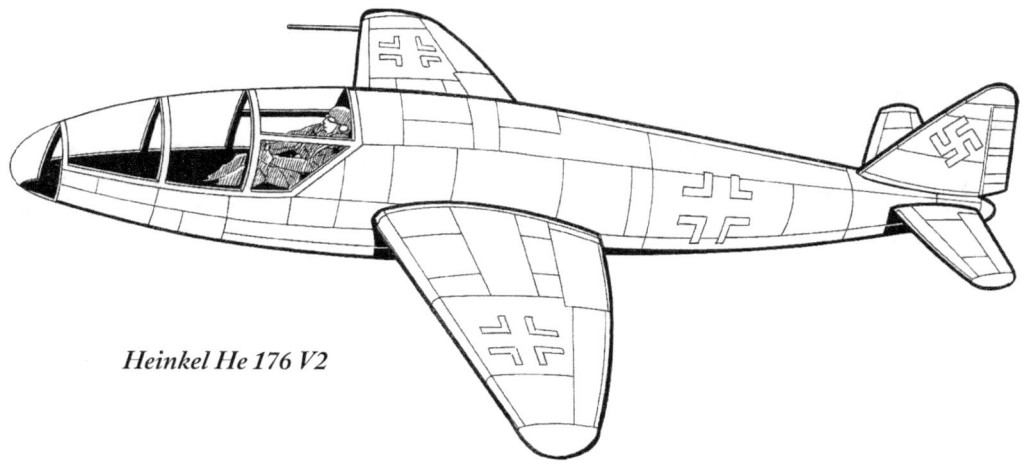

Heinkel He 176 V2

himself and more of the Third Reich leadership. An official order was issued in September 1939 terminating any further work on the He 176 project. The prototype aircraft stayed under wraps for years at the Heinkel factory at Rostock-Marienehe, but was eventually crated up and sent to the Air Museum in Berlin, where it was destroyed in an air raid in 1944.

Lippisch Li P 01 Series

The Li P 01 single-seat fighter series was designed by engineer Alexander Lippisch, a glider designer who had joined Willy Messerschmitt's firm in 1939. All aircraft had a common configuration, namely that of a tailless upper or mid-mounted swept wing, and all fitted with skid undercarriage with pilot in both sitting and prone position. The mode of propulsion varied, including rocket, ram and turbojet engines, as well as hybrid powerplants. The series included the following planned models: the Li P 01-106, designed in April 1939; the P 01-111, designed in October 1939; the P 01-112, designed in February 1940; the P 01-113, designed in July 1940; the P 01-114,

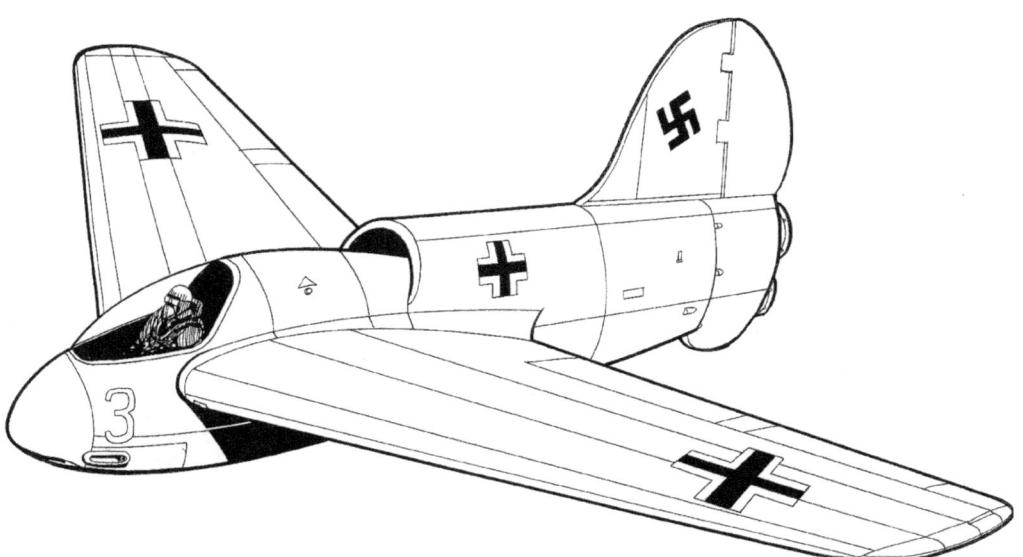

Lippisch Li P 01-115. The Li P 01-115 had a span of 9 m (29 ft 6 in), a length of 6.75 m (22 ft 2 in) and a wing area of 18 square m (192 square feet). The dorsal air intake fed a BMW P 3302 turbojet engine, and additional power was provided by a 1,500-kp Walter HKW rocket engine.

designed in July 1940; the P 01-115, designed in July 1941; two versions of the P 01-116, designed in June 1941; the P 01-117, designed in July 1941; the P 01-118, designed in August 1941; and the P 01-119, designed in Augustus 1941. The Li P 01 series obviously turned toward the layout adopted for the Messerschmitt Me 163.

Messerschmitt Me 163 Komet

The Me 163 *Komet* (Comet) was one of the most radical and futuristic aircrafts to see service in World War II. Designed by engineer Alexander Lippisch, it was based on the concept of the short-endurance local-defense interceptor powered by a rocket engine. The *Komet* stemmed from the DFS 39, the DFS 194 rocket-powered aircraft tested before the war, and the Lippisch P 01 series, and finally the project turned into a combat aircraft. Some ten unarmed prototypes, known as Me 163 A (V4 to V13) were built by Messerschmitt; some were powered by the Walter HKW rocket engine, other were just gliders intended to train pilots. In August 1941 Lippisch put forth an alternative proposal, powered by three HKW rocket engines; this aircraft, known as the Li P 05, was unsatisfactory because of its short endurance. First flown on October 2, 1941, by test pilot Heini Dittmar, the operational and slightly modified Me 163 B had a dramatically unconventional form with no horizontail tail surfaces, and a short bat-like fuselage. The pilot sat in a pressurized cockpit in the nose with a bubble canopy, providing visibility in all directions. Wingspan was 9.3 m (30 ft 7 in), length was 5.69 m (18 ft 8 in), and height was 2.74 m (9 ft). Propelled by a Walter HWK 509 A2 rocket engine burning concentrated hydrogen peroxide (T-Stoff) and hydrazine/methanol (C-Stoff) with a thrust of 1,700 kg (3,750 lbs), it had a tremendous speed of 960 km/h (596 mph). The interceptor took off from a droppable two-wheeled trolley and landed on a sprung skid. It could climb steeply to an altitude of 30,000 ft in just over 2.5 minutes, but the engine consumed fuel at such a fantastic rate that it had a very short range, not exceeding 100 km (62 miles), only about ten minutes of flight. It was armed with two 30-mm MK 108 cannons in wing roots, each with sixty rounds, and later units also had twenty-four R4M rockets. Development of the *Komet* went slow and had been delayed by strife between Lippisch and Messerschmitt.

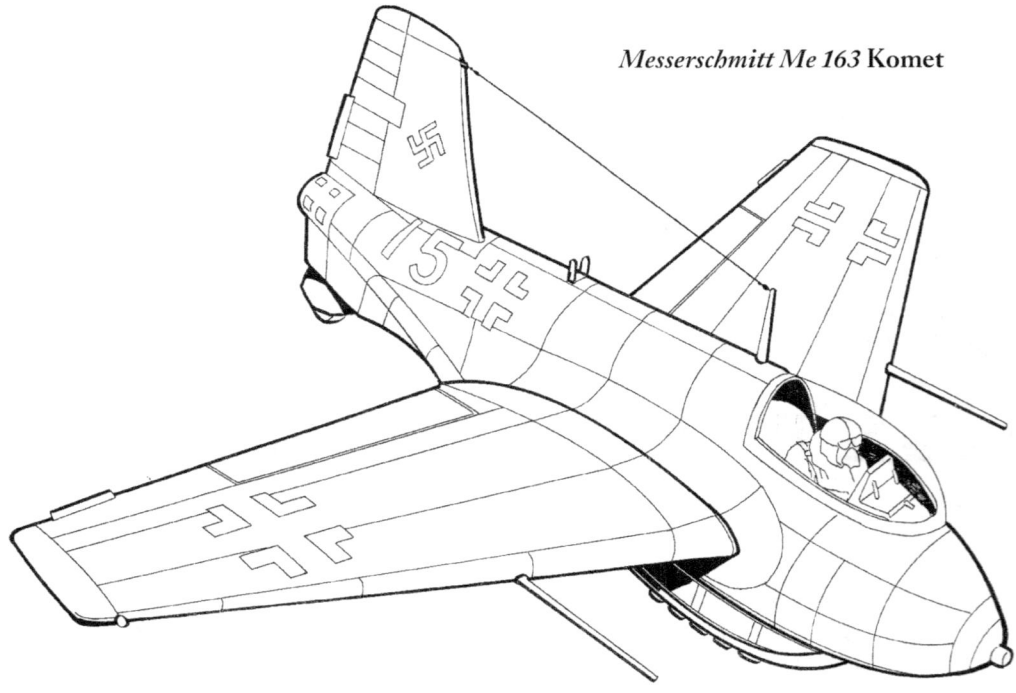

Messerschmitt Me 163 **Komet**

About 370 Me 163 *Komets* were built, and preceded the twin jet-propelled Messerschmitt Me 262 into service by a little over two months. A few of them—flown by a special units known as I/JG 400—were engaged against a U.S. bomber in May 1944. Agile, extremely fast, and difficult to hit in the air, the Me 163 was a remarkable and futuristic airplane in the sky, credited with having downed twelve US B-17s. It was also a great disappointment. The hardest part of the mission was getting back to base alive. The *Komet* was indeed a very dangerous plane on the ground both to the pilots and ground crews. Numerous accidents and casualties were caused by violent explosion on landing, when residual highly corrosive, unstable and reactive rocket propellants sometimes sloshed together as the skid hit the ground. Others exploded on take-off by bouncing into the ground. The engine tended also to cut out as the airplane leveled off from a climb. The extraordinary Me 163, an aircraft of last resort, earned a grim reputation for killing more of its own pilots than Allies.

There existed variants; the Me 163 C had a slightly different engine; the Me 163, D was fitted with a tricycle landing gear and had fuselage length increased from 5.69 m to 8.82 m (announcing the Me 263); and the Lippisch/Messerschmitt 163 S was a training version with enlarged cockpit for pupil and training officer. There was also a non-piloted version of the Me 163 rocket fighter. Known as Messerschmitt *Enzian* (Gentian Violet), this was a radio-guided surface-to-air anti-aircraft missile mainly made of wood. *Enzian* existed in several versions (none of which ever was close to production), and could have carried a 25-kg (55-lb) warhead at a speed of 756 km/h (416 mph) to a maximum ceiling of 10 km (32,800 ft).

The Messerschmitt Me 163 was also the inspiration for the Japanese Mitsubishi J7M1 *Shusui* (Rigorous Sword) or *Ki* 200.

Messerschmitt Me 263

Based on the Me 163 D, the fast interceptor Me 263 was an improved version of the Messerschmitt/Lippisch Me 163 *Komet*. Fitted with a proper retractable landing gear, and a more aerodynamic fuselage, it had a length of 7.88 m (25 ft 10.5 in), a span of 9.50 m (31 ft 2 in) and an empty weight of 2,105 kg (4,640 lbs). Powered by a Walter HWK 109-509C 4 rocket engine with a cruising chamber, it was intended to have a maximum speed of 1,000 km/h (620 mph), a range of 220 km and a maximum endurance of one hour, including fifteen minutes under power. The aircraft could climb to 14,000 meters in only three minutes. Planned armament was two MK 108 cannons mounted in the wing roots. In order to relieve the Messerschmitt company, the Me 263 program was transferred to Junkers in spring of 1944, and ran under the designation Ju 248. Junkers introduced several improvements, namely a circular fuselage, larger trailing-edge flaps and automatic wing nose flaps, pressurized cockpit, and a more powerful rocket engine. After a lot of development work, an unpowered glider prototype with fixed landing gear made a first flight in August 1944. In February 1945 the Ju 248 reverted to Messerschmitt, and engineer Lippisch designed a highly experimental version with swivel wings, in which the outer wings could be made movable. Due to the chaotic situation that prevailed in Germany in early 1945, the promising Me 263/Ju 248 scheme was never completed. The Russians made a

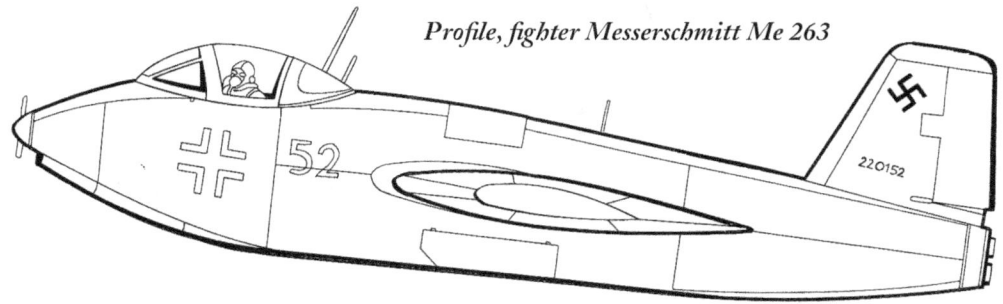

Profile, fighter Messerschmitt Me 263

Interceptor Messerschmitt Me 263

brief further development of the aircraft right after the war.

Von Braun VTO Interceptor

Designed in July 1939 by Professor Wernher von Braun, this aircraft was intended as a VTO (vertical take-off) fast interceptor. It had a conventional layout, a cigar-shaped fuselage with a length of 9.3 m (30 ft 6 in), and low-mounted wings with a span of 8.5 m (27 ft 10 in). The single pilot sat in a pressurized cockpit placed at the front. The aircraft was to be armed with two or four cannons mounted in the wing roots, and powered by a rocket engine, giving a tremendous speed of 700 km/h (435 mph) but only a very short endurance of fifteen minutes. The rocket engine consisted of an A3 missile powerplant burning A-Stoff (liquid oxygen) and M-Stoff (methyl alcohol),

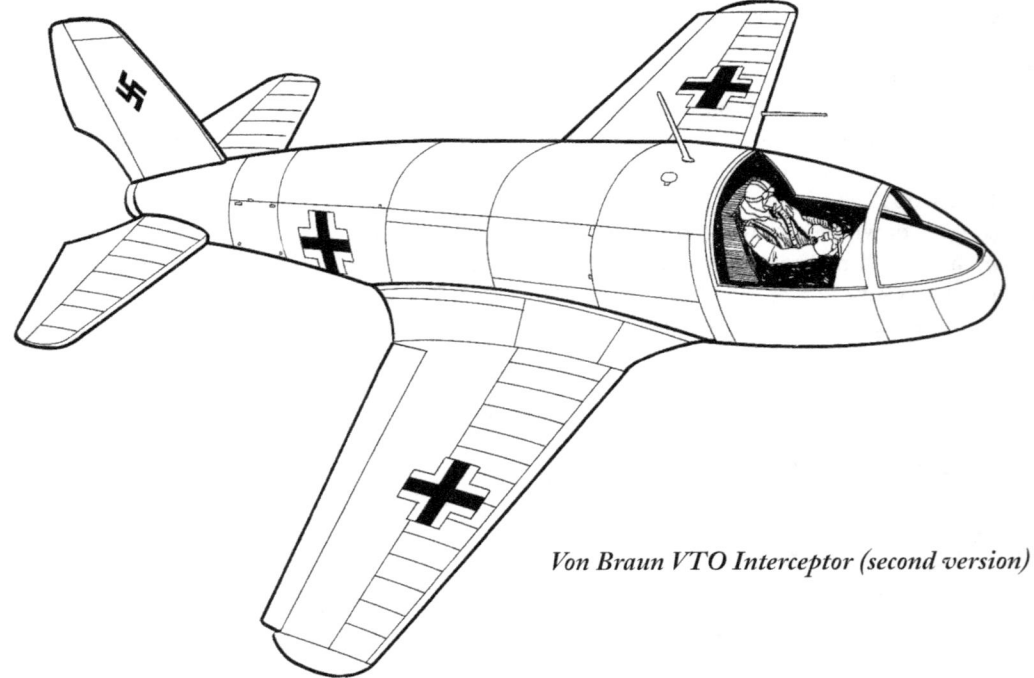

Von Braun VTO Interceptor (second version)

pressure being provided by a nitrogen supply. It was thus a pinpoint interceptor which took off vertically, being launched on two parallel rails. When targets had been detected and identified by radar, the interceptor's optimal flightpath would be calculated by a control center; the fighter would be steered automatically to an altitude of about 8,000 meters; at this point the pilot would take over control, start the aircraft's rocket engine and attack. After attack the plane would go on as a glider and make a skid landing at its home airfield. Two slightly similar versions were planned which differed only by the cockpit arrangement. Although the project was handed over to the Fieseler Company, which in 1941 drew up similar designs known as Fi 166, the von Braun interceptor was not developed. Proposed at a time when the Luftwaffe was preparing for short aggressive *Blitzkrieg*, the defensive design by von Braun was rejected by the Reichsluftfahrtministerium on the grounds that it was "unnecessary and unworkable." The concept was soon dropped, only to be revived several years later by engineer Erich Bachem.

Bachem Ba 349 Natter

Dr. Erich Bachem's Ba 349 *Natter* (Viper) was the world's first manned, vertical take-off, semi-expendable point interceptor. The aircraft was a daring and imaginative solution to a desperate problem but World War II ended before this expedient weapon saw combat.

Bachem, technical director of the Fieseler Company, thought that von Baun's VTO rocket interceptor had merit. At the start of 1944, the Allied bombing offensive began taking a serious toll on the German war machine. None of the conventional methods employed by the Luftwaffe to intercept the bombers seemed to work, so the service began to explore unconventional means. Bachem sought the support of Reichsführer Heinrich Himmler, head of the SS (Nazi Party security forces) who by then had control over all secret weapons. Himmler liked Bachem's proposal for a fast cheap interceptor and signed an order to build 150 *Natter* aircraft using SS funds. Bachem's design was easy to build with cheap plywood, and simple enough to be manufactured in a carpentry workshop. Semi-skilled labor could construct one in about 1,000 hours. The wings were plain rectangular wooden slabs without ailerons, flaps, or other control devices. The cruciform tail consisted of four fins and control surfaces. Bachem's *Natter* was powered by a Walter 109-509A rocket motor. Two liquid fuels combined inside the motor to generate thrust. When T-Stoff (a highly caustic solution of hydrogen peroxide and a stabilizing chemical) mixed with C-Stoff (a hydrazine hydrate/methanol/water mixture), combustion was spontaneous, so extreme care was required to handle both chemicals. The Walter motor generated about 1,700 kg (3,740 lbs) of thrust, but a loaded Ba 349A weighed more than 1,818 kg (4,000 lbs) so lift-off required more power.

Bachem Ba 349 **Natter**

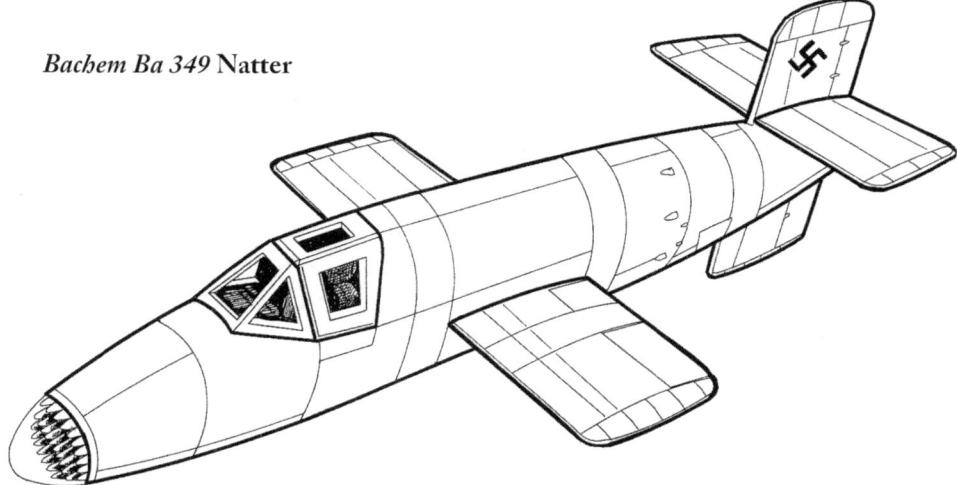

Bachem got the extra thrust from four Schmidding 109-533 solid-fuel rocket motors that he bolted to the aft fuselage, two per side. Each motor produced 500 kg (1,100 lbs) of thrust. At lift-off, all five motors ignited, generating about 3,700 kg (8,140 lbs) of thrust.

Operating the *Natter* required a pilot with nerves of steel. After being launched vertically from a platform (or launched from a mother aircraft, e.g., a Heinkel He 111), the *Natter* climbed on autopilot, even with an Allied bomber formation. Then the airman (by now, it was hoped, having regained consciousness after blacking out under the forces generated at take-off) took over control, steering his machine in close. At a range of about 1.6 to 3.2 kilometers (1–2 miles) from the bomber formation, the pilot jettisoned the nose cone and fired all twenty-four Henschel Hs 217 Föhn 7.3-cm (or R4M 5.5-cm) unguided rockets. By then, rocket fuel would be nearly exhausted, so the machine began to descend. At about 1,400 m (4,500 ft), the pilot released his seat harness and fired a ring of explosive bolts to blow off the entire nose section. A parachute simultaneously deployed from the rear fuselage and the sudden deceleration literally threw him from his seat. The airman activated his own parachute after waiting a safe interval to clear the bits of falling aircraft. Ground crews were to recover the Walter motor to use again, but the airframe was now scrap. Bachem set up a factory to design and build his interceptor at Waldsee in the Black Forest. By November 1944, the first Natter was ready for tests, and on December 22, the aircraft made its first successful launch with solid-fuel boosters. With the end of the war near in March 1945, the Germans erected a battery of ten Natters at Kircheim near Stuttgart. Pilots stood alert day after day but fortunately for them no Allied bombers flew into range. It is safe to assume that the dangerous and even suicidal Bachem Ba 349A Natter, little more than a piloted surface-to-air missile, was a bad and crazy idea from the start, and as a bomber interceptor it probably would have been a total failure.

Zeppelin Rammer

The Zeppelin Rammer, also known as *Fliegende Panzerfaust* (Flying Iron Fist), was a another suicidal, last-resort weapon. Designed in November 1944, it existed in two similar

Zeppelin Rammer

versions, consisting of a small attack aircraft with a length of 5.1 m (16 ft 8.9 in) and a span of 4.9 m (16 ft 1 in). Operated by a single pilot, the Rammer took off and flew to operational altitude towed by an aircraft (e.g., a Messerschmitt Bf 109). In the vicinity of the target (obviously a formation of Allied heavy bombers), it was released, a solid-fuel Schmidding rocket engine was ignited, and—with an optimistic estimated speed of 970 km/h (602 mph)—the aircraft would fire its fourteen R4M air-to-air rockets mounted in the nose. A second attack was planned, this time by ramming the tail of an Allied bomber with wings made of high-strength materials. If the aircraft and the pilot survived this quasi-suicide attack, landing was done on a retractable skid mounted under the fore fuselage; the pilot was ordered to choose a convenient piece of open ground so that the machine could be recovered and reused. The Zeppelin Rammer never received an RLM designation, which is an indication that it was probably not taken entirely seriously. Indeed, this Kamikaze-like scheme was never developed.

Blohm & Voss Bv 40

Designed in 1944 by Blohm & Voss technical director Richard Vogt, the Bv 40 was the simplest and cheapest single-seat interceptor glider. Using no fuel, a minimum of raw materials, requiring few skilled hours for assembly, and operated by pilots hastily trained only to a basic standard, the Bv 40 was a desperate improvisation which had a certain attraction when Nazi Germany found herself in a critical situation. The cockpit was heavily armored and the attack glider was very small in order to reduce the chances of being hit by the hail of fire from B-17 and B-24 formations. It had a length of 5.70 m (18 ft 8.5 in), a span of 7.90 m (25 ft 11 in), and an empty weight of 836 kg (1,844 lbs). The cheap Bv 40 was to be towed by a standard fighter (e.g., Messerschmitt Bf 109), it took off with a jettisonable landing gear/trolley, and was flown to operational altitude in the vicinity of the targets. Then it was released and made a head-on diving attack at Allied bomber formations, firing with its two 30-mm MK 108 cannons (each with 35 rounds) with an anticipated (and probably overoptimistic) dive speed of 900 km/h (560 mph). Finally it was to glide down and away to safety and land on a skid mounted under the fuselage front. Six prototypes were built which underwent tests and flight trials in May 1944, but development was overtaken by lightweight, rocket-powered fighters.

Heinkel He P 1077 Julia

Started in the summer of 1944, the P 1077 Julia was a rocket-propelled, single-pilot fighter.

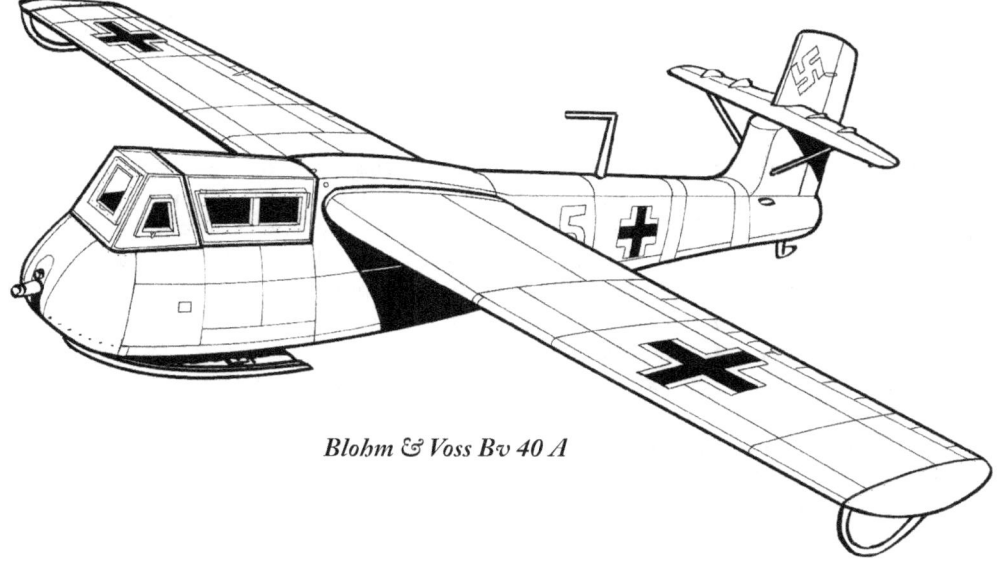

Blohm & Voss Bv 40 A

Heinkel He P 1077 Julia

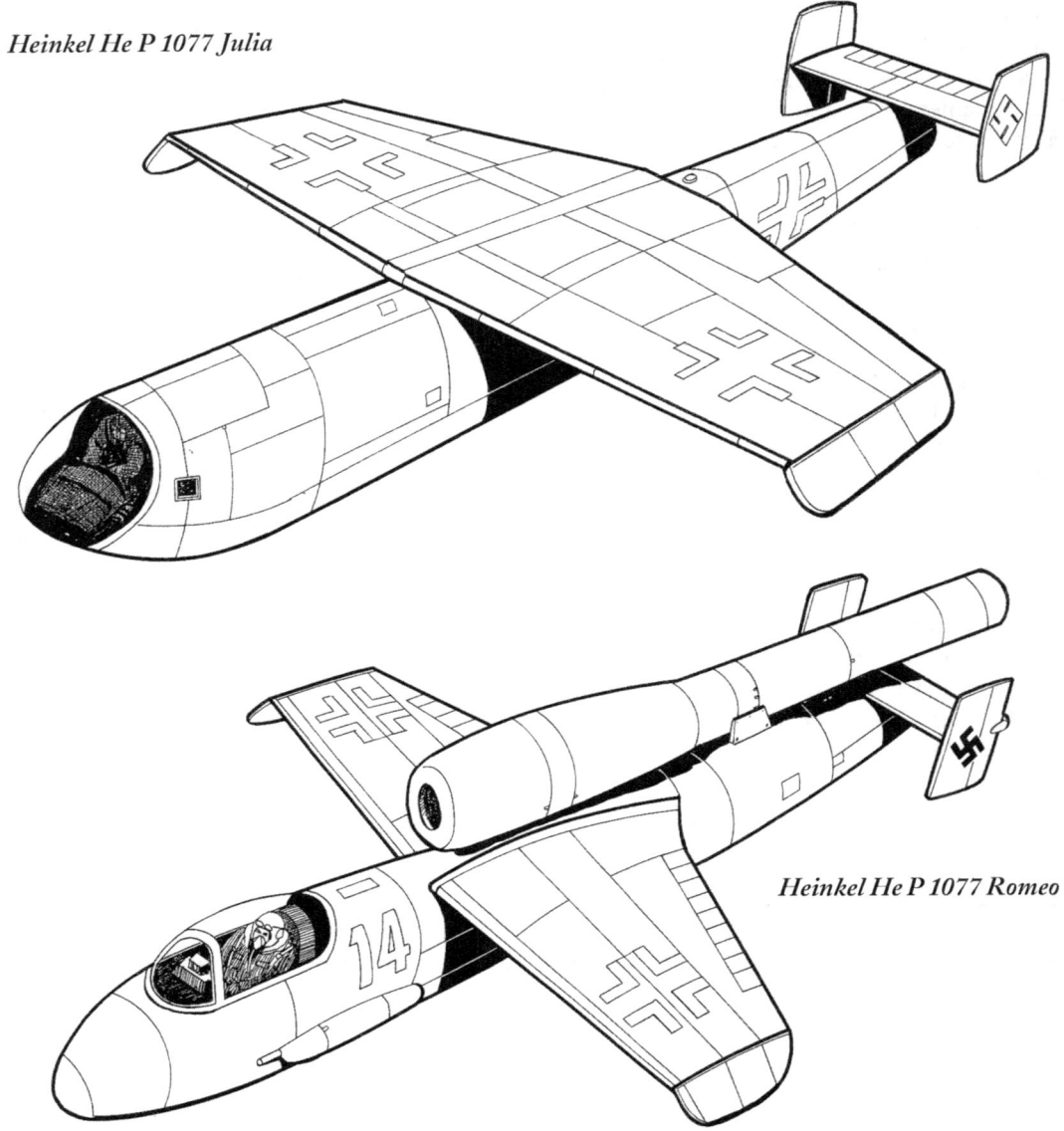

Heinkel He P 1077 Romeo

The fuselage was circular in cross-section with a length of 6.8 m (22 ft 3.9 in). The shoulder-mounted straight wing had a short span of 4.6 m (15 ft 1 in). The pilot lay in the prone position in the cockpit at the front. Julia was powered by a Walter HWK 109-509 rocket engine, and was expected to have a maximum speed of 900 km/h (559 mph). The aircraft was not provided with a landing gear; take-off was to be made vertically, assisted by four solid-fuel rockets, while landing was to be done on a skid. Armament would have consisted of two MK 108 30-mm cannons located on the sides of the fore fuselage. There was a second version of the He P 1077, known as Julia II, with the pilot seated in an upright position. A third variant, known as He P 1077 Romeo, was to be powered by a pulse-jet engine mounted on top of the fuselage, the pilot seating in a conventional upright position. None of these projects were ever completed, as mock-up models, plans and components were destroyed in an air raid at the end of 1944. Two unpowered nearly completed prototypes were discovered when the Heinkel plant was overrun by Soviet troops at the end of the war.

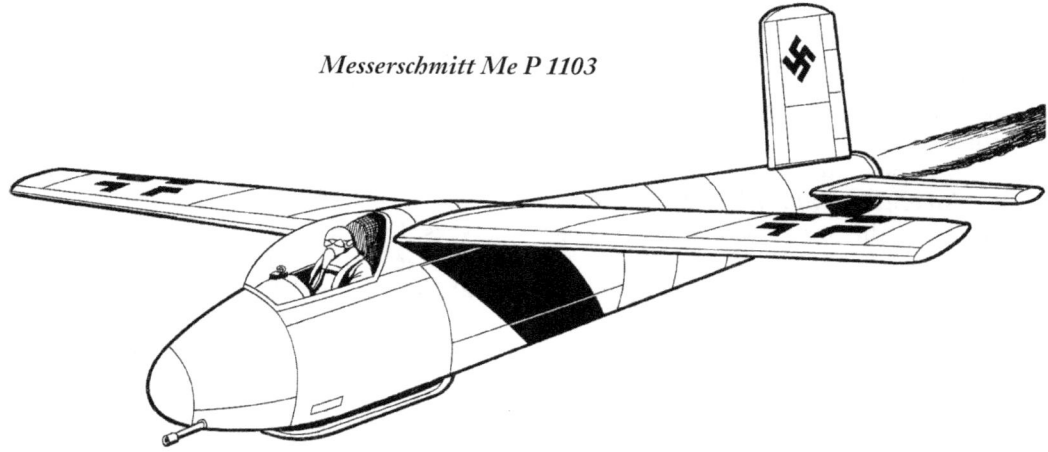

Messerschmitt Me P 1103

Messerschmitt Me P 1103 and Me P 1104

Designed in the summer of 1944, the Me P 1103, Me P 1104 and their variants were small *Bordjäger* launched from a mother aircraft. Cheap, made of wood, piloted by a single airman (sitting upright or in prone position), they were to be powered by various rocket engines, either four Schmidding 109-513, one Walter HKW Ri-202, or a Walter HKW 109-509 A-2. Maximum speed would have been between 840 and 930 km/h. Similar in appearance, they had a typical span of 5.38 meters, an average length of 5 meters, a height of 1.75 meters and a weight of 1.110 kg. They landed on a skid, though some models would have been fitted with two small, retractable, narrow-track main wheels and a nose skid. Planned armament would have consisted of an unknown number of MK 108 cannons or a Würfkorper 28/32-cm rocket launcher. Further work on this scheme was abandoned when it was decided to develop the Bachem Ba 349 Natter.

Messerschmitt Me P 1106 R

A variant of the Me P 1106 series, the interceptor Me P 1106 rocket was designed in December 1944. It was intended to be launched from a mother aircraft and landed on a retractable tricycle landing gear. It was powered by a Walter HKW 109-509 S2 rocket engine developing 2,000 kp thrust (the same one used in the Me 163 *Komet*), in place of the standard turbojet. It was expected to have a speed in the

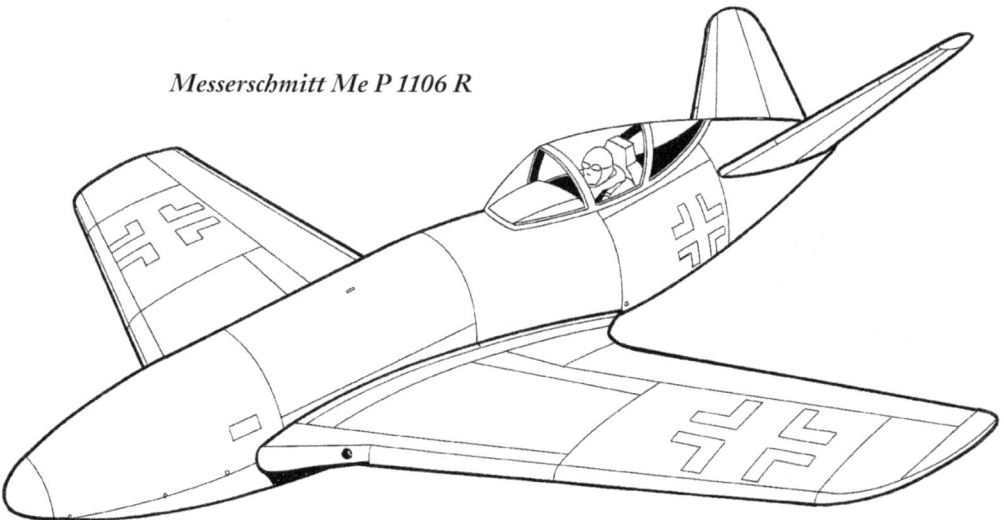

Messerschmitt Me P 1106 R

supersonic region, but an endurance of only twelve minutes. Span was 6.74 m, length was 8.42 m, height was 3.05 m and wing area was 13 square m. The disastrous situation of Germany in 1945 did not allow this scheme to go further than the drawing board. Ultimately it was the American-made Bell X-1, piloted by Chuck Yeager, that made history by breaking Mach 1 on October 14, 1947.

Focke-Wulf Volksjäger

Launched by the RLM, the *Volksjäger* series was a program aiming to design cheap and lightweight fighters which could be mass-produced and engaged against Allied heavy bombers. Arado designed the Ar E 580; Blohm & Voss, the Bv P 210, Bv P 211-01 and -02; Junkers, the Ju EF 123; and Heinkel, the He P 1073 and He 162. Designed in September 1944, Focke-Wulf's response was two prototypes. *Volksjäger* 1 was a modern, small, single-seat jet aircraft with a span of 7.5 m (26 ft 7 in) and a length of 8.8 m (28 ft 9 in). The Focke-Wulf *Volksjäger* 1 was powered by a single BMW 003 A1 jet engine fed by front air-intake and would have had a maximum speed of 820 km/h (509 mph). The planned arma-

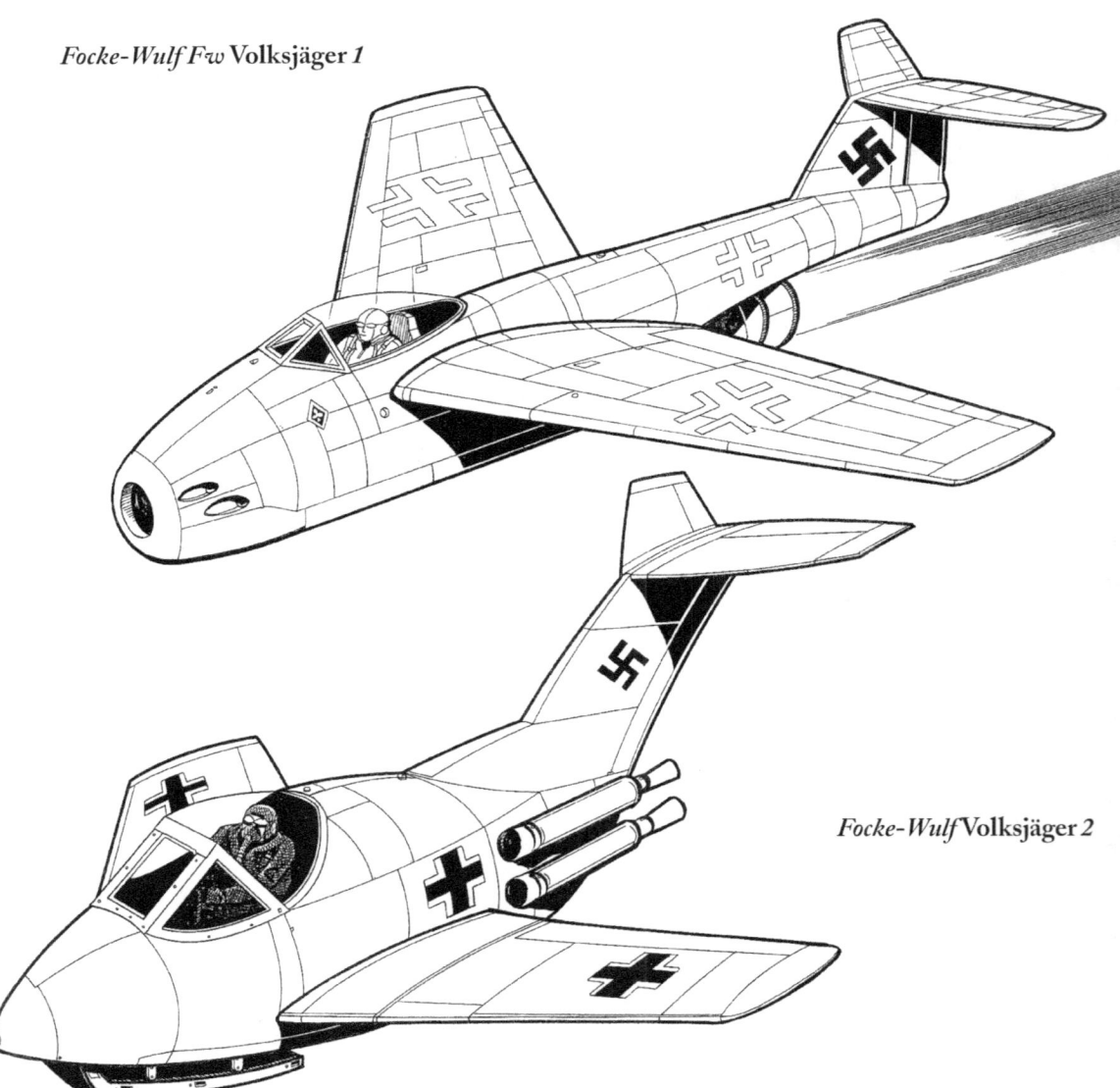

Focke-Wulf Fw Volksjäger *1*

Focke-Wulf Volksjäger *2*

ment would have included two MK 108 30-mm cannons placed in the nose.

The Focke-Wulf *Volksjäger* 2 was a small interceptor fighter with a fuselage length of 5.3 m (17 ft 5 in) and its mid-fuselage-mounted wing had a span of 4.8 m (15 ft 9 in). Built mostly with wood, the aircraft was very light and fast. Powered by a Walter HWK 109-509 A2 rocket engine, it had a maximum speed of 1,000 km/h (621 mph), and could reach an altitude of 5,900 m (19,400 ft) in one minute, but its endurance was short: just fifteen minutes. The *Volksjäger* would have been armed with two MK 108 30-mm cannons. It was to take off on a detachable dolly and land using a ventral skid. Three *Volksjäger* 2 craft were under construction when World War II came to its end.

Of all the *Volksjäger* designs, only the Heinkel He 162 Salamander was produced.

Sombold So 244

Designed by engineer Heinz Sombold in January 1944, the single-seat interceptor So 244 was intended to attack Allied heavy bombers flying in tight combat box formation. The experimental Sombold 344 was actually a mixture of a rocket-powered plane and an antiaircraft mine. It was composed of two sections: a powered piloted section at the rear and an ejectable explosive nose section filled with 500 kg (1,100 lbs) of explosives; this was fitted with stabilizing fins and a proximity fuse. The detachable nose section was to be released into an Allied bomber box formation, thus causing enormous damage to the bombers—at least that was the plan. Span was 5.7 m (18 ft 8.6 in) and length was 7 m (22 ft 11.8 in). The So 344 was carried to combat by a specially converted bomber, then it was released to fly on its own, powered by a single Walter 509 rocket engine for a high approach with unknown speed. After the attack, enough rocket-engine propellant would be retained to escape—at least in theory; the aircraft had an endurance of only twenty-five or thirty minutes. After a glide, the So 344 was to land on the built-in landing skid. Defensive armament consisted of two MG machine guns in the attack version, and two MG machine guns and one MK cannon for the fighter version. A 1/5 scale model was built for aerodynamic tests, but the So 344 was never completed and the project was abandoned in early 1945.

Arado Ar E 381

The miniature Arado Ar E 381, designed in late 1944, had a span of 4.43 m (14 ft 6 in), a length of 4.69 m (15 ft 4 in) and a height of 1.29 m (4 ft 3 in). Powered by a small Walter

Sombold So 344

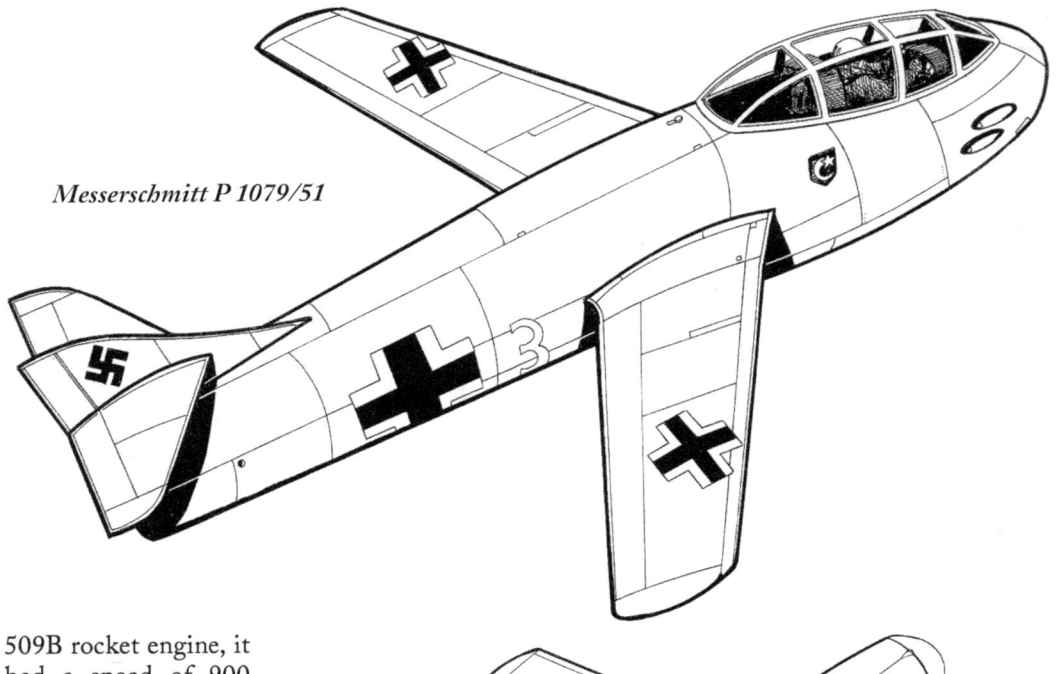

Messerschmitt P 1079/51

Arado Ar E 381/1

509B rocket engine, it had a speed of 900 km/h (559 mph). The pilot lay in a prone position in a very cramped cockpit fitted with a small round window in the nose. Cockpit entry was from a hatch placed above the fuselage, and the pilot had no way to escape in case of emergency. The aircraft, armed with a single MK 108 30-mm cannon with 60 rounds, was planned to be carried and launched from an Arado Ar 234 C3 four-engined jet bomber, and landed on a retractable skid. The Ar E 381 would have existed in three versions (1, 2 and 3) with slight differences.

Pulse-jet-Engined Planes

Messerschmitt Me 328

The small single-seat fighter/interceptor Messerschmitt Me 328 was designed after a prototype known as Project P 1079/51. Work on the Me 328 program began in 1941, and a glider prototype, carried by and launched from bomber Dornier Do 217, flew in the autumn of 1943 (some sources say August 1942 or July 1941). The Me 328 A-version had a length of 6.83 m (22 ft 4.7 in) and a span of 6.40 m (20 ft 11.7 in). Powered tests followed, first with two Argus As 014 pulsejets mounted on the rear fuselage. As this led to problems, the engines were placed under the wings. Speed varied in the versions designed, from 590 km/h (367 mph) to 920 km/h (572 mph). Envisaged

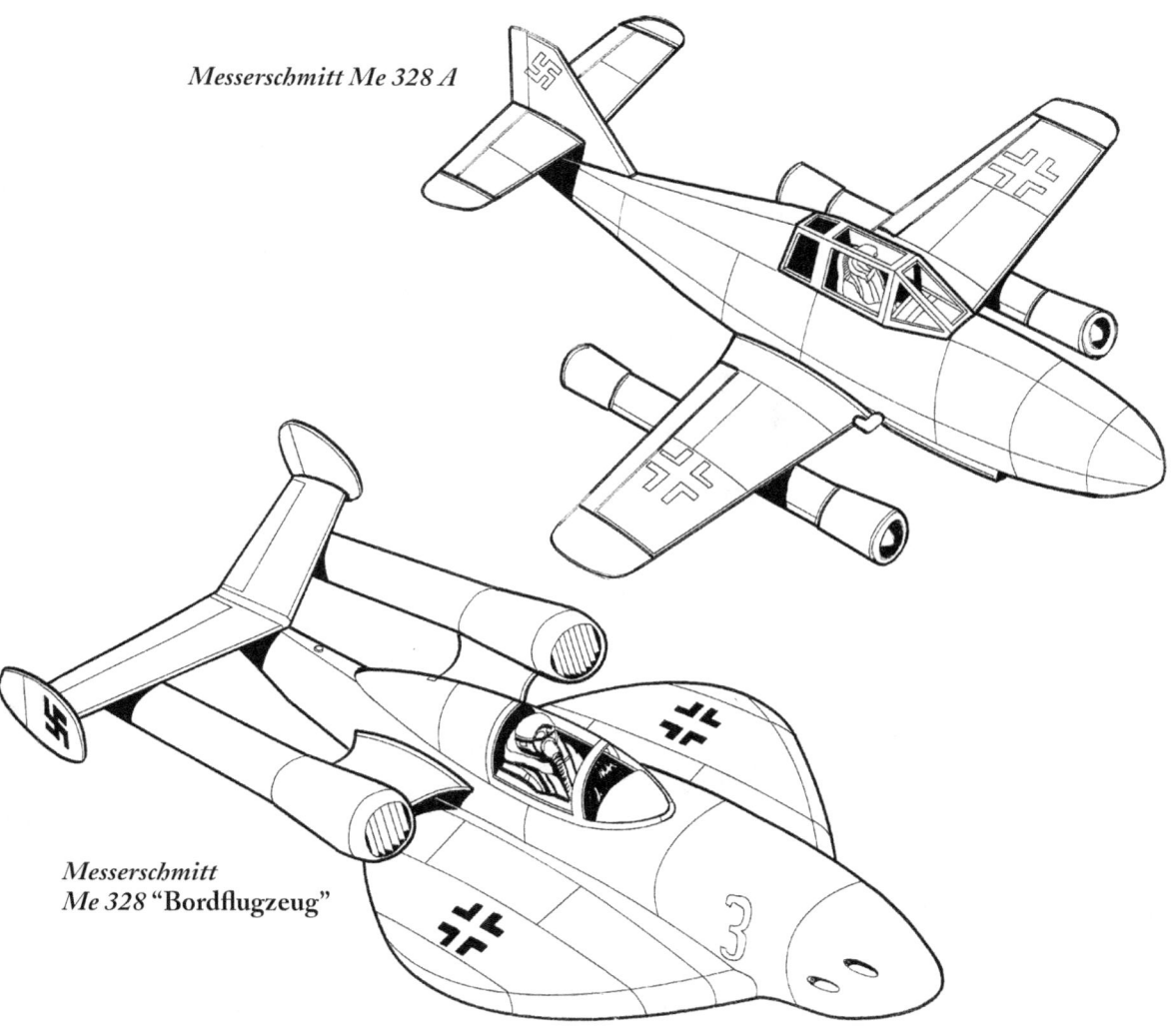

Messerschmitt Me 328 A

Messerschmitt Me 328 "Bordflugzeug"

armament was to be two MG 151 cannons or two MK 103 cannons for a fighter version. A bomb load of 1,000 kg (2,005 lbs) could be carried for a fast bomber variant. The aircraft took off with a jettisonable wheeled trolley and landed on a ventral skid.

One version was planned to be catapulted from submarines. Another version (Me 238 B) was powered by two small ram-jet engines placed on both wingtips. The Me 238 C had a fixed main-wheel landing gear, and was powered by a turbojet engine placed under the fuselage. Another version, intended to be a *Bordflugzeug* (carried by a mother aircraft, e.g., a Heinkel He 111) had almost circular wings. Another project, known as Me 328/Porsche 109-005, had oval wings and was powered by a Porsche 109-005 turbojet in dorsal position delivering 500 kp thrust. The Me 328 series remained a project only; it was not developed into mass production and operational use; the whole program just dragged on, probably due to other priorities.

Messerschmitt Me P 1079

The designation P 1079 was given to a number of experimental, small, and quite different pulse-jet-powered fighters designed in 1942. The Me P 1079/1 was a small fighter with short, swept-back wings, landing gear in ventral skid form, and a pulse-jet engine mounted on top of the fuselage. The Me P 1079/10C was powered by one SR 500 pulse-jet engine

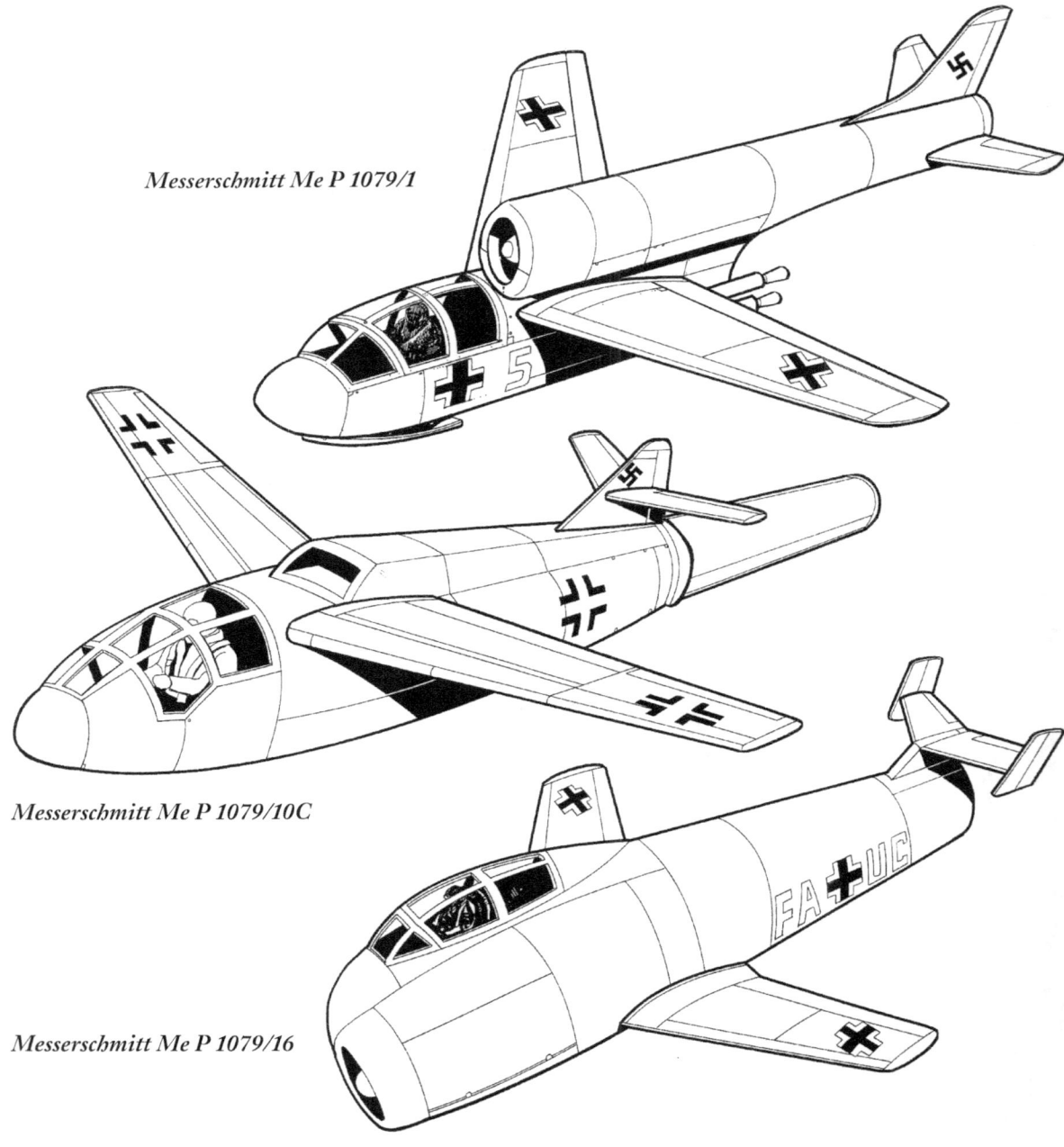

Messerschmitt Me P 1079/1

Messerschmitt Me P 1079/10C

Messerschmitt Me P 1079/16

that projected some half its length beyond the fuselage, with air intake placed in dorsal position; it had a span of 5 m, a length of 7.20 m, and was armed with two MG 131. The Me P 1079/13b was powered by two SR pulsejets mounted on each side of the fuselage. The Messerschmitt Me P 1079/16, designed in June 1941, had an asymmetrical layout; the cockpit for the single pilot was placed on the right side of the fuselage, the Schmidt pulse-jet on the left. The aircraft was to be armed with two MG 151/20 20-mm cannons.

No further details are available, and how these fighters achieved initial speed sufficient to start the pulse-engine is not known. Were they to be catapulted? Launched from a carrier aircraft? Rocket assisted?

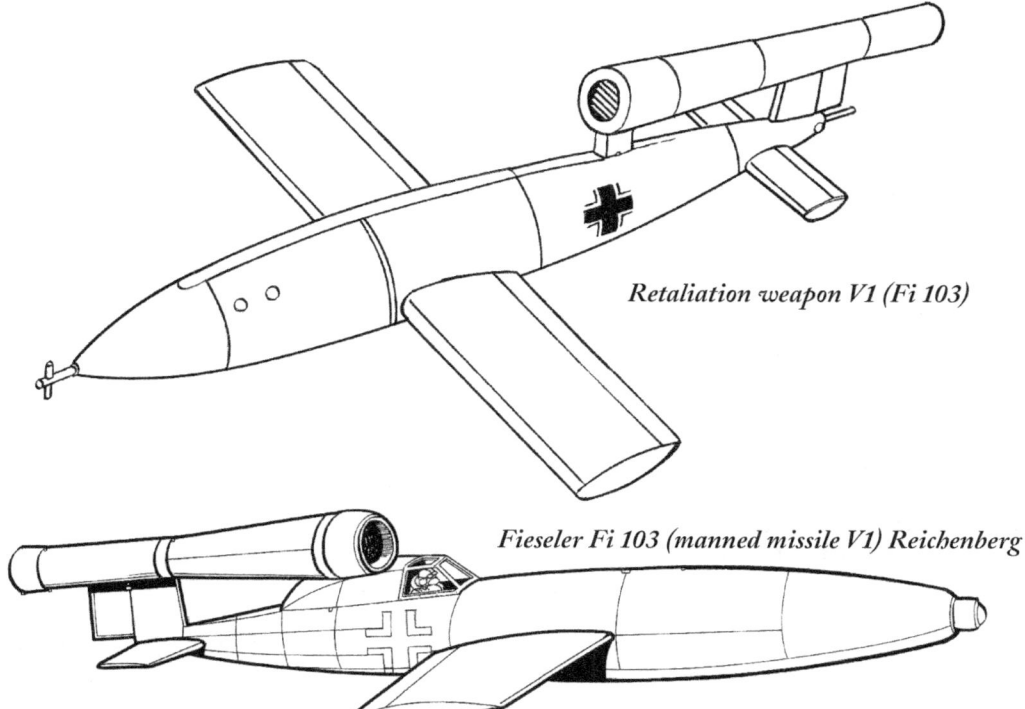

Retaliation weapon V1 (Fi 103)

Fieseler Fi 103 (manned missile V1) Reichenberg

Fieseler Fi 103 Reichenberg

This fast, experimental, manned, jet-engine version of the pilotless "Doodlebug" flying bomb (V1) was known as Fieseler Fi 103 Reichenberg R.IV. Jointly designed in June 1944 by the Gerhard Fieseler Werke GmbH and the DFS glider institute, this single-seat version was sanctioned by Hitler for use against high-priority targets. The manned flying bomb was intended to be launched from a mother plane (e.g., Heinkel He 111 bomber), and aimed at its target by the pilot who would bail out in the final seconds before hitting, with chances of surviving being thus very slim. Span was 5.71 m (18 ft 9 in), length was 8 m (26 ft 3 in), and weight (loaded) was 2,250 kg (4,960 lbs). Like the pilotless V1, the manned Fi 103 was propelled by a pulse-jet engine designed by Paul Schmidt and produced by Argus Motoren Werk company. The jet engine was simple to manufacture and cheap to produce; it was placed above the tail and used a fuel mixture of compressed air and low-grade gasoline. The jet engine developed 335 kg thrust at take-off and carried the craft to a maximum range of about 330 km (205 miles) with a speed of about 560 km/h but later improved machines were planned to reach 645 km/h at 1,200 m altitude. As already said, since pulsejets do not operate at slow speed, the V1 and its manned variants were either launched from a mother aircraft or catapulted for take-off. The pilot's cramped cockpit was located just ahead of the propulsive duct. The instruments were quite rudimentary, consisting of an arming switch, a clock, an airspeed indicator, an altimeter, and a turn and bank indicator. The aircraft was otherwise quite similar to the unpiloted Fi 103. The manned missile was tested by the famed and audacious Hanna Reitsch and the equally renowned SS-Hauptsturmführer Otto Skorzeny (the "most dangerous man in Europe," who had rescued the Italian dictator Benitto Mussolini from his prison). A training program was initiated, and the task of first deployment was assigned to the secret KG 200 squadron. However, the whole program was cancelled in October 1944, after some 175 Fi 103s had been converted to a piloted configuration. None were ever used operationally. The whole Reichenberg scheme was abandoned in favor of the Mistel program

("Mistel" also being a generic term for the lower component of all piggyback aircraft combinations). Like the Japanese piloted suicide craft Yokosuka MXY-7 *Ohka* (Cherry Blossom, also known as "Baka," the Japanese word for fool), the Fi 103 Reichenberg would have been practically unstoppable once it had neared its target; although it was incapable of much evasive action, it was small, fast and difficult to intercept. The best way to stop it would have been to attack and destroy the mother aircraft before the missile was launched.

Junkers Ju EF 126 Elli

The single-seat Ju EF 126, designed in November 1944, was an attempt to create a simple and cheap midget fighter mainly built with wood. It had a span of 6.65 m (21 ft 10 in), a length of 8.46 m (27 ft 9 in) and an empty weight of 1,100 kg (2,420 lbs). Elli had a retractable tricycle landing gear, and was powered by one Argus AS 014 pulse-jet engine (the same as used on the Fi 103 V1). It had a maximum speed of 780 km/h (485 mph), a range of 350 km (218 miles) and an endurance of twenty-three minutes at maximum speed. It was armed with two MG 151/20 20-mm cannons (with 180 rounds) mounted in the nose, and could carry a bomb load of 400 kg (880 lbs). The project was abandoned in March 1945.

Focke-Wulf Fw Ta 283

Designed by engineer Kurt Tank of the Focke-Wulf Company, this single-seat jet-powered fighter had a long, pointed nose and a large vertical fin. The pilot operated the aircraft from a cockpit placed at the rear of the fuselage. The wings were mounted low on the fuselage and were swept back at 45 degrees. Span was 8 m (26 ft 3.2 in) and length was 11.85 m (38 ft 10.9 in). The Ta 283 was powered by two Pabst ramjets once operating speed was reached. Since ramjets do not operate at slow speeds, a Walter HWK rocket engine was used for take-off. The ramjet engines were placed on the tips of the sharply swept tailplanes to avoid any disturbance of the airflow. A maximum speed of 1,100 km/h (683 mph) was expected. The aircraft had a retractable

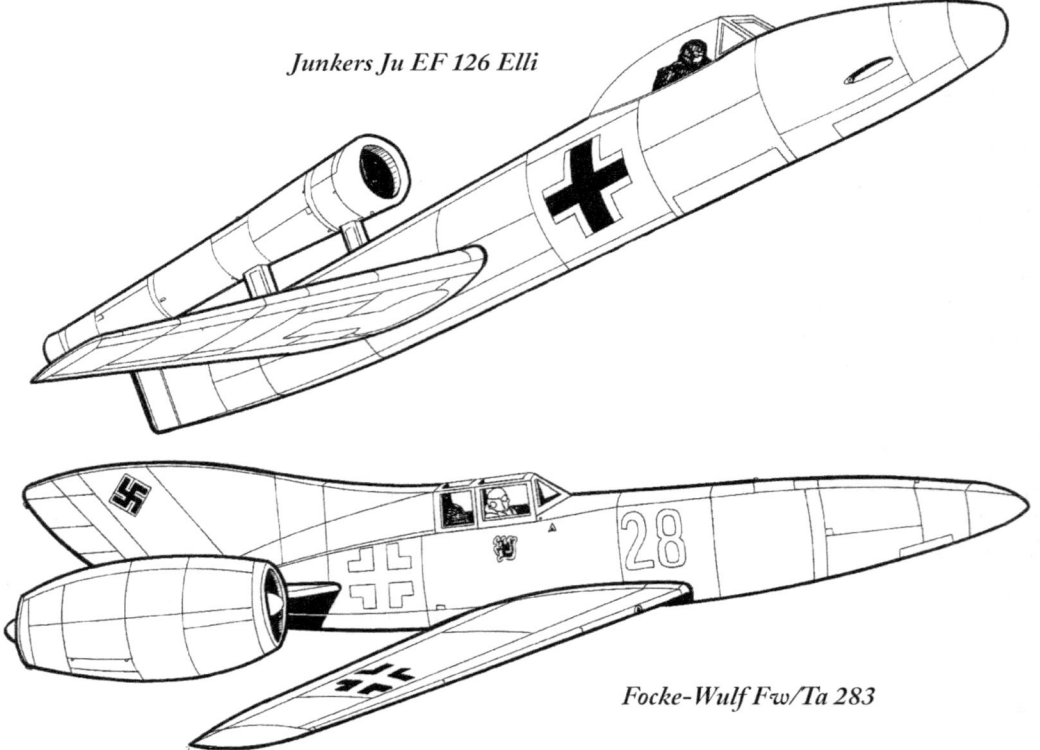

Junkers Ju EF 126 Elli

Focke-Wulf Fw/Ta 283

landing gear with a tricycle arrangement—nose wheel and two wheeled-leg undercarriage. The planned armament would have been two powerful MK 108 30-mm cannons.

Focke-Wulf Super Lorin

This fighter, designed after the Fw/Ta 283 by the engineer Von Halen, was powered by two ram-jet engines (patented by the Frenchman René Lorin in 1908) placed at the tips of the swept-back tailplanes. It had a crew of one and was fitted with a retractable tricycle landing gear. It had a length of 11.6 m (38 ft 1 in) and swept-back wing with a span of 7.6 m (24 ft 11.3 in) mounted mid-fuselage. It would have been armed with two MK 108 30-mm cannons positioned in the nose. This strange project never reached completion.

Blohm & Voss P 213

The Bv P 213 was Blohm & Voss's design for the *Miniaturjäger* (Midget Fighter) program. It was to have a simple fuselage with a span of 6 m (19 ft 9 in), and a length of 6.2 m

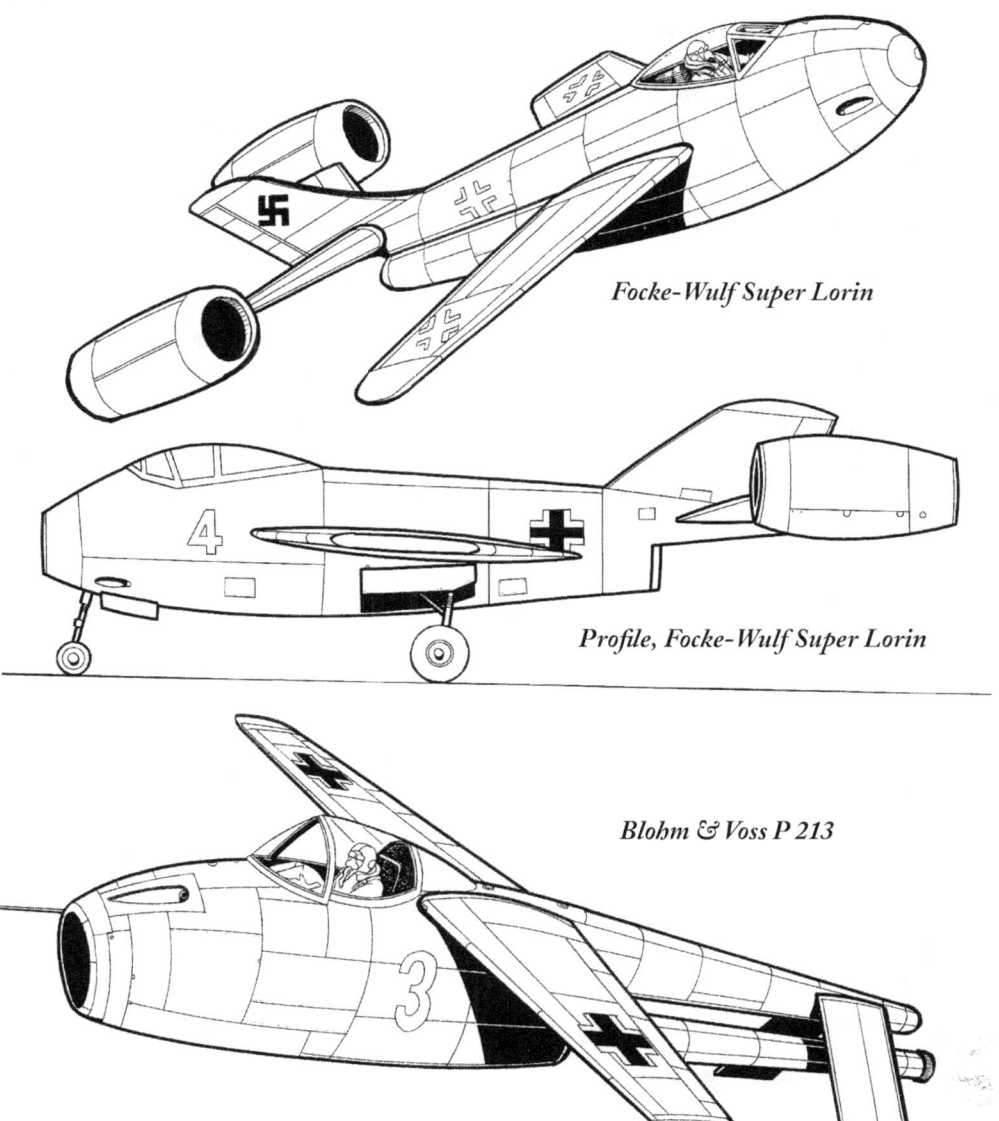

Focke-Wulf Super Lorin

Profile, Focke-Wulf Super Lorin

Blohm & Voss P 213

(20 ft 4 in). Wooden construction was chosen for the shoulder-mounted wing, which had a straight leading edge and tapered trailing edge. The tail unit was also made of wood, and angled down sharply. Behind the fuselage was a tail boom, with the Argus As 014 pulsejet attached by free-swinging brackets. The aircraft was to have a maximum speed of 705 km/h (438 mph) and a maximum flight duration of about twenty-three minutes. To get the pulsejet to operating speed, either a catapult launch or solid booster rockets would be used. The aircraft was to land on an undercarriage that retracted by means of compressed air. Armament was to be a single MK 108 30-mm cannon with 135 rounds, located in the fuselage nose. When the whole *Miniaturjäger* program was canceled in December 1944, work on the Blohm & Voss Bv P 213 was stopped.

Skoda Kauba SK P 14-01

Designed in early 1945, the SK P 14-01 was intended to be a jet interceptor fighter. The aircraft had a length of 9.5 m (31 ft 2 in) and a span of 7 m (22 ft 11 in). It was to be powered by a single Sänger ram-jet engine with an estimated speed of about 1,000 km/h. For take-off, RATO rockets and a jettisonable trolley were used, and the machine was to land on a ventral skid. The aircraft was operated by a single pilot who lay in prone position in a cockpit placed above the engine air intake. It was to be armed with two MK 109 30-mm cannons mounted above the pilot's canopy. There was a similar version with slight differences, known as Skoda Kauba SK P 14-02. None were ever completed.

Heinkel He P 1080

Heinkel designed this ram-jet-powered fighter after receiving ram-jet data from DFS near the end of World War II. Two 900-mm (2 ft 11.5 in) Lorin-Rohr ramjets were mounted on each side of the fuselage with their outer surfaces faired into the wing, so that the large surface area of the ramjets were exposed to the airstream for cooling purposes. To save design time, the swept-back wing with the eleven controls were based on those of the He P 1078, but a single orthodox fin and rudder assembly was used instead of wingtip anhedral. The cockpit was located in the forward section of the fuselage, along with a radar unit and two MK 108 30-mm cannons. The fuel tanks were located in the rear of the fuselage. Four solid-fuel rockets of 1,000 kg (2,200 lbs) of thrust each were used for take-off. An undercarriage that could be jettisoned was used on take-off,

Skoda Kauba SK P 14-01

and landing was done on an extendable skid. Span was 8.9 m (29 ft 2.7 in), length was 8.15 m (26 ft 9.1 in), and maximum speed would have been 1,000 km/h (621 mph).

Stöckel Ram-fighter

Designed in August 1944 by engineer J. Stöckel from the Blohm & Voss Company, this aircraft had a length of 7.20 meters, a span of 7 meters, and a fuselage diameter of 1 meter. It was powered by a mixed-propulsion system featuring a ramjet and a series of rocket chambers that brought the ramjet to operating speed. The machine was to be launched and brought onto its target from a mother aircraft. No landing gear was fitted, as the pilot would have done only one suicide attack mission, ramming Allied bombers with its 200-kg high-explosive warhead. Hitler had (for public relations purposes) forbidden suicide attacks, so Stöckel made a second design in which the pilot would have been able to bail out and escape by parachute right before ramming.

Single-Jet-Engined Fighters

Heinkel He 178

A private venture of the Ernst Heinkel AG Company, the He 178 claims the fame of being the first jet-powered aircraft ever. The small experimental fighter He 178, designed by engineer Hans-Joachim Pabst von Ohain, was suc-

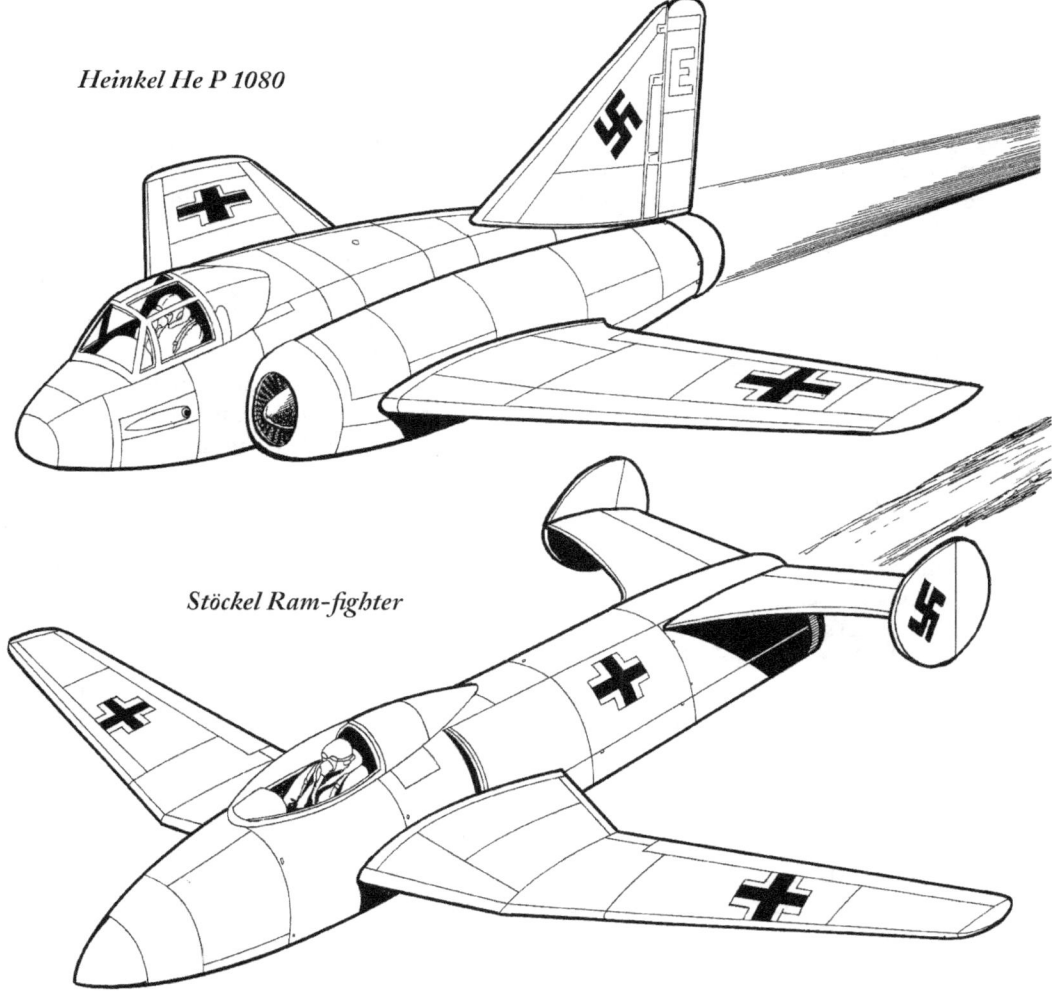

Heinkel He P 1080

Stöckel Ram-fighter

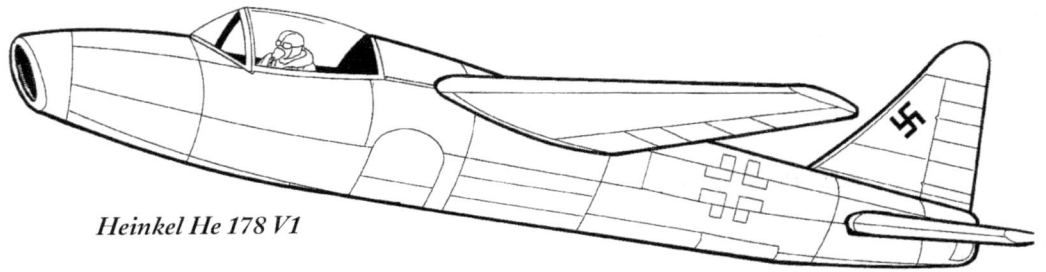
Heinkel He 178 V1

cessfully tested in August 1939. The He 178 was a shoulder-wing monoplane with the cockpit well forward of the wing leading edge. It had a HeS 3 B turbojet engine, a retractable landing gear, a speed of 700 km/h (435 mph), a wingspan of 7.20 m (23 ft 3 in), and a length of 7.48 m (24 ft 6 in). Udet and Milch attended a test flight at the Marienehe base on November 1, 1939, but—in spite of its tremendous potential—the futuristic He 178 did not generate much interest from the RLM. Just like the later Heinkel He 280, a remarkable twin-jet-engine combat fighter from 1940, the He 178 appeared at a time when the RLM showed no interest in new development other than that could be used at once for short *Blitzkrieg* campaigns. Only two prototypes (designated V1 and V2) were built. V1—the aircraft that might have revolutionalized the Luftwaffe before World War II—ended up in the Berlin Air Museum and was destroyed by an Allied bombardment in 1943. Prototype V2, with enlarged wings, never flew.

Heinkel He 162
Volksjäger/*Salamander*

The Heinkel He 162 *Volksjäger* (People's Fighter), designed by engineer Siegfried Günther, was Heinkel's response to an RLM demand for a cheap and expendable jet fighter, fast and armed in such a way to deal with the impact of Anglo-American bombing of German industries. It was the second single-seat, jet-engined fighter to be fielded by the Luftwaffe in World War II. *Volksjäger* was the RLM's official name for the He 162. Other names given to the plane included Salamander, which was the codename of its construction program, and *Spatz* (Sparrow) which was the name given to the plane by Heinkel. A potential rival to the Messerschmitt Me 262, the Salamander had a length of 9.05 m (29 ft 8 in), a wingspan of 7.2 m (23 ft 7 in), a height of 2.6 m (8 ft 6 in), a wing area of 14.5 square m (156 square ft), and an empty weight of 1,660 kg (3,660 lbs). Powered by one BMW 003E-1 or one E-2 turbojet engine placed in dorsal piggyback position, the Salamander had a maximum speed of 900 km/h (562 mph), a maximum range of 975 km (606 miles), and a service ceiling of 12,000 m (39,400 ft). The engine discharged its exhaust between twin rudders, and by that means avoided all the problems of intake and exhaust ducting. The landing gear was a narrow-track tricycle undercarriage, which retracted into the fuselage. Armament included two 20-mm MG 151 guns (120 rounds each) placed in the nose.

The Heinkel He 162 was placed in production in a very short time, a remarkable achievement even by today's standards, at a time when German industry was being pounded to rubble by fleets of Allied bombers, when fuel supplies were inexorably running down to nothing, when experienced aircrew were no longer available, when materials were in short supply, and when time before the defeat was measured not in months but in weeks. The He 162 made its first flight on December 6, 1944, but further tests proved failures, killing several pilots. The type suffered a number of aerodynamic problems as well as a tendency to lose parts of its wooden flying surfaces as a result of poor adhesive bonds. The difficulties experienced by the He 162 were caused mainly by its rush into production, not by any inherent design flaws. The aircraft was quickly improved and in January 1945, the Luftwaffe formed a special *Erprobungskommando* 162 (test pilot evaluation group) to which the first forty-six aircrafts were delivered. It is reported that, although

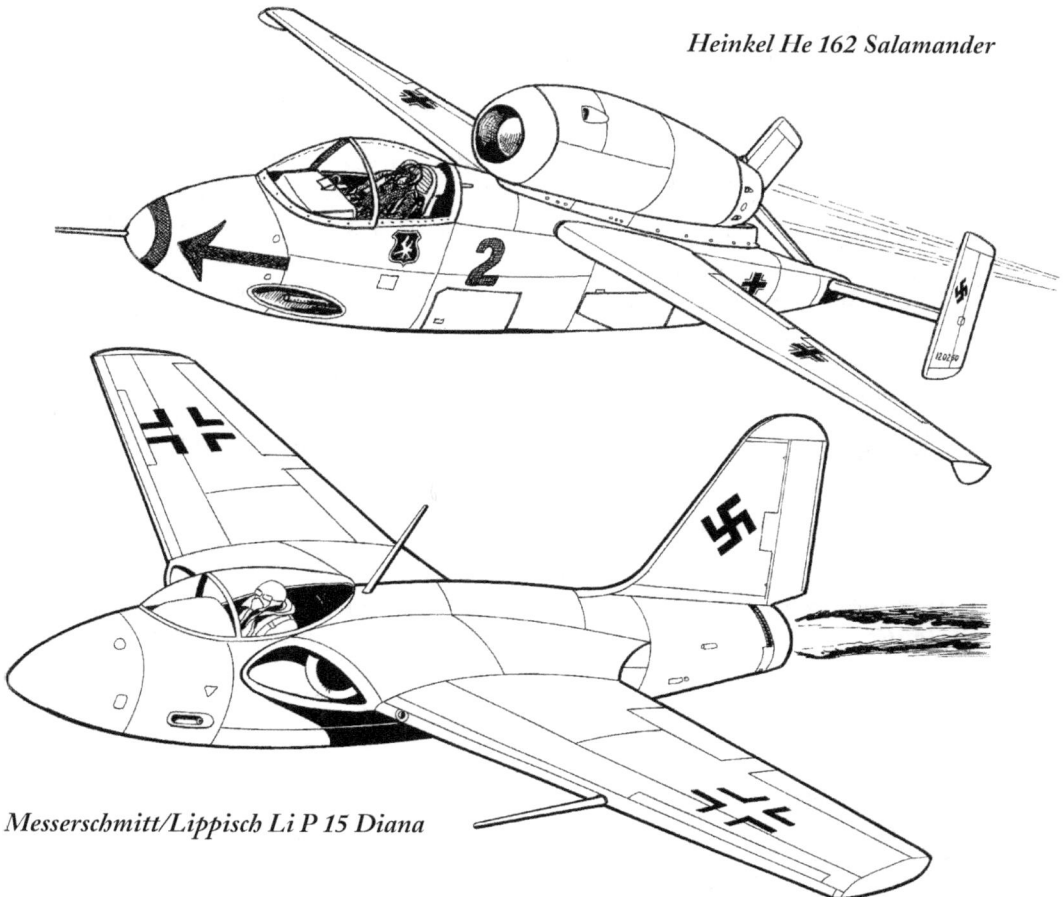

Heinkel He 162 Salamander

Messerschmitt/Lippisch Li P 15 Diana

fuel and trained pilots were desperately lacking, the He 162 probably saw sporadic combat in mid–April 1945. The RLM envision initial production of a thousand aircraft per month, rising to a peak of no less than four thousand. The He 162 was to be manufactured at Heinkel's Rostok-Marienehe factory, the Junkers Bernburg plant and the Mittelwerke GmbH at Nordhausen. To speed up production, the RLM extensively subcontracted component manufacture. The pilots were drawn from the *Hitler Jugend* (Hitler Youth) and hastily trained in primary gliders. By the time of the German unconditional surrender on May 8, 1945, 120 He 162s had been delivered; a further 200 aircraft had been completed and were awaiting collection or flight-testing; about 600 more were in various stages of production. Designed and produced much too late, the He 162 was never a significant threat to Allied bombers. Postwar evaluation by Allied air forces indicated that with a little more time and development work, the He 162 would have been perfectly viable, and would certainly have made a considerable impact on the air war above Germany.

There was a planned version, known as He 162 A-10 and A-11, which was powered by two Argus pulse engines. Experiments were made for a special ejection seat, and also made with the wing configuration: the He 162 B had forward-swept wings and the He 162 C had backward-swept wings.

Messerschmitt/Lippisch Li P 15 Diana

The Diana, designed in March 1945, was intended to provide the Luftwaffe with a *Volksjäger* that would have better performance (namely range and endurance) than the Heinkel He 162. The tailless aircraft with swept wings was a hybrid fighter incorporating the nose and cockpit of the He 162, the fuselage of the Ju 248, and the wings of the Me 163 B. It had a span of 10 m (33 ft 1.2 in), a length of 6.75 m (22 ft 2 in), a height of 3 m, a wing area of 20 square meters and a weight of 3,600 kg. It was powered by one HeS 011A turbojet with two air intakes in the wing roots. The machine was expected to have a maximum speed of 1,000 km/h (621 mph) and an endurance of forty-five minutes. It was to be armed with four MK 108 cannons, two mounted in wing roots and the other pair in the nose. A test model was done in a wind tunnel, but the end of the war prevented any further development.

Blohm & Voss P 211-02

The design of the Blohm & Voss P 211-02 fast jet fighter was refused. It lost out to Heinkel's He 162.

Focke-Wulf Fw 190 TL

In an attempt to improve the Fw 190, a jet-engined aircraft known as Focke-Wulf Fw 190 TL used a T1 turbo jet engine (600-kg thrust) in place of the BMW or DB piston engine. The suffix "TL" was short for *Turbolader Strahltriebwerk* (turbocharger jet engine). This engine included a two-stage radial compressor, single-stage turbine and an annular combustion chamber. Exhaust passed through an annular outlet running around the fuselage. The Fw 190 TL would have had a speed of 830 km/h at an altitude of 8,000 m, and an endurance of seventy-two minutes. The project was cancelled in 1943.

Focke Wulf Fw P1

The Fw P1, intended to become a fast fighter, was designed in March 1943. Basically

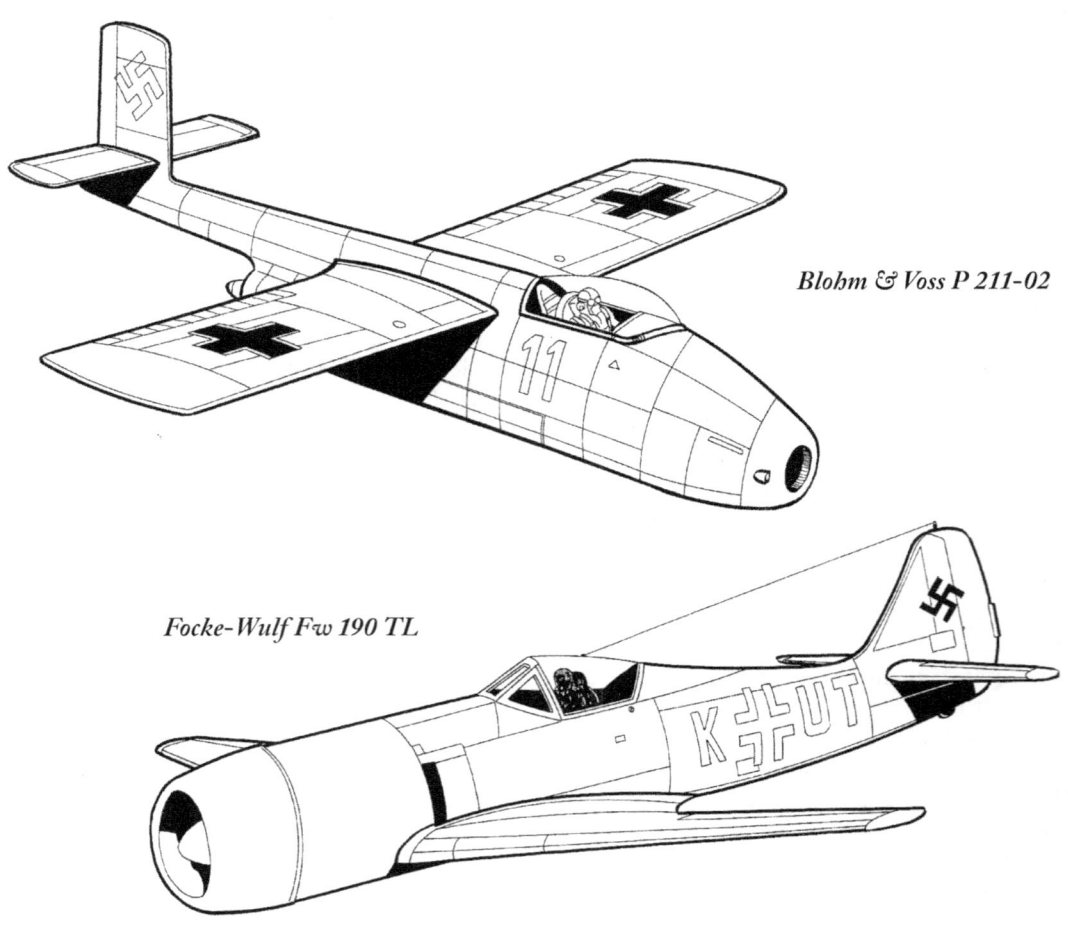

Blohm & Voss P 211-02

Focke-Wulf Fw 190 TL

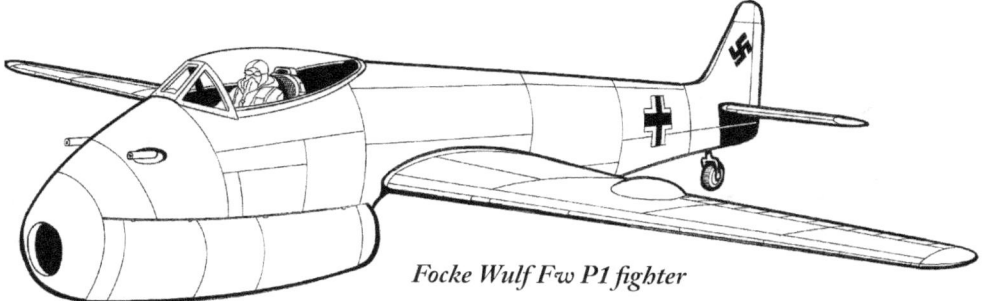
Focke Wulf Fw P1 fighter

a rebuilt Fw 190, it had the same fuselage, tail unit, wings and landing gear, only the front was totally reshaped. Instead of a piston engine, the Fw P1 was fitted with a jet engine with exhaust placed under the fuselage. The pilot sat in conventional position in a cockpit placed above the engine. There is no available data for this fighter which never made it further than the drawing board.

Messerschmitt Me P 1092 series

Designed in 1943, the Me P 1092 project included a series of about eleven proposals featuring the concept of a light but fast, single-seat aircraft powered by jet propulsion, and using different configurations for various roles, including fighter, night fighter, and interceptor. The initial design Me P 1092/1 was powered by a Jumo 004 C turbojet slung under the fuselage. A dive-bomber variant Me P 1092/1a had inverted gull wings for stability in dive.

The Me P 1092/2, designed in mid–1943, had a length of 8.1 m (26 ft 6 in) and an empty weight of 2,626 kg (5,789 lbs). The wings were swept back at 21 degrees, with a span of 7.75 m (25 ft 5 in) and a wing area of 12.7 square m (136 square ft). The fighter was powered by a single Jumo 004C (developing 2,237 lbs thrust) and had a speed of 931 km/h (578 mph) and a range of 870 km (540 miles). It was to be armed with two MK 103 30-mm cannons and two MG 151/15 15-mm cannons mounted in the nose.

The Me 1092/3 had its cockpit moved to the rear and faired into the vertical fin. The Me 1092/4 had its cockpit moved to the front, and weapons mounted on the sides of the fore fuselage. The 1092/5 had slight differences with the Me 1092/2, but with improved per-

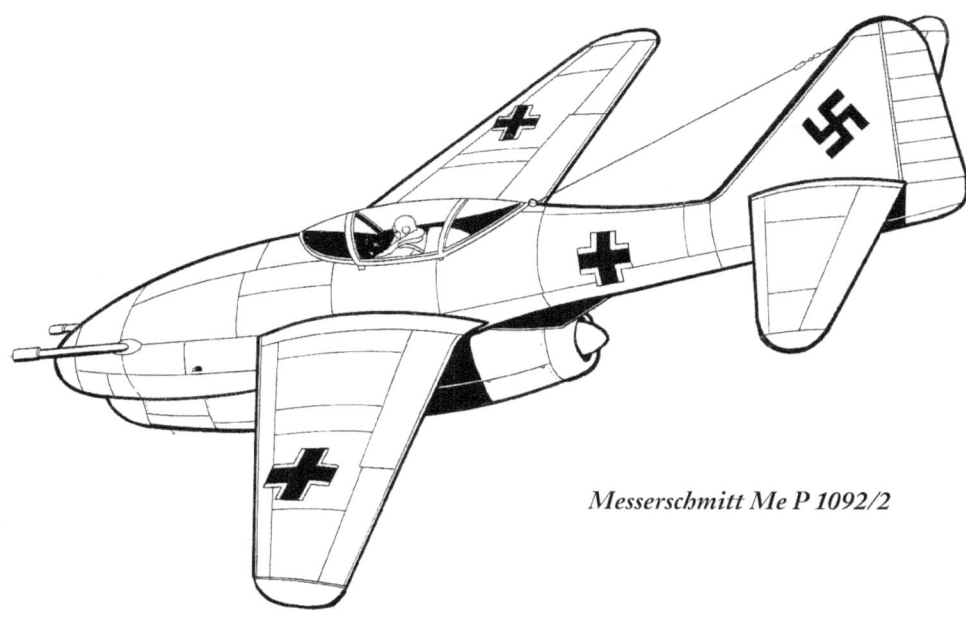
Messerschmitt Me P 1092/2

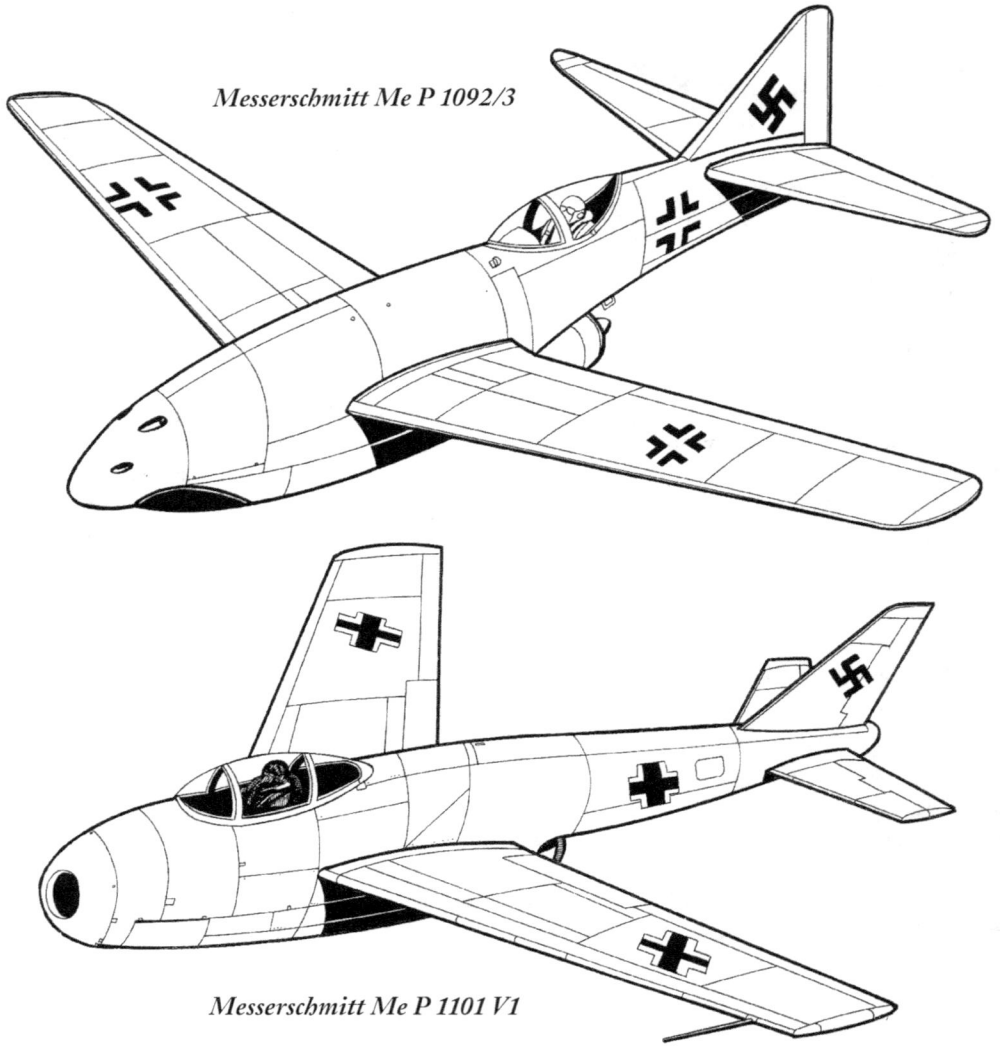

Messerschmitt Me P 1092/3

Messerschmitt Me P 1101 V1

formance. The Me 1092 series was never developed but constituted the forerunners to the Messerschmitt Me P 1106 and Me P 1101 designs.

Messerschmitt Me P 1101 series

Messerschmitt's designation P 1101 included several jet proposals with different configurations intended for various roles such as fighter, interceptor, night fighter, and ground attacker. Anticipating the need for a replacement of the Me 262, the design of the single-seat Messerschmitt Me 1101 prototype V1 started in July 1944. The aircraft, designed by engineer Waldemar Voigt, was intended to be a fast interceptor. It had 40-degree swept-back wings with a span of 8.24 m (27 ft), a length of 9.13 m (30 ft 1 in), and an empty weight of 2,596 kg (5,724 lbs). The initial design was powered by one Jumo 004B turbojet, and later fitted with one Heinkel-Hirth 109-011 turbojet. Maximum speed was 890 km/h (553 mph) at sea level, and 980 km/h (609 mph) at height. Planned armament would have included four Mk 108 cannons mounted in the nose. In March 1945, the jet fighter was almost completed. Captured by U.S. troops, the aircraft was shipped to the United States, and, much modified and improved by Robert Woods, chief designer at Bell Aircraft, it formed the basis of the Bell X-5 that flew in June 1951.

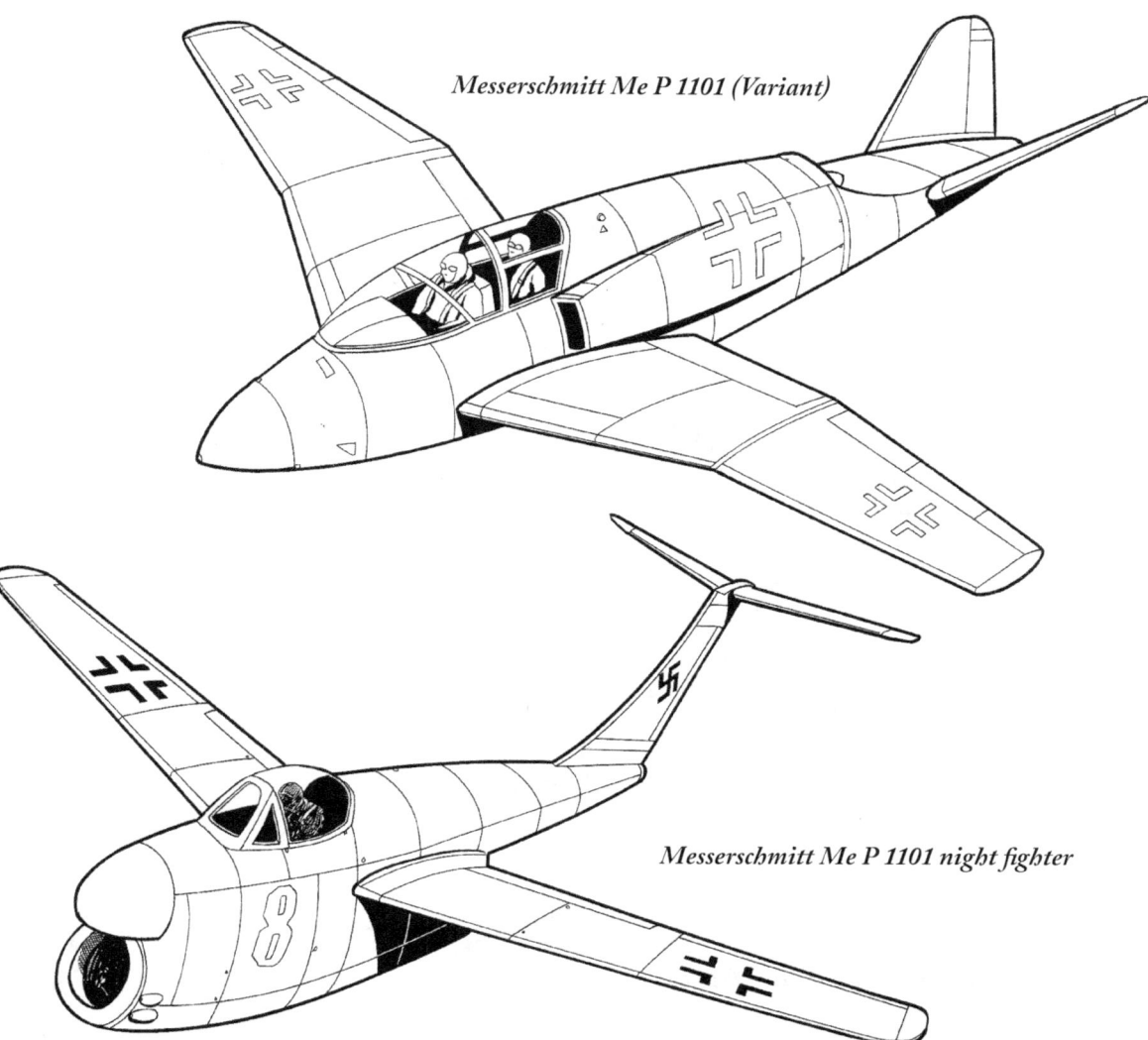

Messerschmitt Me P 1101 (Variant)

Messerschmitt Me P 1101 night fighter

There was a variant totally redesigned with a slender fuselage, compound-sweep wing, V-tail, lateral air intakes and jet engine incorporated in a dorsal position, operated by a crew of two. Another version, known as Me P 1101/XIII-113, had swept-back wings, V-tail and HeS 011A jet engine located under the fuselage. A night-fighter version had a T-tail and nose housing a parabolic antenna.

Messerschmitt Me P 1106

The Me P 1106, designed by December 1944, was basically a modification of the Messerschmitt Me P 1101 single-seat supersonic jet fighter. The air intake's length was reduced to minimize lost thrust, fuel capacity was increased to 1,200 kg rather than the 1,079 kg of the P 1101, the aerodynamic shape was improved, and the cockpit was slid to the rear of the fuselage. The result was a different airplane. The Me P 1106 had a length of 9.12 m (30 ft 2 in) and wings were swept back at a 40-degree angle with a span of 6.65 m (21 ft 10 in); the wings were placed in the pilot's field of vision, making the design highly problematic. To the designers' credit, they placed the horizontal component of the plane's T-shaped tail unit above the wake zone that normally resulted from the separate flow shock of the wing and fuselage. This innovative tail unit was so successful that it can still be found on

Messerschmitt Me P 1106

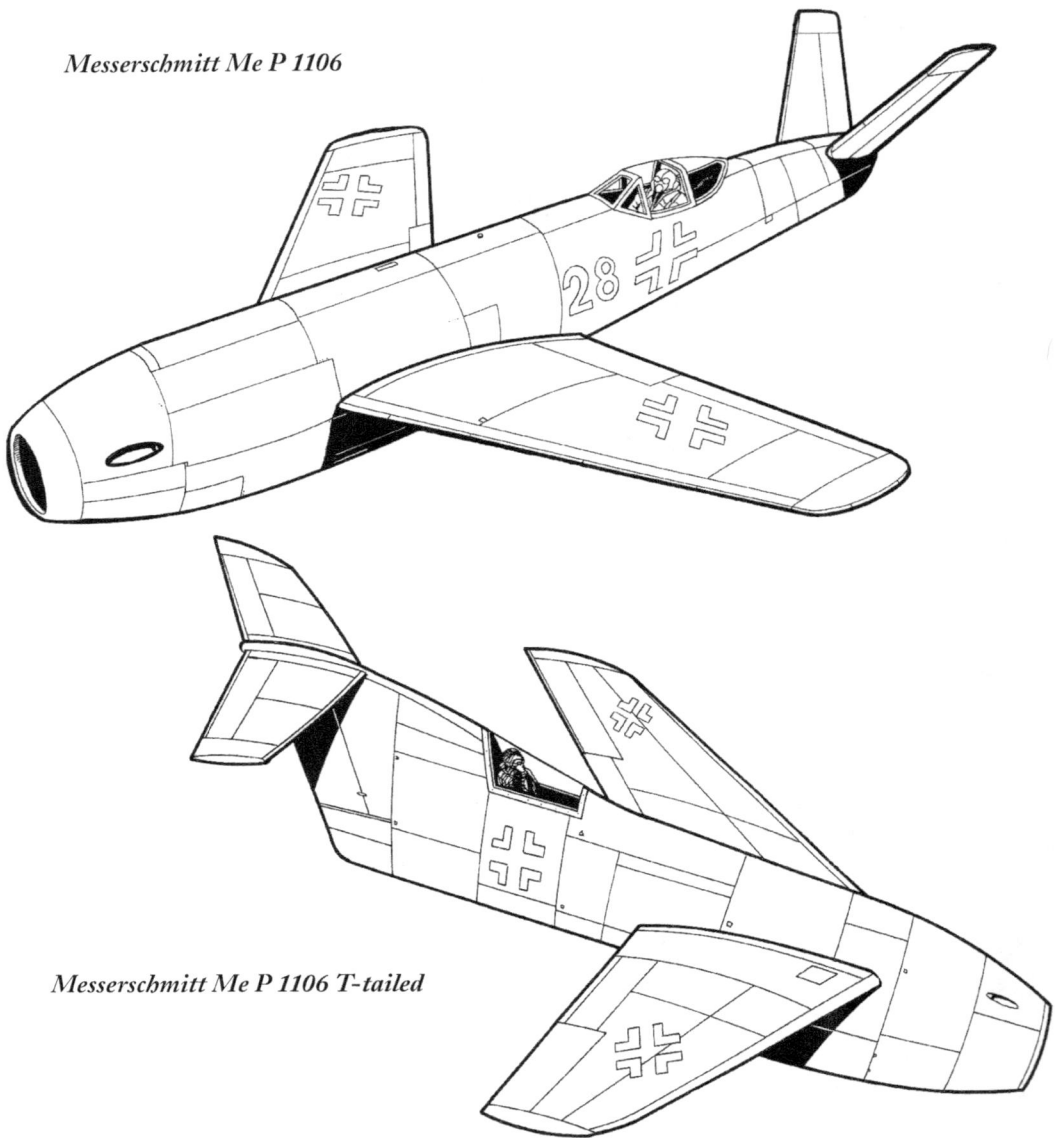

Messerschmitt Me P 1106 T-tailed

many modern aircraft. The P 1106 was to be powered by one Heinkel He S011 jet engine, and would have had a maximum speed of 993 km/h (617 mph). Several designs were made with different tail units and various armament (e.g., two MK 108 cannons), but the project was never completed.

Messerschmitt Me P 1095

Designed by Rudolf Seitz in the end of 1943, the Me P 1095/1 was to be used as fighter, ground-attacker, fast light bomber or reconnaissance aircraft. Using wings, cockpit and controls of the Me 262, and tail surfaces and landing gear of the Me 309, it had a length of 9.71 m (31 ft 9 in), a span of 9.74 m (31 ft 11 in), and a height of 3.38 m (11 ft 1 in). Powered by a Jumo 004 turbojet engine placed under the fuselage, it was to have a maximum speed of 860 km/h (534 mph) at 6,000 m altitude. The planned armament consisted of two MK 108 30-mm cannons mounted in the nose. There were slightly different versions known as Me P 1095/2 and Me P 1095/3 with respectively smaller and enlarged wings.

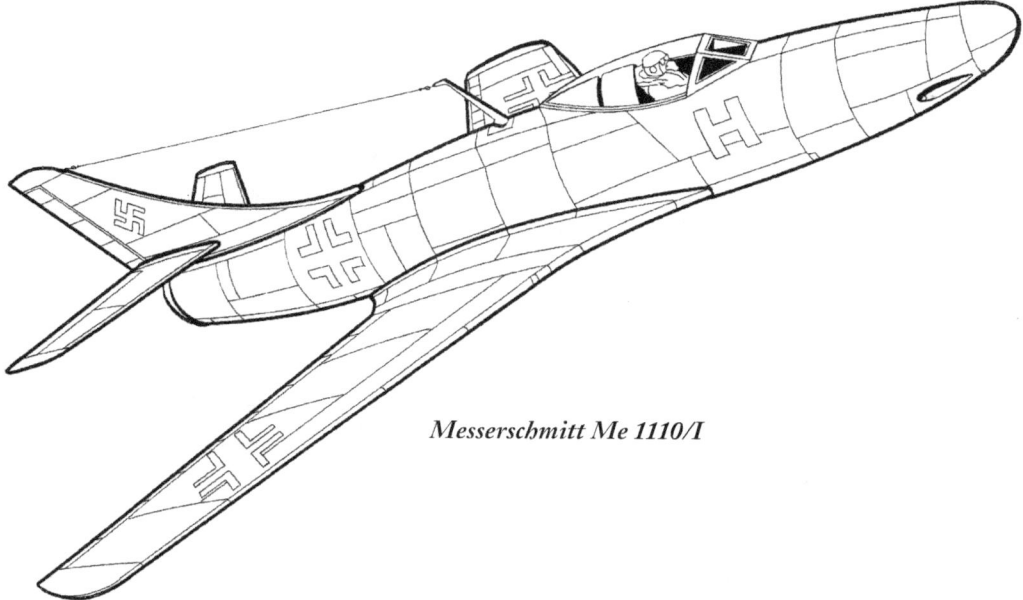

Messerschmitt Me 1110/I

Messerschmitt Me P 1110 series

The Me P 1110 series was essentially a modern design with just about all features of fighter jets of the 1950s. It was designed in early 1945 by the Messerschmitt Company as a high-altitude, single-seat jet fighter. Basically the aircraft had a length of 10.36 m (34 ft), and 40-degree swept-back wings with a span of 8.25 m (27 ft 1 in). It was intended to be powered by one or two HeS 011 jet engines. Projected maximum speed was 1,015 km/h (630 mph). The design did away with the nose air intake: the engine was located much further back in the airframe, with the duct openings placed on the fuselage shoulders, just forward of the trailing edge of the constant-chord swept wings. The Me 1110 would have been armed with three MK 108 30-mm cannons mounted in the nose, with a provision for two more in the wing roots. Two designs were made. The

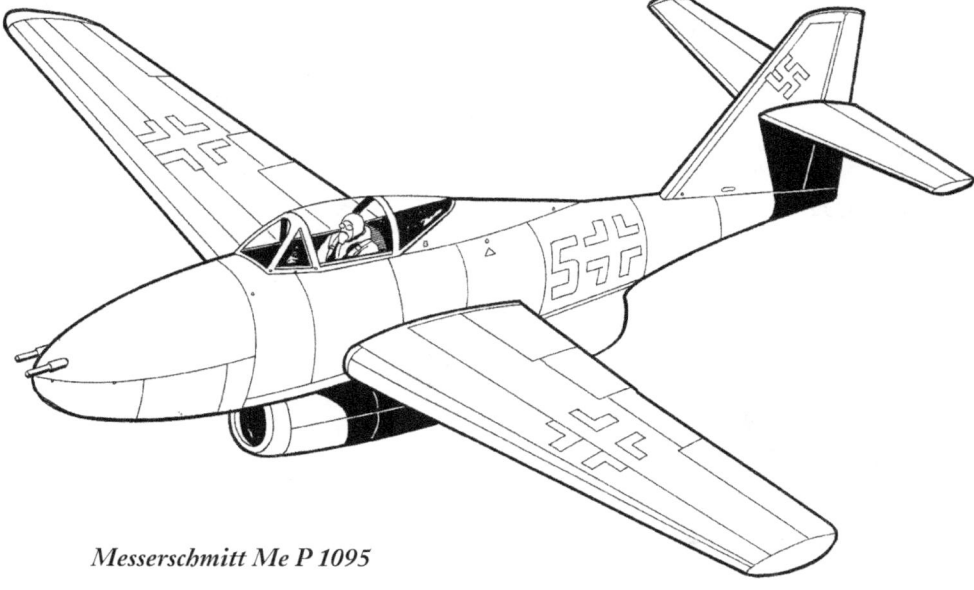

Messerschmitt Me P 1095

Messerschmitt Me 1110/II

Me 1110/I had a conventional tail unit, and the Me P 1110/II had a V-shaped tail unit. Another design, known as Me P 1110/170, had annular air intake around the fuselage behind the cockpit. No versions of the Me P 1110 left the drawing board level.

Messerschmitt Me P 1110 Ente

This project, another variant of the Me P 1110, was designed in mid-February 1945. It had an *Ente* configuration, that was small wings (canard) at the front and main wing at the rear, with a sweep of 52 degrees. The aircraft had a length of 9.67 m (31 ft 9 in), and was operated by one pilot sitting in a cockpit placed in the nose. The Me P 1110 was powered by a single He S011 turbojet engine located at the rear of the fuselage. The aircraft was expected to have a maximum speed of 1,000 km/h, and would have been armed with four MK 108 30-mm cannons mounted in the nose. This futuristic design was not completed.

Messerschmitt Me P 1111

Designed in January 1945, the Me P 1111 was an adventurous, delta-shaped, tailless, modern-looking fighter aircraft with a single heavily swept fin and rudder. The aerodynam-

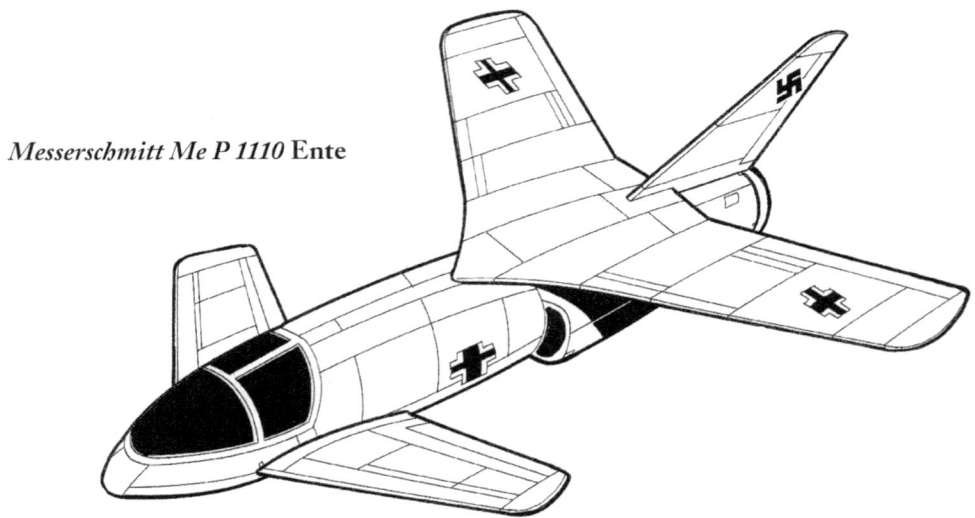

Messerschmitt Me P 1110 Ente

6. Jet Fighters

Messerschmitt Me P 1111

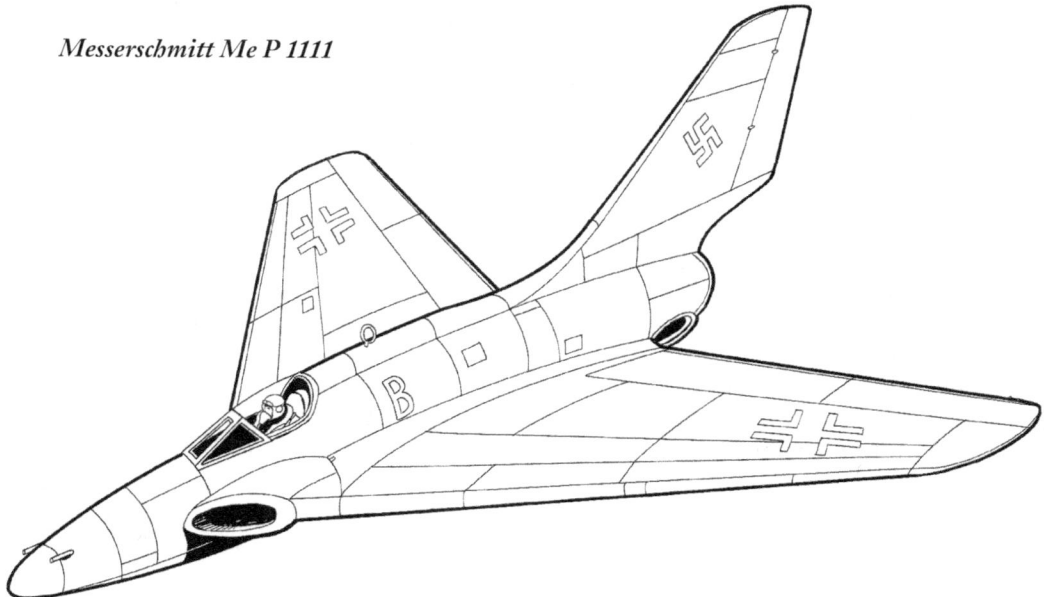

ically refined aircraft had a length of 8.92 m (29 ft 3.4 in) and the wings were swept back at 45 degrees with a span of 9.16 m (30 ft 1 in). The cockpit for a single pilot was pressurized and equipped with an ejection seat. The Me 1111 was to be armed with four MK 108 30-mm cannons (each with 100 rounds), two mounted in the wings and two placed in the nose. Maximum speed was estimated to 995 km/h (618 mph). The design never developed beyond a partially completed wooden mock-up.

Messerschmitt Me P 1112

The jet fighter Me P 1112, designed in March 1945 by engineer Waldemar Voigt, incorporated much experience gained with preceding designs. The tailless aircraft existed in several projected versions, with slightly different air intakes for the He S011 jet engine. It had a length of 8.25 m (27 ft 1 in), the sweptback wings had a span of 8.74 m (28 ft 8 in), and the craft was expected to fly at a maximum speed of 1,100 km/h (683 mph). The tail unit evolved from a conventional large single fin

Messerschmitt Me P 1112 S-2

and rudder to a smaller V-shaped design. The aircraft was fitted with a retractable tricycle landing gear. It was to be operated by a single pilot sitting in a semi-reclined position with an ejection seat in an armored, pressurized cockpit faired into the fuselage nose profile. Armament was to include four MK 108 30-mm cannons mounted in the sides of the fuselage. There was a planned version for a night fighter which was slightly enlarged and powered by two He S011 engines integrated into the wing roots. The Me P 1112 was planned to be ready by mid–1946. A mock-up construction of the forward fuselage section was built, but Allied forces overran the Oberammergau workshops in late April 1945. They captured documents, files and data, and Valdemar Voigt was soon employed by the U.S. aircraft company Chance Vought for whom he designed the postwar U.S. Navy Chance Vought F7U-1 Cutlass.

Blohm & Voss P 209-02

The P 209-02 was a single-seat jet fighter with a length of 8.78 m (28 ft 10 in) and a wing span of 8.1 m (26 ft 7 in). It was powered by one He S011 turbojet engine and was to have a speed of 988 km/h (614 mph). The fighter was to be armed with four MK 108/30 30-mm cannons mounted in the nose. It had

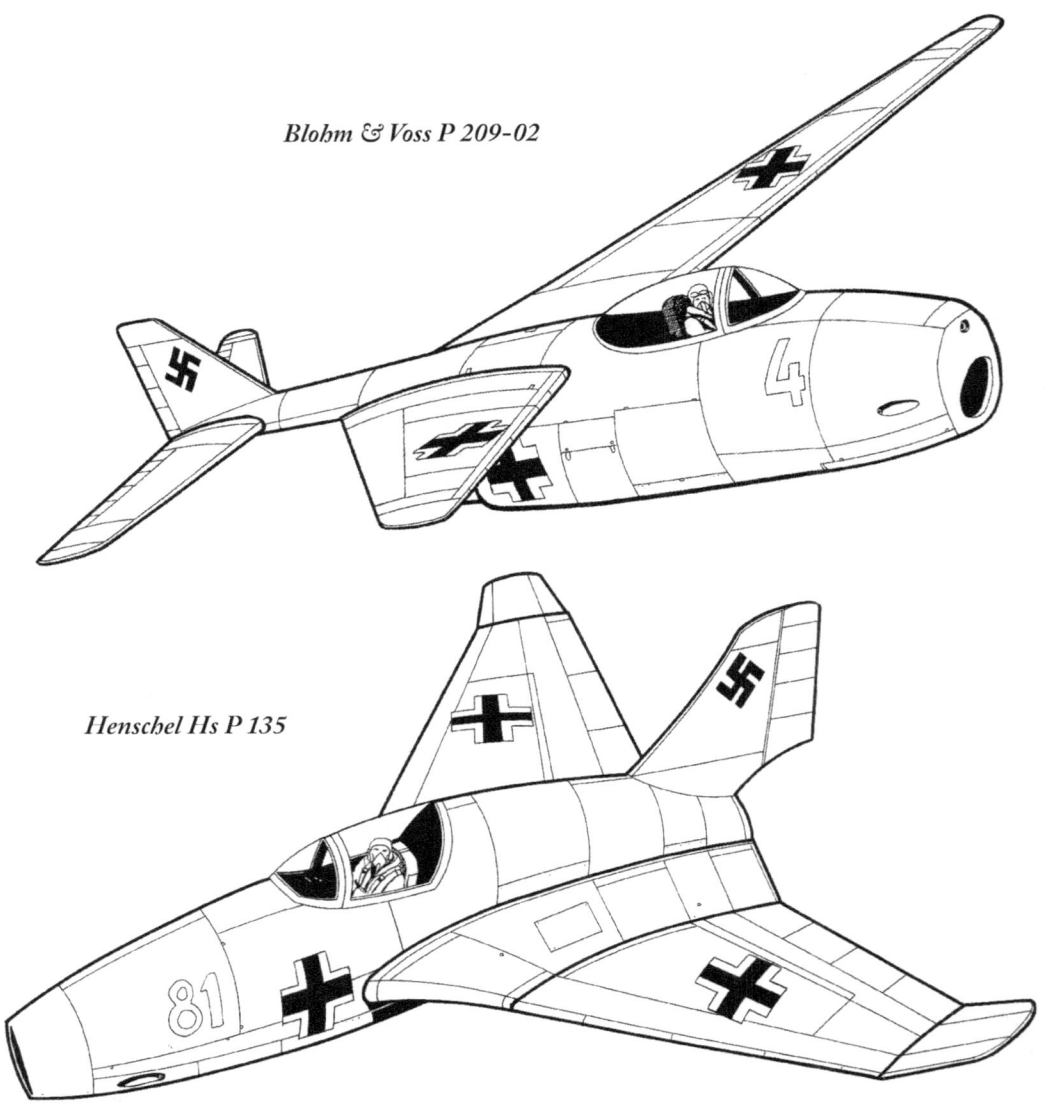

Blohm & Voss P 209-02

Henschel Hs P 135

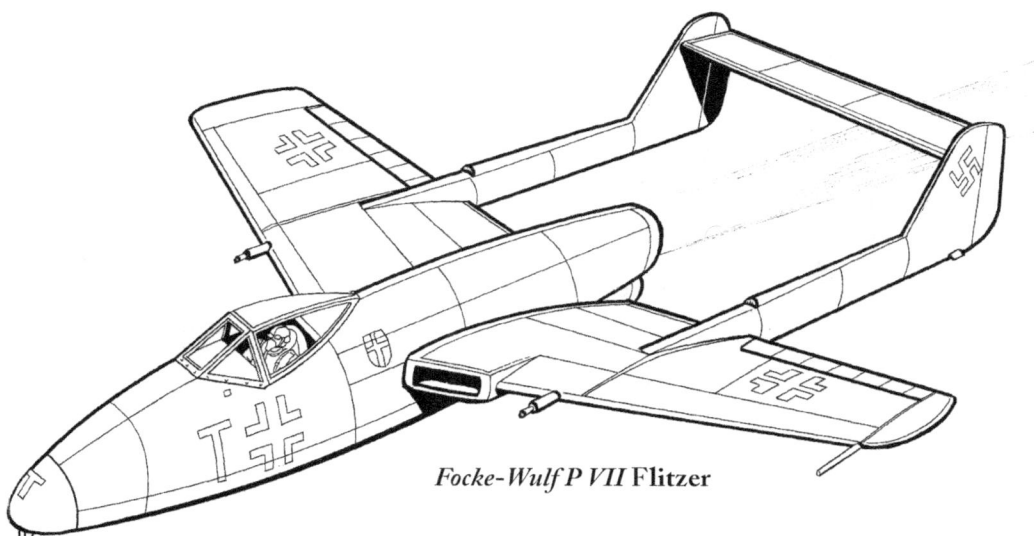
Focke-Wulf P VII **Flitzer**

a retractable tricycle landing gear, and its most striking feature was the sharply forward-swept wings.

Henschel Hs P 135

The single-pilot, tailless Hs P 135, designed in 1944, had a delta wing with a span of 9.2 m (30 ft 2.5 in) and a length of 7.75 m (25 ft 5.4 in). Powered by one He S011 turbojet engine, it was to have a speed of 985 km/h (612 mph). Planned armament consisted of four MK 108 30-mm cannons mounted in the nose.

Focke-Wulf Fw 281 P VII Flitzer

In March 1943, Focke-Wulf in Bremen initiated a series of design studies for single-seat, jet-powered fighters. *Entwurf 6*, also known as Projekt VI, was approved for mock-up construction in February 1944. The designation was later changed to Projekt VII and was given the code name *Flitzer* (Dasher). The mid-fuselage-mounted wings had moderate sweepback (32 degrees), twin booms and a high-mounted tailplane. Span was 8 m (26 ft 3.2 in), length was 9.8 m (32 ft 2.1 in), and maximum speed was 830 km/h (516 mph). The single He S 011A turbojet was to be supplemented with a Walter HWK 509 A-2 bi-fuel rocket mounted below the jet, although this arrangement was later revised, eliminating the rocket engine. Projected armament consisted of two MK 103 30-mm cannons or two MK 108 30-mm cannons in the lower nose and two MG 151/20 20-mm cannons in the wings. The *Flitzer* was well advanced in development, a full-size mock-up and some prototype sub-

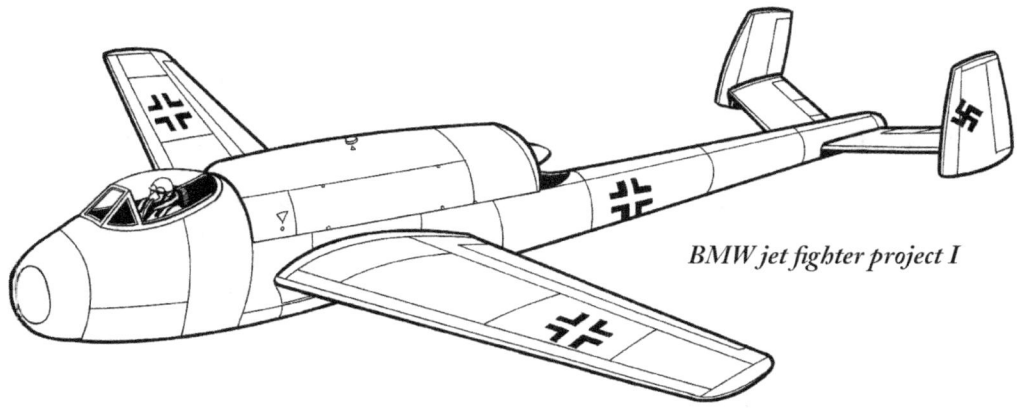
BMW jet fighter project I

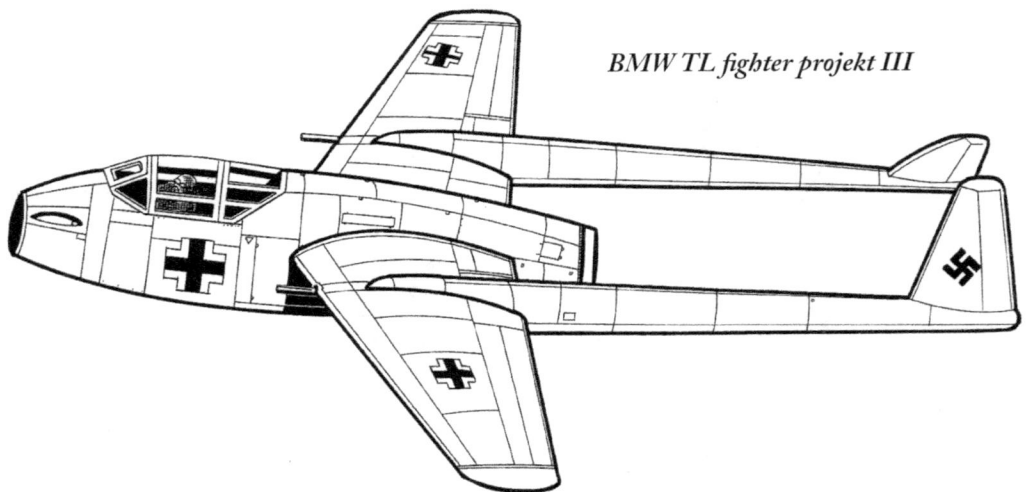

BMW TL fighter projekt III

assemblies being completed. The project was eventually abandoned because, though using only a single turbojet, its performance was no better than the Me 262 which was entering service.

BMW jet fighter project I

BMW's first project for a *Strahljäger* (jet fighter) was powered by a BMW 003 jet engine mounted on top of the fuselage behind the cockpit with a front air intake. The landing gear was planned to be of a tricycle arrangement, the tail included a twin fin and rudder, and planned armament was to include two cannons. Four designs were made under the leadership of engineer Dr. Huber in November 1944 by the EZS, a subsidiary company of BMW. No further data is available.

BMW TL fighter Projekt III

Another project for a fast single-seat jet fighter was developed in November 1944 under the direction of Dr. Huber by BMW subsidiary EZS. The aircraft would have had a short fuselage, with the air intake in the nose and ducting under the cockpit to the rear-fuselage-mounted BMW 003 turbojet. The wings featured a small amount of sweep on the leading edges; the trailing edges were straight. The twin tail booms had a single fin and rudder at the end of each boom, with the rudder canted inward. Armament would have consisted of two MK 103 30-mm cannons mounted in the forward end of the two tail booms. Unfortunately, no further details are available. The project did not develop further than the drawing board.

Focke-Wulf Project II

This was the second design from Kurt Tank of the Focke-Wulf company for a single-jet engine, single-seat fighter, submitted in June 1943. The wing was mounted mid-fuselage and had a slight sweep on the leading edge and straight trailing edges. The Focke-Wulf P II had a wing span of 9.7 m (31 ft 10 in), a length of 9.85 m (32 ft 4 in), a height of 4.43 m (14 ft 6 in), and a wing area of 15 square m (161.46 square ft). Empty it weighed 2,410 kg (5,313 lbs). A Jumo 004B turbojet was slung beneath the fuselage because of fears of operational problems associated with mounting the jet engine on top of the fuselage. The main advantage was to facilitate maintenance, but there were several bigger disadvantages to this design, such as the nose wheel blocking the intake on takeoff and landing, foreign matter being sucked into the intake since it was so close to the ground, and the destruction of the jet engine in case of a belly landing. Maximum speed was 850 km/h (528 mph) and maximum range was 640 km (398 miles). The cockpit was protected by armor of varying thicknesses. Armament was to be two MK 108 (70 rounds each) or two MK 103 30-mm can-

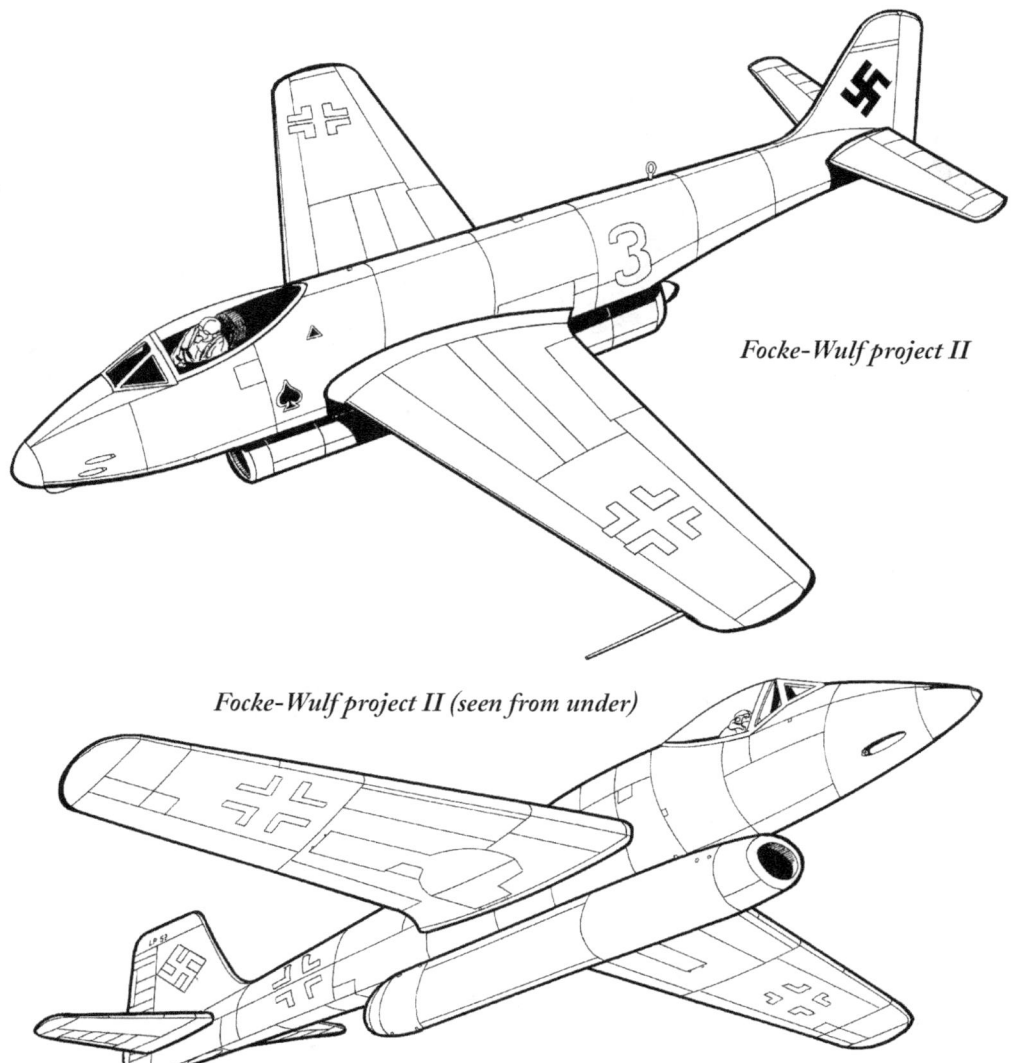

Focke-Wulf project II

Focke-Wulf project II (seen from under)

nons in the fuselage nose and two MG 151/20 20-mm cannons (175 rounds each) in the wing roots.

Focke-Wulf Fw Ta 183

The Fw Ta 183 jet fighter, designed by engineer Kurt Tank, Hans Mulhopp and their team, existed in several main versions. The first version of the aircraft consisted of a short and squat fuselage which was no more than a shroud for the single engine, with the cockpit and armament placed above it. The Ta 183 Design III, the second version, was similar in appearance to the first version, differing by its wings swept back at 40 degrees, cockpit set farther aft, and the tail unit which was of a conventional design, with a curvilinear sweep of the fuselage into the vertical tail. The horizontal tailplanes were mounted lower than on the first design, which were placed atop the vertical fin. The single pilot sat in a pressurized cockpit with a bubble canopy enabling full vision. The Ta 183 was fitted with a retractable tricycle landing gear. Span was 9.5 m (31 ft 2 in), length was 9.1 m (29 ft 10.3 in), and maximum speed was 965 km/h (599 mph) owing to a HeS011 or a Jumo 004 jet engine. Armament would have consisted of four MK 108 30-mm cannons located in the top, for-

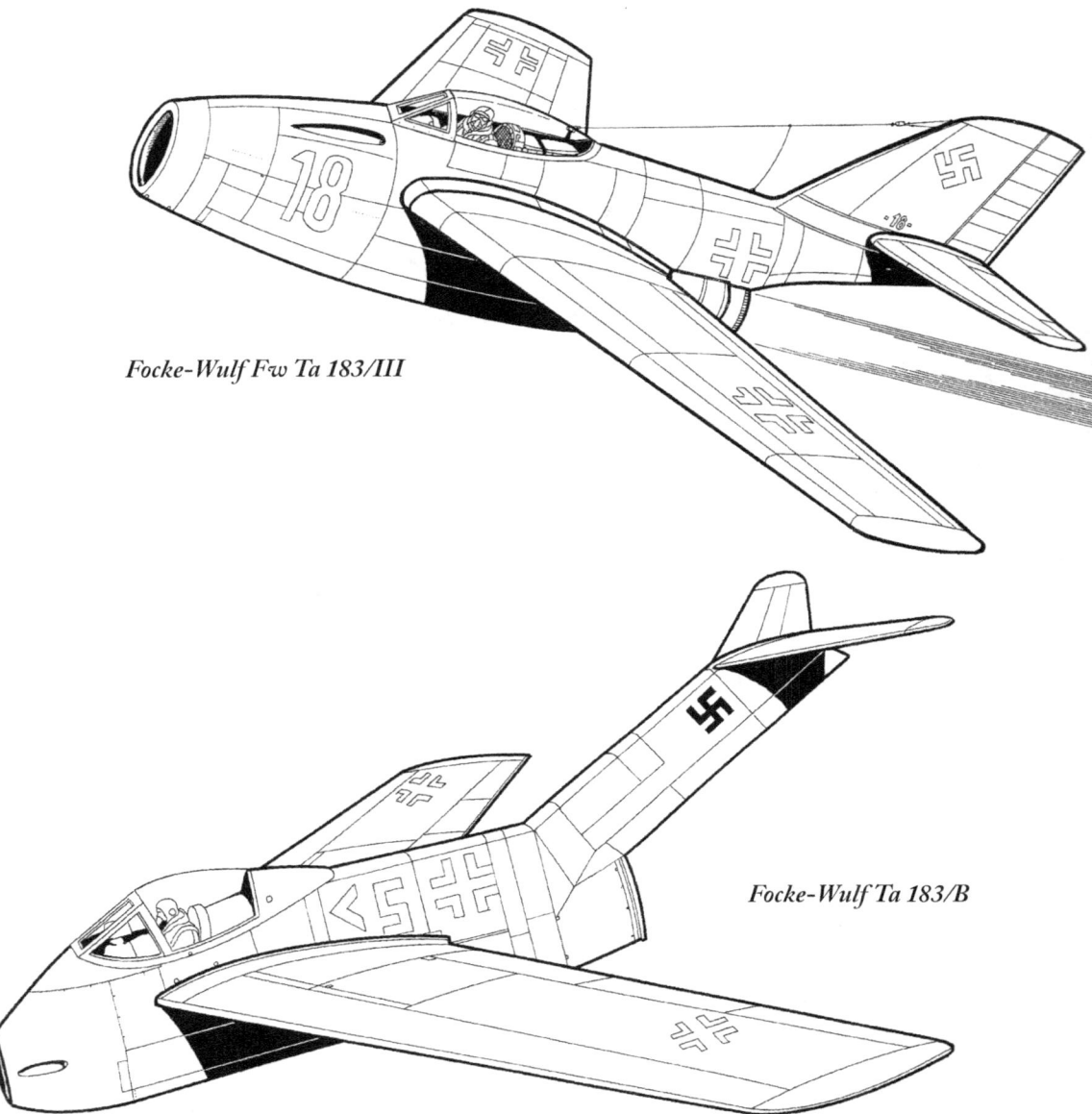

Focke-Wulf Fw Ta 183/III

Focke-Wulf Ta 183/B

ward fuselage. It was also envisioned that the aircraft could carry a bomb load of 500 kg (1,100 lbs) or even four Fritz-X missiles mounted in racks under the wings. Considerable attention was paid to ease of manufacture with the sort of resources which could be expected to be available. The result was that each Fw Ta 183 would require a total of 2,500 hours of labor (compared to 10,000 for the Messerschmitt Me 262). Scheduled to be operational by October 1945, the Fw Ta 183 series went undeveloped due to the ending of the war. The Ta 183's design was probably used by the Russians Mikoyan and Gurevich to develop the postwar MiG-14. A similar-looking aircraft, the SAAB-29, was later produced by the Swedish company Saab.

Focke-Wulf Fw P 127

The Focke-Wulf Fw P 127 was an attempt to create a fast, single-seat, jet-engined fighter. The aircraft was powered by a HeS 021 turbojet engine, placed within the fuselage just

6. Jet Fighters

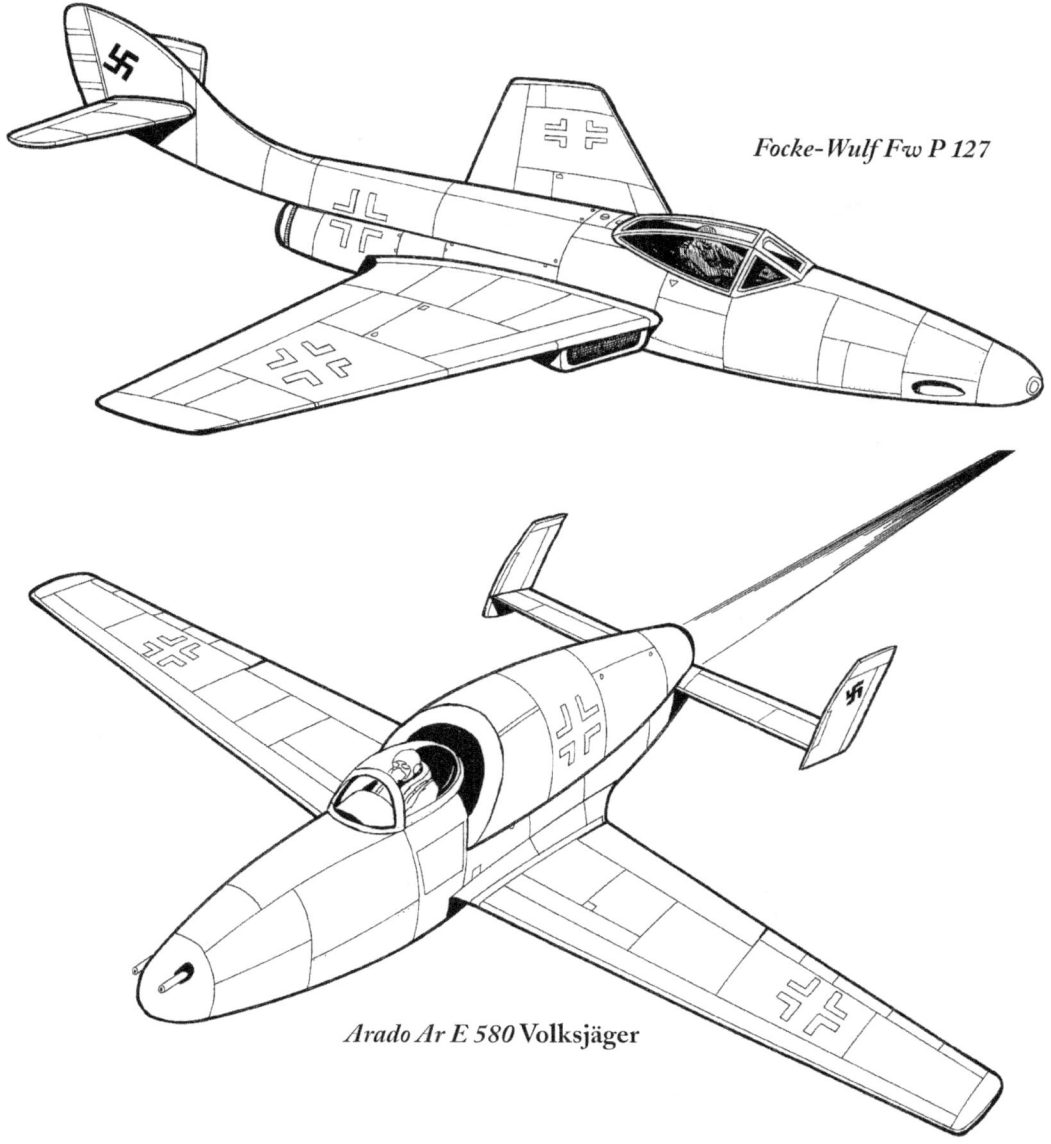

Focke-Wulf Fw P 127

Arado Ar E 580 Volksjäger

behind the cockpit. The engine was fed by two air intakes located in each wing root. The wings (mounted mid-fuselage) and tailplanes were swept back at 31 degrees. The landing gear was a tricycle arrangement. Span was 8.2 m (26 ft 11.1 in), length was 10.8 m (35 ft 5.5 in), and a maximum speed of 900 km/h (559 mph) was planned. Armament would have consisted of a single MK 103 30-mm cannon firing through the propeller hub and two MG 213 20-mm cannons placed in the lower forward fuselage. The project did not go further than the drawing board.

Arado Ar E 580

Based on an earlier 1943 model, the Arado Ar E 580 was designed in September 1944 to be a cheap and rapidly constructed *Volksjäger*. The aircraft had a length of 7.86 m (25 ft 9.7 in) and a span of 7.62 m (25 ft), with unswept wings mounted low on the fuselage. The tail unit included twin fins and rudders. The pilot sat in a cockpit placed right fore the air-intake of the single BMW 003A-1 jet engine positioned on top of the fuselage. The Ar E 580 was expected to have a maximum speed of 744 km/h (462 mph), and its armament would

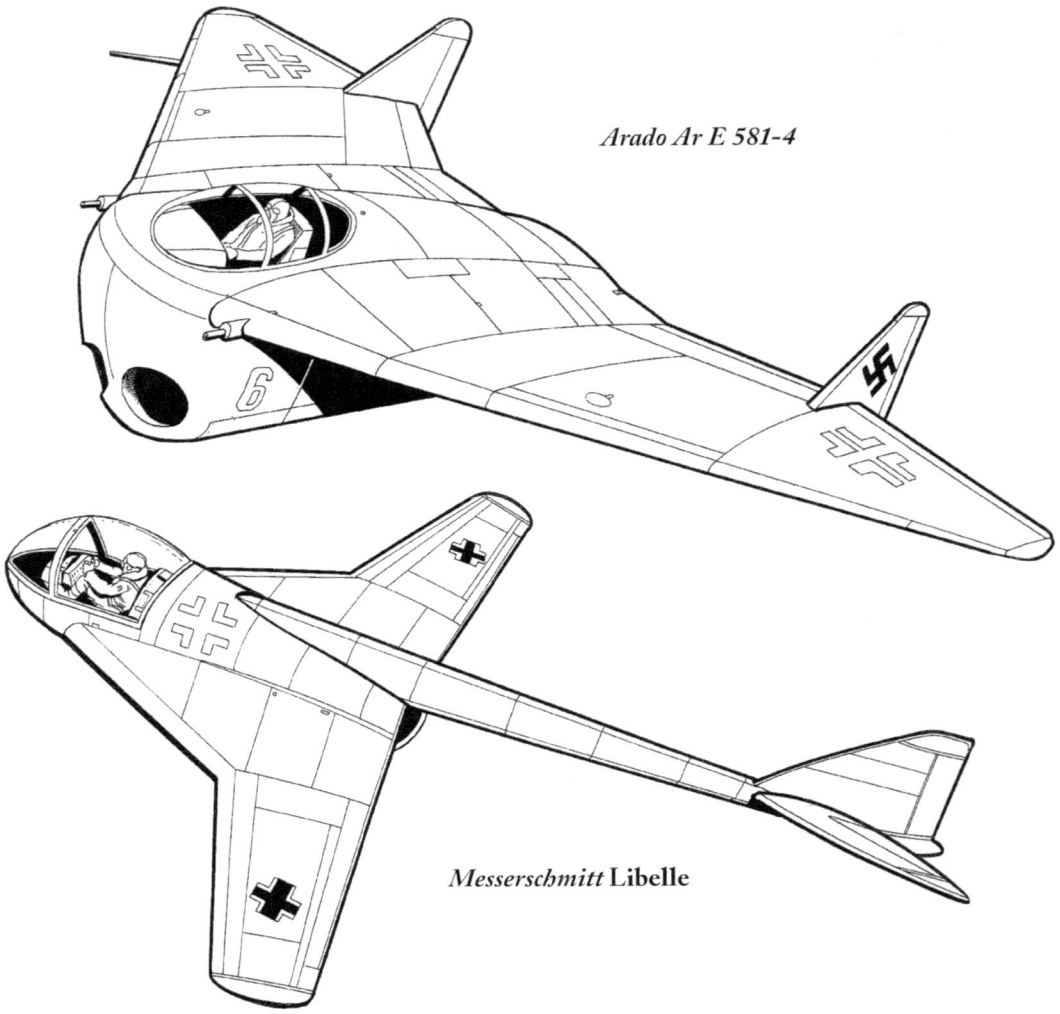

Arado Ar E 581-4

Messerschmitt Libelle

have included two MG 151/20 20-mm cannons or two MK 108 30-mm cannons mounted in the nose. The end of the war prevented any further development.

Arado Ar E 581-4

The Ar E 581-4, designed in early 1944, was to be a single-seat jet fighter. It was a delta-shaped flying wing with fins and rudders on the trailing edge. It had a span of 8 m (26 ft 3.2 in) and a length of 5.65 m (18 ft 6.6 in). It was powered by a Heinkel He S011 turbojet engine fed by two air intakes placed at the front under the cockpit. The aircraft was to have a maximum speed of 854 km/h (530 mph). It was fitted with a retractable tricycle undercarriage and was planned to be armed with two MK 30-mm cannons mounted in the nose.

Messerschmitt Libelle

The midget fighter Messerschmitt *Libelle* (Dragonfly) had an egg-shaped cockpit for the pilot, and a short fuselage with a long tail boom beginning above the jet exhaust and which held the V-shaped tail unit. The miniature aircraft was to be fitted with a retractable tricycle undercarriage and powered by a He S011 jet engine. The *Libelle* had a span of 7 m (22 ft 11.8 in) and a length of 7.3 m (23 ft 11.6 in). No further data is available about this project that did not leave the drawing board.

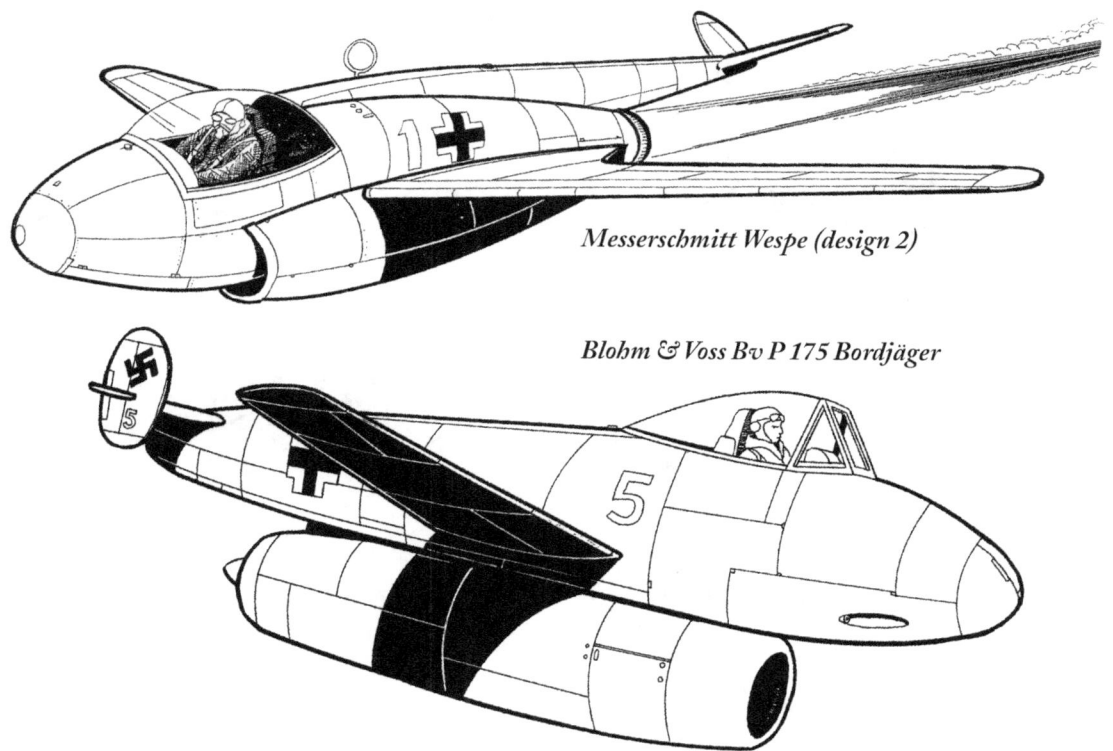

Messerschmitt Wespe (design 2)

Blohm & Voss Bv P 175 Bordjäger

Messerschmitt Wespe

The project Me *Wespe* (Wasp), a fast jet fighter, had a length of 10 m (32 ft 9 in), swept-back wings with a span of 8.65 m (28 ft 4 in) and a wing area of 15 square m (161.46 square ft). Powered by a single He S011 jet engine, the aircraft would have been armed with two MK 108 30-mm cannons. It was fitted with a retractable tricycle landing gear and operated by one pilot. The *Wespe* existed in two different versions. Project 1 had the cockpit placed midway on the fuselage and the jet engine was mounted at the rear. Project 2 had the cockpit placed forward and the engine located mid-fuselage with an air duct placed under the forward fuselage and exhaust below a slender tail boom with a V-shaped tail unit. The Messerschmitt *Wespe* was never completed.

Blohm & Voss Bv P 175

The Bv P 175 was a project for a *Bordjäger* (parasite fighter) which was carried and flown to the vicinity of the target by a larger airplane. It had a wing span of 6.2 m and was powered by a single Jumo 004 jet engine placed beneath the fuselage. It was armed with two M 108 30-mm cannons mounted in the nose. Once released from the launcher aircraft, the Bv 175 would attack its target with a speed of 810 km/h, then fly away to safety and finally land on its belly. This high-risk project was never developed. Similar designs were the Messerschmitt Me 1103 and Me 1104.

Twin-jet-Engined Fighters

Heinkel He 280

The single-seat, two-jet-engine fighter Heinkel He 280 was a remarkable achievement designed by engineer Max Müller from the Jumo Company. The second Heinkel jet aircraft had a span of 12 m (39 ft 5 in), a length of 10.20 m (33 ft 5.5 in), a height of 3.19 m (10 ft 6 in) and an empty weight of 3,350 kg (7,386 lbs). It had twin fins and retractable tricycle landing gear, and was powered by two Junkers Jumo 004A turbojets mounted under the

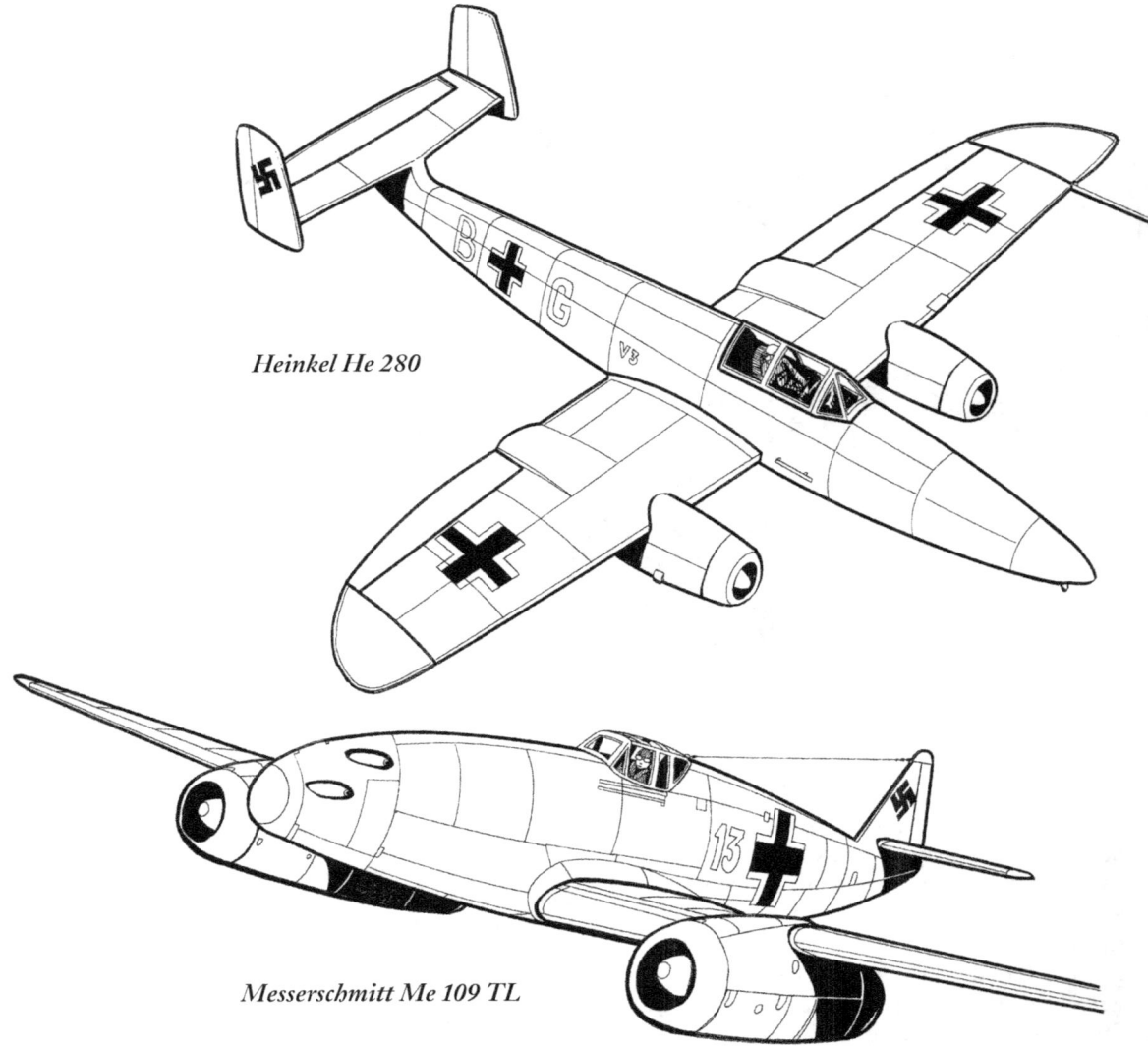

Heinkel He 280

Messerschmitt Me 109 TL

wings which gave a maximum speed of 817 km/h (508 mph) and a range of 615 km (382 miles). Intended armament was three 20-mm MG 151 cannons, and a bomb load of 500 kg (1,102 lbs) for the envisioned He 280B fighter/bomber version. The prototype He 280 V1 made its first flight in April 1941, and proved its excellent maneuverability and tremendous potential during a mock dogfight with a Focke-Wulf 190 in early 1942 which the He 280 easily won. Yet this attractive and advanced craft appeared at a time when the German leadership showed no interest in jet aircraft or any novelty that could not be used at once for a short *Blitzkrieg* campaign. The aircraft was plagued with engine troubles, but there are suggestions that the decision to reject the He 280 was political. In any case, the Heinkel project was abandoned in favor of the Messerschmitt Me 262. Only nine prototypes were built and used in a variety of test flights which greatly contributed to turbojet-powered-aircraft research.

Messerschmitt Me 109 TL

The Messerschmitt Me 109 *Strahltriebwerk* ("TL" indicating turbojet engine) was intended to be a single-seat fast fighter, but, at Hitler's instigation, the aircraft would also be used as a light bomber. Designed in January 1943, it was an interim, patchwork proposal composed of the fuselage of the Messerschmitt 155 B high-altitude fighter with a length of 9.5 m (31 ft 2 in). The wings were taken from the Messerschmitt Me 409 with a span of 12.55 m (41 ft 2 in). As for the carriage, it was borrowed from the Me 309. The aircraft would have been armed with two MG 151/20 20-mm cannons (each with 120 rounds) and two MK 103 30-mm cannons, all mounted in the nose. The Me 109 TL was to be powered by two Jumo 004A turbocharger jet engines placed under the wings; planned maximum speed was 980 km/h (609 mph). This project, for a fighter whose performance was expected to approximate that of the Me 262, was abandoned when all efforts were concentrated on the jet-engined Me 262.

Messerschmitt Me P 65 and Me P 1065

The Me P 65, designed in July 1940, was the initial proposal that led to the famous Me 262. The aircraft already displayed the Me 262's triangular "shark" fuselage cross-section but had unswept, tapered wings. It was to be powered by two BMW P3304 TL jet engines. A further design, known as Me P 1065, had outer wings with moderate back-sweep and jet engines placed above the wings in an attempt to improve the aircraft's center of gravity.

Messerschmitt Me 262

In the Me 262 *Schwalbe* (Swallow), Willy Messerschmitt and his chief designer, Woldemar Voigt, with Robert Lusser, Hans Mauch and Helmut Schlep, created a machine which could have restored to the Luftwaffe command of the sky over the Reich. Despite its tactical misuse and never-solved engine problems, the Me 262 was the first operational jet aircraft to serve in quantity with any air force. It is often described as one of the great "might-have-beens" of World War II. The Me 262 had been on the drawing board since 1938, but Hitler's blindness to technical innovation led to its development being delayed. Another holdup with the Me 262 was the failure of the aircraft company to come up with a reliable jet engine, the key problem being a shortage of the essential metals (nickel and chromium) needed to produce alloys for the engine's fins. The first prototype, fitted with a Jumo 210G piston

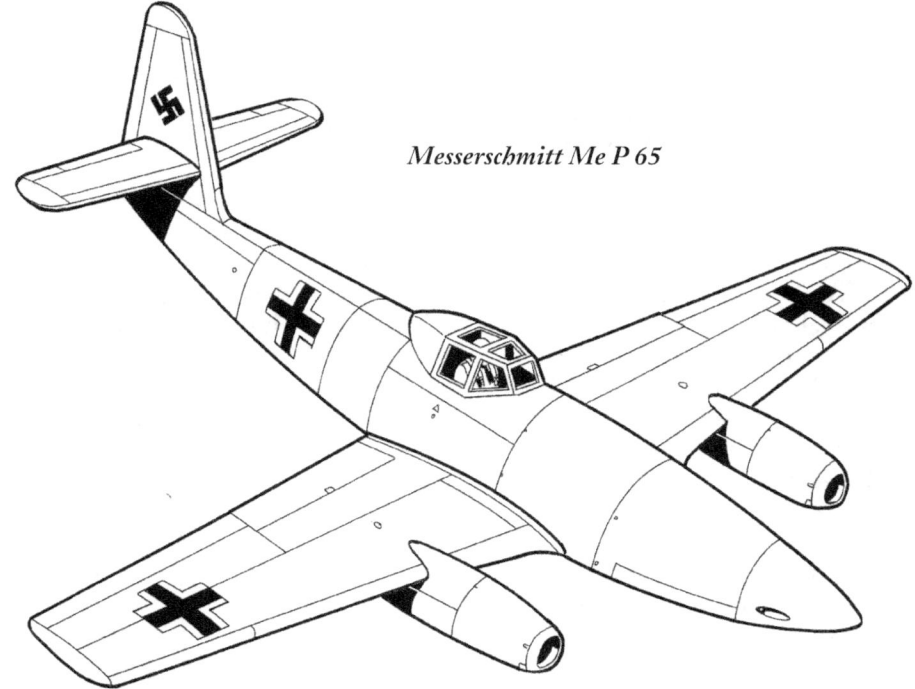

Messerschmitt Me P 65

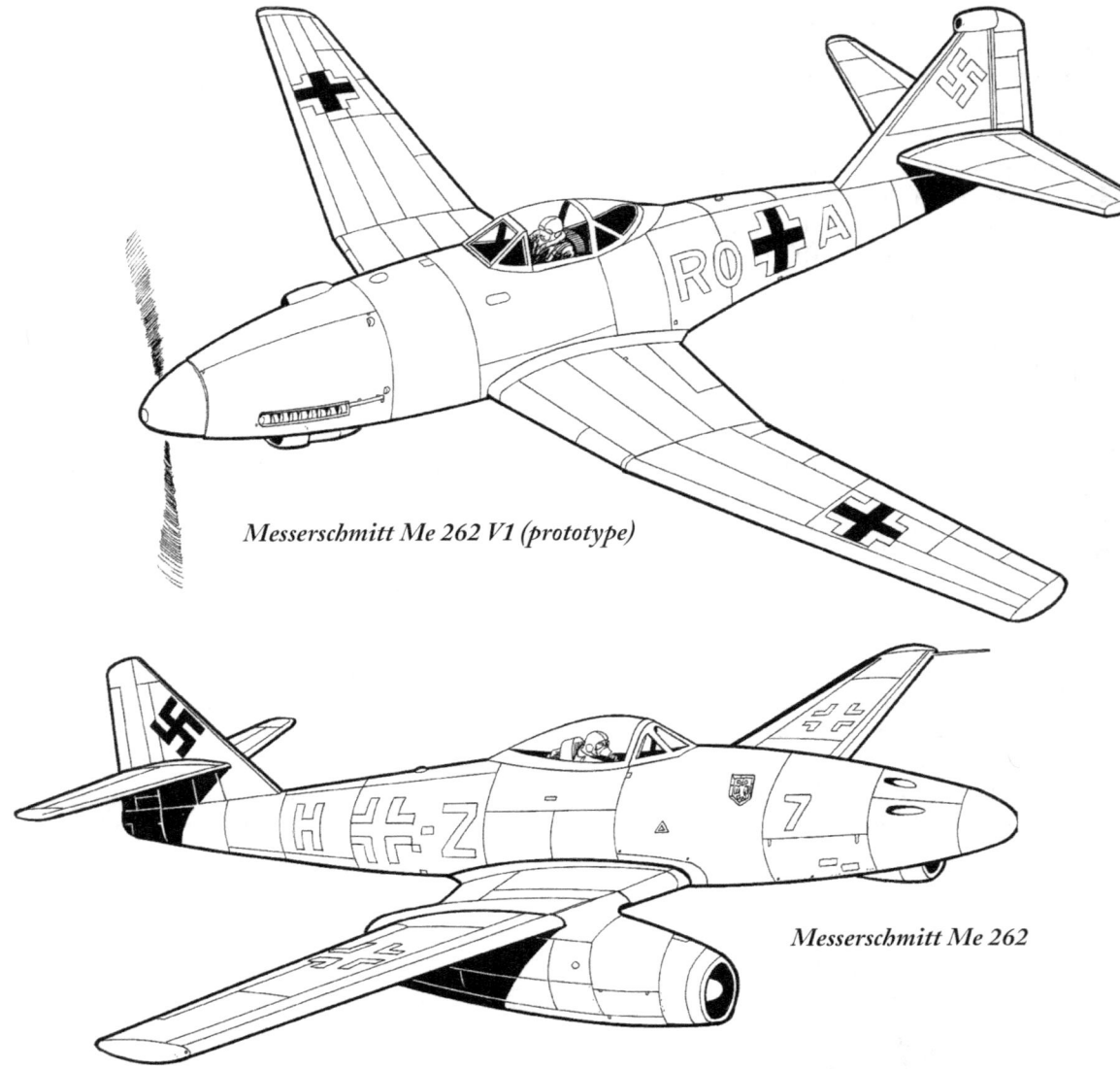

Messerschmitt Me 262 V1 (prototype)

Messerschmitt Me 262

engine in the nose and with tail-down landing gear, flew in April 1941. A third prototype made the first flight on jet power in July 1942, but further development was held back by military leaders' lack of interest. Hitler believed the war would be won soon, and the RLM thought they would not need such an advanced aircraft, and that production of a new model would interfere with the production of existing types.

By modern standards, the Me 262 was a fairly conventional all-metal aircraft with gently swept, low-set, variable-chord wings, powered by twin turbojets mounted under the wings. Compared with Allied fighters of its day, including the British jet-powered Gloster Meteor I, which entered RAF service at the same time, the new Me 262 was much faster and packed a much heavier punch. Both the Messerschmitt Bf 109 and Focke-Wulf Fw 190 could have been supplemented from 1943 and possibly replaced by 1944. Amazingly Hitler refused to consider the Me 262 as a fighter, and instead ordered its development as a bomber. To use the Me 262 as a bomber was ridiculous, as the airplane could only carry an insignificant load of bombs which only lowered its performances. But as a fighter/interceptor it was able, because of its phenomenal speed, to shoot down Allied bombers which in raid after raid were dropping thousands of tons of explosives on German cities. But the Me 262 was best suited to attack fighters escorting bombers, where speed and rate of climb were decisive factors. Hitler's interference delayed production, and ultimately the type entered moderate service, but it was not until July 1944 that a few machines were successfully tested in combat missions. A first regular squadron (8/ZG26) was formed in September 1944. At first there were accidents and casualties, mainly because of engine failure, undercarriage breaking, and complete lack of special training personnel. Nevertheless, although teething troubles were never totally cured, the Me 262 appeared a superb machine, with formidable flying qualities, tremendous speed, excellent maneuverability, and devastating armament against which the Allie had no answer. Finally the Me 262 did enter production, with a large measure of subterfuge in an effort to avoid Hitler's strictures; the Führer reluctantly allowed one in every twenty to be a fighter, but his order was discreetly ignored.

There were several versions of the Me 262, some actually built, others only planned, including a fighter armed with four 30-mm MK 108 cannons in nose; it's a two-seat bomber/dive bomber with 500-kg (1,100-lb) bomb load (some fitted with modified, glazed nose for bomb aiming); a destroyer armed with twenty-four 55-mm R4/M spin-stabilized air-to-air rockets or the large 50-mm MK 114 gun, or the formidable SG 500 *Jadgfaust* (twelve rifled mortar barrels firing heavy rounds up diagonally at Allied bomber formations); a two-seat, radar-equipped night fighter armed with 30-mm MK 108 *Schräge Musik* guns; a reconnais-

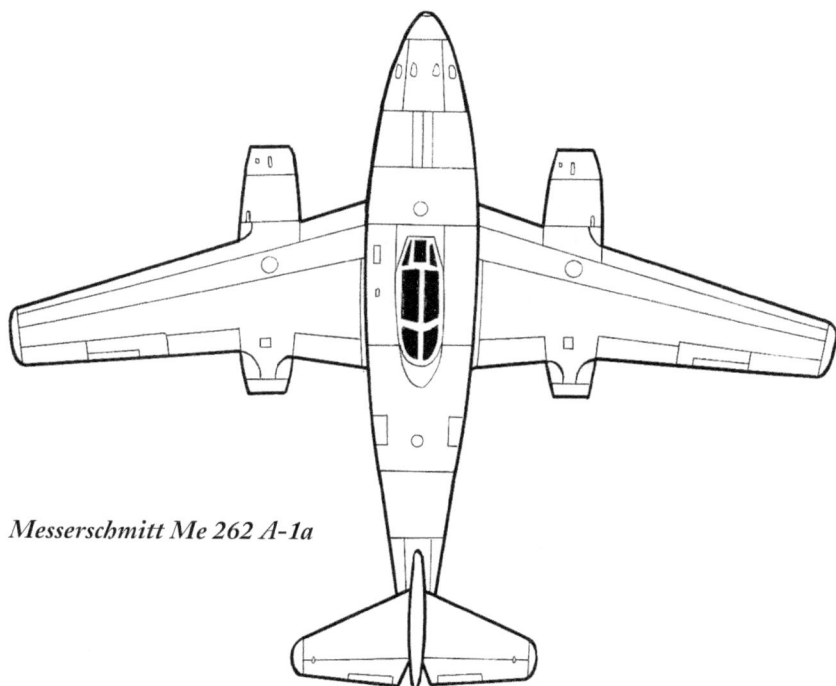

Messerschmitt Me 262 A-1a

sance aircraft fitted with camera and jettisonable fuel tanks; and a two-seat, dual-control trainer. The Messerschmitt Me 262 was fitted with a tricycle undercarriage, it had a span of 12.5 m (40 ft 11.5 in), a length of 10.6 m (34 ft 9.5 in), and an empty weight of 4,000 kg (8,820 lbs). Most versions were powered by two 900-kg (1,980-lb) thrust Junkers Jumo 004B single-shaft axial turbojets hung under the wings; some were fitted with rocket boosters. Engine reliability plagued the Me 262 throughout its short operational career. The Jumo 004 was prone to flame out, it required an overhaul after ten hours, and its total life was no longer than thirty hours. The aircraft had a typical speed of 870 km/h (540 mph) and a typical range of 1,050 km (650 miles), but performance varied according to weapons and equipment carried.

Total production by May 1945 is said to be 1,433 or 1,294 units, of which a majority were hopelessly grounded due to lack of fuel and trained pilots, with hundreds more under construction, damaged or destroyed in the factories by bombing. This was lucky for the Allies because the Me 262 was perhaps the most formidable Luftwaffe fighter of the war. Although the engine problem was never completely solved, there can be little denial that the Me 262 was a generation ahead of all Allied fighters, including their sole turbojet-powered plane, the Gloster Meteor. In capable hands, provided the engine ran smoothly, the 262 was formidable. Its impressive speed advantage could be used to make slashing attacks on Allied bombers, hurtling away faster than the escorts could react. A single burst from its 30-mm cannon or a volley of rockets was often enough to destroy an American B-17 or B-24 or a British Lancaster—or at least cripple it, causing it to fall out of formation where less capable German fighters could finish it off. In one month in early 1945, one Luftwaffe unit (*Jagdverband*—Jv 44, composed of experienced pilots and aces still alive), with an average of only six serviceable airplanes, destroyed no fewer than forty-five Allied aircraft. It must however pointed out that the Me 262's greatest asset, its speed, was often a problem when attacking Allied bombers. Flying some 250 mph faster than its target meant that the pilot had very little time to aim and fire.

The Messerschmitt Me 262 was undoubtedly one of the major landmarks in aviation history but its success was ultimately prevented by the Allied air supremacy. The only moment when the Me 262 was vulnerable to roving Allied fighters, was at take-off and landing. Fortunately, for too few Me 262s were built, and they were deployed in front-line combat much too late to have any effect on the outcome of World War II.

Messerschmitt Me 262 variants

As the famous Messerschmitt Me 262 went into production in 1944, it was only considered an interim type, and several variants were

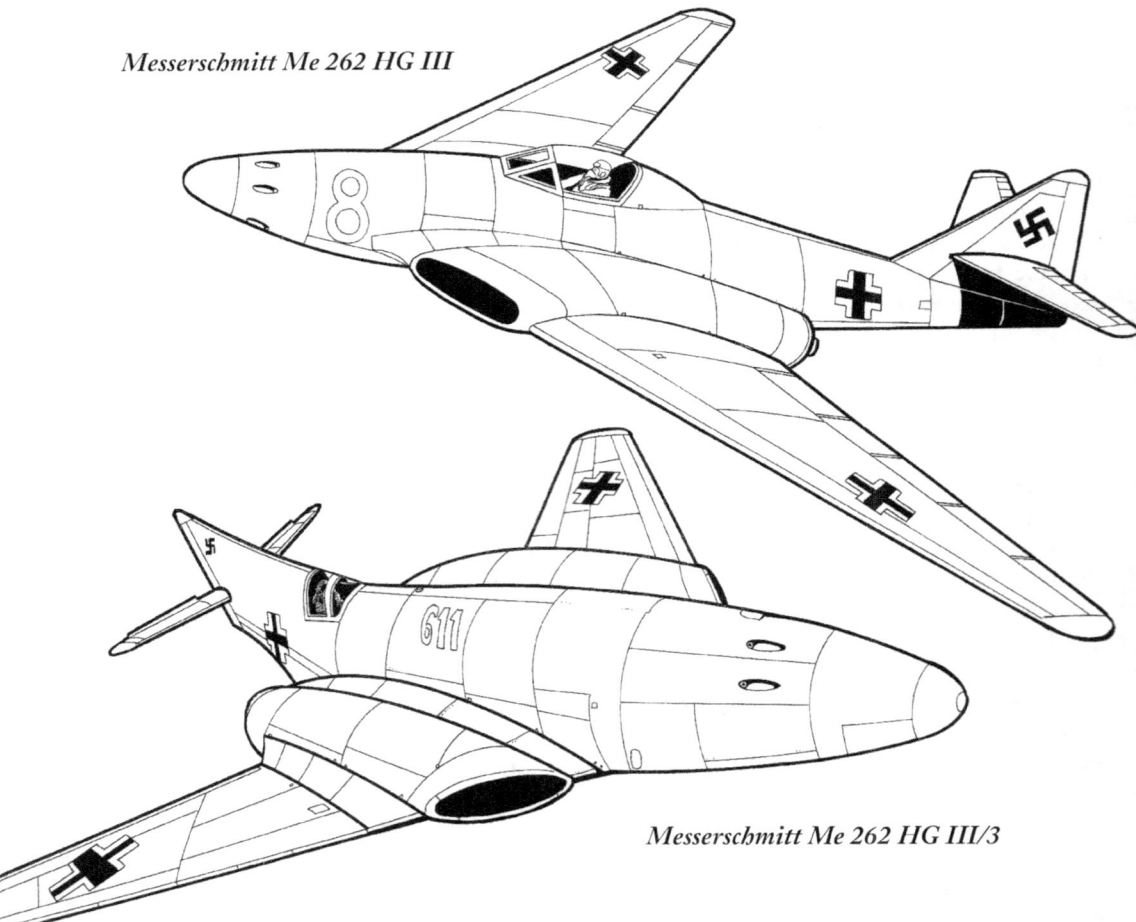

Messerschmitt Me 262 HG III

Messerschmitt Me 262 HG III/3

planned. The *Hochgeschwindigkeit* (HG—high-speed) versions with swept wings were envisaged as early as 1940 on the drawing board. A first version, known as Me 262 HG I, was actually flight-tested in 1944. This had only small changes to the Me 262 combat aircraft, most notably a low-profiled canopy to reduce drag.

One variant of the Me 262 was powered by two turboprop DB 021 engines, each driving a six-bladed propeller for less fuel consumption and thus extended flying endurance. This was designed in February 1945, but no further details are available.

There was also a variant for a night fighter, with a crew of three sitting in an enlarged cockpit; this was to be equipped with radar and armed with four MK 108 30-mm cannons and—in a ground-attacker version—carrying a bomb load of 1,000 kg. Other projected versions, known as Me 262 HG II and Me 262 HG III, were fitted with far more radical features. The Me 262 HG II variant combined the low-drag canopy with a 35-degree wing sweep and a butterfly tail. The Me 262 HG III had a conventional tail, a 45-degree wing sweep and the two He S 011 jet turbines embedded in the wing root. The HG series of Me 262 derivatives was planned to be capable of reaching transonic Mach numbers in level flight, with the top speed of the HG III being projected as Mach 0.96 at 6 km altitude. These projects, which consisted of an almost completely new design, with different appearances

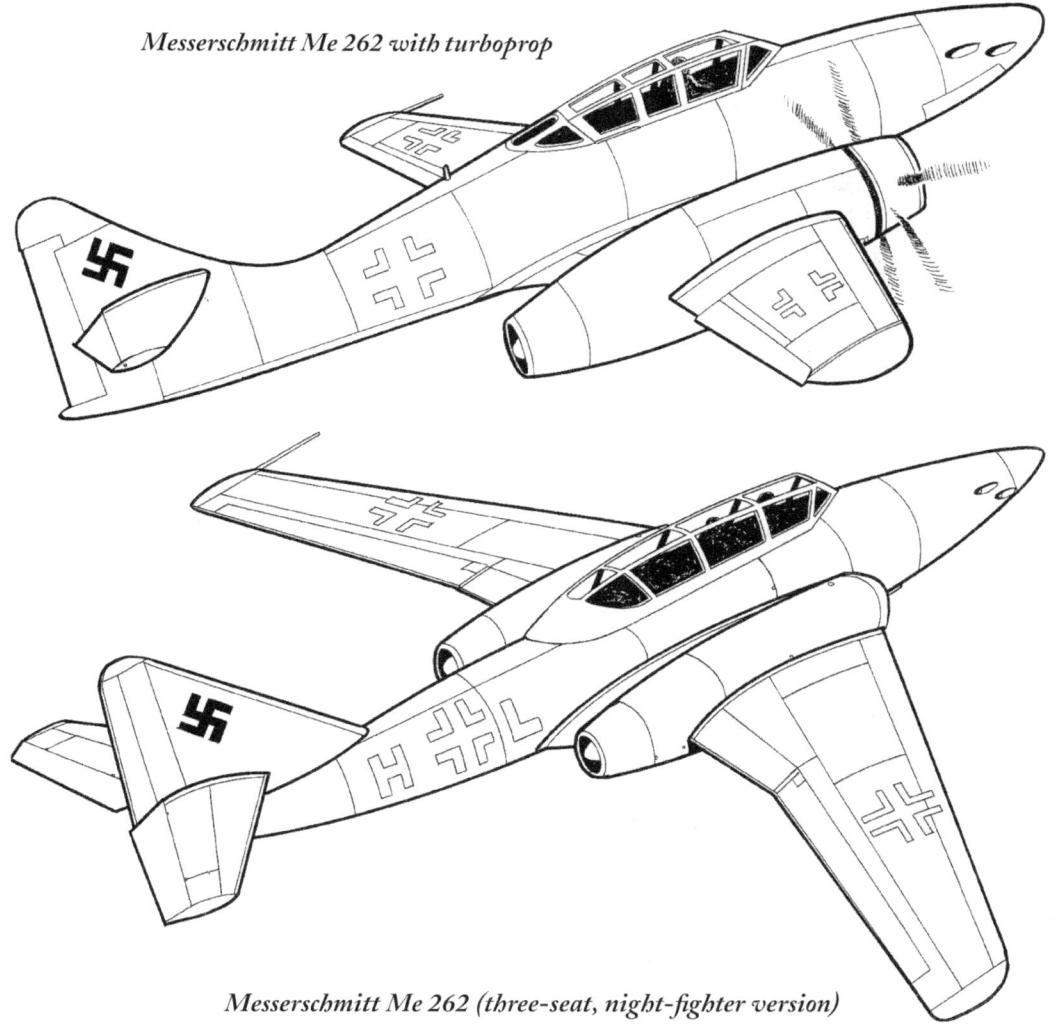

Messerschmitt Me 262 with turboprop

Messerschmitt Me 262 (three-seat, night-fighter version)

and profound structural modifications, were never further than the drawing board.

Messerschmitt Me P 1099 and 1100

Designed in January 1945, the fast fighter Me P 1099-A used many features of the Messerschmitt Me 262, notably the tail unit, landing gear, wings and engines, but the fuselage was redesigned, being slightly thicker. The crew of two sat in a cockpit placed in the totally rebuilt nose. It had a span of 12.58 m (41 ft 3.7 in) and a length of 12 m (39 ft 4.8 in). Powered by two Jumo 004-C turbojets mounted under the wings, the aircraft had a maximum speed of 825 km/h (512 mph). Planned armament was various: four MK 108 30-mm cannons, for example, would be mounted in the nose. There was a variant, designated Me P 1099-B, intended to be a night fighter;

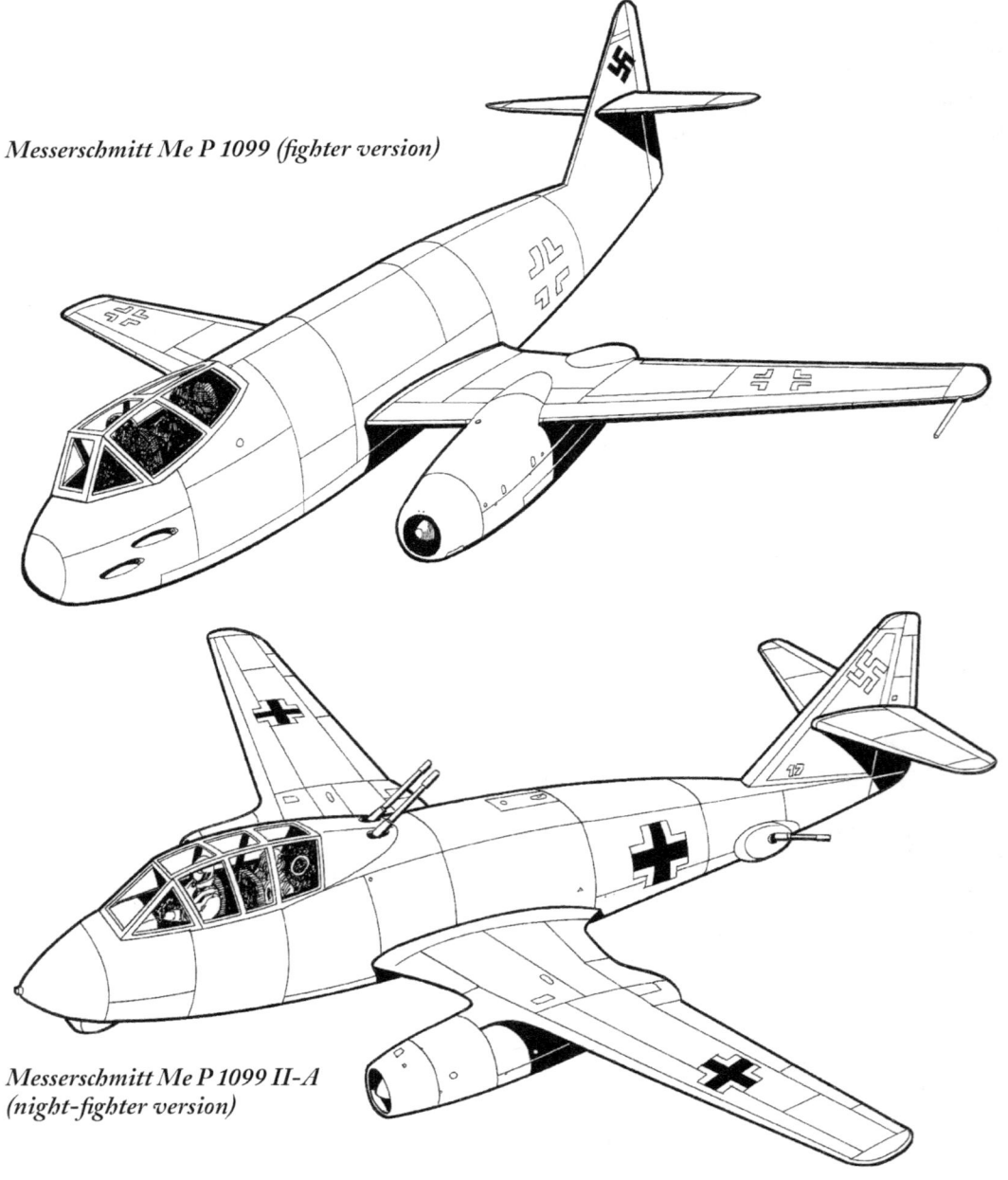

Messerschmitt Me P 1099 (fighter version)

Messerschmitt Me P 1099 II-A (night-fighter version)

this had a slightly different cockpit arrangement, with the crew of two sitting back to back, and would have been armed with *Schräge Musik* (two upward-firing MK 108 30-mm cannons placed behind the cockpit), and four MK 108 cannons firing forward. Another variant, designated Me P 1100, was a *Schnellbomber* (fast bomber) with a crew of one, carrying a bomb load of 2,800 kg. A further variant with swept wings was powered by two HeS 011 turbojet engines. The Me P 1099 and Me 1100 were never built.

Messerschmitt Me P 1101/92 and Me P 1101/99 Pulkzerstörer

The Me P 1101/92 *Pulkzerstörer* (bomber-formation destroyer) was the largest of the P 1101 Series, and fell somewhat out of the orderly lineage. It had swept-back wings with

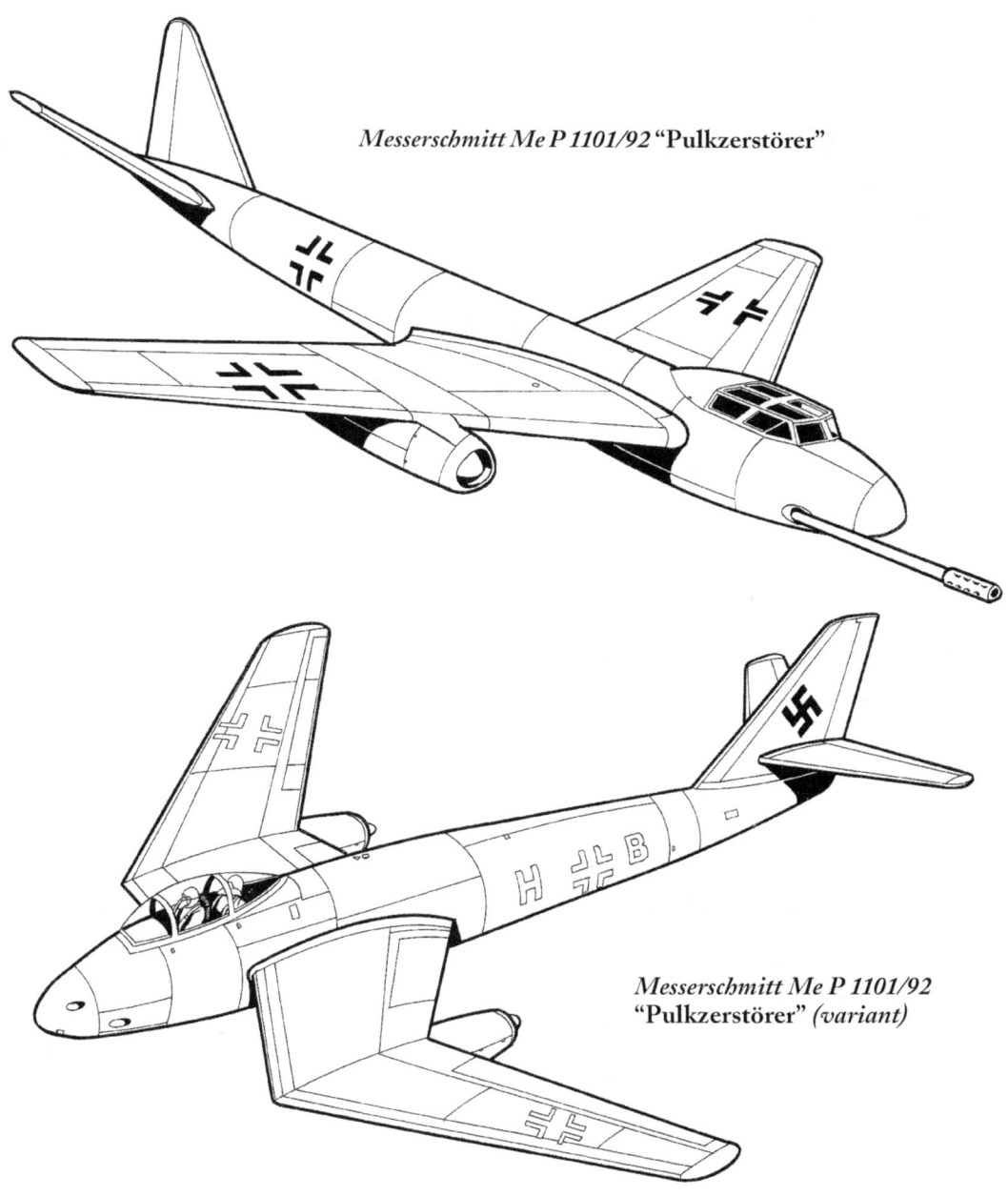

Messerschmitt Me P 1101/92 "Pulkzerstörer"

Messerschmitt Me P 1101/92 "Pulkzerstörer" *(variant)*

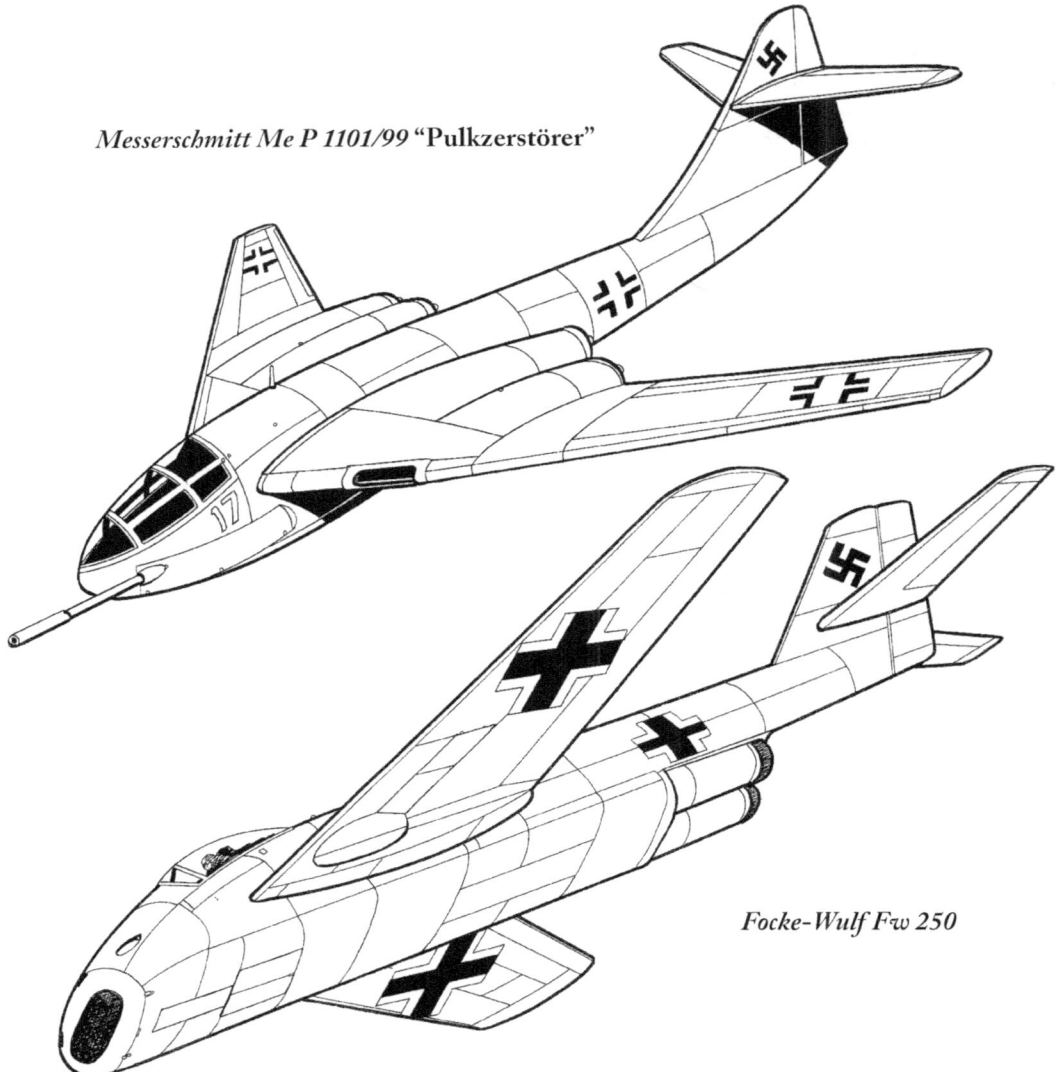

Messerschmitt Me P 1101/99 "Pulkzerstörer"

Focke-Wulf Fw 250

a span of 13.28 m (43 ft 6 in), a wing area of 35 square m (376 square ft), a length of 13.10 m (42 ft 11 in), and a height of 4.10 m (13 ft 5 in). Operated by a crew of two, it was powered by two under-wing Heinkel-Hirth HeS011 turbojets, each developing 1,300 kg (2.860 lbs) of thrust, with an expected speed of 900 km/h (558 mph). The machine had a V-shaped tail unit and a retractable tricycle landing gear. Intended to attack bomber formations, the aircraft was to be heavily armed with one 7.5-cm (3-in) cannon mounted offset on the right of the nose. It was also to carry one SD 1700B bomb. An alternative was a tailless aircraft with piston engine driving a pusher propeller.

There was a paper-project variant with a compound swept wing: sharp forward sweep on the inner third of the wing, and rearward sweep outboard of the engine nacelles.

Another yet more powerful two-seat *Pulkzerstörer*, mounting large-caliber weapons was the Messerschmitt Me P 1101/99. This was to be powered by four HeS011 turbojets located in the wing roots, with an expected speed of 960 km/h. The larger Me P 1101/99 had wing sweep of 45 degrees, a span of 14.50 m, a length of 15.20 m, a height of 4.90 m and a wing area of 47 square m. It was to be armed with one 7.5-cm Pak 40 anti-tank cannon and five MK 112 cannons.

6. Jet Fighters

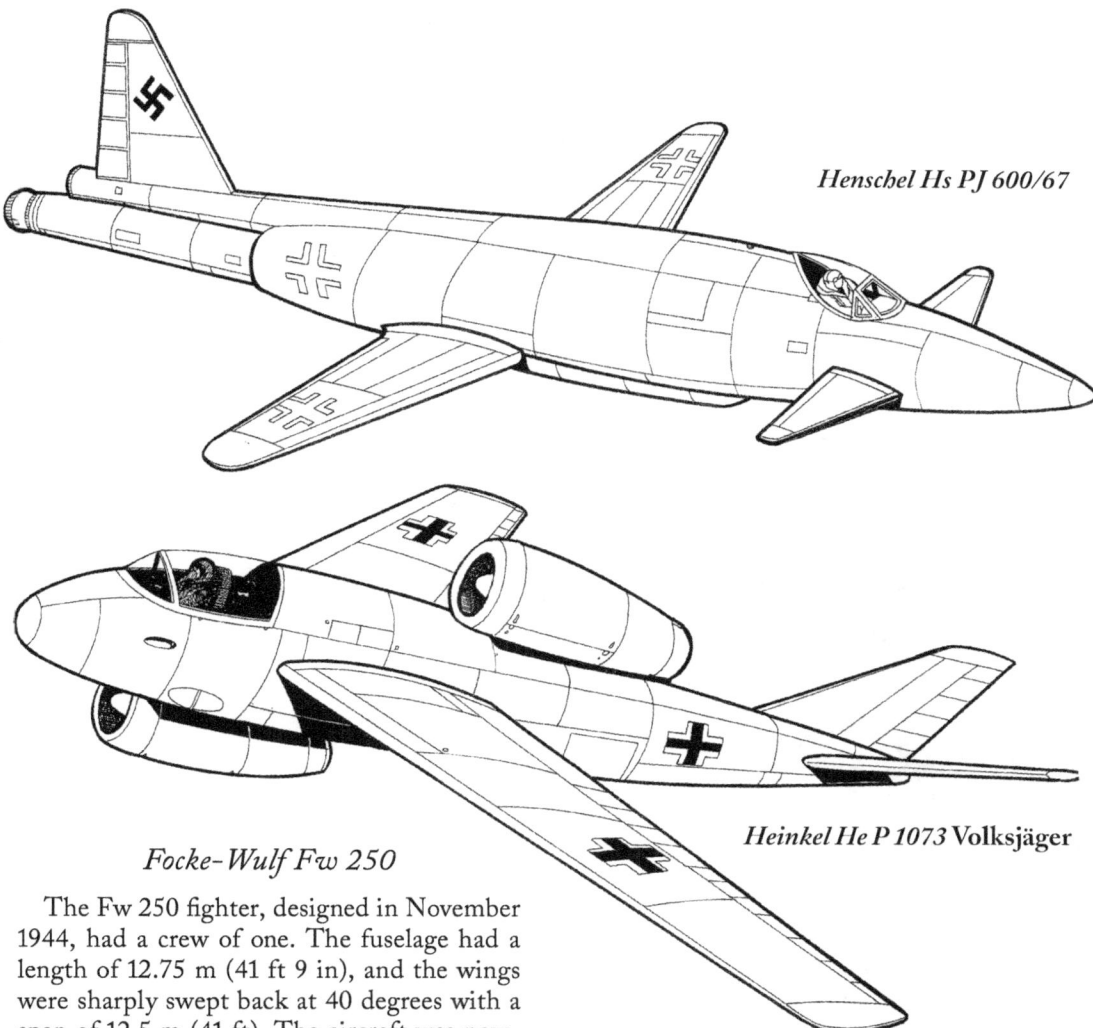

Henschel Hs PJ 600/67

Heinkel He P 1073 Volksjäger

Focke-Wulf Fw 250

The Fw 250 fighter, designed in November 1944, had a crew of one. The fuselage had a length of 12.75 m (41 ft 9 in), and the wings were sharply swept back at 40 degrees with a span of 12.5 m (41 ft). The aircraft was powered by two Heinkel Hirth S011 jet engines with front air intake. It would have had a maximum speed of 1,078 km/h (669 mph) and a range of 1,370 km (851 miles). The planned armament consisted of either four MK 108 30-mm cannons or four MG 213 20-mm cannons positioned in the nose. A fast-bomber version could have carried a bomb load of 1,000 kg (2,200 lbs). The defeat of Germany and the end of World War II prevented any development of this jet fighter/bomber with formidable potential.

Henschel Hs 600/67

This project for a manned "canard"-design aircraft was to be fitted with two Argus-Staurohre As 044 engines developing 500 kp thrust each. Its span was 8 meters and its length 11 meters. The armament would have included two MG 151/20 guns placed in a special belly compartment called *Waffen-Wanne*, similar to those used on Ju 88G and He 219. A wooden scale model of the Hs 600/67 was tested in a wind tunnel, but the further fate of this experimental jet fighter remains unknown.

Heinkel He P 1073

Heinkel's original design of the P 1073 was later redesigned for submission in the *Volksjäger* competition, was a single-seat aircraft with a length of 10.32 m (33 ft 10.6 in) and a

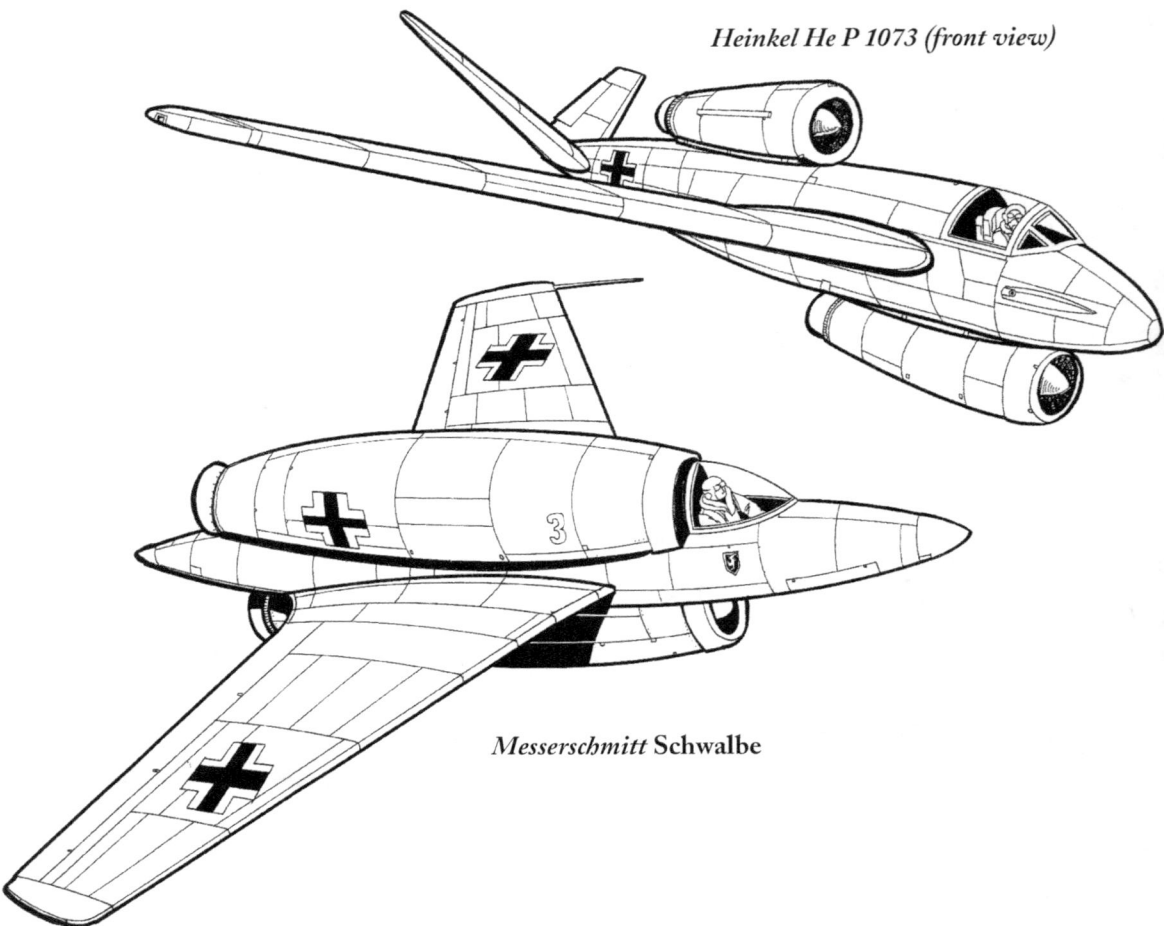

Heinkel He P 1073 (front view)

Messerschmitt Schwalbe

span of 12 m (39 ft 4.8 in), featuring a midwing swept-back wing with a V tail. The experimental fighter was to be powered by two HeS 011 jet engines (or two BMW 003 turbojets) located one on top and one underneath the fuselage in order to keep the wings unencumbered. When using HeS 011 engines, a maximum speed of 1,010 km/h (627 mph) was expected. Armament would have consisted of two MK 108 30-mm cannons.

Messerschmitt Schwalbe

The Messerschmitt *Schwalbe* (Swallow) was a tailless, single-seat jet fighter with a length of 8.9 m (29 ft 2 in), wings swept back at 31 degrees, a span of 9.05 m (29 ft 8 in), and a wing area of 20 square m (215.28 square ft). The most radical of all the experimental configurations designed by Messerschmitt, the aircraft was to be powered by two turbojet engines, one placed above the fuselage and the other below; the aircraft's speed was estimated to be about 950 km/h. A wide-track, retractable, tricycle landing gear would be used. The pilot sat in a cockpit placed at the front between the engines' air intakes. The *Schwalbe* was never built.

Blohm & Voss Bv 197-01

This modern-looking, single-seat fighter aircraft had a length of 9 m (29 ft 6.6 in). The wings, mounted low on the fuselage were swept back, with a span of 11 m (36 ft 5.3 in). Powered by two BMW 003 turbojet engines placed at the rear, it was expected to have a maximum speed of 1,000 km/h (621 mph). Armament would have consisted of two MK 103 30-mm cannons and two MG 151/20

6. Jet Fighters   295

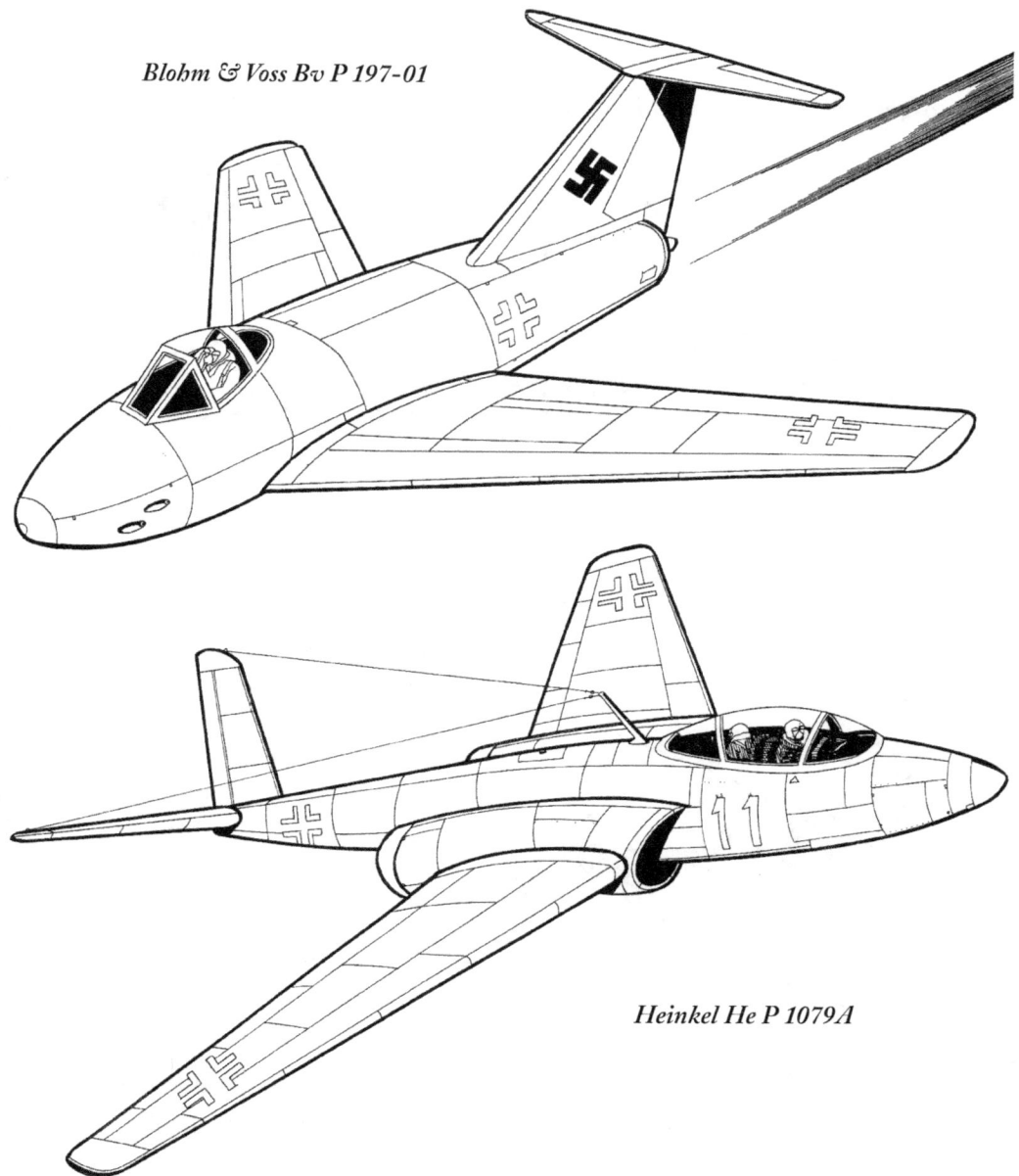

Blohm & Voss Bv P 197-01

Heinkel He P 1079A

20-mm cannons, all mounted in the fuselage nose.

Heinkel He P 1079 A

The first of five designs, the He P 1079A was intended to become a Luftwaffe night fighter. The aircraft would have had a length of 14.25 m (46 ft 9.4 in), a V-shaped tail unit, wings swept back 35 degrees and mounted mid-fuselage with a span of 13 m (42 ft 8.2 in).

The aircraft would have been powered by two HeS 011 turbojets located in the wing roots, and maximum speed would have been 950 km/h (590 mph). Armament was to be four MK 108 30-mm cannons, and the crew of two would have sat back to back in the cockpit which was located near the nose. The very modern design was not developed.

Two variants, known as Heinkel He P BI and He P BII, were flying wings.

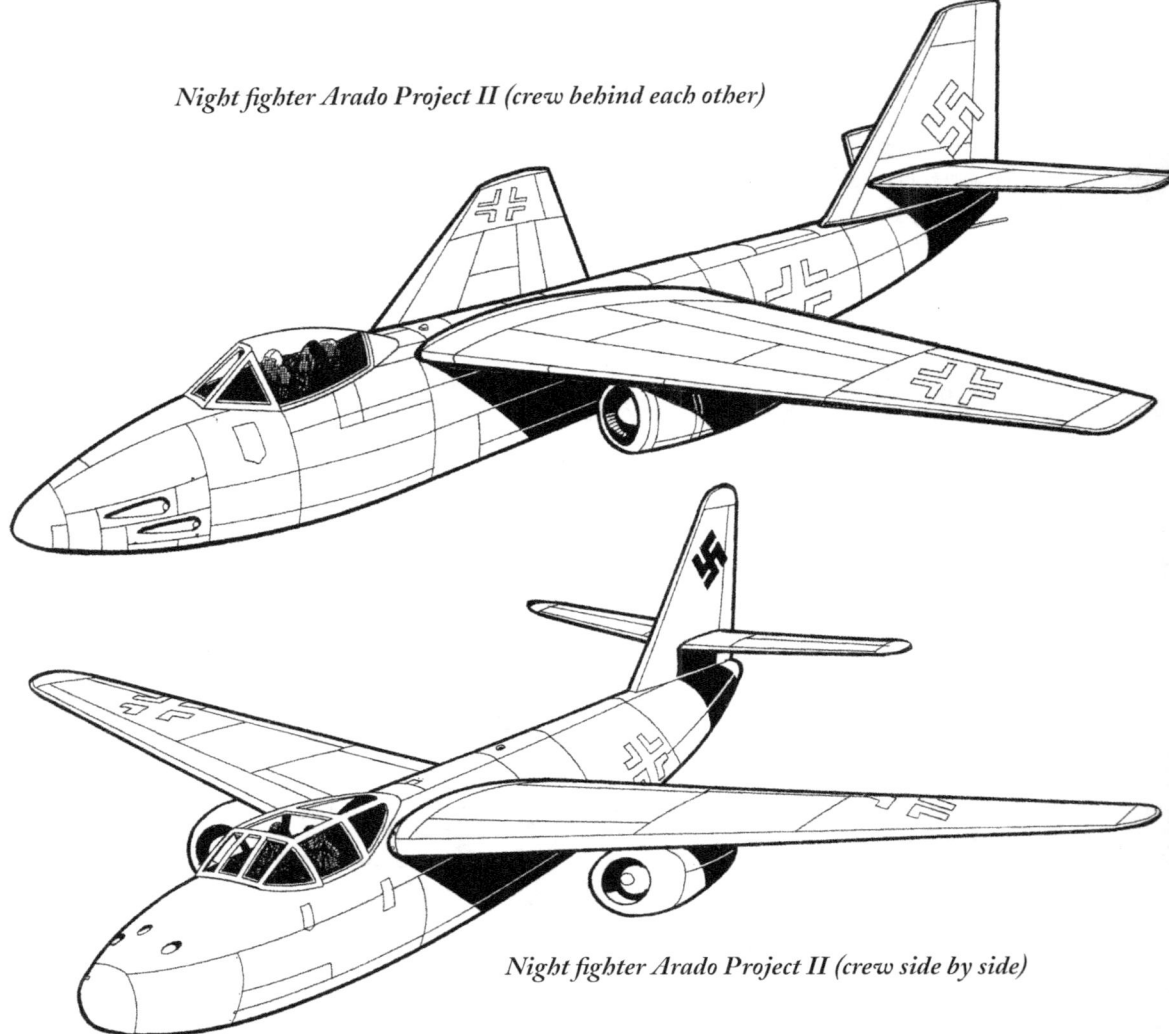

Night fighter Arado Project II (crew behind each other)

Night fighter Arado Project II (crew side by side)

Arado Project II

This second Arado project for a night/all-weather fighter was designed in March 1945. The aircraft was operated by a crew of two who sat in a pressurized cockpit fitted with ejector seats. There were two designs for the cockpit, one with the crew sitting one after another, the other sitting side by side. The experimental aircraft had a length of 17.3 m (56 ft 9.6 in) and a span of 14.98 m (49 ft 2 in). This craft would have been powered by either two HeS 011A or two BMW 003A-1 jet engines located under each wing. With BMW engines, a speed of 750 km/h (466 mph) was expected. The armament would have consisted of four MK 108 30-mm cannons placed in the nose. Due to the ending of the war, this Arado project never reached completion.

Experimental Jet Fighters

Junkers Ju EF 009 Hubjäger

The Ju EF 009 was a rather curious aircraft. The most striking feature was the jet engines, ten of them mounted around the fuselage at the wing's leading edge, six on top and four underneath, hence the name of the fighter—the German adverb *huben* means "at the side." Expected speed was 905 km/h (562 mph). The

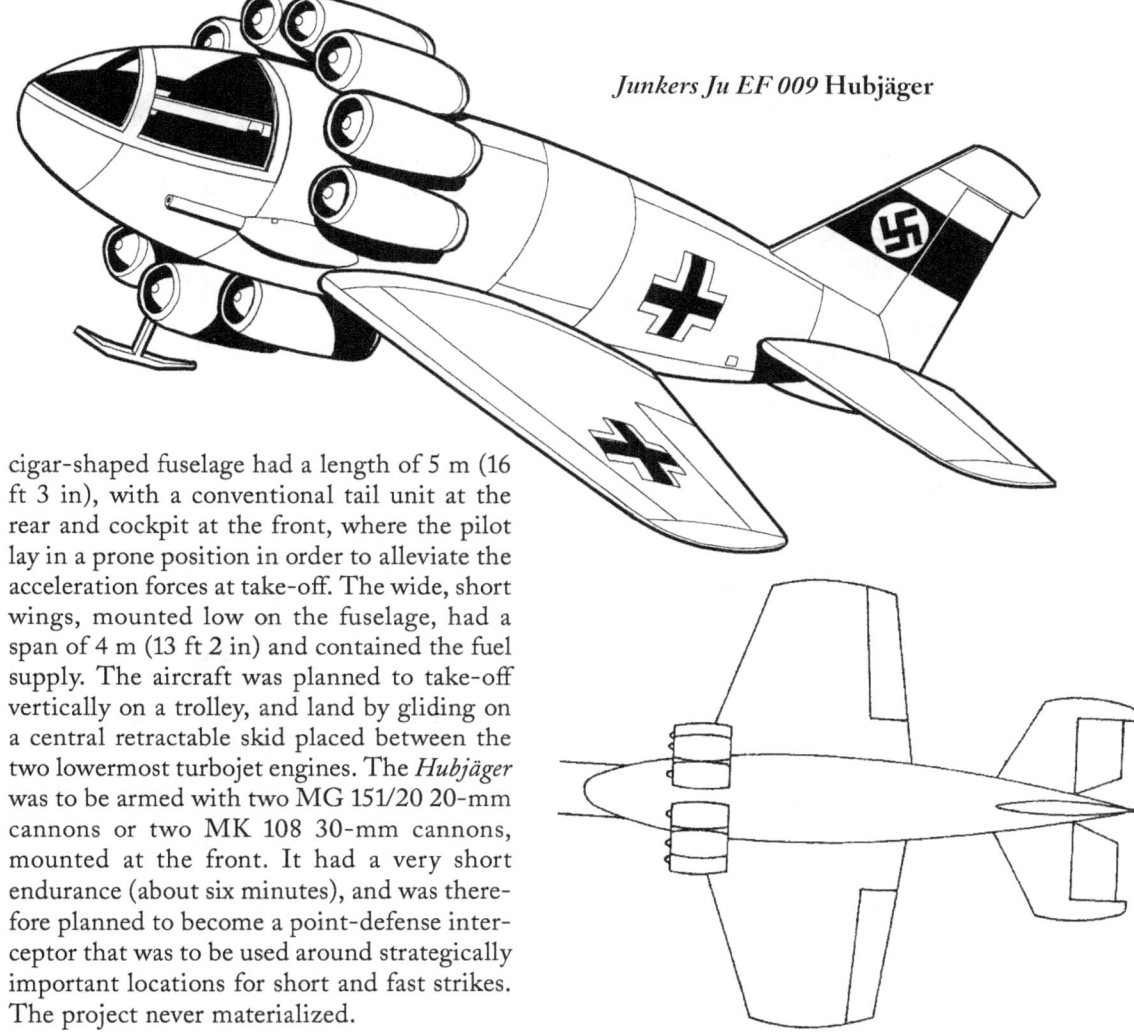

Junkers Ju EF 009 **Hubjäger**

cigar-shaped fuselage had a length of 5 m (16 ft 3 in), with a conventional tail unit at the rear and cockpit at the front, where the pilot lay in a prone position in order to alleviate the acceleration forces at take-off. The wide, short wings, mounted low on the fuselage, had a span of 4 m (13 ft 2 in) and contained the fuel supply. The aircraft was planned to take-off vertically on a trolley, and land by gliding on a central retractable skid placed between the two lowermost turbojet engines. The *Hubjäger* was to be armed with two MG 151/20 20-mm cannons or two MK 108 30-mm cannons, mounted at the front. It had a very short endurance (about six minutes), and was therefore planned to become a point-defense interceptor that was to be used around strategically important locations for short and fast strikes. The project never materialized.

Messerschmitt Me P 1109

The daring concept behind the Me P 1109 designed in February 1944 was the use of variable geometry. A pair of pivoting wings mounted above and under the fuselage were in their normal unswept position for take-off and landing, and swiveled in opposite direction for high-speed cruise flight. The design existed in two similar proposals, both to be powered by two HeS011 turbojet engines placed on each side of the fuselage. Span with wings in unswept position was 9.40 m (39 ft 10 in) and length was 12 m. Projected armament and performance data for this questionable and almost unbelievable project are not available.

Junkers Ju EF 009 **Hubjäger**

Lippisch DM-1

The performance of the Messerschmitt Me 163 Komet encouraged engineer Alexander Lippisch to experiment with high-velocity, delta-winged aircraft flying beyond the speed of sound. In 1943 Lippisch became director of the *Luftfahrtforschungsanstalt Wien* (LFW— Aeronautical Research Institute at Vienna) and began to develop supersonic designs. Several experiments culminated in the design of the Lippisch DM-1 (Darmstadt-Munich model 1) glider. The one-seat, sharply-swept delta-wing DM-1 had a wingspan of 5.9 m

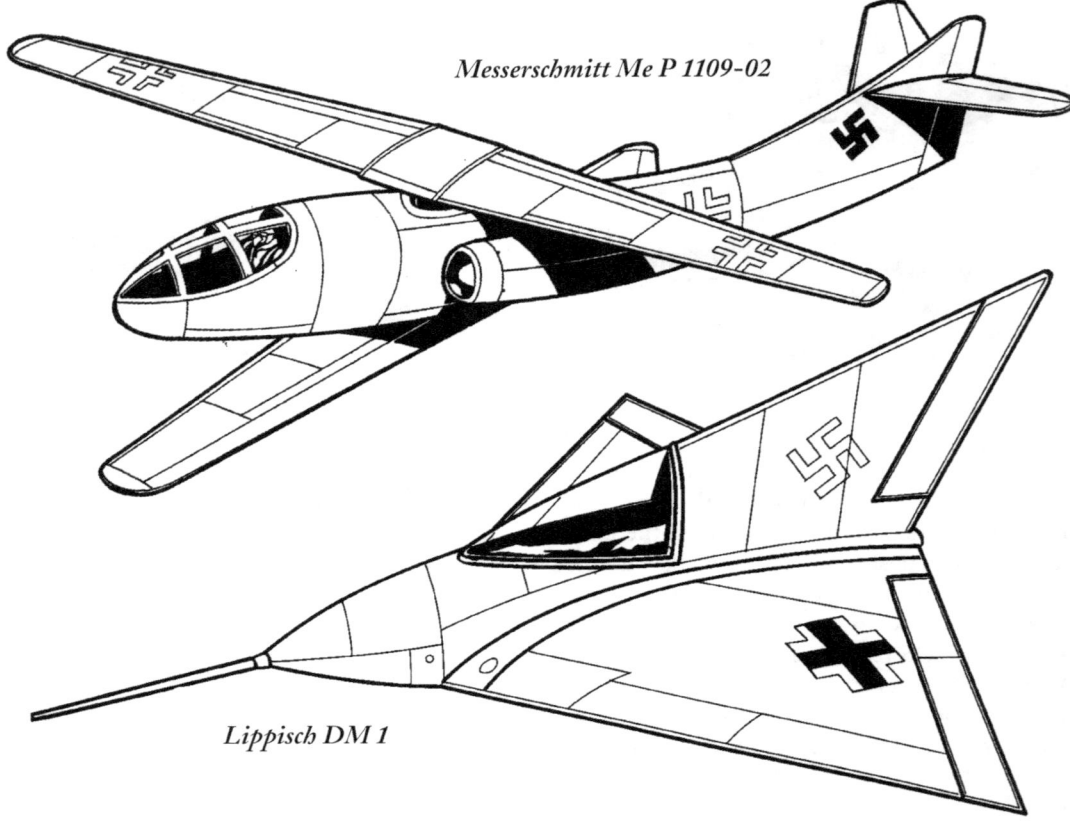

Messerschmitt Me P 1109-02

Lippisch DM 1

(19 ft 5 in), a length of 6.6 m (21 ft 7 in), a height of 3.2 m (10 ft 5 in), an empty weight of 297 kg (655 lbs), and—if properly powered—an anticipated speed of Mach 6, about 6,743 km/h (4,188 mph). In August 1944 one glider prototype was under construction at the Flugtechnische Fachgruppe Darmstadt, but work was interrupted by an Allied air attack. In May 1945 the unfinished airplane was captured by U.S. troops at Prien am Chiemsee in southern Germany. In November 1945 the DM-1 was shipped to the Langley Aeronautics Laboratory in the United States. The aircraft was completed, transformed and improved, and the new design, made by the Convair Company, flew in September 1948 as the world's first delta-wing aircraft under the designation Convair XF-92A. The delta-wing concept was since successfully developed and widely used for modern jet aircrafts, including the U.S. General Dynamics/Convair B-58A Hustler from 1956, the French Dassault Mirage from 1959, and others.

Lippisch Li P 11

Based on work by engineer Alexander Lippisch from late 1942, the Li P 11 (also known as Delta VI) was intended to be a fast jet fighter. It was a broad-chord, delta-wing, turbojet-powered proposal which existed in two main versions: fighter and fast bomber. The wing was swept back at 37 degrees with a span of 10.8 m (35 ft 5.5 in), and the total length was 7.49 m (24 ft 7.1 in). The airframe was planned to be made of synthetic materials (Dynal and Tronal), a feature well ahead of its time. The delta-wing aircraft was fitted with a tricycle landing gear, and double fin and rudder, and was to be powered by two Jumo 004B turbojets with air intakes on each side of the cockpit. A speed of 1,040 km/h (646 mph) and a range of 3,000 km were estimated. Armament would have consisted of two MK 103 30-mm cannons mounted in the wings, with provision for two MK 103 30-mm cannons or one BK 7.5 75-mm cannon placed in an external pack. The planned bomber version could have

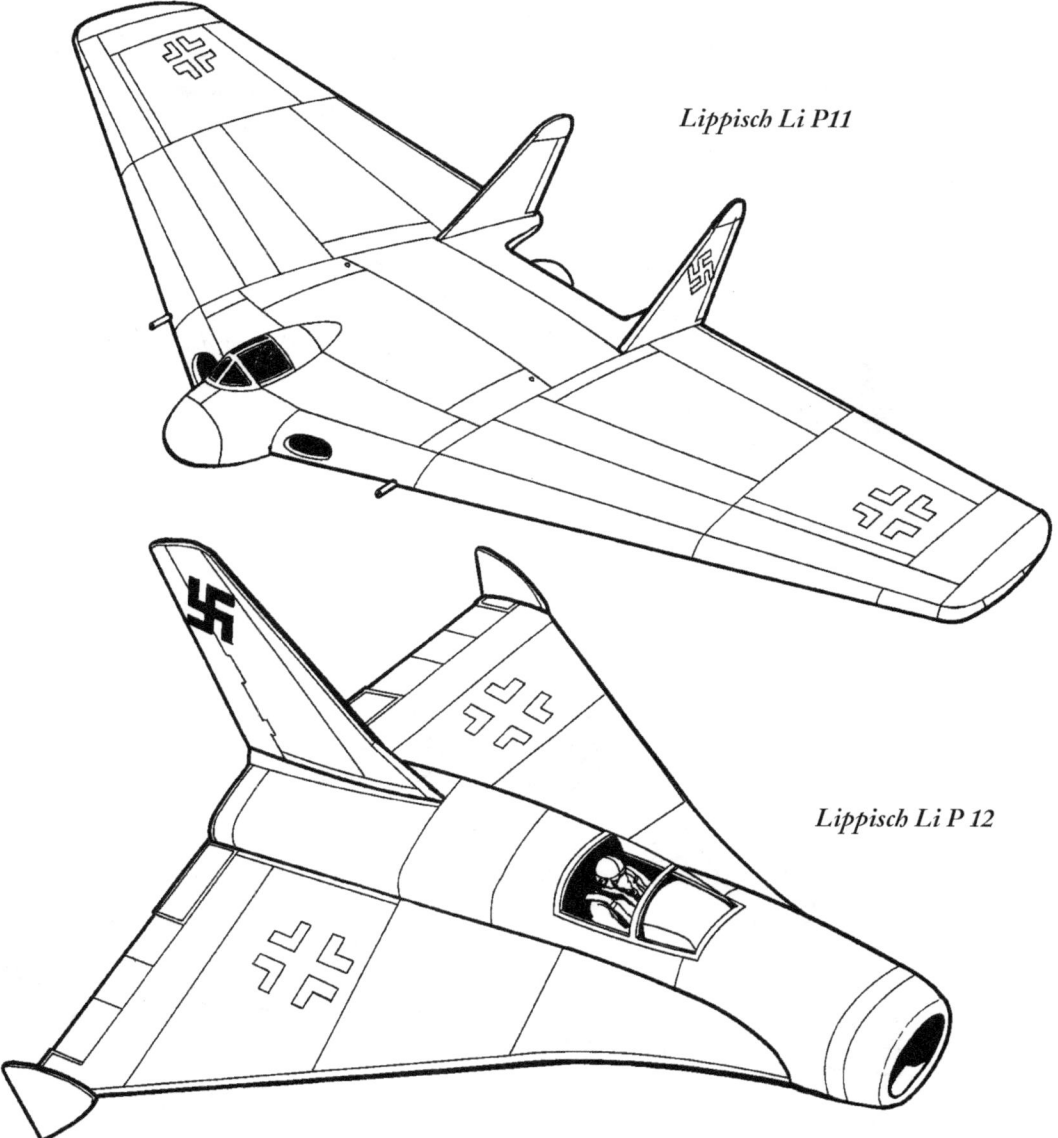

Lippisch Li P11

Lippisch Li P 12

carried a bomb load of 1,000 kg. There was a variant, designed in May 1943, featuring a single fin and rudder, known as Li P 11-121. Wind-tunnel research was carried out in 1944 with models, mock-ups, and a central section of the aircraft, but the end of the war prevented the Li P 11 from reaching completion.

Lippisch Li P 12

The Li P 12 was a delta-winged, ramjet-powered, single-seat fighter. Designed in March 1944, it was to be a small, simple aircraft capable of supersonic flight, armed with two MG 151/20. For landing, a single, central retractable wheel was extended and each wingtip was fitted with a down-turned winglet. It is not known how the necessary pressure was to be produced in order to start the ramjet, perhaps with additional rocket engines or launching from a mother airplane. Various designs existed. Project I was a pilotless test frame. Project II had a wider fuselage, making room for a pilot, but this had too much drag, as indicated by wind-tunnel tests. As a result, Project III included numerous aerodynamic refine-

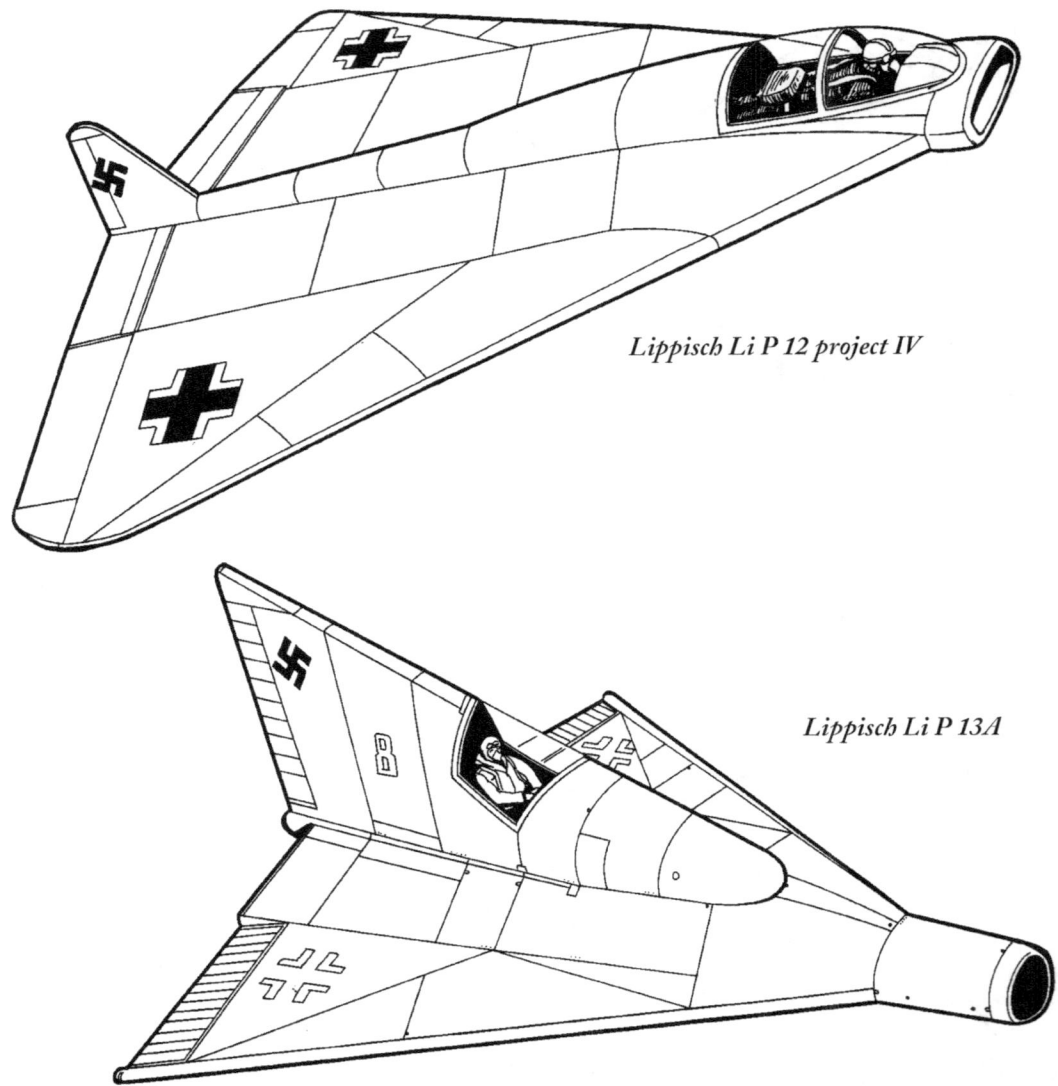

Lippisch Li P 12 project IV

Lippisch Li P 13A

ments, notably the adoption of an elliptical air intake for the ramjet engine, and the wings and tail surfaces being redesigned. The final version, Project IV (often referred to as Lippisch Supersonic Flying Wing) was flatter, with a smaller tail unit, a simplified, elliptical air intake, and operated by a pilot in the prone position. This version also included a variable-geometry rectangular section and was fitted with four hydraulically operated flaps. The plane's landing gear was composed of a retractable main skid and two smaller ones at the wing roots. The end of World War II prevented the promising Lippisch Li P 12 project IV from being produced.

Lippisch Li P 13 A

The Lippisch Li P 13A was a variant of the DM-1. Intended to become a Luftwaffe fast interceptor with an estimated speed of Mach 2, this aircraft was powered by a ramjet fed by a circular intake that protruded from the nose and exhausted beneath the vertical fin at the rear. It had a length of 6 m, a span of 6.70 m, a height of 3.25 m, a wing area of 20 square m, and an empty weight of 1,800 kg. A liquid-fueled rocket motor was planned for take-off and to get the ramjet to operating speed. Various armament was planned, notably two MG 213/20 or twenty-four R4M rockets, or two heavy SG 500 Jägerfaust air-to-air projectiles.

6. *Jet Fighters*   301

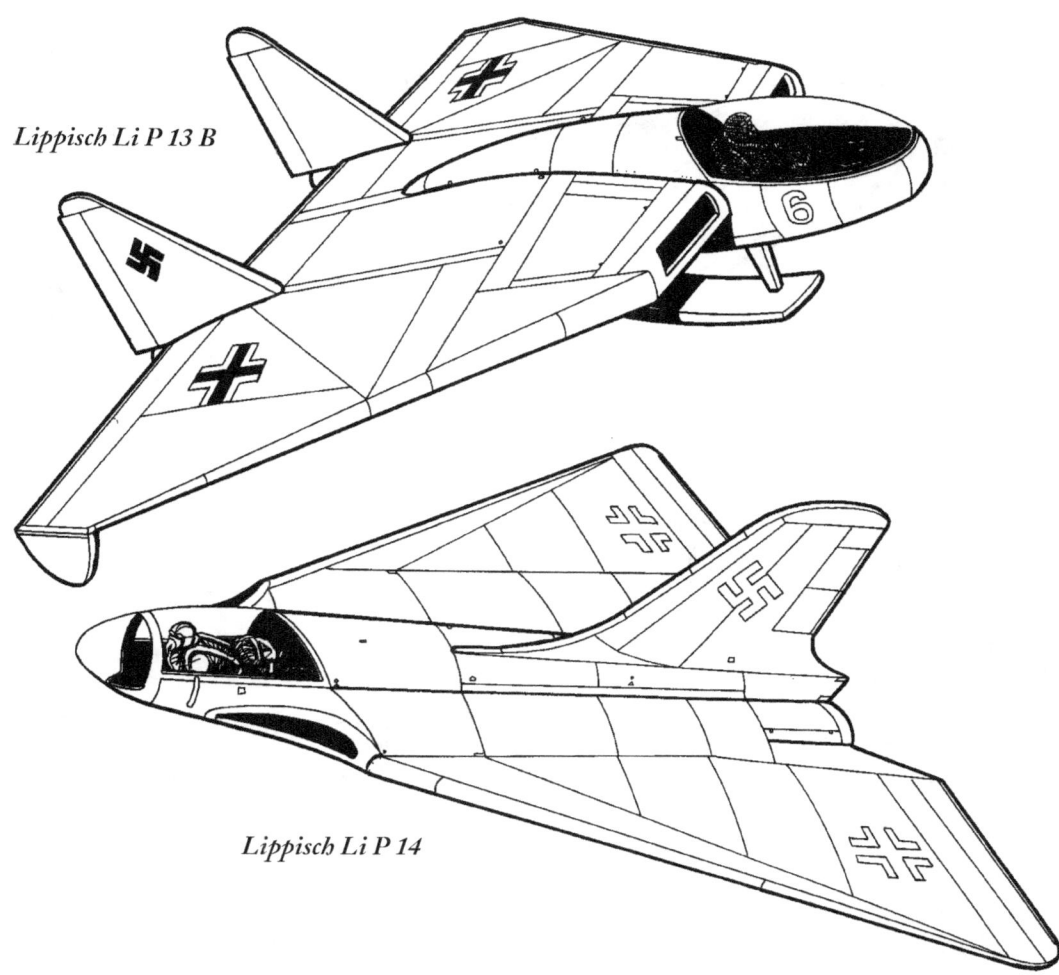

Lippisch Li P 13 B

Lippisch Li P 14

The Li P 13 A did not progress further than the drawing board.

Lippisch Li P 13 B

The Li P 13 B was a further development of the Lippisch Li P 13 A. Designed in December 1944, the P 13 B had a delta-wing layout swept back at 60 degrees with a span of 6.90 m (22 ft 8 in). The wing was fitted with double fin and rudder as well as down-turned wingtips. The single pilot sat in a cockpit at the front. Total length was 7.20 m (23 ft 7 in) and height was 3.47 m (4 ft 10 in). The fighter was to be powered by one ramjet with air intakes placed on both side of the cockpit. As Germany suffered a fuel shortage, the aircraft was to use coal (or paraffin-coated lignite dust) for fuel. For this purpose a round or hexagonal heat-resistant combustion chamber made of ceramic material was installed in the interior of the wing, and this could be filled from above. Take-off and landing were to be done on a retractable skid placed under the cockpit, and with the help of the reinforced wingtips. Speed and planned armament are not known. The project was never developed.

Lippisch Li P 14

Designed in the spring of 1945, there is unfortunately no detail available for the Lippisch Li P 14, a delta-wing fighter project.

Lippisch Li P 15 Project 1

The Lippisch P 14/1 had a span of 10.80 m (33 ft 1.2 in), a length of 6.4 m (21 ft) and an

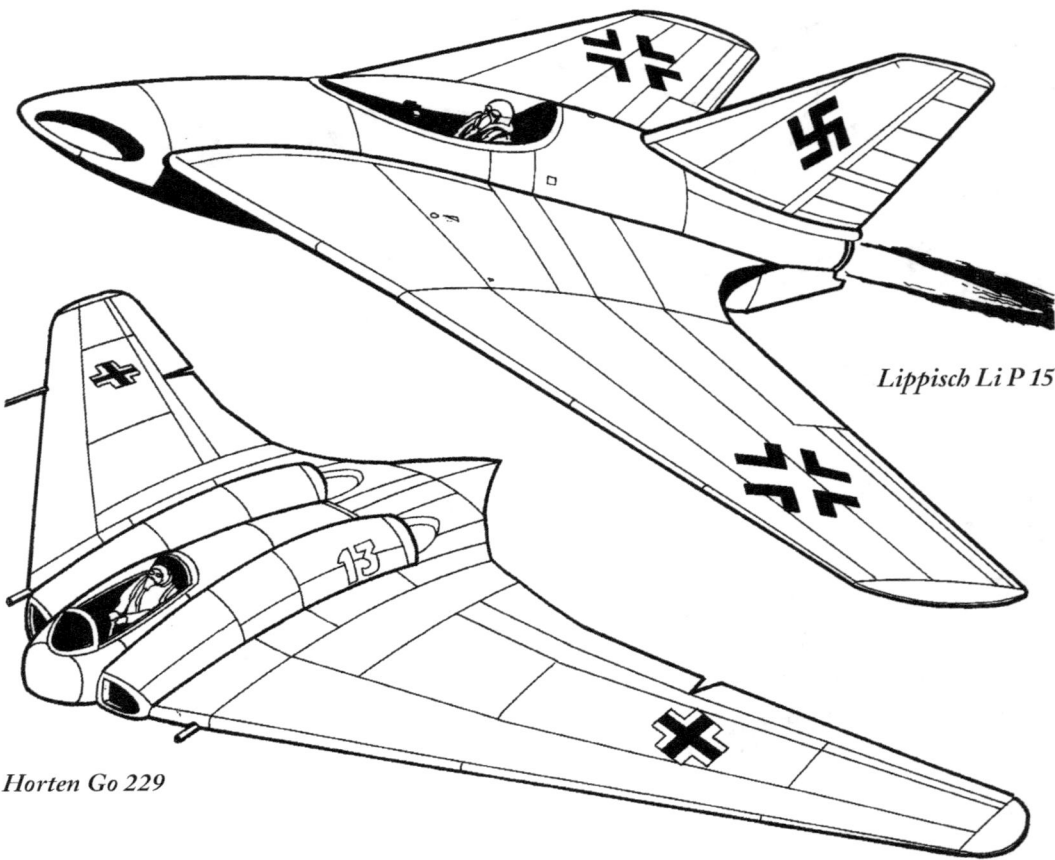

Lippisch Li P 15

Horten Go 229

expected speed of 1,000 km/h (621 mph). Further information and data for this single-jet fighter with sharply-swept wing are not available.

Horten IX/Gotha Go 229

This futuristic flying wing was designed in 1942 by the brothers Reimar and Walter Horten, but because the prototype was built by the Gothaer Waggonfabrik Company, it was also designated Go 229. Since 1933, the Horten brothers had designed several sailplanes and pioneered the concept of tailless *nurflügel* (only-a-wing) aircraft. The Horten IX/Go229, fitted with two Junkers Jumo 004B turbojets, first flew in January 1945 and eventually achieved an astonishing speed of 800 km/h (500 mph). The aircraft was partly made of wood, it had a comparatively slender airfoil, the engines were placed in dorsal humps and the jet exhaust was vented onto the top surface of the wing. The landing gear was of retractable tricycle arrangement. The airplane had a span of 17 m (54 ft 12 in), a length of 7.70 m (24 ft 7 in), an empty weight of 4.600 kg (10.140 lbs) and an estimated range of 635 km (393 miles). The planned armament included four 30-mm MK 103 cannons plus two 1,000-kg (2,205-lb) bombs. The Horten/Go229's potential as single-seat fighter/bomber was obvious, but fortunately for the Allies it never went into production, as the Gotha plant at Friedrichsroda was captured by the American army in April 1945.

Simultaneously, the Horten brothers also worked on another yet more ambitious project, a six-jet-engined flying-wing bomber with a span of 132 ft. Designated Ho 18 Amerika Bomber, this plane was intended to reach and attack the East Coast of the United States. The concept of long-range flying-wing bomber was also developed by the Junkers Company, as already seen in Part 4 (see Junkers EF 130).

6. Jet Fighters 303

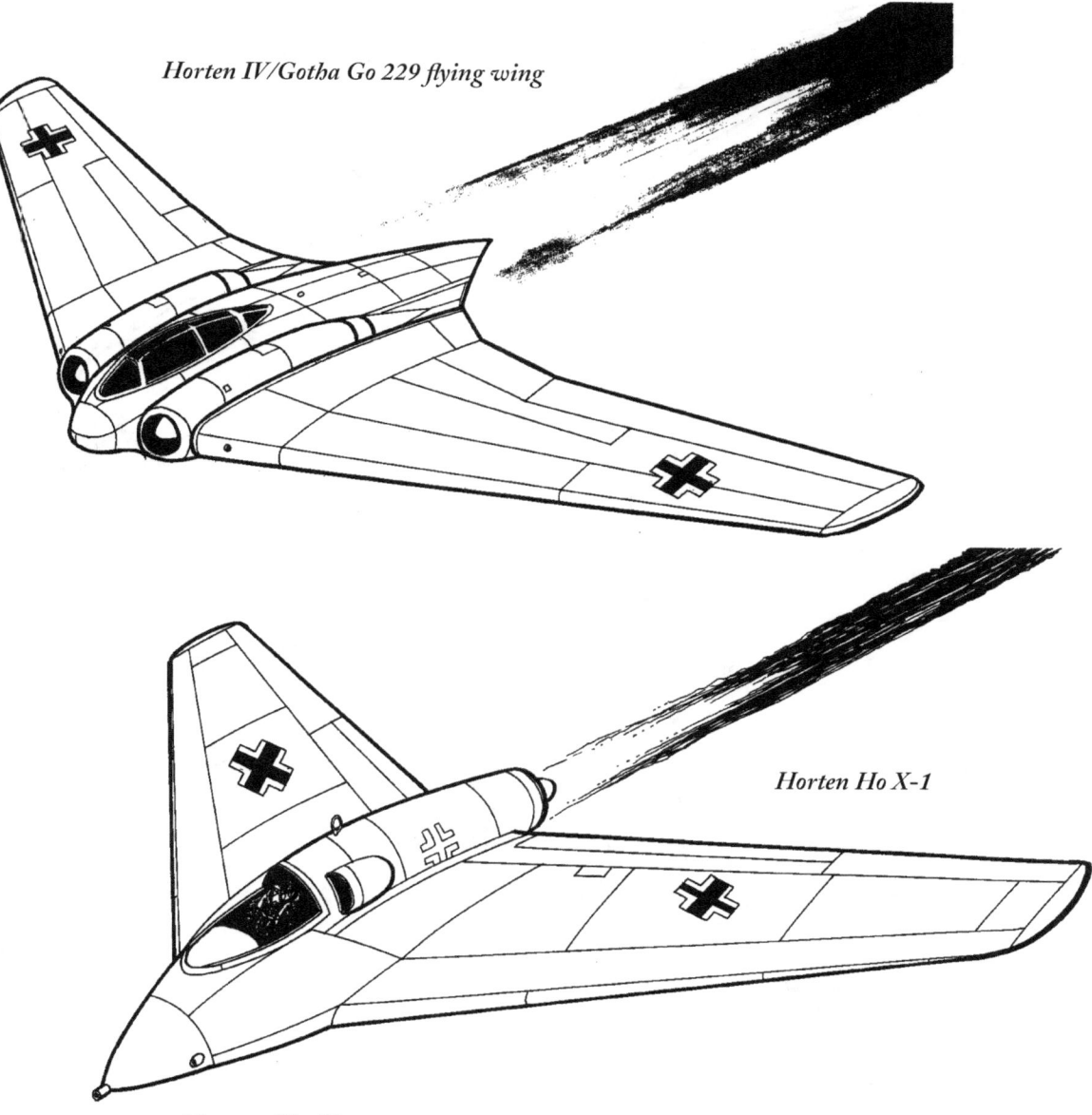

Horten IV/Gotha Go 229 flying wing

Horten Ho X-1

Horten Ho X

Although not chosen to submit a design for the *Volksjäger* scheme, the Horten Brothers came up with the lightweight Ho X-1 that met the specifications laid out by the RLM. The single-seat fighter, based on the Horten IX /Ho 229 flying-wing design, was to be made of steel pipes covered with plywood panels. The Ho X had a length of 7.2 m (23 ft 8 in), a height of 2.3 m (7 ft 6 in), and a wingspan of 14 m (45 ft 11 in). It was to be powered by a single BMW 003E jet engine with 900 kp of thrust, placed at the rear of the fuselage and fed by two air intakes on either side of the cockpit. This design had the advantage that different jet engines could be accommodated, such as the Heinkel-Hirth He S 011 with 1,300 kp of thrust. Maximum speed would have been 1,100 km/h (684 mph) and range 2,000 km (1,243 miles). The landing gear was to be of a tricycle arrangement and the pilot to sit in a pressurized cockpit in front of the engine compartment. Armament would have consisted of a single MK 108 30-mm cannon (or a single

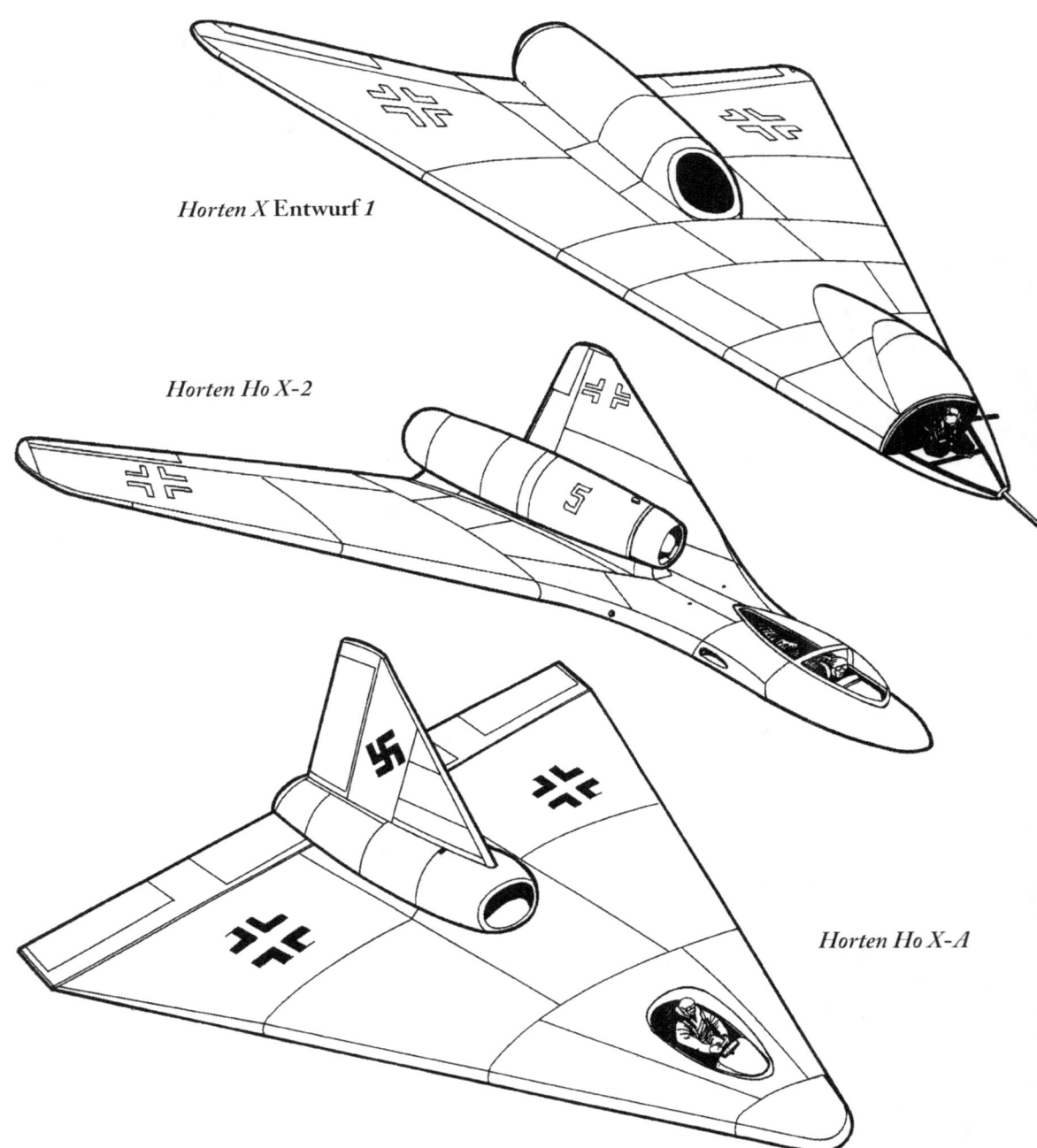

Horten X Entwurf 1

Horten Ho X-2

Horten Ho X-A

MK 213 30-mm cannon) mounted in the nose, and two MG 131 13-mm machine guns, one in each wing root. Scale models with a 3.05 meters (10 feet) wingspan were built, and a full-sized glider was also under construction but was not completed before Germany's capitulation. It was also planned to add a 240-hp Argus As 10C piston engine in a pusher configuration and later the more powerful Heinkel-Hirth He S 011 with 1,300 kp of thrust; this variant—in which the pilot lay in prone position—was known as Horten X-2. There was a planned version with slight differences, notably a vertical fin, known as Horten Ho X-A. The end of World War II prevented any further development of the Horten Ho X.

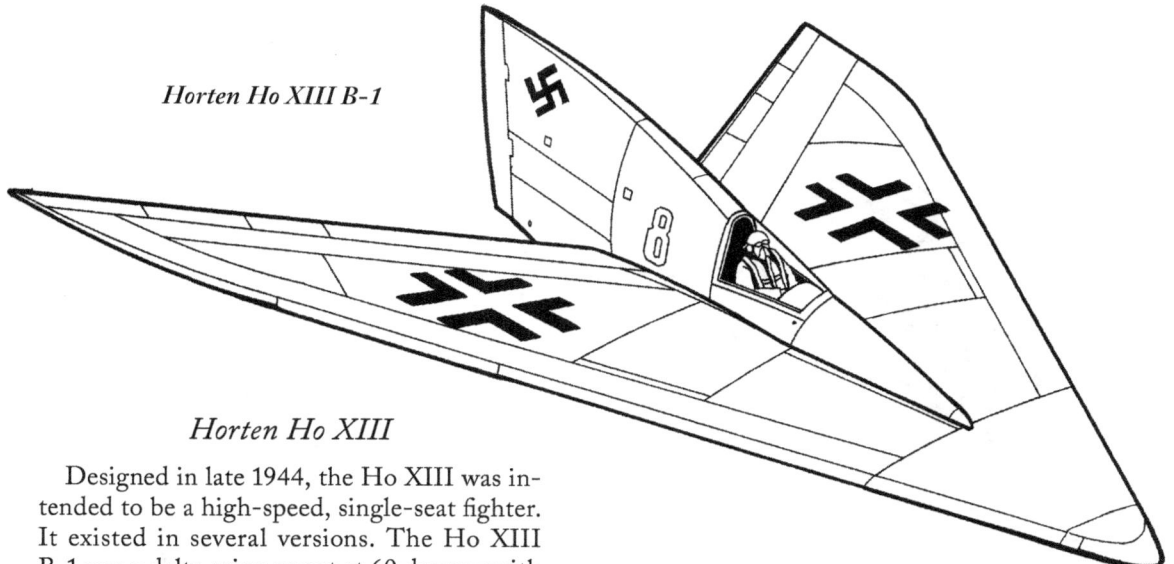

Horten Ho XIII B-1

Horten Ho XIII

Designed in late 1944, the Ho XIII was intended to be a high-speed, single-seat fighter. It existed in several versions. The Ho XIII B-1 was a delta-wing swept at 60 degrees with a span of 12 m (39 ft 4.8 in), a length of 12 m and a height of 3.80 m. It was to be powered by a 800 kp BMW 003R turbojet placed under the fuselage and a 1,000 hp liquid-propellant BMW 718 rocket engine. It was to have a speed of 1,800 km/h (1,118 mph), a range of 2,000 km, and a ceiling of 18,000 m. The tricycle landing gear retracted into the central part of the fuselage. The single pilot sat in a pressurized cockpit (equipped with an ejection seat) placed in the root of the central vertical fin. Armament would have included two or three MK 213 20-mm cannons. The variant Ho XIII B-2 was slightly different, the version Ho XIII B-3 had lateral-wing leading-edge air intakes, and the Ho XIII C was larger but the dimensions, and powerplant and performance data are not available.

Gotha Go P 60

The Gotha P 60 was an improved variant of the Horten/Gotha Go 229. In August 1944 the Gotha Aircraft Company was given the job of series production of the Horten all-wing fighter. After receiving the plans and design data, Gotha engineers, led by Dr. Hünerjäger, found some areas for improvement. The Ho/Go 229 was limited in space to install new equipment or to add more crew members. More importantly, since the engines were to be enclosed in the wing, different engines could not be fitted without extensive aerodynamic testing, which was not possible given the time necessary for that and considering the worsening war situation for Germany. The designers proposed an alternate all-wing design to the RLM in January 1945 which used many of the same construction techniques as the Horten aircraft but had the advantage of being able to be modified with new equipment and engines without changing the flying characteristics greatly. The result was the Gotha Go P 60A, a flying wing that was powered by two turbojet engines near the rear of the wing center section, one above the wing and one below the fuselage. One advantage to this arrangement was that any jet engine could be fitted, and maintenance would be easy. Two BMW 003A-1 jet engines with 800 kg (1763-lbs) of thrust were to be used. Three fuel tanks were enclosed within the wings, one 1,200-liter (317-gallon) tank in each outer wing panel and one same-sized tank behind the cockpit. The pressurized and armored cockpit, located in the extreme nose, held two men who were in a prone position. The prone position had the advantage of allowing the crew to withstand G forces better. The main landing gear legs retracted to the front and rotated 90 degrees to lie flat. The nose gear was offset to the port side and retracted to the rear. The Go P 60 had a span of 12.2 m (40 ft 1 in), a length of 8.82 m (28 ft 11 in), a maximum speed of 915 km/h

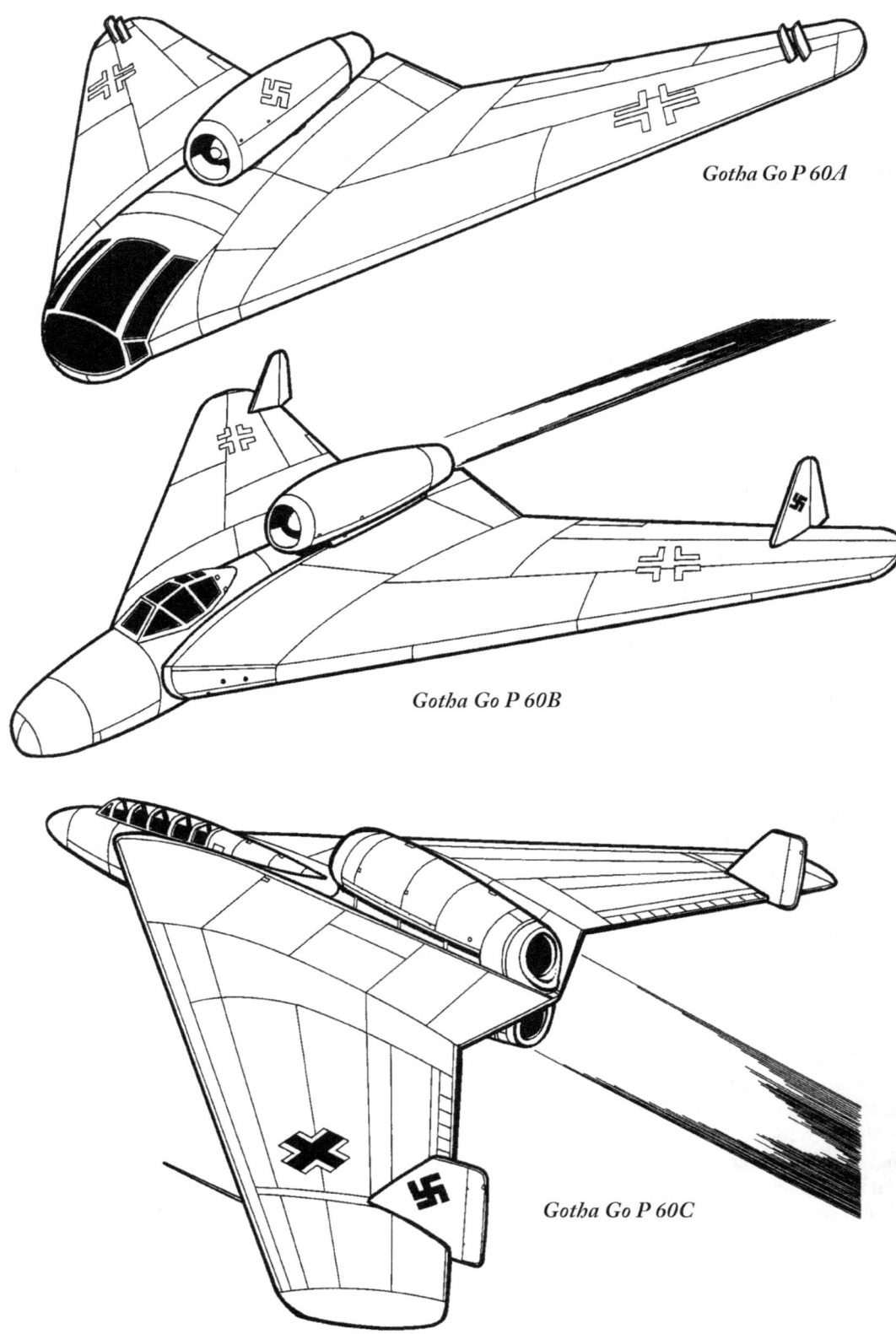

Gotha Go P 60A

Gotha Go P 60B

Gotha Go P 60C

(569 mph) and a range of 1,600 km (994 miles).

Three versions were planned: reconnaissance aircraft, heavy fighter and high altitude fighter. Armament was to be four MK 108 30-mm machine cannons (150 rounds for inner cannon, 175 rounds for outer cannon) for the *Höhenjäger* (high-altitude fighter) version, two MK 103 30-mm machine cannons (175 rounds per gun) for the *Zerstörer* (heavy fighter) version and two MK 108 30-mm machine cannons and two RB 50/18 cameras for the *Aufklärer* (reconnaissance) version. The *Höhenjäger* version could also to be fitted with a Walter HWK 509B rocket engine to increase the ceiling and climb rate, and this variant was designated the Gotha Go P 60A/R .

One of the main criticisms of the Go P 60A was the difficulty for the crew to escape while in flight. One solution was to mount both jet engines side by side below the wing, and this proposed version was known as the Go P 60A-2. Unfortunately, this configuration reduced the roll rate in combat and was eliminated.

The Gotha P 60B was a further development of the previous design. This had two He S011 turbojet engines, increasing speed to 973 km/h (604 mph), the crew was accommodated in a conventional sitting position in a re-designed cockpit, and the fuselage was slightly enlarged.

The Gotha P 60C was the final design. Quite similar to the P 60B in appearance, its fuselage was slightly enlarged in order to house a *Morgenster* (Morning Star) radar set. The end of World War II prevented the completion of the promising Gotha Go P 60 series.

Heinkel He P 1079/B2

Intended to be a night and all-weather fighter, the Heinkel P 1079 was a tailless delta-wing with a length of 9.48 m (31 ft 1.5 in) and a wingspan of 13.13 m (43 ft 1.5 in). It was operated by a crew of two sitting back to back. It was powered by two He S011 jet engines placed in the wing roots, and was to have a maximum speed of 1,015 km/h (630 mph). The aircraft was to be armed with four MK 108 30-mm cannons mounted in the nose. The project was not developed.

Arado Ar Project I

This project for a night fighter consisted of a narrow, tailless fuselage fitted with a 35-degree swept-back delta-wing with twin fins and rudders placed on the wing trailing edge. It had a span of 18.38 m (60 ft 4.2 in) and a length of 12.95 m (42 ft 6.2 in). Powered by two BMW 003 A turbojet engines placed under the rear fuselage, it should have had a speed of 800 km/h (497 mph). The aircraft was manned by a crew of two, sitting side by

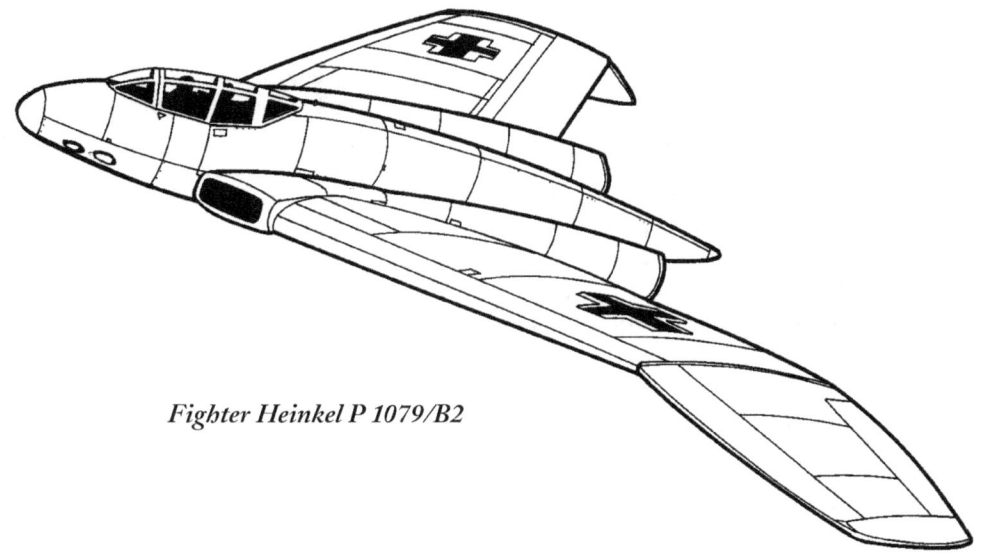

Fighter Heinkel P 1079/B2

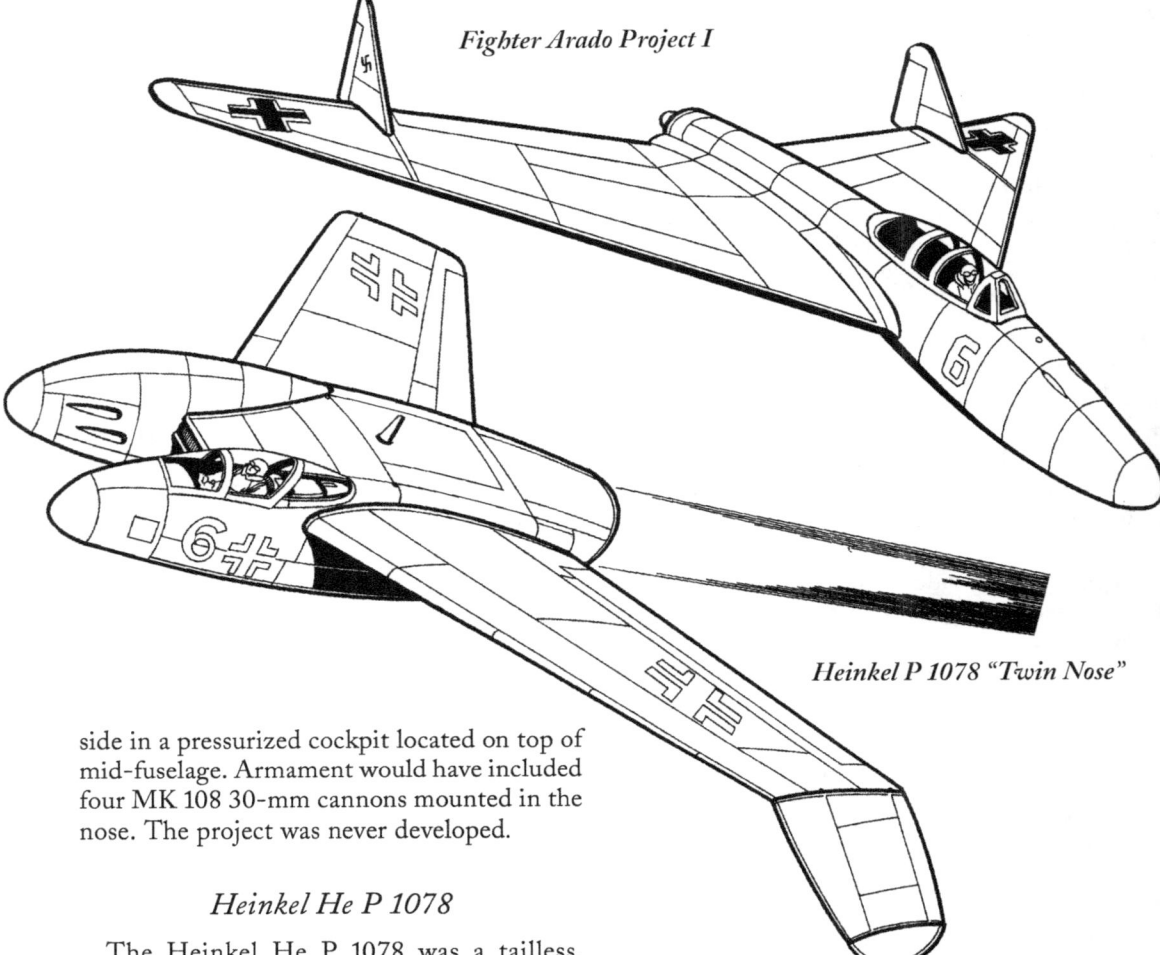

Fighter Arado Project I

Heinkel P 1078 "Twin Nose"

side in a pressurized cockpit located on top of mid-fuselage. Armament would have included four MK 108 30-mm cannons mounted in the nose. The project was never developed.

Heinkel He P 1078

The Heinkel He P 1078 was a tailless, single-seat fighter with a somewhat unusual asymmetrical "twin nose" front arrangement. The cockpit was placed in a gondola on the port side, and another gondola with radar and armed with two MK 108 30-mm cannon was located on the starboard side. Between the two gondolas there was an air intake feeding the single HeS011 turbojet engine. The gull wings were swept back at 40 degrees, with a span of 9.43 m (30 ft 11.5 in). The odd aircraft's length was 6.04 m (19 ft 10 in) and maximum speed was 1,025 km/h (636 mph). This curious project was never developed.

Junkers Ju 128

This Junkers fast jet fighter, designed in February 1945 by engineer Heinrich Hertel, consisted of a short fuselage and wings of wooden construction, swept back 45 degrees, with two small vertical fins and rudders on the wing trailing edges. The aircraft had a span of 8.9 m (29 ft 2 in), a length of 7.05 m (21 ft 3 in), a wing area of 17.6 square m (189 square ft), and an empty weight of 2,607 kg (5,747 lbs). The pilot sat in a pressurized cockpit fitted with an ejector seat and provided with armor (protection from 12.7-mm rounds from the front, and 20-mm rounds from the rear). The Ju 128 was powered by a Heinkel-Hirth HeS 011 jet engine, air intakes were fitted at the fuselage sides to divert the boundary-layer airflow to a vent outlet aft of the cockpit fairing. It was calculated that the aircraft would have a maximum speed of 905 km/h (562 mph). Armament would have consisted of two MK 108 30-mm cannons installed in the sides

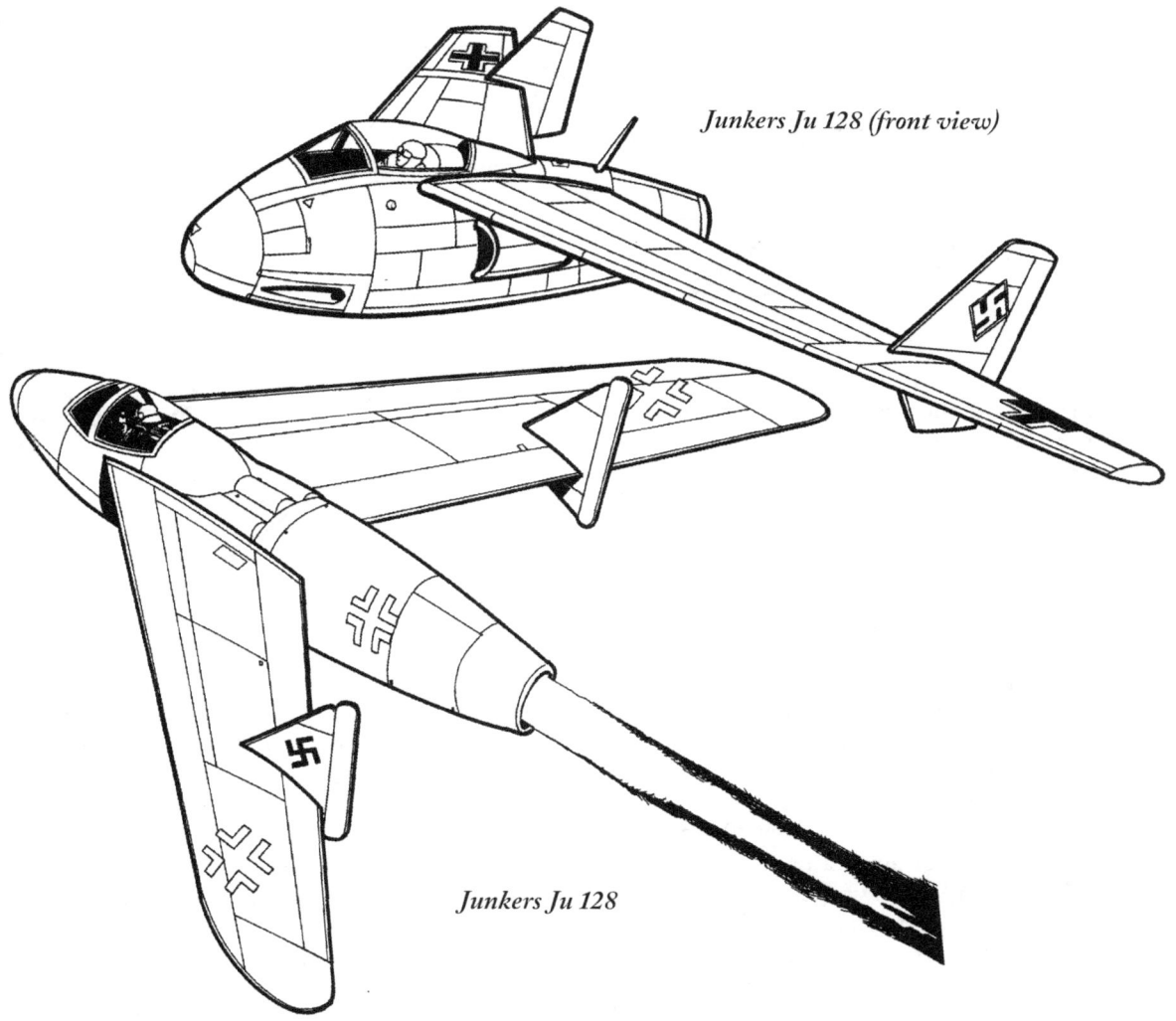

Junkers Ju 128 (front view)

Junkers Ju 128

of the fuselage nose, with 100 rounds each, and with provision for two more. A model of the Ju 128 was tested in a wind tunnel, and a mock-up fuselage was built, both showing promising results. There was also a plan to build a night fighter/all-weather version of this fighter with a lengthened fuselage and room for a second crew member. The war ended before these projects could be further developed.

Blohm & Voss P 212-03

The jet-powered Blohm & Voss P 212-03 had a radical design which shows how far afield the Germans were experimenting with aerodynamics. It was intended to be a fast, high-altitude fighter, armed with two to seven MK 108 30-mm cannons or twenty-two R4M rockets or a bomb load of 500 kg. Designed in February 1945, three prototypes were possibly made, of which one made its first flight in August 1945.

Blohm & Voss BV P 215

A specification was issued by the *Technische Luftrüstung* (Technical Air Armaments Board) in late January 1944 for a jet-powered night fighter. Preliminary requirements were to be a top speed of 900 km/h (559 mph), an endurance of four hours, powerful armament and internally mounted radar. Dr. Richard Vogt used the BV P 212 as the overall basis for the new BV P 215 night fighter. The fuselage was

Blohm & Voss P 212-03

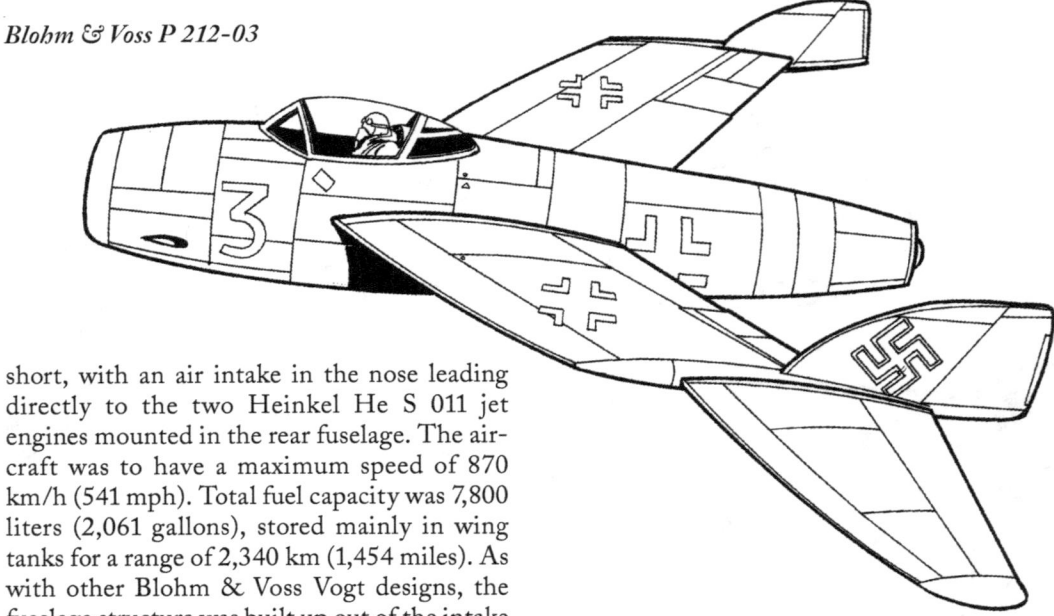

short, with an air intake in the nose leading directly to the two Heinkel He S 011 jet engines mounted in the rear fuselage. The aircraft was to have a maximum speed of 870 km/h (541 mph). Total fuel capacity was 7,800 liters (2,061 gallons), stored mainly in wing tanks for a range of 2,340 km (1,454 miles). As with other Blohm & Voss Vogt designs, the fuselage structure was built up out of the intake tube, and all components attached to this structure; it had a length of 11.6 m (38 ft 1 in) and a height of 5 m (16 ft 5 in). The BV P 215's construction was mainly of metal throughout, except for wooden control surfaces and the aircraft's nose; empty weight was 7,400 kg (16,314 lbs). The wings were backswept 30 degrees and had 6 degrees of dihedral, with a span of 18.8 m (62 ft 8 in) and a wing area of 63 square m (678.13 square ft). The outer wingtips angled down at 23 degrees, and assisted stability and control. There were two small vertical fins and rudders located on the trailing edge of the wings, where the outer wingtips angled downward. The aircraft was fitted with a retractable landing gear taken from the Heinkel He 219. The pressurized cockpit held a three-man crew—a pilot, radar operator and navigator/radio operator—and all three were provided with ejection seats. A wide variety of offensive armament could be carried in the aircraft's nose, and defensive armament consisted of an FHL 151 remote-controlled, rear-facing turret, armed with either one or two MG 151/20 20-mm cannons. A provision was made for possibly mounting two upward-firing *Schräge Muzik* MK 108 30-mm cannons, located behind the cockpit. Two SC 250 250-kg (551-lb) or SC 500 (1,102 lbs) bombs could be carried in a belly recess. The end of the war pre-

Blohm & Voss P 215-02

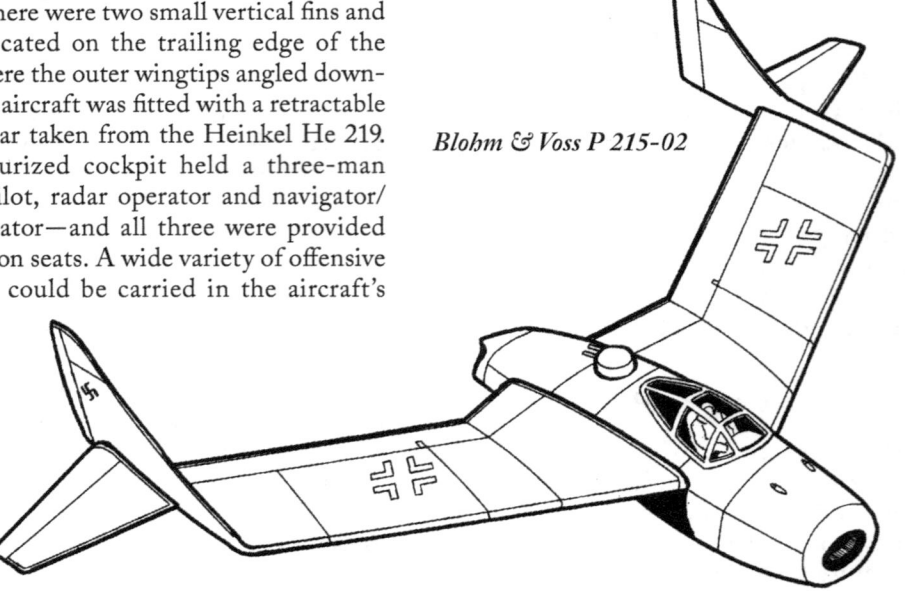

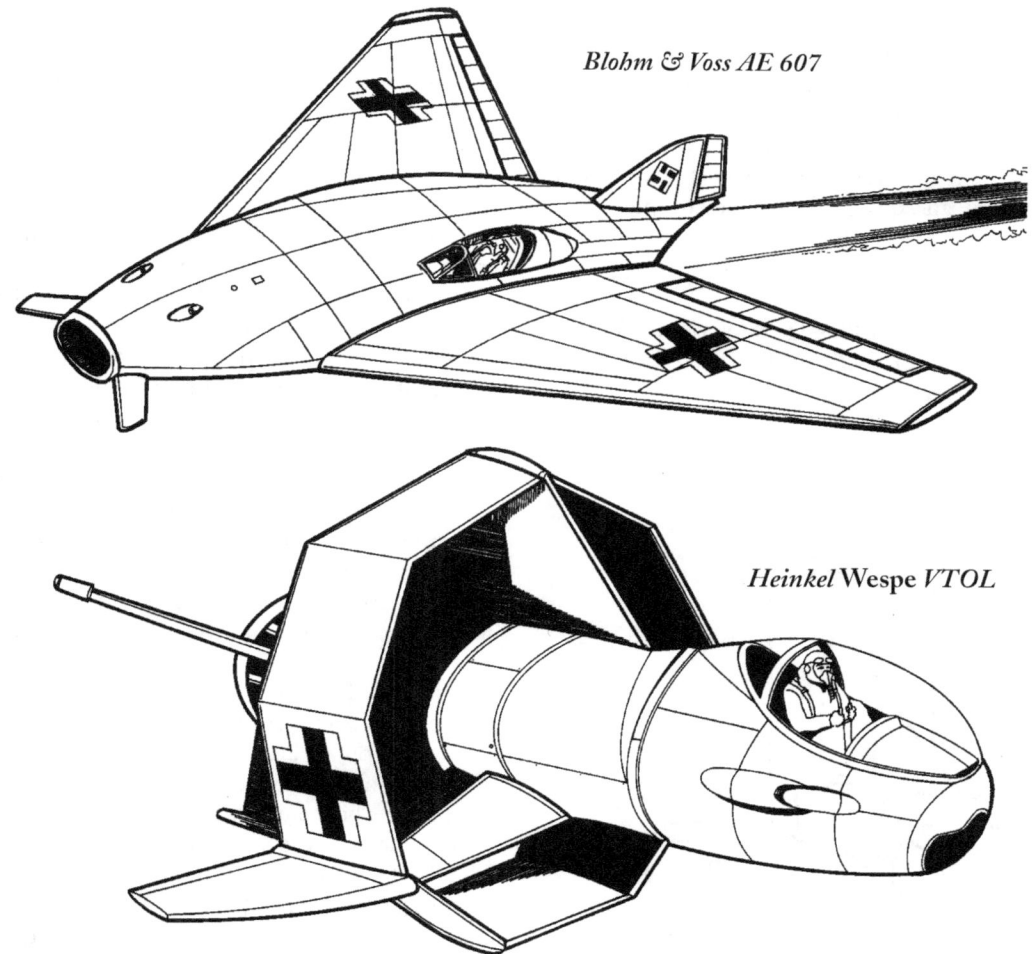

Blohm & Voss AE 607

Heinkel Wespe *VTOL*

vented any further development of this novel aircraft.

Blohm & Voss AE 607

Little is known about the odd and experimental fighter Bv AE 607. Presumably powered by a HeS 011 jet engine, it had a span of 8 m, and a length of 7.1 m. The aircraft presented an asymmetrical layout, as the cockpit was moved off center. The AE 607 would have been armed with three MK 108 30-mm cannons. It did not go further than the drawing board.

Heinkel Wespe

The Heinkel *Wespe* (Wasp) was designed in late 1944 at the Vienna Heinkel works as a VTOL (Vertical Take Off and Landing) interceptor. It was mainly to be used around factory complexes as a point-defense interceptor, much like the Bachem Ba 349 Natter. The *Wespe* was designed around a circular wing, with small wingtips protruding beyond the circular wing at the two lower wing support locations. A single HeS 021 turboprop (the turboprop development of the He S 011 jet engine), driving a six-bladed propeller, provided 2,000 horsepower plus 750 kp thrust and was fed by an air intake located below the cockpit. The *Wespe* had a span of 5 m (16 ft 5 in), a length of 6.2 m (20 ft 4 in) and a maximum speed of 800 km/h (497 mph). The aircraft took off and landed on three landing gear, which in flight were covered for aerodynamical purposes. The pilot sat in a normal seated position in the nose under a huge blown canopy, and two MK 108 30-mm cannons mounted in blisters on each side of the cockpit were envisioned for the armament. Further development was not carried forth due to the approaching end of World War II. A similar project of VTOL aircraft utilizing the same ring-shaped wing was the *Lerche* (Lark). This was powered with two piston engines, and designed as an assault plane.

Focke-Wulf VTOL Triebflügel

The Focke-Wulf VTOL (Vertical Take Off and Landing) single-seat fighter/interceptor, known as *Triebflügel* (gliding wing), was designed in September 1944 by Heinz von Halem based on work and experimentation made earlier by Erich von Holst and Dr. Kuchemann of the Gottingen Technical University. The design was one of the Luftwaffe's most eccentric, as the aircraft was to be powered by what could be termed a ramjet rotary engine. Three untapered wings (attached to a rotary collar located about halfway down the fuselage) rotated around the fuselage and had a gradually decreasing pitch towards the wingtips, thus acting like a giant propeller. At the end of each wing was a Pabst ramjet. Since ramjets do not operate at slow speeds, either the rotor had to be driven by a fuselage-mounted take-off booster or small Walter rocket engines could have been fitted to each ramjet pod. When an operational speed of 150–200 mph was reached, the wings would be spooled up to speed and the ramjets engaged. The wings would then be moved into pitch so that further lift could be generated, supplemented by the ramjets' thrust. Speed would be in the region of 205 m/s (670 ft/sec). The *Triebflügel* had four wheels attached to the tail fins and one big central wheel. All five of them were retractable and covered to increase speed. Thanks to this gear and the fact that the *Triebflügel* did not need much infrastructure to operate, it could take off from small areas. This was an excellent method to have fighters ready close to a newly formed front line almost immediately. The pilot sat in a cockpit near the nose, and the armament would have consisted of two MK 103 30-mm cannons with 100 rounds plus two MG 151/20 20-mm cannons with 250 rounds. The airplane was to have a span of 11.5 m (37 ft 8.8 in), and a length of 9.15 m (30 ft). The Focke-Wulf *Triebflügel* was not constructed and thus never flown—probably a good thing for the test pilot, as the viability of the design is still a matter of speculation. Due to the enormous gyroscopic force created by a rotor of that size, steering would have been really hard. Maneuverability would not have been that good, at least not satisfactory for a fighter/interceptor. Pilots would have needed great courage, skill and luck to set this machine down on its hind legs, as they would have had to do it backwards

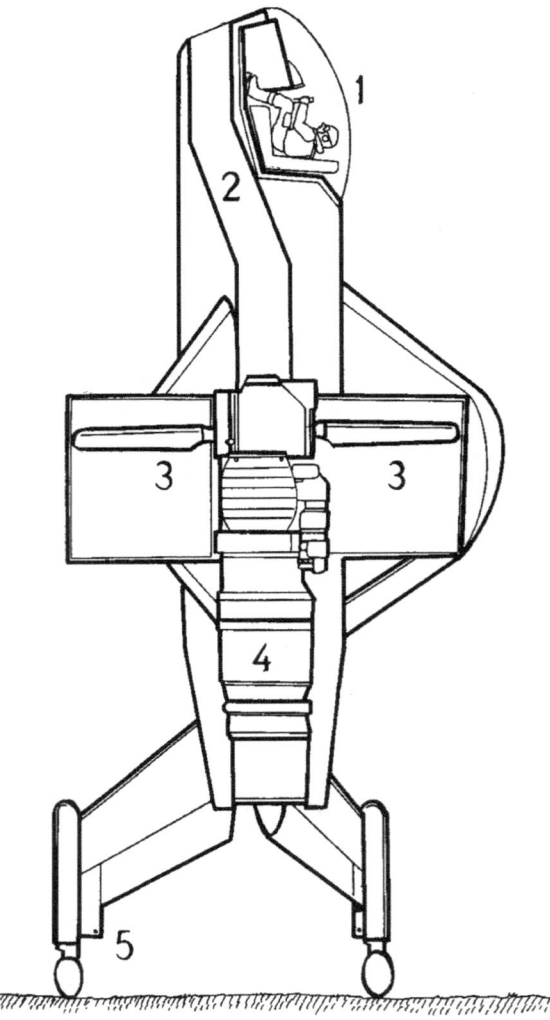

Cross-section, Heinkel Wespe. *The aircraft is shown ready for take-off. 1: cockpit. 2: air intake. 3: propeller (six blades). 4: He S021 turboprop engine. 5: landing gear.*

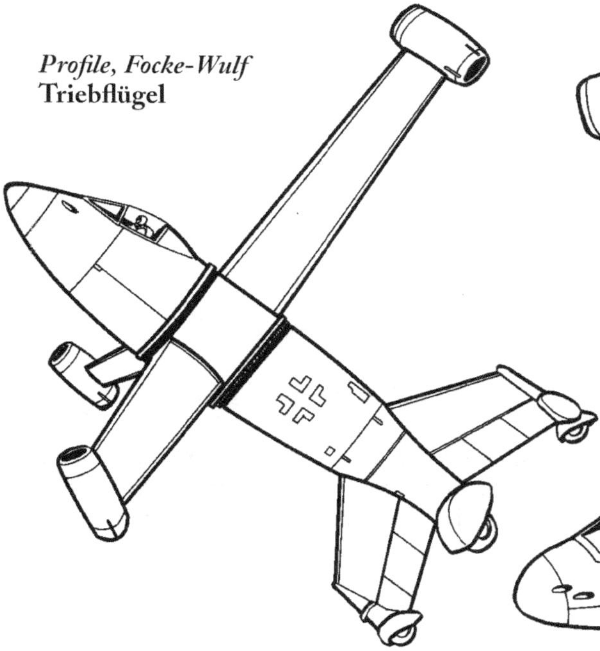

Profile, Focke-Wulf **Triebflügel**

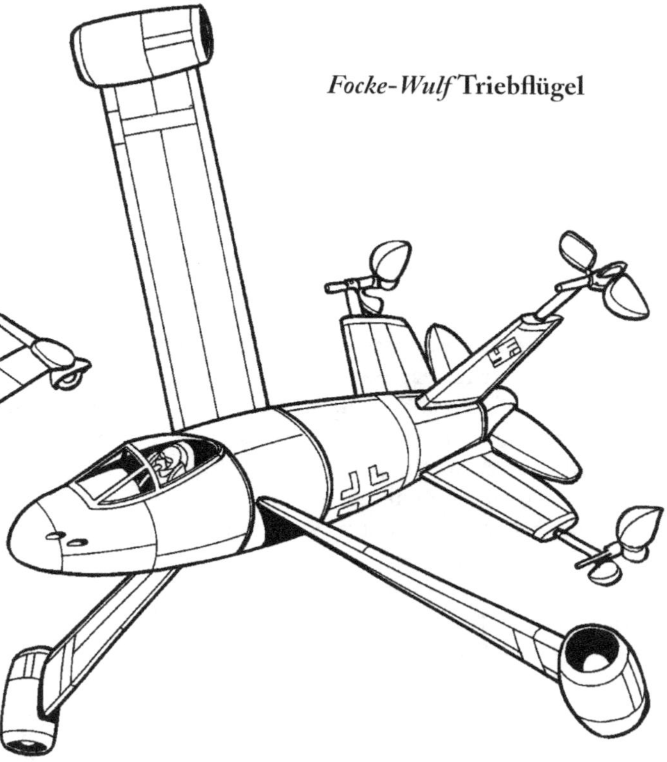

Focke-Wulf **Triebflügel**

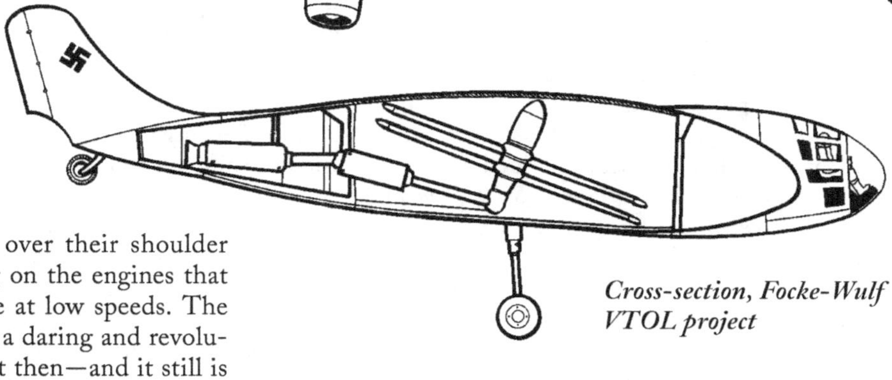

Cross-section, Focke-Wulf VTOL project

while looking over their shoulder and depending on the engines that were unreliable at low speeds. The *Triebflügel* was a daring and revolutionary concept then—and it still is today.

A wind-tunnel model was tested up to a speed of Mach 0.9, about 1,000 km/h (621 mph).

Focke-Wulf VTOL project

A futuristic Focke-Wulf VTOL was planned, consisting of an airfoil section with two large turbojet-driven propellers placed in the center of the oval fuselage. Unfortunately no data is available.

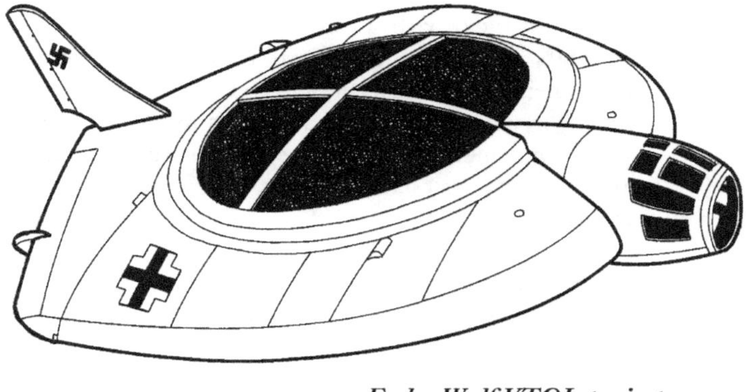

Focke-Wulf VTOL project

7

Seaplanes

The task of a navy in war has always been to keep the seas open for the passage of its country's merchant ships carrying supplies and troops, and at the same time to deny the use of the sea to the enemy. With the adoption and development of airpower, the task remained the same but new materials and methods appeared.

Seaplanes (sometimes known as hydroplanes) are aircraft specially designed to land and take off on water, only in calm water with little or no wave action. The first practical seaplanes were designed and built in the 1910s by the French engineer Henri Fabre and the American aviation pioneer Glenn Hammond Curtiss (1878–1930). Seaplanes developed rapidly in the 1920s and 1930s and for a time were the largest and fastest aircraft in the world. They are usually divided into two main categories. Floatplanes (*Seeflugzeuge*) have a conventional aircraft fuselage under which the wheeled landing gear is replaced by large floats, generally two, fixed to the aircraft by means of several struts. Flying boats (*Flugboote*) have the lower part of their fuselage shaped in the form of a ship hull, providing buoyancy, with additional stabilization floats (or pontoons) fitted under the wings. Their ability to alight on water enabled them to break free from the size constraints imposed by general lack of large, land-based runways, so flying boats could be enormous machines.

The pontoons on floatplanes and the bulky shape of the hull of flying boats resulted in enormous drag, causing poor speed and poor maneuverability. In spite of this disadvantage, the military value of seaplanes was quickly recognized. Launched from a catapult on a battleship or operating from a port, they fulfilled such missions as maritime patrol and reconnaissance, transport, rescue, torpedo carrying, mine laying, and anti-submarine search.

German seaplanes played an unglamorous and unpublicized part in the war, as naval support was not a role stressed by the Luftwaffe. They had only a low priority, and only a few adaptations of aging commercial flying boats finally achieved acceptable combat status. They were used for the typical roles of maritime reconnaissance and observation; they patrolled the waters on behalf of the navy in search of enemy movement and also protected friendly shipping against enemy surprise attacks from the air, on the surface or beneath it. Seaplanes were also useful for transporting personnel and supplies or evacuating casualties to and from areas separated by bodies of water or difficult to access. Other roles included mine laying, allowing the Germans to mine coastal channels and even harbors which no surface or submarine mine-layer could hope to approach; this development added immensely to the labors of the enemy mine-sweeping forces. A few seaplanes were equipped with a large current-carrying degaussing ring for making magnetic mines inoperative. Some were used for bomb or torpedo attack. Although the airborne torpedo was an important anti-shipping weapon, it use was limited by the slowness and vulnerability of German seaplanes. This was recognized and accepted, and little effort was made to produce adequate torpedo-carrier planes. At sea the prime torpedo carriers were the lethal submarines, the U-boats, that carried the war across the Atlantic Ocean, and could strike without warning and remain unseen, whereas seaplanes could make a far less surreptitious attack. Another important role for seaplanes was sea rescue, and for this purpose a special *Seenotdienst* (Sea Rescue Service) was created, at first to take care of German airmen shot down over the North Sea and the English Channel during the Battle of Britain. The service's airplanes were unarmed, painted white with large Red Cross markings, carried inflatable rubber boats, blankets, medicine and everything needed to recover survivors and provide first aid. However, the chief of RAF Fighter Command, Hugh Dowding, was determined to deprive the German air force of valuable aircrews and authorized attacks on the rescue seaplanes, forcing the *Seenotdienst* to arm its machines. Neither bad weather nor British action prevented the Sea Rescue Service from operating, though, and during the Battle of Britain its crews rescued more than a hundred airmen (some of them British) at the cost of twenty-two seaplanes and forty-nine casualties. Sea rescue crews of both sides routinely took pity on each others' ditched aircrews, and would notify their enemy counterparts of the location via Swiss shipping radio. The Luftwaffe Sea Rescue Service was later extended to the Mediterranean, the Black Sea and the Baltic. The Sea Rescue Service was subordinated to the *Luftflotte* within which they operated. The units were organized into *Seenotflugkommandos* (sea rescue commands), each of which was headed by a *Seenotdienstführer* with the rank of colonel. Subordinate to these commands were *Bereichkommandos* (regional commands) which controlled the various detachments.

Despite the splendid new warships built for Germany after Hitler's accession to power in January 1933, the need for a powerful modern naval air arm as an adjunct to the activities of the fleet was never accepted. Seaplanes were maintained and operated by mixed Luftwaffe and Kriegsmarine personnel, but Hermann Göring's paranoid obsession with his private empire produced his watchword, "Everything that flies is mine." The Luftwaffe's technical experience could have given the navy a good fleet air arm but for Göring's jealousy and pigheadedness. It was not that Germany had failed to acquire good seaplanes, but a relative small production run and a lack of development clearly indicate a lack of real interest in naval support, a major German weakness. Interservice rivalry, plus the belated recognition of the strategic meaning of an unanticipated war against Britain deprived the Luftwaffe of any major success in sea warfare. Even when local, promising but limited successes were achieved (such as against Russian convoys or

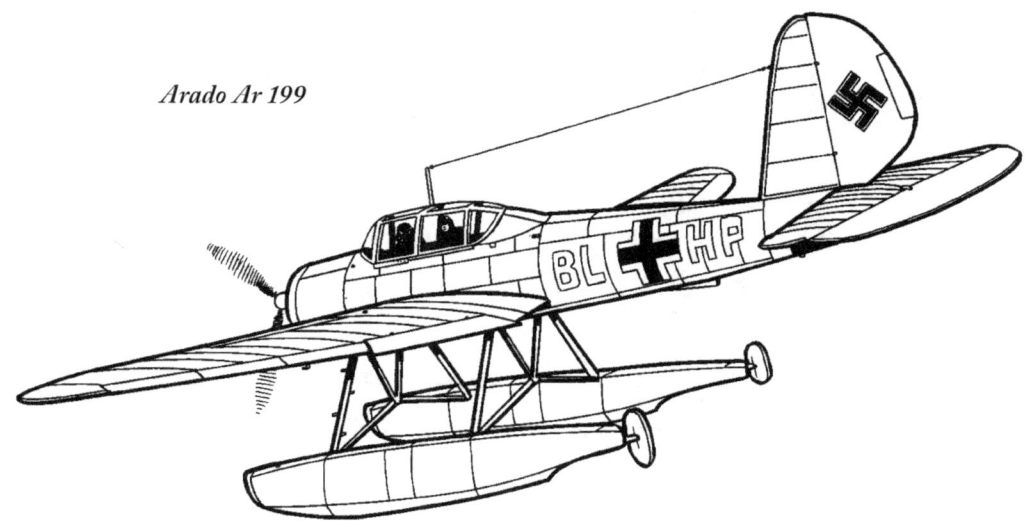

Arado Ar 199

at Malta, for example), these were washed out by the demands of other fronts. Seaplanes were of crucial importance in allowing long-range maritime patrols and rescue, but with the introduction of very long-range land-based aircraft, which had greater flexibility and which could operate from ordinary airfields, they gradually faded from the scene.

Below are discussed the most commonly used Luftwaffe land-based floatplanes and flying boats, plus little-known seaplanes, as well as other sea-warfare-related aircraft: planned carrier-based airplanes intended to arm the one and only (never completed) German aircraft carrier *Graf Zeppelin*.

Floatplanes

Arado Ar 199

The Ar 199 was a monoplane trainer floatplane powered by a 450-hp Argus As 410C inverted-V-12, aircooled engine, with a maximum speed of 260 km/h (161 mph) and a range of 740 km (460 miles). It had a length of 10.57 m (34 ft 8.3 in), a span of 12.70 m (41 ft 8 in), and an empty weight of 1,675 kg (3,693 lbs). The airframe was stressed for catapulting from a ship, and the crew of three sat in a capacious enclosed cockpit. Although a technical success, only two units were built in

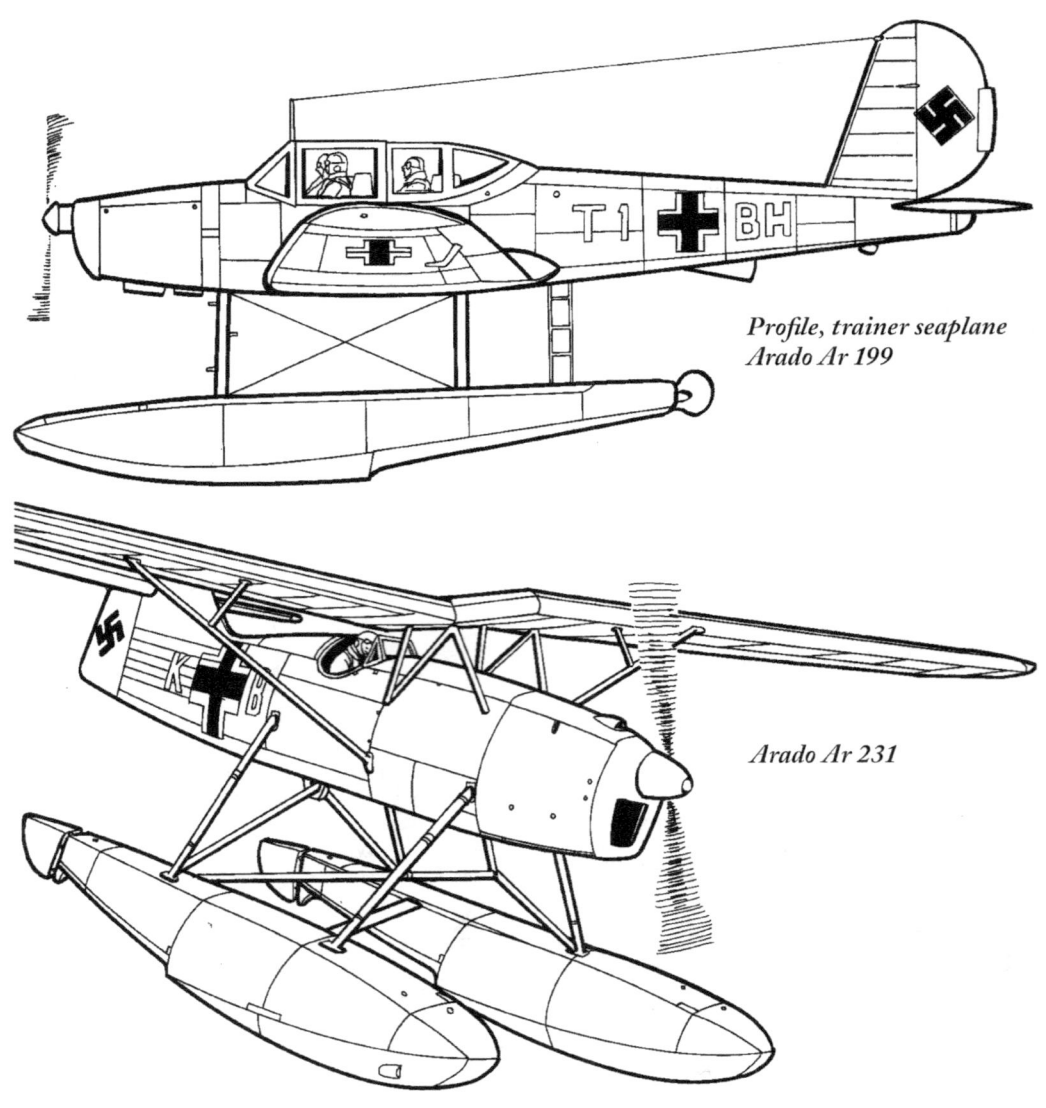

Profile, trainer seaplane Arado Ar 199

Arado Ar 231

1939, as it was decided that the Luftwaffe did not need such a trainer.

Arado Ar 231

The Arado Ar 231 was a small, lightweight observation seaplane. Developed as a single-seat scout plane for submarines, it could be broken into easily detachable sections and stored in a submarine's watertight, cylindrical compartment. It was a parasol-wing design, and for easier storage the right wing was attached lower than the left wing, and the center section was angled. The Ar 231 could be stored in six minutes, after having one wing folded on top of the other. The plane was very difficult to handle in the air, even more so on water since it was so delicate and fragile. The Ar 231 could not take off save in the lightest winds and calmest seas. It was also inadequately powered, with a 160-hp Hirth HM 501 inverted 6-inline, air-cooled engine, and sometimes the radio had to be removed and fuel drained to reduce weight. The plane itself weighed (empty) around 833 kg (1,837 lbs), it had a wingspan of 10.18 m (33 ft 4.5 in), and a length of 7.81 m (25 ft 7.5 in). Maximum speed was 170 km/h (106 mph), range was 500 km (311 miles), and endurance was four hours. Some testing was done on the auxiliary cruiser KMS *Stier*, and two of the six prototypes ever built were taken on one voyage. Proven of little practical use, the program was dropped in 1942.

Blohm & Voss Ha 139

The all-metal floatplane Ha 139 was designed in the late 1930s as shipboard mail plane for the prewar German civilian airline Deutsche Lufthansa. Built by Blohm & Voss/Hamburger Flugzeugbau GmBh (Ha), it was a large monoplane with an inverted gull wing powered by four 600-hp Junkers Jumo 205C diesel engines with twelve pistons in six double-ended cylinders. Maximum speed was 288 km/h (179 mph) and maximum range was 4,948 km (3,075 miles). At the time it was one of the largest floatplanes ever built. Wing span was 29.50 m (96 ft 10 in), length was 20 m (65 ft 10 in), and height was 4.80 m (15 ft 9in). Loaded, the aircraft weighed 19,000 kg (41,888 lb), and could be launched by catapult from a ship when it was near its destination, thus delivering high-priority mail well before the ship reached harbor. Three prototypes were built and given names: Ha 139 V1 *Nordmeer* (North Sea), Ha 139 V2 *Nordwind* (North Wind), and Ha 139 V3 *Nordstern* (North Star). Upon the outbreak of World War II the planes were taken over by the Luftwaffe and converted for reconnaissance work over the Baltic Sea. They were not particularly suited for military use and were not further produced. They were fitted with glazed noses for maritime reconnaissance and transport in the Norwegian campaign of 1940. One of them, known as Ha 139 B/MS, was equipped with a large current-carrying degaussing ring for blowing up underwater mines. By 1942, sub-

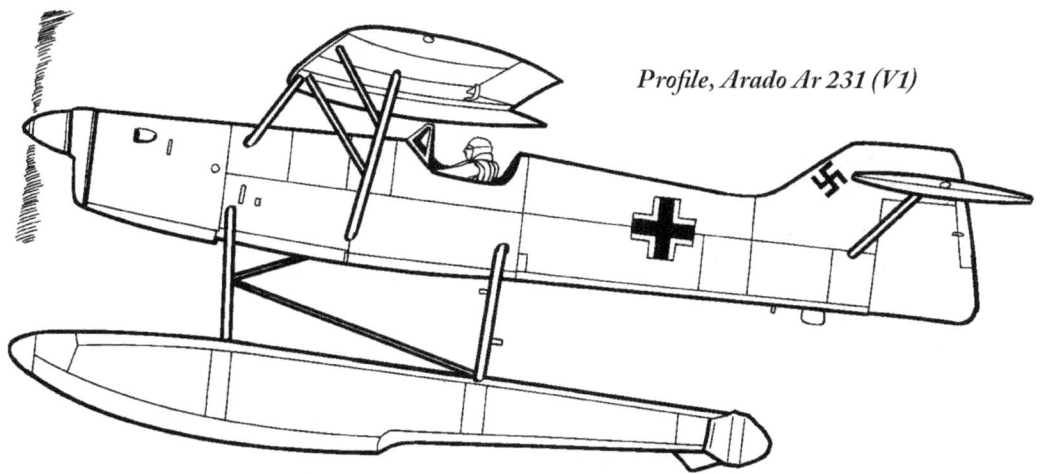

Profile, Arado Ar 231 (V1)

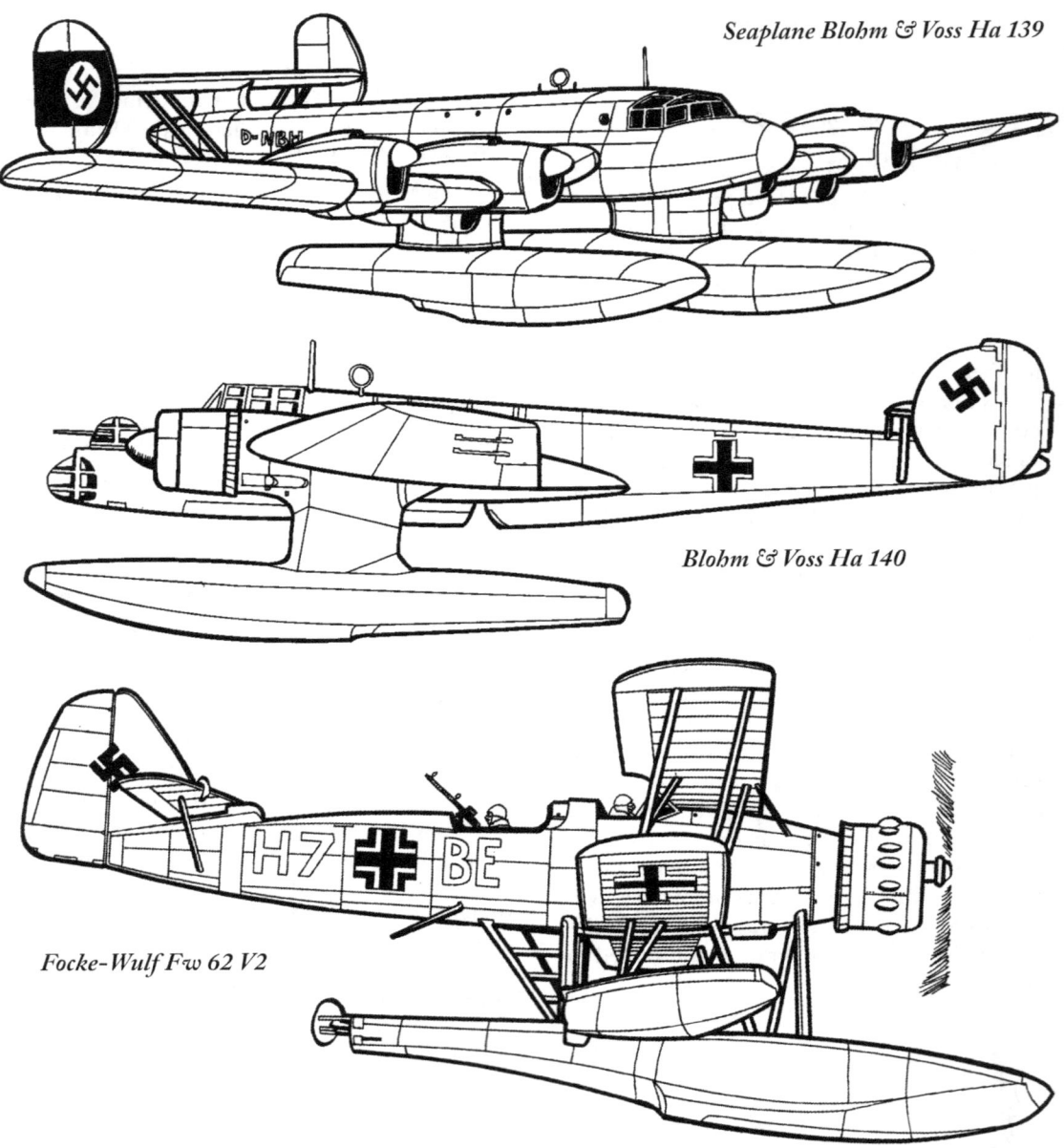

Seaplane Blohm & Voss Ha 139

Blohm & Voss Ha 140

Focke-Wulf Fw 62 V2

sequent use of these aircrafts was discontinued, presumably due to lack of spares.

Blohm & Voss Ha 140

First flown in September 1937, the Blohm & Voss reconnaissance and torpedo bomber floatplane Ha 140 was powered by two 830-hp BMW 132K Hornet 9-cylinder radial engines. It had a maximum speed of 333 km/h (207 mph) and a maximum range of 2,000 km (1,242 miles). It was fitted with two large floats. Wingspan was 22 m (72 ft 2 in) and length was 16.7 m (54 ft 11 in). As the similar Heinkel He 115 had better performances, the Ha 140 project was abandoned after three test units had been built.

Focke-Wulf Fw 62

The Focke-Wulf Fw 62, designed in 1936, was intended to be a shipboard reconnaissance

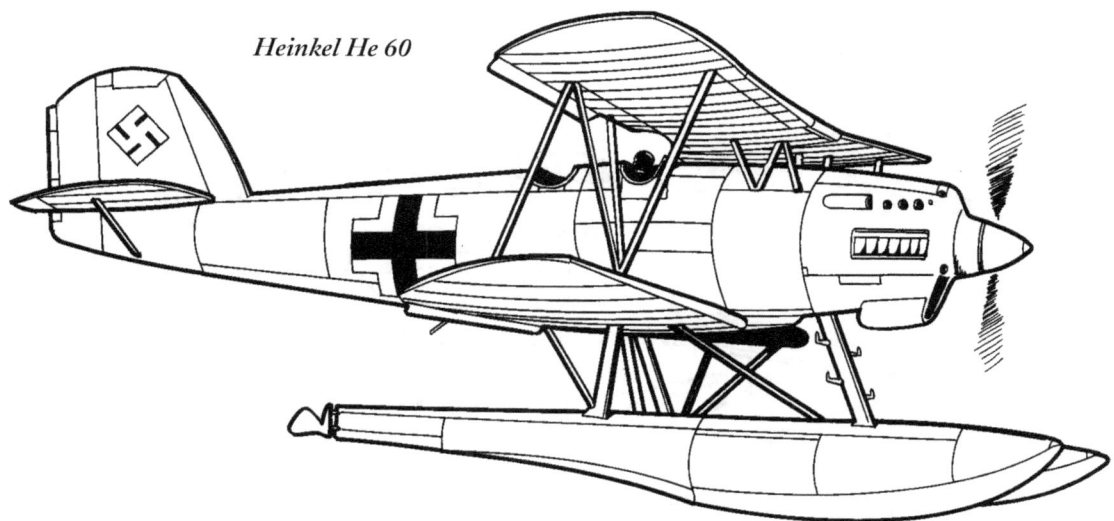

Heinkel He 60

seaplane operating from surface warships of the Kriegsmarine. Two prototypes were built; Fw 62 V1 had twin floats, and V2 had a central float and two additional floats at the tip of the underwing for stability. Both had a crew of two, a wingspan of 12.35 m (40 ft 6.25 in), a length of 20 m (36 ft 7 in), and an empty weight of 2,300 kg (5,070 lbs). Powered by a 880-hp BMW 132Dc 9-cylinder radial engine, the Fw 62 had a maximum speed of 280 km/h (174 mph). First flown in early 1937, the Fw 62 never made it. Although it was quite satisfactory, the RLM chose the rival Arado Ar 196 as standard shipboard floatplane.

Heinkel He 60

The Heinkel biplane He 60 was originally designed in early 1933 to operate from catapults mounted on warships. It had a span of 13.50 m (44ft 4 in), a length of 11.50 m (37 ft 9 in) and an empty weight of 2,730 kg (6,019 lbs). Powered by one 660-hp BMW VI 6-0 V-12, water-cooled engine, it had a maximum speed of 240 km/h (149 mph) and a maximum range of 825 km (513 miles). It had a crew of two (pilot and observer/rear gunner). Armament included a MG 15 machine gun aimed by the observer and some versions were armed with a forward-firing MG 17 placed above the engine. Manufactured by Heinkel, Arado and Weser, it had a sturdy construction and could absorb a great deal of punishment both from enemy fire and heavy seas. The He 60C equipped all major German warships until replaced by the Arado Ar 196, and eventually served from coastal bases in reconnaissance duty until 1943. By that time about 250 had been produced in several versions.

Arado 196

The two-seat floatplane Arado Ar 196 was designed in 1938, in response to an RLM specification for a catapult floatplane to replace the Heinkel He 50. Intended for use on Kriegsmarine capital ships and large surface vessels, it entered operational service in August 1940. Powered by a 960-hp BMW 132 K 9-cylinder radial engine, it had a speed of 310 km/h (193 mph) and a range of 1,070 km (670 miles). Wingspan was 14.4 m (40 ft 8 in), length was 11 m (36 ft 1 in), and height was 4.4 m (14 ft 4 in). The main role was reconnaissance and shadowing of surface vessels, but two 50-kg (110-lb) bombs were carried in underwing racks for attacks on merchant ships or surfaced submarines. For this purpose, the Ar 196 was also powerfully armed with two MG FF 20-mm cannons in wings, one 7.92-mm MG 17 in top decking, and twin MG 15 machine guns manually operated by the observer in the rear cockpit. The aircraft could also be equipped with a *Seilbombe*, consisting of a 20-inch cylinder attached by hook to a seventy-to-eighty foot cable designed to break

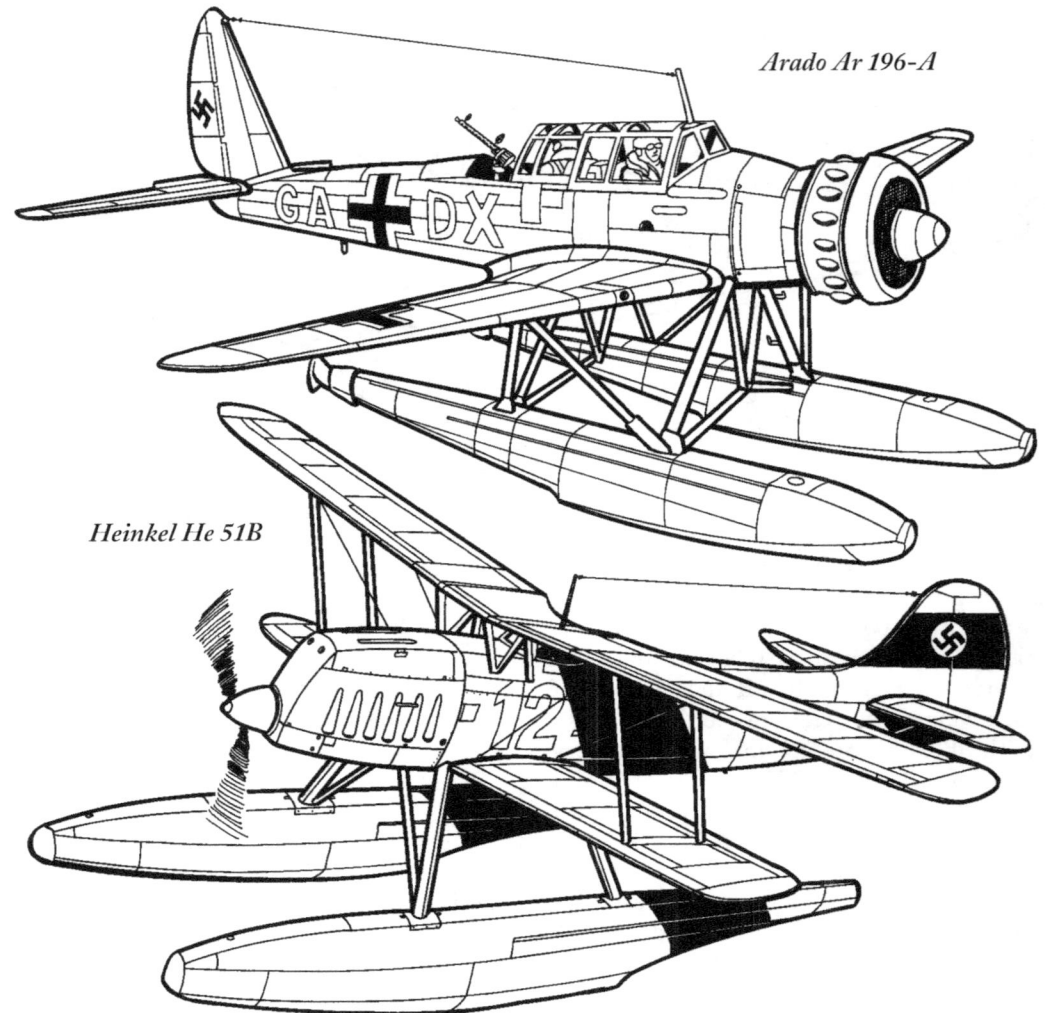

Arado Ar 196-A

Heinkel He 51B

away wireless aerials from merchant ships, preventing them from sending SOS signals. The Ar 196 was never developed as an anti-submarine search-and-strike weapon, despite its obvious potential. Indeed one forced the surrender of the British submarine HMS *Seal* in May 1940. A total of 401 Ar 196s were built, some of which were produced by the French SNCA factory at Saint-Nazaire (Britanny). Though outclassed by modern Allied fighters, the Ar 196 was an excellent design, a versatile multi-role aircraft used as maritime reconnaissance aircraft, sea patroller, and attacker to harass Allied aircraft and small ships over the North Sea, Baltic Sea, English Channel, and Mediterranean Sea. Many flew from catapults in German capital warships (e.g. *Gneisenau* and *Scharnhorst*), but also from coastal bases. About fifty served with co-belligerent Balkan air forces in the Adriatic and Black Sea.

Heinkel He 51 B

Fitted with floats, the He 51 B was the maritime reconnaissance seaplane version of the He 51 fighter (see Part 5).

Dornier Do 22

The Dornier Do 22 was a torpedo bomber and reconnaissance seaplane. It had a crew of three (pilot, observer and rear gunner), a span of 16.2 m (53 ft 2 in), a length of 13.12 m (43 ft), and an empty weight of 2,600 kg (5,733

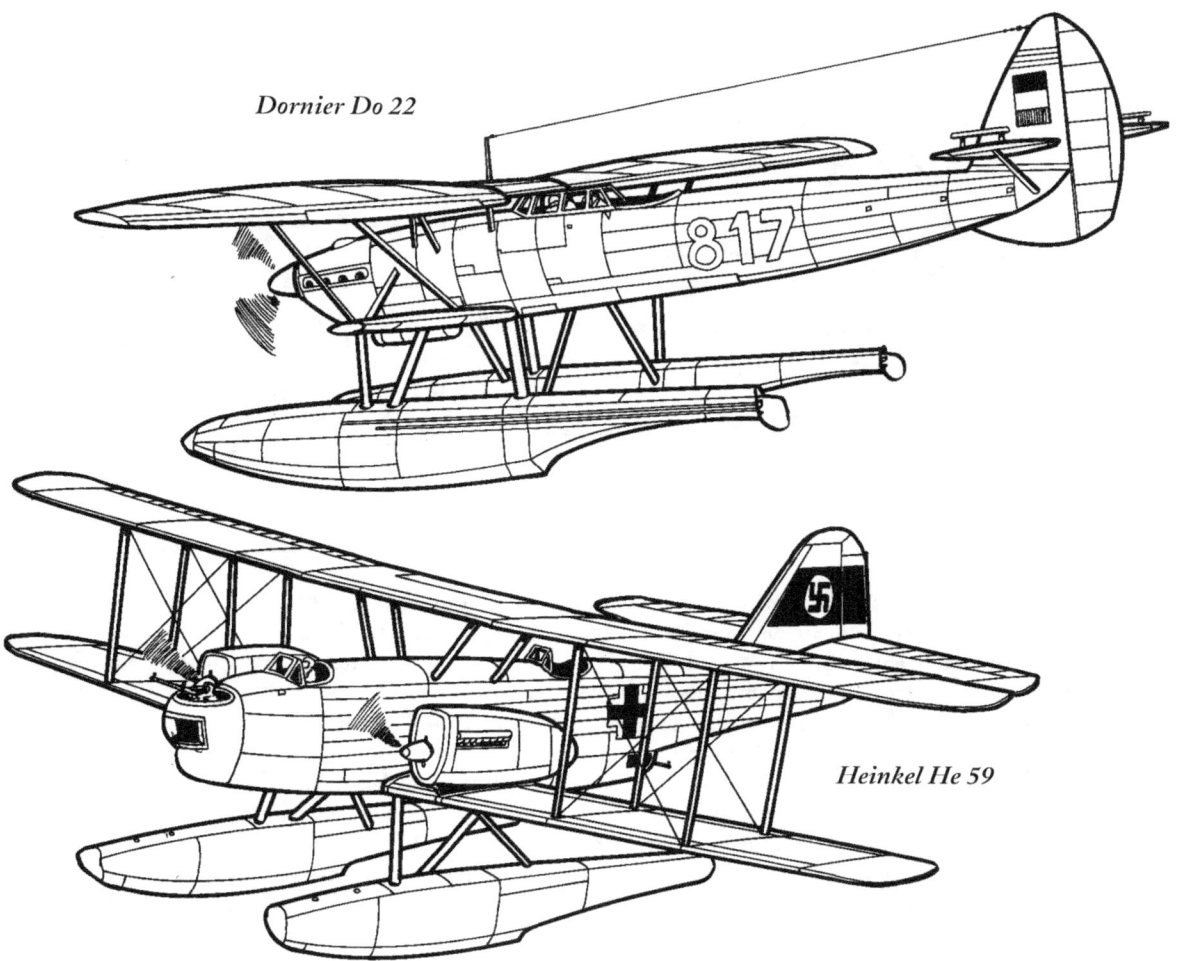

Dornier Do 22

Heinkel He 59

lbs). It was powered by an 860-hp Hispano-Suiza V-12 engine, and had a maximum speed of 350 km/h (217 mph) and a maximum range of 2,300 km (1,429 miles). First flown in 1935, the Do 22 was designed and built in the Dornier factories in Germany and Switzerland, but the aircraft was not ordered by the Luftwaffe. The 31 units produced were entirely all sold abroad in 1939 to Greece, Finland, Yugoslavia and Latvia. A landplane prototype, known as Do 22L, was planned but never put into production.

Heinkel He 59

The Heinkel He 59 made its first flight in September 1931 and entered service in 1932, openly contravening the stipulations of the Versailles Treaty which forbade Germany to have warplanes. As a wheeled reconnaissance/bomber biplane, the He 59 never achieved production status, but it made it as a floatplane. Manufactured by Heinkel which subcontracted the craft to Walter Bachmann AG and Arado, it had a length of 17.4 m (57 ft 2 in), a span of 23.7 m (77 ft 9.5 in) and an empty weight of 6,215 kg (13,702 lbs). Powered by two 660-hp BMW VI V-12, water-cooled engines placed on the lower wings, it had a maximum speed of 215 km/h (134 mph) and a maximum range of 1,750 km (1,087 miles). The He 59 had a crew of four, consisting of pilot, observer, radio operator/gunner and gunner. Defensive armament included three 7.92-mm machine guns manually operated from bow, dorsal and rear ventral positions. An attack version He 59 B2 had provision for a bomb or mine or a torpedo load of 1,000 kg

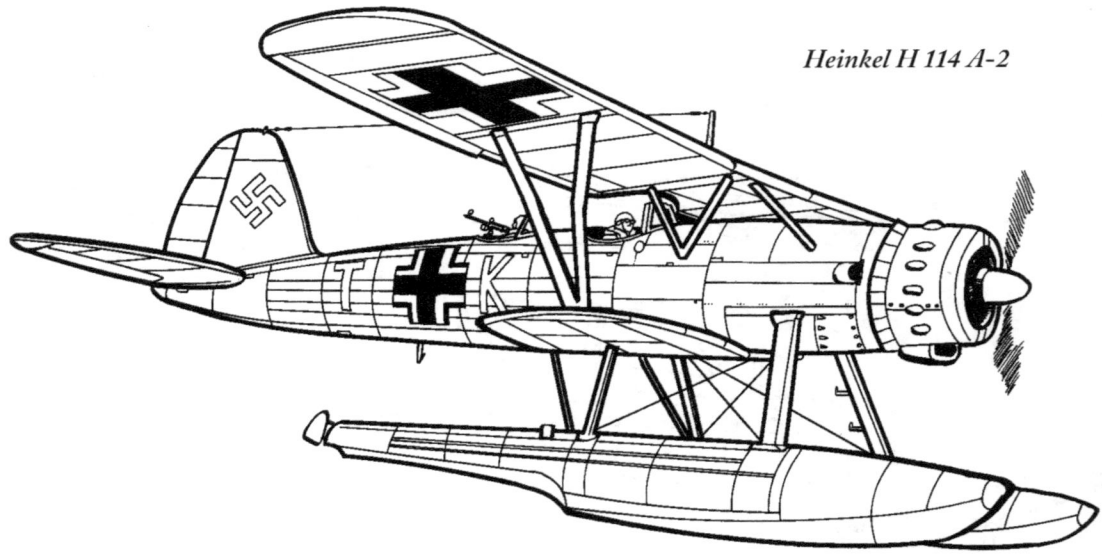

Heinkel H 114 A-2

(2,205 lbs). In spite of its antiquated appearance, the obsolete He 59 was retained and served in many roles during World War II. Produced in a variety of versions, it was used for reconnaissance, air-sea rescue, transport, and training but also as a combat aircraft, torpedo carrier, bomber, mine-layer, anti-shipping craft and even for ground attack. It achieved notoriety at the beginning of World War II when disguised as an ambulance bearing red crosses it carried out reconnaissance and mine-laying missions above the North Sea. An audacious and daring mission was the use of several He 59C-2 rescue transports to land troops on the River Maas to capture the Rotterdam bridges under Dutch fire in May 1940. The He 59 remained in Luftwaffe service until 1943, but it was relegated to second-line duties, mainly as a radio/radar trainer aircraft.

Heinkel He 114

The two-seat reconnaissance floatplane Heinkel He 114 was intended to replace the Heinkel He 60. It had a span of 13.6 m (44 ft 7.5 in), a length of 11.64 m (38 ft 2.5 in) and an empty weight of 2,315 kg (5,104 lbs). Powered by a 970-hp BMW 132K 9-cylinder radial engine, it had a maximum speed of 335 km/h (208 mph) and a maximum range of 920 km (571 miles). The aircraft was armed with one 7.92-mm MG 15 machine gun on a flexible mount, operated by the observer in the rear cockpit, and two 50-kg (110-lb) bombs could be carried on external racks under the wing. The He 114 encountered a lot of early handling troubles both on water and in the air, and never made it as replacement for the He 60. It was outdated when World War II started and saw limited service in the German air force in Latvia, Estonia, Greece and Crete. Small numbers of several versions were sold and operated by Rumania and Sweden. Production ended in 1939 after ninety-eight He 114s had been produced.

Heinkel He 115

First flown in August 1936, the twin-float monoplane Heinkel He 115 was originally developed as a replacement for the aging Heinkel He 59. The aircraft broke various international speed and range records in March 1938, which helped establish its reputation. A militarized version entered Luftwaffe service in 1939 as a torpedo bomber with a crew of three (pilot, observer/torpedo aimer, and radio operator/rear gunner). Length was 17.3 m (56 ft 9 in), wingspan was 22.2 m (72 ft 10 in), wing area was 87.5 square m (942 square ft), and empty weight was 5,290 kg (11,670 lb). Powered by two BMW 132 9-cylinder 630 kW 845-hp air-cooled radial engines, the He 115 had a maxi-mum speed of 349 km/h (217 mph) and a com-

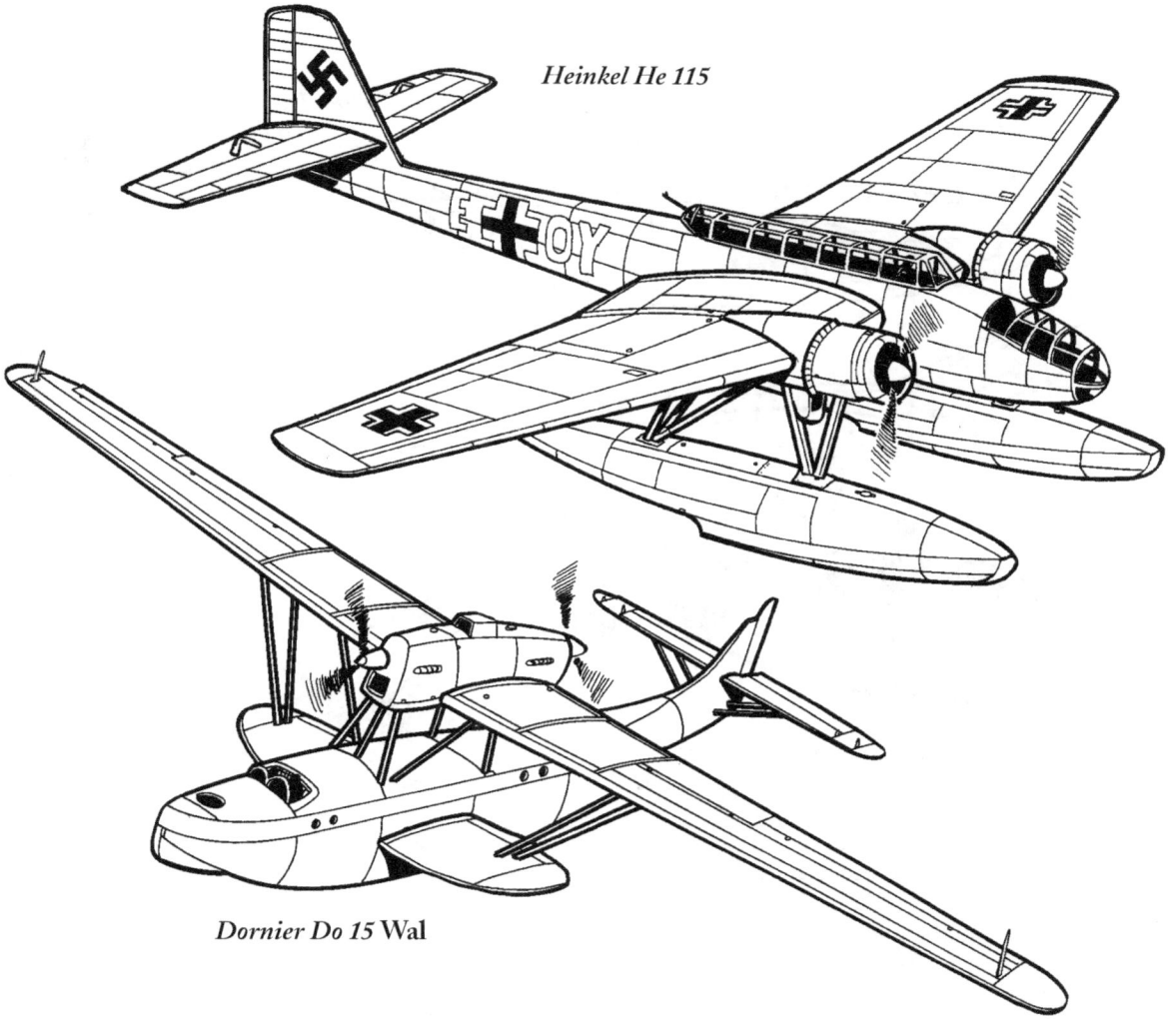

Heinkel He 115

Dornier Do 15 Wal

bat range of 2,100 km (1,305 miles). A load of 1,000 kg (2,205 lbs) of torpedoes, mines or bombs could be carried. Armament varied but generally included two or more MG 15, MG 151, and MG 17 machine guns. A wholly outstanding, sturdy and tough airplane, the Heinkel He 115 was held in high esteem although regarded as obsolete, too slow and vulnerable in the torpedo-attack role by 1942. It was nonetheless one of the most long-lived German general-purpose floatplanes, used and manufactured until 1944. As World War II proceeded, its combat roles, such as torpedo bombing, anti-shipping attack, and even shallow dive bombing greatly diminished, and the He 115 performed more and more valuable general seaplane duties such as utility transport, reconnaissance, rescue, casualty evacuation, and mine laying. Total production was about 400 in several versions, some sold to Norway and Sweden. A later upgraded model, Heinkel He 115 E, could seat four, had more powerful engines, and used different weapon set-ups.

Flying Boats

Dornier Do 15 Wal

Designed in 1922, the Do 15 *Wal* (Whale) was extensively used by both civil and military operators during the interwar period. The flying boat had a span of 23.19 m (76 ft 1.5 in), a length of 18.19 m (59 ft 8.5 in), a height of

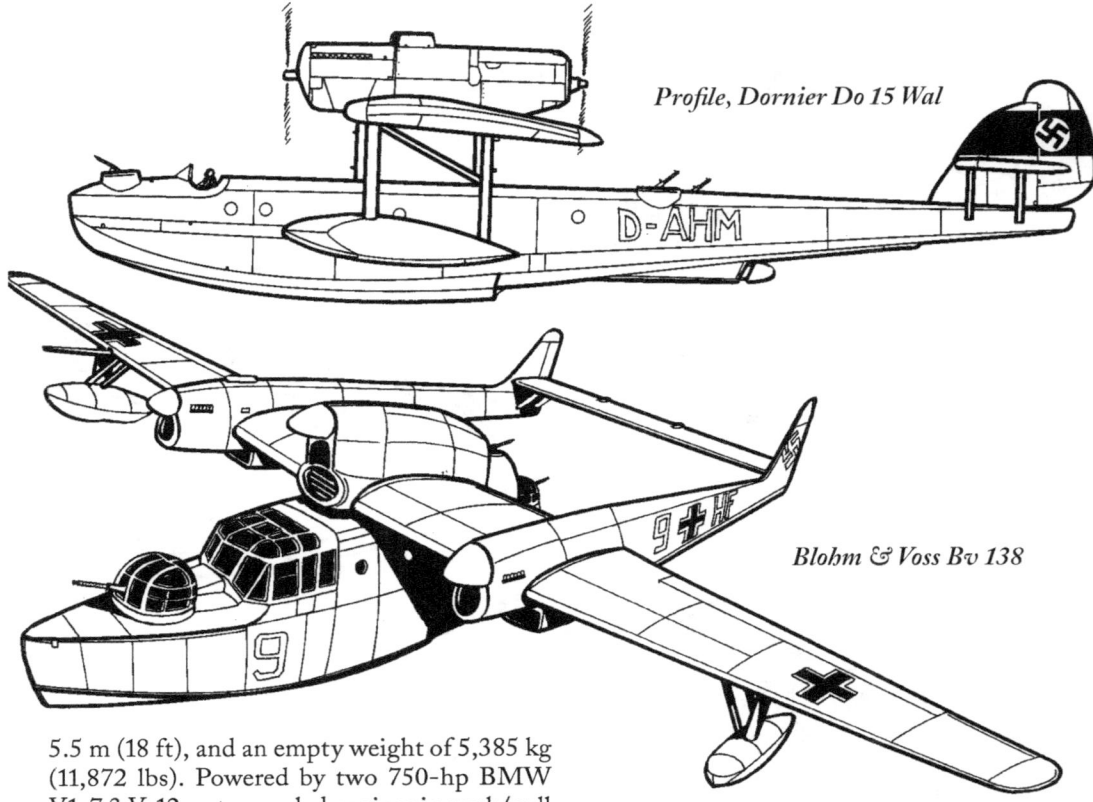

Profile, Dornier Do 15 Wal

Blohm & Voss Bv 138

5.5 m (18 ft), and an empty weight of 5,385 kg (11,872 lbs). Powered by two 750-hp BMW V1-7 3 V-12 water-cooled engines in push/pull arrangement, it had a maximum speed of 220 km/h (137 mph), and a range of 2,200 km (1,367 miles). The *Wal* was much improved in the early 1930s and some thirty units were adopted for Luftwaffe use in 1935 for a maritime reconnaissance and rescue role. The military version was armed with three 7.92-mm MG 15 machine guns in bow and two dorsal positions. A bomb load of 110 lbs could be carried on external racks. It had a crew of four including pilot, observer, engineer/gunner and radio-operator/gunner. By 1938, the aging Do 15 was retired from active service and replaced by the Dornier Do 18, although some were retained for training.

Blohm & Voss Bv 138

The flying boat Bv 138 was first flown in July 1937 and entered Luftwaffe service in January 1940. The plane had a crew of five (pilot, copilot, observer, radio operator and engineer), but for long-range maritime reconnaissance patrols two additional crew members were taken. Length was 19.9 m (65 ft 3in), wingspan was 27 m (88 ft 7 in), height was 5.7 m (18 ft 10 in), wing area was 111.9 square m (1.205 square ft), and weight (empty) was 8,080 kg (17,820 lb). It was powered by three 880-hp Junkers Jumo 205C diesel engines, with one mounted high above the centerline driving a four-bladed propeller, and one on each wing driving three-bladed propellers. Maximum speed was 275 km/h (171 mph), range was 2,400 km (1,490 miles), and service ceiling was 4,880 m (16,000 ft). Despite of an early problem with hull and floats, it was a seaworthy and sturdy aircraft. It had a rather unusual and ungainly appearance with twin-boom tail unit, and gun turrets at the bow and the stern of the fuselage, as well as behind the central engine. Because of its distinctive hull shape it earned the nickname of *Fliegende Holzschuh* (Flying Clog). The Blohm & Voss BV 138 was a long-range maritime reconnaissance aircraft, and sometimes its range could be increased by catapult launching from a ship. The basic armament included two MG 151 20-mm cannons

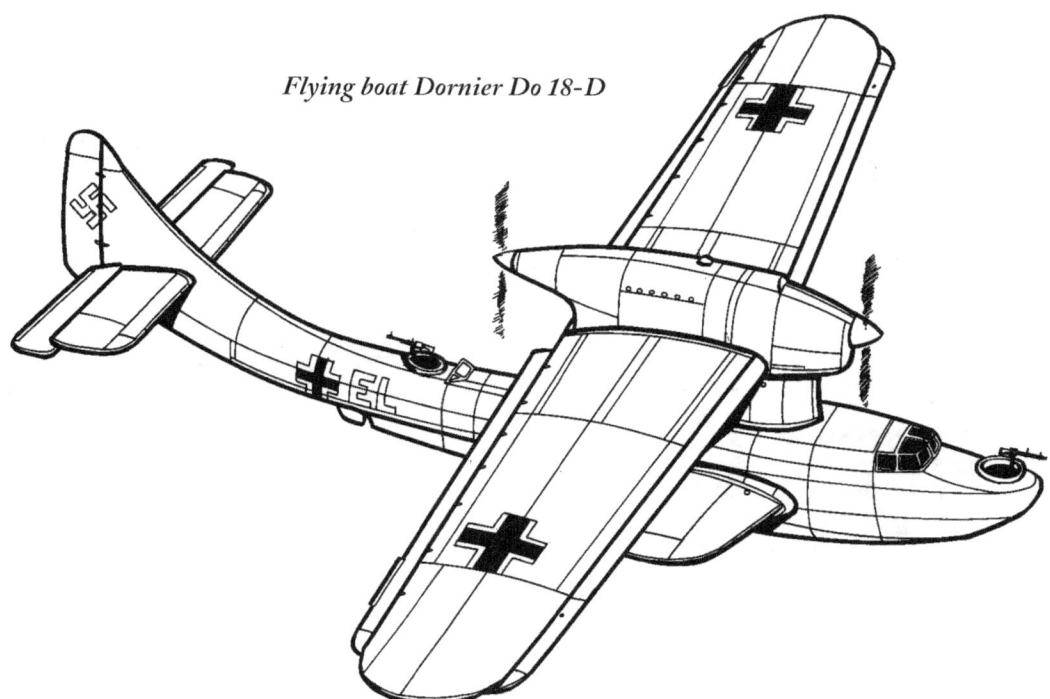

Flying boat Dornier Do 18-D

in front and rear turrets, and one MG 131 13-mm machine gun placed in a cockpit behind the central engine. Various versions of the aircraft carried a variety of bombs and depth charges. There was also a minesweeper variant of the aircraft, known as Bv 138 MS, which carried a degaussing device in the form of a large circular hoop around the fuselage instead of weapons. Some twenty-one Bv 138B-1 craft were built in 1940, and 227 improved Bv 138C-1 versions were produced between 1941 and 1943.

Dornier Do 18

By the middle of the 1930s the Dornier Company had acquired a good reputation for the building of seaplanes. Following a requirement of the German civilian airline Lufthansa, Dornier designed in 1935 the all-metal, high-wing, braced monoplane flying boat Do 18 as a high-priority-mail carrier over the North Atlantic Ocean. The prototype Do 18-E first flew in March 1935, and in March 1938 a Dornier Do 18 established a world record by flying from the Strait of Dover in Britain to Brazil in a nonstop flight of 8,391 km (5,214 miles) in forty-three hours. A military version (Do18-D) entered service in the Luftwaffe in September 1938 as coastal reconnaissance aircraft. The flying boat had good seaworthiness and stability. It was delivered in various versions (Do18-G, Do 18-H and Do18-N) and used for reconnaissance and in an air/sea rescue role during World War II, mainly in the Baltic Sea and North Atlantic Ocean. The Dornier Do-18 versions D, G, H and N had slightly different performances but basically the flying boat was operated by a crew of four, and powered by a tandem of push/pull Junkers Jumo 205 C diesel engines; it had a maximum speed of 260 km/h (162 mph) and a range of 3,500 km (2,175 miles). Wingspan was on average 23.7 m (77 ft 9 in), length was 19.25 m (63 ft 2 in), and weight (empty) was 5,850 kg (12,900 lbs). Defensive armament included one 7.92-mm MG 15 machine gun placed in a bow hatch, and another MG 15 machine gun placed in hatch (later turret) on the back of the fuselage. Some Do 18 craft were fitted with underwing racks enabling them to carry a 500-kg (1,102-lb) bomb load. Others (unarmed) were used for transport or as ambulances. The Dornier Do 18 had the dubious honor to be the

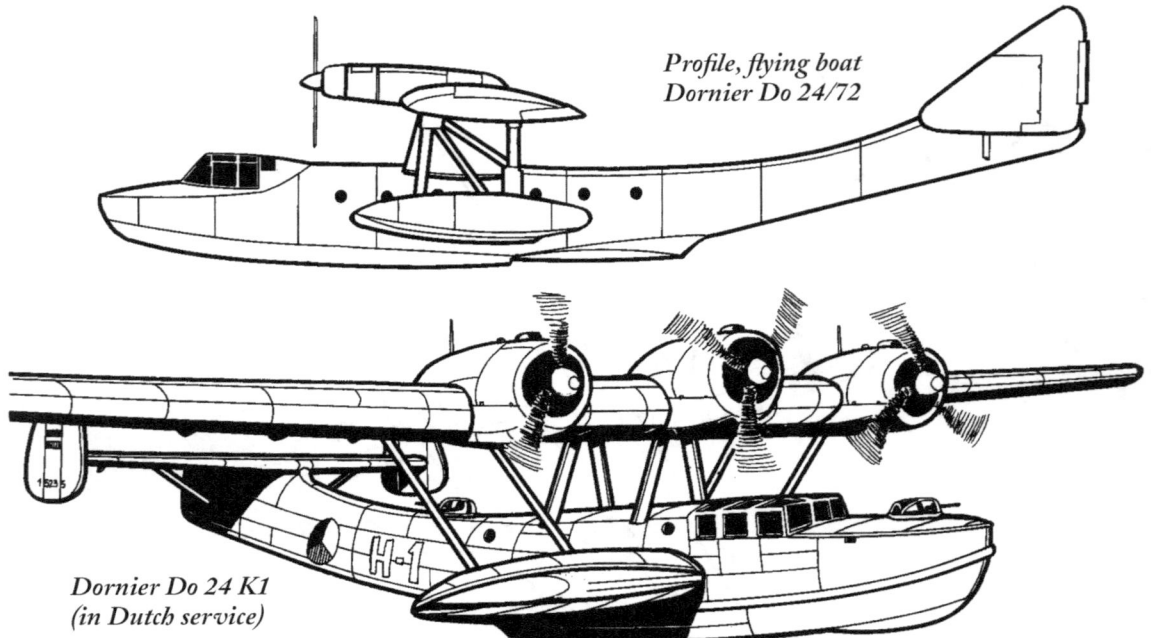

Profile, flying boat Dornier Do 24/72

Dornier Do 24 K1 (in Dutch service)

first German airplane to be shot down at the outbreak of World War II: this happened on September 26, 1939 when RAF Skua fighters from the aircraft carrier *Ark Royal* engaged three of them; the other two flying boats (both Do 18) managed to escape—clearly demonstrating the poor capability of the Blackburn Skua as a fighter aircraft. Production of the Do 18 was halted in 1940 after 152 units were produced.

Dornier Do 24

An all-metal, three-engine, strut-mounted-wing monoplane with a shallow broad-beam hull and stabilizing sponsons, Dornier Do 24 was a transport flying boat. It was built by the German Dornier Company and made its first flight in early July 1937. The customer was not Nazi Germany but the Kingdom of the Netherlands, and the Dutch Aviolanda Company built forty-eight Do 24s under license. In 1940 some thirty-seven units had been produced and served in the Dutch East Indies naval air service. After the defeat of Holland in May 1940, the Dutch Dornier Do 24s were captured and immediately entered Luftwaffe service in reconnaissance and air-sea rescue duty. Production of this excellent and reliable trimotor flying boat was continued in the Low Countries and France by the French aircraft company Potez-Cam. The military Do 24 usually had a crew of six, including pilot, copilot, observer, engineer, radio-operator/gunner, and gunner. It was powered by three 1,000-hp BMW-Bramo 323R-2 Fafnir 9-cylinder, air-cooled radial engines, and had a maximum speed of 340 km/h (211 mph) and a maximum range of 4,750 km (2,950 miles). The aircraft had a length of 22 m (72 ft 2 in), a span of 27 m (88 ft 7 in), a height of 5.45 m (17 ft 10 in) and an empty weight of 13,500 kg (29,700 lbs). In Luftwaffe service, defensive armament included two 7.92-mm MG 15 machine guns in bow and stern turrets, and one 20-mm Hispano-Suiza cannons in a dorsal turret. Twelve 50-kg (110-lb) bombs could be carried in underwing racks. In the air-ambulance role, the Do 24 could carry eight stretchers plus another twelve seated passengers. The aircraft was reportedly easy to fly and had a good all-round view for reconnaissance, with a maximum endurance of about eleven hours. The wartime Do 24, the workhorse of the Luftwaffe air-sea rescue service, was produced by the resurrected Dutch Aviolanda (placed under the control of the German company Weser Flugzeugbau) and by the French SNCA du

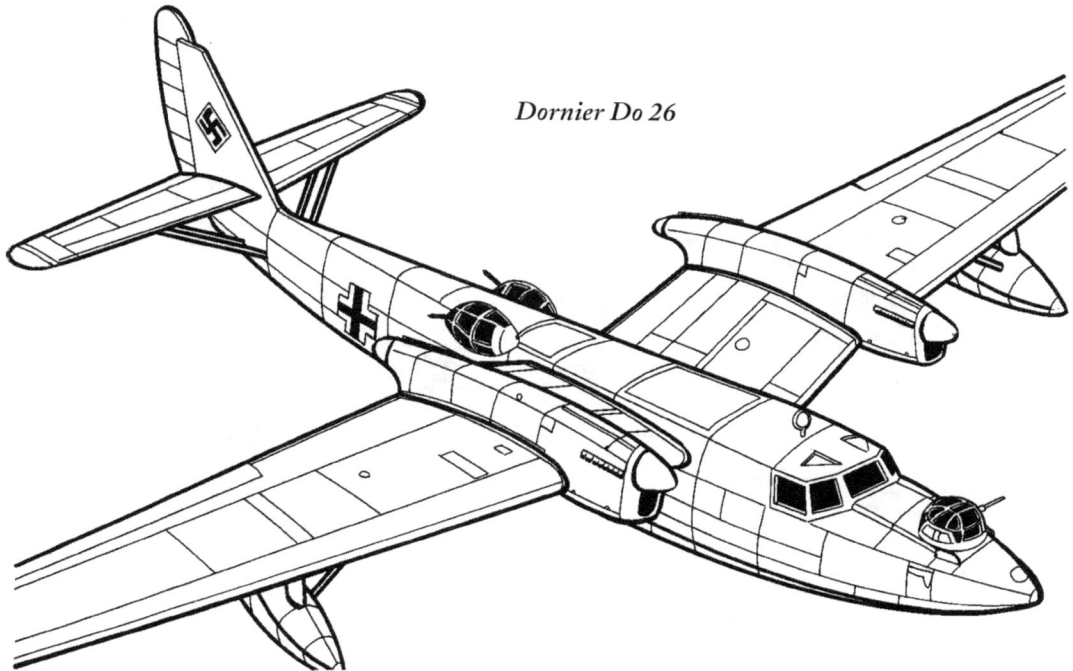

Dornier Do 26

Nord factory located at Sartrouville near Paris. A total of 294 units in several versions were produced during World War II, most of which served in the rescue role. Postwar, license-produced versions were still in service, notably those manufactured by the Spanish aircraft company CASA, until the late 1960s. There was a variant, known as Dornier Do 318; this one and only prototype, designed by Weser Flugzeugbau, was destroyed in Lake Constance near the end of the war.

Dornier Do 26

The Do 26 was originally designed in 1938 as a commercial, civilian, Lufthansa mail-carrier flying boat operating between Lisbon, Portugal, and New York City. Five units were built in total, all were militarized by the Luftwaffe in 1939, and took part to the invasion of Norway in 1940 as long-range reconnaissance and transport flying boats. The Do 25 had a crew of four: pilot, observer, radio operator/gunner, and engineer/gunner. A trim and sleek all-metal aircraft with gull-wing and retractable stabilization underwing floats, it had a length of 24.6 m (60 ft 8.5 in), a wingspan of 30 m (98 ft 6 in), a height of 6.85m (22 ft 6 in), and a weight (empty) of 11,300 kg (24,912 lbs). It was powered by four 880-hp Junkers Jumo 205D diesel engines mounted in push-pull tandem arrangement, each engine with six double-ended cylinders and twelve opposed pistons. Maximum speed was 324 km/h (201 mph) and range was 7,100 km (4,412 miles). Defensive armament included one 20-mm MG 151 cannon in bow turret, and three 7.92-mm MG 15 machine guns in lateral midship blisters and aft of rear planning step. The elegant flying boat had only a short military career. Two Do 26s were shot down by the RAF in May 1940 and the other three operated on communication missions and coast patrol; they were withdrawn from front-line duty soon afterward.

Blohm & Voss Bv 222 Wiking

The Blohm & Voss Bv 222 *Wiking* (Viking) was a large six-engined flying-boat originally ordered in September 1937 by Deutsche Lufthansa as a civil flying boat for use on the Atlantic. The *Wiking* made its first flight in September 1940, and the nine units built were quickly taken over as military strategic transports and maritime reconnaissance planes. The

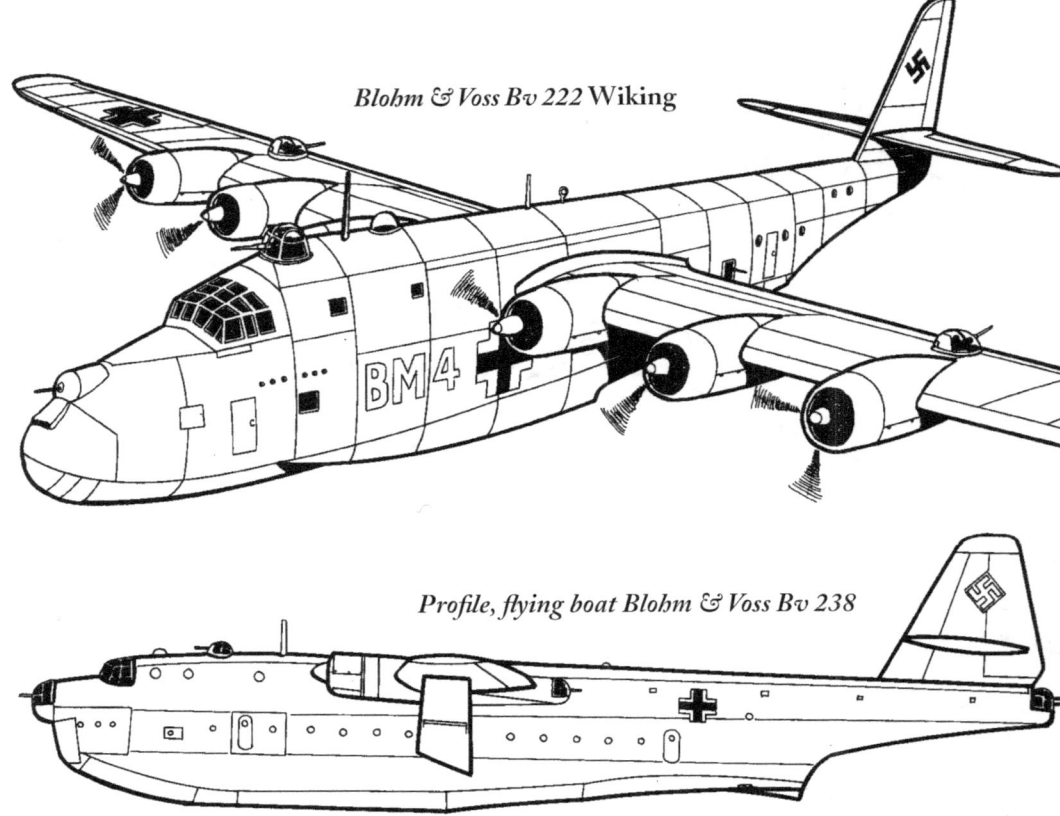

Blohm & Voss Bv 222 Wiking

Profile, flying boat Blohm & Voss Bv 238

transport version was operated by a crew of ten and could carry seventy fully equipped troops. Owing to its good basic quality, thirteen Bv 222s were completed. Early prototypes were identified as V1 to V8. Production examples were designated C-09 to C-13. Length was 37 m (121 ft 4.75 in), wingspan was 46 m (150 ft 11 in), height was 10.9 m (35 ft 9 in), wing area was 255 square m (2,744.89 square ft), and empty weight was 30,650 kg (67,572 lb). Originally the type was powered by six Bramo 323 Fafnir radial engines. Later aircraft were powered by six 1,000-hp Jumo 207C in-line diesel engines. The large flying boat was always underpowered, but the use of diesel engines permitted refueling at sea by surface and U-boats. The Bv 222 C-13 aircraft was a sole example fitted with Jumo 205C engines and later Jumo 205D. Access in flight through the wing was via a tubular wing spar of a meter in diameter. Engineers could also reach the engines in flight via the same spar. Maximum speed was 390 km/h (242 mph), cruising speed was 257 km/h (139 knots), endurance was twenty-eight hours, and range was 6,095 km (3,787 miles). Armament was various. For instance, the Bv 222 A V4 was rather well-armed. One dorsal gun turret was positioned behind the cockpit, another was placed in dorsal position, rear-facing machine-gun turrets were added on both wings, and machine guns were operated from side windows. The Bv 222 *Wiking* was used from northern Norway to North Africa for transport. Most of them were shot down or destroyed at mooring. Four survived the war and were sent to Great Britain and the United States for testing.

Blohm & Voss Bv 238

The Blohm & Voss Bv 238 flying boat was the heaviest aircraft of the whole war, beating out even the giant Boeing B-29 Superfortress by many tons, and physically it was the largest aircraft produced by any of the Axis powers in World War II. Empty weight was no less than

Blohm & Voss Bv 238

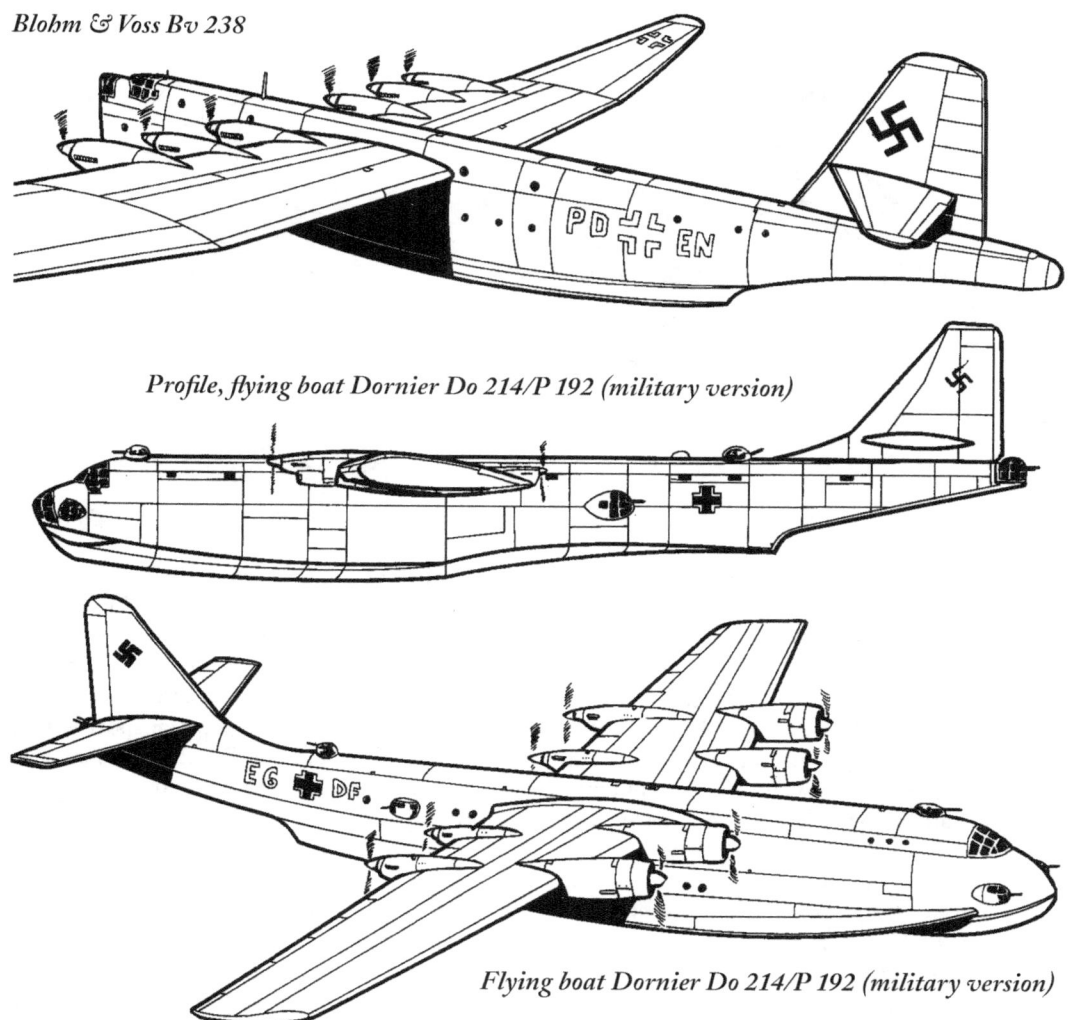

Profile, flying boat Dornier Do 214/P 192 (military version)

Flying boat Dornier Do 214/P 192 (military version)

54,700 kg (120,593 lbs). Total length was 43.36 m (142 ft 3 in), height was 13.40 m (43 ft 11.6 in), wingspan was 60.17 m (197 ft 5 in), and wing area was 362 square m (3,900 square ft). Six 1,750-hp (1,287 MW) DB 603 V engines built by Daimler-Benz were used in total, arranged in three forward-facing integrated engine nacelles in a row on each wing. Maximum speed was 446 km/h (277 mph), and cruising speed was 355 km/h (220.6 mph). Service ceiling was 7,300 m (23,950 ft), and range was 7,200 km (4,474 miles). The Bv 238 V1 prototype first flew in March 1944, and two other units, though started, were not finished. The only completed specimen was destroyed by American fighter attack by the end of the war. Also of note, a large model of the plane was made during development, known as the FGP 227, and used for testing.

Dornier Do 214/Do P 192

The flying boat Dornier Do 214 (originally designated Do P 93) was intended for civilian passenger transatlantic service from Lisbon to New York. Designed in 1941 after successful testing with a scale model, it would have been a huge flying boat with a windspan of 60 m (196 ft 10 in), a length of 51.6 m (169 ft 4 in), a height of 14.3 m (46 ft 11 in) and a wing area of 500 square m (5,382 square ft). It would have been powered by eight Daimler-Benz DB 613 24-cylinder piston engines with a total of 32,000 hp, placed on both edges of the wings

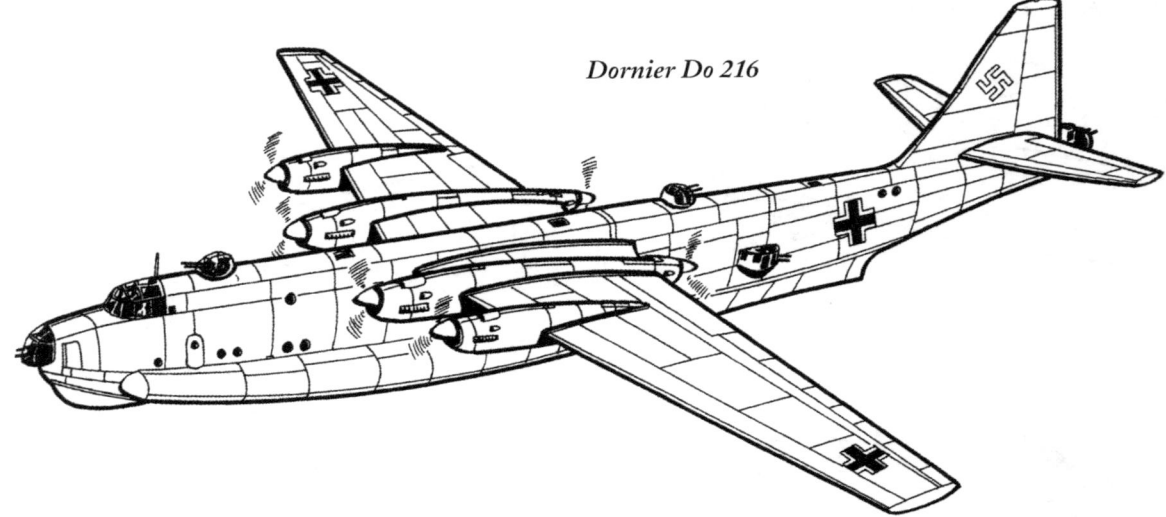
Dornier Do 216

with four engines pulling and four engines pushing, giving the aircraft a maximum speed of 490 km/h (304 mph) and a cruising speed of 425 km/h (262 mph). Fuel tanks with a capacity of 66,000 liters (17,435 gallons) were placed in the fuselage, with additional tanks located in the wings, with a capacity of 1,500 liters (396 gallons), allowing a maximum range of 6,200 km (3,853 miles). The fuselage was streamlined, of a round cross-section, and instead of the usual stabilization floats, a more aerodynamic design was used, consisting of long bulges added along the fuselage bottom. The aircraft had a single fin and rudder, and the tailplanes were of conventional design. The interior was divided into two luxurious decks with seats, cabins, lounge and bar for the comfort of forty (obviously wealthy) passengers. The crew of twelve consisted of a captain, two pilots, navigator, radio operator, two flight engineers, two stewards, and three hostesses. Some 2.6 metric tons of high-priority mail, freight and luggage were to be carried in the lower fuselage storage area, the total loaded weight of the aircraft being about 145,000 kg (319,670 lbs). Work on this civilian project went on until 1942 when the RLM (German Air Ministry) decided that what Germany needed for the time being was war machines and not civilian transatlantic airliners. The Do 214 project was discontinued, and Dornier was ordered to concentrate on a military version redesignated Do P 192. Dornier then proposed nine military versions with various weapon/transport options. P 192 01 was to be a transport variant with a capacity of 33,000 kg and heavily armed with ten manned and remote-controlled machine guns and cannon emplacements; P 192 02 was a troop transport with a capacity of 333 soldiers; P 192 03 was a heavy cargo transport fitted with a large bow door admitting vehicles and bulky freight to the upper deck, with a capacity of 82,000 kg; P 192 04 was to be a U-boat supply flying boat for operation in the Atlantic Ocean; P 192 05 would be a minelayer aircraft; P 192 06 was a fuel transport and flying tanker; P 192 07 was a transport for fully armed and equipped troops; P 192 08 would be an air ambulance; and P 192 09 would become a long-range bomber and guided-weapons carrier. No P 192s were ever completed. By 1943, due to the worsening war situation for Germany, it was realized that long-range flying boats were redundant, and so the Do 214/P 192 project was abandoned.

Dornier Do 216

The Dornier Do 216 was a slightly smaller version of the Do 214/P 192. It was intended to become a transport, anti-shipping and ocean patrol flying boat. The flying boat had a span of 48 m (157 ft 6 in), a length of 42.3 m (138 ft 9 in), a height of 7.9 m (25 ft 11 in), a wing area of 310 square m (3.337 square ft), and an empty weight of 40,000 kg (88,195 lbs). The

7. Seaplanes

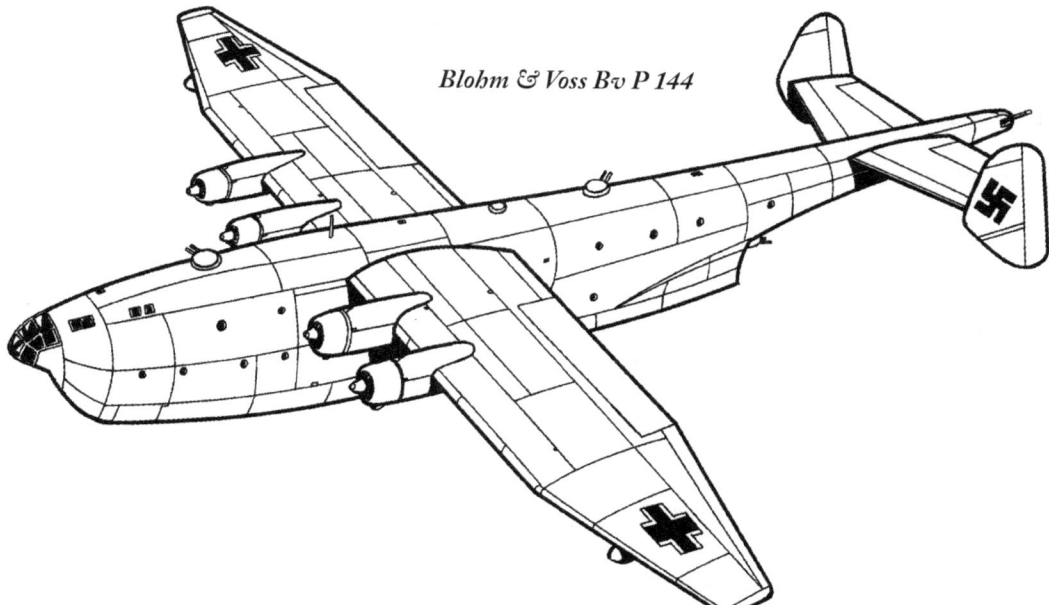
Blohm & Voss Bv P 144

Do 216 was powered by six Daimler-Benz 603C engines, and expected to have a maximum speed of 445 km/h (277 mph) and a range of 6,700 km (3,853 miles). It was intended to be operated by a crew of ten, and powerfully armed with seventeen 151 20-mm cannon placed in eight firing positions and remote-controlled turrets. A bomb load of 5,000 kg (11,020 lbs) could be carried. Its fate was the same as the Dornier Do 214/P 192. As there was no longer any need for this kind of long-range flying boat, the development of the Dornier Do 216 was cancelled.

Blohm & Voss Bv P 144

The Bv P 144 was a huge flying boat with a span of 53 m (173 ft 10 in), a length of 40 m (131 ft 2 in), a wing area of 280 square m (3,014 square ft), and an empty weight of 38,300 kg (84,437 lbs). The aircraft was powered by four 2,500-hp Jumo 223 24-cylinder radial engines. It had a crew of ten, and—with a range of 8,650 km (5,371 miles)—it was intended for several roles, including long-range reconnaissance, U-boat support at sea, long-range bombing, and surface mine-laying. It was to be armed with three remote-controlled turrets, each armed with twin MG 131 13-mm machine guns, two in a dorsal position and one in a ventral position. One FDL MG 151/20 20-mm cannon was planned in the tail. The Bv P 144 was never completed; by 1944 the project was cancelled.

Carrier-Based Aircraft

Another category of plane related to the sea was the aircraft-carrier machine.

It is significant that Germany, with Hitler's basic misconception of naval strategy and neglect of the importance of the aircraft carrier in modern naval warfare, proved woefully inadequate in producing such a weapon system. It is almost incredible to reflect on how much the Allies owed to Hitler's lack of interest and his miserable policy regarding aircraft carriers.

The German navy had two aircraft carriers, the *Graf Zeppelin* and *Peter Strasser*, but only the former made any progress. In the early years of World War II, building the *Graf Zeppelin* carrier was considered imperative to provide air cover to commerce-raiding capital ships and cruisers, but as the war progressed priorities changed, and shipyard capacities were used for more urgent work—notably the construction of U-boats (submarines). Commenced in 1938, the *Graf Zeppelin* was still incomplete in 1945, and thus never saw action.

Even if completed, she would have displayed a poor showing compared to World War II Japanese, American and British aircraft carriers, mainly since the Germans had little experience, no independent Navy air force, and above all no real interest. The *Graf Zeppelin* would have had a displacement of 23,200 metric tons, and would have had a crew of 1,760. Armament would have consisted of sixteen 150-mm guns and twelve 104-cm Flak guns, and she would have carried twelve fighters (Messerschmitt Bf 109 G) and twenty-eight dive-bombers (Junkers Ju 87 C). The unfinished carrier, moored at Stettin in northern Germany, was scuttled in April 1945 by a demolition team to prevent her falling into enemy hands. The hulk of the carrier was raised in March 1947 by the Soviet navy and left Stettin in tow for Leningrad in August 1947. On the way she struck a mine and sunk.

Several carrier-based aircraft were designed to arm the never-completed carrier. These included naval versions of the world famous Messerschmitt Bf 109 fighter, Junkers Ju 87 dive bomber, and the much-less-known airplanes described below.

Arado Ar 95

The Arado Ar 95, designed for use as torpedo/reconnaissance airplane aboard the aircraft carrier *Graf Zeppelin*, existed in two versions, either with twin floats or with fixed, "spatted"-wheeled landing gear. The aircraft

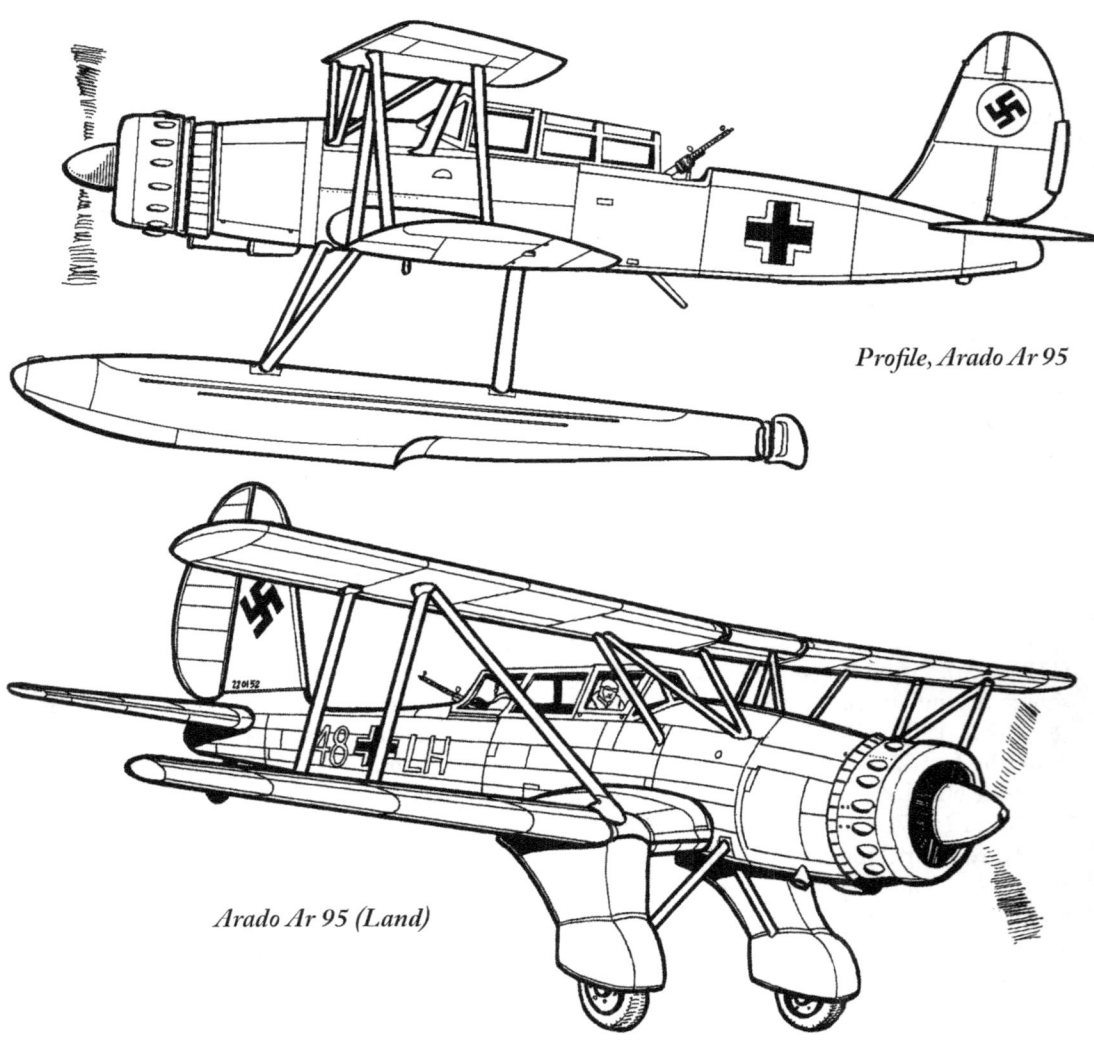

Profile, Arado Ar 95

Arado Ar 95 (Land)

had a span of 12.5 m (41 ft), a length of 11.1 m (36 ft 5 in), an empty weight of 2,535 kg (5,588 lbs). It had a crew of two (pilot and observer/rear gunner). Armament included one 7.92-mm manually-aimed MG 15 gun in rear cockpit, and one synchronized 7.92-mm MG 17 firing forward; a 700-kg (1,540-lb) torpedo or an equivalent load of bombs/mines/depth charges could be carried. Powered by one 880-hp BMW 132Dc 9-cylinder radial engine, the Ar 95 had a maximum speed of 300 km (187 mph) and a range of 1,094 km (680 miles). The aircraft proved rather disappointing. Five prototypes were built, six were produced and sent with the Legion Condor in the Spanish Civil War, and another six were produced and sold to Chile. By 1939, twelve units were manufactured and delivered to the Luftwaffe, equipping a squadron in the Baltic Sea.

Arado Ar 195

The two-seat biplane Arado Ar 195 was intended to become a carrier-based torpedo bomber. It had a wingspan of 12.5 m (41 ft) and a length of 10 m (34 ft 6 in). Powered by a 880-hp BMW 132 M 9-cylinder radial engine, it had a maximum speed of 290 km/h (180 mph) and a range of 650 km (404 miles). Armament included one synchronized 7.92-mm MG 17 firing forward, and a manually aimed MG 15 in the rear cockpit. A load of 700 kg (1,540 lbs) of bombs could be carried. The airplane had excessive drag that ruined its performance, and only three test units were built.

Arado Ar 197

The biplane single-seat, carrier-based fighter Arado Ar 197 had a wingspan of 11 m (36 ft 1

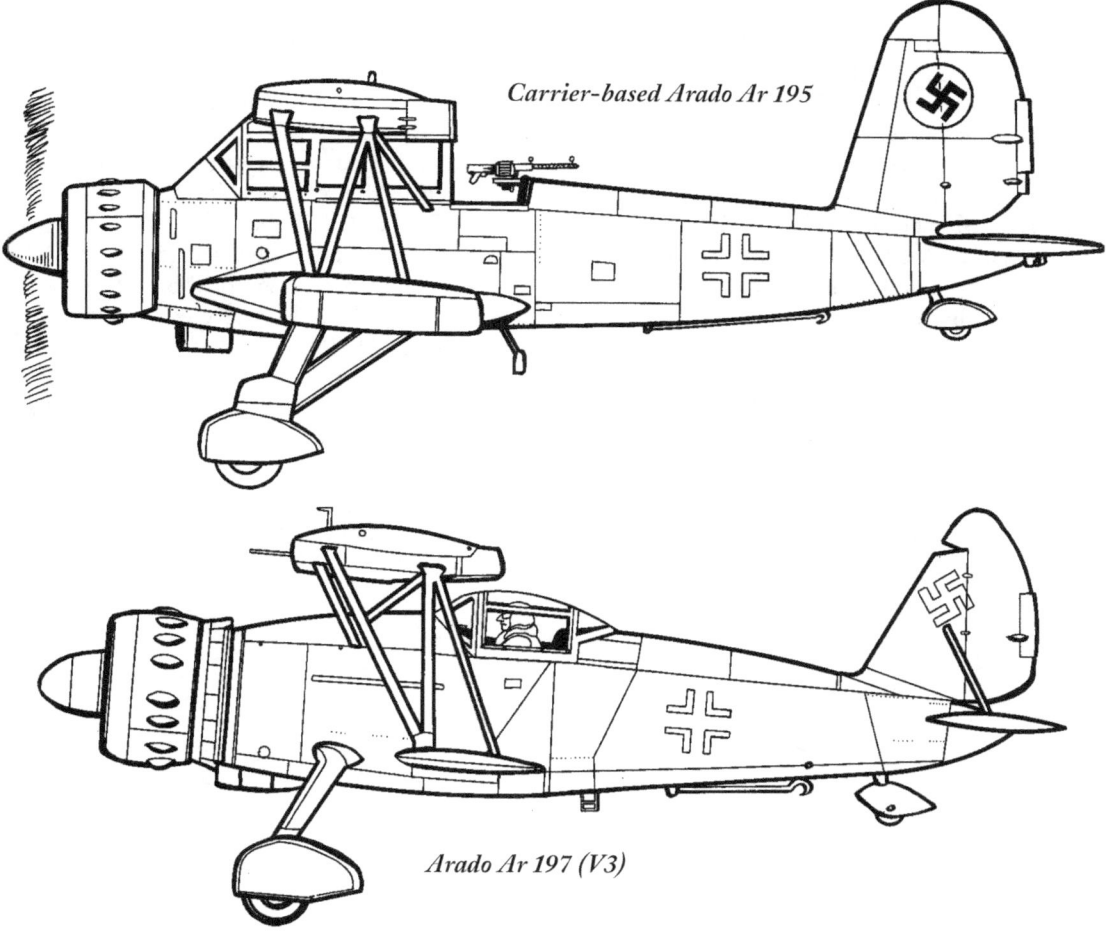

Carrier-based Arado Ar 195

Arado Ar 197 (V3)

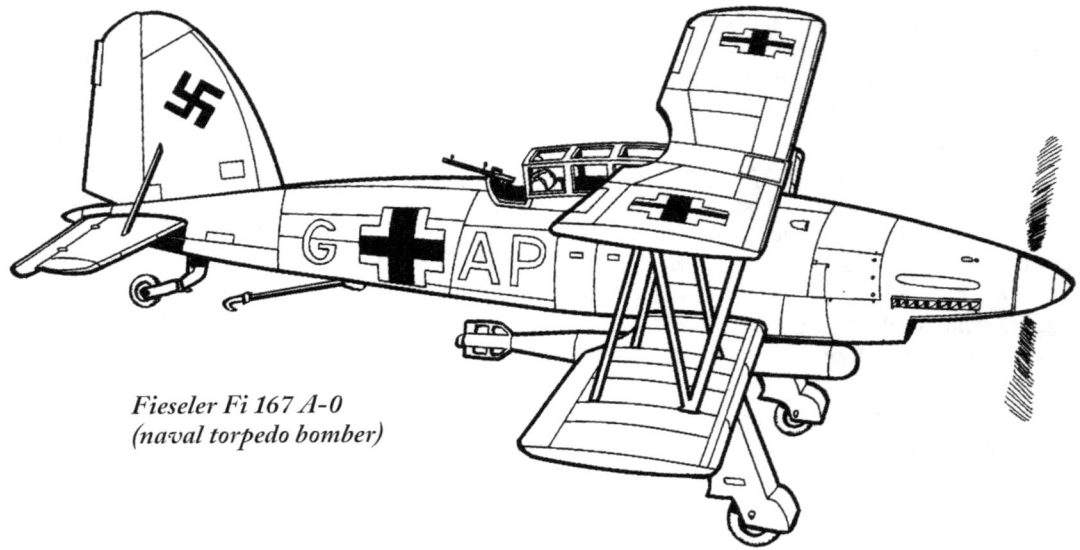

*Fieseler Fi 167 A-0
(naval torpedo bomber)*

in) and a length of 9.2 m (30 ft 2 in). Powered by a 910-hp DB 600 inverted-V-12 engine, it had a maximum speed of 399 km/h (248 mph) and a range of 1,638 km (1.018 miles). Armament included two 20-mm MG FF cannons in wings, two synchronized 7.92-mm MG 17 guns located above the engine, and four 50-kg (110-lb) bombs could be carried. All in all, its performances were rather modest, which put the rival Messerschmitt Bf 109 G2 (the naval version of the well-known fighter) and Fieseler Fi 167 way out in front. Only three test Ar 197s were built.

Fieseler Fi 167

The biplane two-seat Fieseler Fi 167 was the standard torpedo-carrier/light bomber/reconnaissance airplane intended to arm the *Graf Zeppelin*. It had a wingspan of 13.5 m (44 ft 3 in) and a length of 11.4 m (37 ft 5 in). Powered by a 1,100-hp Daimler-Benz DB 601 B inverted-V-12 cylinder engine, it had a maximum speed of 325 km/h (202 mph) and—with a jettisoned tank—a range of 1,300 km (808 miles). Armament included two synchronized 7.92-mm MG 17 machine guns firing forward and a manually aimed MG 15 machine gun in the rear cockpit. A torpedo or a load of 700 kg (1,540 lbs) of bombs could be carried in racks under the fuselage. The Fi 167 was a valuable tactical aircraft, but as no carrier was available, only twelve were produced. In the years 1940–1943, they were used as coastal reconnaissance aircraft in the Netherlands, before being sold to Romania, by the time Nazi Germany's ally.

The other main standard *Graf Zeppelin* dive bomber was the Junkers Ju 87 C, the naval version of the famous Stuka dive bomber.

8

Transport Aircraft

A cargo aircraft is an airplane primarily designed and used for the carriage of goods, rather than passengers. This role demands a number of features that make a cargo aircraft instantly identifiable; a fat-looking fuselage, a high wing to allow the cargo area to sit near the ground, a strong landing gear to allow it to land at unexpected locations, and a high-mounted tail to allow cargo to be loaded and unloaded via a rear ramp directly into and off the aircraft.

Aircraft were put to use carrying cargo in the form of mail as early as 1911. Although the earliest aircraft were not designed primarily as cargo carriers, by the mid–1920s and 1930s airplane manufacturers developed and built dedicated cargo aircraft. Indeed the advantage of using aircraft not only as fighting machines but also to ferry troops and supplies, either around a battlefield or over long distances, was fully recognized during the interwar period. Supply questions have always hampered the more adventurous generals and supply-related short comings have often prevented them from rapid advances. In a tactical setting, transport airplanes could be used to move units in anticipation of a threat, to supply beleaguered units, or to drop specially trained parachutists or gliderborne elements behind enemy lines, to disrupt and weaken defenses and to conquer key positions. In a strategic setting, reinforcements and supplies could be flown from one theater of operation to another to ensure an adequate military effort or to bolster up an ailing defense. Whatever the role, specialized aircraft were needed, combining robustness, reliability and carrying capacity. During World War II, Britain, the United States and Nazi Germany appear to have been the only major combatants to devote time and effort to the transport role. Both transport aircraft and assault gliders made a significant breakthrough, becoming the ultimate expression of mobile warfare, developing the ability to deliver troops, weapons and supplies direct to the battlefield from the air. As the complexion of World War II changed, sustained operations on several fronts forced the Luftwaffe to defensively use aircraft that had previously been spearheading short and decisive victories. The supply situation was so desperate on many occasions that the German army had to rely upon air transportation of personnel, supplies and equipment for its very existence. This was evident in North Africa and Russia, first as an attempt to reinforce the ground forces. When that failed, efforts were made to carry out evacuation by air. Air supply was and still is a very costly business and can be severely limited by lack of airplanes and also bad weather. If aircraft were able to land, more stores could be delivered than by parachute dropping. Air landing of supplies and reinforcements had the advantage that casualties could be evacuated from the battle area. However, it would be mistaken to assume that with air supply only, a besieged garrison could hold out indefinitely, and the fate of the French at the encircled fortress of Dien Bien Phu (Vietnam) in 1954 is evidence of this.

German transport aircraft and gliders were controlled by a general staff department at the

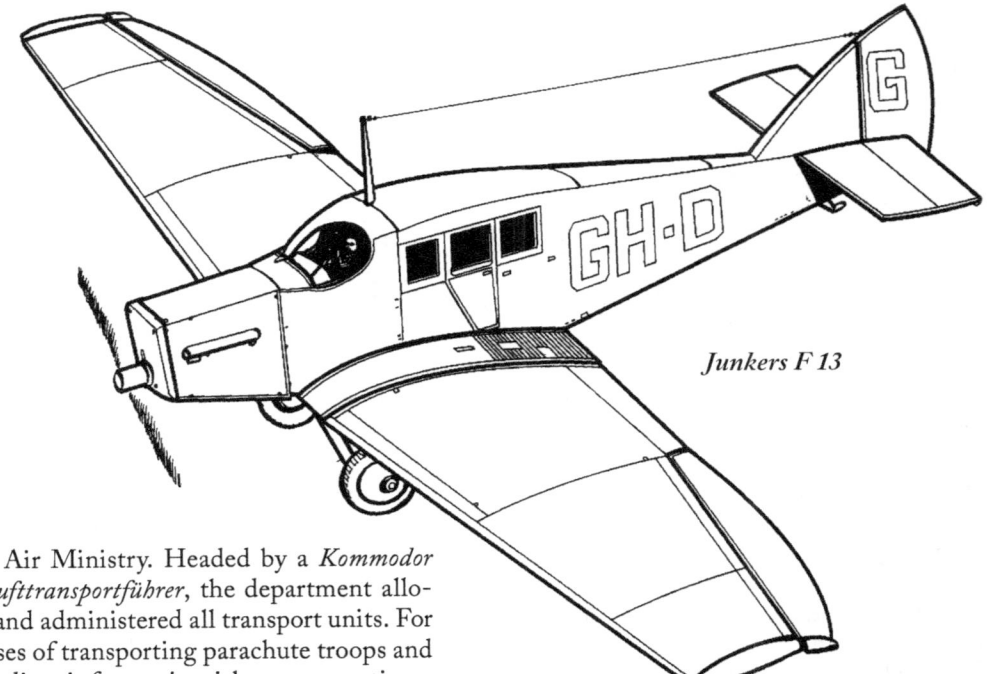

Junkers F 13

Reich Air Ministry. Headed by a *Kommodor und Lufttransportführer*, the department allocated and administered all transport units. For purposes of transporting parachute troops and air-landing infantry in airborne operations, transport aircraft were organized into *Kampfgeschwader zur besonderer Verwendung* (KG zbV—units for special duty). Each such KG zbV unit consisted of about 200 airplanes organized into four *Gruppen* of four *Staffeln* each. For the crews of these airplanes, accuracy was vital. If they dropped paratroops anywhere but in the exact spot selected and at the exact moment selected, the paratroopers would almost certainly become casualties, and the success of the whole operation and the lives of those involved in it would be jeopardized.

By far the most common German transport aircraft was the versatile trimotor Junkers Ju 52/3m, but the Luftwaffe employed many other types, such as the bomber Heinkel He 111 and the Focke-Wulf Condor, which were adapted for extensive employment as freight and personnel carriers.

Transport Planes

Junkers F 13

The Junkers F 13 was a small transport aircraft that exerted a large influence in civilian transport after World War I. First flown in June 1919, the F 13 was one of the first practicable, cantilever, all-metal, monoplane aircraft. It had a crew of two and could transport four passengers. It had a span of 17.75 m (58 ft 2.8 in) and a length of 9.60 m (31 ft 6 in). The F 13 was powered by various engines—either a BMW IIIa, a BMW IV, a Junkers L2, or a Junkers L5; it had a typical speed of 185 km/h (115 mph) and a typical range of 980 km (609 miles). The Junkers F 13 was produced until 1932 when 322 units had been built.

Junkers W 34

Designed in 1926, the Junkers W 34 was a utility/transport/communication aircraft operated by a crew of two (pilot and observer/navigator) with the capacity to transport six passengers or cargo. Derived from the Junkers F 13, the Junkers W 34 had a span of 17.75 m (58 ft 2.8 in), a length of 10.27 m (33 ft 8.25 in) and a height of 3.53 m (11 ft 7 in). The aircraft existed in several versions and was powered by either one 660-hp BMW 132 9-cylinder, air-cooled radial engine, or one 310-hp Junkers L5 inline engine, or a 650-hp Bramo SAM 22B 9-cylinder radial engine. Typical speed was 265 km/h (165 mph) and typical range was 900 km (559 miles). The designers of the later

8. Transport Aircraft   337

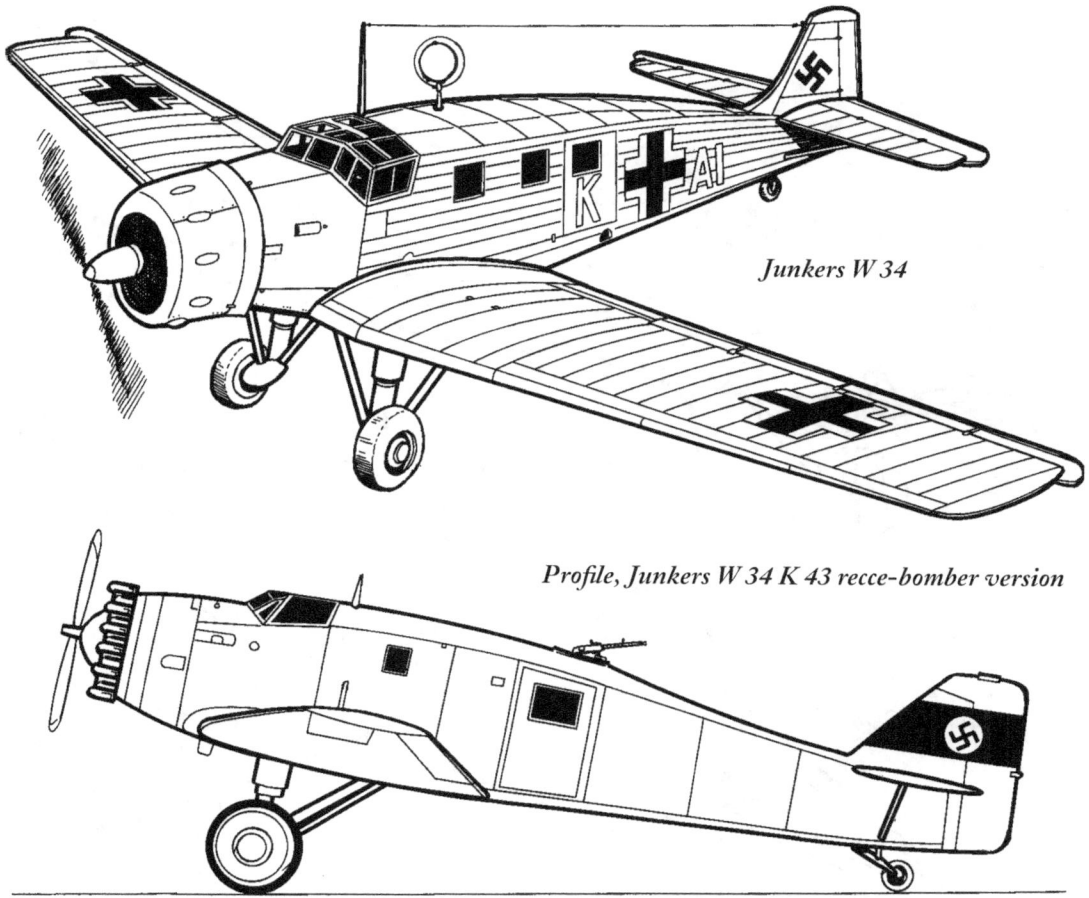

Junkers W 34

Profile, Junkers W 34 K 43 recce-bomber version

and larger Junkers Ju 52 used several of the W 34's design features, namely the general shape and the corrugated skin. The W 34 had a fixed, two-wheel undercarriage that could be replaced by skis or floats. The robust and reliable W 34 saw worldwide service in the late 1920s and 1930s as a civilian transport aircraft, and served extensively with the Luftwaffe and the air forces of Germany's allies during World War II. As a military aircraft, it performed a variety of tasks, including casualty evacuation, communications, liaison duties, training and even reconnaissance and light bombing for a short while. Production ended in 1934 after about 1,990 units had been built.

Messerschmitt M 28

The M 28 was designed in 1931 as a mail carrier. The aircraft had a crew of two, a length of 10 m, a height of 3 m, a span of 15.5 m, a wing area of 25.6 square meters and an empty weight of 1,160 kg. It was powered by one BMW hornet engine, and had a maximum speed of 260 km/h and a range of 2,450 km. Only one M 28 was ever built. It was successfully tried in January 1931, but as requirements for mail carriers had changed, the model was not developed.

Junkers G 38

Before designing the Junkers Ju 52 which became the Luftwaffe main transport aircraft during World War II, the Junkers aircraft company had already acquired experience and reputation. The large four-engine airliner Junkers G 38 made its first flight in 1929. It had a span of 44 m (144 ft) and a maximum speed of 185 km/h (115 mph). The G 38 had a crew of seven and a capacity of 34 passengers, some sitting in the aircraft's thick wing roots behind pano-

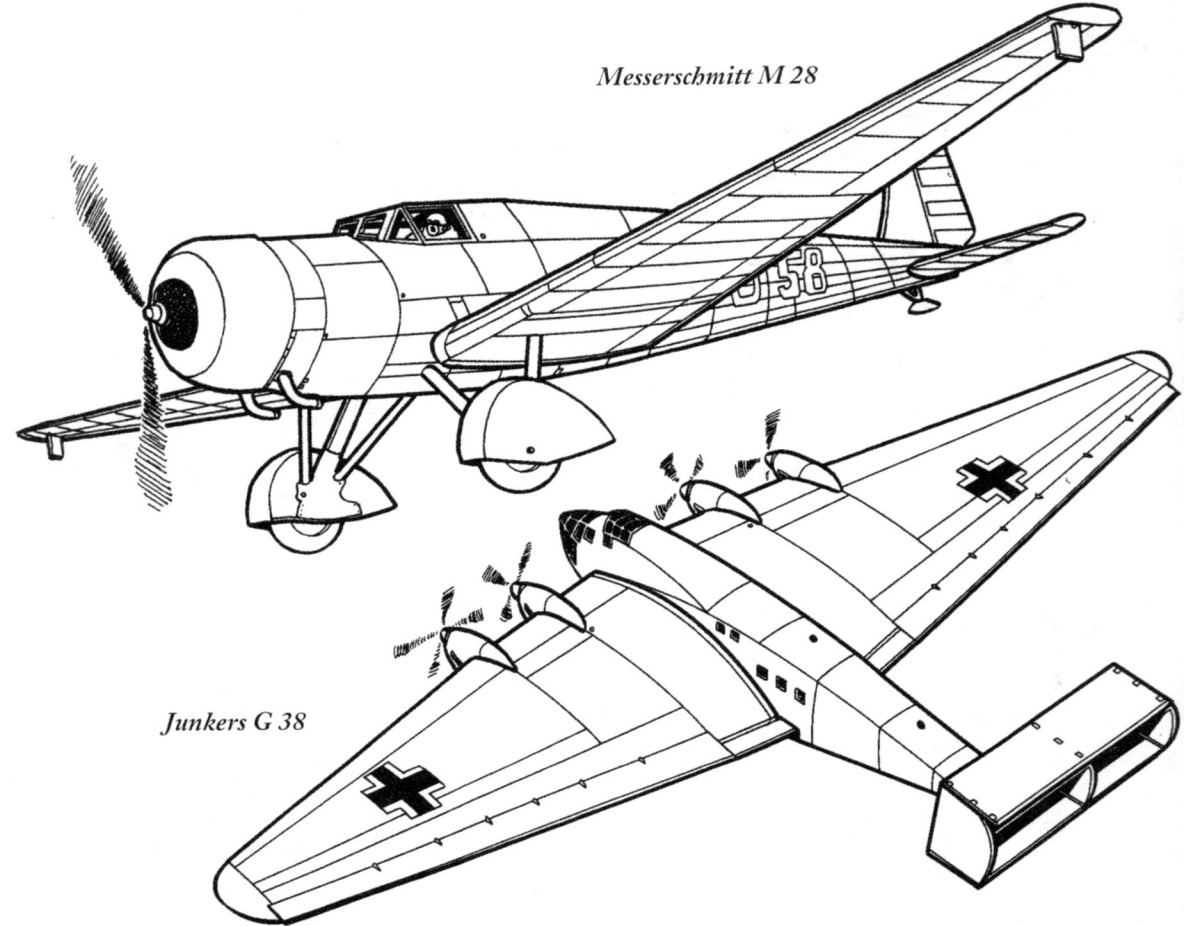

Messerschmitt M 28

Junkers G 38

rama windows. Only two units were built, serving the German civilian airline Lufthansa in the early 1930s and later for a while as Luftwaffe transport airplanes. The Japanese Mitsubishi Ki 20 was a military bomber version of the Junkers G 38, manufactured under license by the famous Japanese company. The Ki 20 was armed with six machine gun positions and could carry a bomb load of 5,000 kg.

Junkers Ju 52

One of the greatest aircraft of history, the Junkers Ju 52 was designed by Ernst Zindel. The prototype first flew in October 1930. As a civilian airliner with a capacity of 15–17 passengers, the Ju 52 sold all over the world and made up 75 percent of the large fleet of Lufthansa before World War II. The aircraft was eventually operated by twenty-eight airlines. Meanwhile the Luftwaffe, still embryonic and clandestine, was evaluating the military capabilities of the airliner. The Ju 52 entered service in the newly formed Luftwaffe in 1935 as an interim bomber with a 1,500-kg (3,307-lb) bomb load, and was employed as such during the Spanish Civil War. Soon the aircraft was discarded as a bomber and replaced by the Dornier Do 17 and Junkers Ju 86. It then started a long-lived and tremendous career as a military transport aircraft. It was a typical low-winged Junkers design with no concessions to elegance. It was operated by a crew of three; pilot and copilot/observer sat side by side and a radio operator/dorsal gunner sat on a jump seat between them. The cockpit was raised above the cabin floor height. When fitted with seats, the Ju 52 could carry up to eighteen passengers sitting in a rather spartan interior. When arranged as an ambulance, the

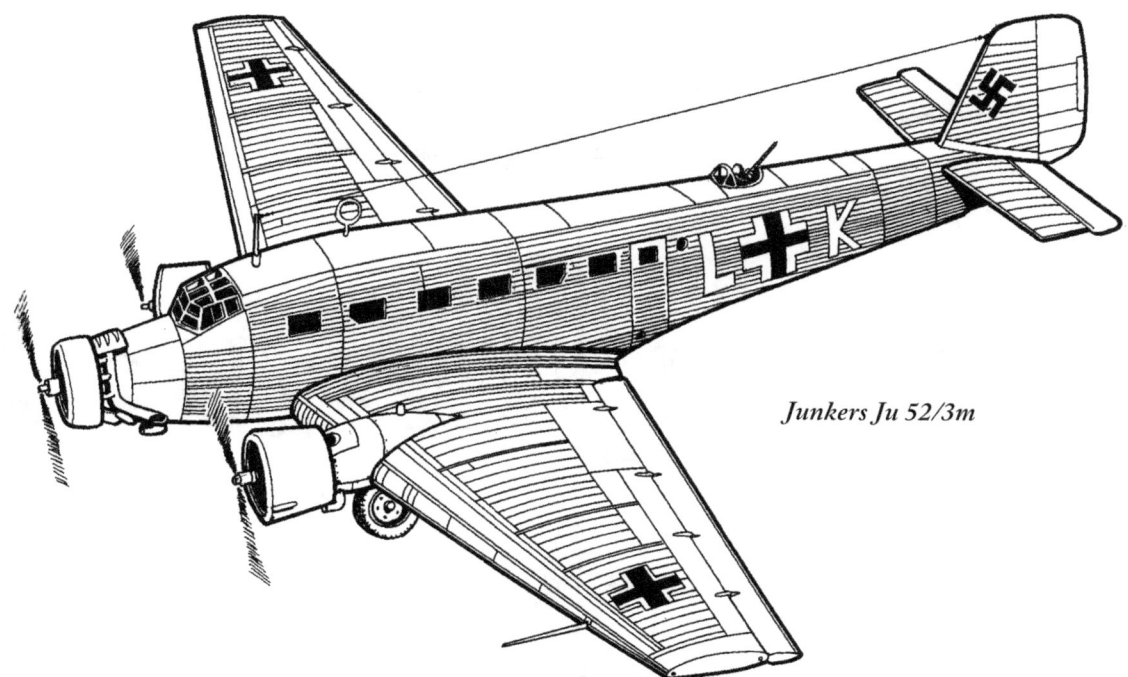

Junkers Ju 52/3m

seats were removed and the aircraft (often overpainted in white with large red crosses) could carry twelve seriously wounded on stretchers, which were fitted with harnesses used to tie them securely for rough take-off and landing. On nearly all wartime versions (Ju 52/3m), power was provided by three 830-hp BMW 132T 9-cylinder radial engines, one in the nose, one on each wing; the wing engines faced slightly outward to reduce yaw should one of them fail. The exhaust gas was collected by annular ducts which gave the Ju 52 its trademark stains. Typical speed was 305 km/h (190 mph) and typical range was 1,300 km (808 miles). Length was 18.9 m (62 ft), span was 29.25 m (95 ft 11.5 in), height was 4.5 m (14 ft 9 in), and empty weight was 5,600 kg (12,346 lbs). The aircraft had a payload of 1,102 pounds. It could transport, for example, twelve fully equipped paratroopers, plus four weapons and ammunitions canisters, or ten oil drums of two hundred liters each. The Ju 52 was usually not armed, but in combat zones it could mount one 13-mm MG 131 manually aimed from an open dorsal hatch, and two 7.92-mm MG 15 guns manually aimed from beam windows. This distinctive and rather ugly trimotor machine had a strong fixed landing gear to cope with repeated landings on rough airfields; spats were issued to reduce drag of the wheels, but these were often dismounted due to clogging up in muddy conditions. The corrugated metal fuselage was a common feature of many Junkers design; that skin was load-bearing and the corrugation gave it considerable strength, for little weight penalty. The Ju 52 was used in all theaters in a wide variety of roles, including bomber, reconnaissance craft, troop and freight transport, ambulance, ski or floatplane, glider tug, and others. There was also a magnetic mine-buster version equipped with a magnetic ring fifteen meters in diameter, and a 12-cylinder, Mercedes-Benz-Nurburg, gasoline-driven dynamo producing a constant 300 amps current used to explode magnetic mines at sea.

The Ju 52 was at the forefront in all German airborne operations in Norway, Holland, Belgium and Crete, as well as in the three major Luftwaffe airlift operations of World War II: Demyansk, Stalingrad and Tunisia. As the war lengthened, demands on the venerable type increased as its losses rose, presenting the Luftwaffe with a major headache, as availability always fell below requirements. As a general workhorse, the Ju 52 was invaluable: it was

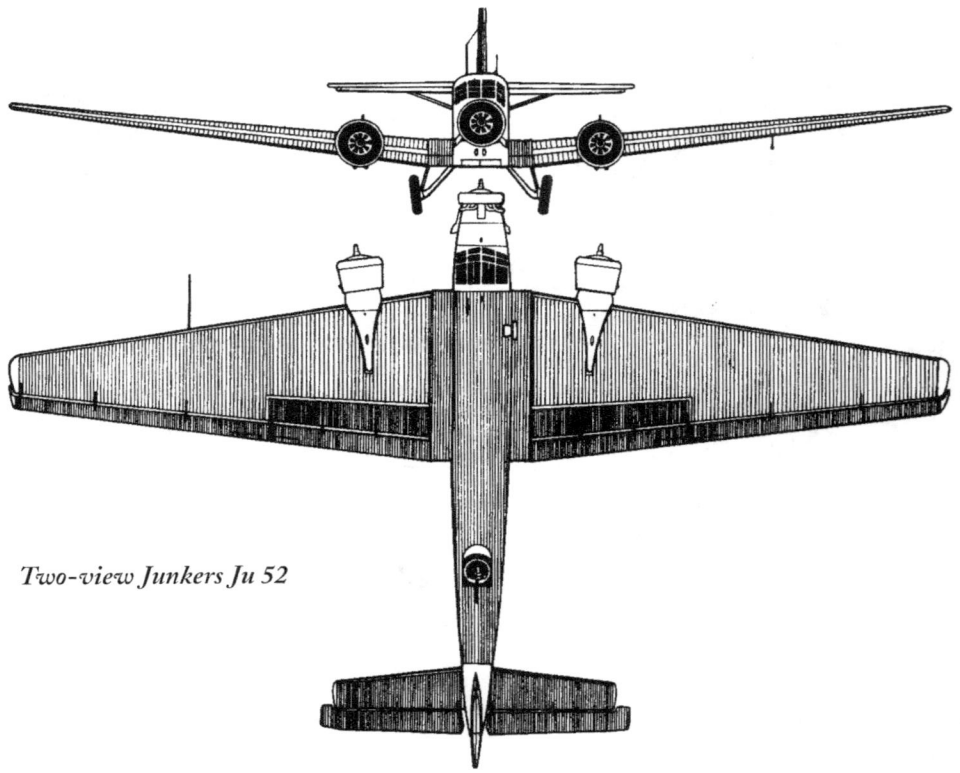

Two-view Junkers Ju 52

cheap to manufacture, simple to operate, and easy to maintain on the field, it could fly with one of its three engine out of commission, had the ability to withstand crash landings with reasonable safety to occupants owing to the ruggedness of construction. It had good STOL (short take-off and landing) performance, robust construction, interchangeable wheel/ski/float landing gear, and great reliability, but it left a good deal to be desired as a transport airplane. Deservedly famous as a German counterpart to the U.S. DC-3 Dakota, the Ju 52 was obsolete by 1939, but continued to serve on all fronts until the end of World War II. It is typical of the Nazi regime that, despite a wealth of later and more capable replacements, the obsolete Ju 52 was kept in production throughout the war. Perhaps the ubiquity and the all-purpose nature of the highly popular *Tante Ju* (Auntie Ju) or *Iron Annie*—as it was nicknamed—tended to preclude the need for replacement designs. Also, there were many of this type on hand at the beginning of the war, engines were widely available, many pilots had been trained to it, and manufacturing facilities were already set up. The Ju 52 was manufactured by Junkers, but also by the French Felix Amiot company located at Colombes near Paris, and by the Hungarian PIRT factory at Budapest. A total of 4,845 were produced by the Germans between 1939 and 1944.

After the war, although totally old-fashioned and obsolete, production of the Ju 52 continued in France by the Amiot aircraft company, and some 400 units (known as Amiot AAC 1) served to drop paratroopers and transport freight for the French army during the early years of the Indochina War (1946–1954). The Ju 52 (designated CASA 352) was also produced for the Spanish air force as multi-role transport until 1975.

Junkers Ju 252

Designed as a replacement for the aging Ju 52, the prototype Ju 252 V1 made its first flight in October 1941. The new transport trimotor aircraft featured a stressed-skin surface replacing the characteristic Ju 52 corrugated metal. It had a length of 25.1 m (82 ft 4 in), a wing-

8. Transport Aircraft

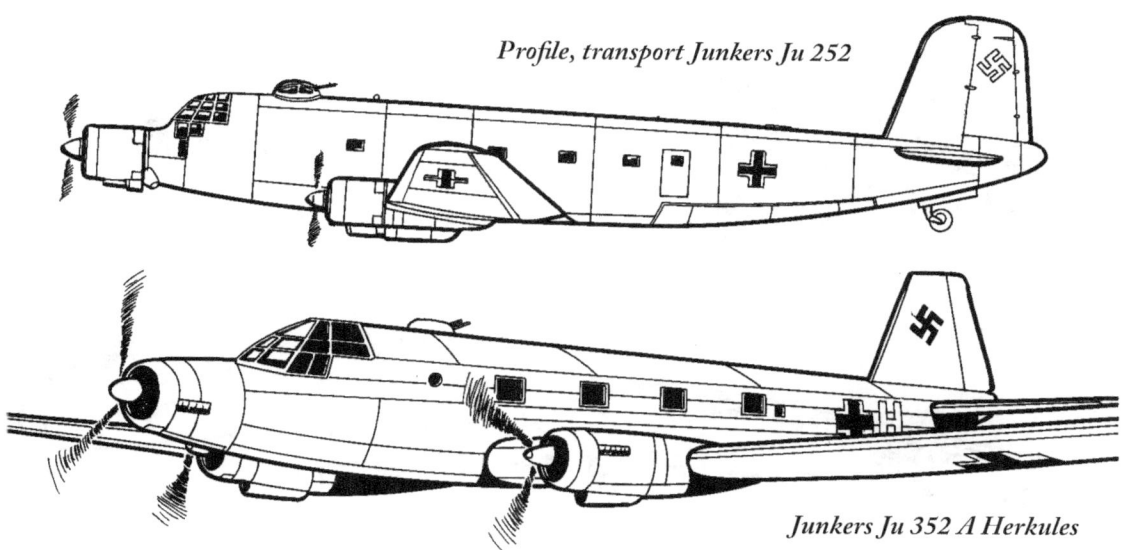

Profile, transport Junkers Ju 252

Junkers Ju 352 A Herkules

span of 34 m (111 ft 10 in), a height of 5.75 m (18 ft 10 in), and an empty weight of 13,100 kg (28,884 lbs). It had a crew of four, including pilot, copilot, observer, and radio operator/gunner. Powered by three Junkers Jumo 211F inverted-V-12, liquid-cooled engines, it had a maximum speed of 439 km/h (272 mph) and a range of 3,980 km (2,473 miles). Defensive armament included a dorsal turret armed with a single MG 131 gun, and two beam-window firing positions each armed with one MG 15 machine gun. With a rear loading ramp allowing easy loading and holding the fuselage level, and with a capacity of 35 passengers or a payload of 11,000 kg (24,027 lbs), the Ju 252 was a great improvement over the old Ju 52. As a result of a low priority given to transport aircrafts, only fifteen units were produced, which entered service in January 1943 with *Lufttransportstaffel* 290. Owing to the shortage of raw materials plaguing late wartime Germany, Junkers was ordered to design a cheaper version (the Ju 352 Herkules), made of wood and using stockpiled engines.

Junkers Ju 352 Herkules

The general-purpose transport aircraft Ju 352 was a redesigned Ju 252. Due to shortage of strategic materials, its construction was of mixed metal (duralumin), wood, steel-tube and fabric. Dimensions, payload, number of crew and defensive armament were rather the same as the Ju 252. The Ju 352 also featured a hydraulically operated loading ramp beneath the rear section of the fuselage; the aircraft could also be raised sufficiently off the ground to enable the carriage of some types of light military vehicles. The rear ramp could be lowered in flight to disgorge paratroopers within one minute. Another feature was its reversible-pitch propellers, designed by Messerschmitt and built by the Vereinigte Deutsche Metallwerke company, which reduced the required runway length for landing by almost 60 percent. Despite its popular name of Herkules, the Ju 352's performances were, not herculean, inferior to the Ju 252's. Powered by three BMW-Bramo 323R-2 9-cylinder, air-cooled radial engines, each developing 1,200 hp, it had a speed of 370 km/h (230 mph) and a range of about 1,800 km (1,120 miles). The aircraft made its first flight in October 1943, and production was stopped in September 1944 after a total of forty-five transport Ju 352s had been built.

Junkers Ju 90

The airliner Junkers Ju 90 was based on the four-engine Junkers Ju 89 bomber, which did not progress beyond the prototype stage (see Part 4). When the Ju 89 project was cancelled, there was a third prototype uncompleted. At

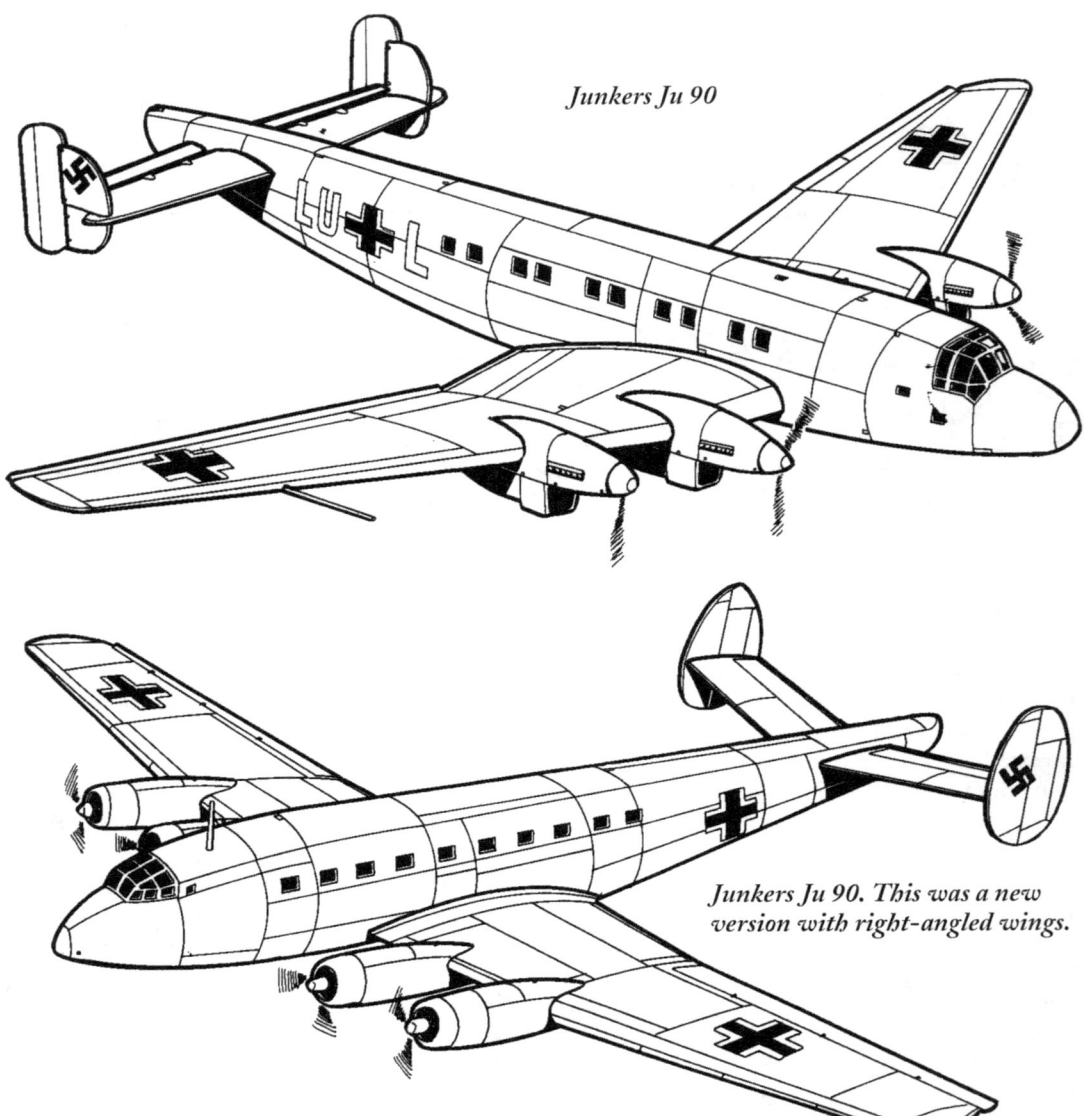

Junkers Ju 90

Junkers Ju 90. This was a new version with right-angled wings.

the request of Lufthansa, it was rebuilt as an airliner, retaining the wings and tail of the original design, but incorporating a new, widebody fuselage. The prototype first flew in August 1937 and was lost in a crash the following February during testing. A second prototype was delivered to Lufthansa in May 1938. This one also crashed during tests, but Lufthansa was satisfied enough to order three aircrafts. The Reichsluftfahrtministerium also ordered one for trials, and South African Airways ordered two units with Pratt & Whitney Twin Wasp engines. Both airliner versions were designated Ju 90A-1. The aircraft was manned with a crew of two and could transport 40 passengers. Length was 26.45 m (86 ft 10 in), wingspan was 35.3 m (115 ft 8 in), wing area was 184 square m (1,979 square ft), height was 7.50 m (24 ft 7 in), and weight (empty) was 19,225 kg (42,295 lbs). The German Ju 90 was powered by four 3,270-hp BMW 132 H-1 engines. It had a maximum speed of 350 km/h (219 mph), a range of 2,092 km (1,308 miles), and a service ceiling of 5,750 m (18,860 ft). With the outbreak of war, the Ju 90s were impressed into the Luftwaffe for a while. They

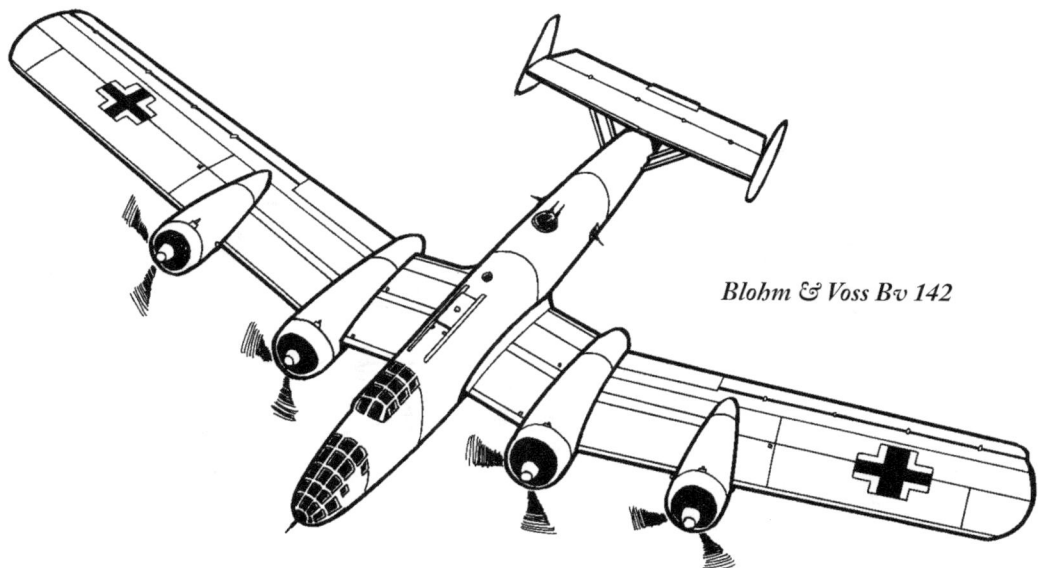

Blohm & Voss Bv 142

took part in the invasion of Norway for troop transport, returned to Lufthansa, and eventually taken back by the Luftwaffe. In late 1939, the RLM ordered prototypes for a military freight-carrier version. One had a loading ramp under the fuselage to facilitate the loading of larger cargoes. Another was equipped with machine-gun turrets and modified as a heavy bomber—ironically, the role for which the Ju 89 had been rejected. These military versions flew in late 1941, but never entered production. Further refinements of the design were suggested, which led eventually to the bomber Junkers Ju 290. In the end, only seventeen Ju 90s of all versions were built.

Blohm & Voss BV 142

The Blohm & Voss BV 142 was basically a slightly improved land version of the seaplane Blohm & Voss Ha 139 (see Part 7). It was at first a civil development for transatlantic postal service, and was intended for the civilian commercial company Lufthansa. First flown in October 1938, the Bv 142 was completely metallic, and had a high horizontal stabilizer and double vertical tail, and low wing with a span of 29.53 m (96 ft 11 in). The fuselage was 20.45 m (67 ft 2 in) in length, 4.44 m (14 ft 6.5 in) in height, and had an approximately round cross section. The main landing gear was double-geared and fully retractable, as was the tail landing gear. The aircraft had a crew of five. It was powered by four 880-hp BMW 132H 9-cylinder radial piston engines, and had a maximum speed of 375 km/h (232 mph) and a range of 3,900 km (2,423 miles). Only four prototypes were built and tested by Lufthansa for use in the postal service. However, the outbreak of World War II prevented the further development of the civilian project. The existing types entered Luftwaffe service and were refurbished for sea-reconnaissance duty. The fuselage nose was extended and glazed, and five MG 15 machine guns were mounted in the nose, in the fuselage floor and on the fuselage upper surface. Four 100-kg bombs or eight 50-kg bombs could be carried. In 1940, the Bv 142s saw service in France, Denmark and Norway. However, performances were not satisfactory, and therefore the airplanes were withdrawn from active service by 1942. They returned to a transport role, with a capacity of thirty fully equipped soldiers over 4,000 km.

Heinkel He 116

The Heinkel He 116 was designed in 1936 as a long-range transport/mail plane for Lufthansa. Eight units of the first version He 116 A were delivered in 1937. The aircraft was operated by a crew of three or four, it had a length of 14.3 m (46 ft 11 in), a span of 22 m

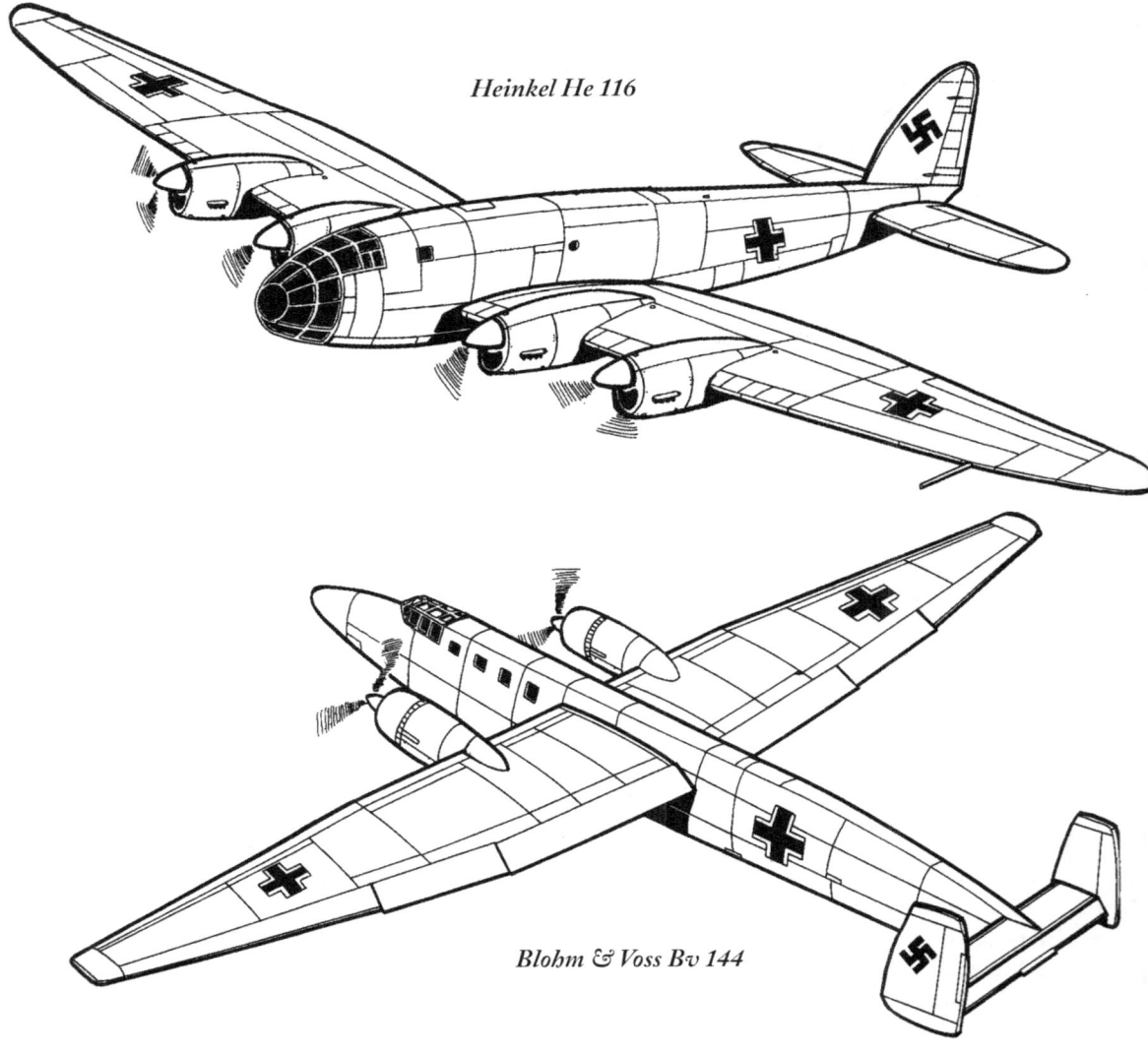

Heinkel He 116

Blohm & Voss Bv 144

(72 ft 2 in), a height of 3.3 m (10 ft 10 in), and an empty weight of 4,020 kg (8,826 lbs). Powered by four 240-hp Hirth HM 508 H inverted-V-8, air-cooled engines, it had a maximum speed of 325 km/h (202 mph), a service ceiling of 7,600 m (24,900 ft), and a range of 3,410 km (2,120 miles). The long-range potential of the He 116 suggested to the RLM that the airplane could have some military application. A militarized version, He 116B, was adapted with glazed nose, and six units entered Luftwaffe service in 1938. The aircraft proved disappointing however, and the Heinkel He 116Bs were confined to carrying out photographic and mapping work over Germany and German-occupied territories during World War II.

Blohm & Voss Bv 144

A fast passenger plane, the Bv 144 was designed as a successor to the Junkers Ju 52/3m as transport aircraft. The project started in 1940 and was reworked in winter 1940-41. Two prototypes were built. Because of the war situation, the design work was made mostly by French engineers in Hamburg. Two aircraft were made in France by the Louis Breguet Aircraft Company at Anglet near Bayonne. The first machine made its first flight in August

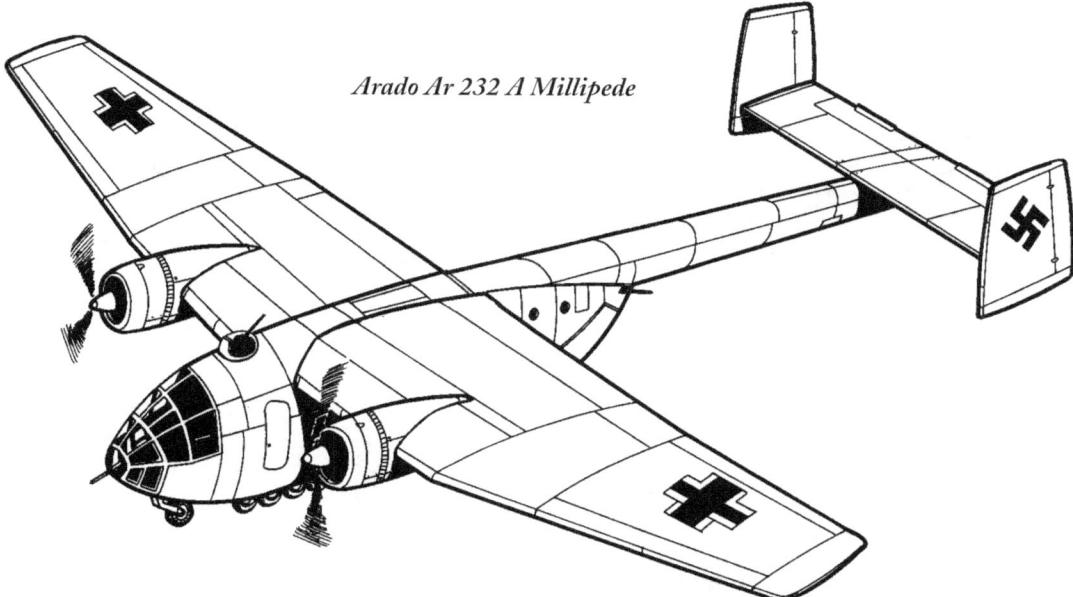

Arado Ar 232 A Millipede

1944, but due to the liberation of France by the Allies in the summer of 1944, all testing was cancelled. Despite the advanced design, both prototype airliners were scrapped after the German withdrawal. The Bv 144 would have had a crew of three and a capacity of eighteen passengers. It was powered by two 1,600-hp BMW 801MA 18-cylinder two-row radial piston engines, would have had an estimated speed of 470 km/h (292 mph), and a range of 1,550 km (963 miles). Span was 26.9 m (88 ft 7 in), length was 21.9 m (71 ft 6.5 in), height was 5.1 m (15 ft 8 in), and empty weight was 7,900 kg (17,416 lbs).

Arado Ar 232

The Ar 232 *Tausendfüssler* (Millipede) was the first truly modern transport aircraft. Intended to replace the legendary but outdated Ju 52/3m, the Ar 232 was designed by engineer Wilhelm van Nes, and made its first flight in April 1941. The aircraft included almost all of the features now considered to be standard to transport aircraft, including a low-slung, boxlike fuselage, rear loading ramp, a high tail for easy access to the hold, and various features for operating from rough fields. It had a length of 23.52 m (77 ft 2 in), a span of 33.5 m (109 ft 11 in), a height of 5.69 m (18 ft 8 in), and an empty weight of 12,780 kg (28,175 lbs). Version Ar 232 A was powered by two 1,600-hp BMW 801 MA 14-cylinder, two-row radial engines, and version Ar 232 B by four 1,200-hp BMW-Bramo 323R-2 Fafnir 9-cylinder radials. Typical speed was 288 km/h (180 mph) and typical range was about 1,050 km (660 miles). A noticeable feature of the 232 was the landing gear. This including a tricycle gear and an additional set of eleven smaller wheels (per side), hence the nickname "Millipede." In flight, the main legs fully retracted into the engine nacelles, while the twenty-two small wheels remained extended and the nose wheel only semi-retracted. Even fully loaded to 16,000 kg the plane could take off in 200 meters. This distance could be further improved upon with the used of RATO (rocket-assisted take off) and RAL (remote area landing). The Arado Ar 232 was operated by a crew of four: pilot, navigator/observer (also manning one MG 81Z mounted in the nose), radio operator (manning another MG 81Z placed in a rotating turret on the roof), and loadmaster (operating another machine gun located at the extreme rear of the cargo bay above the cargo doors). The Ar 232 completely outperformed the Ju 52. It carried roughly double the load over longer distances, operated from much shorter runways and consid-

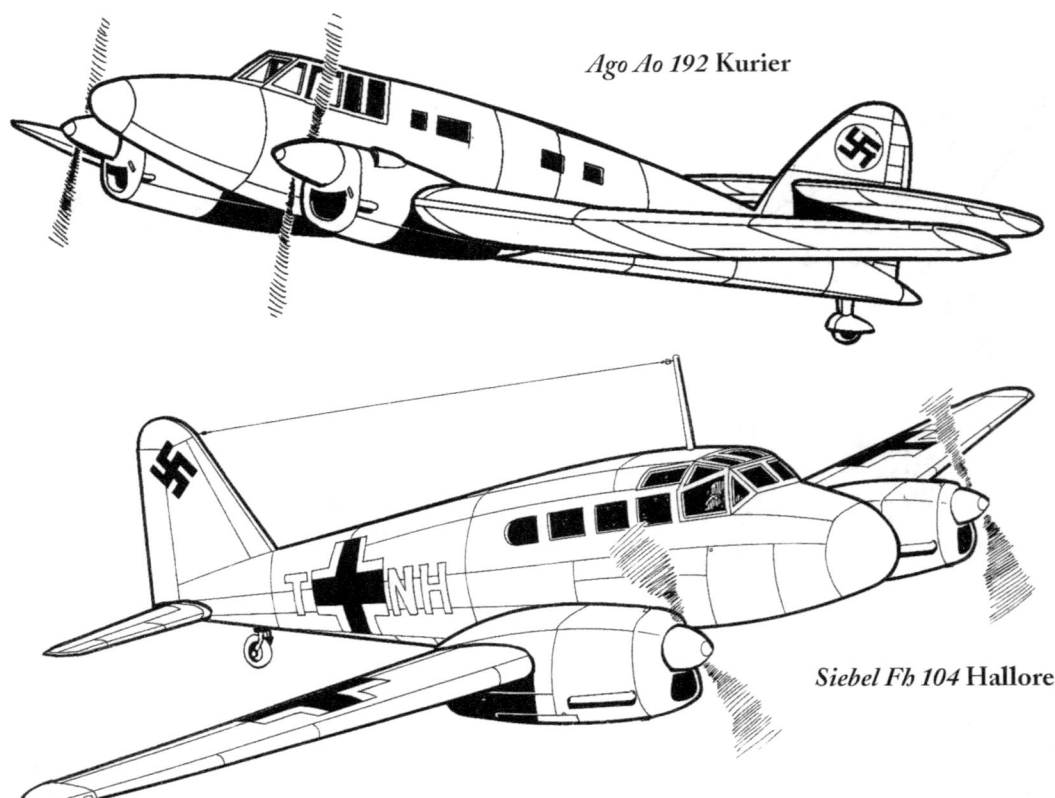

Ago Ao 192 Kurier

Siebel Fh 104 Hallore

erably worse fields if need be, and cruised about 70 km/h faster. Although the Luftwaffe was interested in replacing (or supplanting) their fleet of Junkers Ju 52, they were overloaded with types at the time and did not purchase large numbers of the aircraft. The German transport fleet was never reequipped, as the Luftwaffe gave transport aircraft production a low priority; the trend was not toward modernization by adopting new purpose-built aircraft but toward modification of the existing fleet, so the promising Ar 232 never came close to replacing the Junkers Ju 52. Twenty-four Arado Ar 232 craft were produced and used in an operational role on the Russian front, notably at Stalingrad. A few were used in the *Kampfgeschwader* 200 special mission unit for picking up agents from behind Russian lines.

Ago Ao 192 Kurier

A private venture by the Ago Flugzeugbau Company, the *Kurier* (Courier) was a twin-engine, low-wing, monoplane, multi-purpose, fast, light-transport aircraft. The Ago Ao 192 had a wingspan of 13.54 m (44 ft 5 in), a length of 10.98 m (36 ft ¼ in) and an empty weight of 1,640 kg (3,616 lbs). Powered by two Argus As 10E inverted-V piston engines each rated at 270 hp, it had a maximum speed of 335 km/h (208 mph) and a range of 1,100 km (684 miles). The *Kurier* could transport seven passengers—pilot included. Several variants were proposed, including touring/transport craft, freight or mail plane, aerial survey or fitted with camera and dark room, ambulance (for two litters and attendant), light reconnaissance aircraft armed with three 7.92-mm MG 15 machine guns, light bomber carrying four 50-kg (110-lb) bombs, and smoke-screen-laying combat plane. In spite of its good performances, good capacities and versatility, excellent flying characteristics and advanced features (including a very modern aerodynamic design, retractable undercarriage, and air-conditioned cabin), the promising aircraft did not make it. The small Ago Company was committed to other projects and

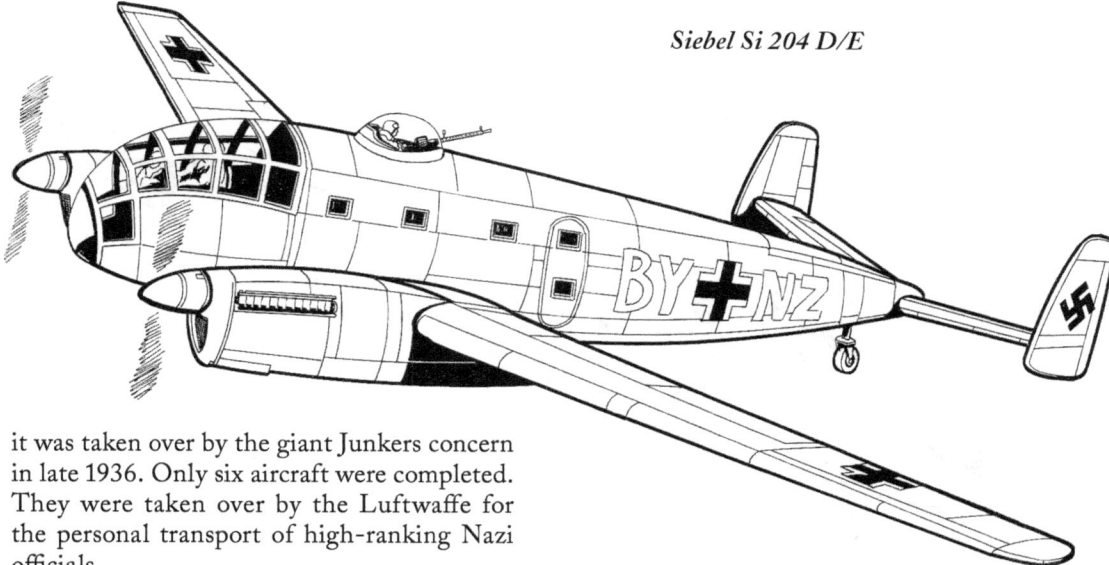

Siebel Si 204 D/E

it was taken over by the giant Junkers concern in late 1936. Only six aircraft were completed. They were taken over by the Luftwaffe for the personal transport of high-ranking Nazi officials.

Siebel Fh 104 Hallore

The Siebel Fh 104, designed by engineer Hans Klemm, was a small communication and liaison aircraft which could transport five persons including the pilot. Span was 39 ft 7 in, length was 31 ft 2 in, and empty weight was 3,330 lbs. Powered by two Hirth HM 508C inverted-V, air-cooled engines, each developing 280 hp, the aircraft had a maximum speed of 217 mph. Some forty-eight units (all unarmed) were produced and used in a communication role and for VIP transport in Germany.

Siebel Si 204

The Si 204 was a slightly enlarged version derived from the Siebel Fh 104 *Hallore*. First flown in May 1941, it had a crew of one or two and could carry eight passengers or 1,650 kg (3,638 lbs) of cargo. Length was 13 m (42 ft 8 in), span was 21.33 m (70 ft) and empty weight was 3,950 kg (8,709 lbs). The aircraft was powered by two Argus 411 A1 engines, each developing 592 hp and each driving a two-blade propeller. It had a maximum speed of 364 km/h (228 mph), a maximum range of 1,400 km (875 miles), and a service ceiling of 6,400 m (20,992 ft). Up to 1945, some 1,175 units were manufactured. As the Siebel factory was being used to manufacture the medium bomber Junkers Ju 88 and had no capacity available for another type, production was therefore allocated to aircraft factories in occupied territories: in Czechoslovakia the BMM factory, and in France the SNCAC company (which manufactured 150 of the craft). The rather unknown Si 204 was thus a leading Luftwaffe light transport and communication aircraft. It served as air ambulance, and was also widely used to train radio, radar, navigation, gunner and bomber aircrew. A few D versions were pressed into combat service in the night ground-attack role. Production of the Siebel Si 204 was continued in Czechoslovakia after the war, under the designation C-103. Many Si 204 served after World War II in French, Canadian, British, Czech and Soviet air forces.

Focke-Wulf Fw 58 Weihe

The Fw 58 *Weihe* (Kite) was a multi-role crew trainer, ambulance, communication plane and transport aircraft. One of the most important Luftwaffe utility aircraft, it made its first flight in 1935 as a six-seat civil transport. The major production version was the military version known as Fw 58C, of which about 4,500 were built and used in 1937–1942. About 2,000 were used in an ambulance role, then known as *Leukoplast Bomber* (Sticking-plaster Bomber). The Fw 58 had a crew of two, including pilot and copilot/observer, plus six

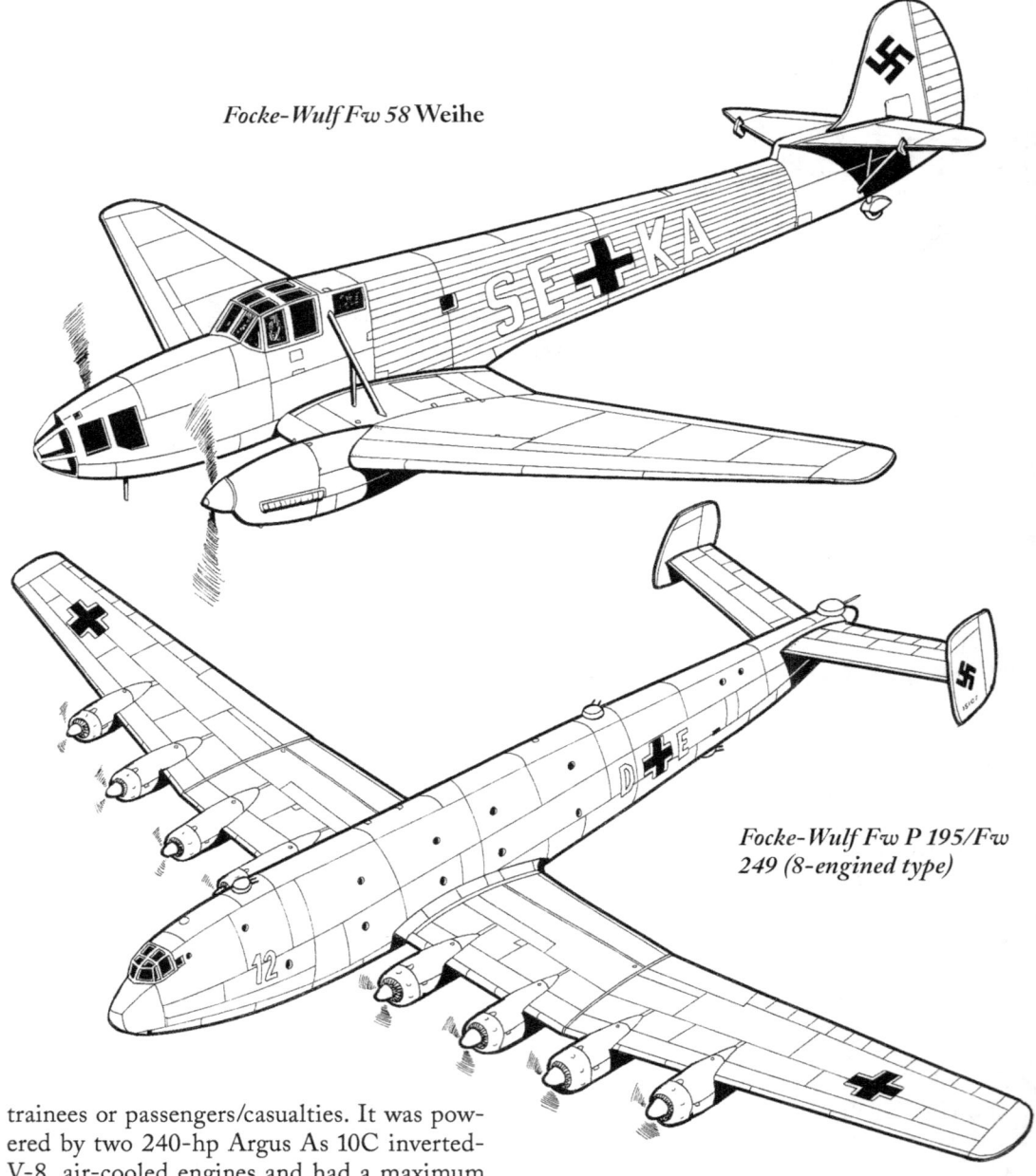

Focke-Wulf Fw 58 Weihe

Focke-Wulf Fw P 195/Fw 249 (8-engined type)

trainees or passengers/casualties. It was powered by two 240-hp Argus As 10C inverted-V-8, air-cooled engines and had a maximum speed of 280 km/h (174 mph) and a typical range of 800 km (497 miles). The aircraft had a span of 21 m (68 ft 11 in), a length of 14 m (45 ft 11.2 in), and an empty weight of 2,400 kg (5,291 lbs).

Focke-Wulf Fw 195

The Focke-Wulf Projekt 195 (also known as the Focke-Wulf Fw 249 or project 0310-2221-15) was intended to be a large-capacity, widebody, all-metal-construction transport aircraft. Submitted to the RLM in August 1941, the Fw 195 was powered with no less than eight 2500-hp Jumo 222 24-cylinder engines mounted on the wing leading edge, the wings being placed low on the fuselage. It would have had a range of 2,100 km (1,305 miles) and a maximum speed of 490 km/h (304 mph). The control unit included a twin fin and rudder

Heinkel He 111 Z Zwilling

configuration. A tricycle landing gear was arranged. With its double deck, the aircraft would have had a capacity of either 52 tons of equipment/freight, or 400 fully equipped troops. A rear loading ramp would have been used. The Fw Projekt 195 was to be manned by a seven- or eight-man crew, but the project never reached production. Due to technical problems with the Jumo 222 engines and no other available suitable engines with the same power, work on the Fw 195 was abandoned. A version with six engines was considered but this, too, came to naught. With a wing span of 58.6 m (192 ft 3 in), a length of 47 m (154 ft), and a wing area of 460 square m (4951.4 square ft), the Fw 192 would have been one of the largest non-seaplane aircraft in the world at that time.

Heinkel He 111 Z *(towing twin)*

While Germany had designed two heavy cargo gliders in 1940, the Me 321 and the Ju 322, the Luftwaffe had no suitable aircraft to tow them. The *Troika-Schlepp* ("Triple-tow," from the Russian three-horse sleigh or troika), using three Messerschmitt Bf 110C-1s, proved dangerous, and types of four-engine transport airplanes such as the Junkers Ju 90 lacked the power required for the task. Ernst Udet conceived the idea of joining two bombers by a common central wing section, and urged aircraft companies to develop such a type. In 1941, two prototypes of the Heinkel He 111 Z (*Zwilling*—twin) were produced. Two He 111H-6 bomber fuselages with complete tail assemblies were joined by a new center section wing having three Jumo 211F-2/S-2 engines, giving a total of five engines. The new airplane had a wingspan of 35.4 m (116 ft 1.66 in), a length of 16.4 m (55 ft 9.66 in), and a wing area of 148 square m (1,587.06 square ft). The He 111 Z soon proved to be an efficient glider tug, with more than enough power to tow the new giant gliders.

Take-off could be assisted by two 500-kg (1,100-lb) thrust JATO rockets beneath each fuselage and two 1,500-kp (3,307 lb) thrust rockets under the center section, one each side of the middle engine. Maximum speed was between 425 and 435 km/h (264–270 mph), but when towing two Go 242, speed was reduced to 250 km/h (155 mph), and 220 km/h when towing a large glider, Messerschmitt Me 321. The He 111 Z entered production early in 1942 and was placed in successful service that year. Although well-liked by crews, the He 111 Z was not easy to control in flight. The aircraft had a crew of seven. The pilot sat in the port fuselage, with five throttles, full instrumentation, and controls for the undercarriage members and radiator flaps for the gear and three engines on his side. The second pilot, in the starboard fuselage, was given dual controls but no throttles, and worked the starboard undercarriage and two sets of starboard engine radiator flaps. The second pilot also served as nav-

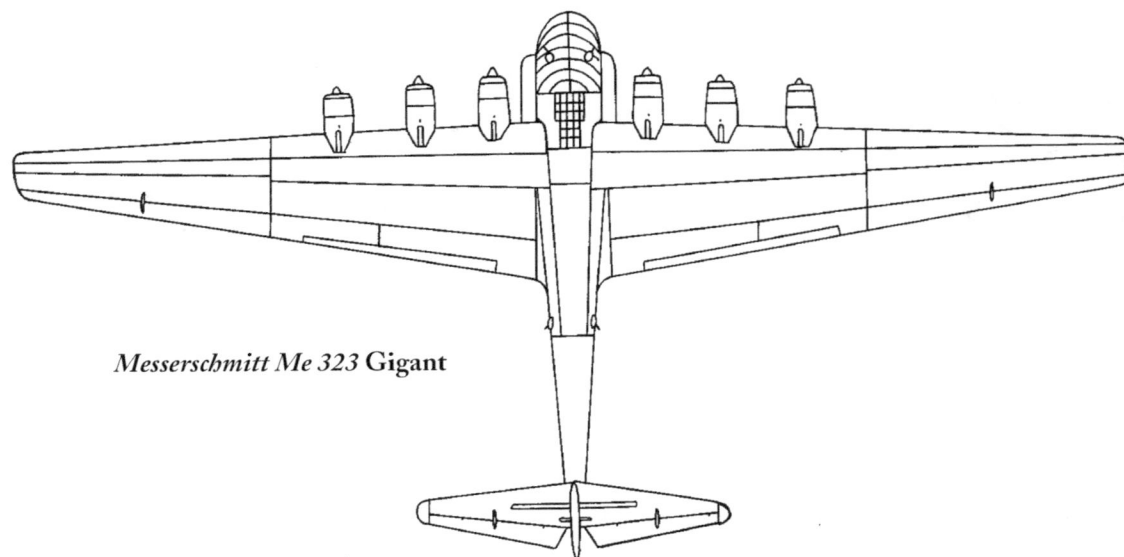

Messerschmitt Me 323 **Gigant**

igator. A mechanic, radio operator and gunner were housed in the port fuselage, and a mechanic and gunner in the starboard. The aircraft could maintain level flight with three engines cut, provided the remaining two supplied symmetrical power. Defensive armament included one 20-mm MG FF cannon in the starboard nose position and one MG 15 in the port nose. Each fuselage had a single 13-mm MG 131 in the dorsal position and a single 7.9-mm MG 15 in the rear of the ventral position and a similar weapon in a beam hatch of each fuselage. Various other armament configurations were tried, including four 13-mm MG 131s, two MG 91Z paired 7.9-mm installations, and five single MG 81J guns. Eight of the twelve He 111 Zs were destroyed in service, being shot down by fighters or destroyed as a result of bombing. The remaining four were presumably destroyed after Germany's surrender.

Messerschmitt Me 323 Gigant

The Messerschmitt Me 323 *Gigant* (Giant), born of desperation, was a powered conversion of the Me 321 glider (see below). The biggest land-based, general-purpose transport airplane of World War II, this monstrosity of limited usefulness (while somewhat more practical than the glider variant) made its first flight in fall 1941 and entered Luftwaffe service in November 1942. The crew of seven was composed of pilot, observer, engineer, radio operator and three gunners. Initially, the Me 323 was to be fit with four engines, but prototype flight testing showed that six engines were necessary to achieve the desired load-carrying capability. Powered by six 1,140-hp French Gnôme-Rhône 14N air-cooled radial engines designed by Gabriel Voisin, the Me 323 had a ferry range of 1,100 km (684 miles), and a maximum speed of 270 km/h (170 mph) which proved exceptionally vulnerable to Allied fighter attack. Booster rockets could be used to assist take-off. Empty, the aircraft weighed 27,330 kg (60,260 lbs). The "powered glider" could carry around 1,625 metric tons (16 tons) and had seats for 130 passengers—though in an emergency about two hundred could be crammed in. Defensive armament was various, including several 7.92-mm machine guns firing from various blister, beam and flight deck positions. A total of 211 craft are recorded as having been made. There was a variant, known as Me 323E-2/WT *Waffenträger* (Weapon Carrier), armored and armed with eleven MG 151 20-mm cannons, intended for use as a gunship. There was a planned conversion for a bomber version with a capability of an 18,000-kg (39,690-lb) bomb load.

The Messerschmitt Me 323 *Gigant* in its transport form was successfully used in North Africa and on the Russian front in a tactical-support role, for evacuation and supplies and reserve-troop transport, but it did have its spectacular failures, as it had never been intended for front-line service. In spite of its defensive armament and escort, the desperately slow Me 323s proved very vulnerable to fighter attack. Many were intercepted by Allied fighters and shot down as a result. For example, on 22 April 1943 near Cape Bon, several squadrons of Spitfires and P 40 Kittyhawks attacked a unit of 14 gasoline-carrying Me 323s and their fighter escort. All Me 323s were shot down, with the loss of about 120 crew and 700 drums of fuel. The Messerschmitt Me 321 and Me 323 were not that popular with operating crews or transported personnel, because of their low speed, vulnerability, and high rate of casualties when shot down.

Horten Ho VIII/ IAe. 38

One example of this flying-wing-shaped transport aircraft was built and flown in 1959. It was designed by engineer Reimar Horten while living in exile in Argentina. The aircraft had a span of 32 m and was powered by four Iae 16 Gaucho piston engines. Named *Naranjero*, it was used to transport oranges. The Horten Iae 38 was based on a wartime project known as Horten Ho P VIII, which was intended to be a large four-engine bomber with a span of 80 m. Unfortunately no details are available.

Gliders

According to the stipulations of the Treaty of Versailles of 1919, Germany had no right to possess a military air force, but no clause forbade gliding. In the late 1920s and early 1930s, gliding was a national German sport which was encouraged by the Nazi Party as a patriotic activity. Germany had already been a pioneer in gliding; the inventor and aeronaut Otto Lilienthal (1848–1896) was the first to establish gliding as a science. He made over two thousand flights before being killed in an accident, and left a valuable book on glider techniques. After the seizure of power by the Nazis in January 1933, all sailplane activities and gliding research came under the supervision of the *Deutsche Forschungsanstalt für Segelflug* (DFS—German Research Institute for Gliding Flight). The DFS was formed by the nationalization of the Rhön-Rossitten Gesellschaft at Darmstadt. It was intended to promote interest and development of air sport and thus became involved in producing training gliders for the Hitler Youth and Luftwaffe. The institute also conducted research on flying wings and rocket propulsion. The DFS and several German aircraft companies produced assault and transport gliders, some of which were fitted with engines, thus becoming proper transport aircraft.

Gliders were used for reasons of economy. Not only were they economical in themselves in that their cost in hours of construction was less than in that of powered aircraft, but they required little or no maintenance and no fuel, and if damaged they could be easily repaired or replaced. In use with a tug aircraft they increased the lifting capacity of the towing plane by 60

Horten IAe. 38/Ho VIII

percent, but at some cost of its speed. After cutting adrift from its tug, a glider could cover great distances under perfect control in nearly complete silence, and could land on almost any type of flat and bare field. Gliders thus combined a high load capacity with comparatively low fuel consumption for the towing aircraft, but a landing operation, accomplished by power-driven airplanes or by gliders, was a safe method of air supply only if proper landing facilities were available—generally a stretch of dead ground adjoining the target. Precise agreements on signals and markers had to be reached, and careful arrangements had to be made as to the time and location of the landing. The use of gliders had an advantage in that less-specialized training was required, and relatively large formations could be delivered with bulky and awkward equipment. In practice, however, the use of gliders in combat was not always a great success, as they depended on surprise. Faulty navigation and a high percentage of crashes on landing caused casualties. Also, a glider lacked any form of motive power once released from its towing aircraft. An important point which is frequently overlooked was that the pilots of the towing aircraft had to be highly trained, determined and courageous. Navigation had to be perfect, for gliders were required to arrive at their goal at the precise moment determined on. To arrive too soon might prejudice surprise, and to arrive too late might jeopardize the lives of those who had landed on time. To be attacked by enemy aircraft or be shot at by enemy anti-aircraft artillery, as well as to drop men at the wrong place was likely to prove disastrous. Today the helicopter has replaced the glider and to some extent the parachutist.

The Germans eventually designed a variety of unpowered gliders for a transport role, in several shapes and sizes, making extensive use of them. Although they met with diminishing success as World War II proceeded, gliders proved a useful addition to the Luftwaffe's logistical fleet.

DFS 230

Initiated in 1933 by Ernst Udet, the DFS 230 was one of the first assault gliders and helped to define the tactics involved in this method of attack. The DFS 230 was first flown in early 1937 by the test aviator Hanna Reitsch. Designed by the gliding institute DFS and constructed by the Gothaer Waggonfabrik Company Erla und Harting and by Mars in occupied Czechoslovakia, the successful glider entered Luftwaffe service in 1939. A conventional, braced-high-wing monoplane of mixed construction, with a large side door for loading and unloading, the DFS 230 had a span of 20.87 m (68 ft 5.5 in), a length of 11.24 m (36 ft 10.5 in), and a maximum towing speed of 210 km/h (130 mph). It had a crew of two (pilot and observer/load-master/machine gunner) sitting in tandem, with optional controls for the gunner. The glider could transport eight fully equipped troops. In a combat zone, the glider could be armed with two swivel-mounted machine guns placed in hatches in the upper fuselage decking. It used a jettisonable landing gear for take-off and landed on a central skid mounted beneath the fuselage. The DFS 230 was towable by a variety of Luftwaffe planes (e.g., Junkers Ju 52, Messerschmitt Bf 110, Heinkel He 45 or He 46, or Henschel Hs 126). If take-off was risky, landing was a downright dangerous operation during which the pilot of the glider played a decisive role. He was responsible for the lives of nine men, and had a difficult decision to make: when to release the seventy-meter cable attached to the towing plane. Generally the line was unlocked at an altitude of 2 km and about 20 km from the target. Then the pilot had to keep the glider above the tug in order to reduce any buffeting by the slipstream from the propeller of the aircraft, and then the pilot had to direct the glider to the objective with an average speed of about 185 km/h. On landing, the speed could be reduced to 85 km/h by using retroactive rockets or a tail parachute acting as a brake, but crashes and serious casualties were not unknown.

A dual-control version (DFS 230-B) existed for training purpose, and it was planned to build an enlarged version (DFS 230-F) with a capacity of fifteen troops. There was also a planned larger version, code-named DFS 203, using a *Zwilling* (twin) arrangement with two fuselages connected by a middle wing. The

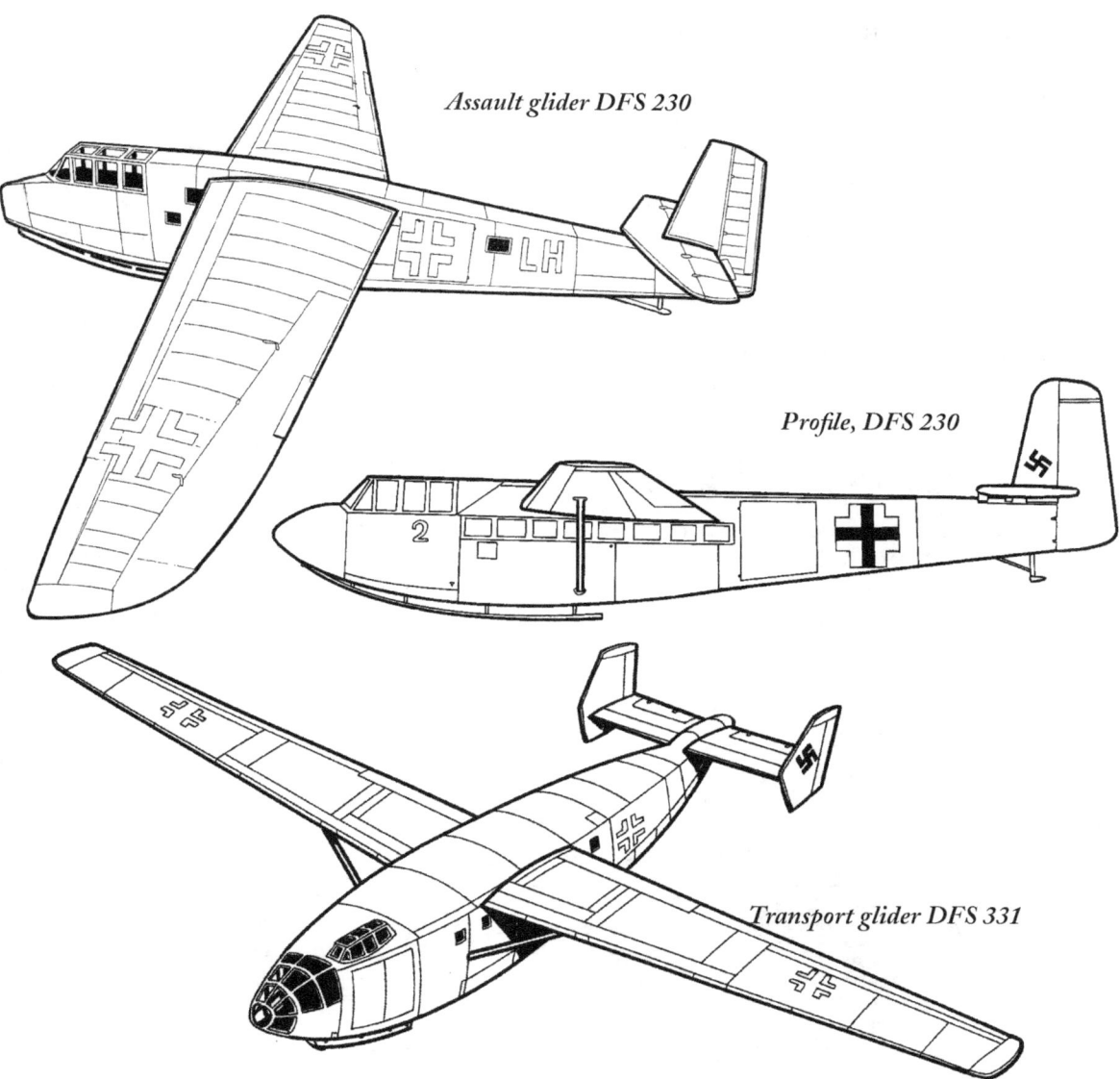

Assault glider DFS 230

Profile, DFS 230

Transport glider DFS 331

fuselage of the DFS 230 was also used to constitute the experimental, unpowered, rotary-wing glider Focke-Achgelis Fa 225.

A total of 1,510 units were built and used during World War II. The DFS 230 was—at least at the start of World War II—a secret weapon, closely associated with spectacular German airborne operations. These included the invasion of the Low Countries and the capture of the huge and heavily armed Fort Eben Emael in Belgium in May 1940. It was also extensively used later in supply missions during the campaign in North Africa, the assault on Crete, and on the Eastern front. The DFS 230's most daring use was without doubt the dramatic surprise rescue of Benito Mussolini on September 12, 1943, when a group of hand-picked commandos led by Otto Skorzeny were delivered on the Abruzzi mountaintop hotel where the deposed Italian dictator was imprisoned.

DFS 331

The transport glider DFS 331 was designed by engineer Hans Jacobs from DFS and built by the Gothaer Waggonfabrik. It was intended to be a larger and more useful version of the

DFS 230 with the capacity to carry a cargo load of 2,500 kg (5,512 lbs). The glider had a length of 15.81 m (51 ft 10.5 in), a span of 23 m (75 ft 6.5 in) and an empty weight of 2,270 kg (5,005 lbs). Maximum speed on tow was 270 km/h (168 mph). Operated by one pilot who sat in a cockpit placed high on the left of the fuselage, the DFS 331 was fitted with a large loading door on the side, and skids for take-off and landing. Only one example was built, in 1941. There was a projected twin variant, the DFS 332, composed of two DFS 331 gliders joined together, with a middle wing section and tailplane.

Gotha Go 242 and Go 244

The glider Gotha Go 242 was designed by engineer Albert Kalkert in response to an RLM requirement for a heavy transport glider to replace the DFS 230 then in service. Two prototypes were first flown in 1941 and the type quickly entered production. A total of 1,528 were built between 1941 and 1943, making the Go 242 the most widely used assault glider produced by the Gothaer Company in World War II. The aircraft was of pod and twin-boom design, with a cross-plane forming the tail and shoulder-wing, a foretaste of the configuration of many postwar heavy-transport aircrafts. It had a crew of two—pilot and navigator. It had a length of 15.81 m (51 ft 10 in), a wingspan of 24.50 m (80 ft 5 in), a height of 4.40 m (14 ft 5 in), and a wing area of 64.4 square m (693 square ft). Empty weight was 3,200 kg (7,056 lb), and maximum speed was 300 km/h (188 mph). There were several variants for troops or cargo, with jettisonable or fixed landing gear, as well as a training version with dual controls. Armament varied with type and consisted generally of four 7.92-mm MG 15 machine guns. The troop

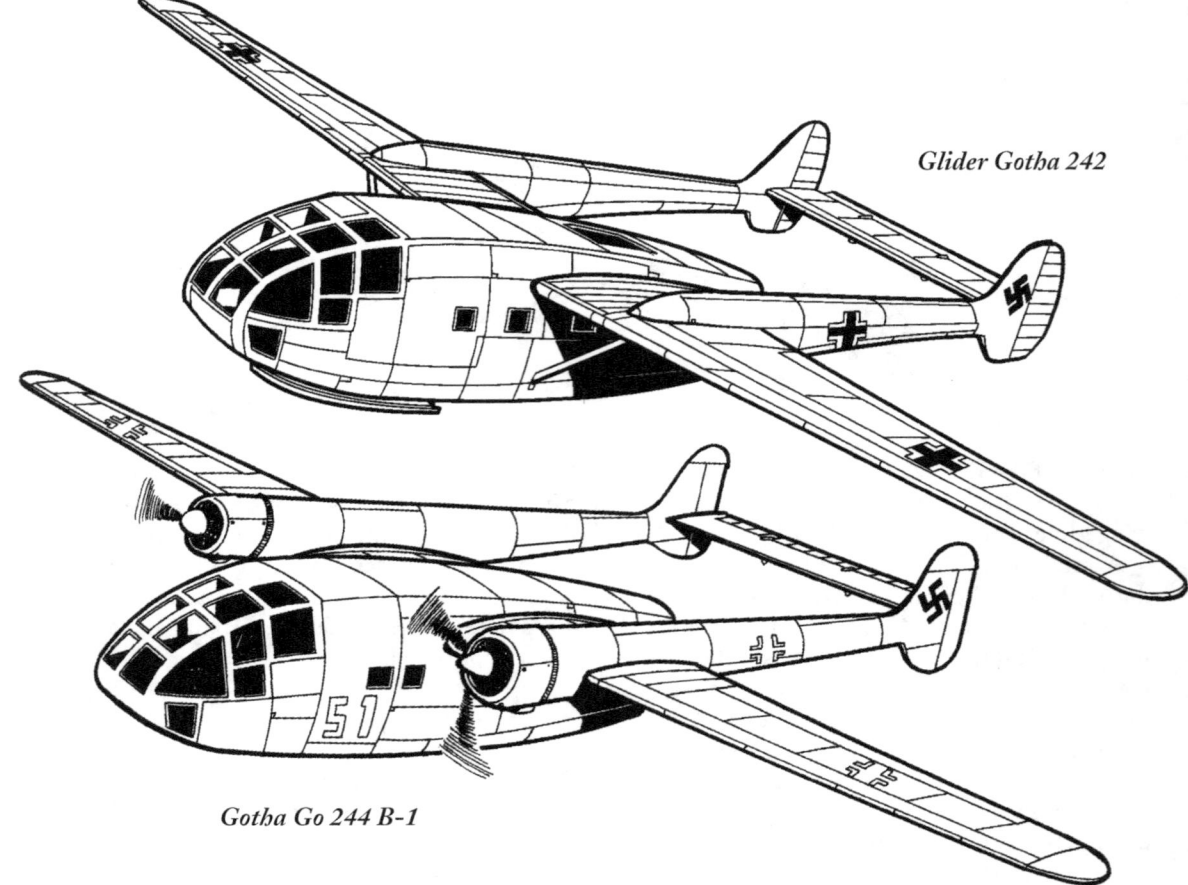

Glider Gotha 242

Gotha Go 244 B-1

transport version had a capacity of twenty-one fully equipped soldiers. Cargo versions of the glider featured a hinged rear fuselage that could accommodate a *Kübelwagen* (a kind of jeep) or loads of similar size and weight. A few Go 242s were converted for use for a daring operation: to alight on water near an enemy ship and capture it by assault. In service, the glider was towed by a Heinkel He 111 or a Junkers Ju 52. Occasionally RATO equipment was used, and landing experiments were done with rocket braking.

The Go 244 was the powered version of the Gotha Go 242. After the fall of France, the German army captured large stocks of the Gnome-Rhone 14M radial aircraft engines, and it was decided to create a motorized version of the glider Go 242. The engines, however, increased the weight of the aircraft and proved to be underpowered, as maximum speed was only 290 km/h (180 mph) and range was 740 km (460 miles). After the invasion of Soviet Union in June 1941, a series of gliders was fitted with captured Russian Shvetsov M-25A radial aircraft engines, but these, too, proved to be just as underpowered as the French engines. The Go 242 was a good glider but the Go 244 a poor airplane. In all, some 133 motorized Gotha Go 244 were produced, entering Luftwaffe service in May 1942 as troop carriers and freight-transport aircrafts.

Junkers Ju 322 Mammut

The Ju 322 *Mammut* (Mammoth) was a giant assault glider that could carry heavy

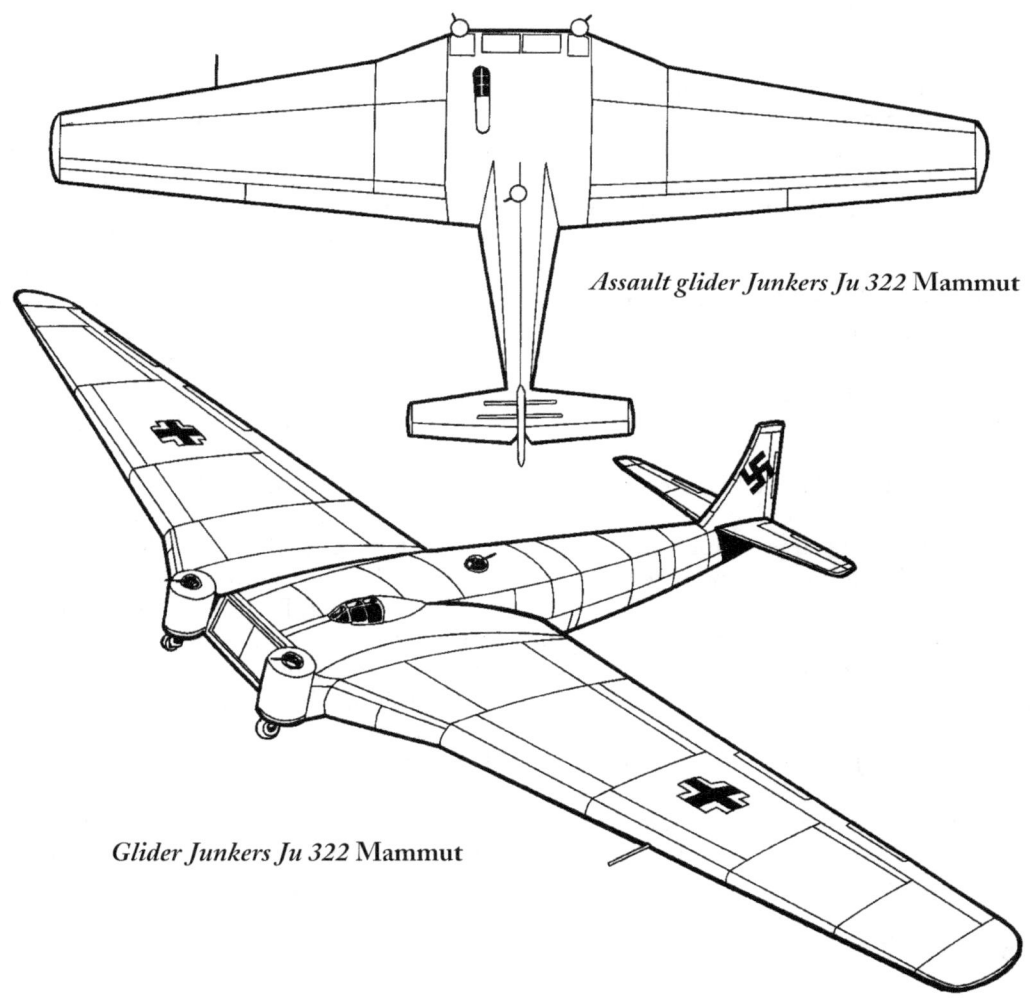

Assault glider Junkers Ju 322 **Mammut**

Glider Junkers Ju 322 **Mammut**

Cargo glider Messerschmitt Me 321 Gigant

Messerschmitt Me 321

When the Junkers Ju 322 was a total failure, the huge transport glider Messerschmitt 321 went into production. The Me 321 was originally conceived to be used in the invasion of Great Britain (Operation Sea Lion) in the summer of 1940, to ferry troops and supplies across the English Channel. The huge glider had a conventional layout with high-set wings (braced by struts to the fuselage), single fin and rudder, and a "rough country," sturdy, fixed, ten-wheel undercarriage. It had a length of 28.2 m (92 ft 4 in), a wingspan of 55.2 m (181 ft), and a height of 10.15 m (33 ft 3.5 in). Operated by a crew of two (five when armed with defensive machine guns), its cavernous interior could carry up to 120 combat-equipped troops, or a similar freight load of about 22 metric tons (22,000 kg—48,500 lbs), three times the lift capacity of the transport trimotor Junkers Ju 52. Besides, its large, swinging, clam-shell front door placed in the nose made loading and unloading easy. To make the Me 321 fit for cheap mass production, it had been designed with a fabric-covered steel-tube framing instead of a conventional light-alloy monocoque structure; it took about 14,000 hours to build it. In spite of this, the Me 321 was well constructed, and able to withstand the rigors of operations in all climates and on all types of terrain. The huge glider made its first flight in March 1941, and entered service in May of the same year. The primitive Mes-

equipment (tanks, heavy guns, vehicles, troops, ammunition and fuel) into combat areas. The craft, made entirely of wood, was anything but conventional: it was basically an enormous flying wing with a tall fin carried on a boom-like expansion at the rear. The machine had a span of 62 m (203 ft 5 in), a length of 30.25 m (99 ft 3 in), a height of 10 m (32 ft 9 in), an empty weight of 26,000 kg (52,900 lbs), and a transport capacity of 10 metric tons. Loading and unloading of cargo was done via a clamshell door located in the nose. Defensive armament included three machine-gun platforms: two placed on each side of the front door and the third positioned on top of the fuselage.

The glider proved a total failure. Problems with stability and ill-balance forced the builders to install two large water tanks in its forward section to make it more nose-heavy. When an armored combat vehicle was first loaded, it crashed through the wooden floor. So the floor was reinforced, thus reducing the glider's payload capacity by 20 percent. Finally, a test flight took place in April 1941. Towed by a four-engined Junkers Ju 90 transport airplane, the monster glider became uncontrollable. The pilot of the Ju 90 was forced to cut the *Mammut* loose and let it crash. The test glider and the other Ju 322s then under construction were sawn up for firewood. The role of giant assault glider was ultimately assumed by the Messerschmitt Me 321.

Assault glider Gotha Go 345. Top: freight carrier Go 345 B. Bottom: troop carrier Go 345 A.

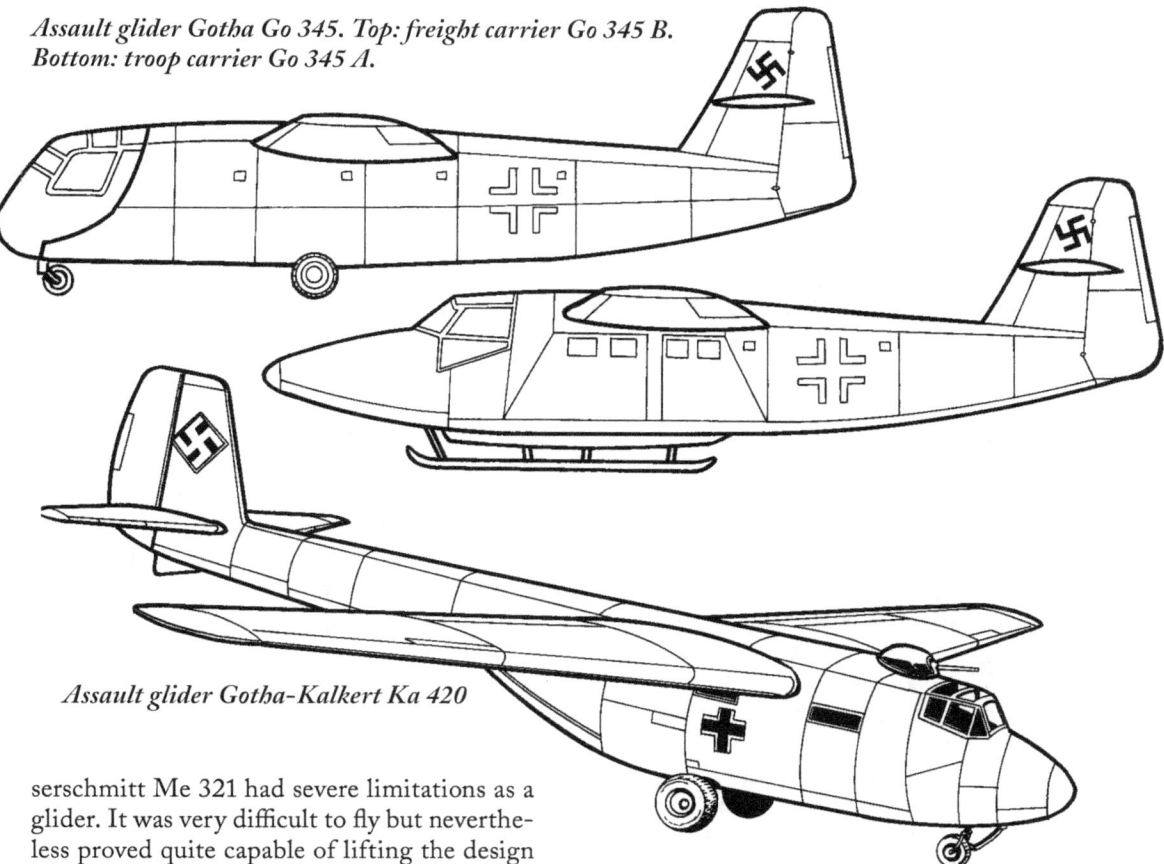

Assault glider Gotha-Kalkert Ka 420

serschmitt Me 321 had severe limitations as a glider. It was very difficult to fly but nevertheless proved quite capable of lifting the design payload. It was so huge and heavy that a special tug arrangement was provided, consisting of either a *Troika Schlepp* (three Messerschmitt Bf 110 craft), or two towing Junkers Ju 52, or one Heinkel He 111 Z (*Zwilling*). A total of 175 glider Me 321 craft were produced. The powered version of this glider was known as Messerschmitt Me 323 Giant.

Gotha Go 345

Designed in 1944 by the Gothaer Waggonfabrik AG, the assault glider Go 345 had a span of 21 m (68 ft 10 in), a length of 13 m (42 ft 7 in), a height of 4.20 m (13 ft 9 in), and an empty weight of 2,470 kg (5,445 lbs). It had a crew of two. The project existed in two variants. The Go 345 A, intended to carry eight troops, had a pointed nose, side loading doors, and landing skids. The Go 345 B, intended to carry freight, had a wheeled landing gear and a stubby nose that could be hinged for loading and unloading. The end of World War II prevented any further development of this glider.

Gotha-Kalkert Ka 430

The Gotha-Kalkert 430 was designed by engineer Kalkert and first built in late 1944. The glider had a crew of two (pilot and co-pilot/navigator/gunner) and could carry twelve fully equipped troops, a small vehicle (e.g., a *Kübelwagen*) or a small cannon, which were loaded through a rear loading ramp. The shoulder-mounted wing had a span of 19.5 m (63 ft 12 in). The boxy fuselage with a conventional tail unit had a length of 13.22 m (43 ft 4.5 in). Empty weight was 1,810 kg (3,990 lbs). One manually operated 13-mm MG 131 machine gun was mounted in a small turret above the cockpit. Tests proved successful and a production order was placed but only twelve units had been built when the end of World War II caused the abandonment of the program.

9

Miscellaneous Aircraft

Reconnaissance and Observation Planes

Airborne reconnaissance goes back to the early era of ballooning in 1794, and the first military use of lighter—and heavier-than-air aircraft was surveillance and monitoring of enemy activity. Air reconnaissance—the active gathering of information about the enemy by physical observation—was (and still is) essential. Virtually all aircraft have a potential reconnaissance capability, and observation was the earliest role in which aircraft were used at the beginning of World War I. Early observation airplanes mainly worked as spotters for the massed artillery, observing shell bursts and correcting range. After World War I, converted bombers were commonly used for air reconnaissance, since these were the only machines with the long range and high ceiling capability required for that type of mission. In the 1930s, specially designed observation airplanes were produced to seek and collect information about types of enemy units, locations, number, intentions, movement and activity. Operating ahead of the main force, either at treetop height or at high altitude, they would provide a bird's-eye view of battle, take photographs, give additional information to those obtained by ground reconnaissance units, contribute to artillery ranging, and help commanders to remain in constant contact with their advanced forces.

Reconnaissance pilots were not just airmen able to handle flying machines, they were highly trained specialists. They were specially trained in map-reading and navigation. They had gone through courses on the principles of land warfare and the weapons used by their own troops and the enemy army. They knew the significance of the formations in which they might see troops. They were schooled to observe significant details, to thwart enemy camouflage techniques, and trained in military intelligence.

The German air reconnaissance service was tactically organized on the basis of the *Gruppe* (equivalent to the RAF wing and the USAF group). A *Gruppe* was divided into *Staffeln* (equivalent to the RAF and USAAF squadrons). The main *Gruppen* were as follows:

- *Aufklärungsgruppe* (fern): reconnaissance wing (long-range)
- *Aufklärungsgruppe* (Heer): reconnaissance wing (army cooperation)
- *Nahaufklärungsgruppe*: short-range tactical reconnaissance
- *Fernklärungsgruppe*: long-range reconnaissance
- *See-Aufklärung*: maritime reconnaissance
- *Küstenfliegergruppe*: coastal flying wing.

The task of a reconnaissance aircraft was to observe, and only to fight if it was forced to do so. However it could also carry weapons in order to damage or destroy the enemy which it sighted.

The standard type of army cooperation and reconnaissance aircraft, typified by the Henschel Hs 126 and Fieseler Fi 156, proved quite vulnerable to modern fighters and anti-aircraft fire as World War II proceeded. This resulted in the employment of converted fighters sufficiently fast, maneuverable and armed to undertake reconnaissance missions without fighter escort. Such conversion usually consisted of replacing some of the armament with cameras. By the end of the war, experimental high-speed jet planes were designed for the purpose of high-altitude reconnaissance.

Gotha Go 147

Developed by the Gothaer Waggonfabrik AG, the Go 147 was a small observation aircraft. Only two units were produced, designated Go 147 V1 and Go 147 V2. The former was powered by a Siemens Sh 14 A radial engine with 140 hp, and the latter by an Argus As inverted V-8 engine with 240 hp. Both were tailless and had gull wings swept back at 38 degrees, with fins and rudders placed on the wingtips. They had a crew of two (pilot and observer/rear gunner), and had a wingspan of 12.22 m (40 ft 2 in), a length of 5.86 m (19 ft 3 in) and a height of 2.93 m (9 ft 6 in). Speed was 220 km/h (137 mph) and weight (empty) was 945 kg (2,083 lbs). Armament was one synchronized MG 17 firing forward and one aimed MG 15 manually operated by the observer in the rear cockpit. The Go 147

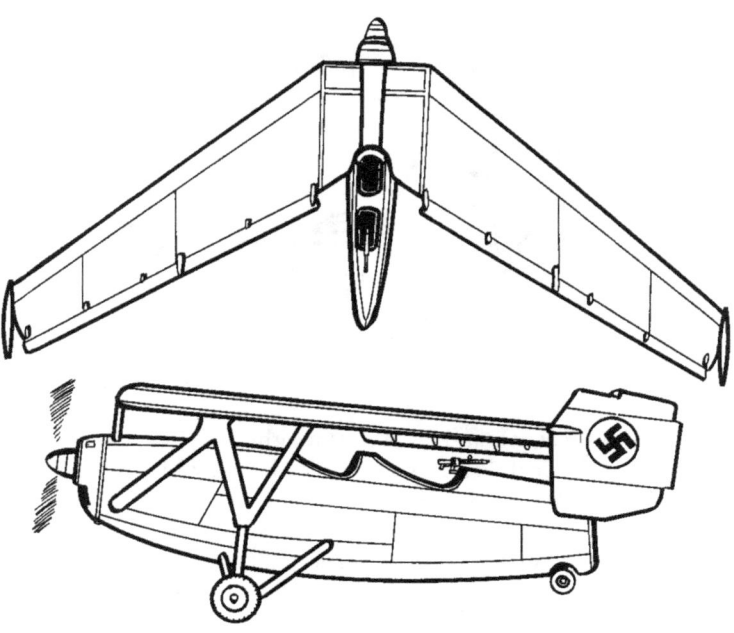

Two-view of Gotha Go 147

first flew in 1936 and proved to have very poor flight characteristics. Soon the project was discontinued and abandoned. An equally unsuccessful and similar British design from 1934 was known as Westland-Hill Pterodactyl.

Heinkel He 45

Designed in 1931, the two-seat biplane He 45 made its first flight a year later. It had a length of 10.59 m (34 ft 9.5 in), a span of 11.50

Heinkel He 45

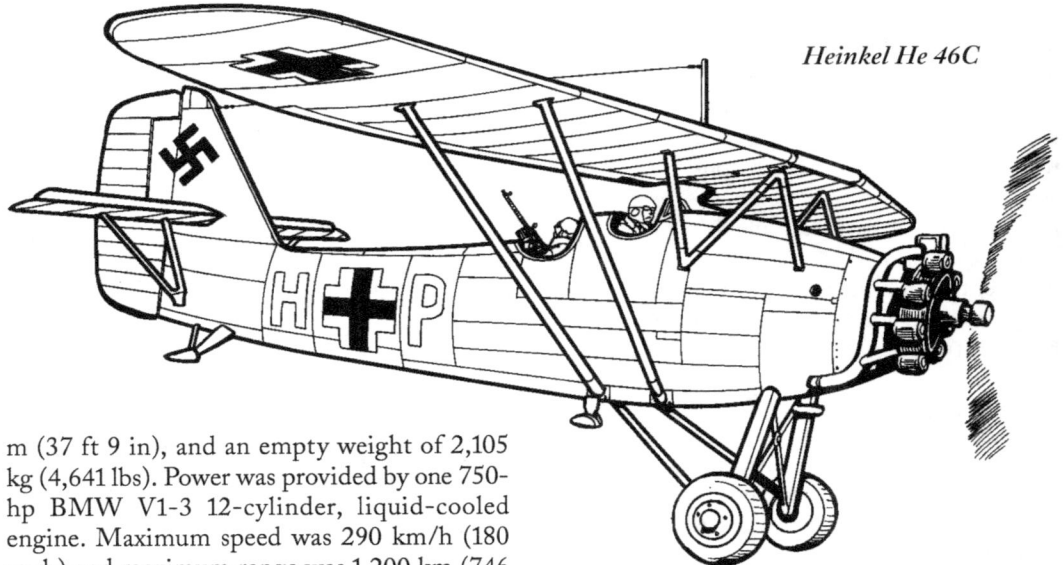

Heinkel He 46C

m (37 ft 9 in), and an empty weight of 2,105 kg (4,641 lbs). Power was provided by one 750-hp BMW V1-3 12-cylinder, liquid-cooled engine. Maximum speed was 290 km/h (180 mph) and maximum range was 1,200 km (746 miles). Armament included one 7.92-mm MG 17 machine gun fixed to fire forward, and one 7.92-mm MG 15 machine gun manually aimed by the observer in the rear cockpit. A bomb load of 200 kg (440 lbs) could be carried. A sturdy and reliable machine, the aircraft was manufactured by the Heinkel Company, and subcontracted to Gotha, BFW and Focke-Wulf. In the 1930s, a total of 512 of all versions was produced, and a number were sold to Bulgaria and some delivered to nationalist China. Some forty units fought in the Spanish Civil War with the German Legion Kondor. When World War II broke out, some twenty-one remained in Luftwaffe front-line service as reconnaissance craft and light bomber/ground attackers. Totally outdated, the Heinkel He 45 was soon relegated to a training and glider-towing role, although a squadron still served as night-attack airplanes on the Eastern front as late as autumn 1942.

Heinkel He 46

The He 46, designed in 1931, was an armed, short-range, reconnaissance and army-cooperation parasol-wing monoplane with a crew of two (pilot and observer/gunner). It was one of the main types chosen for the Luftwaffe expansion program, initiated well before Germany's official announcement of the air force's existence. In its production form, known as He 46C, the aircraft was powered by a 650-hp Bramo SAM 322B 9-cylinder, air-cooled radial engine. Maximum speed was 260 km/h (161 mph) and range was about 1,000 km (621 miles). Wingspan was 14 m (45 ft 11 in), length was 9.5 m (31 ft 2 in), height was 3.4 m (11 ft 2 in), empty weight was 1,765 kg (3,892 lbs). Armament was one 7.92 mm MG 15 or MG 17 on a flexible mount operated by the observer in the rear cockpit. A load of twenty 10-kg (22-lb) bombs could be carried. Some 481 He 46s were produced, manufactured by Heinkel and subcontractors Siebel, Fieseler, Gothaer Waggonfabrik and MIAG. A prominent aircraft in the build up of the Luftwaffe, the He 46 saw service during the Spanish Civil War where it was used both by the German Condor Legion and nationalist forces. By 1939, most He 46s were used as trainers and glider-tugs, but some remained operational with the Luftwaffe on the Eastern front until 1943. It also served with the Bulgarian and Hungarian Air Forces.

Fieseler Fi 156 Storch

The light liaison/reconnaissance high-wing Fi 156 *Storch* (Stork) was designed by Gerhard Fieseler, Reinhard Mewes, and Erich Bachem, technical director of the Gerhart Fieseler Werke GmbH company, in response

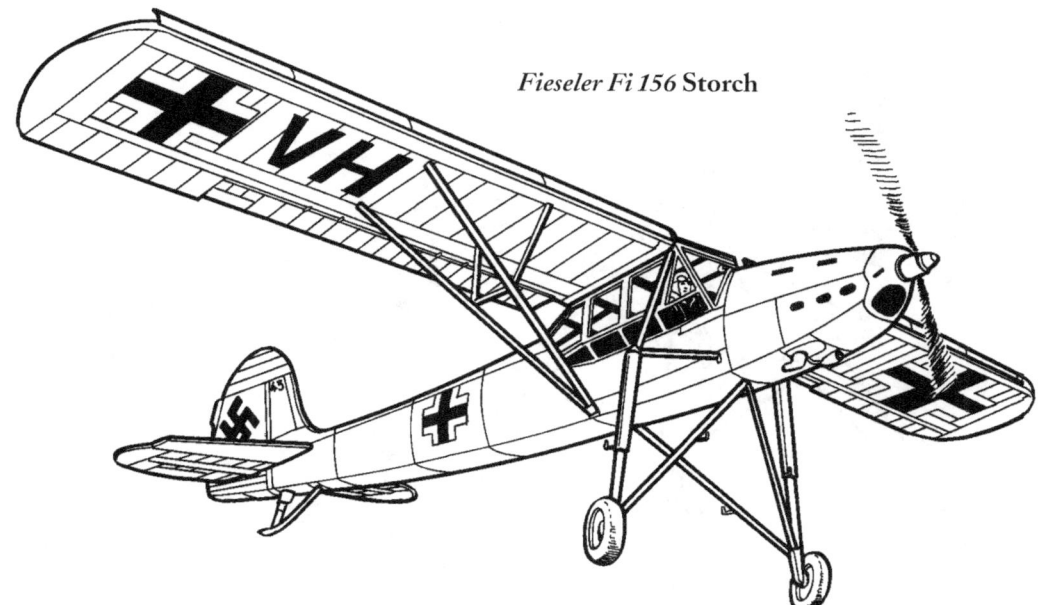

Fieseler Fi 156 **Storch**

to an RLM requirement of 1935. It first flew in early 1936, and proved to be one of the most successful multi-role, "go anywhere" aircraft of World War II. During the war it was built by the French company Morane-Saulnier from Puteaux (near Paris), and the Benes-Mraz company from Czechoslovakia. The lightweight Fi 156 had a length of 9.74 m (32 ft 6 in.), a wingspan of 14.25 m (46 ft 9 in) and a weight of 930 kg (2,050 lb). The Argus AS 100 engine of 240 hp gave a maximum speed of 175 km/h (109 mph) and a range of 380 km (236 miles). The lightweight fuselage was made of rectangular sections of welded steel tubing covered by fabric, overhead wings and tail covered by plywood. The undercarriage consisted of two long legs with shock absorbers and was braced to the center underside of the fuselage; this could be fitted with wheels or skis. The side windows were wider than the fuselage giving excellent vision downward. The craft carried a crew of two (one pilot and one observer/radio operator) with two passengers.

The Fi 156's greatest virtue was its ability to take off and land on the most limited of landing strips. Indicative of its excellent STOL capacities, it could land on just 20 m (61 ft), while ground run to take-off was 65 m (213 ft). It could be used all over the front and even behind enemy lines. A highly versatile aircraft, it was used in many roles, including army cooperation, VIP transport, communications, reconnaissance, casualty evacuation, sabotage, and artillery observation. Marshal Erwin Rommel and many other top Army leaders preferred Fi 156s to their grander official transports when visiting front-line troops. German paratroopers used a Fi 156 in the dramatic operation to rescue the Italian dictator Benito Mussolini from captivity on the Gran Sasso mountain. The aircraft proved such a success that by the end of the war over forty captured Fi 156s were being used by the Allies in preference to their own machines. The famous test pilot Hanna Reitsch and General Ritter von Greim (head of the Luftwaffe for a short period by the last weeks of World War II) flew a *Storch* when they visited Hitler in the ruins of Berlin in late April 1945. A total of 2,700 *Storch* craft were built and they were used on every World War II front. After the war, until 1949, the French company Morane continued production of the *Storch* under the designation *Morane-Saulnier MS 500 Criquet*, which was used in the French Indochina War.

Henschel Hs 126

First flown in August 1936, the Henschel Hs 126 was produced by the Henschel Flug-

Aircraft of the Luftwaffe, 1935–1945

Henschel Hs 126

zeugwerke AG in Schönefeld, and entered Luftwaffe service in June 1937. Very much like the British Lysander, the Hs 126 was a parasol-winged light reconnaissance aircraft with fixed landing gear. It had a crew of two (pilot and observer/radio-operator/rear gunner). Span was 14 m (47 ft 7), length was 10.85 m (35 ft 8 in), and weight was 2,032 kg (4,408 lb). The powerplant was usually a 9-cylinder radial 830-hp Bramo Fafnir 323A with a maximum speed of 355 km/h (221 mph), and maximum range of 580 km (360 miles). Armament included two MG 17 machine guns, and eventually a bomb load of 110 lbs could be carried. The Hs 126 had excellent STOL capacities and good flying characteristics. Production was halted in January 1941 after about 800 units had served in the German reconnaissance squadrons. The Hs 126 was replaced by the Focke-Wulf Fw 189 *Uhu*, but continued in service behind the lines, particularly in anti-partisan and night harassment operations in the Balkans and on the Russian front.

Arado Ar 198

The Arado Ar 198 was intended to replace the Henschel He 46 as a tactical reconnaissance and army-cooperation aircraft. Designed in 1937, the parasol-winged monoplane had a length of 11.8 m (38 ft 8.5 in), a span of 14.9 m (48 ft 10.5 in), a height of 4.50 m (14 ft 9.5

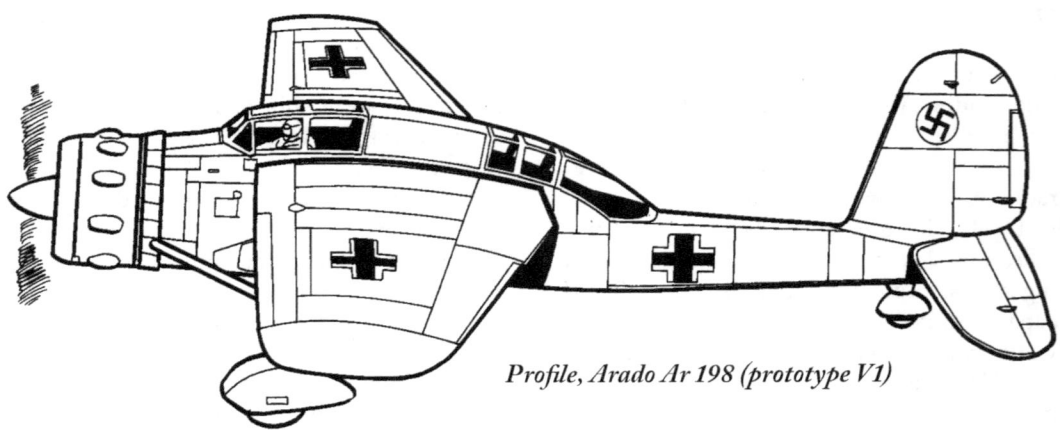

Profile, Arado Ar 198 (prototype V1)

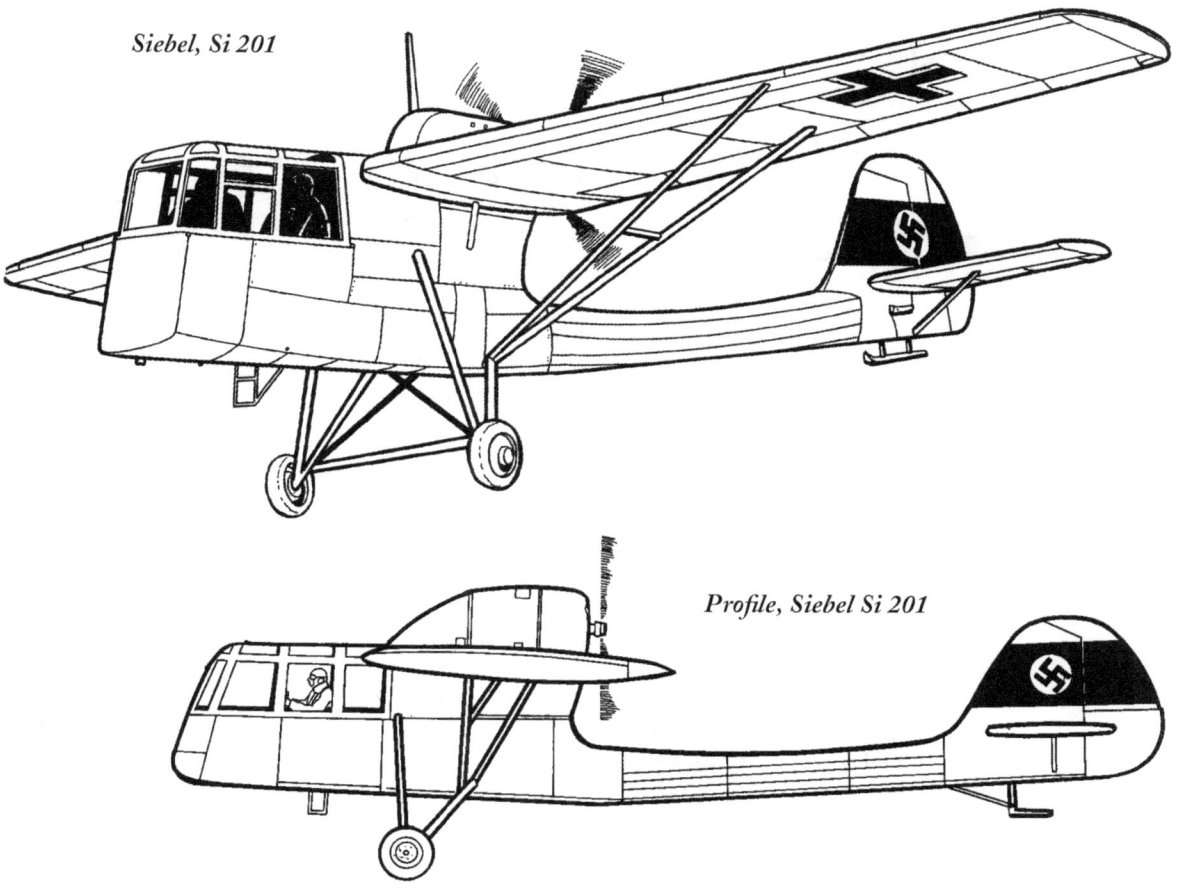

Siebel, Si 201

Profile, Siebel Si 201

in), and an empty weight of 2,400 kg (5,290 lbs). Powered by a 900-hp BMW Bramo Fafnir 323A 9-cylinder radial engine, it had a maximum speed of 359 km/h (223 mph) and a range of 1,081 km (672 miles). The Ar 198 was to be armed with two 7.92-mm, manually aimed, rear-firing MG 15 machine guns (one dorsal, the other ventral) and two fixed, forward-firing 7.92-mm MG 17 machine guns. Four 50-kg (110-lb) bombs could be carried on wing racks. Judged by the RLM too conventional, old-fashioned and unattractive, the Ar 198 was rejected after only three prototypes were built. More advanced recon aircraft with higher performance were ordered instead (e.g., Focke-Wulf Fw 189 and Blohm & Voss Bv 141).

Siebel Si 201

The Si 201 was designed by the Siebel Flugzeugwerke KG company. It was a light small observation/reconnaissance aircraft with a weight of 1,120 kg (2,469 lb) and a fuselage length of 10.4 m (34 ft 1.5 in). The wings were slightly swept back, with a span of 14 m (45 ft 11 in). Powered by a 240-hp Argus As 10C inverted-V-8, air-cooled engine driving a pusher propeller, the Si 201 had poor dynamics and thus a maximum speed of only 185 km/h (115 mph) and a range of 450 km (280 miles). The crew of two—a pilot and an observer/radio-operator—sat in a large square-shaped cockpit at the front, with excellent 360-degree vision. Flight testing, however, revealed various deficiencies, and the Si 201, which was intended to replace the Fieseler *Storch*, never entered production.

Focke-Wulf Fw 189 Uhu

In response to a 1937 RLM specification for a reconnaissance aircraft, the Focke-Wulf Fw

Focke-Wulf Fw 189 A-2

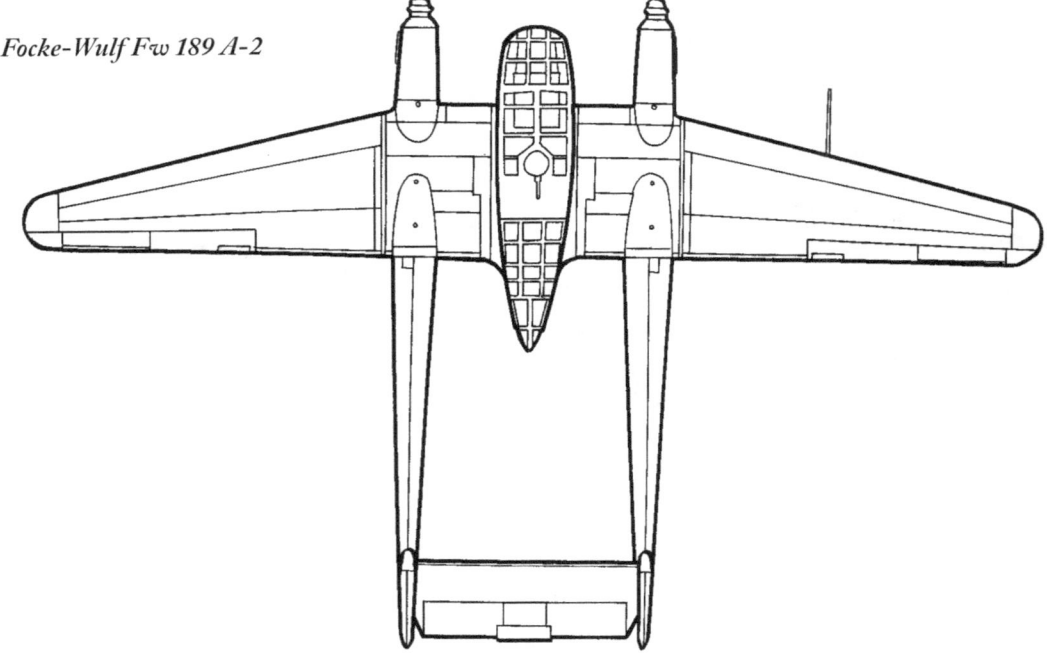

189 *Uhu* ("Owl," nicknamed "the Flying Eye" by the Allies) was designed in 1938 by engineer Kurt Tank from the Focke-Wulf Flugzeugbau GmbH. It was a reconnaissance aircraft with twin 465-hp Argus As 410A-1 12-cylinder, inverted-V, air-cooled engines located on twin-boom fuselage. Today the diversity of aircraft layout makes us forget how odd the Fw 189 seemed. The twin-boom configuration was employed to maximize the field of view in the cockpit pod. Maximum speed was 350 km/h (217 mph), range was 670 km (416 miles), and the aircraft could climb to 4,000 m (13,120 ft) in only eight minutes. The crew, including three airmen (pilot, navigator/observer, and radio-operator/machine gunner), sat in a glazed cockpit placed in a capacious central nacelle between the booms. Wingspan was 18.4 m (60 ft 4.5 in.) and length was 12 m (39 ft 4 in). Armament included two 7.92-mm MG 17 machine guns placed in each wing root, and twin 7.92-mm MG 81 guns manually operated in dorsal rear cockpit. The Fw 189 could also be used as close-support bomber thanks to underwing racks for four 50-kg (110-lb) bombs. A number were converted to night fighter, fitted with the vertically firing 15-mm MG 151 cannon known as *Schräge Musik*. The aircraft was

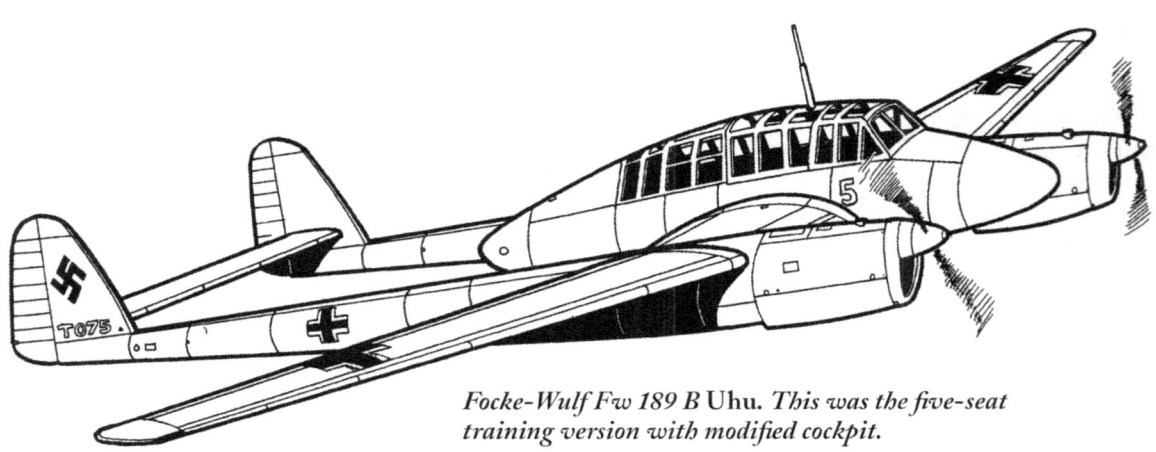

Focke-Wulf Fw 189 B Uhu. This was the five-seat training version with modified cockpit.

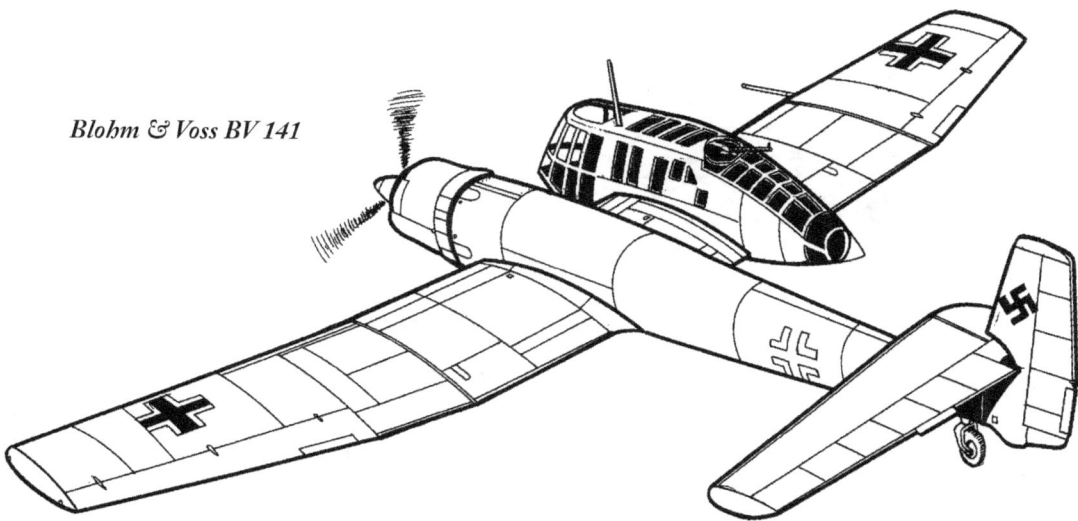

Blohm & Voss BV 141

rather unsuccessful in those armed versions, but performed beyond all expectation in the reconnaissance role, its basic simplicity and stability with twin-boom showing a remarkable toughness and outstanding maneuverability. A few were converted for VIP transport and regularly used by Field Marshal Albert Kesselring and Colonel-General Hans Jeschonnek. Produced between September 1940 and August 1944, and manufactured—under German control—by the French company Breguet in Bordeaux-Merignac, 846 Fw 189s were built in several different versions (designated A-1, A-2 and A-3) and sub-variants, operating in North Africa and on the Russian front. A variant, the Fw 189 B, was a five-seater training aircraft, of which only thirteen were built. A heavily armored ground-attack variant, the Fw 189C, was designed, but its two prototypes (V1b and V6) were not satisfactory, and it was not produced.

Blohm und Voss BV 141

The Blohm und Voss BV 141 was one of the oddest airplanes ever built, as the crew was placed in a nacelle mounted beside the engine/tailboom. The asymmetric aircraft made its first flight in February 1938, and improved versions appeared in September and November of the same year. A total of thirteen Bv 141s were built, including the prototypes and the slightly different A and improved B series. The aircraft, intended for tactical reconnaissance and army cooperation, had a span of 15 m (50 ft 8 in), a length of 9.95 m (39 ft 10 in), and an empty weight of 3,167 kg (6,982 lbs). The prototypes and A series were powered by one 960-hp BMW 132N 9-cylinder radial, and the B series by one 1,560-hp BMW 801A 14-cylinder, two-row radial engine. Maximum speed was 400 km/h (248 mph) and maximum range was 1,139 km (708 miles). Armament included two fixed forward-firing 7.92-mm MG 17 machine guns, one dorsal manually aimed 7.92-mm MG 15, and one MG 15 mounted in the rear tail cone. Four 50-kg (110-lb) bombs could be carried on underwing racks. In spite of its curious asymmetrical design, the Bv 141 was a fast, easy-to-handle, good and reliable airplane. Its separated-from-the-fuselage, all-glazed nacelle gave an excellent vision but there was a blind spot to the left of the cockpit. The crew included three airmen: pilot, navigator/observer, and radio-operator/machine gunner. Despite the Bv 141's bizarre look, the RLM decided the project was worth pursuing, but the program was dogged by minor technical problems, and lack of resources at Blohm & Voss. The Luftwaffe did not like the concept, on the grounds that it was underpowered. Instead, the Focke-Wulf Fw 189 was chosen as reconnaissance airplane. Nonetheless engineer Vogt and the Blohm & Voss designers never lost their enthusiasm for asymmetrical layouts as we have already seen.

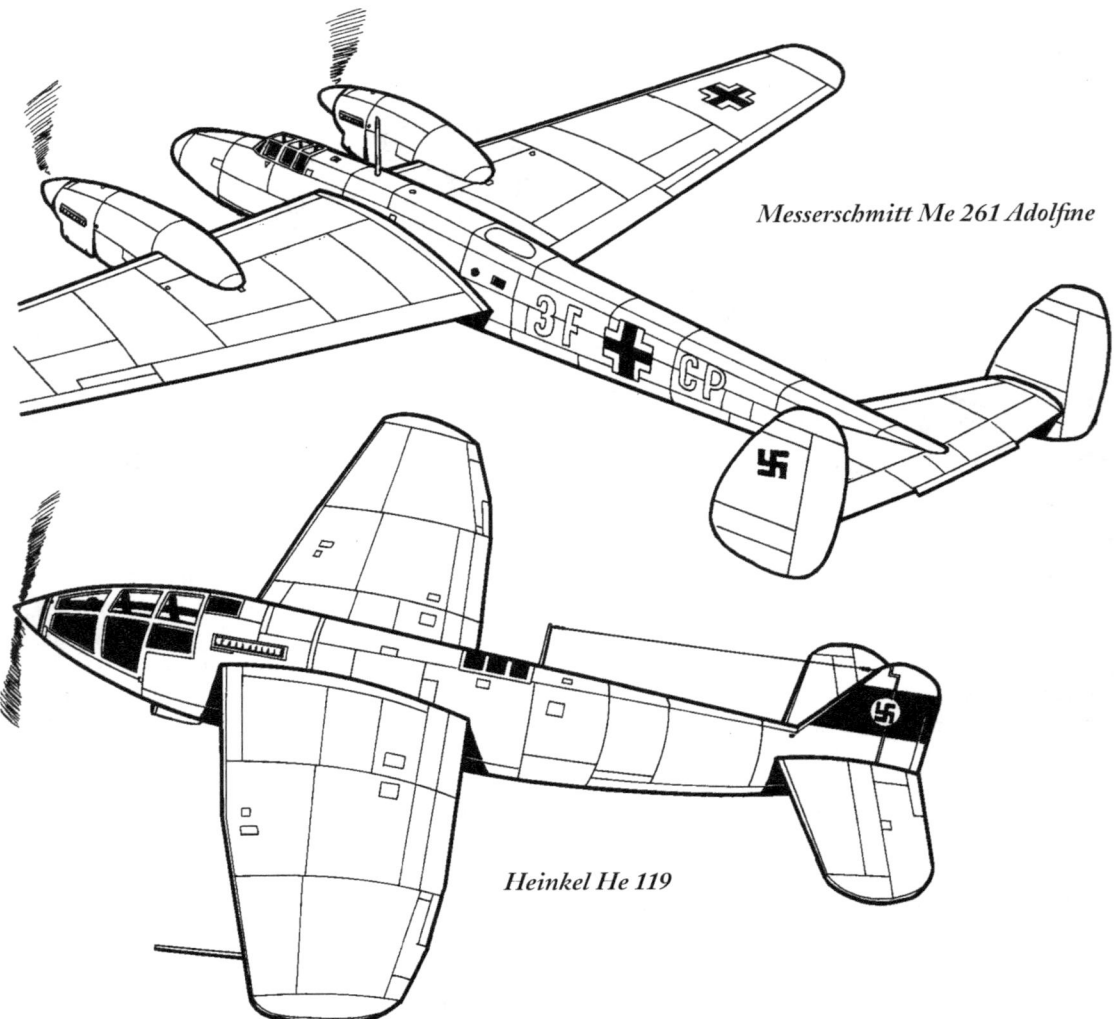

Messerschmitt Me 261 Adolfine

Heinkel He 119

Messerschmitt Me 261 Adolfine

The Me 261 was a long-range aircraft named Adolfine in honor of Adolf Hitler. Originally designed to fly the Olympic flame from Tokyo to Berlin for the Games of 1936, the aircraft was, however, a low-priority work, and prototype V1 did not fly before December 1940. The fuselage had a length of 16.67 m (54 ft 8.7 in), and a height of 4.72 m (15 ft 5.7 in). The wings had a span of 26.87 m (88 ft 1.7 in) and were very thick as they formed an integral fuel tank. In all, only three Me 261s were built. Prototypes V1 and V2 were powered by two 2,700-hp Daimler-Benz DB 606A/B, and V3 by two 2,950-hp DB 610A-1 engines. Typical speed was 620 km/h (385 mph), and range was about 11,000 km (6,835 miles). Adolfine was fitted with a retractable carriage but no armament was planned. During the war, the three Me 261s were occasionally used for ultra-long-range reconnaissance missions. They were destroyed in 1944 by Allied bombardments.

Heinkel He 119

The Heinkel He 119, a private venture by the Heinkel company, was a curious and rather advanced airplane. Designed before World War II by the Günter brothers to test radical design, the aircraft had an unusual feature and layout. The engines (two coupled 2,350-hp Daimler-Benz DB 606 inverted-V-12, liquid-

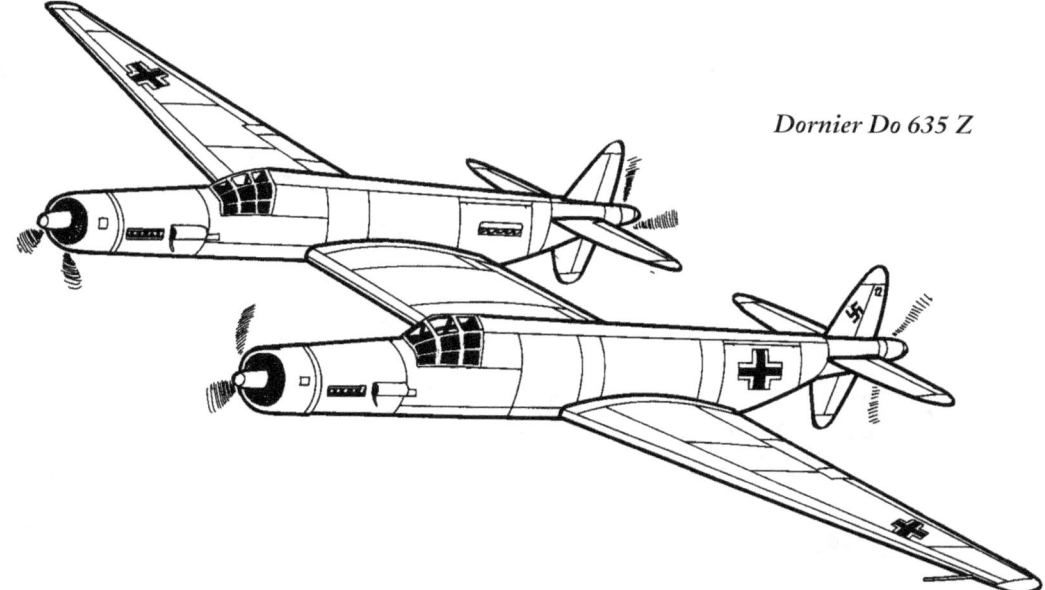

Dornier Do 635 Z

cooled) were mounted in the fuselage behind the cockpit; they drove a tractor propeller placed in the nose via a long shaft. On each side of this shaft sat the two pilots in a glazed nose cockpit. The He 119 had a retractable landing gear, a length of 14.8 m (48 ft 6.5 in), a span of 15.9 m (52 ft 2 in), and an empty weight of 5,200 kg (11,464 lbs). The aircraft had a maximum speed of 590 km/h (367 mph), and a range of 3,120 km (1,940 miles). First flown in mid–1937, several He 119 prototypes were built including a project for a seaplane, a high-speed long-range reconnaissance craft, and a fast bomber version with a bomb load of 1,000 kg (2,205 lbs) carried in a bomb bay. Owing to its high speed, the aircraft was considered not likely to be intercepted and thus not armed. The Heinkel He 119 never entered production and the few units built were used to test engines.

Dornier Do 635 Z

The Do 635 Z (twin) was composed of two Dornier Do 335s (see Chapter 5) joined by a center wing section which held the fuel tank. Intended to become a long-range reconnaissance aircraft, the Do 635 would have had a crew of three (eventually four). It had a length of 18.5 m (60 ft 8.3 in) and a span of 27.45 m (90 ft). The landing gear was retractable and an additional (jettisonable) fifth wheel was mounted in the center section. The aircraft was to be powered by four Daimler-Benz 603 E-1 piston engines, two pushing and two pulling. Wind-tunnel tests were effected and a mock-up cockpit was built but the project was abandoned in February 1945.

DFS 228

Designed by the *Deutsches Forschungsinstitute für Segelflug* (DFS—German Institute for Sailplane Flight), the DFS 228 was intended to be a high-altitude reconnaissance aircraft. Almost entirely made of wood, it had a span of 17.56 m (57 ft 7.5 in), a length of 10.58 m (34 ft 8.5 in), and an empty weight of 1,642 kg (3,650 lbs). The DFS 228 was towed to an altitude of about 10 km and released. Then it was powered by a Walter 109-509 rocket engine, with a maximum speed of 900 km/h (559 mph), a range of 1,050 km (652 miles), and a ceiling of 25 km (82.021 ft). The engine could be used intermittently to save fuel and increase range. The machine was operated by one pilot who sat in a prone position in a pressurized cockpit placed in the nose; in an emergency, the pilot's compartment could be detached and descend by parachute until the cone reached life-supporting air pressure; then the pilot and his seat would be ejected from the

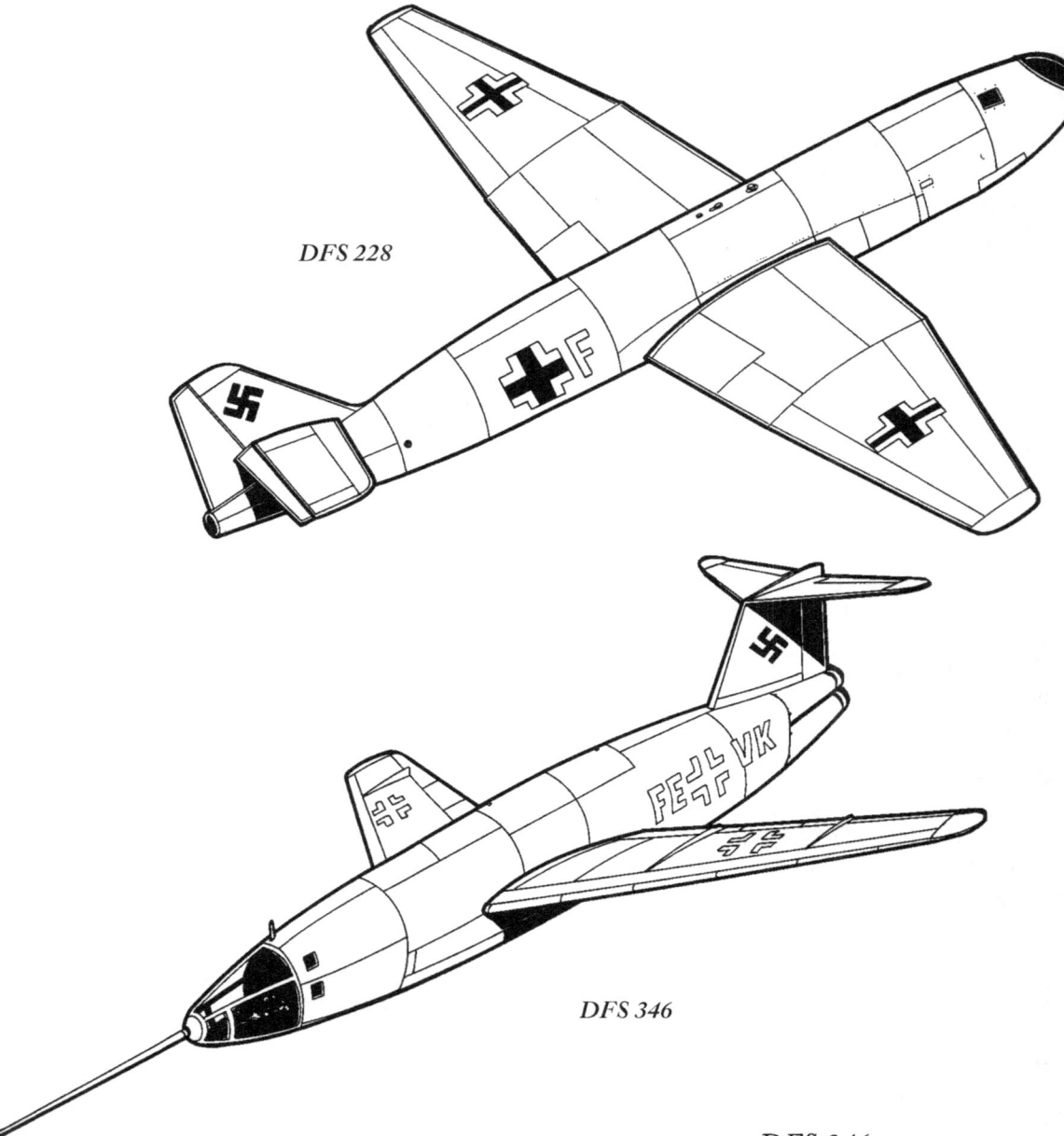

DFS 228

DFS 346

compartment make a normal parachute descent. The machine was not armed but fitted with infrared cameras. The project was started in 1940 but soon shelved by pressure of other work, and finally reactivated in 1943. Two prototypes were built, and several gliding flights where made without rocket engine. The DFS was attached on struts and launched from a bomber, Dornier Do 217K. It landed on a skid after fuel was exhausted. The aircraft never went further than the test level.

DFS 346

The DFS 346 was another design by the German Institute for Sailplane Flight for a fast, high-altitude, single-seat, reconnaissance airplane. Its used several features of the previously discussed DFS 228, notably the jettisonable pressurized cockpit, and the take-off (from a bomber) and landing (on skid) procedure. The aircraft had a length of 11.65 m (44 ft 1 in), and swept back wings fitted with small aerodynamic fences, with a span of 8.9 m

9. Miscellaneous Aircraft

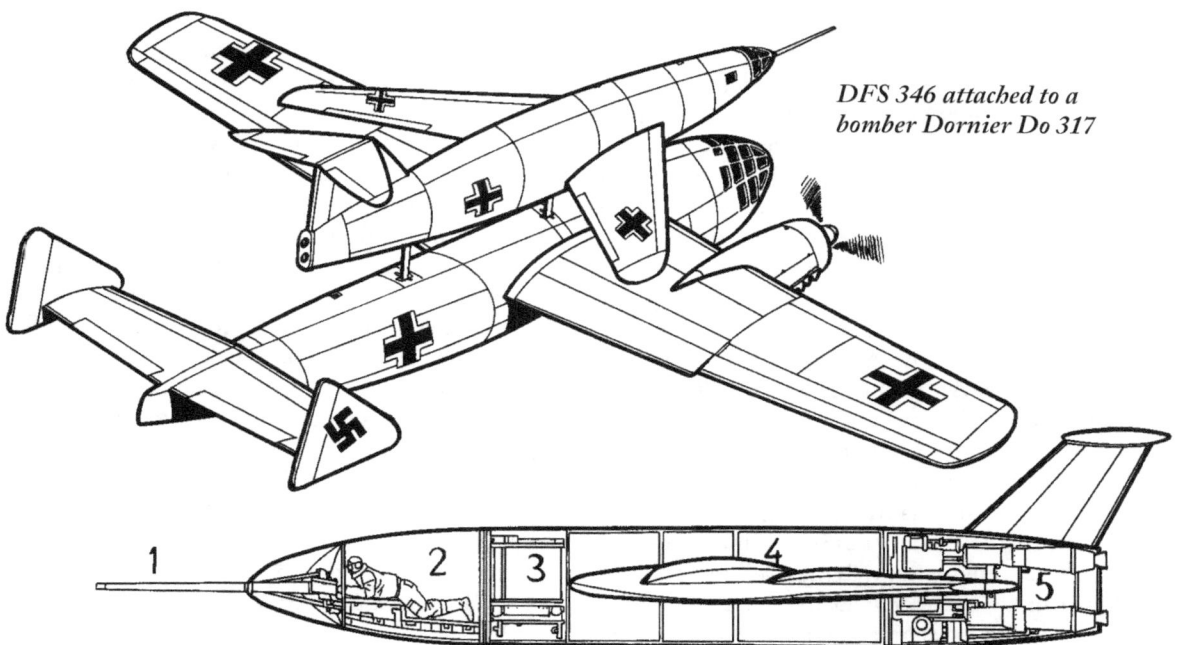

DFS 346 attached to a bomber Dornier Do 317

Cross-section DFS 346. 1: Pitot tube. 2: Jettisonable nose cockpit with pilot in prone position. 3: Instrumentation. 4: Fuel tanks, one containing T-Stoff (a highly caustic solution of hydrogen peroxide and a stabilizing chemical) and the other filled with C-Stoff (a hydrazine hydrate/methanol/water mixture). 5: Walter HMK rocket engine (two units).

(29 ft 6 in). It was powered by two Walter HWK 109-409B liquid rocket engines (2000 kg thrust each) and was to have an astonishing supersonic speed of 2,765 km/h (1,723 mph). Weapons were not mounted, as the aircraft was too fast to be intercepted, but it was intended to carry cameras. In 1945 one prototype was under construction at the Siebel factory at Halle. It was captured by Soviet troops and documents seized. After the war the Russians built three prototypes, designated Samolyot 346. Various tests were carried out in the postwar period until 1948 when the program was abandoned. There was a yet more advanced project, known as the DFS 346 III; except for a wooden mock-up, this too was never developed.

Trainers, Liaison and Utility Planes

As all other air forces of World War II, the Luftwaffe had a fleet of trainer, liaison and utility aircrafts. Many were obsolete discarded machines, but some were designed, built and used for these specific purposes. Some of them acted as progenitors to a wide variety of postwar military and civil light-aircraft designs. Within each *Fliegerkorps* there was a *Kurier-Staffel* primarily intended for liaison with army commanders. These aircraft were at the disposal of army personnel as well as the Luftwaffe. The higher commands, OKW (Army), OKH (ground forces) OKM (Navy) and OKL (air force), each had their own *Kurier-Staffel* to carry mail and personnel. These airplanes operated on a fixed schedule over all of Germany and the occupied territories. The civilian airline company Lufthansa continued to maintain transport operations under strict military supervision for high-priority communication.

Light airplanes were used for all manner of tasks, including operational missions. A number of transport aircraft were designed for highly specialized services such as ambulance with an airborne medical unit. Some were fitted with skis for transporting personnel and supplies into areas made inaccessible by snow. Light transport planes were also involved for covert operations, flying clandestine flights behind enemy lines, even in remote, confined sites, for example, to bring or pick up secret agents, rescue personnel, deliver weapons or documents. The light aircraft was also the obvious solution to rescue airmen who had been shot down over enemy territory.

Light airplanes were, of course, widely used for training. Luftwaffe training was the responsibility of the Air Ministry Training Inspectorate. All prospective Luftwaffe personnel were sent to *Fliegerausbildungsregimenter* (Air Force Initial Training Regiments) where for six weeks to three months they received military basic infantry training. Upon completion of the initial training, pilot candidates entered elementary flying training schools. Personnel to be trained for the aircrew positions of flight engineer, gunner, wireless operator, and observer were enrolled in their respective individual schools.

Pilot candidates proceeded to and began their actual flight training in the *Flugzugführerschulen* A (Elementary Flying Training Schools). All pupils took Course No. 1, a brief glider course, followed by Course No. 2, a preliminary course in powered aircraft. Unsuitable trainees were eliminated, and those acceptable were assigned to bomber or fighting training upon determination of their qualifications. Students in single-engine, fighter-pilot training continued through Course No. 3 for preliminary instruction in fighter aircraft, including aerobatics and formation flying. Then they progressed to specialized *Jagdschule* (Fighter School) where they learned to fly operational fighter types, but also received instruction in gunnery, blind flying and formation flying. Pilots then received intensive combat training prior to joining an operational unit. The total time necessary to train a fighter pilot was from seven to eight months, with a flying time from 107 to 112 hours.

Bomber, reconnaissance, ground attack, and twin-engine pilots were sent to a *Flugzeugführerschule* B (Advanced Training School). Here they were instructed in the handling of multi-engine aircraft, in blind flying, instrument flying, and the use of direction-finder apparatus. This period lasted for two or three months. From the advanced training school, bomber pilots were sent to a specialized bomber school where, during six to seven months, they learned gunnery, blind flying, bad-weather flying, and techniques for day or night attack. Ground-attack students went to a *Schlachtschule* (ground-attack school) where for about five months they were trained in dive bombing, strafing, aerobatics, and navigation. Students in reconnaissance aircraft proceeded to *Fernaufklärerschule* (reconnaissance school) where they were instructed in aerial photography, visual reconnaissance, map reading and navigation.

From the initial training regiment, prospective aircrew members proceeded to their respective specialist schools for a one to two months training: *Aufklärungschule* (observer's school), *Luftnachrichtenschule* (wireless telegraphy school), *Fliegerschützenschule* (air gunnery school), and *Fliegertechnischeschule* (flight engineer's school). Upon completion of their various courses, the specialist personnel were assembled with pilots to form combat aircrews.

Heinkel He 72 Kadett

The He 72 *Kadett* (Cadet) was one of the most important Luftwaffe primary trainers. The biplane aircraft made its first flight in 1933, and a year later some 100 He 72A (powered by one 140-hp Argus As 8B inverted, in-line, air-cooled engine) were built and used by civilian flying clubs and the NSFK (Nazi Flying Corps). By early 1934, a more powerful version was designed, known as Heinkel He 72 B with one 160 hp Siemens Sh 14A 7 cylinder radial engine. The production of the He 72 B continued well after 1936 and totaled several thousand in various, versions including the improved He 72 B3, the He 72BW (seaplane fitted with float), and the He 172 with engine in a slim NACA cowl. The He 72 remained one of the standard German air force training airplanes until 1944, and it was also used for military communications, liaison duties, and reconnaissance work. Some units also served as a flying testbed for the development of the liquid-fuelled Walter rocket engine. The Heinkel He 72 had a crew of two, consisting of train-

9. Miscellaneous Aircraft

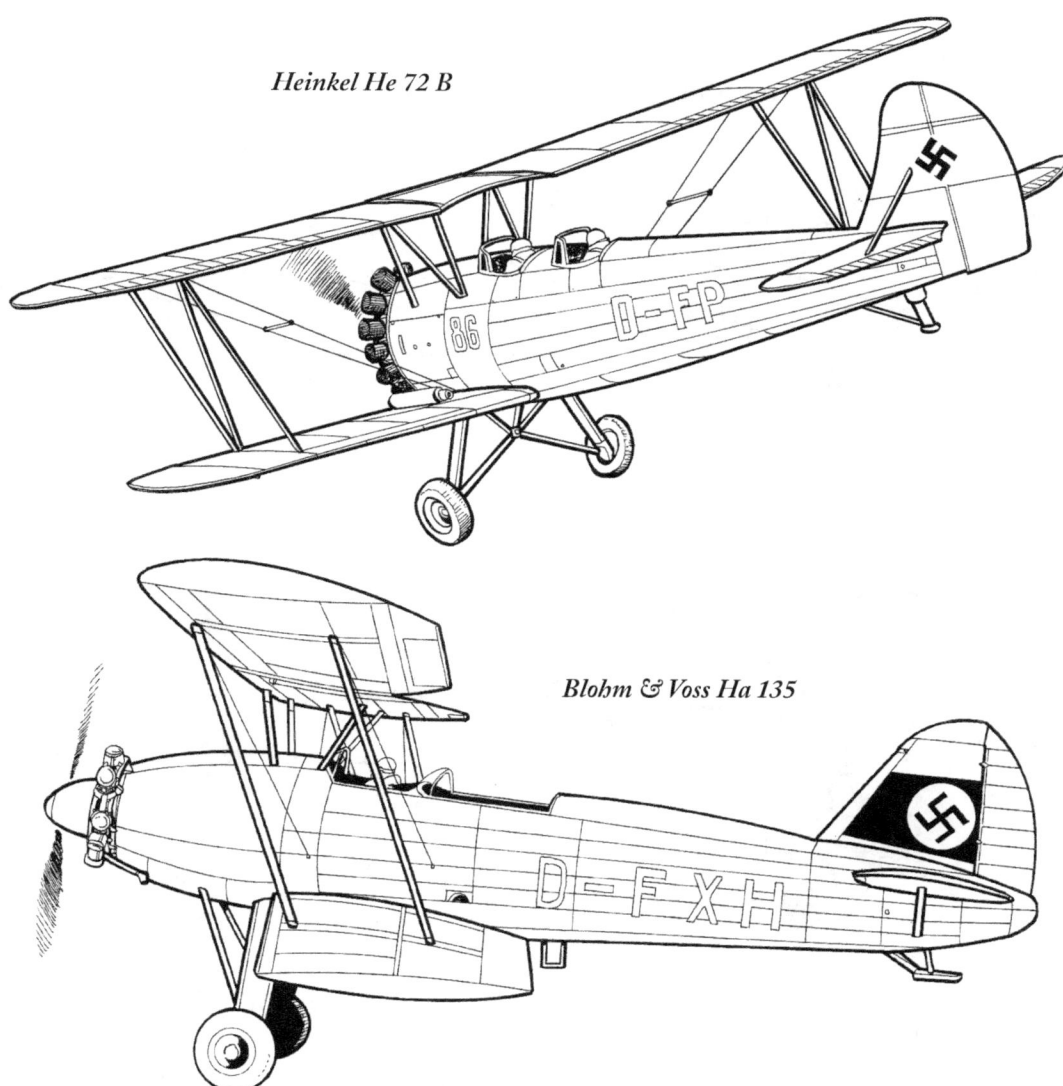

Heinkel He 72 B

Blohm & Voss Ha 135

ing pilot and pupil. It had a span of 9 m (29 ft 6 in), a length of 7.5 m (24 ft 7 in), a height of 2.7 m (8 ft 10 in), and an empty weight of 540 kg (1,191 lbs). Maximum speed was about 185 km/h (115 mph) and typical range was 820 km (510 miles).

Blohm & Voss Ha 135

The Ha 135, designed by engineer Rheinhold Mewes of the Hamburger Flugzeugbau (later Blohm & Voss Company), was a two-seat biplane trainer with sturdy fixed landing gear. First flown in the late spring of 1934, it was powered by a BMW-Bramo Sh 14A radial engine rated at 160 hp. The aircraft had a maximum speed of 205 km/h (127 mph), a service ceiling of 5,750 m (18,865 ft) and a range of 795 km (494 miles). Wingspan was 9 m (29 ft 3.5 in), length was 9.6 m (31 ft 6 in) and empty weight was 520 kg (1,146 lbs). It offered accommodation for instructor and pupil in open cockpit. Made of metal and wood, covered with fabric, the Ha 135 was an unremarkable aircraft. Only one prototype was made.

Klemm L25 and 35 D

The L 25 was designed in 1927 by the Klemm Leichtflugzeugbau (Light Aircraft

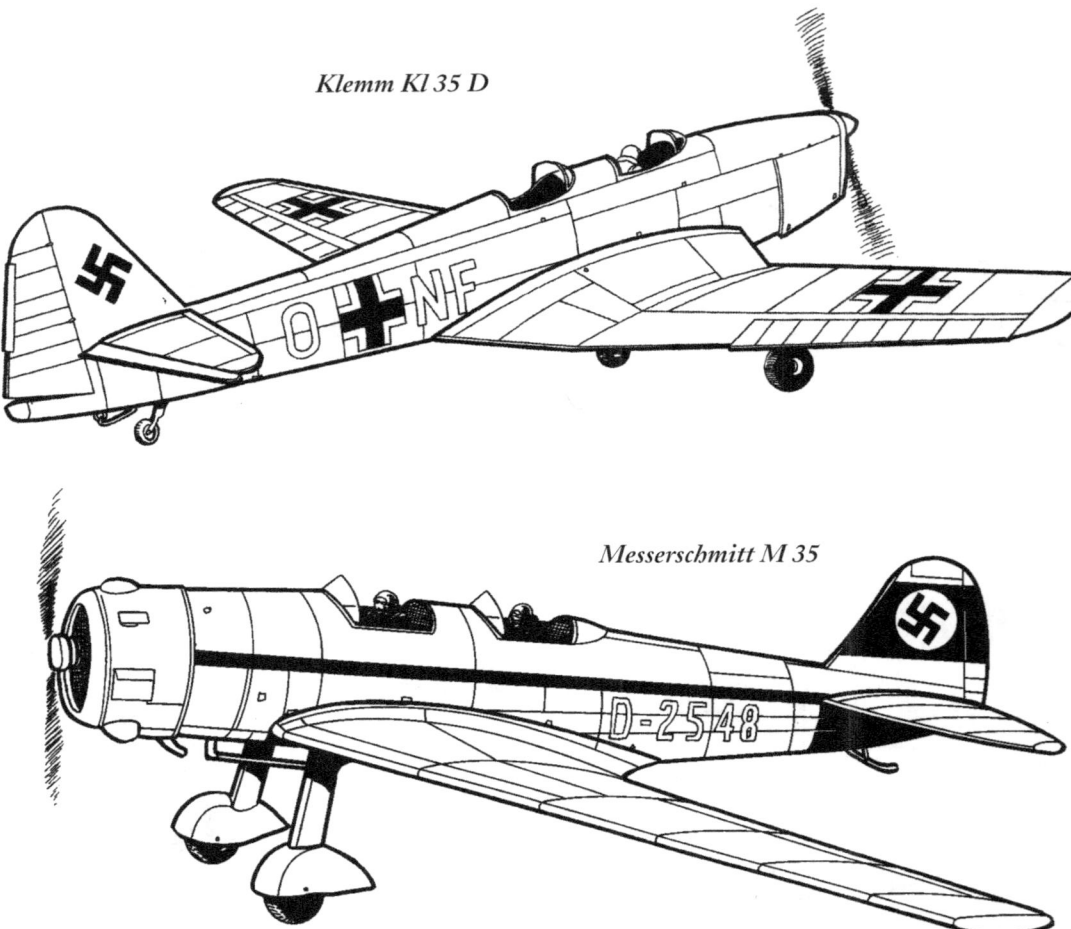

Klemm Kl 35 D

Messerschmitt M 35

Company) led by Dr. Hans Klemm, located at Boblinggen. It was a small low-wing monoplane with a span of 42 ft 8 in used as a trainer and liaison airplane operated by a crew of two (pilot and pupil). It was powered by a Hirth HM 60 R air-cooled radial engine developing 80 hp, and had a speed of 99 mph. It had a fixed landing gear which could be replaced by skis or floats. Six hundred units were produced for civilian and military use. The series was continued with the improved Klemm Kl 35 from 1935 and the Kl 35D from 1938, which had a more powerful Hirth HM504 A-02 engine. The Kl 31 and Kl 32 were four-seat cabin monoplanes used for liaison duties. The Klemm aircraft played a notable role as Luftwaffe trainers. They were also extensively exported and built under license in Sweden and Britain before World War II.

Messerschmitt M 35

First flown in March 1935, the trainer M 35 had a length of 7.7 m, a height of 2.75 m, a span of 11.57, a wing area of 17 square m, and an empty weight of 500 kg. Powered by one Argus As 8 or a Sh14A, it had a maximum speed of 218 km/h, a range of 740 km and could climb to 1,000 m in 3.9 minutes. Only fifteen units were built, one sold to Rumania and another sold to Spain.

Junkers Ju 60 and Ju 160

The Junkers Ju 60, which made its first flight in November 1932, was intended to be a light transport aircraft. Its overall concept was similar to the Junkers W 34. The aircraft was powered by a Pratt & Whitney Hornet A2 9-cylinder radial engine. At first the Ju 60 had a

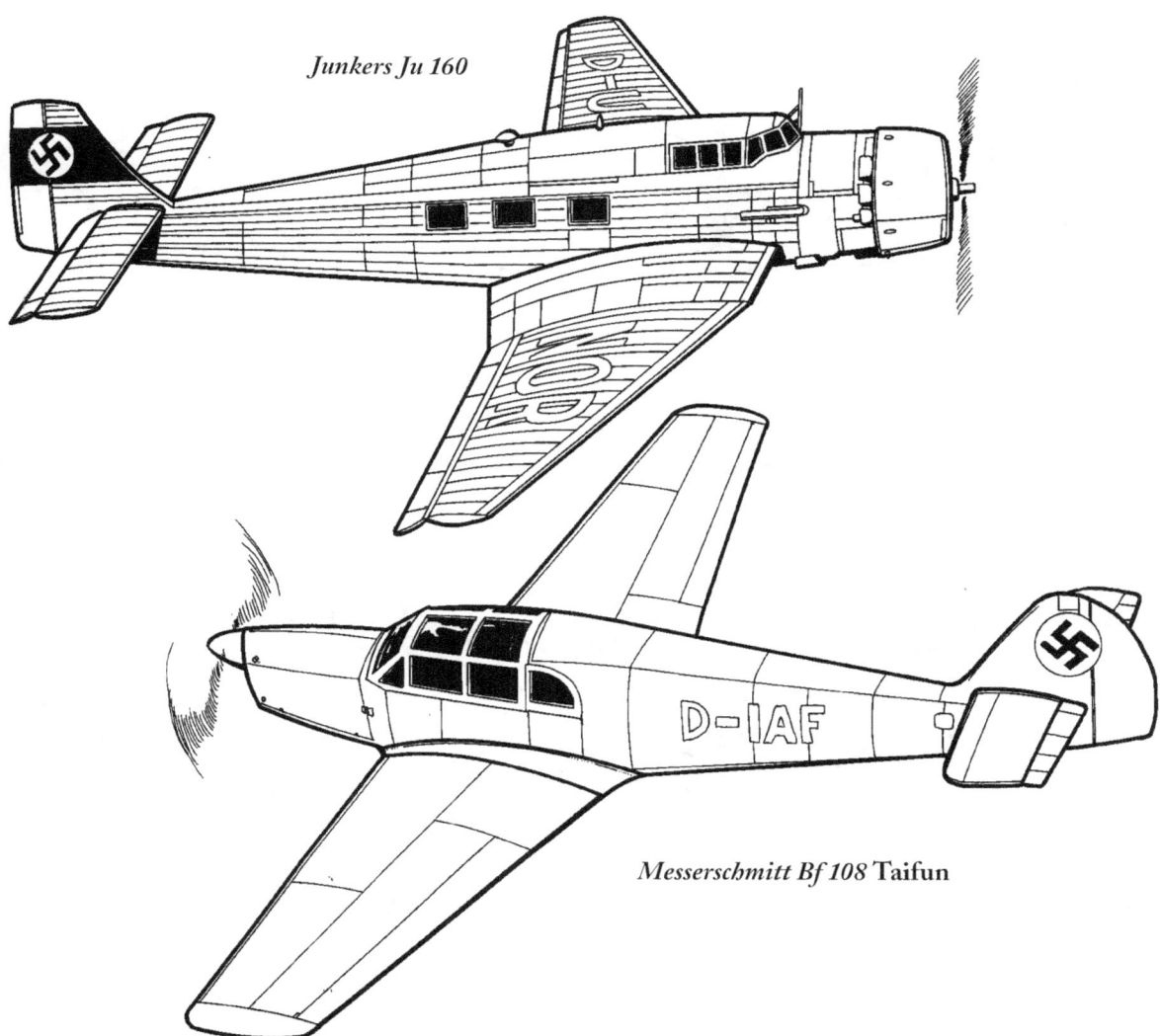

Junkers Ju 160

Messerschmitt Bf 108 Taifun

fixed main landing gear, later modified to be retractable into bulging wing fairings. It had a crew of two and could transport six passengers. The production model, known as the Ju 160, was slightly improved, thanks to being powered by one BMW 123 E radial engine. Forty-eight were built and used by the civilian airline company Lufthansa in 1936. In 1939, fourteen Ju 160 were militarized and used in the Luftwaffe in the liaison role.

Messerschmitt Bf 108 Taifun

The cabin monoplane Bf 108 *Taifun* (typhoon) was a liaison and communication aircraft designed by Willy Messerschmitt's Bayerische Flugzeugwerke (Bf). A very advanced design with numerous innovations, it was probably the best and most modern four-seater before the outbreak of World War II. The Bf 108 was the machine that established the Messerschmitt Company's name in aircraft design. Originally built to compete in the Challenge of Tourism Internationale race in 1934, the successful aircraft attracted RLM's attention. It was operated by one pilot and could carry three passengers. It had a length of 8.29 m (27 ft 2.5 in), a span of 10.62 m (34 ft 10 in), and a height of 2.3 m (7 ft 6 in). It was powered by one 240-hp Argus As 10C inverted-V-8, air-cooled engine. Maximum speed was 315 km/h (196 mph) and range with four passen-

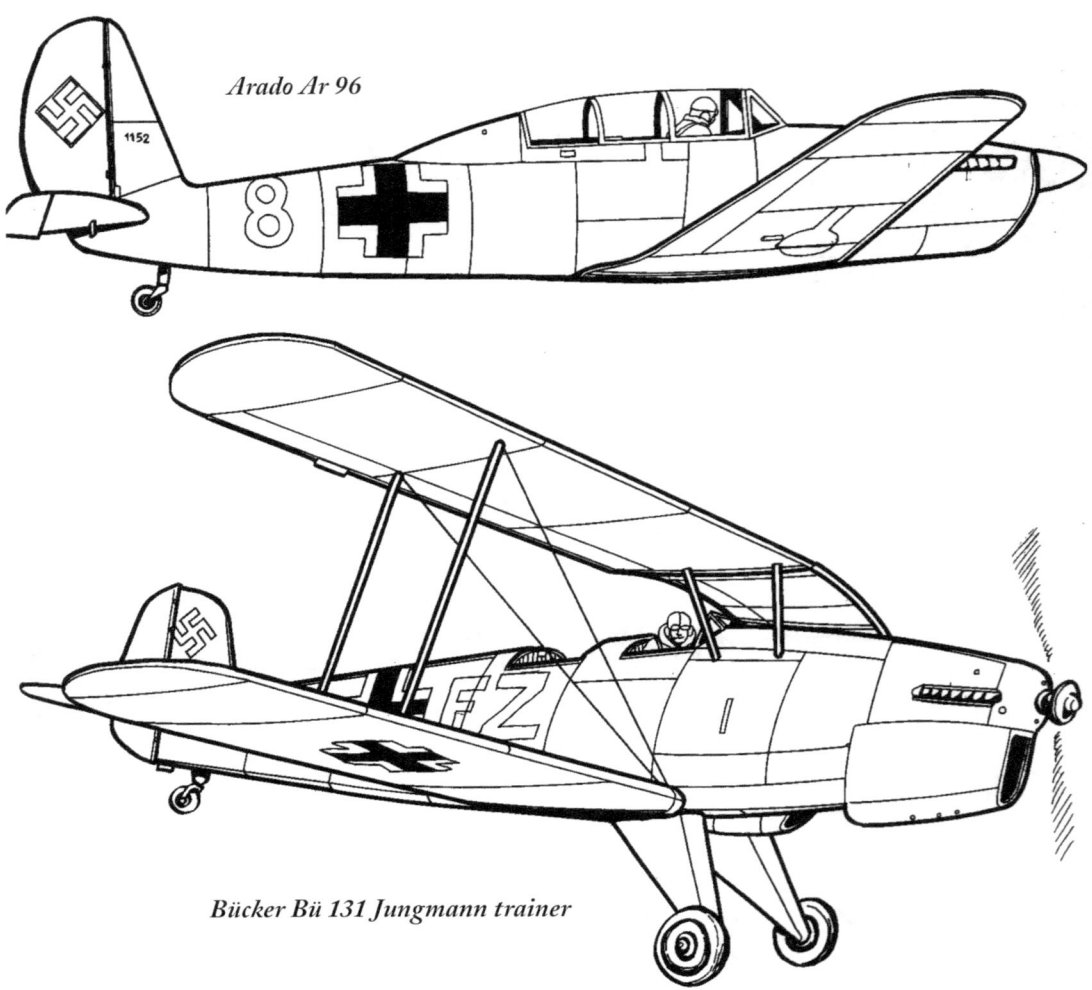

Arado Ar 96

Bücker Bü 131 Jungmann trainer

gers was 1,400 km (870 miles). The *Taifun* served extensively with the Luftwaffe with a variety of tasks, including target towing, rescue, VIP fast transport, and communications. A total of 887 were built. Production was continued after the war in France by the Nord Company, and some examples are probably still in flying condition today.

Arado Ar 96 and Ar 396

The Arado Ar 96, designed by engineer Walter Blume, was the most important advanced trainer to serve with the German air force. The Ar 96 A version entered service in 1939, followed by the bulk production type B, which was intensively used after 1940. The aircraft had a crew of two: pilot and pupil. A typical Arado product with distinctive tail, clean stressed-skin structure and retractable landing gear, the B version was powered by one 465-hp Argus As 410A-1 inverted-V-12, air-cooled engine, and had a maximum speed of 330 km/h (205 mph) and a maximum range of 990 km (615 miles). It had a span of 11 m (36 ft 1 in), a length of 9.13 m (29 ft 12 in), a height of 2.6 m (8ft 6 in), and an empty weight of 1,295 kg (2,854 lbs). There were five main Ar 96 B subtypes of which a few could be used for bombing training and gunnery—in this case armed with one 7.92-mm MG 17 machine gun. Over 11,546 Ar 96s were produced during World War II, and the aircraft remained in production in Czechoslovakia until 1948. An advanced version, the Arado Ar 396, was manufactured by the French SIPA Company where

Bücker Bü 133 Jungmeister

it stayed in production as the S11 (wooden) and S12 (metal) after the war.

Bücker Bü 131 Jungmann

Designed by Carl Bücker and Anders Anderson, the Bü 131 *Jungmann* (Young Man) prototype made its first flight in April 1934. Delivered to the *Luftsportverband* (German Sport Aviation Association) in late 1934, the aircraft entered Luftwaffe service in 1935 as a primary trainer. A sound design, the Bü 131 had a crew of two, a span of 7.4 m (24 ft 3.5 in), a length of 6.62 m (21 ft 8.5 in), a height of 2.25 mm (7 ft 4.5 in), and an empty weight of 390 kg (860 lbs). The A-series was powered by a 80-hp Hirth HM 60R inverted four-inline engine, and the B-series by a 105-hp HM 504A-2 engine with a speed of 183 km/h (114 mph) and a range of 650 km (404 miles). Large numbers of subtype 131-B were produced during World War II, used by the Luftwaffe as trainers, but also as ground attackers on the Russian front in 1942. The Bü 131-B was also built under license in Czechoslovakia (known as C-104 or Tatra T 131), and manufactured by Japan which used it as army trainer (Kokusai Ki-86) and navy trainer (Watanabe K9W). Production of the successful *Jungmann* continued some years after the end of World War II.

Bücker Bü 133 Jungmeister

In 1935 Bücker and Anderson designed another aircraft: the single-seat, advanced, aerobatic trainer biplane Bü 133 *Jungmeister* (Young Master). The Bü 133 utilized many components of the Bü 131; it had a crew of one, a span of 6.6 m (21 ft 7.7 in), a length of 6 m (19 ft 9 in), a height of 2.2 m (7 ft 2.5 in), and an empty weight of 425 kg (937 lbs). After successful test flight in 1935, the Bü 133 soon earned itself a wonderful aerobatic reputation, went into production and entered Luftwaffe service in 1936. The C-series, the most produced, was powered by a 160-hp Siemens Sh 14A 4-cylinder radial engine, with a maximum speed of 220 km/h (137 mph) and a range of 500 km (311 miles). The aircraft was also manufactured by the Dornier company. Several hundred were produced during the war, and production went on after the war, notably a refined version built by the Spanish CASA aircraft company. Many private-owned vintage postwar Bü 133s still fly today in aerobatics competitions.

Bücker Bü 181 Bestmann

Designed as a sports and touring aircraft, the monoplane Bü 181 *Bestmann* (Best Man) made its first flight in February 1939, and became the standard basic Luftwaffe multi-

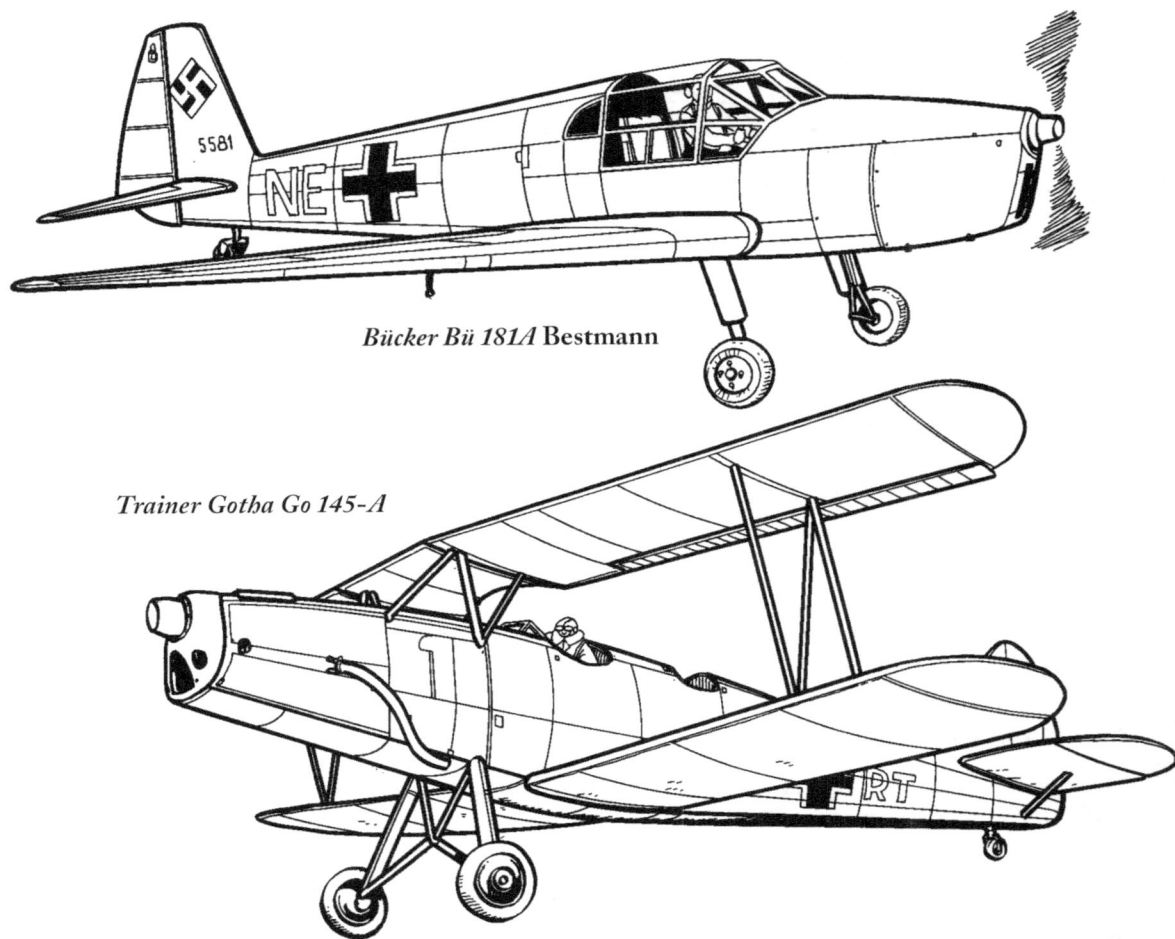

Bücker Bü 181A Bestmann

Trainer Gotha Go 145-A

purpose trainer in late 1940, gradually replacing the biplane Bü 133. The *Bestmann* was not armed, and it had a crew of two sitting side by side in a comfortable enclosed cockpit. It had a retractable carriage, a wingspan of 10.6 m (34 ft 9 in), a length of 7.85 m (25 ft 9 in), a height of 2.06 m (6 ft 9 in), and an empty weight of 480 kg (1,056 lbs). It was powered by a 105-hp Hirth HM 504 inverted 4-inline engine with a speed of 215 km/h (133 mph), and a range of 800 km (497 miles). The *Bestmann* was also used in a communication role, as a glider tug and a tactical weapons-transport aircraft. Some 5,900 units were produced during the war including 708 built by the Dutch Fokker Aircraft Company in Amsterdam. The *Bestmann* had a remarkably long, active life, as production continued after the war in Czechoslovakia and Sweden. The aircraft, in a slightly modified version known as Gomhouria, was still manufactured by the Egyptian Heliopolis Aircraft Company in the 1950s.

Gotha Go 145

A little-known and almost forgotten aircraft, the Gotha Go 145 was a biplane that made an important contribution to the Luftwaffe before and during World War II. Designed and built by the Gothaer Waggonfabrik AG, production was subcontracted to Ago, BFW/Messerschmitt, and Focke-Wulf. It was also built under license by CASA in Spain and Demag in Turkey. No less than 9,965 units were produced in Germany between 1935 and 1943, and more than a thousand in Spain and Turkey before and after the war. The Go 145 was a very conventional two-seat biplane made of wood with fabric covering. It had a length of 8.7 m (28 ft 6.5 in), a span of 9 m (29 ft 6.5

9. Miscellaneous Aircraft

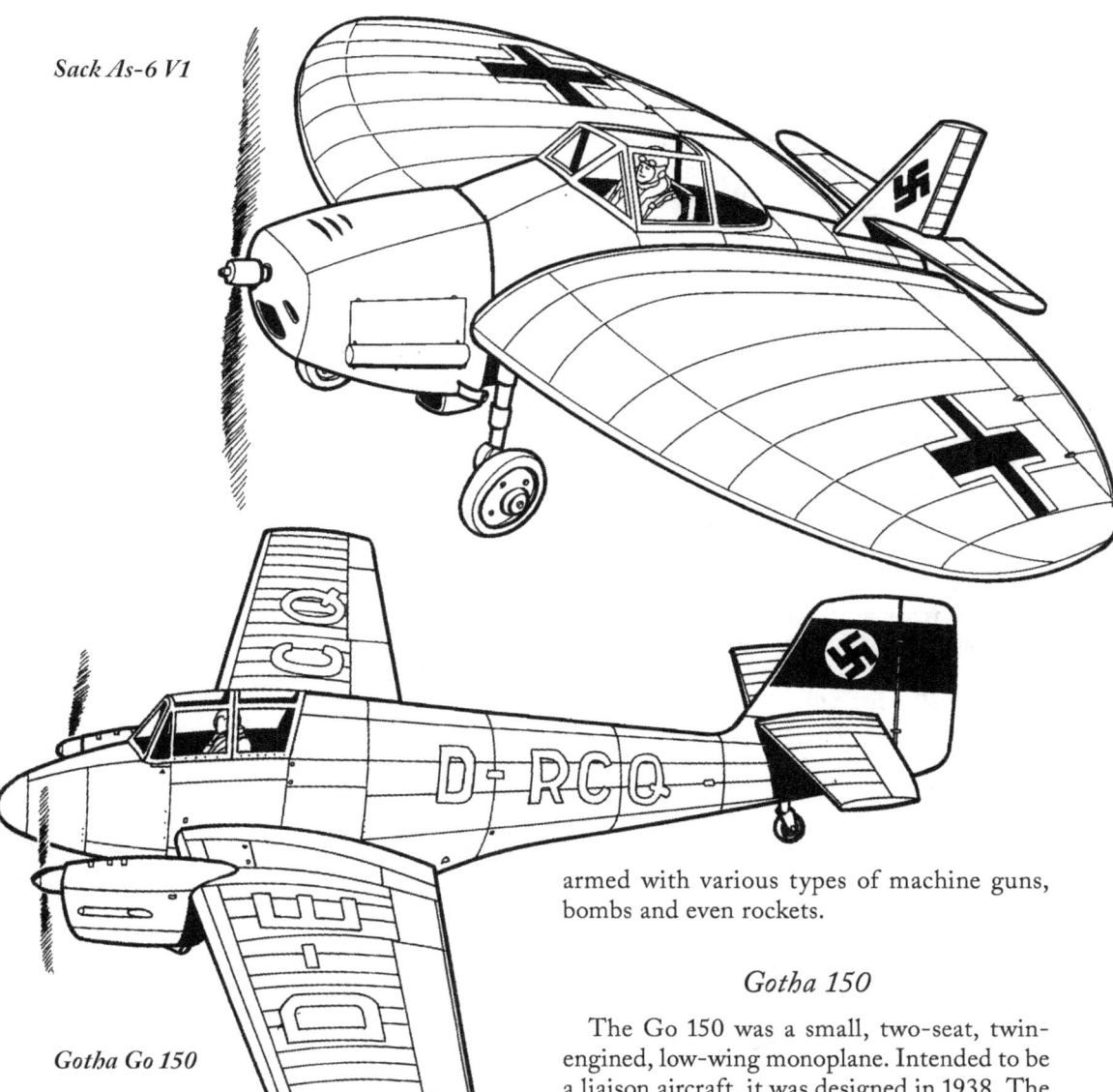

Sack As-6 V1

Gotha Go 150

in), a height of 2.9 m (9 ft 6.5 in), and an empty weight of 880 kg (1,940 lbs). Powered by one 240-hp Argus As 10C inverted-V-8, air-cooled engine, it had a maximum speed of 212 km/h (132 mph) and a typical range of 650 km (404 miles). First flown in February 1934, it entered service in the Luftwaffe in 1936 as a trainer aircraft. During World War II, the Go 145 remained a major Luftwaffe training aircraft, but a large number were also used as night harassment/ground attackers armed with various types of machine guns, bombs and even rockets.

Gotha 150

The Go 150 was a small, two-seat, twin-engined, low-wing monoplane. Intended to be a liaison aircraft, it was designed in 1938. The aircraft was fitted with an enclosed cockpit for the crew of two and a retractable landing gear. It had a span of 11.8 m, a length of 7.15 m, a height of 2.03 m, and an empty weight of 535 kg. It was powered by two Zündapp piston engines, and had a maximum speed of 200 km/h. Two prototypes were produced and a series of ten units was planned but not developed.

Sack As-6

Designed by engineer Arthur Sack, this odd little aircraft had a length of 6.4 m (21 ft). Operated by a single pilot, it used elements of cockpit and landing gear of the Messerschmitt Bf 109B and the 240-hp Argus As 10C-3 piston engine from the Messerschmitt Bf 108 *Taifun*. The most striking feature was the wing which was circular, made of plywood, and had a span of 5 m (16 ft 5 in) and an area of 19.62 square m (211 square ft). All-up weight was 900 kg. Flight tests, made in February and April 1944, proved unsuccessful, and the project was abandoned. The only prototype ever built was destroyed during an air raid in the winter of 1944-45.

Helicopters and Convertiplanes

A helicopter is a heavier-than-air craft powered by an engine that drives a rotary wing. The first flight with such a vertical take-off machine was made in November 1907 by the French bicycle maker and engineer Paul Cornu. The concept was further developed by Igor Sikorsky in Russia in the years 1909–10, and in the late 1930s after Sikorsky had emigrated to the United States. An autogyro is an aircraft with an unpowered rotary wing which autorotates as the machine is propelled through the air by a conventional power plant; it derives its lift from its own forward momentum, but it can take off only with a run, and cannot fly except in a forward direction. Autogyro was a trade name for that sort of aircraft made by the designer Juan de la Cierva who made the first major breakthrough with it in the 1920s in Spain.

The mid-1930s was a period of intensive research with the concept of rotary-wing flight, STOL (short take off and landing) and VTOL (vertical take off and landing). Right before the outbreak of the war, the Germans held most of the helicopter records for duration, distance, speed and height. Helicopters were hardly secret weapons, they were developed very publicly, and the army was quick to appreciate the operational possibilities the type opened up. Although World War II is not associated in the public mind with the use of helicopter, a number of designs was made by the major combatants. Several military helicopters were designed for use with the Luftwaffe but none saw widespread action. Active service was restricted but German World War II designs opened a new dimension of air warfare. Today the helicopter has replaced the glider and to some extent the parachutist. Originally seen in the transport, rescue and communication roles, the helicopter has now become a formidable fighting machine. It is most interesting that this apparently cumbersome, fragile, slow-flying means of transport has become so successful, even in the face of a determined enemy. The main reason is that the helicopter can land vertically in a small space

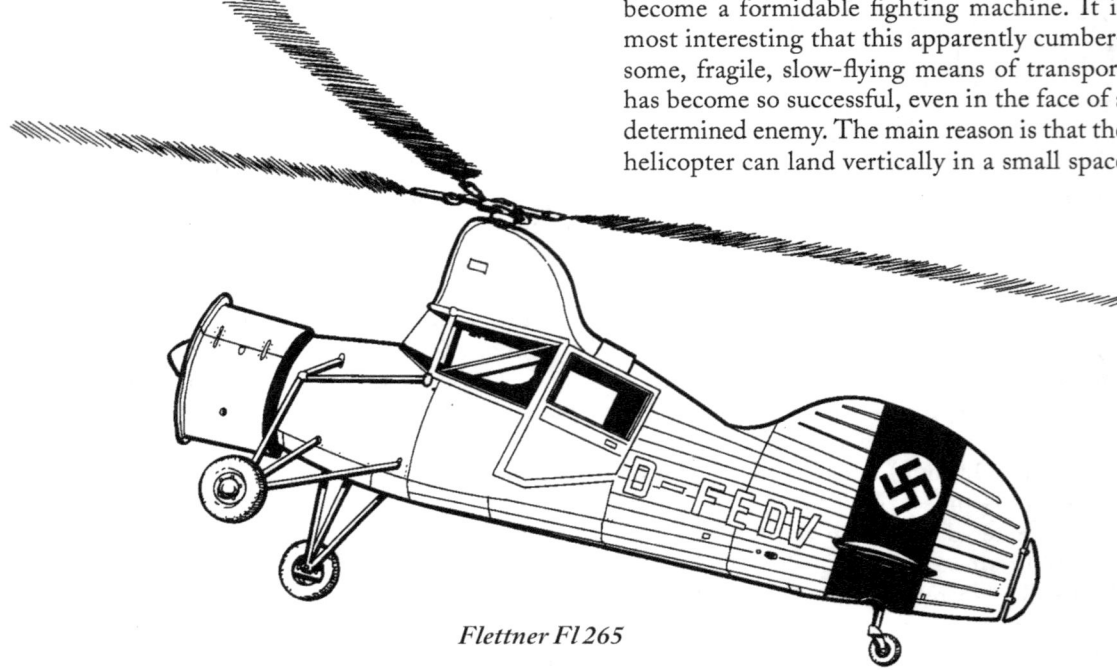

Flettner Fl 265

and take-off again. The introduction of the sky cavalry has undoubtedly given much increased tactical flexibility to the armies of today.

Flettner Fl 265

Designed by Anton Flettner, the Fl 265 made its first flight in May 1939. The single-seat helicopter was powered by one 160-hp Bramo SH 14A 7-cylinder radial engine. Six prototypes were built, and, in spite of accidents during tests, the results were encouraging and led to the design of the Flettner Fl 282.

Flettner Fl 282 Kolobri

Designed by the Anton Flettner Company, the Kolibri (Hummingbird) was derived from the Flettner Fl 265. The *Kolibri* was the first mass-produced helicopter in the world, and the only machine of that kind to have played a modest military role in World War II. Twenty-four units were built; they entered service in 1942 and proved useful and satisfactory machines used for transport and liaison as well as for land or sea observation from surface ships. A production order for 1,000 units was placed in 1944 but was terminated as a result of Allied bombardment. The Fl 282 was extremely maneuverable and very stable. It was powered by a 160-hp BMW-Bramo SH 14A 7-cylinder radial engine (located behind the pilot's seat), and the diameter of each two-blade main rotor was 11.96 m (39 ft 2 in). The length of the fuselage with open cockpit for the single pilot was 6.56 m (21 ft 6 in), height was 2.2 m (7 ft 2 in), and empty weight was 760 kg (1,675 lbs). Maximum speed was 60 km/h (37 mph) and range was about 300 km (186 miles).

Focke-Wulf Fa 61

Heinrich Focke and engineer Gerd Achgelis started the design for this autogyro/helicopter in 1932. One year after its maiden flight in June 1936, the Fa 61 achieved world records for duration, ceiling and average speed, beating comparable constructions by a wide margin. The Fa 61's fuselage and engine were practically identical to the well-known training aircraft Focke-Wulf Fw 44 Stieglitz. The Fa 61 was powered by one 7-cylinder rotary engine with 160 hp, it had a maximum speed of 120 km/h (75mph) and a range of 230 km (143 miles). Empty it weighed 800 kg (1,760 lbs), and could carry a load of 150 kg (330 lbs). The rotor diameter was 7 m (23 ft), length was 7.3 m (24 ft), and height was 2.65 m (9 ft). The small propeller in front of the engine was exclusively used for cooling purposes, whereas speed and direction were controlled by rotor tilt. The craft was already equipped with an emergency rescue system that allowed the pilot, in case of an engine failure, to switch the rotor to idle, enabling him to sail back down

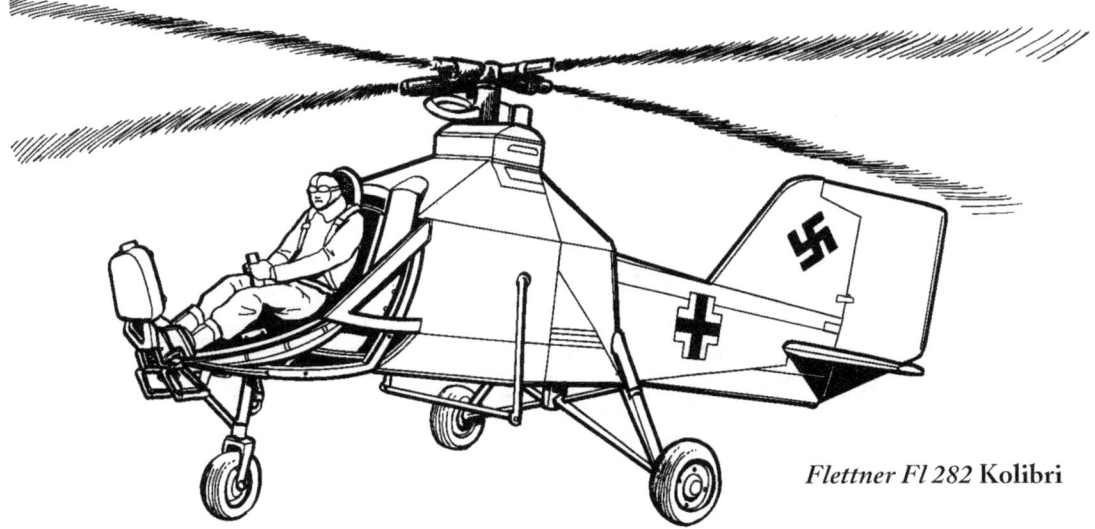

Flettner Fl 282 **Kolibri**

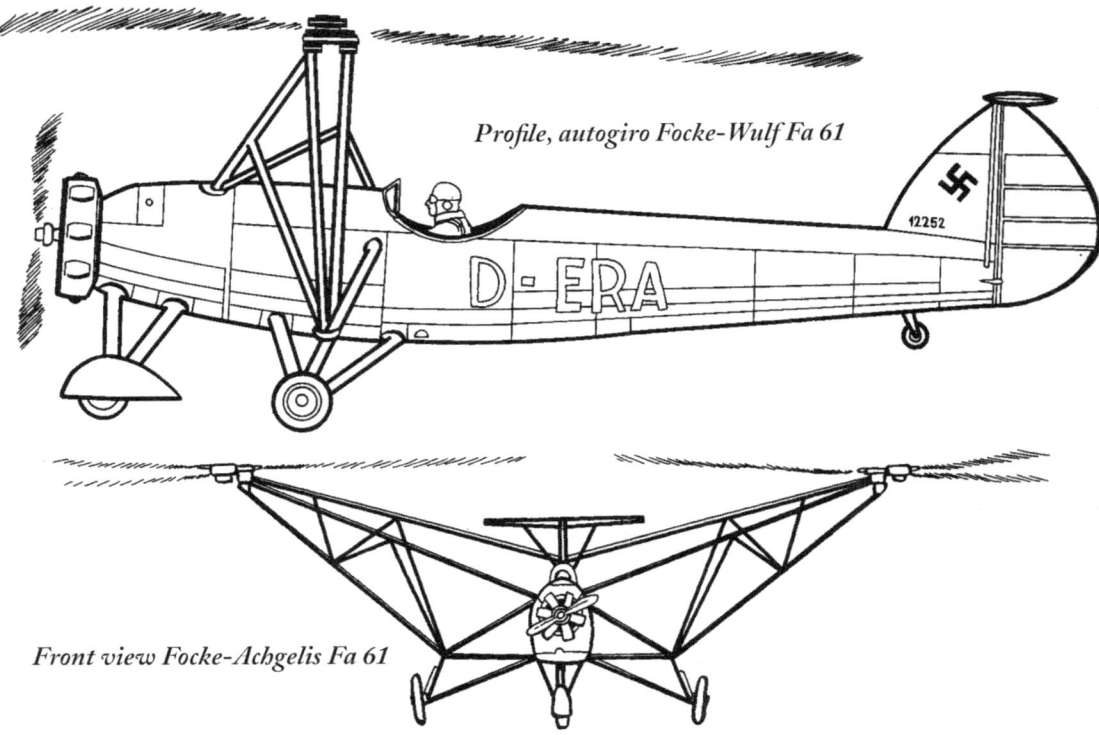

Profile, autogiro Focke-Wulf Fa 61

Front view Focke-Achgelis Fa 61

to the ground. To demonstrate the safety of the design, the famous Hanna Reitsch flew the Fa 61 in an indoor flying show in the Deutschlandhalle in Berlin in 1938.

Focke-Wulf Fw 186

Designed in 1937 by Professor Heinrich Focke, the Fw 186 was intended to be a Luftwaffe observation and army-cooperation autogyro. The Fw 186 was powered by one 240-hp Argus As 10C inverted-V-8, air-cooled engine, and had a speed of 180 km/h (112 mph). The aircraft was composed of the fuselage of the fighter Fw 56 Stösser with wings removed and fitted with one three-bladed rotor enabling vertical take-off and landing. Two prototypes were built, but the Fw 186

Autogiro Focke-Wulf Fw 186

Focke-Achgelis Fa 223 **Drache**

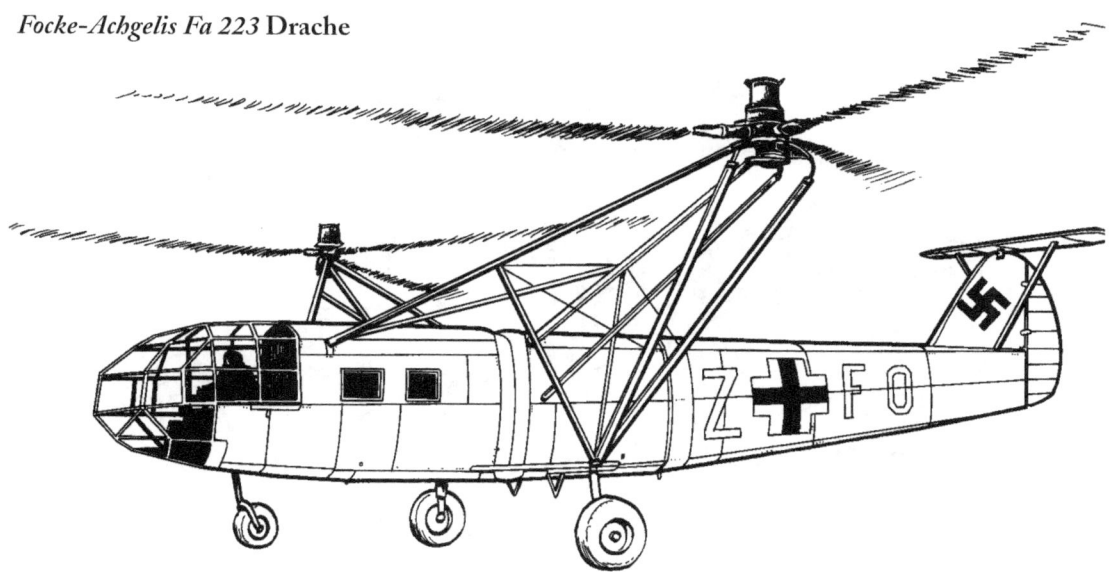

was not adopted. The Luftwaffe finally chose the Fieseler *Storch* as its STOL (short take-off and landing) standard observation aircraft.

Focke-Achgelis Fa 223 Drache

Designed in late 1940 by Heinrich Focke and engineer Gerd Achgelis, the Fa 223 *Drache* (Kite or Dragon) was a twin-rotor helicopter intended for transport, rescue, antisubmarine patrol, reconnaissance and training. The largest and most capable type of helicopter of its day, the wingless aircraft had a conventional tail unit and fuselage with a length of 12.25 m (40 ft 2.5 in) comprising the load compartment, fuel tanks, engine bay, and glazed cockpit for the crew of two (pilot and observer). It was powered by a 1,000-hp BMW 301R 9-cylinder radial piston engine which drove two large, side-by-side, three-blade rotors, each with a diameter of 12 m (39 ft 4.5 in), placed on large outriggers right and left of the fuselage; the total span was 24.5 m (80 ft 4.7 in). The helicopter had a maximum speed of 175 km/h (109 mph) and a range of 700 km (435 miles) with auxiliary fuel tank, and could carry a maximum cargo load of 1,280 kg (2,820 lbs). Thirty units were produced and tested for various roles in 1942. Equipment varied according to role, including a rescue winch and cradle, reconnaissance camera, auxiliary fuel tank and a MG 15 machine gun aimed by hand from the cockpit. Mass production was ordered—per month, but this program was interrupted by Allied air attacks, and only a few Fa 233s were used operationally, notably by *Lufttransportstaffel* 40. One Fa 223 acquired particular fame for a daring rescue mission on Mont Blanc (French Alps), the highest mountain peak in Europe (4,807 m). Development of the Fa 223 continued after the end of World War II in France (known as SE 3000) and Czechoslovakia.

Focke-Achgelis Fa 225

The experimental Fa 225 was a non-powered rotary-wing glider which consisted of the fuselage of a DFS 230 glider, the wings of which had been replaced by a three-blade Fa 223 rotor mounted on a structural pylon. The idea exploited the almost vertical or very steep descent to be obtained from rotary wings in autorotation, thus making possible landing in areas which were restricted by natural or artificial obstacles. Besides, the glider's landing run could be shortened by nose braking rockets. The rotor diameter was 12 meters. With a gross weight of 905 kg, the Fa 225 was to be hauled at a speed of about 190 km/h by a Ju 52, and would then be able to land within not more than 18 m (59 ft). Tested in 1943, this glider was never put to practical use, probably

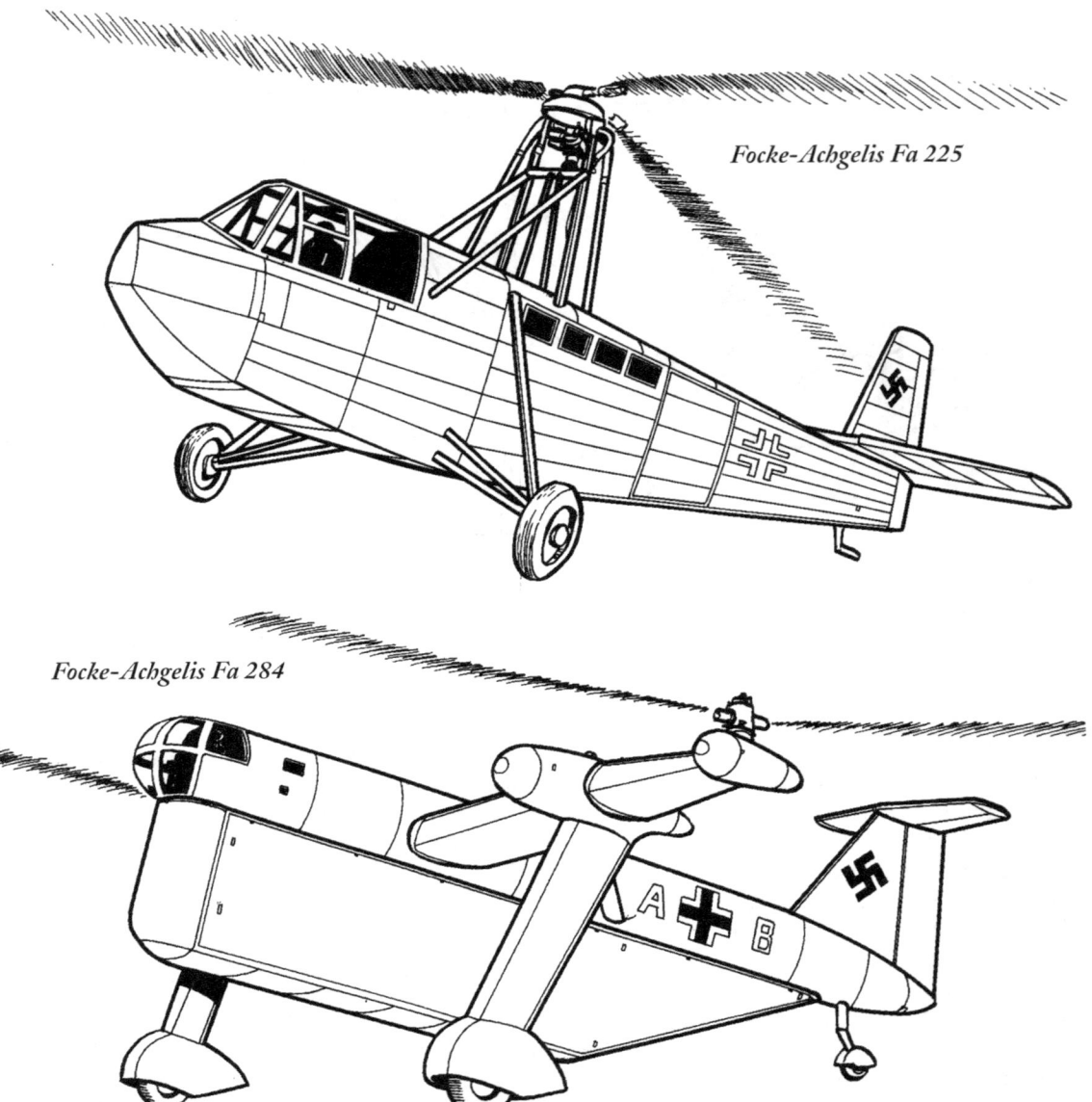

Focke-Achgelis Fa 225

Focke-Achgelis Fa 284

because of changing operational requirements, and possibly because its advantages were counterbalanced by the fact that the towing speed was considerably lower than that of the standard DFS 230, and it would have been more vulnerable to attack.

Focke-Achgelis Fa 284

Designed in 1943, the Fa 284 was a large transport helicopter. The machine had a conventional fuselage and tail unit with a length of 18.6 meters. It was fitted with two small wings, each mounted with a BMW 801 piston engine (1600 hp each) which drove two huge opposite-rotating rotors, each with a diameter of 16 meters. Total span of the Fa 284 was 37.3 m and speed was to be 230 km/h. A maximum load of 3,000 kg could be carried, housed in a large detachable container located under the fuselage. This made necessary the use of a long fixed landing gear composed of two strong wheeled legs and a tail-wheel. The project was never developed but this advanced design was

9. *Miscellaneous Aircraft* 383

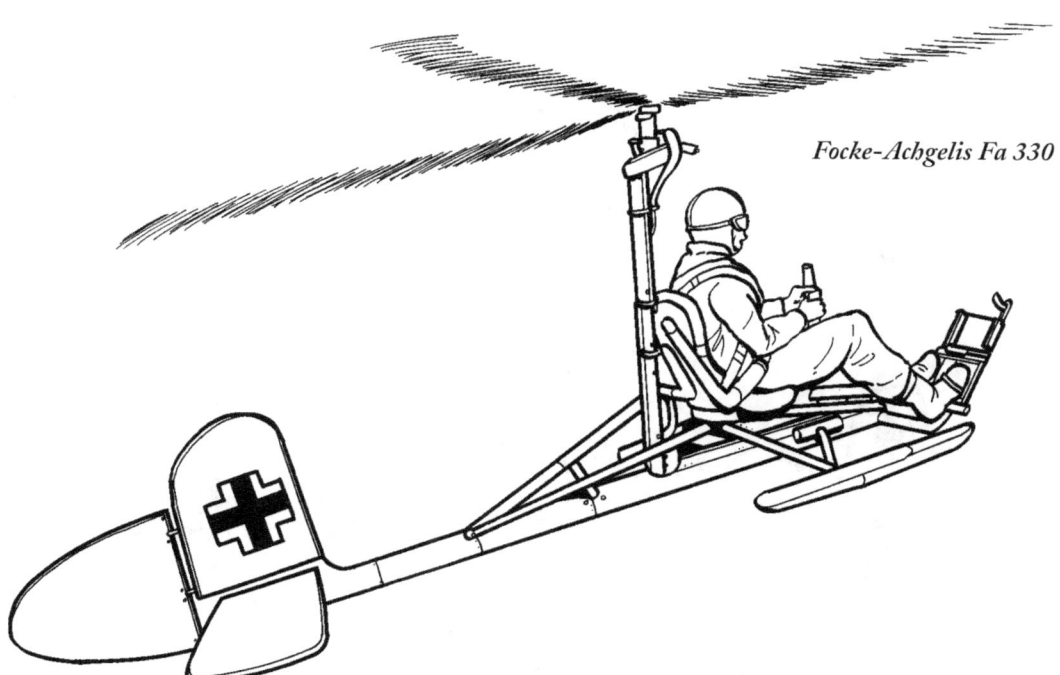

Focke-Achgelis Fa 330

probably the inspiration for a number of post–World War II sky cranes.

Focke-Achgelis Fa 330

The Fa 330 *Bachstelze* (Wagtail) was not a true helicopter but an unpowered gyro-kite. It consisted of a seat for the pilot, a frame made of steel tubes, a landing gear composed of two small skids, and an unpowered overhead rotor. The three-blade pitch was such that the wind produced the lift. The machine had a weight of 75 kg (165 lbs), and a length of 4.5 m (15 ft 8 in); the diameter of the three-blade rotor was 8.5 m (28 ft). The unarmed, one-person gyrokite Fa 330 was intended to serve as an observation machine launched from a submarine. It was stored in a metal container built into the submarine conning tower, assembled in a few minutes, and made airborne by the combination of wind and the speed of the surfaced submarine. It was attached to a cable and the pilot, flying at approximately 400 ft and a maximum towing speed of 25 mph, could scan the horizon for targets; he communicated with the U-boat crew by mean of a telephone. The machine was designed by Focke-Achgelis in 1942, and the production was in the hands of Weser Flugzeugbau in Hoyenkamp. About 112 (some sources report 200) were produced. The Fa 330 was a cheap and ingenious method to increase visibility from a surfaced submarine. Details about combat service are not available, but it seems that the machine was used in the South Atlantic, Gulf of Aden and Indian Ocean. However, problems encountered with rapid recovery of pilot and machine in the event of surprise attack led to its eventual withdrawal from active service.

Heliofly III/57

Designed in 1941 by the Austrian engineer Paul Baumgärtl, Heliofly was a portable "one-man backpack copter." The machine was powered by a 16-hp 8Ps Argus As 8 engine carried in a backpack held by straps and harness. The small engine weighed 35 kg and could lift a load of 120 kg. It drove two blades controlled by a rod swinging over the shoulder from the pack (throttling and tilting the engine). The diameter of the rotor was 6.1 meters. The "flying suit" was easy to assemble, don, and fold up after the flight. The end of World War II prevented further development and use of this project.

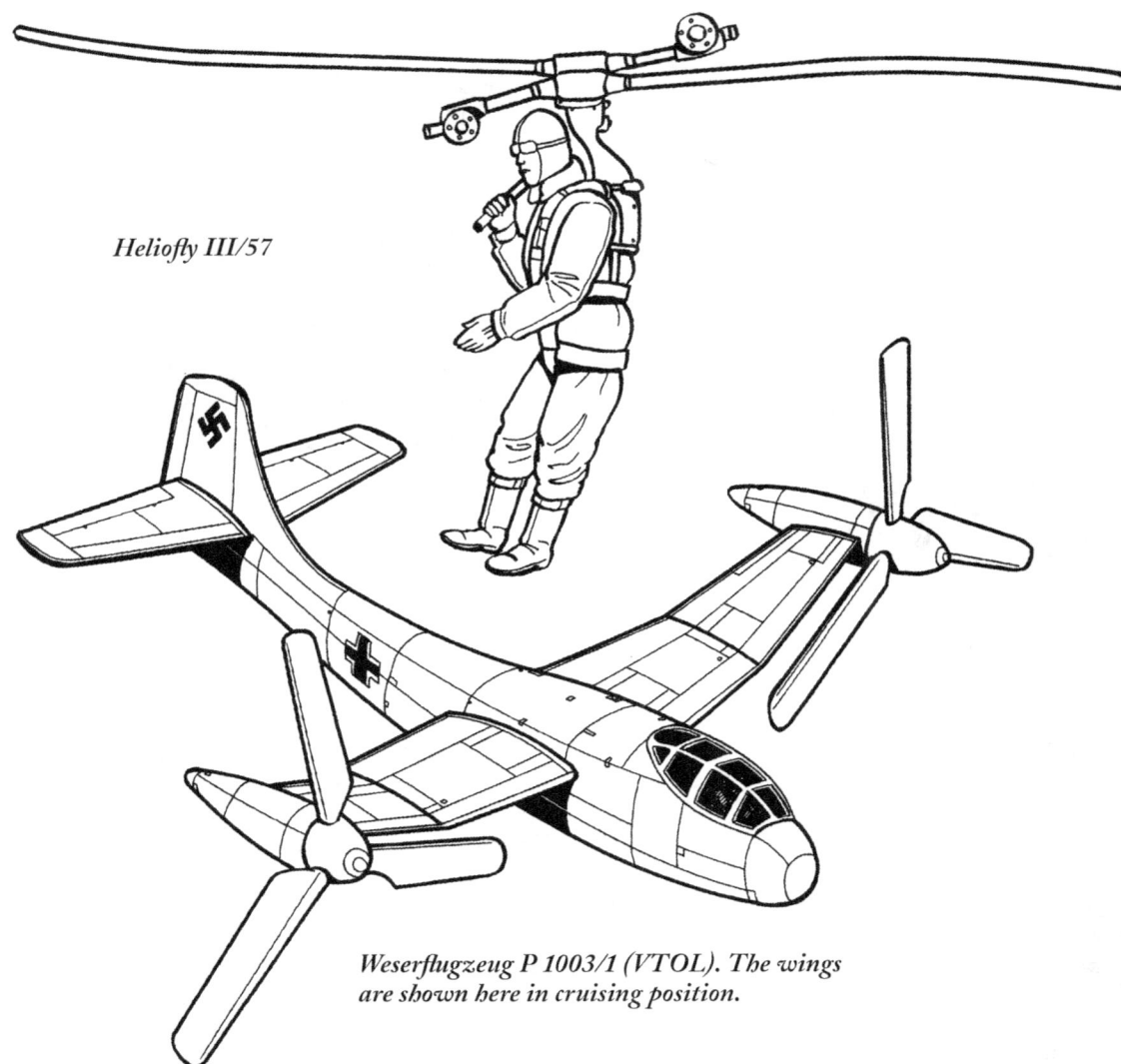

Heliofly III/57

Weserflugzeug P 1003/1 (VTOL). The wings are shown here in cruising position.

Weser P 1003/1

This experimental design from 1938 by the Weser Flugzeugbau Company was a "convertiplane" which was an attempt to combine the vertical take-off and landing of a helicopter with the high cruising speed and fuel economy of a normal aircraft. The P 1003/1, operated by a crew of two who sat in a cockpit located at the front, had a conventional fuselage with a length of 8.3 m (27 ft 3 in). The aircraft had two short, tiltable, hinged wings with a span (without propellers) of 7 m (22 ft 11 in). The power was provided by one Daimler-Benz DB 600 piston engine placed in the fuselage, which drove two large propellers with a diameter of 4 m (13 ft 2 in) placed at the end of each wing. For take-off and landing the wings pivoted in a vertical position and they moved into a horizontal position for flight, with an estimated speed of 650 km/h (404 mph). Due to the considerable and expensive development involved, the P 1003/1 project was abandoned in 1944. This novel design that never left the drawing board was the inspiration for a postwar development: the tilt-wing Boeing Vertol 76 (or VZ-2) that made its first flight on July 15, 1958, the Dornier Do 31 developed in 1967 to meet a NATO requirement, and the American-made Boeing V22 Osprey that flew in 1989.

9. Miscellaneous Aircraft

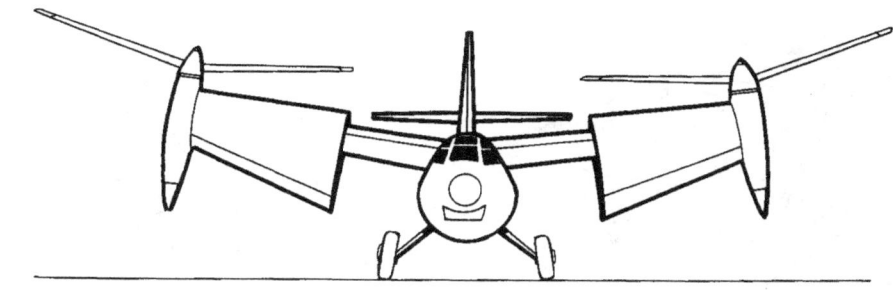

Weserflugzeug P 1003/1 (wing position for take-off and landing)

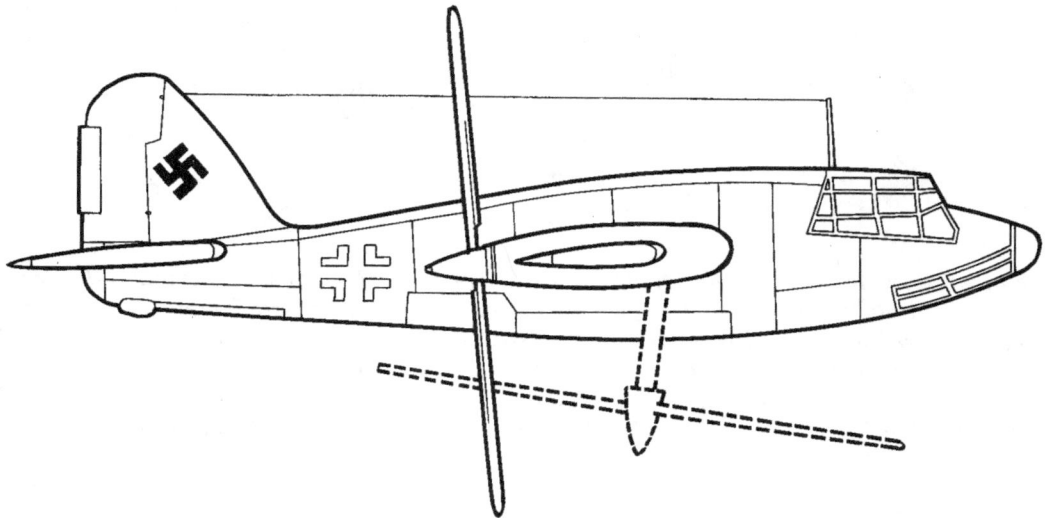

Focke-Achgelis Fa 269. The dotted line indicates the position of the propellers for take-off and landing.

Focke-Achgelis Fa 269

Designed in 1943, the Focke-Achgelis Fa 269 was another ambitious German "convertiplane" project. The twin-engined aircraft had a conventional fuselage and tail unit with a length of 8.9 m (29 ft 2.7 in). The wings had a span of 10 m (32 ft 10 in) and each of them carried either a Daimler-Benz DB 601 or a DB 605 piston engine, which drove a very large pusher propeller. A maximum speed of 600 km/h (373 mph) was expected. For take-off and landing, the propellers swiveled downward through about an 85-degree arc to a vertical position to lift the aircraft off the ground, and in flight they were moved upward into a normal rear-facing position. Very long landing-gear legs and tailwheel, which were retracted into the fuselage, were provided to give ground clearance to the propellers when the airplane was on the ground. The Fa 269 was to be operated by a crew of two sitting in a glazed cockpit placed at the front. Wind-tunnel tests were made, but the complicated project was abandoned in 1944.

Captured Foreign Aircraft

The employment of captured military material was a favored practice in the German army during World War II. Captured military equipment, including vehicles, artillery, tanks, weapons, uniforms, and, aircraft were collected, sorted, repaired and issued for further use by the Wehrmacht. Civilian aircrafts were also commandeered, but they were often flimsy by German military standards.

Captured Czech Avia B 534. The Avia B 534 was designed in 1933 and entered service in the Czech air force in autumn 1937. It was a single-seat biplane fighter with enclosed cockpit and fixed landing gear. It existed in several versions and the 534/4 had a span of 9.4 m and a length of 8.1 m, and was armed with four 7.92-mm Mk 30 machine guns. Powered by an Avia-built Hispano Suiza 12 Y DRS engine developing 830 hp, it had a maximum speed of 300 km/h and a range of 600 km. A total of about 445 were produced, a number of which were used by the Luftwaffe as trainers.

Captured Dutch Fokker G-1. The twin-boom, two-engined heavy fighter Fokker G-1, designed in 1936, was powered by either two Pratt & Whitney PW S B4 or two Bristol Mercury VIII piston engines. Maximum speed was 475 km/h and range 1,520 km. Flown by a crew of two or three, the aircraft had a span of 10.9 m, and was armed with four 7.92-mm machine guns mounted in the nose and one machine gun manually aimed by the radio operator in the rear cockpit. About 30 Fokker G1s were seized by the Germans after the capitulation of the Netherlands in May 1940, and used as trainers by the Luftwaffe.

Captured French Morane-Saulnier MS 406. The MS 406 fighter, designed in 1937, was powered by a 860-hp Hispano-Suiza 12 Y-31 engine. It had a maximum speed of 486 km/h, a length of 8.17 m and a span of 10.61 m.

Captured Lioré et Olivier LeO 451. The medium strategic bomber LeO 451, designed by engineer Pierre Mercier and manufactured by the SNCASE company, made its first flight in January 1937 and entered service in the French Armée de l'Air in 1938. The all-metal monocoque had a retractable landing gear, and double fin and rudder. It was operated by a crew of four (pilot, bomb aimer/radio operator/nose gunner, ventral gunner, and dorsal gunner), and had a length of 17.17 m (56 ft 4 in), a span of 22.52 m (73 ft 11 in), and a height of 4.24 m (17 ft 2 in). The two Hispano-Suiza 14 Aa 6/7 radial engines were on later models replaced with two 1,030-hp 14-cylinder, air-cooled Gnome-Rhône 14 20/21 radial engines. The aircraft had a maximum speed of 480 km/h (480 mph), a maximum ceiling of 9,000 m (29,530 ft) and a maximum range of 2,900 km (1,800 miles). Although mainly relying on high speed and altitude, the LeO 451 was armed with one 20-mm Hispano-Suiza Hs 404 machine gun placed in dorsal turret, one forward-firing 7.5-mm Mac 34 machine gun mounted in the glazed nose, and one 7.5-mm Mac 34 machine gun placed in a retractable "dustbin" ventral turret. The aircraft could carry a load of 1,500 kg (3,305 lbs) in bombs, stored in fuselage and wing root bays. Produced between 1938 and 1942, 561 LeO 451 were built. After the defeat of France, a number were captured by the Italians and the Germans and mainly used as unarmed transport and trainer aircraft. A few were used by the Free French Forces and by the U.S. Air Force in the North Africa campaign, in the role of ground attacker/bomber—soon replaced by more modern Martin B-26 Marauders. A few LeO 451s remained in service in the French Air Force until 1957.

Latécoère 298. The Laté 298 was designed by the Latécoère factory in Toulouse (southern France). The single-engined, mid-wing, cantiliver monoplane made its maiden flight in May 1936 and entered service in the French Marine Nationale in October 1938 as a torpedo bomber/dive bomber and reconnaissance floatplane. Operated by a crew of three (pilot, radio-operator and rear-gunner), the Laté 298 was powered by one 880-hp Hispano-Suiza 12 Y 12-cylinder, liquid-cooled piston engine, and had a maximum speed of 300 km/h (165 mph). Length was 12.56 m (41 ft 2.5 in), height 5.25 m (17 ft 1.75 in), and wingspan 12.56 m (50 ft 10.5 in). The aircraft was armed with three 7.5-mm machine guns: two fixed forward-firing, and one rear-firing placed in the rear cockpit and manually operated by the rear gunner. The Laté 298 could carry either one type 1926 DA torpedo, or a load of 680 kg (1,500 lbs) in bombs, or an equivalent payload of depth charges. About 121 units were built and served in the French Navy, a number of which were captured by the Germans after the defeat of 1940. The aircraft also served in the Free French Forces. It was retired from active service in 1947 but continued to be used as a trainer until 1951.

Aircraft taken over from defeated enemies alleviated the German army's desperate shortages but, on the whole, they played a negligible role in the World War II German Luftwaffe. Using captured foreign airplanes was indeed a mixed blessing, as the huge variety of them would have led to problems. Hundreds of different models of aircraft, either manufactured or plundered from all over Europe, would have created insolvable problems of maintenance, and would have required the acquisition and stocking of countless different spare parts, a situation which would have been almost impossible to administer. Some captured foreign aircraft were exhibited in the Aviation Museum in Berlin, others were sold to Germany's allies, for example, Bulgaria and Croatia. Most of them were used as trainers and only a few saw combat. They were modified to German standards, repainted in typical German camouflage, and given Luftwaffe markings.

The bloodless annexation of Austria and Czechoslovakia as early as 1938 and 1939 had given the Germans a huge production capacity. Czechoslovakia, particularly, had an ad-

Opposite, bottom: *Captured Italian Macchi C-202. Designed in 1941, the C-202 had a span of 10.58 m and a length of 8.87 m. Powered by a 850-hp Fiat engine (later version by a 1,200-hp Daimler-Benz 12 cylinder), it had a maximum speed of 530 km/h.*

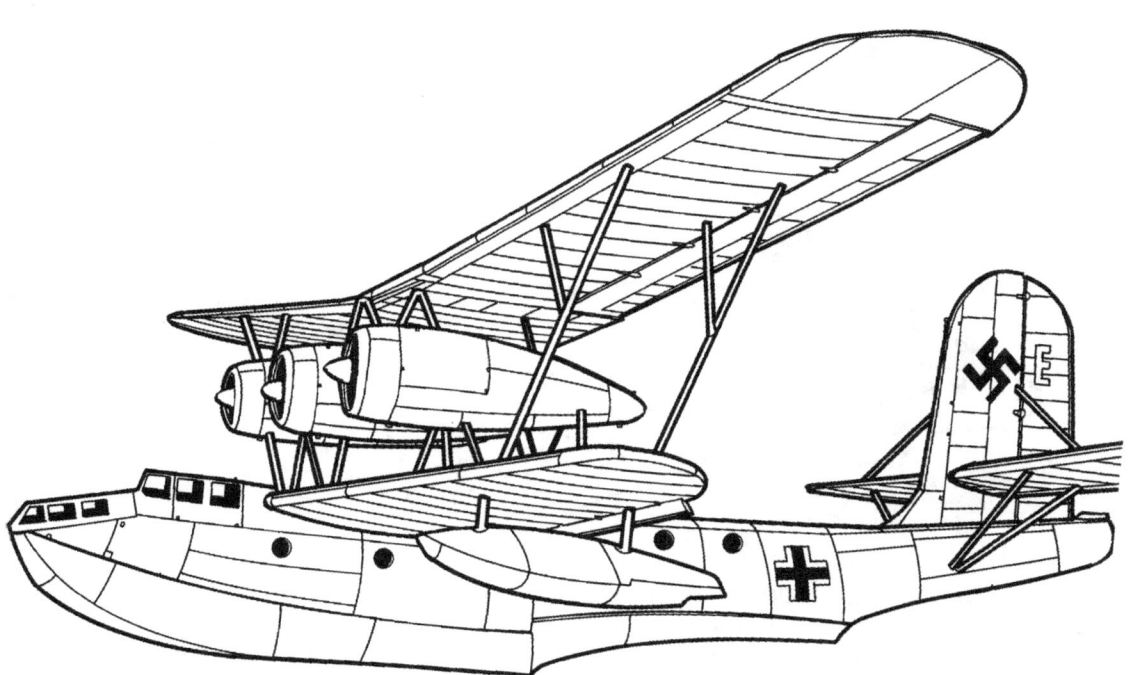

Bréguet Br. 521 Bizerte. Work on the three-engined Br 521 flying boat started in 1933. Derived from the Short Calcutta, the Br 521 was intended as a maritime patrol and reconnaissance seaplane for the French navy. It made its first flight in September 1933. Operated by a crew of eight, it was powered by three Gnome & Rhône 14 Kdrs radial engines each developing 850 hp. It had a maximum speed of 243 km/h (151 mph) and a range of 2,100 km (1,134 miles). Length was 20.33 m (66.99ft) and span was 35.13 m (115.25 ft). The flying boat was armed with six 7.69-mm Lewis machine guns. About thirty-four were built, serving in the prewar French navy, and with the Vichy Air Force during World War II. After the fall of France in 1940, seventeen units were captured by the Germans and used in the Luftwaffe rescue service.

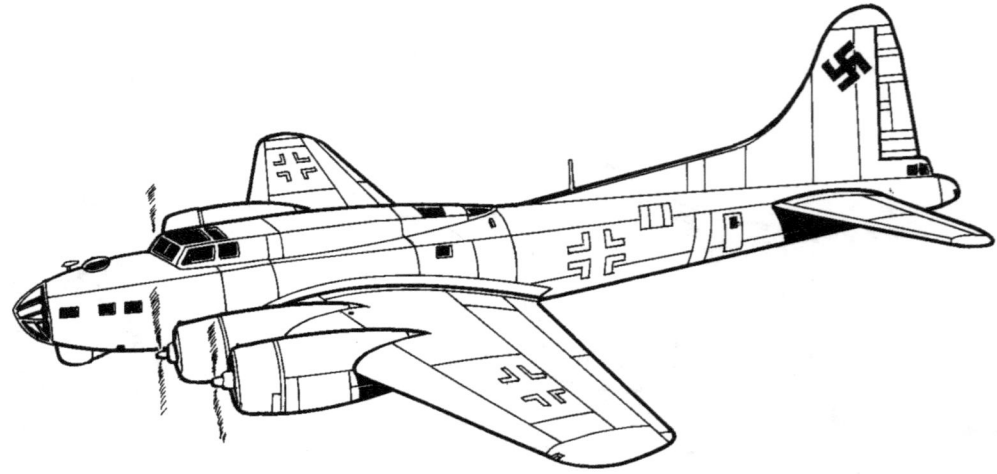

Dornier Do 200. The Do 200 was actually a code name for the American Boeing B-17 Flying Fortress. The Germans indeed had several B-17s which had been downed above their territory. As the B-17 was an extremely sturdy plane that could stand astonishingly heavy punishment, the Germans were able to repair a number of crashed bombers and put them back into active service. Repainted in German colors, they were operated by a special secret unit known as I/KG 200, created in January 1944. The shadowy activities of KG 200 included the use of captured aircraft for transport, reconnaisance and penetration, and special missions, such as dropping secret agents behind enemy lines (notably in Jordan in October 1944). It is reported that on one occasion a Do 200/B-17 (painted in USAF colors) discreetly joined an Allied bomber formation, posing as a crippled straggler, and radioed information such as altitude, speed and course estimates for attacking German fighters and Flak batteries. A few captured four-engined Consolidated B-24 Liberators were also used.

vanced aviation industry and a number of aircraft fell intact into German hands (e.g., Avia B-534 and Avia BK-534 fighters). The defeat and occupation of all industrial European nations after 1940 enabled the Germans to capture, confiscate or produced several types of military airplanes. From the Poles they used a number of PZL P7a fighters, the PZL P 37B bomber and Potez 24 light bombers. From the Netherlands, the Fokker G1 ground attacker and Fokker D XXI fighter were pressed into service. From the French they captured some Morane-Saulnier MS 406 and Dewoitine D 520 fighters, as well as Breguet, Bloch, Lioré et Olivier, and Potez medium bombers.

During the war on the Eastern front, the Germans managed to capture some Russian-made aircrafts, such as the Ilyushin Il-2 Stormovik ground attacker, and they pressed into Luftwaffe service Anglo-imported planes such as the Hawker Hurricane. From Italy they seized several models, including Macchi MC 202 Folgore fighters.

Many British and later American airplanes operating above Germany were shot down and captured, and in some cases repaired and reused, including, a number of British Gloster Gladiators, Spitfires, and Hawker Typhoons. From the United States they reused a number of Boeing B-17s, Republic P 47 Thunderbolts and Martin B 26 Marauders.

Retaliation Weapons (*Vergeltungswaffen*)

As we have seen, Germany was more advanced than the Allies regarding development of rockets and missiles. As early as 1937, a special center was created at Peenemünde, near Stettin on the Baltic Sea shore. Theorical researches and experimental works were directed by engineer Werner von Braun (1912–

1977). Between 1960 and 1972, von Braun was director of the American research center *National Aeronautics and Space Administration* (NASA) and greatly contributed to the exploration of space, and Flight Apollo 11, the landing on the moon in July 1969.

Before those peaceful achievements von Braun carried out many military projects for the Nazis, and several programs were launched concerning secret weapons.

Among those so-called *Vergeltungswaffen* (retaliation weapons), the most effective and best known were the so-called V1 and V2, which were used—not for defensive purposes—but for offensive operations meant to break the Allies's morale in a campaign of terror causing many casualties among innocent civilians populations, notably in Britain and Belgium. The secret V-weapons were thus intended as a retaliatory measure to pay back the British for the devastating air raids on German cities. Hitler's original plan was to discover by experiment which of the secret weapons was the more effective, but eventually he decided to order both V1 and V2. *Vergeltungswaffen* were produced by the Ministry of Armement directed by Albert Speer, they were served by selected Luftwaffe personnel but strictly controlled by the Reichsführer-SS Heinrich Himmler. Luftwaffe colonel Max Wachtel had constituted Flak Regiment 155 with specialists and technicians specifically to operate the V1. Later this unit was reinforced by an army formation and a training division; these units formed the special and secret LXV Corps which operated all V-weapons.

Hitler had hoped to launch his new terror weapons early in 1944, but science was a difficult mistress to hurry. The dictator hoped that those revolutionary "wonder" weapons would enable Germany to win the war as the havoc they would cause would force the Allies to call off their air raids on Germany and perhaps withdraw their forces from Europe and consider a compromized peace. He was almost right: the *Vergeltungswaffen* caused serious casulties and had the V-weapons offensive been launched against Southern England six months earlier or directed against military objectives, D-Day might have had to be postponed perhaps cancelled indefinitely. Fortunately, the chief delay was caused mostly by the natural technical difficulties incurred by both these highly complex experimental projects in the course of their research and development. As already said German technologists saw their achievements often come to nothing through inter-service rivalries and an utter lack of vision at the top. To the great failures of Hitler's strategy—his underestimation of British doggedness, of Russian fighting prowess, and of American productive capacity—one must add his failure to mobilize the scientific talent of his own people until it was too late. In the end the V1 and V2 launching campaign came to late. In no way did they affect the June 6, 1944, Normandy invasion, and have any effect on military operations. Owing to Allied bombing of the launching sites and later the overrunning of them by land forces, the impact of Hitler's secret weapons was comparatively limited. They only diverted valuable German resources and killed many innocent people in a pointless last-ditch resistance. The Führer's ultimate effort to turn the tide of the war by terrorizing Britain and Belgian civilian population was a failure. The V2, however, played an important part in the development of post–World War II missiles and rockets.

Flying bomb Fieseler 103 (V1)

The flying bomb *Fieseler 103*, better known as the V1 or Doodle-bug, was produced by the Gerhard Fieseler Aircraft company. The V1 was a small unmanned self-propelled plane, the precursor of modern cruise missile (see page 261). Measuring 8.32 m in length, 5.30 m in wingspan, and weighing about 2,180 tons at launch, the V1 was propulsed by a pulse-jet placed up on the tail. It used a fuel mixture of compressed air and low grade gasoline. The jet-engine developed 335 kg thrust at take-off and carried the bomb to a maximum range of 240 km or 300 km with a speed of about 560 km/h but later improved machines reached 670 km/h at 1,200 m altitude. The V1 was launched from a pneumatic steam catapult placed on a 40 meters long metal ramp using a piston mechanism to give thrust and propel the device into the air at a speed sufficient to allow the duct engine to function and keep the V1 airborne. The V1 was an inaccurate weapon that was not remote controlled. Its trajectory could not be altered once it was airborne. Its course was preset and regulated by an automatic pilot and a magnetic compass and thus the flight was secure against any form of electronic interference or jamming. A small propeller on the nose drove on an air-mileage counter which, when the set mileage was reached, turned the fuel off, locked all the controls and thus caused the bomb to dive on its target with a limited accuracy, within an 8 miles circle of the selected target. The V1 carried a formidable 850 kg impact-fused high explosive warhead causing enormous, if indiscriminate, ravages.

The V1 was, on the whole, a cheap weapon, using little scarce material, being mostly made of mild steel and wood to save weight. It has been estimated that each unit cost £115; as a comparison, a Volkswagen car cost £125 each. The low-altitude flight path of the V1 cruise missile and its comparatively small size meant that it had a good chance of escaping observation by the Allies's air defence; moreover its cruise altitude was between 3000 and 4000 feet, a zone which was particularly difficult for Allied anti-aircraft fire since the V1 flew too low for the heavy guns to engage effectively, and at the same time too high for the light anti-aircraft guns. Although very noisy, relatively vulnerable and short-lived the V1 was ideal for its purpose taking only about 50 man-hours to build and having remarkably reliability in very ardous circumstances. In late 1943 the flying bomb V1 was ready to become operational. Mass production began in March 1944 and about 35,000 V1s were produced. Between June 1944 and begin 1945, about 10,500 flying bombs were launched over Belgian towns (notably Antwerp), south-east England and London—a few British northern cities becoming targets to V1s—of which some 3,531 succeed to penetrate the air defence. About 4,500 V1s were downed by combination of balloon cables, fighter aircrafts, and anti-aircraft guns using the revolutionary "proximity fuse"; the remaining others fail either on launch or in flight.

Rocket A4 (V2)

The A4—more commonly known as V2—was an immensely portentous invention. It was planned as early as 1936 as a rocket to supplant heavy artillery. It was an unmanned self-propelled long-range bombardment spacecraft. It had a 14 m long cylindrical bullet-shaped body fitted with stabilizers and vanes. The tail-fins span was 3.56 m; its total weight was 13 t at launch, it carried a war-head containing 975 kg impact fused high explosive. Its range was about 350 km and its sophisticated rocket engine gave a tremendous speed of 6,400 km/h. The power of the engine was given by liquid fuelled rocket motor running on liquid oxygen and 3:1 alcohol-water mixture. The guidance was preset, employing integrating accelerometers to measure the velocity at which the motor was shut down. The V2 was an expensive weapon. It has been estimated that each rocket cost about £12,000 (as a comparison a British Lancaster bomber fuelled and bombed up cost £37,000). It was also a complicated project—often erratic and inaccurate—but with immense potentiality. The V2 contained no less than 30,000 parts, and completion-time required 4,000 man-hours in early 1945. First tests in the summer of 1942 were failures, but in September of that year came the first successful flight, and after some technical delay, production began in Peenemünde. After a severe Allied bombing attack in August 1943 the production plant was moved to an underground factory in the Harz Mountains where production eventually reached 900 pieces a month. Operational use of this terrifying weapon began in September 1944, and the effect was shattering as the world had never experienced such a formidable weapon. By the end of the war some 5,000 V2s were launched. Of these 1,115 come down over England and 2,050 over Brussels, Antwerp and Liege (Belgium).

For the firing of V2s gigantic bunkers were built in northern France, at Eperlecques and Wizernes. These were spotted, heavily bombarded and put out of use by Allied air raids. Then V2s were fired from the southern Netherlands by small and mobile launching units. Rapidly put in position, and quickly withdrawn, such a launching train was difficult to

Rocket A4 (V2)

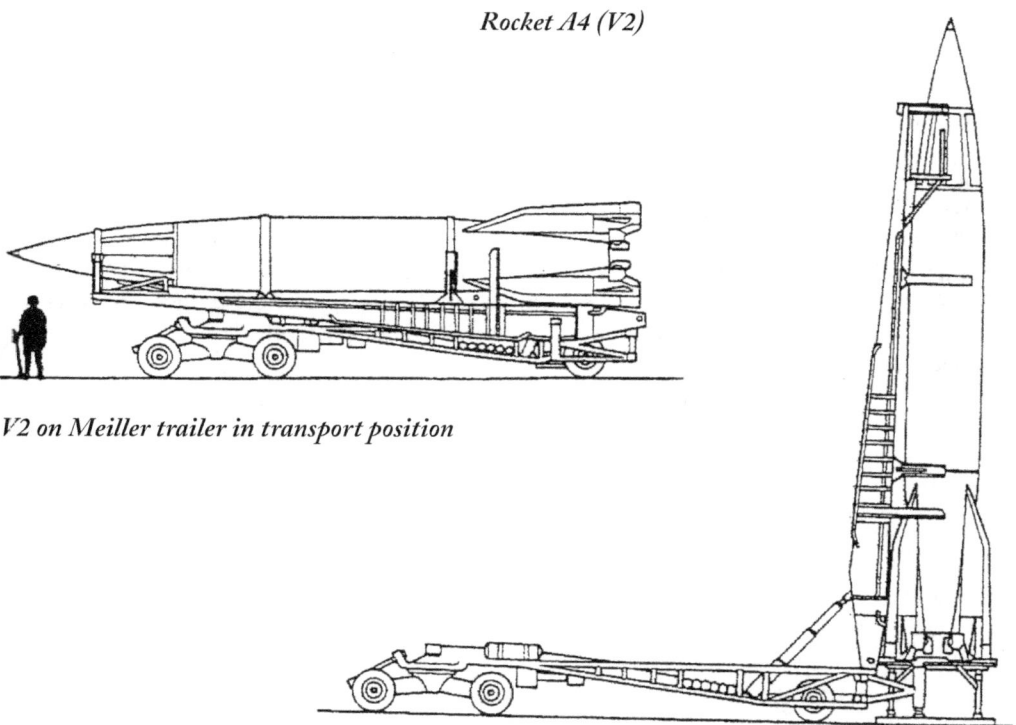

V2 on Meiller trailer in transport position

V2 in launching position

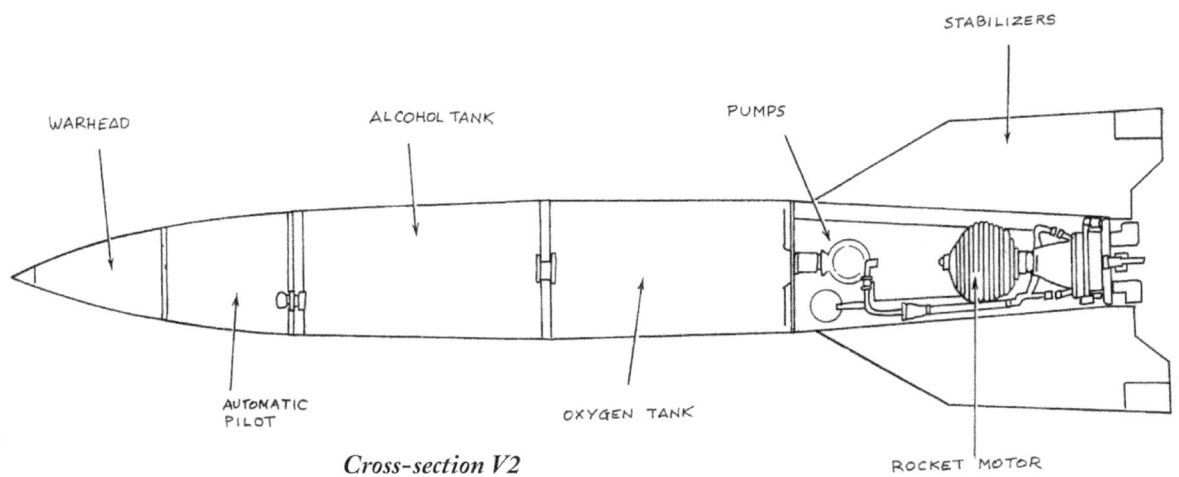

Cross-section V2

locate and destroy. The V2 was verticaly fired from a platform and its trajectory was regulated by a gyroscope control mechanism. For example, a V2 launched from Walcheren in the Netherlands reached a peak trajectory height of about 96 km then dived and exploded about 5 minutes later in London placed at a distance of 260 km. On the other hand, its accuracy in the area of the target left much to be desired, especially considering the non-nuclear character of its warhead. The V2 could be aimed against a city, but, especially at maximum range, hardly against anything less extensive. In spite of this disavantage, the rocket V2 represented a very serious menace for the Allies. Indeed when a flying bomb V1 could be shot down by planes or by AA-guns, nothing could stop a V2 once it had been launched. Against this rocket with its tremendous speed the Allied defenses were absolutely helpless. A huge explosion was usually the first indication that a V2 had been on the way. The only method to oppose to this formidable supersonic weapon was to destroy—or capture—structures where it was manufactured, assembled, stored and launched. Capture and destruction of the V2 launching bases were therefore given top priority. Had not the invasion of Europe already been successful before the V2 launching began, the invasion preparation—according to some opinions, included that of General Dwight D. Eisenhower—might well have been seriously hampered. The significant V2 was a forerunner of modern ballistic missiles and space vehicles.

Bibliography

Anderton, D. A., and J. Bachelor. *Jet Fighters*. London: Purnell & Sons Ltd, 1975.

———. *Straal Bommenwerpers*. Phoebus Publishing Company, 1978.

Connaissance de l'Histoire 18 (1979).

Cook, C., and J. Stevenson. *Weapons of War*. London: Artus Publishing Company, 1980.

Deighton, L. *Fighter*. New York: Ballantine Books, 1978.

———. *Bomber*. New York: Harper & Row, 1970.

Fitzsimons, B. *Warplanes and Air Battles of World War 2*. London: BPC Publishing, 1973.

Frischauer W. *Rise and Fall of Hermann Göring*. New York: Ballantine Books, 1951.

Ginston, B., and T. Wood. *Hitler's Luftwaffe*. London: Salamander Books, 1978.

Griehl, M. *Rohrwaffen in Flugzeugen der Luftwaffe bis 1945*. Wölfersheim-Berstadt: Podzun-Pallas-Verlag, 2001.

Historia Magazine (Paris).

Humble, R. *War in the Air, 1939–1945*. London: Salamander Books, 1975.

Keegan, J. *Encyclopedia of World War II*. London: Bison Books, 1977.

Lowe, V., and J. Bachelor. *Geïllustreerde Encyclopedie van de Luchtvaart 1939–1945*. Lisse: Rebo International Productions, 2004.

Maynard, C. *Lucht Gevechten*. Harderwijk: Deltas. 1990.

McInnes, C., and G. D. Sheffield. *Warfare in the 20th Century*. London: Unwin Hyman, 1988.

Philpott, B. *The Encyclopedia of German Military Aircraft*. London: Bison Books, 1980.

Price, A., and D. L. Uyt den Bogaard. *De Luftwaffe*. Antwerp: Standard, 1994.

Schellens, J. J., and J. Mayer. *Histoire Vécue de la Seconde Guerre Mondiale*. Verviers: Editions Gérard & Co, 1962.

Tagg, M. *De Wereld in Oorlog*. Harmelen: Ars Scribendi, 1993.

Index

Aces 72, 73, 82
Achgelis, Gerd 24, 379
Achselklappen 77
Adlers, Erwin 25
Aerowerke Gustav Otto 20
Afrika Korps 8
Ago Aircraft Company 20
Ago Ao 192 Kurier 20, 346
Air Force field regiments 96
Air-to-air weapons 65–69
Air-to-ground projectiles 62–65
Air warfare 60, 61
Airborne radio and radar 60–62
Airbrake 40
Airfoils 40
Alter Kämpfer 12
Anderson, Anders 22
Anhedral angle 40
Anti-Aircraft Artillery 3, 17, 20, 91, 92, 97, 103, 104, 105
Anti-aircraft medal 73
Anti-partisan war badge 95
Apollo 11 flight 391
Arado Aircraft Company 20, 21, 29
Arado Ar 65 208
Arado Ar 67 and 76 208
Arado Ar 68 210
Arado Ar 76 208
Arado Ar 80 213
Arado Ar 81 111
Arado Ar 95 332
Arado Ar 96 and Ar 396 374
Arado Ar 195 333
Arado Ar 196 319
Arado Ar 197 333
Arado Ar 198 362
Arado Ar 199 316
Arado Ar 231 317
Arado Ar 232 345
Arado Ar 234 Blitz 21, 185
Arado Ar 240 128
Arado Ar 396 374
Arado Ar E 340 158
Arado Ar E 377 flying bomb 160, 161
Arado Ar E 381 257
Arado Ar E 500 130
Arado Ar E 530 131
Arado Ar E 555 196
Arado Ar E 580 281
Arado Ar E 581-4 282

Arado Ar Tew 16/43-19 182
Arado Ar Tew 16/43-23 187
Arado Project I 307
Arado Project II 296
Argus engine 33, 261
Arm of service color 75
Armament (aircraft) 52–56
Armored plate 43
Asymmetric design 43, 138
Atrocities 2, 3
Automatic cannon MK 103 54
Automatic cannon MK 108/30 54
Automatic cannon MK 112/55 55
Automatic cannon Oerlikon MG/FF 20 mm 59
Avia B 534 386

Bachem, Erich 251
Bachem Ba 349 Natter 251, 311
Bachstelze (Focke-Achgelis Fa 330) 383
Badges 73, 95; ex-airmen commemorative 73; ground assault 72; observer 73; specialty 74; wound 72
Balkenkreuz 49
Bandenkampfabzeichen 95
Bär, Heinrich 71
Barbette 58
Barkhorn, Gerhard 72
Battle of the Bulge 9
Batz, Wilhelm 72
Basic flight data 33
Bauer, Hans 169
Baumgärtl, Paul 383
Bayerische Flugzeug-Werke 21, 27, 29, 69
Bayerische Motoren-Werk (BMW) 21, 34
Beer Hall Putsch 11
Bell X-5 270
Belt buckle 74
Benz, Carl 34
Berlin 240 radar 61
Bestmann (Bücker Bü 181) 375–376
Biplane 40
Blacky 87
Blitzkrieg 7, 50, 106, 251
Blohm, Hermann 21
Blohm & Voss AE 607 311

Blohm & Voss Aircraft Company 21, 265
Blohm & Voss Bv 40 glider 253
Blohm & Voss Bv 138 324
Blohm & Voss Bv 141 365
Blohm & Voss Bv 142 343
Blohm & Voss Bv 144 344
Blohm & Voss Bv 155 228
Blohm & Voss Bv 179 230
Blohm & Voss Bv 222 Wiking 327
Blohm & Voss Bv 237 138
Blohm & Voss Bv 238 328
Blohm & Voss Bv 246 Hagelkorn 66, 67, 138
Blohm & Voss Bv P 144 331
Blohm & Voss Bv P 163 231
Blohm & Voss Bv P 168 138
Blohm & Voss Bv P 170 132
Blohm & Voss Bv P 175 283
Blohm & Voss Bv P 178 183
Blohm & Voss Bv P 184 169
Blohm & Voss Bv P 188 195
Blohm & Voss Bv P 192-01 132
Blohm & Voss Bv P 193-01 132
Blohm & Voss Bv P 196-01 185
Blohm & Voss Bv P 197-01 294
Blohm & Voss Bv P 203 137
Blohm & Voss Bv P 204 137
Blohm & Voss Bv P 207/02 238
Blohm & Voss Bv P 207/03 238
Blohm & Voss Bv P 208/02 239
Blohm & Voss Bv P 208/03 240
Blohm & Voss Bv P 209-02 276
Blohm & Voss Bv P 211-02 268
Blohm & Voss Bv P 212-03 309
Blohm & Voss Bv P 213 263
Blohm & Voss Bv P 215 309
Blohm & Voss guided missile 69
Blohm & Voss Ha 135 371
Blohm & Voss Ha 137 111, 112
Blohm & Voss Ha 139 317
Blohm & Voss Ha 140 318
Blohm & Voss/Isacson Zerstörer 140
Blume, Walther 21
BMW engines 34
BMW fast bomber project I 186
BMW fast bomber project II 158
BMW jet fighter project I 278
BMW jet fighter project II 278
BMW Strahlbomber 1 197

Index

BMW Strahlbomber 2 198
Boeing B-17 390
Boeing V22 Osprey 384
Bong, Richard 73
Bombers, medium 142–144
Bombing methods 64
Bombs 62–64
Bone-bag 93
Bordkanone BK 3,7 cm 54
Brain drain (postwar Germany) 31
Braun, Wernher von 31, 391, 215
Bréguet Br 521 Bizerte 389
British Air Intelligence 44
Buchenwald 3
Bücker, Karl Clemens 21, 22
Bücker Aircraft Company 21, 22
Bücker Bü 131 Jungmann 22, 375
Bücker Bü 133 Jungmeister 22, 375
Bücker Bü 181 Bestmann 22, 375

Cabin pressuration 43
Canard design 41
Camouflage 46–49
Campaign medals 72, 74
Captured foreign aircraft 385–390
Cargo aircraft 335
Chord of wing 40
Churchill, Winston 166
Clogs 90
Cockpit 40–43; positioning 43
Collar patches 77
Command controls 40, 41, 42, 44
Convertiplane 378
Cooling 35, 36
Cornu, Paul 378
Crooked legs 60
Cuff-titles 74
Curtiss, Glen 314

Dachau 3
Dagger 74
Daimler, Gottlieb 34
Daimler-Benz engine 34
Daimler-Benz carrier project B and C 177, 178
Daimler-Benz DB Jäger 232
Daimler-Benz parasite fighter 178
Darmstadt Akademische Fliegergruppe 22
Dassault-Bréguet Aircraft Company 22
Delta wing 41
Desert Fox 8
Designs, unconventional 230, 231
Deutsche Forschunganstalt für Segelflug (DFS) 6, 22, 351
Deutsche Luft Hansa (DLH) 10
Deutscher Luftsportverband (DLV) 5
DFS 39 (Lippisch Delta IV) 242
DFS 40 (Delta V) and DFS 194 243
DFS 194 243
DFS 228 367
DFS 230 glider 352
DFS 331 glider 353
DFS 346 368
Dien Bien Phu 335
Diesel, Rudolf 36
Diesel engine 36
Dihedral angle 40
Dinghy 85

Dive bomber 67, 107–109
Division Hermann Göring 97–99
Il Dominio dell'Aria 161
Dönitz, Karl 13
Dornier Aircraft Company 22
Dornier, Claudius 22, 29
Dornier Do X 22
Dornier Do 11 162
Dornier Do 15 Wal 323
Dornier Do 17 149
Dornier Do 18 325
Dornier Do 19 164
Dornier Do 22 320
Dornier Do 22 L 213
Dornier Do 23 163
Dornier Do 24 326
Dornier Do 26 327
Dornier Do 200 (B-17) 390
Dornier Do 214/Do P 192 329
Dornier Do 215 149, 150
Dornier Do 216 330
Dornier Do 217 66, 150
Dornier Do 335 Pfeil 233
Dornier Do 435 234
Dornier Do 635 Z 367
Dornier Do P 252 235
Dornier Do P 256 185
Douhet, Guilio 161
Dowding, Hugh 315
Drache (Focke-Achgelis Fa 223) 381
Dreidecker 205
Drillichanzug 87, 102

Einstein, Albert 65
Eisenhower, Dwight 392
Elektro Mechanische Werk (EMW) 203
Emblems 51, 52, 70
Emergency transmitter 60
Empennage 40
EMW A4 (A9/A10) 203
Engine manufacturers 33–34
Entenbauform 140, 272
Enzian 249
Eperlecques bunker 392
ERLA Aircraft Company 23
Ex-airmen commemorative badge 73
Experimental jet fighters 296–313
Experte 72, 73

Falke (Focke-Wulf Fw 187) 129
Fallschirmjäger 15, 20, 93, 94, 95
Fallschirmjäger Gewehr 42 94
Fabre, Henri 314
Fatigue suit 86, 102
Feldgendarmerie 99–101
Feldregimenter der Luftwaffe 96
Fieseler, Gerhard 23
Fieseler Aircraft Company 23, 391
Fieseler Fi 98 112
Fieseler Fi 103 Reichenberg 261
Fieseler Fi 103 (V1) 67, 102, 261, 391
Fieseler Fi 156 Storch 360
Fieseler Fi 166 251
Fieseler Fi 167 334
Fighter 205–208
Fire Brigade 18
Fixed landing gear 45
Flak 3, 17, 20, 91, 92, 97, 104, 103, 105

Flak Regiment 155 391
Flensburg radar 61
Fliegende Panzerfaust 252
Fliegerdivision 18
Fliegerhorst-Feuerwehr 18
Fliegerkorps 17
Flettner, Anton 23
Flettner Aircraft Company 23, 24
Flettner Fl 265 379
Flettner Fl 282 Kolibri 379
Flight dress 81, 82
Flight helmet 83, 84
Flitzer (Focke-Wulf Fw 281 P VII) 277
Floatplane 314, 316–323
Flugboote 314
Flying boats 314, 323–334
Flying wing 39, 135
Focke, Heinrich 24, 380
Focke-Achgelis Company 24
Focke-Achgelis Fa 223 Drache 381
Focke-Achgelis Fa 225 381
Focke-Achgelis Fa 284 382
Focke-Achgelis Fa 269 385
Focke-Achgelis Fa 330 383
Focke-Wulf Aircraft Company 24
Focke-Wulf Fa 61 379
Focke-Wulf fighter project 226
Focke-Wulf Fw 42 144
Focke-Wulf Fw 56 Stösser 212, 380
Focke-Wulf Fw 57 120
Focke-Wulf Fw 58 Weihe 347
Focke-Wulf Fw 62 318
Focke-Wulf Fw 159 212
Focke-Wulf Fw 186 380
Focke-Wulf Fw 187 Falke 129
Focke-Wulf Fw 189 Uhu 363
Focke-Wulf Fw 190 223–225
Focke-Wulf Fw 190 D Long Nose 224
Focke-Wulf Fw 190 TL 268
Focke-Wulf Fw 191 156
Focke-Wulf Fw 195 348
Focke-Wulf Fw 200 Condor 166, 167
Focke-Wulf Fw 238 173
Focke-Wulf Fw 250 293
Focke-Wulf Fw 261 172
Focke-Wulf Fw 281 P VII Flitzer 277
Focke-Wulf Fw 1000 × 1000 × 1000 198
Focke-Wulf Fw P 1 268
Focke-Wulf Fw P 0310-25-1006 236
Focke-Wulf Fw P 03-10251-13 236
Focke-Wulf Fw Super Lorin 263
Focke-Wulf Fw Twin boom fighter project 236
Focke-Wulf Fw Volksjäger 256
Focke-Wulf Fw/Ta 183 279
Focke-Wulf Fw/Ta 283 262
Focke-Wulf Fw/Ta 400 171
Focke-Wulf P 127 280
Focke-Wulf Project II 278
Focke-Wulf Ta 152 225
Focke-Wulf Ta 154 Moskito 226
Focke-Wulf VTOL project 313
Focke-Wulf VTOL Triebflügel 312
Fokker, Anthony 26
Fokker Aircraft Company 21
Fokker DR1 triplane 205
Fokker G-1 386
Footwear 80

Index

Foreign aircraft, captured 385–390
Forward sweep 41
Fritz-X 67, 68
Fuel, liquid 39
Fuel tank 34; jettisonable 34
Fuselage 39, 40

Galland, Adolf 72
Geodesic fuselage 39
Gerät 105 56
German Air Association (DLV) 5
German Institute for Glider Flight (DFS) 6
Geschwader 18
Gestapo 11
Gigant (Cargo glider Messerschmitt Me 321) 356
Gigant (Messerschmitt Me 323) 350
Glazed nose 43
Gliders 351–357
Goebbels, Josef 30
Goggles 85
Göppingen Gö 9 233
Göring, Hermann 2, 3, 5, 6, 8, 10, 11, 12, 14, 20, 27, 30, 91, 96, 97, 102, 175, 225, 227
Gotha G4 bomber 107
Gotha Go 145 376
Gotha Go 147 359
Gotha Go 149 213
Gotha Go 150 377
Gotha Go 242 and Go 244 24, 354
Gotha Go 244 24, 354
Gotha Go 345 357
Gotha Go P 60 305
Gotha-Kalkert Ka 430 357
Gothaer Rolling Stock Manufacture (GWF or Gotha) 24, 26
Graf Zeppelin carrier 331, 334
Greif (Heinkel He 177) 58
Ground assault badge 72
Ground attack 110
Ground-attack aces 73
Gruppe 18, 358
Guernica 7
Günter, Siegfried 266
Günter, Walter 266
Gurttrommel 52

Hagelkorn (Blohm & Voss Bv 246) 67
Hahn, Otto 64
Hallore (Siebel Fh 104) 347
Hamburger Flugzeugbau see Blohm & Voss Aircraft Company
Harris, Arthur 8
Harth, Friedrich 27
Hartmann, Erich 72
Headgear 79, 80, 83, 84, 85, 88, 89, 93, 94
Heavy bombers 161, 162
Heinkel, Ernst 25, 215
Heinkel Aircraft Company 225
Heinkel He 8 5, 6
Heinkel He 45 359
Heinkel He 46 360
Heinkel He 50 110, 111
Heinkel He 51 209
Heinkel He 51 B 320

Heinkel He 59 57, 321
Heinkel He 60 319
Heinkel He 70 114
Heinkel He 72 Kadett 370
Heinkel He 74 210
Heinkel He 100 215
Heinkel He 111 25, 147–149
Heinkel He 111 Z 349
Heinkel He 112 214
Heinkel He 114 322
Heinkel He 115 322
Heinkel He 116 343
Heinkel He 118 115, 116
Heinkel He 119 366
Heinkel He 162 Volksjäger/Salamander 25, 266
Heinkel He 176 246
Heinkel He 177 Greif 174
Heinkel He 178 265
Heinkel He 219 Uhu 227
Heinkel He 274 176
Heinkel He 277 175
Heinkel He 280 283
Heinkel He 343 193
Heinkel He P 1065/IIC 140
Heinkel He P 1068-01-80 192
Heinkel He P 1068-01-83 192
Heinkel He P 1073 293
Heinkel He P 1076 229
Heinkel He P 1077 Julia 253
Heinkel He P 1077 Romeo 254
Heinkel He P 1078 308
Heinkel He P 1079 A 295
Heinkel He P 1079/B2 307
Heinkel He P 1080 264
Heinkel-Hirth Engine Company 25, 34
Heinkel Jet Engine Company (HeS) 25
Heinkel Wespe 311
Heisenberg, Werner 64
Helferinnen 104, 105
Helicopters and convertiplanes 378–385
Heliofly III/57 383
Helmet model M38 103
Henschel, Georg Christian Karl 25
Henschel, Karl-Anton 25
Henschel Aircraft Company 25, 30
Henschel Hs 121 and 125 211
Henschel Hs 122 As 231
Henschel Hs 123 56, 112, 113
Henschel Hs 124 120, 121
Henschel Hs 125 211
Henschel Hs 126 361
Henschel Hs 127 151
Henschel Hs 129 56, 127
Henschel Hs 130 156
Henschel Hs 132 183
Henschel Hs 217 Föhn rocket 252
Henschel Hs 293 65, 66
Henschel Hs P 87 140
Henschel Hs P 122 195
Henschel Hs P 135 277
Henschel Hs P 1073 293
Hermann Göring Division 20, 97, 98, 99
Hertel, Heinrich 25
Hess, Rudolf 27
High wing monoplane 40

Himmler, Heinrich 2, 12, 65, 91, 95, 251, 391
Hirth, Helmut Wolf 25, 34
Hitler, Adolf 1, 7, 8, 9–14, 26, 27, 30, 65, 71, 74, 96, 102, 167, 179, 227, 245, 246, 284, 285, 287, 331, 391
Hitler Youth 93, 104, 267, 351
Hogan's Heroes 91
Hohenzeichen 70
Holzbauer, Siegfried 159
Hornung, Hans 180
Horten brothers 24, 26
Horten IX/Gotha Go 229 302
Horten Ho X 303
Horten Ho XIII 305
Horten Ho XIII/IAe. 38 351
Horten Ho XVIII A and XVIII B 199
Horten Ho XVIII B 199
Horten Ho 229 24
Hubert, Josef 141
Hubjäger (Junkers Ju EF 009) 297
Hugo Junkers Company 10, 26,
Hurricane rocket 55
Hütter, Ulrich 131, 233
Hütter, Wolfgang 131, 233
Hütter Hü 136 131

Immelmann III 166
In-line engine 34–35
Individual emblems 51
Iron Cross 71

Jackboots 80
Jagdfaust (SG 500) 56
Jagdkorps 18
Jäger (Daimler Benz DB) 232
Jeschonnek, Hans 13
Jet-assisted take off (JATO) 39
Jet bombers 179, 180
Jet engines 37–39
Jet fighters 244–246
Jettisonable fuel tank 34
Jettisonable landing gear 45
Jungmann (Bücker Bü 131) 375
Jungmeister (Bücker Bü 133) 375
Junkers, Hugo 26
Junkers Aircraft Company 26
Junkers Aircraft Engine Company (JUMO) 26, 34
Junkers/DFS long range bomber 201
Junkers EF 009 Hubjäger 296
Junkers EF 61 145
Junkers EF 112 133
Junkers EF 125 (Ju 287) 189
Junkers EF 126 Elli 262
Junkers EF 130 201
Junkers EF 132 191
Junkers F 13 336
Junkers-Fokker Aircraft Company 26
Junkers G 38 26, 337
Junkers Ju 52 10, 26, 338–340
Junkers Ju 60 and Ju 160 372
Junkers Ju 86 145
Junkers Ju 87 42, 109, 115–119, 138, 334
Junkers Ju 88 63, 152–154
Junkers Ju 89 165
Junkers Ju 90 341
Junkers Ju 128 308, 309

Junkers Ju 160 372, 373
Junkers Ju 187 120
Junkers Ju 188 154
Junkers Ju 248 249
Junkers Ju 252 340
Junkers Ju 287 188
Junkers Ju 288 155
Junkers Ju 290 57, 167
Junkers Ju 322 Mammut 355
Junkers Ju 352 Herkules 341
Junkers Ju 388 155
Junkers Ju 390 168
Junkers Ju 488 172
Junkers Motoren (JUMO) 34
Junkers W 34 336

Kadett (Heinkel He 72) 370
Kamikaze scheme 245
Kammhuber, Joseph 61, 227
Kauba, Otto 28
Kesselring, Albrecht 13, 162
Kill tally 52
Kittel, Otto 72
Klemm, Hans 26
Klemm L 25 and 35 D 371
Klemm L 35 D 371
Klemm Light Aircraft Company 26
Knemeyer, Siegfried 11
Knockensack 93
Kolobri (Flettner Fl 282) 379
Komet (Messerschmitt Me 163) 248
Koppenburg, Heinz 26, 152
Kozhedub, Yvan 73
Kraft, Heinz 168
Kragenspiegel 77
Kübelwagen 355
Kurier (Ago Ao 192) 346

Landing gear 44–46; fixed 45; jettisonable 45
Landing skid 46
Latécoère 298 388
Leading edge 41
Lebensraum 2
Legion Condor 7, 14, 50, 71
Lehrdivision 18
Libelle (Messerschmitt) 282
Lichtenstein BC radar 61
Lichtenstein 220 SN2 radar 61
Lielienthal, Otto 351
Life vest 82, 83, 85
Lioré & Olivier Leo 451 387
Lippisch, Alexander 22
Lippisch DM-1 297
Lippisch Li P 01 Series 247
Lippisch Li P 04–106 135
Lippisch Li P 09 135
Lippisch Li P 11 298
Lippisch Li P 11-05 181
Lippisch Li P 11-92 and Li P 11-05 181
Lippisch Li P 12 299
Lippisch Li P 13 141
Lippisch Li P 13A 300
Lippisch Li P 13B 301
Lippisch Li P 14 301
Lippisch Li P 15 project 1 301
Lippisch/Messerschmitt bomber glider 142
Liquid fuel 39

Lorenz beam 60
Lorin, René 37, 263
Lörzer, Bruno 5
Lübbe, Heinrich 21
Luftflotte 17
Luftgau 17
Lufthansa 5, 10, 25,
Luftwaffe: *der Adler* (newspaper) 31; crew training 370; emblem and flag 70, 71; field infantry divisions 20, 95, 96, 97; figures 31–32; flag 70, 71; history 5–9; lack of heavy bombers 161, 162; leadership 11–16; organization 16–20, 336, 358; production of aircraft 30; ranks 75, 76, 77; uniforms 77–105
Lusser, Robert 27

Macchi C-202 388, 389
Machine guns: MG 15 52; Mauser MG 81 53; MG 131 53; MG 151/15 53
Mammut (Junkers Ju 322) 355
Mantel 79, 88, 100, 104
manufacturers, aircraft 20–29
Marschstiefel 80
Maschinegewehr (MG) 53
Manhattan Project 65
Markings 49–52
Marseille, Hans-Joachim 52, 72
Medal for bravery 72
Medals 71–74, 95
Medium bombers 142–144
Meier 12
Meiller trailer 392
Meitner, Lise 64
Messerschmitt, Wilhelm Emil 21, 27
Messerschmitt Aircraft Company 27, 30
Messerschmitt Bf 108 Taifun 373
Messerschmitt Bf 109 216- 220
Messerschmitt Bf 110 121, 122
Messerschmitt Bf 161 124
Messerschmitt Bf 162 123
Messerschmitt-Bölkow-Blohm Company 25, 27
Messerschmitt Libelle 282
Messerschmitt/Lippisch Li P 15 Diana 267
Messerschmitt M22 144
Messerschmitt M28 337
Messerschmitt M35 372
Messerschmitt Me 109 TL 284
Messerschmitt Me 163 Komet 248
Messerschmitt Me 209 220
Messerschmitt Me 210 and Me 410 124, 125
Messerschmitt Me 261 Adolfine 366
Messerschmitt Me 262 and variants 9, 285–290
Messerschmitt Me 263 249
Messerschmitt Me 264 270
Messerschmitt Me 265/Lippisch Li P 10 125
Messerschmitt Me 309 221
Messerschmitt Me 321 356
Messerschmitt Me 323 Gigant 350
Messerschmitt Me 328 258
Messerschmitt Me 329 125
Messerschmitt Me 334 238

Messerschmitt Me 410 124, 125
Messerschmitt Me 509 221
Messerschmitt Me 609 222
Messerschmitt Me P 08–01 176
Messerschmitt Me P 65 and Me P 1065 285
Messerschmitt Me P 1065 285
Messerschmitt Me P 1079 259
Messerschmitt Me P 1092 Series 269
Messerschmitt Me P 1095 272
Messerschmitt Me P 1099 and 1100 290
Messerschmitt Me P 1100 290
Messerschmitt Me P 1101 180
Messerschmitt Me P 1101 Series 270
Messerschmitt Me P 1101/92 and Me P 1101/99 Pulkzerstörer 291
Messerschmitt Me P 1101/99 Pulkzerstörer 291
Messerschmitt Me P 1102/5 183
Messerschmitt Me P 1103 and Me P 1104 255
Messerschmitt Me P 1104 255
Messerschmitt Me P 1106 271
Messerschmitt Me P 1106 R 255
Messerschmitt Me P 1108 190
Messerschmitt Me P 1109 297
Messerschmitt Me P 1110 Series 273
Messerschmitt Me P 1110 Ente 274
Messerschmitt Me P 1111 274
Messerschmitt Me P 1112 275
Messerschmitt Schwalbe 294
Messerschmitt Wespe 283
Messerschmitt Zerstörer project II 183
Military police 99–101
Milsch, Erhard 6, 10, 13, 27
Miniaturjäger program 244, 263
Minister of Aviation (RLM) 6, 10, 11, 17, 25
Missile 65–69
Mission clasp 74
Mistel 62, 63, 158–161, 261
Mitchell, William 161
Mölner, Werner 72
Monocoque fuselage 39
Monoplane 40
Morane-Saulnier MS 406 387
Moskito (Focke-Wulf Ta 154) 226
Musician 90, 91
Mussolini, Benito 261, 353, 360

National Aeronautics and Space Administration (NASA) 391
National markings 49, 50
Nationalsozialistische Fliegerkorps (NSFK) 5, 9
Nationalsozialistische Kraftfahrkorps (NSKK) 101
Natter (Bachem Ba 349) 251
Navigational equipment 60
Nazi feast days 71
Nazi Flyers Corps (NSFK) 5, 9
Nazi Motorized Corps 101
Neptun 218 radar 61
Newton, Isaac 37
Night fighters 61, 207
Nomenclature 29–30
Normandy Invasion (June 6, 1944) 8, 15, 32, 161, 391
Novotny, Walther 72

NSKK Transportregiment Luftwaffe 101, 102
NSKK foreign volunteers 101
nuclear weapon 64, 65

Oberkommando der Luftwaffe 16
Oberkommando der Wehrmacht 16
Observer badge 73
One-man backpack copter 283, 384
Operation Barbarossa 7
Operation Market Garden 15
Operation Paperclip 31
Operation Sea Lion 356
Organisation Todt (OT) 102
OT Einsatz Luftwaffe 102, 103
Overcoat 79, 88, 100, 104
Oxygen mask 85

Pabst von Ohain, Hans Joachim 181, 265
Panzer uniform 98
Panzerfaust 99
Parachute 85
Parasol monoplane 40
Paratrooper 15, 20, 93, 94, 95
Paratrooper helmet 93
Payen, Nicolas 243
Payen Pa 22 243
Peeckhaus, Wilhelm 73
Peenemünde 391
Peter Strasser carrier 331
Pfeil (Dornier Do 335) 233
Photo Reconnaissance Unit (PRU) 49
Picasso, Pablo 7
Piston engines 33–36
Pitch 44
Pitot, Henri 43
Pitot tube 42
Pohl, William 28
Polizeigruppe Wecke 97
Positioning of cockpit 43
Positioning of weapons 57–60
Postwar German Brain Drain 31
Power-driven turret 57, 58
Prone position 43
Propaganda 30, 31
Propeller 36, 37
Pulse-jet engine 38, 391
Pulse-jet-engined planes 258, 259
Pusher propeller 36

Raab-Katzenstein Aircraft Company 23
Radar 60–62; *see also* Airborne radio and radar
Radio *see* Airborne radio and radar
Radial engine 35, 36
Radio equipment 60
Rakete 4 Minenkopf (R4M) 55
Rall, Günther 72
Ram-jet engine 37, 38
Ranks 75–77
Reciprocated engine 34
Reconnaissance units 358
Reconnaissance and observation planes 358–369
Red Baron 51, 205
Regalia 70–71
Reich Air Ministry (RLM) 10, 11

Reichsluftfahrtministerium (RLM) 10, 11
Reitsch, Hanna 12, 14, 261, 352
Retaliation Weapons 245, 391
Rethel, Walter 21
Retractable undercarriage 44
Richthofen, Manfred Baron of 51, 205
Richthofen, Wolfram Freiherr von 14
Ritter von Greim, Robert 12, 13
Rocket A4 (V2) 102, 392
Rocket-assisted take off (RATO) 39
Rocket engine 39
Rocket-powered aircraft 246, 247
Rocket nozzle 39
Roll 44
Rommel, Erwin 8, 13, 14, 15, 361
Root of wing 40
Rotte 19, 206
Ruak, Matthew 34
Rudel, Hans 73, 74
Ruhrstahl-Kramer X-4 68, 69

Sack, Arthur 377
Sack As-6 377
Sänger, Eugen Albert 202
Sänger Silverbird 202
Sauckel, Friedrich 2
Schlageter, Leo 51
Schmidt, Paul 38, 261
Schönert, Rudolf 60
Schräge Musik 59, 60, 123
Schwalbe (Messerschmitt) 294
Schwalbe (Messerschmitt Me 262) 285
Schwalbennester 91
Schwarm 19
Schwarze 87
Scourge of the Atlantic 166
Sea Rescue Service 315
Seaplanes 314–316
Seeckt, Hans von 20
Seeflugzeuge 314
Semi-monocoque fuselage 39
Serno, Erich 21
Service dress 79
7.5 cm Pak cannon 56
Shark's mouth 52
Shoulder straps 77
Siebel, Friedrich Wilhelm 28
Siebel Aircraft Company 28
Siebel Fh 104 347
Siebel Si 201 363
Siebel Si 204 347
Sikorsky, Igor 378
Single-jet-engined fighters 265–283
Skoda-Kauba Aircraft Company 28
Skoda-Kauba SK P 14-01 264
Skoda-Kauba SK V6 239
Skorzeny, Otto 261, 353, 360
Solid fuel 39
Sombold So 244 257
Sombolt, Heinz 257
Sonderführer 75, 77
Span 40
Spanner-Auflage 61
Special Commando Elbe 245
Specialty badge 74
Speer, Albert 8, 11, 30, 65, 102, 207, 391

Speerle, Hugo 14
Staffel 19
Stamer-Lippisch SG 38 glider 9
Standard bearer 70, 71
Startwagen 45
Steel helmet type 1935 97, 98, 105
Stöckel ram-fighter 265
Storch (Fieseler Fi 156) 360–361
Stösser (Focke-Wulf Fw 56) 212
Straight in-line engine 35
Straw boots 90
Stressed skin fuselage 39
Student, Kurt 15
Stuka (Blohm & Voss Bv 237) 138
Stuka dive attack 108, 109
Sturkampfflugzeug (Stuka) 64, 108, 130
Sturmgruppen 245
Survival aids 85, 86
Swallows' nest 91
Swastika 50, 70

Tactical markings 50, 51
Taifun (Messerschmitt Bf 108) 373
Tail assembly 40
Taildragger 44
Tailless aircraft 40
Tank, Kurt 24, 30, 171, 212, 225, 262, 278
Tausendfüssler (Arado Ar 232) 345
Technical personnel 85–87
Todt, Fritz 102
Torpedo 64
Trailing edge 41
Trainers, liaison and utility planes 369–378
Transport aircraft 335, 336–351
Treaty of Versailles 5, 6, 9, 20, 24, 25, 29
Trenchard, Hugh 161
Tricycle landing gear 45
Triebflügel (Focke-Wulf VTOL) 312–313
Trimtab 44
Triplane 40
Troika Schlepp 349
Tropical uniform 87–89, 98
Trouser press 61
Tsiolkovsky, Konstantin 37
Turbo-jet engine 38
Turbo-prop engine 38
Turret 57, 58, 59
Twin fuselage 39
Twin-jet-engined fighters 283–296

Udet, Ernst 5, 15, 27, 30, 108, 349, 352
Udet Aircraft Company 28
Udet U-12 Flamingo 28
Uhu (Focke-Wulf Fw 189) 363–364
Uhu (Heinkel He 219) 227
Uniforms: flying personnel 77–85; Luftwaffe ground forces 91–105; Panzer 98; winter 89, 90
Unit emblems 51
Ursinus, Oskar 24

V-in-line engine 35
Valenki 90
Variable-geometry wing 40

Vergeltungswaffen 391, 392
Vertical Take off and Landing
  (VTOL) 311, 312, 313, 378
Vogt, Richard 21, 137, 138
Volksjäger program 244
Von Braun VTO Interceptor 250
Voss, Ernst 21

Wachtel, Max 391
Waffenfarbe 75
Wagenführ, Felix 21
Wal (Dornier Do 15) 323
Watt, James 34
Weapons positioning 57–60
Weihe (Focke-Wulf Fw 58) 347
Weser Aircraft Company 29, 384
Weser P 1003/1 29, 384

Wespe (Heinkel) 311
Wespe (Messerschmitt) 283
Wessel, Horst 51
Wever, Walther 15, 162
Whitehead, Robert 64
Wiking (Blohm & Voss Bv 222) 327–328
Wild Boar 206
Window 61
Windschutzbrillen 85
Wing 40
Winter uniform 89, 90
Wizernes bunker 392
Wocke, Hans 31
Women auxiliaries 104, 105
Wood, Robert 270
Work clothing 85, 86

Wound badge 72
Wulf, Georg 24
Würger (Focke-Wulf Fw 190) 223
Wurster, Hermann 137

X-device 60

Y-device 60
Yaw 44
Youth auxiliary 103, 104

Zeppelin, Ferdinand, Count of 29
Zeppelin Manufacture 29
Zeppelin Rammer 252
Zerstörer 110, 130
Zindel, Ernst 165, 201
Zwilling (Heinkel He 111 Z) 349

www.ingramcontent.com/pod-product-compliance
Lightning Source LLC
Chambersburg PA
CBHW081533300426
44116CB00015B/2615